WOMEN WHO
RUN THE SHOW

How a Brilliant and Creative
New Generation of Women
Stormed Hollywood

ST. MARTIN'S PRESS 〰 NEW YORK

WOMEN WHO
RUN THE SHOW

Mollie Gregory

www.stmartins.com

Library of Congress Cataloging-in-Publication Data

Gregory, Mollie.
    Women who run the show : how a brilliant and creative new generation of women stormed Hollywood / Mollie Gregory.—1st ed.
        p. cm.
    Includes bibliographical references (p. 433) and index (p. 437).
    ISBN 0-312-30182-0
    1. Women motion picture producers and directors—United States—Biography.
I. Title.

PN1998.2 .G74 2002
791.43'023'0820973—dc21
[B]
                                                                    2002017775

First Edition: August 2002

10   9   8   7   6   5   4   3   2   1

Joe: You hit it! The truth's no good to me, Polly! History just isn't practical ... We can't stick to history. History's unbelievable! And it's up to us to make it seem real.

Polly: Honest to God, Joe, you must have a brain of solid popcorn.

—RUTH GORDON,

OVER TWENTY-ONE, ACT III

For the unremarked, taken-for-granted status of women's work applied equally to their lives, and both combined to ensure that what women did went largely absent from the historical record.

—ROSALIND MILES,

WHO COOKED THE LAST SUPPER:

THE WOMEN'S HISTORY OF THE WORLD

A man would never get the notion of writing a book on the peculiar situation of the human male.

—SIMONE DE BEAUVOIR, *THE SECOND SEX*

CONTENTS

ACKNOWLEDGMENTS   ix

INTRODUCTION   xi

I: Beachhead—The 1970s   1

  1. I Don't Want to Watch, I Want to Play   5

  2. We Don't Want Anything Itsy-Poo   24

  3. She's Young, She's Pretty, and—She's a Producer!   40

  4. The Start of a Wonderful Heyday for Women   57

  5. Get Me a Woman!   80

  6. You Don't Meet Boring People in This Business   99

  7. I Don't Know Any Women—Getting Organized   112

  8. I Was Supposed to Be Hedda Hopper   126

II: Securing the Perimeter—The 1980s   151

  9. Yes, Sir, Giving Way to Yes, Ma'am   155

  10. Chutes and Ladders—Executive Games in the 1980s   170

  11. More Ladders Than Chutes—The Newcomers   190

  12. Women Make Good Producers—Movies   209

  13. Getting on the Yellow Brick Road—Producing for Television   224

  14. A Different Take on the Set   242

III: Breakthrough—The 1990s   271

  15. The Suit with Legs   275

16. Don't Ever Take It Personally   291

17. Hiring a Woman (Writer) Is the Hip Thing to Do   309

18. This Is What Men Do   327

19. Making the Whole Frame in the '90s   342

EPILOGUE: HOW FAR IS FAR?   361
AUTHOR'S NOTE   379
ENDNOTES   381
LIST OF WOMEN INTERVIEWED   423
BIBLIOGRAPHY   433
INDEX   437

ACKNOWLEDGMENTS

I consider this book a collaboration with the women I interviewed who candidly, humorously, sometimes painfully shared their work experiences in the motion picture and television industry. It is their book far more than it is mine.

Many people helped the effort to trace this history from the 1970s to the present. The members of the boards of Women in Film and its foundation were a tremendous support in every way. I particularly wish to thank Iris Grossman, president at that time, succeeding president Hollace Davids, and board members Beth Kennedy, Carol Savoie, Debra Hill, and Arnold I. Fram; from the foundation, Irma Kalish, Patricia Barry, and WIF cofounder Nancy Malone, who gave me noble help from the beginning. On the staff, my gratitude to Diane Conforti, Holley Hankinson, and Deena Wonders.

Women in Film provided funds for additional research and this book could not have been written without that assistance. I am just as indebted to the foundation for an early research grant from a fund donated by Rand Marlis, Creative Licensing Corp., in the memory of Annette Welles. Annette was vice president of creative affairs at Universal Pictures and served on the board of Women in Film. She was lively, smart, and knowledgeable, and I liked her very much.

I am indebted to many other friends who also read and reread sections of the manuscript, offering informed comments, perspectives, or rare bits of history they recalled as they read: Diane and Richard Baer, Andrew Griffin, Bernard Gordon, Adele Scheele, Milly Loeb, Richard Goggin, Jon and Nancy Wilkman. Many friends and acquaintances contributed in a variety of ways, including information, good counsel, and enthusiasm: Michael Black, Mackenzie Green, Judee Flick, Billie B. Jenkins, Pola Miller, Rochel Blachman, Judi Davidson, Norman Fox, Catherine Finnegan, Dr. Martha M. Lauzen, Linda Loe, Larry Mole Parker, Kayla

Garen, and Sybil Niden Goldrich. At the Writers Guild of America, Karen Pedersen, librarian at the James R. Webb Library, Angela Kirgo, executive director of the WGA Foundation; John Sheridan; Michael Franklin, former executive director; scholars Denise D. and William T. Bielby; and former WGA presidents John Furia and Del Reisman.

I depended on the substantial assistance of Sue Terry of Sue Terry Research Associates; Destiny McCune for her prompt and able transcriptions; and Hunter L. Hughes, who served for months as a cheerful and tireless assistant.

Every writer owes debts to friends who selflessly help them along the way, through one book that, once published, leads to another, and for me Maria Stratton was one of these early supporters before my first novel was published. Others who came later are Tammy Gold and Bernard Gordon. For my agent, Loretta Barrett, words are not enough. She saw the value of this book from its inception and never quit in her efforts to get it into print. My first editor, Brenda Scott Royce, also understood this kind of history from a bare-bones proposal, never lost faith, and helped in numerous ways, above and beyond. To my second editor, Elizabeth Beier, I am so grateful for her rescue, her splendid competence, and her good humor.

INTRODUCTION

What we failed to say yesterday, no one will know tomorrow. This book chronicles women's readmission to film and television in the last third of the twentieth century and the changes they have caused to be made and have experienced in their work. Women now have some access and influence. Not since the days of silent movies (1910–28) have women worked in any real numbers in the industry. Yes, women worked from 1930 to 1970, mainly as actresses, some of the best, or as writers, like Sonya Levien (*Bhowani Junction, Quo Vadis*), Madelyn Pugh Davis (*I Love Lucy, Alice*), Leigh Brackett (*The Big Sleep, Rio Bravo*), Marguerite Roberts (*True Grit, Ivanhoe*), Virginia Van Upp (*Gilda, Here Comes The Groom*), Joan Harrison (*Suspicion, Rebecca*; also producer of *Alfred Hitchcock Presents* television series). In the 1950s, actress Ida Lupino wrote and directed *The Hitch-Hiker* and *Outrage*. But during that forty-year period, women were not a movement of numbers or influence.

In January 1996, the Writers Guild of America moved into new quarters in Los Angeles. The entire membership was invited. Guided tours were offered. I joined a guide and three young men, and we went from floor to floor, where helpful staff members showed us their working space and told us what they did for us. An easel parked outside the Employment Access office displayed gaily colored graphs depicting the employment status of female and minority writers from the 1970s to the present. One of the guys in our group said to the guide, "Is this *right?*" The graph showed that women in the 1990s were writing 17 percent of the film scripts and 24 percent of television scripts. The guide said it was right. "Gee," the writer said, "I thought it was all equal now."

Despite published statistics, the widespread perception of equality at the turn of the millennium is one reason I wrote this book. I wanted to know what the women themselves had experienced in these thirty years. Did it feel equal now? If not, why not?

Around the time of the Writers Guild move, I went to the Larry Edmunds Bookshop in Hollywood. It is famous for its remarkable collection of new and used books on film and television. Inside, every wall bristles with books on shelves that rise to the high ceiling. I was looking for Dawn Steel's autobiography, *They Can Kill You but They Can't Eat You.* Steel had been head of production at Paramount Pictures and, in 1987, the first woman to run a studio as president of Columbia Pictures.[1]

The man behind the counter moved into one of the shelf-lined aisles. About two feet from the back wall, he stopped and pointed skyward, where a small handwritten sign proclaimed: WOMEN IN FILM. A shelf and a half. He stood on a stool and reached for Steel's book. "Are these the only books you have on women in television or film?" I asked. He nodded. Most were biographies or scholarly texts.

I bought Steel's book. At the door, I turned and looked at the book-crammed room. Were all the rest of the books "Men in Film"? Somewhere in this sea of biographies, histories, memoirs, autobiographies about the art and commerce of films and television, there *had* to be women's experiences told in their own words. Of course, there were batallions of biographies of actresses like Mary Pickford, a founder of United Artists, but little information about women like Lois Weber or Frances Marion. Weber, the highest-paid director at Universal from 1912 to 1917, was as famous as D. W. Griffith at the time.[2] Frances Marion was the most prominent screenwriter then, writing scripts for Norma Talmadge and Greta Garbo, and particularly for Mary Pickford.[3] In 1930 and 1932, she won Academy Awards for her screenplays *The Big House* and *The Champ.* The next woman to pick up a solo Academy Award for screenwriting was Ruth Prawer Jhabvala for *A Room with a View* in 1985.[4]

The image of that short shelf in the Larry Edmunds Bookshop stayed with me as I began work on this book.

I began to refer to the period from the 1920s to the 1970s, when women in numbers began to reenter film, as the long desert. But the details of the changes that came after it which encouraged women to become part of the industry again had not been recorded. I wanted to know about their behind-the-camera experiences in the 1970s. I wondered if the experiences of younger women who started in the late 1980s or mid-1990s had been truly different.

Several things became clear in the research: most women starting in the 1990s knew that things "had been tough" for women in the 1970s, but had no real knowledge of any history of women in television or film, how comparatively new women were to the field, what kind of challenges women had surmounted, or how few women had produced films or TV series in the late 1970s compared to today. In short, they had no idea of their own history. But then, neither did women whose careers had started in the 1970s.

By the mid-1990s, it was "in the air" that women had become equal in this industry . . . or if they weren't totally equal, they would be tomorrow. When I began this book in 1997, this perception was so widespread that it was unpopular to question its accuracy.

Shortly after I picked up Dawn Steel's book, I attended a board meeting for the Women in Film Foundation. I had known most of the members for years, but I realized as I looked around the table that though I knew which film that one had produced or which television show this one had written, I did not know much about their personal career experiences—the struggle, the humor, the joy. I called one the next day and asked her out to dinner. "Tell me all about your working life," I said. We talked for three hours.

I began the interviews in 1997, planning on sixty or seventy, ending with more than 130. The accounts in this book come from women who work in both film and television. They came to this region of dreams from poverty or wealth, from indifferent or loving parents, with trepidation or with confidence, from San Antonio, New Orleans, Minneapolis, New York City—Harlem, the Lower East Side, the Bronx, Manhattan—St. Louis, and Portland. A few even came from Los Angeles. They are the daughters of immigrants from Russia, Germany, Cuba, England, and China. Their parents were middle-class executives, pharmacists, shopkeepers, dancers, housewives, surgeons, dressmakers. Very few had any family links to the film or television industry.

The first group of women chronicled here arrived in Los Angeles in the 1960s and 1970s during a momentous cultural shift that changed practically everything. American society was being transformed by the civil rights movement, the women's movement, and the rousing 1960s—the Beatles and the Stones, Joan Baez, protest music, folk music, the Pill, and the new youth-is-great era. The social tidal wave brought profound economic and creative alterations in the business and art of American entertainment. Television, about twenty-five years old in 1973, was a muscular, aggressive, omnipresent institution; the older film studio system was collapsing—tents waiting for the next act, their absorption into huge conglomerates. The "big" movies of the 1970s—*Mean Streets, Jaws, Star Wars*—were comparatively low-budget films but caused an artistic and economic firestorm. They were made by young new directors who changed the face of our cultural icons.

Women had little to do with those changes, yet women were about to advance on the industry. Through an accident of the times, and by dint of will, they were going to be an integral part of it.

During the process of the interviews, I had a number of surprises. Most are noted in the following chapters, but two are not. When I first telephoned people to ask for an interview and told them the book was about women working from the 1970s to 2000, a few began to talk about work experiences twenty or even thirty years before, incidents that lingered like an ache. I was just calling for an appointment; I hadn't even asked any questions. Sometimes they kept talking, spilling out memories like a fountain. I realized they had not been asked to think about their lives in this way in a long time, if ever. I learned to jot down the outlines of the passionate flood.

My second surprise was recognizing the role of organizations. We take them for granted today, but in the formative years of change, the 1970s and 1980s, organizations played a vital role for which they have received little or no credit. (The American Film Institute's Directors Workshop for Women in Hollywood was not, of course, an organization of this kind, but it was important to many women, and still is.) I am focusing here on the women's committees of the Writers, Directors, and Screen Actors guilds, and Women in Film.

When the guilds (and unions) were formed in the 1930s, the industry was already predominately male. Guilds had female members, but not many until the 1970s, when the women's committees within the guilds were formed. To their credit, the boards of the guilds supported these committees when the injustice of women's working situations was demonstrated. The committees often provided the only forums where women could talk with other women professionals; they became seed beds for change, and the women who started and worked inside them instigated change for other women.

Women in Film was another organization that, despite its famous annual Crystal Awards luncheon, comes in for criticism from some quarters as "the women who lunch." When viewed in the longer historical perspective gained from the interviews, particularly those during the 1970s and 1980s, Women in Film becomes extremely important. Only when one understands now how isolated women were from each other professionally, and from the natural contacts a woman needed to begin a career, which she could not fashion in any other way, does the merit of that organization become evident.

The women whose experiences appear in this book were selected for a number of different reasons: their professional profile in film or television; the type of work they do, which makes a big difference in a woman's experiences; and the decade they began working, because women's opportunities, trials, and perceptions in the 1970s differ sharply from their experiences in the 1990s.

The interviews show that a woman's own attitude toward herself, her work, and its possibilities for her are crucial. Optimism and persistence count as much as talent. Other aspects include the joy of work, the influence of films and television in our culture and, now, the world's culture, the challenges of being a mother in a tough profession, problems with self-promotion, changes in observations about the industry over time, and the differences between the ways men and women function in the world of work.

Women have struggled to gain admittance to this global arena, to survive and flourish in it with grit, determination, and humor. They fought for it, they're winning, and the size of the victory, depending as always on the size of the challenge, has to be admired.

This book cannot include all the women who played important roles in this history. If it had been up to me, the book would be much longer, plump with more accounts of many other women as well as many men. Some women I wanted to interview were, for various reasons, unavailable, but included here or not, they played a role in the evolution of women in Hollywood, and paved the way for those who followed. Nor does this chronicle try to encompass the variety of experiences of women all over the world, or the crucial and complex history of women in other media centers in the U.S., such as New York City. However, it does note the penetrating influence New Yorkers and others brought with them to Los Angeles.

I wish it had been possible to include more interviews with a variety of women who began their careers in the 1990s, but time and space intruded. That's reserved for a second volume, built upon the foundation of the first, perhaps. Some will ask why men's accounts do not make up at least fifty percent of these pages. During the last third of the twentieth century, men of course had experiences relating to women's increasing numbers and visibility in the workplace, but only a few are quoted here. I look to a second volume because male and female history related to working with each other seems to be different. Once again, it was a matter of time and page count, but it was also a matter of choice: men's experiences in film and television have been recounted roundly and frequently, while women's had not. So for this book, I stuck to women's stories. Finally, space also abbreviated fuller accounts of some women I interviewed at length. However, their experiences echo through the book for they provided rich and instructive background, and I am very grateful.[5]

Painful, hilarious or triumphant, women's experiences during this period are reports from the trenches. There is no better way to describe what happened in these decades than through the metaphor of war, where events tumbled forward as in a strategic battle.

Many mentioned the connection between their ability to dream and their ability to approach or do the work. In our youthful dreams, we can do anything; only later do we see the difficulties of turning dreams into deeds. But difficulties stopped no one in this book.

"My brother and I used to sit under the dining room table listening to the radio stories of Tom Mix and Gene Autry," says one television producer. "I was really young. I closed my eyes and saw myself riding across the range as Tom Mix's sidekick. I told my brother and he said, 'You can't do that because you're a girl.' That was the first time in my life I realized there was anything different about me from my brother. We could not accomplish the same dreams. I remember this so vividly. I didn't want to be a boy, but from that moment I was not going to be undercut by any guy."[6]

"It never occurred to me that I couldn't be anything I wanted," says one film producer, speaking of her youth. "You can call it drive or ambition or ego, but I was blessed with encouragement from my family. If I can dream it, I can do it."[7]

For the famous women and for the comparatively unknown—the generals and the foot soldiers—the battle continues. That fight, reported from many different angles, shows a side of Hollywood no one knows much about except the women who won or who lost, the women who lived through it.[8]

ℬEACHHEAD: THE 1970S

"An area on hostile shores seized and defended to secure further landing of troops and supplies."

—WEBSTER'S THIRD NEW INTERNATIONAL DICTIONARY

I

It felt like a beachhead. Certainly each woman fought and struggled hard in different ways in a kind of war. "Women working today have never been in battle, but we were," one woman, an entertainment lawyer, said. "I deserved war pay."

1973 might as well be a century ago, so much has changed.

Before 1973, employment want ads were separated into jobs for *men* and *women*. In some states women could not invest in stocks without their husband's written approval. Most women went to work in high heels and skirts. Society still frowned on women and men living together without benefit of a marriage license, "single parent" and "significant other" were unknown tags to define your personal setup, and baby boomers were a long way from retirement. Abortion was illegal and often dangerous. Face-lifts were something only movie stars did.

There were three networks—ABC, NBC, and CBS—and seven major film studios (Paramount, Warner Bros., 20th Century Fox, Columbia, United Artists, MGM, and Universal). A few independent producers turned out shows and films so constantly they resembled mini-studios. We went to movies in theaters and watched shows on television. If we missed a TV show, it was gone until rerun time. Video cassettes, VCRs, and personal computers did not exist; neither did CDs, laser discs, Home Box Office, CNN, or Blockbuster.

In January 1973, the Supreme Court made two momentous decisions: ruling on *Roe v. Wade*, the Court made first trimester abortions legal; it also declared in another case that job advertisements could not specify gender. Imagine scanning an ad for a mechanic that did not specify men only—or a cosmetics sales position not restricted to women. Reading those ads, imagination began to wander outside traditional limits for, perhaps, the first time.

That January, President Nixon started his second term in office as the Watergate shadow neared the White House. OPEC imposed an oil embargo and gas prices soared. The average annual salary for male college graduates was $19,000; for female graduates it was about $12,000. "Ego trip" was a new phrase; pet rocks, CB radios, and bell-bottom trousers were *in*. Mickey Mouse watches were out. As we waited in long lines for that high-priced gasoline, "Tie a Yellow Ribbon Round the Old Oak Tree" streamed from our car radios. Inching toward the gas pumps, we listened to the tumultuous national debates about women's rights under the law as the Equal Rights Amendment to the U.S. Constitution moved toward what seemed to be an assured ratification. That was not to be. However, the effects of the 1972 Equal Employment Opportunity Act prohibiting discrimination in the workplace were just beginning to be felt. The statute and its many amendments would open the doors of law, medicine, sports, and other fields to women and minorities. It would, through law, change attitudes and behavior as new attorneys, many of them women, began exploring what the statute meant in terms of gender and equal protection.

At home, we watched *The Carol Burnett Show*—skits, singers, acts, guests, jokes—which the ebullient Burnett had hosted since 1967. Or we watched powerful and popular TV specials like *The Autobiography of Miss Jane Pittman*, starring Cicely Tyson, the memoirs of a fictional 110-year-old slave reliving her life from the Civil War to civil rights, and Marlo Thomas and Friends in *Free to Be You and Me*, which had new music and a new message for women.

The women's movement was no longer the seismic news it had been in the late sixties, but the effects of Betty Friedan's book, *The Feminine Mystique*, and the lessons of the civil rights and antiwar protests had sunk deep into women's consciousness, stirring up trouble. Congresswoman from New York, Shirley Chisholm, was the first black American woman to run for president of the United States. *Ms.* magazine's Preview Issue appeared in January 1972 and sold out in eight days.[9] Letters to the editors in the next issue brought reactions to writer Jane O'Reilly's "The Housewife's Moment of Truth," the consciousness "click," which permanently entered the language. It was (is?) "The shock of recognition when a woman first realizes the injustice of her housewifely role in life ... The awakening has begun."[10] ("Why didn't you iron my shirts?" *Click.*) The label "bra-burners" turned into "women's libbers" when a woman said "chairperson" instead of "chairman." Women's libbers were "difficult women" and everyone seemed to know they were aggressive, shrill, and dissatisfied.

Feminists or not, most women working in film or television were secretaries, script supervisors, and publicists. Only a few were editors, like Dede Allen and Verna Fields; only a few were agents, like Sue Mengers. Though women had produced, directed, written, and acted in movies since 1910, by 1973 women did not *make* movies. They *acted* in them. Major female film stars did not have their own production companies. Women were not heads of networks. They did not run studios. From the 1920s to the 1970s, only a handful produced films. Almost no women directed, they did not run cameras or sound, they did not carry equipment or shout into walkie-talkies. No one said women couldn't do these things. It was assumed. It was the way things were. The business and art of entertainment reflected society, and the roles of women and men were sharply drawn.

Then the invasion, a reentry, really, began—first in television, then in motion pictures.

I DON'T WANT TO WATCH, I WANT TO PLAY

"Bitch, bitch, bitch."

Even though Joyce Perry was sick of all the negativity in the Writers Guild Women's Committee, she was on her way to the monthly meeting.

On that autumn day in 1972, Perry wasn't thinking about women's lib, George McGovern's campaign for president against Richard Nixon, the Paris Peace Talks to end the war in Vietnam, or the movie she'd seen last night, *The Godfather.* Perry was thinking about the new low in her life—she had credits as a television writer but she couldn't get a script off the ground. Working as a secretary in 1960, she'd written stories for the producers of *Laramie,* which had gotten her into the guild in 1962, and for the next ten years pretty and vivacious Perry had hammered and sawed her way into a television writing career—*Room 222, Mickey Spillane, Ironside,* and others. She had dreamed of being an actress but began writing as a way to augment her secretarial salary and support her two children.[11]

She parked her car on Beverly Boulevard in front of the dun-colored two-story Writers Guild building in West Hollywood. She marched to the guild's front door, flung it open, nodded at the receptionist, and climbed the stairs to the boardroom.

Inside, committee cochairs Noreen Stone and Jean Rouverol and about a dozen other women, including a Screen Actors Guild liaison to the committee, were already clustered at one end of the giant oval table. Sue Grafton, now a well-known mystery writer, was a member of the guild's committee until late 1973. The Women's Committee had been "the brainchild" of screenwriter Diana Gould in 1971. "She was from New York, a very strong feminist," says Stone.[12]

As usual, the committee was debating how women writers could get better access to prime-time television shows. Westerns and dramas like *Ironside* and *Marcus Welby, M.D.* dominated television. *The Mary Tyler*

Moore Show had started in September 1970, *All in the Family* in January 1971. A few women—Gail Parent, Ann Marcus, Joanna Lee, Lila Garrett, D. C. (Dorothy) Fontana, and M. (Margaret) Armen—worked steadily, but in general, networks and producers were reluctant to listen to women's ideas for episodes—their "pitches"—believing that women were not funny and therefore could not write great comedy, and that women couldn't write action shows or dramas either. "When the networks sent out invitations to members of the Writers Guild to come in and pitch ideas for the new season," says Jean Rouverol, "the only women I ever heard of to receive that notice were D. C. Fontana and M. Armen, because from their names they were assumed to be men."[13]

"I was working with Gene Roddenberry at MGM, had some westerns under my belt, and was trying to get other material sold," says Fontana. "I was always being told, 'Women can't write these things.' I changed my name from Dorothy to D. C. Fontana on a script I wrote on speculation, a spec script for *Ben Casey*. It landed with one of the producers, who liked it and wanted to meet the writer. He was really surprised to see me walk in. That name change really worked for me because when I submitted scripts or stories they'd at least get a reading because they didn't know if a man or a woman wrote it."[14]

"Sometimes you got in to pitch ideas because they wanted a female slant on a story," says Fontana, "which happened to me on *The Streets of San Francisco* when they wanted a woman writer to do a story about a policewoman. We were all used to pitching to a man or a couple of men. We had to look better for the pitch than the guys who were writers; they could get away with wearing a T-shirt or a casual top and jeans. Women had to look nicely dressed, and it helped if you had your perfume and makeup on. I never thought that was a drawback, though. I always thought if they're looking at you, they're paying attention and they're listening.

"See, the women's movement did open up possibilities for us. It made people aware that a woman writer walking in the door on an action show was not necessarily Miss Priss or Miss-Doesn't-Understand-Which-Way-a-Gun-Works, that we could write those stories. It did do that for us. But I don't think it's raised the glass ceiling very much, actually."[15]

At the monthly meeting of the WGA Women's Committee, members were asking, "How do we convince the industry that we've got real problems even being considered for these shows?"

"It's more than that," said another. "How do we convince *our own guild* that we're being discriminated against?"[16]

Joyce Perry had joined the committee because she'd felt "so very isolated."

"It's really hard to describe," she says, "how bleak and depressed I
felt. Deep down, most of the women in that room felt—I know I did—
that we weren't getting work because we weren't good enough."[17]

Other members of the committee joined it because as writers and as
people they needed new connections. "I was a widow. My children were
grown," Rouverol says. "I was looking for political usefulness. I found
it on that committee, and I miss the human quality in the relationships
we had there. We were not competitors. We had rapport and respect."[18]

The meeting wore on. Horror stories, gripes, and gossip shot around
the room. An ongoing committee skirmish swirled around the Guild, the
Viking Club, a men's social group, and Scandia, a restaurant on Sunset
Boulevard. At that time, the Viking Club met regularly at Scandia, offering members of the Writers Guild a free lunch if they gave blood
during the club's semiannual drives. One member, a lawyer, says the
club also distributed toys for children and donated food on holidays, and
that he had brought a female staff member to donate blood and she got
the free lunch. However, women WGA members who had donated blood
but were unescorted by a Viking Club regular had been excluded from
the free Scandia lunch.[19]

"What is it with them?" someone muttered at the women's committee
meeting. "Our blood's as good as theirs. Why can't we get lunch, too?"[20]

The Survey

Though the media hailed 1973 as the Year of the Woman, virtually
all theatrical films and television shows were produced, written, and
directed by men, the crews were men and the corporate structures were
overwhelmingly male. Television had been based in New York, but in
the 1970s, programming was moving to the West Coast, and that meant
jobs. In 1973, most women in "the industry" worked in television, and
it's in television that this story begins.

"I'd probably had one too many martinis," Perry recalls. "I came up
with the idea because I couldn't stand the frustration of all that bitching."
At the meeting of the Women's Committee, she said, "We know women
are underemployed but we haven't *proved* it. Let's get into the damned
guild files and do a survey. Let's get some statistics!"[21]

At the time, the Writers Guild had 2,978 members; 411 were women,
2,567 were men. The Women's Committee wanted to know how many

women had written how many episodes of how many prime time television shows in the 1972–73 season.

This kind of statistical survey had never been done before by any
guild. The executive director of the WGA, Michael Franklin, was reluctant to open up the files to the Women's Committee. According to
Perry, he said, "That's confidential! Those files have financial information
in them."[22] But Franklin was a friend of the Women's Committee and
saw the value of what they were proposing.

The committee had to get the permission of the board (or "council,"
as it was then called). John Furia[23] was president; Fay Kanin was vice
president. Board member Howard Rodman, a respected screenwriter,
was the only male member of the Women's Committee. "Howard was
always so great when it came to supporting women," says Noreen Stone.
"He really helped get the board to go along with our survey."[24]

The files were opened up and the committee began combing the credit
lists, marking how many women had written *Barnaby Jones* or *Adam 12*
in the 1973 season. "We got lucky," says Gloria Goldsmith, a member
of the committee. "A woman employee of the WGA helped us check the
records."[25]

"It felt like it took forever," Perry says. "We didn't have computers.
We used Howard's big, clunky calculator and legal pads and pencils.
After a while, we just couldn't believe what we were finding."[26]

"The numbers were mind-boggling," says Stone.[27]

"I remember sitting with Howard, Noreen Stone, and Jean Rouverol,"
says Perry, "and staring at those numbers." *The Mary Tyler Moore Show*
had the highest number of women writers of all the shows surveyed—
50 men and 25 women. To anyone today looking at the rest, *I Love Lucy*
(written by 116 men, 4 women) or *The Partridge Family* (69 men, 7
women) would look like a situation that cried for a lawsuit. But to Perry
and the statistics committee, these figures were "great successes! Those
were good!" Why good? "Because most shows had no women writers at
all; some had a half, denoting a woman working with a male partner.
We stared at the number of shows with no women writers that confirmed everything we'd ever said or imagined and we thought, This
cannot be true," says Perry. Hadn't one woman written *Love Story* (Esther Shapiro was the story executive) or *Medical Story*? "We had to
double-check our figures." They went back and counted again. They got
the same results. "At least we knew it wasn't that we weren't good
enough," says Perry.[28]

A survey of real figures attached to actual television shows charting
the underemployment of women in cold statistics caught everyone by
surprise. Noreen Stone and Jean Rouverol took the statistics report to

the guild's board. "We had copies for everyone," says Stone. "We told them that women were underemployed. They said, 'Nonsense.' We read them the statistics, they looked at the report, and they gasped. See, the biggest hurdle in the 1970s for our committee was to be taken seriously. The gents figured we were just a bunch of complaining women—until we brought in the statistics."[29]

Sue Cameron was the "Coast to Coast" columnist for the *Hollywood Reporter* on Sunset Boulevard in Hollywood, one of the two daily trade papers of industry news. Tichi Wilkerson-Miles had headed the *Reporter* since the death of her husband in 1963.

Cameron always looked younger than she was, and back then, she looked like a teenager. She had started the job three years earlier, just out of college, a brash neophyte who was not afraid to pick up the telephone and call anyone. She had become an experienced observer of the entertainment scene, but though her youth protected her from trepidation it gave her no awareness of the political or corporate turmoil she was about to stir up.

"The women's movement was just being felt in Los Angeles," Cameron says. "Women were angry about everything. I had become good friends with Marlo Thomas, and we talked constantly about the need of women to support other women. The situation in the entertainment industry was particularly bad. It was so unequal, something had to be done, but no one knew what. We had no evidence. We only had our anger."

Never revealed until now, Sue Cameron says: "In November 1973, Joyce Perry slipped me a copy of the WGA Committee's survey of the '72 to '73 shows. I was truly amazed. That survey shocked me. I printed it word for word without anyone's permission, just slapped it in there and sent it off."

"The day it appeared, November 27, a Tuesday," Cameron says, "our phones at the *Reporter* started ringing off the hook. They were calling Tichi and calling me—outraged men and women who were just as shocked as I'd been or producers trying to defend themselves, like a producer from *The Carol Burnett Show*, someone I love dearly. 'Oh, but we have a woman, we hired so and so.'

" 'Yeah,' I said, 'but what about the other eight positions?' "[30]

Perry had not given the survey results to Cameron lightly. It was risky; she had done it without the guild's permission, without in fact telling anyone except a trusted friend on the committee. She was scared. "What if people found out I'd made it public?" she wondered. "Would I work again?"

At seven o'clock on the morning after Cameron's column appeared,

Joyce Perry got a call. "It was from a very successful person in the business," says Perry. "She said to me, 'How dare you do this?' She was really in a rage."

Perry asked how the woman knew she had any connection to the report. She responded that she had called the guild and learned that Perry was a member of the committee.

Perry recalls, "I said something like, 'Well, I'm sorry but that's what we found in the files.' "

The woman yelled back, "For your information, we just hired a bunch of women writers! You'll never work here!"[31]

She was right. Perry never worked her shows.

"That survey was an explosion," Cameron says with a smile. "It woke up the city. Then people started being careful and the press releases I got tried to emphasize which woman they'd just hired on which project."[32]

The survey that *Hollywood Reporter* and *Variety* made public threw a bright light on a subterranean stream, an unspoken, unacknowledged reality. Those women writers who'd been complaining that "things aren't equal"? Well, they were right.

In December 1973, *WGAw News,* the monthly publication of the Writers Guild, reprinted the article by Bill Greely that had appeared in *Variety* in November. Like Cameron, Greely cited some of the more damning statistics, such as mega-producer Quinn Martin "with four action adventure series going for a total of 346 episodes, has used 345 male scripters and one female." Greely concluded, "The current rise in women execs at the networks and production companies is sure to eventually ease the apparent discrimination. But for now, primetime scripting is a man's game."[33]

Michael H. Franklin, executive director of the Writers Guild, fired the next shot when he sent a letter and a copy of the statistics to all the signatories to the guild, production companies, studios, and networks in April 1974. He pointed out what the statistics showed and asked eleven questions, such as "Have you ever communicated to a literary agent a preference for male writers over female?" and "Have you ever employed a woman as a writer? If not, why?" Reporting on Franklin's mass mailing, the *Hollywood Reporter*'s headline was, "WGA Scores Sexist Bias in Scripting." The article led with: "Possibility of wholesale violation of federal and state laws prohibiting sexual discrimination in hiring was raised Friday as the Writers Guild of America, West, revealed the results of an employment survey showing a disproportionately low use of distaff writers on current prime time television shows."[34] Franklin's letter was in perfect synchronization with the boiling times. Title VII had banned gender discrimination in education and Title IX in school sports. In New York, media women had filed and were continuing to file sex discrimination complaints with the EEOC.[35] Moreover, the one-sentence Equal Rights Amendment was lurching toward what looked like ratification by the states. Though few remembered its words, everyone knew what it would mean—discrimination in any form would be unconstitutional.

In Hollywood, the testy problem of "what to do about the women" now hung in the air. Something had to be done. The women were restless. The industry came up with the first motions they hoped would quiet everyone down. But like the crack in the dike, a few changes slowly led to others, which continued into the mid-1980s when the trend became well established.

Women in Casting Are Promoted to Vice President

"I'm really not sure why they made me vice president," Ethel Winant says. "I guess someone in corporate decided they wanted a woman, which probably had to do with the women's movement."[36]

In the spring of 1973, Ethel Winant was promoted to vice president of talent and casting at CBS. Winant's striking face blends ease and determination. She is one of the most respected people in television, and in 1973 was the highest-ranking woman at CBS.

"I don't think [CBS] paid much attention to women before or after I was a vice president," says Winant. "At the top levels of the network, the corporate people probably said, 'What are we doing about women?' " Winant did not think the question had been raised before. "When they looked around," she says, "they had to say, 'Not much.' " In fact, there were no women officers at CBS.

"Today," Winant says, " 'vice president' is just a title. Anyone is a vice president because he says he is. Back in 1973, CBS didn't have that many VPs because the position was elected by the board of directors."

Winant was in Ireland making a movie when she got a call urging her to return.

"CBS never asked me if I wanted to be a vice president," she says. "They surprised me by announcing my new title, an incredible honor, at the affiliates meeting. The affiliates liked me. I worked well with them, and in those days the network courted affiliates. It never occurred to me that I'd be a vice president. I wasn't interested in climbing the corporate ladder. I just wanted to make shows.

"Afterwards, I said to them, 'What if I'd said no?' That had not occurred to them. 'It's really nice,' I said, 'but you wouldn't have treated a man like that. You'd have negotiated a new salary, you'd have made a deal.' It seemed to me that on the few occasions somebody was going to be made a vice president, the guys usually had a lot of meetings."

Winant said to the CBS brass, "Nobody has ever mentioned money to me."

"You're sure?" they asked.

"Yeah, I'm sure, nobody's ever discussed it."

"Of course, there must be something."

A call was placed to New York. "Ethel feels that she should be recompensed as the men are when they get to be vice president." The word came back from New York that they would look into it.

"I could have gone out and said it was all a fraud," Winant says, "that I'm not really a vice president, nobody's paying me, but that wouldn't have looked very good. They just hadn't thought about it." In the end, Winant says, "they did give me a little more money."[37]

The women who got these early vice presidencies were usually in talent and casting, not production. Casting was one area of the industry where companies thought it was safe to put women, and where they thrived.

The Men Kept Swearing and Begging My Pardon

In 1973, Renée Valente moved up to vice president of talent at Columbia/ScreenGems, which was a major supplier of television shows to the networks. Four years before, Jackie Cooper, vice president of television production for Columbia, asked Valente, already working for the studio in New York, to come out to California. She did not want to do that.

Valente's manner is alert and crisply direct. Like most producers, she appears to be a woman well acquainted with battle. "I didn't want to come out here because California at that time did not want women producers, and everybody knew that," Valente says. She had already produced a short-lived television show, *Hawk* (1966), for Burt Reynolds.

"It was a strange time," she says. "When I got here, I was the only woman in the meetings and the men kept swearing and begging my pardon. Finally I said, 'Listen, screw this, you can't walk on eggs like this. I'm one of you. I'm here. You have to say what you think.' The men were uncomfortable. This transition period shocked them, and that's what it was, a transition." Valente says she asked one executive, "What is it that you don't like about women in business?"

"Women in business," he answered.

"The key to working then with men," says Valente, "was understanding what they were going through. In a way, they were like kids, and to help them get through it you had to find a way to show them that you were not out to take their jobs. I could see the insecurity in their eyes. They were trying to get used to hearing a woman say something of merit.

"When I was head of development at Columbia, a nice young man had been hired to sell our pilots. I couldn't get him to do anything. 'Listen, have I done anything to upset you?' I asked him. 'I'm development. You have to come to me. Have I created a problem for you?'

"He said, 'No, but you could. When something happens that offends women, they cry.'

" 'Have you ever seen me cry?'

" 'No, but you could. Also, women use their sexuality.'

" 'Have I used my sexuality?'

" 'No, but you could.'

"A few years ago, we had lunch together and laughed about it."[38]

The promotions to vice president were as sensational (or as oddball or as craven, depending on your view) as the times. Kate Millett's *Sexual Politics*, Marjorie Rosen's *Popcorn Venus*, Germaine Greer's *The Female Eunuch*, Robin Morgan's *Sisterhood Is Powerful*, and Susan Brownmiller's *Against Our Will* helped ignite the social understanding of what was occurring. Movies became targets. In late 1972 at a screening of *A Clockwork Orange* in New York, poet Sandra Hochman "flung herself in front of the screen, arms outstretched in a cross silhouette, protesting a picture that was being called a masterpiece of its time." Her message was passionate and brief. "I am Sandra Hochman. I am a poet. I think that all of you people getting off on this male violence are sick."[39] You couldn't go to a dinner party on either coast where the subject of *Clockwork Orange* or *Straw Dogs* (another controversial film considered by some to be antifeminist) vs. the context of women's issues did not come up. By 1975, it would be *The Stepford Wives*. "Violence against women" and "women as victims" had been stock story lines practically since *Beowulf* but the early 1970s transformed them into new and sizzling symbols. Movies and TV shows raised a whole new set of social responsibilities when it came to the use and portrayal of women and minorities.

The protests in the early 1970s were direct offshoots of the civil rights movement and the Vietnam War demonstrations. Speeches, marches, rallies, and mini-demonstrations broke out in every major city to draw attention to the Equal Rights Amendment and to the exclusion of women as professors, lawyers, doctors. Women insisted that language perpetuated sexism—firemen should be called firefighters, policemen should be police officers or the even more radical, often ridiculed "police person." All the areas from which women had been virtually barred were under siege—even sports. Who can forget Billie Jean King vs. Bobby Riggs in September 1973? Billed as "The Battle of the Sexes," the game squarely set one contest of the 1970s: could a woman beat a man at a "man's game"?

Women were closely examining and deploring the depiction of women on TV and in film. Attorney Florynce Kennedy, founder of the National Feminist Party, said publicly, "Alcoholics love alcohol and junkies love dope and brainwashed female addicts crave media poison in the same way. But it is criminal to keep feeding the habit."[40] Kennedy felt, as many did, that the ways women were portrayed gave women a totally false model of behavior—in fact, addicted them to such behaviors. Steve Mills, a vice president of ABC Entertainment, felt the networks should lead society: "Break down barriers, update the system. Cast women in strong roles."[41] One feminist group objected to segments of *The Dean Martin Show*, carried picket signs, and chanted, "Dino's the real ding-a-ling," as they marched from Buena Vista Park to the NBC studios in Burbank protesting sexist stereotypes. The Ding-a-Ling Sisters, a regular feature on his show, were dropped.

A handmaiden to depiction was women's lack of access to work in the business, which was seen as a white male club. Joanne Woodward said, "If the door is opening, it is not opening enough." One of the few female studio VPs, Monique James, in casting at Universal, said, ". . . the number of women who are producers and directors . . . You can count them on the fingers of one hand . . . A woman has to be ten times better." MCA Inc. president Sid Sheinberg was also quoted: "I feel strongly that we must be very forceful in moving women into executive capacities, whether or not some of our men like it . . . The dam is long since broken. The waters are flowing."

"Long since?" he was asked.

"Well, no," he replied, "short since."[42]

Brianne Murphy was running a news camera in the early 1970s. "This is what it was like," she says. "Mayor Yorty was signing our press passes, and he looks up, sees me in the line, sees the camera, and says, 'Shouldn't you be home making cookies or something?' "[43]

Where the Help Came From

The rocky launch of women's reentry into the industry in the 1970s was built on nothing, really, except that inside the turbulence, women had the energy of the excluded. Their support came from the nature of the times and the help of some of the men in the business.

The women's movement was restructuring the landscape judicially, legislatively, economically, socially. The winds of the movement—"the largest social movement in the history of the United States, and probably in the world,"[44] the "first in history to have been planned and executed by women"[45]—blew from east to west by the 1970s, sweeping women in Hollywood into, first, the television industry.

I call it the beachhead. No one could stop women from gaining shelter in studios or a foothold in agencies despite the withering fire. The first women were promoted to vice president, and by the 1980s, as Ethel Winant says, "everyone was a vice president,"[46] as if the title had been declassified or demoted, not an unknown occurrence when women enter a field.

Though the entertainment industry was an all-male structure like nearly every other industry in the country at that time, many men provided a climate that incubated women's work. Men hired them, advised them, promoted them. Almost every woman in this book names at least one man who helped make their careers possible—Norman Lear, James Brooks, Steven Bochco, Steven Spielberg, Roger Corman, Lindsay Law, David Susskind, Allan Burns, Warren Beatty, Barry Diller, Jeffrey Katzenberg, Fred Silverman, David Begelman, Michael Eisner, Peter Guber, Frank Wells, Ned Tannen, Grant Tinker, Mike Medavoy are mentioned as well as others in these pages. When a man hired a woman from the new, untested group in the 1970s and 1980s, it went against all the usual hiring codes—work with the people you trust and have worked with before. The only reason a woman began working in the 1970s was that some guy gave her a chance.

An incubator maintains a favorable environment for hatching or developing—in this case talent, ideas, and drive. Around Hollywood in 1973, a few corporate and creative environments, primarily in television, actually nurtured women's careers: Tandem Productions, MTM Enterprises, Tomorrow Entertainment, New World Pictures, and the West Coast division of ABC. These "incubators," owned and run by men, gave dozens of women their start. The 1970s were the golden age of incubators. By the 1980s, the chicks had hatched.

The Companies Hiring Women

"Tomorrow Entertainment was a lovely company," says Fay Kanin, a distinguished writer of plays, films, and movies for television.[47]

Its West Coast production offices were at 9200 Sunset Boulevard, on the cusp between West Hollywood and Beverly Hills, conveniently near agents, and practically next door to the landmark Cock and Bull restaurant.

Tomorrow was formed by Thomas W. Moore, who had headed ABC through the 1960s, and Roger Gimbel, a respected and well-liked producer. They produced feature films and Emmy Award–winning movies for television that tried to raise the bar of quality, including *A War of Children* and Truman Capote's *The Glass House* (both in 1972); *I Heard the Owl Call My Name* (1973); *Tell Me Where It Hurts, The Autobiography of Miss Jane Pittman,* and *I Love You, Goodbye* (all in 1974); *In This House of Brede* (1975) and Maya Angelou's *I Know Why the Caged Bird Sings* (1979).

Tomorrow hired women from the outset, and most of them had long careers. Marcy Carsey, Nancy Malone, and Marian Rees were among those who landed on staff there in the early 1970s; Fay Kanin and Diana Gould were among the writers and producers.

Through Tomorrow Entertainment, Gould's script, *I Love You, Goodbye*, found a home at ABC, where Deanne Barkley, another early VP, was in charge of movies for television.

"It was one of the first television movies to come out of the women's movement," says Gould about her script. "I'd read an article in *Life* magazine about a woman who had left her husband and children. That's what I pitched. I don't think you could get that movie made today or at any point in between. It was not rewritten, though it was toned down a bit. I was quite radical and the script I wrote was not quite the movie that was made. Nonetheless, it was unusual for its time."[48]

Gould grew up in New York City. Though her father was in a business unconnected to movies or television, some of his childhood friends had become blacklisted writers. "Knowing those writers made it possible, I think, for me to become a writer," says Gould. "I had examples. Even though none were women, I saw people who were writers."

Right out of college, Gould sold her first script when a well-known television star became interested in it. "I got one lump payment and then X amount per week to do rewrites with the director," says Gould. "The television star wanted to work with a foreign director, Agnes Varda, but it didn't happen. Instead, a man from another country was hired to direct. I knew the script was incipiently feminist, the story of a woman's journey from dependency to autonomy, the obstacles she overcame, her relationship with her mother. These were some of the elements the television star responded to in the script that was going to be her first feature.

"I was flown to New York for rewrites with the director but I soon realized he wanted changes that were antithetical to the script. I was very young and I didn't know anything in any area. He asked me to do things I couldn't do . . . One Sunday morning I went to see him to try to explain to him what my script was about and started telling him about where the movie had come from, my relationship with my mother and how I had envisioned the script. I was very emotional.

"The next day I was fired for 'being too close to the material.' He hired a male friend and in a matter of weeks they rewrote the script from beginning to end. They changed the name of every character, changed what the movie was about. It became a guy's story. The girl was reduced to one more kooky, crazy girl. When the movie came out I went to see it in the theater and I was so upset I ran out in tears. I wasn't able to watch the movie for a long time. It was so painful. My debut into the movie business, very telling both as a woman and as a writer."

Undaunted, Gould created the WGA Women's Committee in a Hollywood still untouched by the women's movement, and kept writing. She clearly saw that being a woman could be an obstacle, "but I never let it stop me or define me and I was not going to be victimized by it."[49] She had already sold three more scripts by the time Tomorrow bought *I Love You, Goodbye*.

■   ■   ■

Marcy Carsey's substantial career as a television executive and producer began at Tomorrow. "When I moved from New York to California around 1971," Carsey says, "I heard that Roger Gimbel was starting this production company called Tomorrow Entertainment, and that he had a room full of scripts and books piling up. I also heard he had nobody except one wonderful assistant to pore through this stuff.

"To get the job with Roger Gimbel, I pestered him unmercifully. I just kept calling him for an interview. A couple of times he had to cancel after I got there, but I kept on calling. I took some material home and wrote synopses and evaluations for him to read because you ought to prove that you can do it."

Gimbel called Carsey and asked if she could just come in and help out for one day. She recalls, "I went in and it stretched to three years. It was my first real job in Los Angeles. I started as a reader and became story editor. What a lovely time."

Carsey always seemed to know where she was heading, a drive seasoned by a jubilant spirit and eager enthusiasm. "The quality that helped me the most," Carsey says, "was courage. No question about it. Balls. It hurt me, too. But it mostly helped me. I wasn't afraid of being fired. I wasn't afraid of what my boss thought of me, of what my peers thought of me, of making a mistake."[50]

■ ■ ■

By 1970, Nancy Malone was at the top of her performing career, with extensive Broadway theater, film, and television credits. Her face was well known from her starring television roles in *Naked City* and *The Long Hot Summer* on ABC. Tom Moore, the president of ABC, was a gentleman with courtly manners and a southern accent. Malone often saw him at ABC parties but on this night, they were having dinner at LaScala on Little Santa Monica in Beverly Hills. She was complaining to him about the image of women in the media and the "trashy, awful dialogue" actresses had to learn.

"I just can't wrap my mouth around 'How-do-you-want-your-coffee-darling?' once more," she told him, referring to the dialogue in the two television movies she'd just completed.

Moore suggested she learn to write and produce.

"Why would I do that?" she asked. "I'm employed. I do very well."

"Then don't complain," Moore said.[51]

Moore was leaving ABC to form his own production company, Tomorrow Entertainment, which General Electric was financing. He said to Malone that if she wanted to learn something else, he'd offer her a job in his new company. She would read scripts and learn how to produce.[52]

She couldn't see where Tomorrow Entertainment would lead her. "Acting isn't something you drop and then pick up again; you have to work while you're hot. And I was hot. If Tomorrow failed in a couple of years, where would I be? It was very risky."

Malone accepted a role in a play, *The Catonsville Nine*, then a movie with Burt Reynolds, *The Man Who Loved Cat Dancing*. But she and Moore continued to talk about Tomorrow Entertainment, and at one point, she recalls, he asked her, "What's going to happen in another twenty years, Nancy? Where will you be, what will you be doing? You won't be acting, because older actresses are not in demand."

"That question stopped me cold," Malone says. "I'd seen actresses getting to the age of forty-five, having nowhere to go except Bloomingdale's or regional theater. I had a mother to look out for. I was head of the family. What would happen if I couldn't cut it?"

In a complete career reversal, Malone joined Tomorrow Entertainment on the low-level staff position, director of motion pictures. One of the first scripts that came her way was called *American Graffiti*.

"I read it and begged Tom and the board to do it, but they turned it down. I will never know why."[53]

· · ·

"Tandem, the production company where I'd worked for fifteen years as head of development, had just fired me," Marian Rees says, "...so 1973 was a major transitional time for me, and a dark time. I had been at Tandem through its beginnings, its successes with *All in the Family* and all the inherent problems of sudden success."[54]

Rees, a serious, thoughtful woman with silver hair, can sit quietly in a meeting for an hour and then, in a low voice, draw all the scattered chatter into one statement that points to a path of action.

"Roger Gimbel at Tomorrow was looking for someone," Rees recalls. "I went over as a corporate development executive. I stayed for about four years. Then G. E. put *The General Electric Theater* back on CBS, and I was in charge of that. I hadn't been working there very long when I came across an article about a women's consciousness-raising group. We sent it to Fay Kanin, who is a wonderful writer and a friend, and that movie for television became history."[55]

The film was *Tell Me Where It Hurts*. It was about a housewife who becomes increasingly dissatisfied with her lot in life. She organizes a discussion group among her close friends that changes all their lives.

"I don't remember who gave me this tiny little article," Fay Kanin says.[56] "She thought there might be a movie in it. I embraced it. It dealt with some women in the East, an unlikely group of housewives and women blue-collar workers who lived in the same neighborhood and just started talking together really candidly. I wanted to find out more about them. I went east and asked a friend, a teacher in Queens, if she'd contact some of the women in the article who were in a parent/teacher association."

The teacher got the women together at her house. "I want to ask you some questions," Kanin said to them, "because I want to write about you. You may recognize yourselves in some of the attitudes or expressions in what I turn out, but I will never use your names. I want what I write to be true." She asked them about their feelings toward their husbands, whether they wanted to work or if they'd given up work, and she asked them about sex.

Kanin recalls, "At first they were very diffident. 'Be honest and speak up,' I said. They did not. But then suddenly someone spoke, then another, and soon the floodgates opened. I don't think they'd ever said these things to anyone before, not even to other women. My God, the stuff that came out, the feelings, the anxieties, the fears. I loved writing the script because the material was so great."

In *Tell Me Where It Hurts*, Maureen Stapleton played the leading woman, Paul Sorvino, her husband. Paul Bogart directed, and Roger Gimbel produced. "Marian Rees had a lot to do with that production, too," Kanin says. "I think of her as one of the producers."

Amazing as it seems now, that movie was the first time a story had been made about women talking together, sharing important feelings. "I think men appreciated it," Kanin says, "because it did not put them down. I screened it at my home and invited all my friends. I thought the men in the audience might resent the women saying some very open things about their relationships with men, but they didn't. Their reaction was quite positive."

In 1974 Kanin says she was astonished to win two Emmys for *Tell Me Where It Hurts* (Best Writing in Drama-Original Teleplay and Writer of the Year). "I never got over it. That movie was not a big activist piece. It was about ordinary women who have to work out their relationships with men and with each other. I've always said, though, timing is very important. The women's movement was stirring that year and the timing was just right for that movie."[57]

Fay Kanin has written scripts and plays since the 1940s—some with her husband, Michael, and some alone. She is lively without being showy, a really good sport, a writer who was part of the old and is part of the new Hollywood, quite a feat.

▪   ▪   ▪

Other women working at this time were not on staff; they were freelance. One such woman chose an area where no woman had ever been accepted—cinematography.

My Camera Weighs Less Than a Kid

The glass ceiling, says the *Oxford Dictionary of New Words*, "is an unofficial or unacknowledged barrier to personal achievement in the workplace." It adds that it is "something which constitutes a barrier to ascent but which cannot be seen because it is made of glass."

In 1973, "glass ceiling" was a genteel term for the cement walls confronting minorities or the steel door Brianne Murphy had been pounding on for a dozen years: Local 659, the cameraman's union in Los Angeles. Each time Murphy beat on the door, the union boss yelled, "You'll get in over my dead body!"

"You know what?" Murphy says. "He died and I got in."[58] She was the first woman to be admitted to the camera union as a director of photography.

Murphy had started working in B movies in the 1950s doing practically anything, then learning camera. She was also the only woman shooting news film for NBC in southern California (her first news job was during the Watts riots in Los Angeles). She recalls a telling incident when she was running a news camera, trying to get footage of a gubernatorial candidate leaving a press conference. Outside the press club, the politician was shaking hands with people right and left as he approached Murphy. Murphy says, "He gets up to me and puts out his hand and realizes that I've got both hands on a camera. He said, 'Oh, excuse me, I didn't realize you were a woman.' I didn't want to talk to him, I'm trying to get a nice shot of him. He said, 'That camera must be heavy, what does it weigh?' I said, 'I don't know, less than a kid.' I was trying to get him to keep going, you know, but by that time the other network cameras had turned on him talking to me, and that's what was on the news that night, 'Less than a kid.' "

In 1975, Murphy wanted to show that she was a good union member. She went to the next meeting, which was held in the musicians' hall on Vine Street in Hollywood.

"As I came in, the crowd grew totally silent and parted right down the middle of the hall," says Murphy. "It was so terrible. I felt like a leper, someone with a disease you can catch. They gave me lots of room on both sides. I was the only woman in the hall and there must have been a hundred men there who knew me, but they weren't going to talk to me. No one said anything. I was mortified. I felt afraid, but I wasn't going to let on. Usually I never felt uncomfortable being the only woman. But that was really horrible."

By 1980, Murphy was admitted to the American Society of Cinematographers, an honor society, after prolonged and vigorous debate among the members. In 1983, she was voted onto the executive board. "I'm no longer the only woman in the ASC, and I just hope those women can hang in there."[59]

Just getting into the local is still tough. "If you're working and people like your work, you figure work will arrive," says Amy Halpern, gaffer and lighting cameraman. "But you would be wrong to think that. Most people assumed I'm in the union and I should have been in it fifteen years ago. Every time I had enough days, some of them were disallowed. I've trained about thirty guys who are in. This work deselects women. Part of [the problem] is that when guys see you carrying equipment, it still doesn't compute for them. When I started, I thought it was exotic to be the only girl on a set, fun but unnatural to work with all these guys. I thought I'd better enjoy it because in fifteen minutes there'll be lots of women. That was in 1974. I'm still one of the very few women doing this. The show I'm on now has a best boy grip named Shipley. She's the first woman best boy grip I've ever met. You almost never meet a woman grip."[60]

When Brianne Murphy first got into the local union, everyone told her she would never get a job assignment from them—ever. One day, NBC called the union. "We're doing a story on breast cancer and we'd like very much to have a woman. Do you by any chance happen to have one?"

"As a matter of fact . . ." And they sent Murphy out. In the beginning, Murphy says, her only assurance was getting hired on Jewish holidays when the number of potential candidates dwindled. They'd go down the list of available names and stop at hers. "Murphy, get him." Amy Halpern recalls, "Brianne told me years ago she was absolutely convinced most of the first jobs she got were because she has a low voice and people assumed her name was Brian."[61]

Murphy says she called the harassment and the difficulties on the job "hard times" or "different opinions."

"Just about every night, I went home hurting from the slurs I'd get. Over and over again I realized that men just did not want to accept a woman in that position.

"Once a male friend of mine on a camera crew said, 'Bri, you've got to realize it's very hard for us to go home and tell our wives that we work for a woman because we've convinced them that we're top dogs and we do a very difficult, complicated job. Our wives would never understand it.'"

Murphy is convinced that attitude was a key reason she had so many problems. If a woman could do the job as a director of photography—a position in filmmaking that has always had a technical and artistic mystique—then what was so special or unique about the men's ability to do that job?

Still, Murphy always liked working with the guys. "There was a lot of really filthy language that I'd have to pretend not to hear, and some of the men wore T-shirts with dirty words on them. After I got more secure, I'd send someone out to get them another T-shirt and ask them to change. They did, but at first I had to pretend I couldn't read."

As word got around that the local had accepted her, some of the old-timers would approach her and ask, with some curiosity, "Do you have your own light meters?"

"What could they have been thinking?" Murphy laughs. "That I borrowed a few when I got a job? It was insane. I had so much to learn from them but they never talked to me about what I needed to know. It was always, 'Do you know how to read a light meter?' It's like saying to someone whose job is driving, 'Does your car have tires?' "[62]

2

WE DON'T WANT ANYTHING ITSY-POO

It didn't seem so in 1973, but television as a medium was quite limited. There were the networks, ABC, NBC, CBS, big-city "flagship" stations that produced for their networks, and "educational" television, the Public Broadcasting System. That was it.

The prime-time dramatic shows on television were *Columbo, Cannon, The Waltons, The Streets of San Francisco, Kojak.*[63] The top comedies were *All in the Family, Maude, The Mary Tyler Moore Show, M*A*S*H, Sanford and Son.*[64] No hour-long dramas were headed or "carried by" women, but women played important roles in a few situation comedies, which, at the time, made a crazy sort of cultural sense: drama is serious, comedy is light and fun, ergo, male characters headed drama, women and minorities carried comedies.

On NBC, Dan Rowan and Dick Martin's *Laugh In* (produced by George Schlatter) was a completely original, often sidesplitting comedy/variety show that made many performers famous, including Goldie Hawn and Lily Tomlin. It ended a stupendous five-year run in May 1973. Two months earlier, on March 16th, while members of the WGA Women's Committee hunched around a table, marking down how many women had written how many shows, Lily Tomlin and her characters—Edith Ann, Ernestine, Judith Beasley, and Bobbie-Jeanine, cocktail organist extraordinaire, many mined from her Detroit childhood—made her first two specials on CBS.

Everyone in television has painful or hilarious stories about battles with the networks around the content of their shows, which derive from performers', producers', or writers' experiences. In the 1970s, it became clear that women had different experiences to relate and these began surfacing in comedy written by Jane Wagner, Lily Tomlin, Treva Silverman, Susan Harris, Gail Parent, Susan Silver, Barbara Corday, Barbara Avedon, Linda Bloodworth, and Mary Kay Place.

Lily Tomlin says that her 1973 television specials were pilots. "But I didn't relate to that. I didn't think about designing a show that could be replicated every week, or even how to make a show the network would like. I just tried to make something that *we* would like and be proud of."

The network insisted she have a producing partner and assigned Bob Precht, Ed Sullivan's son-in-law. "You can attribute their insistence to my never having produced a television show like it before," Tomlin says. "Bob was a nice guy but we weren't really in sync—it was a style thing. He was much more an establishment guy, which was why they wanted me to pair with him."[65]

Her guests on the show were Richard Pryor and Richard Crenna. Crenna is a witty, fun-loving, reliable actor who at the time had starred in and survived *The Real McCoys* and other sitcoms. Pryor, one of the foremost comedians of his time, sailed into mainstream media with a ribald African-American brand of humor that transformed American comedy. He was terribly funny and extremely provocative. Many at the network considered him and his views objectionable if not downright dangerous. Tomlin virtually guaranteed his good behavior.

The Peabody Award–winning writer Jane Wagner had collaborated with Lily Tomlin since 1971. "Jane wrote a piece for this special about a soul food diner—I ran the diner, Richard Pryor was a junkie on methadone," says Tomlin.[66] "[Pryor] and I wrote another called 'War Games'; he was much more responsible for it than I was. In 1973, the Vietnam War was ending but was still fresh. In this piece, Mrs. Beasley, my Middle American housewife, goes out to call her son to supper and finds there's a war going on in her backyard, you know, rocket launchers, grenades going off. Mrs. Beasley yells to her child, 'Come on, leg or no leg, supper's on the table.'

"It didn't dawn on me that I'd be stopped at anything, but I found out the 'soul food' piece was taken out of the script before it even got to CBS. We filmed 'War Games' but the network insisted it couldn't go on the air. The special was okay but it wasn't what I thought it could have been. But that special got such a high rating, I guess the network didn't know what to do with me. So they gave me another special, which aired in November of 1973, *Lily*. I told them I'd only do it if I personally didn't have to have a producing partner. We wanted the show to be more biting, more reality-based.

"On it, my guest was Alan Alda, the star of *M*A*S*H*. We put 'Soul Food' back in and filmed 'War Games' again. By this time, I was educated to the network system. I wanted both pieces, but we ended by trading 'War Games' for 'Soul Food.' Fred Silverman, head of CBS programming, called it a three-hundred-sixty-thousand-dollar jerk-off.[67] The network wasn't going to air it but they finally did."[68] It won an Emmy for Best Comedy/Variety and a second one for Best Writing.[69]

I Was the "Half" in the Statistics

Tandem and MTM were prolific production companies that gave many women writers, producers, and directors their start in the 1970s.

Tandem Productions, founded and run by Norman Lear and Bud Yorkin, liked timely, controversial material that took chances—*What's Happening, Sanford and Son, All in the Family, Diff'rent Strokes. Maude*, a spin-off from *All in the Family*, starred Bea Arthur as an outspoken liberal who was on her fourth husband.[70]

"Our idea for *Maude*," says Irma Kalish, "was to take a relevant topic and see how we could apply it to that show because the Bea Arthur character, Maude, was exactly the kind of liberal woman who might have an abortion.'[71]

Tandem was in the Metromedia Building on Sunset Boulevard. "We went over there and broached the idea to them," says Irma. "It was seized upon and elaborated into a two-parter where she then persuaded her husband to have a vasectomy."

The second episode was written by Susan Harris.[72] Maude became the first prime-time TV character to have an abortion.

"There was no firestorm that I recall around this episode," Irma says, "though the Population Institute jumped on it and gave us an award. The Supreme Court was deliberating on the case of *Roe v. Wade* or had just come down with its *Roe v. Wade* ruling, which may have inspired our idea. Many newspaper stories were written about the subject and that's where we often went for inspiration, knowing, of course, that Norman Lear liked controversial stories on his shows. It's strange, but today I don't think you could do a show like it without a great deal of brouhaha. If we took one of the *Friends* characters and wrote an episode about her having an abortion, the hue and cry would be outlandish. Yet today, we're supposedly more liberal and liberated."

Short and energetic, Irma Kalish cracks jokes often, with a stony face, followed by a delightful smile. She and her husband, Austin "Rocky" Kalish, have written over three hundred scripts for comedy series: *Family Affair, My Three Sons*, and *The Bob Newhart Show*, among others. Irma served as story editor for *Family Affair* and *The Brian Keith Show*, and in 1979 began producing *The Facts of Life*.

"The first statistics the Writers Guild put out," she says, "listed thirty-nine and a half men writing *The Brian Keith Show* and one-half woman. I was the one-half!" She says there's no question that writing with a male partner made it easier to sell scripts and to produce, particularly in the 1970s. But it's wrong to think that either partner "carries" the other, she says. They may work differently, splitting the tasks, but they do work jointly.

"If I think a joke is funny and Rocky doesn't," Kalish says, "once we get past my crying about it, we really try to think of a third way we're both happy with. It's not a compromise, it's better than either of the ideas we each had before."

They had been writing for *All in the Family*, attuned to coming up with story ideas that were relevant and topical. "Norman Lear was a great guy for that," she says. In 1973, the Kalish team wrote the *All in the Family* episodes about Gloria's molestation ("Gloria the Victim") and Edith's breast cancer ("Edith's Christmas Story").

"For the show with Gloria," says Irma, "we wanted to punch home the idea that a person who is the victim of molestation is also the victim of the aftermath. In those days, it was a very common belief that women who wore short skirts were inviting trouble. That's what we wanted to get into. We were also intrigued by having Archie (Carroll O'Connor's role) and his son-in-law Mike Stivic (Rob Reiner) switch roles when they learn of Gloria's ordeal. Very much a law-and-order establishment guy, Archie did not want to report it to the police, he wanted to bury it, whereas Mike, Gloria's husband, who hated the police and was always antiestablishment, wanted to report it and bring it out in the open. Sally Struthers, who played Gloria, was upset that, as she put it, Gloria was not actually penetrated, or raped. It was my opinion that she wanted us to take it further."

Irma Kalish was nominated twice to run for president of the Writers Guild. During her first campaign, in the 1990s, she got a death threat over the phone. "That's where I first felt discrimination, that the Writers Guild was still an old boys' organization, that some could not stand a woman president. I lost by four votes, which is still referred to as 'the four fucking votes.'" (In 2001, Victoria Riskin was elected president of the Guild.)

In the 1960s in television, most women worked as secretaries. "But there was Selma Diamond," Irma says, "a tough writer and a wonderful woman. She worked with men and held her own. She'd kid around and say, 'Hey, guys, let's knock off work and go look for some broads.' There was also Madelyn Davis, who created *Lucy*. But you didn't say, 'Boy, there are a lot of women writers out here,' because there weren't. I was working with Rocky, protected to a degree, but it took a while for me to be treated as a writer on my own merit. At first, I was Rocky's wife, and I suspect many people thought I was just doing the typing. When we got on staff, people realized I was a person in my own right.

"I was almost always the only woman in the room with quite a few men who treated me like one of the boys, throwing four-letter words around. Once, and I remember this vividly, a secretary came in the room and one of the men actually said, 'Okay, guys, hold it, there's a lady in the room.' I'd been there all along! But you know, I was willing to be one of the guys just to stay in the industry, to be an acknowledged presence in it."[73]

See? We Have This Woman

Gail Parent says she came from "the curse of the happy family," and always saw things as funny.

"My parents were actually not depressed people. He was the prince, a Wharton School graduate on Wall Street, and she was the showgirl because she'd been Miss Atlantic City. There was confidence in my family. I mean, you either laugh or you cry, and the people who made it to Hollywood in comedy writing were the ones who laughed. For instance, Arnie Rosen, the head writer on *The Carol Burnett Show*, once said that when he was young he asked his mother for a goldfish and she said, 'Just what I need, another mouth to feed.'

"Norman Lear called me," says Parent. "He wanted to do a soap opera with a funny slant. I brought in the cover of *Life* magazine which had a male factory worker on it. We said these are the people we're going to use, and that's where we started. I created most of those characters, Mary Hartman, her husband, the slut sister and the father. I have a treatment that says 'The Life and Times of Mary Hartman,' and that's crossed out and in Norman's handwriting it says 'Mary Hartman, Mary Hartman.' He said it would be funny if her mother keeps calling her by her full name."

Parent doesn't look like a comedian, she seems demure and sensible. She got her start as a television comedy writer in 1967 on *The Carol Burnett Show*. She says of those days, "There weren't a lot of women working. There were ten variety shows on the air and approximately ten writers on each show. I was the only woman. Out of a hundred. The first show I was up for—*The Smothers Brothers*—they told my agent they didn't want a woman working on the staff. At the time, I thought, 'Okay, that's a good reason.' I was not enlightened. I was really young.

Years later I produced their show, so they're forgiven. Back then they thought if a woman invaded the writers' room, they wouldn't be free to speak and be dirty. They'd be inhibited.

"I had a male partner, Kenny Solms, and he is the reason I worked on *Carol Burnett*. Kenny was pushing to get an agent, get hired. I wouldn't have had the guts to get an agent. A woman comedy writer was very unusual but I didn't have the battle getting in because at the time it was very valuable to have a man as a partner. Kenny was the key, even though we did the material equally and the male-female combination was perfect from the creative perspective."

Parent felt privileged to work on *The Carol Burnett Show*. "CBS used to drag me out for publicity, saying, 'See? We have a woman,' like I was this totally rare creature. I felt terrific. Later, I realized that I should not be thrilled to be the only woman on the staff. Actually, it wasn't a thrill, it was more like *amazing*. I'd come from this really traditional family, so writing that show made no sense at all. On top of that, we were writing for stars I'd seen on television. Half the time, I was speechless to see Lucille Ball and all these other big names. The show was not expected to be a hit and neither were we. We stayed five years."

And, while writing for Carol Burnett, Parent wrote for Tandem and MTM, and the best-seller *Sheila Levine Is Dead and Living in New York*.

By the mid-1980s, she had her first half-hour sitcom staff position, on *Golden Girls*. "For three years, it was eleven men and me," says Parent. "They needed a woman. It was probably the one time in my life they actually sought out a female. They'd do a line like a football term, 'Ma, go deep,' and I'd say, 'No, women are not going to understand that.' But they were very good. Mitchell Horowitz came up with the line, 'I'm not feeling well, I'm expecting my little friend.' And Bea [Arthur] says, 'You haven't had your little friend in years.' That's a twenty-eight-year-old man doing a menopause cycle. At that point, I knew you don't need men or women, you just need good writers."[74]

■   ■   ■

Norman Lear was central to television and to women's opportunities during this period. Anyone, male or female, who was not working with Tandem did everything they could to make that happen. Ann Marcus's career began on the *New York Daily News*, "the first copy 'boy' with a D cup," as she says.[75] In the 1960s, she wrote sitcoms, sometimes partnered with her husband, Ellis (*Gentle Ben, Please Don't Eat the Daisies*). By 1972, she was head writer on *Search for Tomorrow*. But she wanted to work with Norman Lear. Lear was in the early stages of developing what was to become the groundbreaking comedy satire *Mary Hartman, Mary Hartman.*

"Lear had gone through just about every comedy writer in town for his blue-collar soap, a real cutting-edge kind of thing with very controversial stories that would also satirize how TV was destroying America. I don't think he thought I'd be able to hack it, but I saw him after a long line of people who'd told him he could never get it off the ground. For instance, in the first week of the show, he wanted Mary Hartman and her husband to live near a family of five who are murdered along with their goats and chickens, and he also wanted her father to be arrested for flashing. I'm listening as Norman reels off his ideas, absolutely rapt.

"He asked me what I thought. I said, 'What a wonderful idea!' I just lied through my teeth."[76]

She says it was the hardest job she ever had, five shows every week. She was given material already created by Gail Parent, the original characters and the *Mary Hartman* concept of dramatizing the everyday lives of a dysfunctional auto worker's family. "One," Marcus recalls, "was a hilarious and defining scene between the housewife and a door-to-door salesman that totally captured the essence of the Mary Hartman character.

"Working with Norman," she says, "was very difficult because at first he was very chauvinistic. I can swear with the best of them, but the language there was really bawdy and rough. Remember, this was a daily show, two-and-a-half hours of comedy a week. We'd spend hours in story conferences with Norman—he loved the show and he wanted to contribute. After one of these marathon sessions, I was in the conference room gathering up my papers, and Norman was in the bathroom. He came out and said, 'Annie, you were so terrific today I could fuck you.' I thought that was one of the nicest compliments I'd ever been paid by a boss. Now, today you wouldn't think of saying something like that.[77]

"But it was a different time then. Norman changed, too, and became one of the major backers of the women's movement, giving thousands of dollars to the Equal Rights Amendment battle. He came from the same place my husband came from, both wonderful guys, moral, ethical, sweet, good fathers, but they felt their careers came first and that the woman stands behind the man."

Marcus says she enjoyed working in story conferences as the only woman. "I used my being a woman. In the early seventies, I was hired to write a TV movie for Aaron Spelling and Len Goldberg. You entered the office on one level and went down three or four steps. They had liked what I'd written. I was coming in for notes. I entered on the upper level, did a Loretta Young thing, and I went 'Dah, dah, dah, dum, dah, dah, dum,' dancing down the stairs, and swirled around. I loved being flirtatious, which was terribly antifeminist, I'm sure, but it was such fun."[78]

Everyone Bitched About the Male Execs

"I was probably the only person in this town who wasn't dying to work for Norman Lear's company," says Fern Field, an exuberant woman whose eclectic interests have taken her into many different kinds of jobs.

Rod Parker, the executive producer of *Maude*, hired Field as a secretary. The only thing she knew about television she'd learned in a course at Hunter College.

"One day Rod came back from a meeting with Norman," says Field. "He told me he wanted me to do some research because they were going to do a sitcom about handicapped people. I thought that was the worst idea I'd heard." Parker told Field to find him a factory with an assembly line that employed people who were handicapped.

"In the course of this research," says Field, "I met some people at a committee on the disabled in the South Bay who wanted to do an informational tape to be used when they spoke to prospective employers about the benefits of hiring people with disabilities. By this time, Tandem was on hiatus and I had time on my hands. I agreed to put something down on paper. 'We'll get a friend of mine who has one leg to play tennis with Norman Lear,' I said shamelessly, 'and we'll get John Denver to do the music, and we'll go for an Academy Award.' The light went on in their eyes—showbiz.

"They did not leave one stone unturned." Field was back working as an assistant on *Maude* when they called her about applying for a government grant; they needed a proposal and a budget. Field enlisted the help of Jim Belcher, a comedy writer who had written industrial films. She says, "He put the budget together and we both wrote the proposal and sent it off to the government, which incredibly gave the little outfit in South Bay the money—forty thousand dollars. Fortunately by that time, at Tandem, we were into hiatus again."

Field produced *A Different Approach* in 1978, and it was nominated for an Academy Award. "Everybody in South Bay said, 'This is easy, let's make another film!' I said, 'No, guys, you don't understand. This is very unusual.' Anyway, the film won awards and it broke some ground by really helping to change attitudes about disabilities on a worldwide basis. It was one of those magic projects where everything fell into place."

When it screened at the Directors Guild, Field was no longer working for Tandem, but Norman Lear saw it and offered her a development position, director of off-network projects.

"I didn't know what development meant," says Field. "I found out it meant sitting in an office saying no to mostly bad projects. I hated it with a passion. I was housed in Century City, which immediately sucks all the creative energy out of you. Then there was all the office politics, so different from the politics in production." Field recalls that one day as Lear was leaving her office, he said, "Do you think this company is chauvinistic?"

"I thought, 'Hmmm.' Everybody always bitched about the male executives—it was an old boys' and young boys' network. 'Norman, let me put it to you this way. You're very comfortable with women, but not all the executives here are.' I thought that was diplomatic.

"In production at the studio," Field explains, "it was better for women. In corporate quarters, it was all guys. I might have added to Norman that the guys don't pal around with women, that if they went to lunch, they went with each other. It probably wasn't their intention to exclude women, but we were not part of the club. I think Norman was getting feedback from women in corporate that the company was chauvinistic. In production, it was different."

Many, like Field, say that by the late 1970s, it was an advantage to be a woman. "But in the early seventies, women were not getting any directing work," says Field. "However, Norman Lear was hiring women before it was fashionable—Joan Micklin Silver, who was directing episodes on *All That Glitters*, and Joan Darling."[79]

At Least I Can Earn a Living

In 1973, actress Joan Darling, who had played on and off Broadway and had been a series regular on *Owen Marshall, Counselor at Law*, went to see Norman Lear to pitch a ninety-minute movie on the life of Golda Meir.

"I wanted it to go from the time she was sixteen until she retired—starring me!" says Darling. After she finished her passionate pitch, Lear said, "Joan, how would you like to be a director?"

"I'm not a director," she replied.

"I think that's what you really are." Lear pressed her into duty and gave her the scripts of the pilot for *Mary Hartman, Mary Hartman.*

"There was no place back then for a woman even to think about being a director," says Darling. "If Norman hadn't thought it up, it would not have happened. I had no directing ambitions, there were no role models. Meta Rosenberg, who was producing *The Rockford Files*, directed an episode once in a while. Elaine May [*A New Leaf, Mikey and Nicky*] was such a complete auteur, I didn't think of her as just a director, I thought of her as a painter doing a whole painting.

"The one thing I knew I could do was direct actors," Darling says, "which I had done before. I told Norman I couldn't be a journeyman director delivering someone else's concept, but I could deliver my own and if he liked it, I'd try to direct it. We took eight weeks to cast. We showed him the two half-hours as a stage presentation, which was the only direction I knew anything about—stage. He liked it. He hired someone to do the camera work and set up the show. All through that day, I was thinking, 'My God, I'm not a director, how do I get out of here?'

"At the end of the day, Norman said to me, 'What do you think of this camera work?' I told him that I didn't know anything about it but it felt awful to me. He said, 'It is awful. I want you to do the cameras.' I protested that I didn't know anything about directing with cameras. 'I think you do,' he said."

Darling directed the pilots. She has focus and passion. She listens deeply. "When I finished, Lear said, 'I want you to have your own crack at editing because that's where you're really going to learn about directing.' He left me alone to edit it.

For a while, it seemed that *Mary Hartman* would never see air time. "Norman couldn't sell that show," Darling says. "He took it to all the networks and the comments he got were amazing. Fred Silverman at CBS said it was the best-directed, best-acted, best-written show he'd seen and it would never in a million years see the light of day as a television show."[80] Darling's agents started sending out the *Mary Hartman* pilot as her directing sample.

She was amazed when they called to tell her that Grant Tinker wanted her to direct an episode for MTM. "'At last, I can earn a living,' I thought. I also believed that since no women were directing, if I did this well enough I could establish the idea in people's minds that women *could* direct. I knew if I focused on the story I was trying to tell," Darling says, "I'd be able to direct the show."

As she drove to the set that first morning, she had to pull her car off the road and stop. "I said to myself, 'Joan, you lived through your childhood, you can do this.' My childhood was horrible. We were neglected. My father died when I was very young and my mother went to bed for six years. I had two brothers and a sister. I was very frightened all the time because I felt I didn't know anything but I was busy doing it as if I knew it.

"I came to camera-blocking day, a rehearsal. I knew exactly how I wanted to shoot it but I didn't know who to give the camera shots to. I was absolutely terrified. I really didn't want to make a fool of myself."

The next MTM episode show she directed was "Chuckles Bites the Dust." For that show, Darling was the first woman to be nominated for an Emmy for Outstanding Direction.[81]

"About a year later," says Darling, "my mother told me, 'You were lucky your father died, because if he hadn't, you'd probably have ended up stuck'—her exact words—'living in Newton, married to a lawyer with four children.' She was describing her life to me."[82]

After that year, Darling got a lot of work as a director. Others remember her from this period as one of very few who was proving women could direct. Some still say of her today, "This is the kind of script Joan Darling directed," or "Joan Darling helped me when I was starting out," or "Back then, there was Joan Darling." By 1976, she was directing her first feature film, *First Love*.

She's Going to Make It After All

Powerhouse MTM Enterprises, a company owned by Mary Tyler Moore and her husband, Grant Tinker, an influential television producer, created *The Mary Tyler Moore Show* in 1970. MTM produced alone or in partnership many other shows—*The Betty White Show, The Bob Newhart Show, Hill Street Blues, Remington Steele, Rhoda, St. Elsewhere*. Marlo Thomas's show, *That Girl* (1966–71), has been called a prototype for the independent woman on 1970s television, though the girl, Ann Marie, was still deferring to Daddy as other female characters on TV deferred to husbands or boyfriends.[83]

The Mary Tyler Moore Show ran from 1970 to 1977, a wildly popular, literate sitcom that aired on CBS on Saturday nights. Mary Richards (Mary Tyler Moore) was a *single* career woman, a rarity on the small screen. She worked as an assistant producer in the news department of a Minneapolis television station. She was an ambitious, independent woman, ready for marriage, but not bending every effort to make it happen. Mary's neighbor and friend, Rhoda Morgenstern, played by Valerie Harper, was also single, thirtysomething, a department store window dresser. Unlike Mary, Rhoda desperately wanted to be married.

"The female characters on *Rhoda* and *Mary*," says Valerie Harper, "were created and written as multifaceted human beings with all kinds of talents, frailties, quirks, and virtues. The women were not written as foils or props for men. The producers, Jim Brooks and Allan Burns, were hilarious and truthful, and they made a concerted effort to include, nurture, and support female comedy writers, like Treva Silverman, Charlotte Brown, Gail Parent, and others."

Valerie Harper began her career as a dancer, working in a chorus, which taught her perseverance. She developed a flair for comedy while working in the famed Second City improvisational theater group. "For years," Harper says, "the Second City cast was made up of four to five guys and 'the girl'—Barbara Harris was 'the girl,' Elaine May, Melinda Dillon, Mina Kolb, and later on, I was 'the girl.' That readily accepted configuration was weird—as if the world was divided up that way, five men to every one woman, as if women weren't over half the world's population. I think it came from a myth that women weren't funny or interesting except sexually.

"I remember going on retreat as a young Catholic girl," Harper says, "and listening to the father at St. Adens Church in Jersey City as he talked about Saint Paul or Saint Thomas Aquinas, one of those two equally nonfeminist thinkers. The father said, 'You have to know your proper relationship to God. God is the man's head and the man is the woman's head.'

"I raised my hand. 'Excuse me, Father, are you saying that men created God?'

" 'Oh, no, you pray to God, it's your God, but in the family your husband is your master. You serve God through serving your husband.' "

Harper says, "That was the end of the Catholic church for me. I quit. I had a big click."[84]

The problem at the outset of *The Mary Tyler Moore Show* was that they couldn't cast the role of Rhoda. "We were at our wit's end," says Ethel Winant, then head of CBS casting. "We saw hundreds of women and nobody was right."[85] Finally, she saw Harper in an improv group from New York at a theater on Melrose. "I told my secretary to call the theater and get a phone number for this Valerie Harper." But the theater management didn't know anything about the acts. Winant checked all the guilds, SAG, AFTRA, Equity. No Valerie Harper.

A week later, Winant's secretary came into the office carrying an envelope. "Is this who you're looking for?" The envelope had come from the man who had put the show together. He had enclosed the pictures and resumes of the people who had been in the company.

Valerie Harper read for Winant that afternoon. "She told me she was Italian," says Winant, "and I told her 'Just don't mention that. Everyone's nervous. If nobody asks you if you're Jewish, don't volunteer that you're Italian.' I took her over to read for the producers of *Mary*.

" 'My God, it's Rhoda!' they said.

"That was such a happy show," Winant says. "I loved that show so."[86]

Gail Parent says she can pinpoint the moment women were incorporated into the comedy sitcom world. "I was at MTM when a woman came in—maybe it was Charlotte Brown—and suggested a story about how much it cost to be a bridesmaid. Allan Burns and Jim Brooks and the rest of the staff looked at each other and realized they would have never come up with that story. That moment is still so vivid in my mind, and that's when I date the doors really opening for women. I give those guys real credit, too, for realizing that comedy could also come from experiences only women have."[87]

"There were oceans of comedy material," Harper says, "that men didn't have automatic access to. During the first season, Jim Brooks told me, 'We don't come up with that nail polish and panty hose stuff.' The attitude on that show was never 'Oh, God, now we have to do a scene for the girls.' The comedy was not based on sexuality or breast size. I still see shows that put a woman in a scene just to imply something sexual. The MTM shows were about human beings being funny with specific attention to the reality of women's lives. *Mary* did something in comedy that was really different: it showed women as distinct individuals who didn't defer to Daddy or hubby. I think that's part of its popularity and its staying power. Treva Silverman, one of the writers, was very important in the early days of *Mary* in terms of the female sensibility she brought to the writers' room."

In a famous episode, Mary asked her boss, Lou Grant, for a pay raise. "No," said Lou.

"Mr. Grant, why am I getting less?"

"Because you're a woman."

"That was good writing," Harper says, "a major click. The Lou Grant character was being honest, so were the writers, and it was funny to boot!"[88]

Mary did defer to her boss and always called him "Mr. Grant." The men on the show called him "Lou."

I've Never Worked with a Woman Before

Charlotte Brown began her writing career with MTM. "Episodic comedy grew out of variety shows, which created this template of the typical sitcom writer. They were the guys with the cardigan sweaters and pinkie rings," says Brown. "They stayed up all hours, smoking cigars with the other guys, swearing and writing—an all-male domain. I date the end of the stereotype to *The Mary Tyler Moore Show*, which changed that old image by hiring and developing women comedy writers."[89]

Charlotte Brown was celebrating in 1973. She'd just finished her first successful year as a freelance writer on *The Partridge Family*, *All In The Family*, and *The Mary Tyler Moore Show*. The year before, she'd been living leanly off unemployment, submitting spec scripts to comedians. She also wrote a spec *Mary* episode. "I had no idea about how to do it," Brown says. "The idea of an outline never occurred to me. With his typical enthusiasm, Jim said, 'Gosh, it's the worst thing I ever read!' But it showed a good sense of comedy."

"You need to learn plot construction," he told her.

Most producers were reluctant to hire a woman because they'd never done it before. Brown says, "A lovely man, Ed Feldman, producer of *The Doris Day Show*, liked my sample *Mary* script, but said, 'Gee, I don't know, I've never worked with a woman before.' We heard that a lot. 'No, I don't think it will work,' he went on. 'I've got all these guys around here.' But I kept bugging him until he finally said, 'Okay, okay, I'll give you a chance.' I got that work because I just kept wearing him down. Then Jim Brooks bought a *Mary* script of mine, and it was filmed."

At the Writers Guild annual meeting in 1973, Brown met Susan Harris (who in just a few years would create *Soap* and then *The Golden Girls*). "Susan and I began the same year—she was over at the Tandem track (*All in the Family*, *Sanford & Son*) and Treva and I were on the MTM track. I don't know how Susan and I got in touch, but there were so few women then, we heard about one another and met in person at that meeting. She was a single mother, and she'd started out as a secretary. The meeting began but Susan and I were whispering, comparing notes, practically giggling about how much money we made that year. Compared to now, it was nothing, but we felt it was terrific. We'd started at scale, about fifteen hundred per script."[90]

A Woman Isn't as Funny

Treva Silverman wrote the first script of *The Mary Tyler Moore Show* after the pilot, then went on staff as executive story consultant. She is one of the reasons MTM received such high marks in the Writers Guild survey.

She says of her promotion to executive story consultant, "Jim Brooks and Allan Burns told me, 'We need another head. We don't care what your title is, whatever you like.' So there were the four of us, Jim Brooks,

Allan Burns, Ed Weinberger, and me. We were pretty much accountable for everything from story ideas to writing to rewriting and casting. My title was pretty arbitrary. It meant I couldn't say 'they' anymore. I became 'they.'"

To Silverman, *The Mary Tyler Moore Show* traces the women's movement. For example, at the beginning, Rhoda was self-deprecating; her image of herself needed improvement. "Her jokes were insults about herself, how unwantable she was. That decreased as she became more confident, and then a year or two into the series, she had a sort of breakthrough.

"During that same time, in my own life," Silverman says, "I was close to an agent in New York and I'd see him from time to time. After one lunch, he said, 'Congratulations!'

" 'What for?'

" 'I've known you for years and this is the first time we've had an entire lunch and you didn't do any self put-downs.'

"I really believed I had to be better than the people around me," Silverman says, "because it was so rare for a woman to be hired, and no one seemed to think women could be funny. Just before MTM, when I was writing with a male partner, we were up for a pilot. We met with the executive and he asked, 'How do you split the work up?'

"My partner said, 'Treva does the story and—'

"The executive interrupted, 'And you do the comedy?' There was no convincing him I could be funny, too. Another time I was up for something alone. The producer called my agent. 'Tell her we don't want anything itsy-poo. We don't like itsy-poo.'

" 'Tell him I don't either,' I said."

Producers usually said to her agent, "We feel uncomfortable around a woman," or "A woman isn't as funny," or "Don't even bother. No women." That's why Silverman felt she had to be better than anyone else.

"In the early 1970s," she says, "I found that because I was a woman in charge I was expected to hire women. So I started to, and I found that at that time a lot of women weren't prepared. They hadn't worked as long as the men had. It was very difficult because here I was, like a beacon to show that woman were getting ahead, that I could open doors, and trillions of women could troop in. And I wanted to open those doors. But what kept me up nights was rewriting them and rewriting them and rewriting them. I was caught between a philosophical place and a do-I-really-want-to-rewrite-someone-so-another-woman-can-have-her-name-on-this-script? I let practicality win out, but I never let practicality win out to the extent that a woman new to the work had to be as good as a guy. I'd give them more of a chance, but if there was more than a 20 percent difference, I just wouldn't bother. I felt shitty about it, but not that shitty. This was not part of the pressure of being one of the first women to do 'X,' it was my own self-pressure, and it also came from women expecting things from me.

"It's impossible for me to separate the women's movement from what was happening in the business," Silverman says. "Even though I felt isolated in a profession dominated by men, before the mid-1970s I'd never once thought of women writers or men writers, only of good writers and bad writers. Then, suddenly, on *Mary Tyler Moore*, when we started hiring women (and other shows did, too) a subtle and sometimes not-so-subtle change occurred in the stories."

For instance, Silverman wrote "The Lou and Edie Story" episode for *The Mary Tyler Moore Show* in 1973, for which she won an Emmy. The story reflects the decade.

Lou Grant's wife, Edie, is leaving him because she's never experienced being on her own. "She kept saying to him, 'It's not about you, Lou.' The Ed Asner character, Lou, is totally confused by her desire to leave," Silverman relates, "but *at that time* women were examining their lives and where they wanted their lives to go. Instead of taking it for granted that she, Edie—or we—would do this or that, we were asking, 'Do I have to? Is this what I want?' That was very seventies. It was an absolutely wonderful time."[91]

"I wasn't aware in those days that we represented a historical change," Charlotte Brown says, "or that we were at some historic crossroads. I was just thrilled to be working. I didn't know until later that MTM was a safe but very idealistic place to be."[92]

On May 28, 1974, the number of Emmys won by women dramatically increased for their work behind the camera. Treva Silverman and Fay Kanin both took home two Emmys. Silverman won Best Writing in Comedy, and Writer of the Year—Series for "The Lou and Edie Story" of *The Mary Tyler Moore Show*; Kanin won Best Writing in a Drama–Original Teleplay, and Writer of the Year–Special for *Tell Me Where It Hurts*. Lily Tomlin's special, *Lily*, won Best Writing in Comedy–Variety and for Outstanding Comedy–Variety of the year. Joanna Lee, one of the few women writing hour-long drama, won an Emmy for an episode of *The Waltons*, "The Thanksgiving Story." Marlo Thomas and Carola Tart won Outstanding Children's Special, *Free to Be You and Me*. And, a story about a woman, *The Autobiography of Miss Jane Pittman*, won the Emmy for Outstanding Special and eight other awards, including one for its star, Cicely Tyson.

3

SHE'S YOUNG, SHE'S PRETTY, AND—SHE'S A PRODUCER!

What was possible in the early 1970s in television for talented and extremely determined women was almost impossible in motion pictures. Moreover, movies and television were separated by a deep divide, and no one skipped freely from one to the other and back again.

From the 1920s to the 1970s, few women stars produced or directed, but between 1912 and 1920, about twenty companies were controlled by female stars. Mabel Normand, Chaplin's first leading lady, directed some of his first films at Keystone; Gale Henry wrote, directed, produced, and costarred in two-reel shorts for Century Comedies; Mary Pickford (the only woman involved in the establishment of the Academy of Motion Picture Arts and Sciences in 1927) headed her own production company, as did Nell Shipman, Lois Weber, Dorothy Davenport (often credited as Mrs. Wallace Reid), and Norma Talmadge.[93]

In 1971, Elaine May, with Mike Nichols in the comedy team Nichols and May, never hung back. She produced and directed her first movie, *A New Leaf,* followed by *The Heartbreak Kid* in 1972.[94] Barbra Streisand began producing in 1976, followed by other producing performers like Jane Fonda, Lee Grant, Goldie Hawn, and Sally Field.[95]

The films nominated for Best Picture for the 1973 Academy Awards were *Cries and Whispers, The Sting, The Exorcist, A Touch of Class,* and *American Graffiti.* Verna Fields and Marcia Lucas were nominated for editing *American Graffiti.* No women were nominated for writing that year. One woman produced a major box office hit—Julia Phillips, with her husband, Michael, and their partner, Tony Bill. *The Sting* won seven Oscars, including Best Picture, Best Screenplay, and Best Director. Julia Phillips was the first woman ever to produce a film that won the Oscar for Best Picture.

If You Want a Job that Sucks, Try Pioneer

Julia Phillips says she felt excluded when she was producing *The Sting*. "I was pregnant. That's one way I felt excluded from that film." She worked on *The Sting* all through her pregnancy. After her daughter was born, she worked on *Taxi Driver* and *Close Encounters of the Third Kind*. "I didn't mind being off the set, frankly," Phillips says, "because *The Sting* was a big love story being done on sets and stages. Our biggest decision had been committing to director George Roy Hill. There was no question that anyone was going to have any kind of real input after that. David Ward had written a fucking perfect script but he wasn't allowed on the set either. My husband, Michael, and our partner, Tony Bill, were pretty laid-back types and a lot of times I pushed them, which made them hate me."[96]

Julia and Michael Phillips had no credentials when they took their first project, a script by David Ward titled *Steelyard Blues*, to Tony Bill, who did know his way around. He and they cofounded Bill/Phillips Productions in 1971. *Steelyard Blues* starred Jane Fonda and Donald Sutherland. Meanwhile, David Ward had written another script, *The Sting*, which the Bill and Phillips team took to Universal, where Richard Zanuck and his partner, David Brown, had a deal. *The Sting* would be Zanuck-Brown's first Best Picture Oscar. Two years later, they produced *The Sugarland Express* and *Jaws* with Steven Spielberg..

"If you want a job that sucks, try pioneer," Phillips once said. "There is nothing to recommend it . . . Nobody believes in you, you're the first of your kind, you have an idea whose time hasn't come yet. It's a terrible job."[97]

She recounts an exchange with Ray Stark that reveals how many women were generally perceived at the time. Stark had just produced *The Way We Were* with Barbra Streisand and Robert Redford; he was also a major behind-the-scenes power at Columbia Pictures. Phillips was new to the business, but she had produced one film and was producing *The Sting* at Universal with the Zanuck-Brown company. Stark offered her a job as a reader, "something to do in my spare time while I sat at the beach with my baby. 'I have this movie coming out, it's called *The Sting*. I have points. I expect to make zillions. . . . I expect to make other movies, some great movies.' *My* movies, not some dick love story."[98]

Julia grew up in the fifties in New York, the child of Russian-Jewish parents. Her mother gave up a career as a radio writer when Julia was born. "I inherited low self-esteem," she says. "I guess that's what you'd call it now."[99] She married Michael Phillips, got a job as a story editor for Paramount's First Artists (Barbra Streisand, Sidney Poitier, and Paul Newman's production company), where she met agents Freddie Fields and David Begelman. Phillips described Begelman as a "gambler and an embezzler" but also gave him credit for his "high-rolling instincts" that helped her keep two film productions together.[100] When she and Michael formed their partnership with Tony Bill, Julia asked First Artists for a leave of absence from her job to go off and produce *Steelyard Blues.* She was fired. "They gave me the job as a way up and when I used it, as any man would, they got mad," she says.[101]

Ten months after *The Sting* won its seven Oscars, Julia and her husband divorced. Phillips went on producing. She became friendly with Nessa Hyams at Columbia Pictures. Though a few women in the studios' corporate hierarchies were vice presidents, none were in production until November 1973 when David Begelman, then president of Columbia Pictures, named Warner Bros. casting executive Nessa Hyams vice president of creative affairs, a newly created (and, in this case, some say politically inspired) post at Columbia Pictures.[102]

Some thought the promotion put Hyams in competition with Rosilyn Heller, the only other ranking woman at Columbia in production. Phillips wrote, "Nessa (concert empresario Sol Hurok's granddaughter) looks down her nose at Roz because Roz came up off the street. Roz feels the same way about Nessa because she's always been handed the things Roz has to struggle for. They put me right in the middle."[103] Phillips decided to talk to Heller about *Taxi Driver* and to Nessa about the other movie she wanted to make, *Fear of Flying.*[104] To an extent during this period, Phillips and her ex-husband split up the production chores; he concentrated on *Taxi Driver* and she on *Close Encounters.*[105] Both films were made for Columbia.

"I didn't have any problem with Julia at all," says Rosilyn Heller, who worked on both films. "She and I were totally on the same wavelength. We were very close friends. Everybody thinks that drugs made Julia excitable or erratic, but she was always like that. She had very little patience and she was really smart. What people forget is how extremely frustrating it was for women then because we knew we were smart and in many ways we weren't getting anywhere. We were dead in the water and had to fight for everything. At Columbia, it was absolutely fine with Peter [Guber] if women were smart—that's why he hired us."[106]

Heller describes *Taxi Driver* as a battle to get it made. "It had a 'down and dirty' budget but we still had to fight because nobody else believed in it." Heller went to bat for Julia and Michael with Guber and Begelman. "After a point," Heller recalls, "Michael [Phillips] did more on *Taxi Driver* because Julia was doing everything on *Close Encounters.* We made the deal in 1973 for *Taxi* but production was postponed until 1975. We got the budget increased a little because by then, Marty [Scorsese] was a becoming a hot director and so was Steven Spielberg—*Jaws* was out. Every budget was bigger."[107]

Close Encounters of the Third Kind had come from an idea of Steven Spielberg's, a friend Phillips had known for several years. She sold it to Columbia Pictures and fought for three years for bigger budgets as the special effects escalated. By the summer of 1976, as *Taxi* won the Palme d'Or at Cannes, Julia was on location with *Close Encounters*. Budget and other battles continued, not unusual; the pressure on Julia was intense. By this time, Columbia was in trouble and facing bankruptcy. Julia Phillips inveigled and bullied and got tougher. "She paid a big price," said producer Howard Rosenman. Facing the same problems all producers face, when she said the same things a man would have said, the men at the studio called her "a woman and a bitch." Rosenman said, "I'm sure it was very painful to her. She medicated her pain."[108]

Phillips's use of drugs, a subject she writes candidly about in her book, *You'll Never Eat Lunch in This Town Again*, was increasingly evident during this time. When she cut an important merchandising meeting, David Begelman, Steven Speilberg, and her former husband fired her. Speilberg brought Michael Phillips in as the new producer of *Close Encounters*.[109]

"It was crushing," Julia says of that time. "If I had been ten years older, I wouldn't have been crushed. I was only thirty-three. I was an outsider. I didn't grow up in the business and didn't know its ups and downs. There were so many things I didn't understand."

"I didn't understand how people could abscond with credit for something somebody else did. To me, that was embarrassing. My parents, for all their intellectualism and cynicism and coolness, were actually good people with a strong moral code." Most important, she did not understand that a man who'd produced an Oscar-winning picture might be forgiven for using some drugs and for missing a meeting. She would not be.

Phillips made an easy target. She acknowledges that in many ways she "did it to herself." She did not understand the double standard at work, and she did not produce again for almost ten years. "But there are guys who do it to themselves over and over," she says, "who hadn't produced the work I had, and they're protected." She wanted to know where the old girls' club was. It wasn't there at all yet. It was far too early.

"As the years have gone by and it's post all that . . . Michael thinks he produced *Taxi Driver*," says Phillips. "He was on the set for seven weeks.

The movie took four years from beginning to end. I line-produced *Close Encounters of the Third Kind*, which was certainly equivalent to both *The Sting* and *Taxi Driver*. It was an equal exchange. I don't understand the desire among them to erase me. I really had very little option but to write a book because they did try to erase me. I think that there's a great deal of revisionism in these guys' heads about who did what, and over the years they've redone the stories for themselves so that they actually believe them. I'm not supposed to take it personally, but it feels personal, because their objective is to minimize my effect as much as possible. I don't think they got in a room and said, 'Let's bury her.' Rather, I think it's sort of a male instinct . . . which goes back to that thing about credit, who did what. Now I'm sorry I made all those people feel so good about themselves. That was one of the things I was so good at. I was the only woman there with all those guys. I tried to make every meeting or each day shooting as much fun [as I could], I tried to make it easy for them, I tried to make people know I understood the contribution they were making, without being a kiss-ass. I was like this cute peppery girl who could be one of the boys, not swearing or being gross, just like hang with them."[110]

"I was a young publicist, just starting out at Columbia," says Cheryl Boone Isaacs, "when I met the ever-famous Julia Phillips. I saw her often because she was the producer. I was a little dippy, one of the many publicists working on the *Close Encounters* junket. What I remember is her grandness. She was fabulous. You'd see this woman out there, a true producer, and she was so confident. I thought she was great."[111]

"No matter who's on your team, producing is hard," says Phillips.[112] She was a flamboyant, eccentric, dramatic dynamo with an unusual mind and an unusual way of doing things. There have been exotic or unstable producers before, but clearly, Phillips was dealing with more than her drug habit, which was bad enough; she was young, a single mother, surrounded by the same producing pressures, learning on the job, as many do, and going where almost no woman had gone before. That she produced four terrific films, three of them classics, is a miracle.

※　※　※

Almost no other women were producing—certainly not on the scale of Julia Phillips's films. But there were a few others working in feature films in the early 1970s.

Editor Verna Fields was one of the best known and best liked. Executives and filmmakers sought her guidance for everything—cinematography, editing, casting. She edited *American Graffiti*, *Paper Moon*, and later *Jaws*, for which she won the Oscar. Internally, at Universal, she was credited as "the savior of Steven Spielberg" on *Jaws* and for that reason, among others, was made the first female VP of Post Production in 1975.[113]

Fields's picture editing career started in 1960 on low-budget movies like *Studs Lonigan*, produced by Philip Yordan, moved forward with difficulty all through the 1960s, then flowered in the 1970s. In some ways, Verna Fields was the quintessential woman, "trapped" in sound editing for years, as Dede Allen describes, yet Fields helped many men and women, the most famous being Steven Spielberg, but others as well like Julia Phillips, Debra Hill, Dede Allen, Deborah Kavurick, Beth Kennedy, and many others who recall her in these pages.

At the time, women worked mainly as performers, costume designers and script supervisors, but industry folklore has it that women always edited, that in editing women were equal.

Of all the senior editors working today, Dede Allen and Anne V. Coates are the best known. Coates, born in Surrey, England, won the Oscar for Film Editing for *Lawrence of Arabia*, and was nominated for *Beckett*, *The Elephant Man*, and *In the Line of Fire*. Dede Allen, born in Cleveland, Ohio, was nominated for an Oscar for *Reds* and *Dog Day Afternoon* (she got the BAFTA award, the British "Oscar"). Carol Littleton, born in Oklahoma, started out editing commercials; in the 1970s, she edited Karen Arthur's first two films, *Legacy* and *The Mafu Cage*, and Lee Grant's first, *The Stronger*. In 1981, she edited *Body Heat*, advanced to *E.T.* (for which she was nominated for an Oscar), *The Big Chill*, *Places in the Heart*, *Silverado*, and *The Accidental Tourist*, among others. Susan E. Morse, nominated for an Oscar for *Hannah and Her Sisters*, has edited all of Woody Allen's films. Marion Rothman was editing *The Boston Strangler* in 1968, *Beneath the Planet of the Apes* in 1970, *Funny Lady* in 1975, *Starman* and *All Night Long* in the 1980s. Thelma Schoonmaker started in the late 1960s, edited *Raging Bull* in 1980, *The Color of Money*, *The Last Temptation of Christ*, and many of Martin Scorsese's films through the 1990s. Claire Simpson was an assistant editor on *Reds*, won the Oscar for *Platoon*, and went on to edit *Wall Street*, *Mambo Kings*, and *Jakob the Liar*. Sally Menke was nominated for an Oscar for *Pulp Fiction*; she also edited *Reservoir Dogs*, *Teenage Mutant Ninja Turtles*, and *Mulholland Falls*. Mia Goldman edited *The Big Easy*, *Something to Talk About*, and *Choose Me*.[114]

Sounds like a lot of women editing big films, but the reality is, the vast majority of feature films are edited by men. By 2000, the number of women editing the top one hundred pictures was 13 percent, down from a "high" of 15 percent in 1997, which was up from 13 percent a decade before.[115] Thirteen percent is about fifty-two films out of the approximately four hundred made every year in the U.S. Eighty-seven percent of the top one hundred films had no female editors. The figures for television (pilots, series, dramas, and specials) are almost the same.[116]

Robert Wise Said He'd Never Worked with a Woman Editor Before

"Editing," says Dede Allen, "has long been considered a woman's work, but it isn't."[117] Editing became known as "women's work" from a much earlier generation of women, such as Viola Lawrence, Anne Bauchens, Rose Smith, and Margaret Booth. "Viola Lawrence cut Goldwyn's [first sound film]; Anne Bauchens had a lifetime position cutting all of DeMille's epics from 1919 on, and he would not sign a production contract without her being included."[118] Smith edited *The Birth of a Nation* with her husband, James. Booth, who started as a cutter with D. W. Griffth, was editing *The Way We Were* in 1973.[119]

"In *my* generation in the '50s, '60s, and '70s," Allen continues, "no women were getting in. In California, women like Verna Fields were totally stuck in sound editing for years after I was already cutting pictures in New York. Very few women of my generation managed to get features. Even though I started at eighteen in the studios, I was thirty-three before I got my first feature, *Odds Against Tomorrow*, directed by Robert Wise. He told me he'd never worked with a woman editor before. I don't remember when Verna finally got her first picture. I think it was *Studs Lonigan*.[120] Verna came back into the field after her husband died and she had to regain her union card. She used to tell the story about how hard it was for her to get back into the union. She had to sit there and just demand and demand because they didn't want to let her back in. It was very much a closed boys' club. Later, Verna had a lot to do with helping me get my card back."

Dede Allen is the revered editor of films like *Serpico, Dog Day Afternoon, Slap Shot, Alice's Restaurant*, and *Reds*, which she also executive-produced, working with Warren Beatty, for whom she had edited *Bonnie and Clyde* in New York.

"Arthur Penn, the director, and Warren, the producer," says Allen, "brought *Bonnie and Clyde* to Warner Bros. in Los Angeles to shoot the car chase sequences. Arthur was really uptight about having to go to Warner Bros. because of the way they had totally taken control of [Penn's 1958 film] *Left-Handed Gun.*

"The first morning, I drove on the lot behind Arthur. The guard, a wonderful skinny, old man I got to know very well, said to Arthur, 'Is that a woman behind you?'

" 'That's my editor,' Penn replied.

" 'A lady editor?'

" 'Yes.' "

As Allen recalls, the guard smiled and said, "We haven't had a lady editor on this lot in a long time."

Getting on the lot was the least of Allen's problems. She says, "Jack Warner looked at the picture and he was horrified. We hadn't even gotten our fade-outs and fade-ins. 'You mean you're going to'—he put up his hands—'fade out and cut in?' "

That was precisely what they planned to do.

"Jack Warner hated that movie," says Allen. "The head of editorial almost lost his job because he loved the movie and he went around saying so. It was that kind of an atmosphere.

"The day after we'd screened it for Warner, I wasn't allowed on the lot. I went across the street to the Smoke House and called Warren Beatty's office. He told me to wait there. He picked me up, drove me onto the lot. I was on Warren's personal payroll for the last eleven and a half weeks. Warren wasn't rich in those days, but he was very determined. The more they tried to put our credits or put me down, the more Warren would put me up.

"It's always taken certain men to help women," Allen says. "Thank heavens, I also had Verna to help me. I had male mentors all along who kept pushing me forward, helping me in an era where it was really really hard."[121]

In 1973, as Dede Allen edited *Serpico* and *Visions of Eight*, Verna Fields was editing *Paper Moon*. Peter Bogdanovich was directing, Lazslo Kovacs was the director of photography, and Polly Platt was designing the production.

It's Like Being Thrust into a War

"I call myself a confused careerist," says Polly Platt, who moved from production design into writing, producing, executive producing, and directing.

When Platt was about ten years old, her mother took her to a summer stock theater for a performance of George Bernard Shaw's play *Arms and the Man*. During the act break, they wandered behind the theater.

"My mother was smoking a cigarette, and some of the actors in costume were there too, smoking. I'll never forget the image. The light from the theater streaming into the dark space, the smoke resting on the air, moths flying around. I realized that these actors were actually ordinary real people just like me. They came offstage and became real people. In that instant, I decided that I could work in the theater. It was possible."[122]

Platt could paint and draw, longed to be a painter, and went to art school. "It's aberrant in a certain way to want to be an artist. I had the skill and a lively imagination. These make you different, they set you apart. None of my other friends wanted to do paint. They wanted to get married. Now the world has changed. But one thing that disturbed me when I was studying painting in college, I didn't learn about any women painters. I began thinking I couldn't be a painter because there weren't any women in the history of painting. Of course, later I discovered there were women, but very few. Even so, I consider myself first an artist, then a woman, and then a mother."

She began as a production designer, working with her then husband, Peter Bogdanovich, on a low-budget film, *Targets* (1968). Written and directed by Bogdanovich, *Targets* was about a Vietnam vet who uses his training as a sniper at home on people in the malls. In one of his last roles, Boris Karloff played a horror film actor. The film was produced by Roger Corman. Platt and Bogdanovich's most celebrated collaboration was *The Last Picture Show* (1971), which was followed by the also successful *What's Up, Doc?* (1972) and *Paper Moon* (1973).

"A production is like being thrust into a war," Platt says. "Nothing else matters. Children can get sick, parents can die, accidents can happen, but you must go on directing [or producing] that movie. A production shoot is like an army, the production staff is the quartermaster corps, and it supplies its own cars, communication system, radios, food, trucks—we carry it all with us. A production has the same mentality as an army."

During the production war of *The Last Picture Show*, Bogdanovich's father had a stroke. "Peter," says Platt, "had started his well-publicized affair with Cybill Shepherd, who played Jacy. It was awful because we had these two little children . . . it was simply awful. Peter was directing the movie and he didn't want to go to Phoenix to see his father in the hospital. I understood—the budget was very low-budget, the schedule was very tight, we'd already lost two weeks, and I was desperately trying to figure out how to cut two weeks' work out of the shooting script. I insisted that he go. His father was a Serbian, a painter, and a very proud man. I'd grown up in Europe and there are certain things you just have to do as a European. 'If he lives and finds out you didn't come, he'll never forgive you.' Frank Marshall, my location manager, drove him to the Dallas airport. We missed one day of shooting. Peter's father died a few days later. We just went on shooting. It's amazing the kind of sacrifices people make during filming." It's part of the war.

Only later did Platt realize she was, in effect, producing the pictures she'd worked on as production designer with Bogdanovich. "My overview of the films, working closely with Peter, made me a far better production designer," she says.

"One of the odd things about being a woman in the industry, especially in the 1970s and 1980s, as a production designer or writer or producer you don't meet other women doing the same work you were doing. You just did the work and moved on to the next."

Around the time she was designing *What's Up, Doc?* Platt became the first woman production designer to be inducted into the Art Directors Guild. More often, women were art directors. "There was a lot of resentment toward me from the union, the Art Directors Guild," says Platt, "because it was known that I rode the camera car and hung around for the shooting, and that I talked to Peter about how a scene was shot." After she was voted in as a member, nominated by Tambi Larsen, a well-known production designer, the head of the guild called her. "You're a lucky girl," he said to her.[123]

"Confused careerist" could apply to almost any woman tracing the vicissitudes of careers started, stopped, restarted, delayed, or sidelined by family responsibilities. "Confused careerist" also sheds light on the strengths women often bring to careers as mutliskilled individuals who only *appear* confused.

"I could always recognize great material," Platt says. "For instance, Peter had never read *The Last Picture Show,* but I felt it would make a wonderful film. When he read it, he said, really angrily, 'This isn't about old movies.' It was also my idea to make *Paper Moon*—he didn't want to make it. I found Tatum O'Neal, but Peter had the idea of casting Ryan O'Neal, and that's a great example of the true collaboration we had then." *Paper Moon* was originally set in Georgia but when Platt went there, it seemed to her it wasn't right visually for the picture she had in mind. She drove across the country, passing through Kansas, which she and Bogdanovich had once crossed "in a very old car with a bad radiator. I realized the picture needed this vast, empty plain with these two people—father and daughter—lost, alone, and isolated. We didn't have to show breadlines, we just had to show how barren and cold their world was. Peter accepted what I said without even seeing the space."[124]

Paper Moon was the last film collaboration between Platt and Bog-danovich. Afterward, Bogdanovich's bright career began to disintegrate as his films started failing (*Daisy Miller, At Long Last Love, Nickelodeon*).

"The loss of Peter as my creative partner was the most traumatic part of our divorce. It was hard for me to work in Hollywood without the same kind of confidence from the director that I'd had with Peter. I never had to explain myself to him or fight for anything. My ideas were good, Peter accepted them, and utilized them brilliantly."

In 1976, divorced and supporting two small children, Platt was hired to design *Bad News Bears*. It starred Tatum O'Neal and Walter Matthau; Michael Ritchie directed; Stanley Jaffe produced. The story is about an inept Little League team with a stumbling coach (Matthau) and a girl who pitches (O'Neal). It's a movie with heart that travels from defeat to triumph.

"I was really excited about that movie," says Platt, "but when I came on the picture, I remember noticing—I don't know why—that it was all men—production manager, director, cinematographer, the writer, Bill Lancaster. They had sort of an attitude, 'Gee, what does Polly know about baseball?' I didn't know much but I sensed they didn't think I could design it *because* I was 'a girl.' Girls couldn't possibly know about baseball!"

They couldn't use the existing Little League baseball diamonds be-cause in Los Angeles they're on public land next to freeways, which makes shooting next to impossible. Platt had to find a location and design the baseball diamond somewhere else.

"There was a lot of talk that I wouldn't be able to do that because I didn't know anything about baseball. I got the Little League booklet and read about the diamond, how many feet from first to second base, from second to third. I found a wonderful park in Chatsworth about fifteen miles from L.A. I convinced Lancaster, the young screenwriter, to cut the scenes about the children's families in their homes and make the baseball diamond the world of the movie." But the grumbles about girls and baseball kept on coming. Platt got sick of it.

"Just to be funny, as a joke, I took the director, the cinematographer, and the production manager out to the park. 'This is where we're going to do it,' I said. 'Here's where the diamond is going to be. Here's home base, here's first, second base is there . . . I laid it out so the sun would go not from home base to the outfield but across the diamond so we'd have better shooting. The movement of the sun can really be a problem when you're shooting outdoors. I'd plotted it out with strings in a kind of crazy way. They looked at each other as if they'd known all along, 'Yup, we were right, she can't do it, she doesn't know what a baseball diamond looks like.' It was a joke! It got a lot of laughs. Of course I knew what the diamond looked like. Why should anyone doubt that?" she asks. "But for a moment the layout dismayed them and that was wonderful."[125]

It Was Like Running a Film School Out of Our Company

Beside the ocean in Santa Monica, New World Pictures was the place many people began long careers in Hollywood, including Peter Bogdanovich, Polly Platt, John Sayles, Jack Nicholson, and Martin Scorsese. In the 1970s, the Corman school began matriculating a few female graduates: Gale Anne Hurd, Terry Schwartz, Tamara Asseyev, and Alexandra Rose.

Celebrated maverick producer Roger Corman and his wife, Julie, functioned outside the Hollywood studio system making a number of low-budget, usually high-profit films a year. Their company, New World Pictures, was one of the most commercially successful independent film enterprises in Hollywood history, churning out hundreds of films. How did they do it? Roger established the model in the 1950s when he began giving young people yearning to get into the movies their first break. Julie Corman says, "It was like running a film school out of our company. Somebody would wander in and just be talented and we'd say, 'Do it, just go do it.' "[126]

The other "adult" at New World was Barbara Boyle, the Cormans' lawyer. In 1973, among her other duties, Boyle had just acquired the U.S. distribution rights to Ingmar Bergman's film, *Cries and Whispers.* Boyle has worked on motion pictures as a producer, an executive, and as an attorney since 1960. Her entry into the business, long before she met Roger Corman, is worth recording.

When she was just out of UCLA law school, one of Boyle's professors sent her on her first Hollywood interview for a job at a major studio that involved labor law. "The guy at the studio gate said, 'Oh, yes, they're expecting you, Building B,' " Boyle recounts. "The gates open and I drive my beat-up old car inside. I thought I was supposed to go to Building A, but I go into Building B, and there are three absolutely gorgeous, completely color-coordinated women sitting there. I see the women in the room and I'm thinking, 'This is real affirmative action.' There were so few women law students that I knew every woman at every law school in southern California. I think these women must be from the East Coast.

"The receptionist said, 'Oh, honey, I don't have your name down.'

" 'We made this appointment at the last minute.' Unlike the beautiful women there, I'm dressed in a T-shirt and jeans, have long straight hair down my back, and no makeup.

" 'Don't worry, sit down, I'll get you in.'

"Every interview is really short, so I thought the man inside really knew what he wanted. I finally got my turn and go into the office. A guy is sitting with his feet up on the desk, smoking a big cigar.

" 'Take off your jeans,' he says.

"I completely flip out. I go on for ten minutes about Hollywood and women and I'm shocked at my professor for sending me, that 'you're supposed to be a UCLA graduate, too . . .' He's just looking at me, smoking his cigar. Finally, after this diatribe, he says, 'Do you ever think you're wrong about anything?'

" 'What do you mean?'

" 'I'm casting a beach party movie. Who are you supposed to see?'

" 'Sam Arkoff, American International Pictures.'

"The man picked up his phone. 'Sam, if you can ever keep her quiet, she's probably really smart.' "[127]

Boyle worked at American International Pictures for five years as corporate counsel, business affairs. She then started her own entertainment law practice, Cohen & Boyle. Roger Corman was one of her clients. She joined New World Pictures, his company, in 1974.

"There were always women at New World," Boyle says, "because we were cheaper and more loyal. People talk about being color blind? Roger was gender blind."[128] Julie Corman says about her husband, "I don't think discrimination ever occurred to him. He was really just thinking about getting the films made."[129]

Boyle says that when she was Corman's lawyer, she and Roger once drove into the hot, dusty hills of San Bernardino to meet with the Hell's Angels. "Roger wanted to make a deal with them to be in a movie about a destructive motorcycle gang. The Hell's Angels was a very, very hierarchical society, and women had a fixed place in it." Boyle recalls that after chatting for a few minutes, a Hell's Angels leader said to Corman, "Let's get down to business. We'll leave the women out here."

"This is my lawyer," Corman said, pointing at Boyle.

"She's a girl."

"Oh, really?" Roger said. "I never noticed."[130]

A picture of the decade of the 1970s, says Boyle, is a picture of the golden years of Corman—Jonathan Demme, Joe Dante, Jonathan Kaplan. They were coming out of NYU Film School, sent by Marty Scorsese, who was filming *Mean Streets*. But Scorsese's first Hollywood movie was

for Corman, *Boxcar Bertha* (1972). Julie Corman, Roger's wife, coproduced it.

"It was my first production," Julie Corman says. "Roger made *Bloody
Mama* for American International Pictures, and it had done very well.
They wanted another 'woman gangster' picture. I went looking for one
and I had a hard time. I called a friend in the district attorney's office.
'What's going on here? Why do I find only men gangsters? Are women
that good?' "

Corman says she was told that there was an unwritten law that the
crimes of women and children are not reported. Only the most egregious
come to light.

"To me," Julie Corman says, "that smacked of the stereotype that
women were chattel or childlike—basically characterized as property, to
be maintained or protected, so of course it wouldn't be decent to report
on women serial killers. I found a book called *The True Story of Boxcar
Bertha*, as told to Dr. Ben L. Reitman. I never found him or the publisher,
but I did find Boxcar Bertha living in a kind of hotel in San Francisco.
She was extremely reclusive. Though I never saw her, I got her release.
I loved her story because it was about a woman living outside the system. In a way, at the time, I felt I was outside, too, looking at the social
system pretty critically, saying, 'Hey! Women can do that! Give me the
chance.' In the early 1900s, when Bertha wanted to see the guy she
loved, an IWW worker [Industrial Workers of the World—the 'Wob-
blies'], she hopped on a boxcar. I felt her story was very much worth
telling.

"Then," says Julie Corman, "the writer entered the picture, Bill Corrington, who wrote with his wife, Joyce. Bill's grandfather had been an
IWW worker and he saw this as the story of Big Bill Shelly, Bertha's
boyfriend. In fact, one day he announced the title should be *Big Bill
Shelly*. I'm sitting in the meeting with Roger, Bill, Joyce, and our story
editor, Frances Doel, and I heard that and I dissolved in tears and left
the room, showing how mature I am."

It remained *Boxcar Bertha* because the distributor wanted a woman
gangster picture.

"As in all productions," Julie relates, "other people enter. I began to
see that my brilliant idea about a woman outside the social norms was
not going to stay pure. That was hard for me to deal with because by
then I felt this was *my picture*. Barbara Hershey was the star and she
was living with and pregnant by, at the time, though we didn't know,
David Carradine, and they brought their own needs or connections to
the movie. Then Marty Scorsese came on board and he saw dynamics
in the picture which had to do with him and his brother."

Not only did Julie feel the picture wasn't hers anymore, she was also wondering what else would be stirred into the mix. "I'm kind of wondering where everything went wrong. We got to Camden, Arkansas, for the shoot, a location I'd found that was dictated by the presence of a narrow-gauge railroad, an important story point. Marty had already sketched every single shot in the picture and had tacked them all over the walls of his motel room in Camden. From that moment on, it was a Marty Scorsese film."

The making of *Boxcar Bertha* was nerve-wracking and exhausting, Julie Corman says, but she found she liked producing. Her second film, *Night Call Nurses*, was produced for $115,000 and made $1 million. "I kept on producing because I realized that it was solving problems, my strong suit. My question always was, 'Why aren't we shooting?' A simple question, and the answer is also very simple: *We're not shooting because . . . there's no script. We're not shooting because . . . there's no money.*"[131] By 1973, Julie Corman had produced three more. By 1997, she'd produced twenty-six pictures.

Despite some Hollywood disdain for the larky but highly profitable films New World produced, Roger Corman built an enterprise that turned out cult classics, brought European films like *The Story of Adele H* to the American market, and functioned as a company truly open to women (and men) who had no experience but a lot of drive and talent.

"No one else would hire women to do anything responsible," Boyle says, "and no one, *no one*, would hire women to learn the ropes on features by actually working on a production. Gale Anne Hurd, Terry Schwartz, Frances Doel, Alexandra Rose, Tamara Asseyev—they all started with Roger."[132]

"When I produced my first film at twenty-three," recalls Tamara Asseyev, "the *Los Angeles Times* wrote an article that said, 'She's young, she's pretty and—she's a producer!' That sort of sums [that time] up."[133]

One of the first films Asseyev worked on for Roger Corman was *Prehistoric Woman*. "He'd come back from a science fiction festival in Russia with some science fiction footage and gave Peter Bogdanovich and Polly Platt and the actress Mamie Van Doren enough money to shoot for one week and turn it into a science fiction project," says Asseyev. "Roger just threw people into the soup, which was great because that's how we learned the nuts and bolts of producing low-budget movies."[134]

Asseyev was thrown into *The Wild Racers*. Though she is credited as an associate producer, "I produced it," she says, "because the person hired to do it ended up in a Spanish jail the first week. It was a Formula II race car film, starring Fabian and Mimsy Farmer, directed by Dan

Haller. We went to Europe and followed the race cars in five different countries for two hundred thousand dollars. We did it in six or seven weeks. I'd worked for Corman only about a year."[135]

Dan Haller and Asseyev worked so well together they decided to try to make something with a little better content, *Goodbye to the Hill*, a novel set in Dublin. "We called it *Paddy*. Corman invested in it. Danny and I took off to Dublin, where we made the film with actors from the Abbey Theater. I took it to New York to sell it to a distributor. I remember bending over a phone book, calling film companies and asking to speak to the president of the company. They actually took my calls and many said, 'Come over tomorrow and I'll look at it.' That's how different the film business was then. I sold it to Allied Artists. Barbara Boyle, Corman's lawyer, flew in and drew up the contract. Allied Artists put me under contract for a year.

"It was strange working then," says Asseyev. "A lot of times it was, 'Listen, honey, you don't understand . . .' and I'd say, 'But I do' or 'This is what I think.' I was raising some tax shelter money and I had to really know what I was doing. For two years I went to law school at night and I learned how to think, to isolate an issue and stick to it. I look back on that whole period as a wonderful time. I was doing what I really liked. I was experiencing the creative process fully. But you have to have a deep belief in what you're doing. Otherwise, it's too difficult to get a movie going."

Sweet Kill, a thriller starring Tab Hunter and Isabel Jewell, was Curtis Hanson's first film. He wrote and directed it; Asseyev produced it in Venice, California. When the Embassy Pictures deal fell through, Corman released it through New World Pictures. "In his typical fashion," Asseyev says, "Roger changed the title to *The Arousers* and made Curtis shoot a sequence of a young woman being stabbed in the shower.

"That was pivotal for me," says Asseyev. "I looked at this scene and although Curtis did a good job directing it, the treatment of women personified by this girl being stabbed was so offensive to me. I decided I'd work only on films that I had an emotional rapport with, that somehow reflected my sensibility as a woman, politically and creatively. I wanted to try to show a human condition, or show women coping in a positive way, that didn't denigrate them.

"This turning point had a parallel to my own life at that stage. I was sort of a fish out of water, I was beginning to realize that I was one of the very few women producing in the film business, I was coping with it. Trying to work in a man's world was not easy. Today," she adds, "it doesn't seem to make much difference if you're a man or a woman."[136]

School was out and some of the women working at New World were graduating. Julie Corman was producing children, four in all, as well as pictures. "Out of all my films, the line that sums up women's attitudes in the 1970s was written by Barbara Peters in *Summer School Teachers:* 'I don't want to watch, I want to play.' Early in that decade women knew we were going to do more than we had before. Battles were raging around the Equal Rights Amendment. 'Equality of rights under the law shall not be denied or abridged on account of sex.' That was the entire amendment! The opposition said, 'You already have provisions to take care of it.' We didn't have anything in the law like it. We knew we could work but in the 1970s we knew we were going to do more. We felt that. We wanted equality not just for ourselves but for our children."[137]

That was the mood. As one woman, a documentary producer, says: "I remember the instant when, on a street in San Francisco in 1973, the word 'cameraperson' came out of my mouth. It was wonderful to be a woman then—wonderful and arduous."[138]

For women in motion pictures it was going to get easier and harder. Boosted by the phenomenal success of Coppola's *Godfather* in 1972, Spielberg's *Jaws* in 1975 and *Close Encounters of the Third Kind* in 1977, and George Lucas's *Star Wars*, also in 1977, film budgets ballooned. "Blockbuster" and "high concept" began driving and defining the film industry. Trusting women with budgets that big was not in the social context of the times. As usual, women found a way.

4

THE START OF A WONDERFUL HEYDAY FOR WOMEN

On February 3, 1974, the Hollywood trade papers, *Variety* and the *Hollywood Reporter*, carried small articles: "Heller Appointed Col Creative Affairs V.P." Rosilyn Heller, a sleek, smart, dramatic woman, had been promoted to vice president in charge of Columbia Pictures' worldwide literary operations. Actually, it was pretty much the same job she'd been doing at the studio since 1971—evaluate scripts, books, and other properties, and supervise their course through the studio with actors, directors, and producers on the lot.

At Columbia, Peter Guber was VP of worldwide production. "I just went in to Peter," Heller says, "and asked him, 'Why aren't I a vice president?' He said something like, 'Well, I didn't know you were interested in that.' It was like it would never occur to anybody or that no woman had dared to ask before.[139]

"When they made me vice president," says Heller, "they gave me a car. When I called about it, the guy in charge of the cars couldn't believe it. He kept saying, 'Who is it for?'"

"I kept saying, 'For me!'"

"'But who do you work for?'"

"'Me! It's for me! I'm vice president of creative affairs!'"

"'No, no, who's your boss, what's his name?'"

"I tell you," Heller says, "it was quite a contest. Women today don't live with that. They need a car, they get a car. The simplest thing brought on a skirmish. Every time I came in from lunch, I'd ask if there were any messages for me. They'd shake their heads. I'd say, 'No?'"

"They'd say, 'Who do you work for?'"

"'I work for me.' They were used to secretaries asking 'Are there messages for me?' meaning 'Are there messages for my boss?' I felt my vice presidency was slightly illicit, like I was having an affair with somebody off-limits and everybody knew but nobody was talking about it to me. I felt that no one officially recognized that I was a vice president, but I'm sure they talked about it a lot.

"What did women do in the 1970s?" she asks. "We were there to make men look good. It became more threatening to them when we began to want our own careers.

"The change during this period in the 1970s was incredible. Most women at the studios were secretaries, and even great agencies like Adams, Ray, Rosenberg had no women. But Peter Guber, head of production at Columbia, wanted access to New York, which I supplied—I came from publishing and from ABC Pictures there."

A self-described "uppity woman," Heller says she never took no for an answer. "Lynda Obst[140] said that to be in the studio system, you've got to ride the horse in the direction it's going," Heller says. "A perfect metaphor. I'm never riding the horse in the direction it's going, I'm always taking the horse and going the other way—that's who I am."

Heller stayed at Columbia until 1980, through a rocky corporate period that saw regular regime changes and the explosive departure of president David Begelman for embezzlement. "I survived [outlasted] them all," she says, "Guber, Begelman, Stanley Jaffe, all of them."[141]

That period also saw a stream of first-rate, now classic releases—*Close Encounters of the Third Kind, Taxi Driver, Tommy, Shampoo, The China Syndrome.* "They were one-of-a-kind movies," says Heller. "It was a thrilling time. Then the 1980s hit and all that totally changed. It was about blockbusters.

"But the fact is, the favors [women got] from the men—positions, titles—were eked out penuriously. They were like gifts to us despite the fact that we worked harder and deserved them more. Every vice presidency, every promotion, every moment of recognition had to be wrested from them."[142]

It's Easy to Leave When They Treat You Bad

"That," says Marcia Nasatir, "is why so many women quit."[143] It was much harder to stay.

In the spring of 1974, Nasatir was a literary agent. She ran into good-looking Mike Medavoy in the dark, paneled Cock and Bull restaurant on Sunset Boulevard. Medavoy had just become vice president of West Coast production at United Artists, a solid move up from his position as Hollywood agent representing hot talent like George Lucas and Francis Coppola.

"Mike! How are you? And how come you haven't asked me to come to work with you?" Nasatir asked him.

Later, she says, "We made one of those confidential breakfast meetings at the Bel Air Hotel, where he offered me the job of story editor, a very conventional job in Hollywood for women. At least he offered me more money than I'd ever made, fifty thousand a year.

" 'I won't take it,' I said, 'unless I'm a vice president.' This developed into a big battle."

"But there's never been a woman vice president at UA," Medavoy said.

"I may have pointed out to him that Roz Heller had just been promoted to VP at Columbia," Nasatir says, "and maybe that's why I got the idea. All I know is that I wouldn't take the job without the title. We went round and round with them saying, 'Why don't you come to work and in six months we'll reevaluate?' and I was saying, 'No, no, no, no, I won't, no, no.' "

In New York, many women were editors and agents. When Nasatir came to Los Angeles in 1969 as a literary agent for Everett Ziegler, she was shocked that she didn't work with women as agents or executives or producers. "Looking back," she recalls, "women were subsidiary characters, the second story line. We had no real power and we were isolated. I remember a lawyer from 20th Century Fox who had just started with Ziegler. At his first meeting with us, we were discussing what we'd read over the weekend. He said he couldn't figure out what I was doing in the meeting, that I seemed to know too much to be a secretary. He said he'd never been in a meeting with a woman."[144]

Nasatir has a wry, understated sense of humor. Her manner seems as comfortable as that of a favored relative; beneath that surface, she's pragmatic, sharp, experienced, and insouciant. "She was like a god to me," says Lucy Fisher, a former cochair of Columbia TriStar, now a producer with Red Wagon Productions. Fisher began as one of Nasatir's readers. "When I got to know her, she always was very homey and approachable and funny. I thought of her as a friend's mom. She was very maternal. She'd say, 'You didn't go out looking like that, did you?' She was sort of a tough-love type—free with the compliments, free with the criticism. Everybody wanted to be just like her. Filmmakers loved her."[145]

Nasatir grew up in San Antonio, Texas, where her father ran a yard goods store. Both parents had come from Russia. Her mother arrived in the 1920s and became a member of the ILGWU—the International Ladies Garment Workers Union in New York. "She was very much a socialist free spirit," Nasatir says, "and my father thought his children were the best, especially his two daughters."

Nasatir was still wrangling back and forth with United Artists about her job title when Dr. Matilda Krim weighed in. She was an MD who would later become well known for starting the American Foundation of AIDS Research. Her husband, Arthur Krim, was an entertainment attorney who, with his partner, Robert Benjamin, had bought United Artists in 1951 and had been running it successfully for twenty-five years since the release of *The African Queen.* According to Nasatir, Dr. Krim told her husband, "Arthur, it would be good for your business to hire her as a vice president." She gave him the same argument Nasatir had been making: "If someone meets with a woman who has a title, and that woman turns something down, it has more meaning. They don't have to feel ashamed that it was turned down by a story editor. It was turned down by a vice president."[146]

Finally, in July 1974, United Artists hired Nasatir as a vice president of West Coast motion picture development.[147]

"And we began."

As a motion picture studio, United Artists had the distinction of being created not by businessmen or entrepreneurs but by three actors and a director—Mary Pickford, Douglas Fairbanks Jr., Charlie Chaplin, and D. W. Griffith—in 1919. They created it to distribute their independent productions. Upon hearing the news, one studio head groused the famous line, "The inmates have taken over the asylum." UA was always a maverick studio. The 1920s were good, mainly because Joseph M. Schenck was at the helm. The studio went into a tailspin in the 1940s when Chaplin and Pickford agreed to sell to Krim and Benjamin. In the 1960s, UA was enormously profitable, partly because of the talent who wanted to work with them, and also because of the James Bond and Pink Panther series of movies they released. There was no reason to expect the 1970s to be different, and for a while, from 1974 to 1978, according to Nasatir, the glory years kept coming. Nasatir worked on films such as *Bound for Glory, Rocky, Coming Home,* and *One Flew Over the Cuckoo's Nest.* "There was Mike Medavoy, Mark Canton, Mike's assistant who'd just come from UCLA, and me," says Nasatir. "It was a very stable company, probably the best experience I had. They were men of integrity. And they were men who read."

When the script of *Rocky* (1976) came in, Nasatir and Medavoy read it and both thought it was terrific. "Ziggy [Everett Ziegler] had told me that boxing and submarine movies always made money. We sent *Rocky* to New York, but Arthur [Krim] and Eric [Pleskow] didn't want to do it. The agent had told us that [Sylvester] Stallone wouldn't sell the script unless he was in the title role, and New York didn't know some guy called Stallone. Mike and I had seen him in *Lords of Flatbush,* which we sent on to New York. After they screened it, they called us. 'Okay, if it can be made for one million.' So Talia Shire, Burt Young, Carl Weathers, Burgess Meredith are hired, and John Avildsen, the director, and the movie gets made. Mike and I saw it, liked it a lot, and sent it on to New York. The guys see it and call us up. 'Where's our lead actor in this?'

" 'Stallone's there,' we told them. 'He's Rocky Balboa.'

" 'But that guy wasn't in *Lords of Flatbush*.'

"We finally figured out that the guy they'd thought was Stallone had been a good-looking blond guy, Perry King, who played Chico in *Flatbush*. Picture this: the whole *Rocky* movie is made and where is Perry King? That to me said what it was like to work in Hollywood."

Lagging behind New York in terms of being conscious of women's liberation, in Los Angeles, women's groups were just beginning to spring up. Former New Yorkers like Nasatir, Heller, and fledgling executive Paula Weinstein joined a group that met monthly for lunch purportedly to discuss women's rights. "Marilyn Bergman, Julia Phillips, Nancy Harden, a Paramount producer, and others," Nasatir says. "One month somebody was getting married. We all had to bring a recipe. I don't recall any discussion about this but I remember thinking, *This is a group of liberated women?* I cut something out of the *New York Times* and put my name over the name that was there, like Betty Lou's Coffee Cake. Some of the women there got mad at me. I wasn't going to do a recipe! I didn't have time! That whole recipe thing would not have happened in New York."[148]

Producer Paula Weinstein recalls of the gathering, "I remember walking out of this with Marcia, and I'm saying to her, 'What the hell are we doing here? This has nothing to do with us!"[149] Fresh from New York and from intense political demonstrations around civil rights, the Vietnam War, and women's rights, Paula Weinstein was about to begin a sharp ascent through the studios, beginning with Warner Bros. in 1976, at the precise time the industry was actually looking for women. Weinstein has character; she is outspoken and frank about her beliefs. She is the only woman in the business whose mother, Hannah Weinstein, had been a producer and studio head in England, after leaving America during the McCarthy blacklist period. In the 1970s, she was back home, still producing, still radical and respected.

We Are Invisible

Suddenly, every studio wanted a woman as a vice president. It was trendy. Not many women were chosen but for those who were, it changed their lives forever.

When Jack Haley Jr., president of 20th Century Fox Television, and vice president Sy Salkowitz called Nancy Malone, she had left Tomorrow Entertainment to set up her own production office. She had produced and directed a short film,[150] and had sold a movie-of-the-week to NBC, *Winner Take All*, the story of a compulsive gambler, starring Shirley Jones, Joan Blondell, and Sylvia Sidney. She knew Salkowitz and Haley. "They said they'd heard of my work at Tomorrow Entertainment and about the movie-of-the-week I was producing."[151] At Fox, Malone was offered a position as director of television development.

"I was excited, challenged, and delighted. I knew I could do it," Malone says. She developed dramas, comedies, and specials for television, supervised existing shows (*M*A*S*H* was Fox's hit), and executive-produced an MOW, *Sherlock Holmes in New York* (1976). "I'd never done anything like this job before so I didn't know you didn't take on everything. Most nights, I didn't leave until ten or eleven o'clock. It was very lonely."

Malone says she wasn't promised a promotion, but she was promoted to vice president within a year by dint of hard work, selling mainly comedy shows and a highly visible special, *That's Television*, to NBC. Malone's years of experience as a performer in films, on the stage, and as an Emmy-nominated actress in television usually worked for her, as did her corporate experience with Tomorrow.

In 1975, after she was promoted, she was invited with all the other execs to a meeting with Dennis C. Stanfill, chairman and CEO of 20th Century Fox. "It was held in the conference room, and we were there to present our shows for the following year, report on what our divisions' profits were, and discuss our 'management by objective,'" says Malone. "I'd never heard that term before. I had no background in business management. I hadn't graduated high school (I'd been touring in a play during my high school graduation). I never went to college. But I'd spent years acting in theater, movies, and television; I could perform when I had to and I knew how to prepare. But I was very nervous."

They were sitting around a huge oval table when she realized with a snap, as all women do, that she was the only woman there; there wasn't even a female secretary in the meeting. Malone also knew what was about to happen. "We had to go around the table and report. I was hoping something would happen like a fire that would break up the group. One by one, around the table each man finished, and then the next one talked, and the next, and it was rolling toward me like a train coming around the bend, and all of a sudden it was on me.

" 'I think we did great!' I said, all bouncy and cheery. 'We made a lot of money, and I think we've made this division happy, and I expect a big bonus.'

"I had a certain amount of charm and my Irish humor, but those men didn't know what to make of this opening. They just muttered to themselves. Then I presented my report. Even though I didn't know the business jargon, I *was* prepared and knew exactly what my division had sold. We *had* done very well and we did make a profit. I was selling my heart out."[152]

Though it was becoming chic to have one female vice president on every corporate tree, there were still very few, and the scarcity led to one of Malone's signal memories. It was 1975, and Deanne Barkley, well remembered by many for her competency and her support of women, was vice president of movies at NBC (she would later move to ABC). Malone was in New York pitching Fox's new pilots to the networks. One night, during the selling binge, everyone was invited to 21 for a big party.

"I'll never forget it," says Malone. "I think I was the only woman television executive selling for a studio and Deanne was the only woman heading a movies-for-television buying arena. I know we were the only single women there. The guys had their wives. I didn't have a girlfriend, a boyfriend, a monkey, or a husband and neither did she. We talked to each other because no one at that party talked to us. She was a buyer, and people should have been talking to her, selling to her. At the end of the party, Deanne and I looked at each other and said, almost simultaneously, 'We are invisible.' "

Sometimes we are all trapped in the amber of short moments in our lives, trying to figure out what we could have done differently. Malone says that she would have tried harder to find social connections with the men because "this business is based on relationships." But she didn't realize it then. The single men at the studios who were Malone's counterparts were often "fixed up by the heads of divisions with dates," says Malone, "but single women execs didn't fit in and we weren't supplied with dates."[153]

Most of the real business in Hollywood is carried on at social functions. The social scene was set up to accommodate the working preferences of men. Married men had wives who cared for the children, packed their clothes for sudden trips, called the baby-sitters, and accompanied them to receptions. Women executives, who, after all, had only been around a couple of years, had to be invited to the parties to get to know the key players, but they had no social network in place to make this happen.

"A lot of the networking has to do with the wives," observed Ethel Winant, VP of casting at CBS from 1973 to 1980. "The town is built around the dinner party . . . [the wives] are smart, highly motivated and have a view of the business . . . They can see who needs to be courted, who should sit next to who. I think 'the club' is of husbands and wives. It's harder for a woman working in the industry because her husband is usually in another club if he's successful . . . A woman doesn't have somebody carefully working to make sure she is moving as cleverly as she could . . ." Winant said she felt she needed a wife for two reasons: "When the phone rang and I was told we all had to be in New York tomorrow morning and needed to be at the airport at six P.M., the guy down the hall would pick up the phone and call his wife and tell her to pack the blue suit. I had to be out of there because I had to lay out my own blue suit, put the dog in the kennel, make arrangements [for the children] to be at the plane by six o'clock. If I had a dinner party, I'd have to be home to talk to the caterer, not working in the office saying, 'I'll be home in twenty minutes, dear.' "154

Divorced women with children had the hardest challenge of all to make a stream of screenings, dinner parties, or tennis games. But for ambitious women, their appearances were a mandatory part of the social-commercial fabric of Hollywood. For many single women, the best solution was to align themselves with unmarried, ambitious male executives.

■   ■   ▩

In West Los Angeles, 20th Century Fox had sold off its back lot, which created the Century City high-rise office complex and mall. To the north, just over the Cahuenga Pass on the edge of the San Fernando Valley, the sprawling Universal back lot was already being turned into a theme park. All the studios were engaged in the same general effort, but each was a city with its own history and distinct character. Some were liberal, some conservative, a few had women executives, and some were more receptive to increasing those numbers than others.

No One Knew How a Woman Exec Should Behave

Beth Kennedy landed at Universal in 1975, between degrees at UCLA. "I belong to the generation between the women who were told, 'Get your teaching certificate so you'll have something to fall back on' and those who were told, 'Get your MBA/JD and go into business.' "[155] Kennedy is a doer—brisk, smart, confident, impatient. At UCLA in the early 1970s, her post-master's fellowship in folklore and mythology included work on UCLA's first automated archives, her introduction to computers. When the Ph.D. program she wanted didn't get funded, a family connection suggested she get a job "in the real world" and referred her to Universal Studios. She designed and supervised the implementation of the first on-line computer system to track the distribution of Sensurround equipment to theaters around the world. Her experience in technology, an area in which few women worked, brought her to the attention of the studio manager. He placed her in charge of reviewing various studio operations on Universal's back lot, where virtually no woman, except Verna Fields in postproduction, had gone before.

Kennedy was twenty-four, had long straight hair down her back, wore wire-rim glasses, and dressed casually in the fashion of the times (one observer suggested she looked like "a hippie"). She appeared in the transportation department to "study and review" the domain. The grizzled old guard there must have thought management had lost its mind. Undeterred, Kennedy analyzed the twenty-four-hour-a-day operation, noting they were hiring more than 750 drivers a day *manually*. She asked lots of questions, made pages of notes, and went away. The Teamsters probably felt they'd seen the last of her.

When she gave the studio manager her recommendations for reorganizing and automating their hiring procedures, he said, "Can you fix it?" The challenge intrigued her. "I didn't think to ask for a raise or a title."

The department head looked up one day. That girl was back.

"Transportation was the ultimate men's club, decorated with nude pictures from *Playboy* and *Hustler*," Kennedy recalls. "It had no women's bathroom—they finally built one. I redesigned the drivers' trip tickets, the captains' reports, so drivers had to get approvals on rate changes, account for nondeductible breakfasts, and report specific mealtimes. They hated me. My new car was trashed, my tires were slashed regularly, I got threatening, obscene phone calls. It was *awful*. Much later, one guy told me why: I took five thousand dollars a week out of his check."[156]

Kennedy's role models were the male executives at Universal. No one knew how a woman executive should behave; few studio execs had ever worked with a woman. "They didn't like it when women behaved the same way they did," Kennedy says. "Many of them were tyrants who yelled and screamed regularly. One time, in a meeting with another executive, one questioned my integrity. 'If that's the way you feel,' I said, 'we have nothing to talk about.' I got up and started to walk out.

" 'Wait a minute!' he yelled.

" 'You pay me to tell you the truth,' I told him. 'I wouldn't be doing my job if I don't tell you what I think, or if you're making a mistake. Don't expect me to sit here and play dumb.'

"Later, in private, he muttered to me, 'This is not a business for grown-ups!' "

The other executive in that meeting was sure Kennedy was going to be fired. "We all learned something," Kennedy says. "I became more sensitive about what to say and how to say negative things to male executives. They got used to women who were not their wives, mothers, daughters, or bimbos telling them what to do."

One day Kennedy asked her boss for a performance review and received a blank look. "How am I doing?" she asked. Another blank stare. "There must be something I'm doing you want to change? Is there anything I can do to improve?"

Relief washed over his face; he understood. "Did you get your check?" he asked. She nodded.

"You're doing fine." That was the end of her performance review.[157]

The following year, the studio manager gave her a second review. "You know Joan's a lawyer," he said of one executive, "and Joanie's a CPA, but when your name comes up, it's 'she does something with computers.' I want you to become an important woman executive." Kennedy laughs as she recalls the scene. "I told him I knew what a production executive does and what a studio executive does. But what's an 'important woman executive' going to do here? He didn't think that was funny," she says. "He said, 'Pick a school, we'll pay. Go to law school or get an MBA.' I did, the company paid for law school and I went nights after work. Getting the degree and getting married—I met my husband the first night of law school—did make a difference in my career. It changed their perception of me."[158]

■   ■   ■

It's hard to imagine today how bewildering it was for women to be thrust into corporate jobs, and for many men to adjust to women in

positions other than as their secretaries, but in some instances, like the
following, everyone was trying. Humor always helped.

While Kennedy was replacing the tires on her car, Willette Klausner
was working inside the Universal tower as director of marketing research, a position created for her. Though in very different areas, Kennedy and Klausner knew of each other because, as Klausner says, "there
were so few women in management back then."

A tall, dignified woman given to dramatic apparel and bold jewelry,
Klausner grew up in Santa Barbara, the daughter of a caterer. She was
one of the few black teenagers in her high school in the 1950s, where
she was the first black vice president of the student body. She majored
in economics at UCLA. Just before she joined Universal, she had been
vice president of Audience Studies, Inc./Preview House, the largest national testing service for advertising and television programs in the
country. Before that, she'd been a statistical analyst.

"I worked with the finest man in the business, Clark Ramsey, executive vice president of marketing services for MCA," says Klausner. "Marketing movies was quite new and was basically done in prerelease
screenings. It used to be called *exploitation.* Marketing is reaching the
maximum number of the target audience with the minimum expenditure
of dollars. You want the target audience on a cost-effective basis. However, the approach used in the movie business was to spend a lot of
money in a very short window of opportunity—in and out of the theaters
in less than a month.

"Movie marketing executives often have to take into consideration
stars' egos, which may require a double-page ad in the *New York Times*—
even though they may know it's ineffective. A lot of things were done
in the name of marketing that were not really marketing."[159]

Klausner's promotion at the end of 1975 made her the first African-
American woman vice president of marketing research.[160] At the time,
Klausner had no sense of the significance of her promotion. "I found out
after I left Universal. I walked into the publicity offices at Warner Bros.
Joe Hyams ran it, and he said, 'Oh yes, I remember you.'

Klausner was surprised. Hyams explained, "A while ago, I was asked
to do an announcement for Lucy Fisher about her appointment as vice
president.[161] and [someone] came up with the headline, 'First Female
Vice President at Major Studio.' I told them, 'No, because there's a
woman VP at Universal by the name of Willette Klausner. But how
about this: 'First *White* Female Vice President'?"

"I burst out laughing," says Klausner. "With that comment, he forever
endeared himself to me. How many people would tell *me* that? Most
people are so uptight about race."

Once a year, the heads of MCA divisions around the world attended a management meeting at a resort for a weekend. "Before I attended these meetings," says Klausner, "invitations were addressed to 'executives and wives.' That was changed to 'executives and spouses,' largely because of my husband, Manny Klausner. He said that he'd go on the shopping tour, to the art galleries, and even the fashion shows, but he would not play tennis with the wives because he didn't want to get beat."

Like so many other women at this time, Klausner was usually the only woman in meetings, "and the guys kept apologizing to me for their language. These men were from a different era," Klausner says, "and seemed to be somewhat uncomfortable working with women executives. The big difference in those days was this: We didn't ask the guys to adjust their behavior for us. We tried to fit theirs. We women executives simply wanted to be treated like the male executives."

At her first management meeting in the resort, all the male executives and Willette were sitting around the table in a session. Klausner was describing the marketing strategy that had been used for *Smokey and the Bandit.* "I told them that we had recruited an audience for the film that predicted its success in the U.S." Lew Wasserman, president and CEO of MCA/Universal, asked how that could be. 'If we tested the film in Los Angeles, how can you say that it was predictive? The film did not do well in the Los Angeles market.'

"I replied, 'Although the test was conducted in Los Angeles, we only recruited people who were in the target audience for this type of film—a shit-kicker audience.' Everyone at the table gasped. I immediately put my hand to my head and said, 'Oh, I'm sorry, I forgot there are men present.' There was silence, everyone looked at Lew, and then he laughed and everyone laughed. It was perfect. The guys never apologized about their language to me again."[162]

What Do You Guys Do?

Anthea Sylbert is jolly and thoughtful, a great combination. She's perhaps the only costume designer who became a studio vice president, and then a film producer in the 1980s.

"My father wanted me to be an architect or a lawyer," Sylbert says. "When I told him I wanted to go to design school, he said, 'To do what?'

" 'To become a designer.'

"He actually said, 'Isn't that what women do?'

"He was Greek," she says, "and it was atypical for a man of his generation to deal with a daughter that way, but he always thought I was smart. He wasn't treating me like a son—he had a son, too—but he thought I should choose a path equal to the brain I had. I think now his radical ideas about me came from his polytheism. Being Greek, the heavens for him were populated with male and female gods, each powerful in different ways. Women, especially bright women, were expected to be powerful. Those were the myths I grew up on."[163]

Working with Roman Polanski spoiled her. "*Chinatown* was thrilling not just because the ending was written the very last night we were shooting but because we were all sort of young, and not necessarily always playing by the rules. I never knew when I was breaking the rules or when I wasn't. I didn't know costume designers were not supposed to have an opinion on a script," Sylbert says. "I probably got my first costume job because I worked cheaper than anyone else."

Chinatown was different. One day she realized that Faye Dunaway's character, Mrs. Mulwray, a widow, had to be in black for most of the movie. It was not a design choice; it was a historical, sociological fact. "I argued with Roman about it, told him that somebody of that class, at that time, wouldn't wear dark red nail polish."

As Sylbert recalls, Polanski said, "I don't care. Every movie I know they're wearing dark nail polish."

"Okay, I lost that one," Sylbert sighs.[164]

In 1977, she was designing *Julia*, and directly after it, *F.I.S.T.*, a United Artists picture directed by Norman Jewison. She began wondering why she'd chosen costume designing. "I liked working with people who were inspiring, who gave me that buzz, and I liked costumes. Then I started not to like it." She had just finished *F.I.S.T.* when John Calley, one of three top execs at Warner Bros., called her. He knew that she'd worked with his good friends, Mike Nichols and Elaine May.[165]

"I got the sense," Sylbert says, "that he believed I might be more valuable than just your costume designer. He asked me to have breakfast with him, which I thought was very weird. When you're making movies, breakfast is that swill they pass off as coffee, and in those days, before health arrived, we had doughnuts with jelly in the center. That was breakfast on the set. He asked me to meet him at the Polo Lounge. There, I discovered, breakfast was somewhat different.

" 'Anthea,' he said to me, 'Frank and Ted and I have been thinking.' He meant Frank Wells and Ted Ashley, the other two prongs of the triumvirate running Warner Bros. 'We think maybe it would be not a bad idea for you to join our creative team.'

" 'But you're the enemy,' I said.

" 'That's the whole point. We think it would be a good idea to have somebody like you on our staff who can explain them to us and us to them.' "

Sylbert thought that another, unstated reason was her phone book with Warren's [Beatty] home number and Jack's [Nicholson] home number. She could call them and they'd pick up the phone.

Sylbert told him she'd think about it. She talked to some friends. She says that Warren Beatty told her the move would be "traitorous." But she'd been thinking about making a change, even about producing, and here were these crazy men at Warner who were trying to change her life.

"Who else was going to let a costume designer do that? Why would I say no? So I said yes!"

In 1977, she became vice president in charge of special projects at Warner Bros. "I was in charge of the loonies," she says. "I was in charge of getting Warren to lunch with Ted Ashley and Frank Wells—they'd had a big fight and he wasn't speaking to them. That's what I was in charge of."[166]

In the 1980s, Sylbert was going to be in charge of more than "the loonies."

The Pie Was Tiny

A portrait of the MGM story department in the mid-1970s describes the industrywide competition among women for the very few positions (mainly in Story) open to them.

MGM had long been the centerpiece of Culver City, a pleasant, small-town suburb slightly southwest of Hollywood. The studio was famous for its musicals, its beloved stars like Mickey Rooney, Fred Astaire, Judy Garland, and for its lion. In the early 1970s, it was making its last big musicals[167] and the old lion was fighting its last fight; the jackals would tear it apart before the decade was out. Wild-man entrepreneur Kirk Kerkorian from Las Vegas had bought the studio and was busy selling off the library, the prop department, and other organs. As its assets and reputation dwindled, studio heads changed almost yearly. The glory days were definitely gone.

Susan Merzbach started as a file clerk at MGM in 1972, a dreary job anywhere else but exciting to her because she worked on the ground floor of the Irving Thalberg Building, named for the legendary production prince, Irving G. Thalberg.[168] "I had access to every piece of MGM material ever written, memos from Louis B. Mayer or *Gone with the Wind* producer David O. Selznick, complete with little notes: 'Judy's being troublesome today.' It was part of history. When someone quit, I inherited their work for a while, stacks of it. But I remember being dreadfully sad Friday nights because I had to go home," says Merzbach. "I couldn't wait for Monday mornings when I could drive back on that lot and wave at the guard. I knew I belonged, and that was my great joy."[169]

The inner sanctum of the story files, where Merzbach worked, stood at one end of a long hall lined with story analysts, the readers' little cubicles where they "covered," read and synopsized scripts submitted by writers. The story editing executive suite was at the other end of the corridor where the head of Story, Carl Bennett, occupied Samuel Marx's old office.[170] Bennett supervised everything connected to scripts, story development, and the story files; his assistant, Pat Falkenhagen, supervised the readers. From all accounts, MGM had almost no women executives, though the fabled editor Margaret Booth, who is credited with helping develop the classic and fluid Hollywood cutting style, had been there since the 1920s.[171] Fifty years later, women were still filing clerks, readers, assistant story editors, or secretaries. There was almost no other position they could aspire to hold.

Before Merzbach arrived, Donie Nelson was Bennett's secretary. She was supporting herself and trying to finish college at night. She had had other secretarial jobs, but a film studio was a whole new world to her.

"I was efficient and organized, I could spell, I knew shorthand," Nelson says. "My parents had raised me to work hard and be honest. If you were good, you would be rewarded. Of course, those precepts didn't prepare me for Hollywood." She recalls her boss, Bennett, as a distinguished-looking man; he spoke with a British accent, wore black slacks and black turtlenecks and a monocle. "This was so long ago that men were story editors, and the job was important," says Nelson. "Nobody had ever heard of D-girl."[172]

The term "D-girl" (development) came into use late in the decade, reaching full flower in the 1980s. D-girls became a caste of young women of various titles on the track to higher executive regions who looked for material, shaped it, worked with story analysts and writers. In short, they "developed." This entry-level position opened up because the industry was being forced to hire women. The joke at that time was "Of *course* women are in development because development is foreplay!" The quip neatly distinguished between preparing for production and the action of the main event. Men produced, women developed. In less than fifteen years, that would change.

"As Carl's secretary, I sat at my desk wearing micro-miniskirts up to my ass," says Nelson, "hair down past my shoulder blades, and go-go boots. On Fridays, Carl invited the staff into his office for sherry and we'd listen to Monty Python on records. Carl was the last of a type. He was admired and had quite an influence. He protected the women in Story from the predators on the third floor."

At this time, before computers, the area Merzbach worked in contained all the MGM files; everything ever submitted to or owned by MGM was recorded on file cards and cross-referenced. "Leota presided over the story files," recalls Nelson. "She'd been with the studio for years, was about five feet tall, rather curvaceous. If we weren't wearing hot pants and miniskirts, we were wearing long granny skirts with the buttons up the front. Leota wore those; she left the skirt unbuttoned up to above her knee. Peek of leg. Leota gave me practical advice: Always be nice to everyone because you never know who's going to be your boss."

Ten months later, in 1972, Nelson in effect became Leota's boss when Bennett's assistant story editor, Pat Falkenhagen, resigned.

In any corporation, a departmental opening means that if you can't fill it with your person, someone above you is going to fill it with *their* person and you'll end up working with somebody who owes you no allegiance. "Carl had seen the executive movements above him," Nelson says, "and I think he sensed the changes converging on the studio and on Hollywood." Bennett promoted his secretary, Nelson, into the assistant story editor position and, to ensure her loyalty, he gave Nelson a raise. "He told me I had to change my wardrobe and wear my hair in a bun." No more miniskirts. The next day, Bennett said to her, "I was right! The execs were stirring around trying to come up with somebody's nephew for your job."[173]

In 1974, Congress had passed the Equal Employment Opportunity Act and established the EEOC, the commission, which was to prove decisive in the treatment of women and minorities in the workforce. In 1975, the EEOC began to investigate the entertainment industry. In Hollywood and elsewhere, the hunt was on to hire or promote women.

"Carl had told Personnel I was not only a woman but a Native American," Nelson says. "I had heard a family story about some Native American blood in our background. It had never been verified, but I'd mentioned something about it months before. Carl ran with it. Nobody could replace me with somebody's white nephew out of Harvard."[174]

In 1975, two young women arrived at MGM, Sherry Lansing in Story and Mary Ledding in Legal.

Frank Rosenfelt was president; Frank Davis was head of business affairs. The highest ranking woman on the corporate side of the studio was Karla Davidson, the associate general counsel. Davidson hired Mary Ledding. "I was her first hire," says Ledding, who was right out of UCLA law school. "She was very much a mentor to me. It was stupendous to see Sherry there, too. I only worked a little with her, but her presence and Karla's gave us the sense that things might be changing."[175]

Ledding, born in Portland, Oregon, has an unvarnished sense of reality mixed with an enthusiastic sense of fun. Like many of the women in these pages, she was the first person in her family to go to college.

"I started off in TV business affairs," says Ledding. "Our business likes to cubbyhole people, and lawyers are legal, not creative. Period. Then Frank Davis, 'Mister Yep, Nope,' who became my other mentor, asked me to come over and do minimal feature business affairs. Television and features are as separate as legal and business affairs. Business affairs makes the deal and legal drafts the deal. Today the business is all about the deal, not the movie. I was at a seminar recently where a lawyer was talking about pickup deals. The word 'picture' or 'film' never crossed his lips. For the studio, it's all about business, not art. I'm not sure it was ever about art."

A unique ritual took place at MGM. A group of executives *liked* to eat lunch together every day. "They lunched together at a big round table in the commissary. If you didn't have a lunch date you just showed up there and heard about everything that was going on. After they finished, they'd walk around the lot."

When Ledding was promoted to vice president, Karla Davidson brought her to the round table. "That was the first time I realized that women really needed to know about sports because that's what these guys talked about. I didn't even know which sport they were discussing, much less which team. Then we walked around the empty back lot because there was almost nothing being shot there. When a flock of analysts from the stock market flew in to visit, the studio actually hired extras, put them in costume and spotted them around the lot. When the Wall Street analysts went from one building to another, someone cued the extras to fly into action and talk about how busy the lot was. If an analyst asked a question, the extra shouted, 'That picture's shooting over on the north end. This lot is so busy!' There was nothing happening. I think they were shooting on one stage."[176]

Meanwhile, back in the MGM story files, Susan Merzbach had been doing some script coverage for Bennett and looking around to see how she could better herself. When a reader's job opened up, she jumped at it. "We had one male file clerk. I'd been there a little longer," she says, "but he got the job."

The new reader didn't work out. Two weeks later, Bennett offered it to Merzbach. "But you have to sign your work 'S. Merzbach' because they want a guy," he told her.

When Daniel Melnick became the new head of the studio, he noticed her coverage and once said to Bennett, "That guy Merzbach is okay," at which point Bennett told him that Merzbach was "a girl." "I was allowed to stay on," Merzbach says, "and after that I was allowed to sign my full name to my work."[177]

Meanwhile, new leadership brought more changes. "Bennett was trying valiantly to get along with Melnick," says Donie Nelson, "but Carl's roots went back to old Hollywood, hanging out with Errol Flynn, and Dan Melnick was new Hollywood." Bennett was allowed to retire. In 1975, Melnick brought in Sherry Lansing as story editor, to whom everyone in Story reported.

Lansing is a beautiful woman of enormous energy. She started as a reader while teaching high school math in the Watts district of Los Angeles, then became an actress briefly before landing at Talent Associates in 1974 as an executive in charge of West Coast development.

"Carl escorted Sherry around to show her the offices," says Nelson. "When he came back, he was grinning. I couldn't understand it. We all knew he was being forced out. 'What are you so happy about?' I asked him.

" 'I pointed out to the dear girl,' he said, 'that all the important people were on the third floor where there happened to be an empty office— Saul David's old office when he was executive story editor. She couldn't wait to leave me and go upstairs to get Danny's [Melnick's] ear. Don't worry, Donie, she won't be down here to bother you.' He was trying to protect us and by suggesting the office up there he felt her sights would be set up instead of down—on us," says Nelson.[178]

Within a few months, Melnick promoted Lansing to executive story editor. "This was just a year after Marcia Nasatir went to United Artists as a vice president, a rank that was comparatively new," says Lansing, recalling that the two or three other executive women at MGM were not in the creative area.

Lansing recalls that at one point, when she asked for a raise, she was told, "You're earning quite enough for a woman. There's no reason for you to earn more. A man has to support a family."

She says, "Without hesitation, I said, 'Oh, okay.'

"Looking back, I'm dismayed at my reaction, but at the time, that's the way we saw such things. I was conditioned by the way I was raised— that a woman ought to be wife and mother, or if we sought careers we could become a nurse or a teacher. They are wonderful professions but they were practically the only ones open to women. I sort of accepted the fact that in the movie business a woman would never run a company. I was really conditioned to believe we could go just so far and I should be grateful for what I could achieve. I was supporting myself in an interesting job, but I sort of accepted second-class citizenship. I had to start to believe I could ask for more before anyone was going to give me more."[179]

"We had no template for our aspirations as working women at that stage," says Merzbach. "I had seen women acting like men just as I'd seen them be flirtatious, and I knew I couldn't be either one. Then I saw Sherry in the corridors. She was direct, open, generous, and hard-working. Aha! I can relate to that."[180]

On the fourth floor of the Thalberg Building, Louis B. Mayer had built a private suite as big as a villa. It held a dining room, an executive gym, and a steam room. Screenwriter Harriet Frank Jr. was there during the MGM heyday. "It was like a country club," she said. "They had a sports club for men on the top floor . . . It was opulent . . . the fairy tale dream of what a Hollywood studio was like."[181]

In 1975, assistant story editor Donie Nelson received a call from Mary Ledding. Nelson recalls, "Ledding asked me, 'Do you know there's an executive gym on the fourth floor?' I did know that. 'Do you ever use it?'"

"No," Nelson answered. "My boss used to."

Ledding told Nelson that she'd asked around and had been told that women couldn't use the gym because there were no separate dressing facilities. When Ledding pointed out that excluding women from the gym wasn't legal, she had been told none of the women who were eligible wanted to use it. So she asked them for a list of all the eligible women.

Ledding was going down the list, calling the eligible MGM women to ask if they'd be willing to use the gym, free the gym. Nelson said she'd be willing to use it. Ledding asked her if she could use her name. Nelson said she'd be willing to use it. Ledding asked her if she could use her name.

"Sure," Nelson said.

"Oh, good. I just got through talking to your boss."

"What did Sherry say?" Nelson wondered.

"She said that she would use it, too." Ledding recalls that Lansing, at her level, helped get them into the gym. Nelson recalls that Lansing did not want her name used though she was willing to state for Ledding's purposes that she was in favor of women using the gym.

Having collected a few women's names, Ledding gave the list to the studio manager, who wanted to allot Tuesday mornings before 8:00 as women's time in the gym. According to Nelson, Ledding said, "We'll use it whenever we want but we'll put a sign on the door, 'Beware, Women Present.'"[182]

That's what they did—Mary Ledding, Deanna Wilcox in publicity, Patt Healy in the television legal department, and Nelson. Nelson recalls,

"It was our routine on Tuesday nights before the executive screenings. We'd work out, have our steam, and then go to whatever the studio was screening that night. That's where we forged our friendship because we rarely met anywhere else—we were all from different parts of the studio. When United Artists moved into the ground floor of the east wing of the Thalberg Building, once in a while Marcia Nasatir joined us."[183]

"It was gorgeous up there," Ledding recalls. "The entire top floor used to be a private dining room, and below that, the gymnasium. There was a steam room, showers, glorious old tile, and an old leather medicine ball that was coming apart, a remnant of the glory days." It was the studio's attic, where the Oscars gleamed dully from glass cases in storage.

"When we sat in the steam room, we talked about what was going on," says Ledding. "You have no idea how unusual that was." There was no other way a couple of women lawyers could hear regularly from women in Story or Publicity.

"Liberating the gym," Ledding says, "was the butt of many jokes. If you give on one front, the others tend to collapse, which they knew, and *that* inspired the guys with the keys not to give in. But they had to give in. It was just another thing that we were in their face about."[184]

When Bennett left, Nelson, as assistant story editor, was supervising veteran readers who made more money than she did, and they all knew it. (Nelson did not become story editor until months later.) "Sherry had a more open approach to managing the story work," Nelson says. "Somebody once said her motto was always, 'Be sincere whether you mean it or not.' That sounds flip, but she made writers feel we gave their scripts careful attention, that they were the most talented people in the world, and to please submit anything else. In the past, story editors were noted for writing long, detailed reasons why the studio was passing on a script. Her letters were brief. She telephoned everybody. She really was an AT&T ad. To her credit, she was compulsive about doing that. When she'd clean off her desk she'd go into Melnick's office and clean off his desk because he had a tendency to sit on things for weeks. She'd call people back, tell them we were passing, and then they'd get a letter saying, 'Per your conversation with Miss Lansing, the script so-and-so is enclosed, look forward to reading anything else...' That way there were no awful memos to haunt you, and people felt they could come back with another script."

Lansing's approach freed Nelson from agonizing every time she rejected scripts. "I learned a lot from her," Nelson says, "even though she was up on the third floor and I couldn't look over her shoulder. But I could see the stuff coming through, because everything that went to her went through me and everything that came down went through me." But Nelson wasn't used to managing people. The only management style she knew was Bennett's, and she had problems he'd never had—such as interruptions from the women in the secretarial pool who insisted that she show them how to change a typewriter ribbon. "They would never have asked Carl to do that."[185]

Merzbach wanted to move up. She admired Lansing and wanted to find a way to work more closely with her because Lansing's style made sense to her. "Shortly after Sherry arrived at MGM, a silly thing happened," Merzbach says. "Someone at work had a 'psychic' friend and I got a free reading. The psychic took my ring and said, 'I'll tell you about your love life.' She was holding the ring to her forehead, frowning and saying, 'I see nothing, I see nothing.' A note had fallen out of my purse. 'Susan can you see me at 4:00?' No signature. The psychic picked it up and started screaming. 'I see diamonds! Oh my God, this is going to be such a famous person!' It was a note Sherry had sent me. When I got back to the studio, I told Sherry about it. She laughed. 'Ridiculous,' she said. 'In our lifetime we're not going to see a woman as head of a studio.' "

In 1975, no one had any question about where the glass ceiling started. "Sherry worked in a sea of men," Merzbach says. "Jack Haley Jr., Ray Wagner, Dan Melnick. There were no women at that level. I was in a sea of men, too, because all the people above me in the structure, except for Sherry, were men."

Women's slice of the pie was tiny. If a woman could not grab the one or two positions open to her in a studio, her only solution was to move to another studio, as the contest that developed between Nelson and Merzbach shows.

Nelson didn't want to be executive story editor; she wanted to hang onto the position she had, story editor. Merzbach wanted Nelson's job, but Nelson was not likely to quit, so Merzbach asked Lansing to help her find another job. Lansing said she would. In the meantime, she let Merzbach sit in on some of her meetings. At that time, a reader like Merzbach wrote an opinion of a script and the story editor wrote a second opinion. Lansing let Merzbach do some second opinions for the experience. Nelson did not like that. To make matters worse, the legal department asked Merzbach to translate a letter from German. Merzbach knew the language; her father had been a doctor in Germany before escaping to Holland in 1936.[186]

The translation of the letter caused more friction between Merzbach and Nelson because, as Merzbach admits, she did the translation without Nelson's permission. Nelson saw herself as the "nonambitious person in the middle of two ambitious women. I did not understand them at all," she says. "Susan wanted, I felt, to do the fun things of my job, sit in on Sherry's meetings, meet the writers, while I got to do budgets and the paperwork. The people in my department knew that Susan could go over my head to Sherry. I was very angry. In ordinary circumstances I could have fired Susan, but Sherry respected her work." Moreover, Nelson did not owe her job to Lansing but if Lansing made Merzbach story editor, Merzbach would owe Lansing. "I didn't realize it but in Hollywood you can't stay in one place or you disappear," says Nelson. "You have to keep moving, preferably up."[187]

"Nelson stumbled," Merzbach recalls. "In some way, she went over Sherry's head. By that time, Dan Melnick, Sherry's mentor, had moved to Columbia and Dick Shepherd had come in to run MGM. He was Old Hollywood, had married Louis B. Mayer's granddaughter, had been president of Warner Bros. Shepherd let Sherry know that Nelson had some complaints. Sherry fired Nelson." According to Merzbach, Nelson's parting words were, "I hope the first thing the new story editor does is fire Susan."[188] Lansing made Merzbach the story editor.

Nelson doesn't remember her parting words but confirms that they were probably along those lines.

"Sherry gave me great references," Nelson says, "but I was devastated. Shepherd had seen a memo of mine and had written on it 'I agree with Nelson 100 percent,' which gave me a lift, and he had yanked me into a production meeting while Sherry was out of town. But I did go to him after she got back. I think he didn't want to be in the middle of a catfight.

"I'd never had to look for a job in the business before," says Nelson. "I thought you got ahead by doing good work and by being honest. I found out that had nothing to do with it. It permanently changed the way I looked at the business. Even though I'd been at MGM six years, I realized how little I knew about how things actually worked in the industry. Carl's paternal approach kept us all in the dark. Sherry was how it really worked."[189]

"Being a woman did not help me when I started out," says Mary Ledding. "Women were completely absent from most areas. I got my break because I was hired by a woman. But for Karla, I could not be where I am." Ledding recalls an incident related to her by one of the most successful women on the corporate side of the business. The woman was being interviewed at a law firm, and during that interview the lawyer made sexual advances. "I never went through anything like that," says Ledding. "I was very lucky. I got my break from a woman, and second, I was always chubby. Overweight women are treated differently. Third, I was married. Married women are treated differently. I know single women really, really had problems. One woman in business affairs told me about being accosted by a star when she took him a contract to sign. In seconds, he had her against the wall. That's what many women went through every day."

At MGM, Ledding was introduced to the remote-controlled door closer. She was in a budget meeting with the head of physical production. "He was a very nice man," Ledding says. "The offices at MGM were really spacious, maybe thirty feet long and twenty feet wide. When I came in, he was sitting at his desk on the far side of the room. I sat down in the chair and behind me, miraculously, the door closed. It was funny and shocking. 'How did you do that?' I asked.

" 'Oh, there's this little switch by my desk.'

"That's old studio," Ledding says, laughing. "I'm sure in many cases as soon as the door shut, the unlucky girl was chased around the room and she couldn't get out. It was creepy. Offices at old studios still have those switches, private bathrooms and private everything. Being married protected me."[190]

By 1977, Dan Melnick was president of motion pictures at Columbia. Lansing was vice president in charge of production, supervising *Kramer vs. Kramer* and *The China Syndrome.* In 1978, Merzbach became executive story editor at Columbia. Ledding remained at MGM, promoted to VP of Business Affairs in motion pictures. Donie Nelson landed a job with writer-producer-director Joanna Lee's company, Christiana Productions, as director of creative affairs.[191] By the 1980s, Ledding and Nelson both had children and would soon be single mothers.

Every studio in town had a group of women like these, usually clustered around Story or Marketing. In the mid-1970s, television was a little more adventurous than film. Young women eager for network careers—not just jobs—streamed through the opening doors, a tide witnessed by a few "grande dames," as the trades dubbed them, who had been working for years.

5

GET ME A WOMAN!

ABC was a scrappy, new-kid-on-the-block network that took chances its more staid and conventional competition, CBS and NBC, wouldn't dream of. Its West Coast programming offices were in a high-rise at 9255 Sunset Boulevard just past Doheny at the junction that connects Beverly Hills with Hollywood. Barry Diller, a tough trader whose pithy observations, such as "This business is all about will," are still quoted today, was in charge of the West Coast ABC entertainment operation. Legend has it that Diller had jumped on an idea called the "Movie of the Week" (first promulgated by producer Roy Huggins)[192] and had run with it for ABC.

Like Tomorrow Entertainment, Tandem, and MTM, ABC in the mid-1970s was known for hiring women and seemed genuinely open to promoting them. Lillian Gallo had been a production assistant in the theater and on the *Twilight Zone* television series. Diller hired her as director of Movies of the Weekend, as the programming segment was called then, making her one of the first women executives in that area. By 1971, she moved from development executive to producer of films for ABC Entertainment, the in-house unit of ABC movies for television.

How Would You Like to Produce?

"Working with Barry Diller was an amazing experience," says Gallo, "though I wasn't as aware of it then as later, when he moved so quickly as a young man, and so high. Barry was a risk-taker. He would move on an idea, and he had wonderful vision. It was easy to work with him, not hard. In those days, the networks had a simpler structure. It was just me reporting to Barry, and he made the decision on the spot. So the working relationship was close. Now the departments are so large.

"I used to drive Barry in my Corvette to Universal or Paramount, whichever studio was doing shows for ABC. During that time, I saw thousands of hours of dailies, read scripts and 'developed' stories, and tracked their progress through script to final product. After you've worked on the development of hundreds of shows, you have a little black book—in my case, a little black book of names. You know who's good at doing what."

Gallo, dignified and smart, chooses her words with precision. Rambling enthusiasm is not her style. "Barry Diller gave me my big break when one day he said, 'Lillian, how would you like to produce?' "

Her first in-house ABC movie for television, *Haunts of the Very Rich* (1972), starred Cloris Leachman, Ed Asner, Lloyd Bridges, and Anne Francis. The story was about a group of vacationers who arrive in a tropical paradise to find that their destination gives each of them what they've always wanted. They are euphoric until someone theorizes that they have all died.

"Our first day was scheduled as a long day of shooting on difficult terrain in Florida. When we'd completed it, the network representative said to me, 'You did a very good job. There isn't a man who could have done it better.' Men were not accustomed to working with women. It was the nicest thing he felt he could say.

"Anne Francis wrote a letter to ABC, which was passed on to me. She said it was the first time in her career that she'd worked for a woman producer, that it was a 'wonderful experience,' that working on the set was 'different,' the crew's language was 'different,' and that the tone I'd set as the producer was 'different.' I was touched by her sensibilities. Consciously or unconsciously, women do bring different things to the workplace. Diversity is good for all of us."[193]

I Had a Feeling Women Had an Advantage

"I knew ABC was the only place to go if you were a woman," Marcy Carsey says, "because it certainly wasn't CBS or NBC, where people were still wearing pin-striped suits and had gray hair."[194] One of the many jokes circulating about ABC was that "the reason nobody could find Patty Hearst was that she was on ABC at eight o'clock Friday night."[195] But ABC would soon become the number one network and make history.

One of the reasons, which Carsey observed, was the energetic leadership at ABC. Still shy of forty, Barry Diller had worked in every facet of programming for ABC since 1966. In 1974, he leaped to chairman of Paramount Pictures, when the irascible Charlie Bluhdorn, chairman of

Gulf & Western, the conglomerate that owned Paramount, hired him. Michael Eisner became head of the West Coast entertainment operation, reporting to ABC Entertainment president Martin Starger in New York.

Marcy Carsey first became excited by television when she was working at Tomorrow Entertainment. "I learned that I loved television. It seemed like a wonderful place to me. It was [also] at Tomorrow that I first had a sense women could do well, that there were no limitations because of my gender. We were selling to the networks. I looked around; we were selling to Deanne Barkley, who was head of the movies-for-television division at ABC. I saw how great she was—what a hoot she was—I saw how much Barry Diller listened to her and how much power he gave her. I saw the women around me, Nancy Malone and Marian Rees and a few women at other production companies like Lillian Gallo, and I saw the women writers we dealt with. It never entered my mind that women would be anything but equal, and I had a feeling they might have an advantage.

"I knew I wanted a career, if there was such a thing in television, and network television was the hub of the business then. I knew I could really learn there. So I chose to go to ABC. I was still kind of a kid—well, thirty, but I was a kid."

Her final interview for the job at ABC as a general program executive in comedy was with Michael Eisner. "I was pregnant, though it didn't show yet," Carsey said. "When I met with Michael I told him, 'I can stay at Tomorrow and come back and talk with you after the baby is born if that would make you more comfortable.'

"He looked at me as if I'd said something really weird. 'How does this relate to what we're talking about?' he said. 'My wife's having a child, too, and I'm coming to work. Are you coming to work?'

" 'Yeah.'

" 'Well, then, this isn't a factor. Why are we talking about this?'

"I thought that was so fabulous," Carsey says. "I knew I had chosen the right place to work."[196]

One reason Carsey felt so at home was that feisty ABC was not like the other networks. People dressed casually, even sloppily. No one cared about style except show style; no one cared about going to the right parties. Almost no time was spent analyzing or strategizing or researching or polling; ideas could come from anyone anywhere—the waitress down the block, a program exec stuck in a snowbound airport. Carsey says Eisner taught her that her job wasn't about making friends; it was about getting a couple of hit shows on the air every year.

"We ran a casual shop," she says. "Instead of using the intercom, I'd scream down the hall . . . We had babies at home so half the time we were covered with throw-up. I often brought my baby to work . . . I'd take her to run-throughs in the screening room and nurse her through reruns. We used to be warned that the guys from New York were coming, Leonard [Goldenson] and Elton [Rule] and those guys. Somebody would slide in and yell, 'Leonard and Elton are in town!'

" 'Holy shit! Maybe I better go home and change . . . maybe I better not be caught . . . with my makeup mirror in front of me and my hair dripping wet.' [But] it was okay if they came in and the baby was crying beside you. The whole office was a little chaotic but as long as you got your work done, everything was fine."[197]

When Carsey did not like the shows she was assigned, she was very blunt in voicing her opinions. At one point, she went to Eisner and offered to trade him all the shows she had for one gem that she'd found on the shelf that had been passed over. It was a pilot about a character called Barney Miller. (*Barney Miller* was picked up as a midseason replacement in 1975, Carsey was assigned to it, and it ran for almost eight years.)

"Very soon after I'd started at ABC, I said to my husband, 'I think network TV is a mad whirlwind.' 'I'm going to get fired very soon or be made vice president!' I wore blinders when I worked. I did the very best job I knew how, and sometimes I butted up against management. But I was never afraid of that. In fact, I relished it. I'm this New England kid with a stubborn streak a mile long. I rather enjoy being a maverick or an iconoclast. I was never afraid of being fired. And the people who hired me at ABC, especially Michael Eisner, encouraged that."[198] By 1976, she was vice president of prime-time comedy program development.

Let's not lose sight of the fact that in 1974, all of the eighteen top executive positions at ABC Entertainment were occupied by men, except for VP of movies for television, a post then held by Deanne Barkley (Brandon Stoddard took over in 1975). Esther Shapiro, who would later create *Dynasty*, did not become VP of novels and limited series until 1979.

ABC headquarters were in New York. Leonard Goldenson was founder and chairman of the board. Martin Starger, the president of ABC Entertainment, was crazy about the theater. The Shubert Theater was in the ABC Entertainment Center in Los Angeles (Century City), a complex still so empty in the mid-1970s that a woman leaving ABC at six o'clock at night could hear only the sound of her high heels echoing on the marble walkways. The Shubert Theater was in trouble. Starger wanted to know more about the productions going into it and the business terms under which the Shubert operated. But who on staff at ABC knew about the inner workings of the theater? Someone remembered an entry-level lawyer named Johnna Levine.

Levine and her husband Joe had been Broadway producers for years[199] until their financing dried up in 1973, forcing Levine to look for work as a lawyer, which landed her at ABC as a program attorney—a position she terms "the lowest of the low."[200] After she'd been there a while, she was assigned to write a report about the Shubert situation. "I hate legalese," she says, "so I wrote the report in a very direct manner to explain how theatrical productions often worked; the sharing terms between the theater, the producer, and investors; what shows might be expected to come in to the Shubert; and the various ramifications for ABC. That report redounded to my fame in the circles around Marty Starger."

The hierarchy at ABC began talking to her directly about topics other than the legal problems of television programming. "I became a denizen of the thirty-seventh and thirty-eighth floors. I wrote reports on what plays were coming in and recommending certain ones, which made some of the executives happy and gave me entree. My knowledge of the theater pulled me out of the lineup of the program attorneys and made it possible for me to get the very next open spot as associate director of business affairs in 1975."

The business affairs departments at ABC, NBC, and CBS had no female vice presidents. "Women," Levine says, "were used as the lower-level troops, the noncoms." Levine was not a typical program attorney. She was in her forties, had years of experience as an entertainment attorney producing in the theater, was married and at that time supporting her husband and two children. She was a knowledgeable professional with specialized information, but she says she often took the position of somebody who asked for assistance or who looked for leadership, maybe for protection.

"It may have been artifice," says Levine, "but at the time I never worried about getting recognition. If I was put on a task, I was a loyal helpmeet, the woman who wouldn't get the credit but who would make it all happen—that was the role I filled. And it worked! I must say the men above me at ABC often treated me not as someone behind the scenes, but as a doer. The only problems I ever had with men occurred later when I was in direct and difficult competition."

By 1975, Levine was ABC's director of business affairs, East Coast, based in New York. But as more programming responsibilities shifted to Los Angeles, she traveled back and forth and was finally transferred there for movies for television and miniseries, a promotion. Logically, Levine believed she was destined to be a vice president.

After a year, she came back from vacation to find that her successor as director of business affairs on the East Coast, Tony Farinacci, had been promoted to vice president. Levine's predecessors in the job had been vice presidents, and now her successor was also a vice president, but she was not.

Levine says, "Tony was comparatively new, a sweet, competent man who worked on programs that had not moved to the West Coast—children's and late night. I had a tremendous amount of programming to deal with. I had a much larger staff."

Such things happen—often. Levine was not in the creative area of the business, but in the corporate sector.

"I was absolutely devastated," says Levine, "but I was not in a position to quit. What I did was imbecilic, but I couldn't help myself. ABC's headquarters in Los Angeles is all glass—the windows, the interior walls of the corridors, and all the executive offices. On Monday, for the first time since I'd been there, I drew the blind across the corridor window wall in my office. Very few people ever did this. A statement. I did my work. I talked, tersely, only about business. I was sulking with a capital *S* and with such a vengeance that in ABC's easy, freewheeling atmosphere my action was conspicuous."

On the fourth day, Levine was called into conference with the two heads of business affairs. They told her, "This is ridiculous, Johnna. You cannot carry on this way. Why are you doing this?"

"Because this is horrific," she replied. Levine recalls, "I didn't want to say that Tony didn't deserve the promotion. He didn't compared to me, but he was a nice guy. 'I'm not going to argue that you shouldn't give him an increase and the stripe. But why pass over me?'

" 'What do we do if we have just one vice presidency to give?' they kept saying.

" 'You decide what you should do as long as it doesn't mean I don't get it,' I kept saying. I was outraged beyond any belief. Finally, I wept. I tried not to but couldn't help myself.

" 'What does it matter?' they kept saying. 'You're doing the same work, you have the same number of people under you.'

" 'You gave me this giant department,' I kept shouting back, 'and not one thing has ever hit the floor and I handle movies airing twice a week. There are one hundred twenty-five films on the development list. I keep all of these, all the rights, make all the deals, and not one has exploded.' "

At the end of two or three hours, the head of business affairs said, "I'll go upstairs and tell them they should give you the vice presidency."

"He didn't say I had it, he said he would fight for it," Levine says. "About two months later, I got the vice presidency. No salary increase or anything else. But I only had it for a few months because Warner Bros. made me an offer, which I accepted." Levine says that the executives at ABC were astonished when she jumped ship—after all, her salary at Warners wasn't much higher, and she was a VP at ABC. But by then, Levine says, "I'd been disillusioned about what it had taken to get ABC's grudging recognition."[201]

Come and Be Director of Daytime Programs! Children's Specials!

Sue Cameron, the *Hollywood Reporter* columnist who had broken the story of the Writers Guild statistics about the inequities of women writers, picked up her phone one day and found herself talking with the head of CBS, Fred Silverman. "He flew me to New York during the television season, took me to lunch at 21," says Cameron. "At the end of a pleasant meal, he said, 'I want you to leave *The Hollywood Reporter* and come to CBS and be director of children's specials in New York.' I did not realize the significance of the offer. 'I don't know anything about children,' I replied, 'and I don't want to live in New York.' I thanked him for a lovely time and went back to L.A."[202]

Cynical or sincere, the hunt was on for women at the networks.

"For the next year or so," says Cameron, "when [Silverman] was in Los Angeles, he'd call and we'd have breakfast or lunch. I suppose the reason he kept meeting with me was that I didn't want a job or to sell him a show."

One day Silverman took Cameron to breakfast at the Polo Lounge. He told her that he was leaving CBS and going to ABC. "This time," he said, "you're not saying no to me."

Cameron recalls, "He offered me three different jobs at ABC—director of daytime programs, daytime comedy, and late night. 'You should take daytime,' he said, 'because that's where I started and that's the profit center of the network. When you start there you will learn everything.'"

Cameron is not sure why Silverman offered to hire her. "This was 1975," she says, "and the EEOC had subtly put out the word to the networks that it was about to come down on them because they had so few women vice presidents. I was in my twenties, naive about such things, and I don't remember even asking him [why]."[203]

In a move that startled many, Cameron quit her highly visible job at *The Hollywood Reporter* and drove over to ABC in Century City—as a director of daytime programming.

"The day I arrived at ABC, because my column had been very popular, there were twenty-three flower arrangements sitting in my office from executives and stars. Those bouquets were not helpful. They singled me out," says Cameron. "In some quarters, I was not liked at all. One reason may have been that at that time no network had ever hired a television critic or editor in an executive position. Plus, I was a woman, I was single, and I was really young. A lethal combo." Moreover, when she got the job, strong rumors were circulating that Cameron and Silverman were secretly dating. "Absolutely false," says Cameron. "God forbid a woman might get a job on ability."[204]

Cameron had no experience as an executive at the network. However, "director of" is an entry-level post in most quarters, one in which determined people can learn on the job. But on this job, she says, "I had little to do. They seemed to want me to stay in my office. My suggestions were not listened to, I got little support. Half the men openly resented me; the other half thought I was nice, if something of an oddity. Of the few women who worked at ABC then, only Marcy Carsey and Loreen Arbus spoke to me.

"We had meetings around a fifty-foot table with all the guys, including Fred Silverman and Michael Eisner, talking about the shows for daytime or nighttime. One we discussed was *Neighbors*," Cameron recalls, "about two teams of feuding neighbors. Someone asked me if I thought it should go on the air. I'd only been there about six weeks. I didn't know that a smart executive avoids answering questions by asking questions back— what is the research, what kind of demographics do we have for the time slot, what's the budget? I didn't know that dance. I just said, 'I think it's great, let's put it on the air.' Its host was Regis Philbin. After six weeks, it was canceled, and I felt sandbagged. I was blamed because I'd spoken up about it in the meeting."[205] In the idea's second incarnation, *Family Feud*, it became a hit.

"I still had a lot of the reporter in me. A producer took me to lunch one day and during the meal, he tried to bribe me. He offered me five thousand dollars for a pilot commitment, ten thousand for a series commitment, fifteen hundred a week for every week the show aired. Then he named other executives at ABC who had taken the money. I was shocked, but I realized what a potentially dangerous situation it was. I didn't chastise this guy. I went on talking about the eggplant parmigiana and told him I'd get back to him.

"I never got back to him." She immediately reported it, offered to set up a dummy account, take the check, and then call the police. The man she reported this to objected. "We'd have a scandal at the network," he said.

"He told me to make out a report and put it in the safe.

"I was then 'promoted' to Honolulu to supervise the Don Ho show, a one-hour daytime variety show. In reality, ABC wanted me away from home base. A corner suite in Royal Hawaiian had been reserved for me; I had an unlimited expense account. It was a gilded prison. To the credit of the man I reported it to, over time he quietly replaced all the execs who were receiving fees from producers.

"After six weeks in Hawaii, I was ready to do anything to get off the island. Finally, I was ordered back to the mainland. Shortly after I'd returned, I was in my office, crying at my desk, when Brandon Stoddard opened the door without knocking. 'What's the matter?' he said. I looked at him and said, 'I hate it here.' "[206]

Cameron resigned. She'd been at ABC for three years.[207]

Other young women took to network television with alacrity. The arenas usually open to women without previous experience were daytime, story development, and children's programming. When it came to television fare for children, ABC was imaginative and inventive, turning out programs like *Richie Rich, Scooby Doo, The Flintstone Kids*, and a new form, AfterSchool Specials such as *Rookie of the Year* (Jodie Foster's first role). Children's programming and women went together, and After-School Specials gave some women their start as executives or as producers.

At the ABC flagship station in Detroit, Bonny Dore created and produced a new children's series, *Hot Fudge*. "At the station, women worked primarily as secretaries," she says, "but one or two were just starting as on-camera reporters. The entire sales force was male. No women in the editing rooms or the booth, so when I came in as the producer of my own show it was noted with skepticism. 'Who is this short person with blond hair and why is she bothering us?' I was about twenty-three, and so was the only other woman who had just been made an assistant program manager. We were closely observed for how we handled our 'high-level' positions."[208]

In 1976, the success of *Hot Fudge* and the legal winds from Washington, D.C., blew Dore into Los Angeles as the manager of children's programming, ABC West Coast. Other young women were arriving, too, like Loreen Arbus, from New York, who landed in Story at ABC in Los Angeles after a short stop in on-air promotions. These slightly younger women met others like Marcy Carsey or Johnna Levine (already vice presidents, though only by a few months) or Lillian Gallo, an independent producer making movies of the week for ABC.

"For many years there were only a few spots we could go for," says Dore. "Women were put in a competitive position against each other instead of a supportive position. You'd be the woman on the department, the woman in the production team. Competition among women for any position was fierce.[209] One of the ways women gained a competitive advantage was by working longer and harder.

"In retrospect, as women in a man's world," Loreen Arbus says, "we wanted desperately to prove ourselves—we worked through lunch, came in earlier, left later, and were often the most reliable resources in the work force."[210]

Arbus's manner is direct and warm. "Women at the networks were found in story development," she says. "We put our opinions on paper and that was a kind of inoffensive way for people to deal with because they didn't have to be in a room and listen to us. They just saw what we wrote on the paper."

Most of the women who were starting out at ABC say they knew they were paid less for the same work. "But it was hard to ferret out what people were making," says Arbus. "We just didn't know." One day, she was in the ABC conference room with Christine Foster, who was the director of development at the Wolper Organization, which in 1977 had just wowed the world with *Roots*. She recalls Foster saying, "Look, I'm sick of everyone being so secretive about what they make. How will we get ahead if we ourselves don't tell what we're making?" Then Foster blurted out what her salary was.

"I would have been mortified to talk about mine," says Arbus, "but in that moment I knew how wrong it was to keep quiet. Knowing comparative figures gave us a baseline for subsequent negotiations."

Around a year later, Arbus was promoted to program executive. Lillian Gallo, by then an established television movie producer, gave Arbus some advice: "You're part of the establishment now. You're not a creative supplier. You need to make opportunities for yourself, to be accepted in the executive world. You've got to think about your physical presentation." Arbus has a style all her own, and still wears her thick black hair in a braid down her back, bright clothes, and clusters of large silver and onyx jewelry.

"Lillian took a risk, as anyone does who tells the truth," Arbus says, "but I heard her. I bought some business suits and put my hair back. I like my freedom of expression in my personal style but I realized I would pay a price. I had to decide how much of that price I was willing to pay."[211]

Suddenly acknowledging the legal pressures streaming from the Equal Employment Opportunity Act, ABC's human resources department began posting job openings on a bulletin board.[212] "This made it possible for us to at least see what was open—before it was closed!" Arbus says.

She saw that Wally Weltman, West Coast head of late night television, had an opening. Late night was low-budget, airing a different show each night: rock and roll concerts, Wide World of Entertainment, drama, mysteries, and documentaries. "No one really wanted to work low-budget in those days," says Arbus. "It was pre-*Nightline* and other talk shows, but a crowd applied for that job. I was one. I campaigned for it by keeping my name in front of him, I sent him my story coverage, I had people call him on my behalf. Finally, he offered me the job of supervisor of late night programming. I was thrilled, but now I had a new problem I knew he'd resent if he found out from someone else."

Arbus went to Weltman and said there was something she needed to tell him. She recalls, "He sort of changed color as if I was going to tell him about being pregnant or a drug problem." Instead, she said, "My father is the founder and chairman of the board of ABC. Leonard Goldenson."

Weltman was taken aback. He told Arbus, "I can't say it doesn't make a difference. I'll have to think about it."

Arbus understood his reaction. "He'd spent time looking for someone and I'd just thrown in this big monkey wrench."

As a teenager, Arbus had wanted to be a radical underground journalist, but her first job as an intern was at *Cosmopolitan*. She had taken her grandmother's maiden name, Arbus. Now, years later at ABC, her father was on the East Coast, she was on the West, and only one person in administration knew her real name. "I didn't want anyone to think I'd been given a job because of my father," she says.

Two days later, Weltman called her into back his office. "I have one condition: If you can meet it, I'll have no problems working with you. I've had a long career, twenty-seven years. Your direct line to the top management of the network can affect my career. I need to know that what we talk about is between you and me, that it goes nowhere else."

" 'Wally,' I said, 'you have my word of honor.'

"We had the best of friendships," she says. "He was a remarkable man, and a true mentor. And I learned how important it is to deal honestly and openly, even in those things you fear most.

"If I had been Leonard Goldenson's *son*," Arbus says, "I think everyone would have just assumed I was there to take over, rather than assuming my employment was a favor. To me, going up the ladder at ABC was not my birthright or my destiny—I was a woman. Had I been a man, I would not have felt concerned about putting others in awkward positions when they had to evaluate my work. It would never have occurred to me to anticipate or take care of everyone's feelings."[213]

Some sons don't want anyone assuming they got their positions because of their dads until they've made their reputations on their own.

Others, like Lachlan Murdoch, the son of media mogul Rupert Murdoch, can't help but be known. Sons have been following their fathers into the entertainment industry, or law or medicine or shoemaking, since the beginning of time. But daughter nepotism? The children of Hollywood's production crews or of famous parents sometimes become respected professionals, sometimes sink without a trace. The daughters rarely became producers or writers or directors until the late 1980s.[214]

Given the time Arbus worked at ABC, it is not strange that neither she nor her father ever considered higher positions in ABC might pave her career. Today, it's not beyond anyone's imagination that daughters can be groomed to head networks or armies. It just hasn't happened enough yet.

■   ■   ■

For young women just starting and for a few of their older sisters, television in the mid-1970s was shouting, Get me a woman!

Treva Silverman, head writer for *The Mary Tyler Moore Show*, parodies the executives of this period: "We're going to do a story about women and we're going to have women writers and women producers and women actresses. It's women, women, women. Get Barbara, she's a woman! Get Linda, get Mary . . . !"[215]

But there weren't that many experienced women around. Some became writers "for a minute and a half."[216] Many failed. One who succeeded was Susan Harris, an experienced writer on the Tandem track, who created the hilarious and controversial satire *Soap* (1977–81) on ABC. In 1979, she created the spin-off *Benson*, starring Robert Guillaume. In the 1980s, her prolific and popular work brought forth *The Golden Girls* and *Empty Nest*.

Barbara Corday started as a publicist before becoming Barbara Avedon's partner in 1972. Avedon had written shows like *Bewitched* since the 1960s, then married and had a child. She started the organization Another Mother for Peace during the Vietnam War years. "Barbara was one of the earliest comedy writers," says Corday. "She told me that she and Selma Diamond were like the two women writing alone at the time, without partners. There was a famous joke that when Barbara was about to marry her first husband, Phil Sharp, also a comedy writer, Selma quipped to Phil, 'Why *her?* I've got more credits.' " Corday says, "Barbara was my first mentor, and Marcy Carsey was my second. They were so important to me.

"When Barbara and I started," Corday says, "the handful of women television writers were in half-hour comedy, and the same three or four teams (we were mainly in teams) would show up for the same job. Women were the new group. Producers, networks, studios were being given bad marks for not having more women.

"One of our agents, Sam Adams, a partner in the Adams, Ray, Rosenberg agency, got us our first break by sort of sneaking us in. One of Universal's new shows, *Senior Year*[217], was a drama, a form for which virtually no women writers were considered. Sam pointed out to the producers that *Senior Year* was about a high school, and 'Women,' he said, 'can write teenagers.'"

A new concept! They wrote three or four episodes; then other dramas followed, including *Lucas Tanner* and *The Doctors.* "We were treated quite well, but with sort of a question mark," Corday says. "We were writing an episode of *Maude,* and at a meeting we'd cleared the story line with Norman Lear and Bud Yorkin. One of the producers of the episode walked us to the elevator with his arm around both of us. As the elevator doors opened and we stepped inside, he said, 'You know, we've started a lot of secretaries on this show.' He was rather smug about giving another team of secretaries an opportunity to write. The elevator doors closed. Barbara and I looked at each other. 'What is he talking about? Did he mean *us?*' We'd been writing for years!

"The theme at that time," says Corday, "was that any woman writing for television was just breaking in. I remember a night at a Writers Guild meeting when a male writer whispered to Barbara, 'Why don't you girls get out of the business and let people who have to support a family have the job?' Barbara and I were divorced and we both had children. The tenor of the times was that women were advancing in a movement big enough to be perceived and reckoned with. And we all knew it."[218]

Avedon and Corday pitched a feature film idea to Ed Feldman, the president of Filmways (which was later reincarnated as Orion Pictures). Filmways had had some success with a movie called *Fuzz,* a police buddy comedy starring Burt Reynolds, Jack Weston, Tom Skerritt, and Raquel Welch. "Barbara and I pitched a female buddy comedy about women cops called *Newman & Redford*—later to become *Cagney & Lacey.*"

Feldman loved the idea. Corday recalls, "He sent us to New York. We researched and wrote the script. At that time, Filmways was developing its own movies but had to get studio financing. Ed was never able to get *Cagney & Lacey* made." The idea was that Cagney and Lacey, because they were women, didn't just battle the bad guys on the show; they also fought sexism, their captains, their relatives, and each other.

"The only executive in town who ever wanted to make that movie was Sherry Lansing," Corday says. "She was working as a development executive for Dan Melnick at MGM. She was a huge fan of the script, and drove Dan so crazy about it that at one point he barked at her, 'If you'll get Ann-Margret and Raquel Welch, I'll give you a million dollars to make the movie.' I've always been glad that we did not waver for a second. 'No, thank you very much,' we said, 'we'll wait.' "[219]

They waited for years. No one could get *Cagney & Lacey* made.

In 1979, Corday and Avedon dissolved their partnership—Avedon wanted to concentrate on writing but Corday wanted to produce. Corday's then husband, producer Barney Rosenzweig (*Charlie's Angels, Daniel Boone*), was still having difficulty getting the *Cagney & Lacey* script off the ground as a feature. So, Corday says, "he and I took it to CBS and sold the idea as a television movie. Could I have sold it by myself? Barbara and I were a pretty successful writing team. Barney had a good relationship with Ed, which helped, but also the idea was right for that company at that time. Yes, I think we could have sold it to TV without him. Barbara and I rewrote it. It aired in 1981 and was picked up as a one-hour series in 1982.[220] It took six years for the movie *not* to get made, then sold as a TV movie, then to be rewritten into a series, then to get cast and on the air."

Just before *Cagney & Lacey* was sold to CBS, Corday took her little girl (now a Hollywood agent) to the beach in Malibu. Tony Thomopoulos, then president of ABC Entertainment, had rented a house a few doors away. "What are you going to do now?" he asked her. She said she had no idea, but she was thinking of producing.

"Have you ever thought about being a network executive?" he asked.

"No, I never have."

"Well, come in Monday morning and meet with Marcy Carsey, and let's see if we can make you a network executive."[221]

By this time, Marcy Carsey was senior vice president of prime time series at ABC. She hired Corday to do comedy development. "I loved doing that job from the first minute!" Corday says. "I also discovered, which amazed me, that I loved the business part of the business, the deal-making, putting people together." Corday stayed at ABC until 1982.

"I had a terrific working relationship with Marcy and I'd worked for years with Barbara. When Marcy left [to form her own company, Carsey-Werner, with Tom Werner, who had also worked at ABC], I suddenly found myself with all these men," says Corday. "It's very odd when you don't know any better, though in the beginning it didn't feel as odd as it did later. As time passed, I realized, 'Gee, I'm *still* the only woman sitting at this meeting...' A lot of us used to think that men were purposely excluding us. It took me a while to focus on what was really going on and still does in many places—that people want to be with like people. It's the same reason I hire women wherever I am and why men hire men. When they have an available job, they pick up the phone and call a buddy. When I have an available job, the women I've worked with are the first who cross my mind. It's the same impulse. I've come to believe there's less maliciousness and more comfort level involved in those decisions than we all thought a long time ago. It's hard for me to be angry at men for it, but we have to continue to point it out—a lot."[222]

Tell Me Where It Hurts Meets Hustling

One of the first female producing teams was Lillian Gallo and Fay Kanin. Kanin had been writing motion pictures since the 1940s and 1950s but had never produced. Gallo began producing television movies in 1971.

Around 1974, Gallo was reading Gail Sheehy's book, *Hustling*, about prostitutes. "Being a girl from Springfield, Illinois, I was fascinated by a subculture of women I knew nothing about," Gallo says. "As I read it, I realized it connected, in a way, with Fay Kanin's impressive script, *Tell Me Where It Hurts*. I knew she'd be right for *Hustling*."[223]

Tell Me Where It Hurts, about working-class women in a consciousness-raising group, was certainly the flip side of *Hustling*. However, both were about segments of women in American society that at that time had only been seen on television in the most cursory ways.

"Lillian was a producer and a strong lady," says Kanin. "I mean, she could give me lessons! She and I became good friends. Around that time, a college offered a course—there was a word for it then, like self-confidence, self-realization, speaking-up-for-yourself course. Lillian and I decided to enroll. Lillian's husband, Lew, burst out laughing. 'If there were ever two women who don't need that course, it's you two!' "[224]

Hustling covered the entire New York prostitution scene. Kanin was only interested in the street girls, about talking with them as she'd talked and listened to the women in *Tell Me Where It Hurts*. In New York, Kanin says, "I'd seen the girls just off Sixth Avenue marching around in those little skirts, back and forth from the Fifty-ninth Street hotels. I wondered, 'Where did they come from? How can they do this and I can't? What's the difference between them and me?' "

Gallo and Kanin met with Brandon Stoddard, the new vice president who had replaced Deanne Barkley in motion pictures for television at ABC. "I told him I'd do *Hustling* if the network wouldn't make me make it into a pantywaist movie," Kanin says. She wanted to make a real movie about what went on with these girls.

Stoddard said, "You write the movie you want to write and I promise you I'll protect you to the best of my ability."

Kanin says, "He did."[225]

Gail Sheehy took Kanin out to meet "the girls" and the cops from Midtown North, the main station where arrested prostitutes on the West Side were booked. At Midtown North, Gail was well liked; her articles had been truthful and tough. Kanin was welcomed. "My husband, Michael, and I went to New York and stayed two or three weeks at a time. We'd go to the theater, I'd come back to the hotel, put on what I called my 'pro's clothes,' and go to Midtown North, where the cops drove me around with them on their sweeps, picking up the girls.

"I sat outside the cages or cells where they were kept until they were bailed out or released, usually in a few hours. The girls were very suspicious of me. 'Who's this straight lady? What's this straight doing?' They'd yell at me, try to shock me. 'You fucking bitch, what're you doing?' None of that fazed me. I just sat there. Finally, they got me to talk. 'I'm doing a movie about you,' I said, 'and I want it to be true. I want to see what you're really like so I can write you honestly.' That got through. They asked the cops if I could come in the cage with them. So I went inside the cage. Often, the same girls were arrested and detained repeatedly; the cops joked with them, and it was just a big scam. As I wrote the script, I decided to make the Lee Remick character find out about the girls much as I had. Jill Clayburgh played the prostitute the story follows, and she was wonderful."[226]

Many writers are not allowed on the sets while a movie is being shot. Kanin had been writing films for years, and now she wanted to produce. Her agency made a deal for Kanin to be associate producer so she could see the budget and be there, authorized, at every stage in the process.

Gallo and Kanin were a strange sight for the crew. "They'd see us standing there together on the set," says Kanin, "these two women, these two producers, talking quietly to each other. Lillian had produced quite a few movies, most unusual for a woman then. Lillian and I were women without men as partners on this film. Also, we had some power over the film—which I'm sure the crew was not used to seeing. We were the bosses, ABC was the boss over us, and the director, Joe Sargent, a terrific director, was the boss on the set. We stayed out of his way, but when we disagreed with him, we called him into a Winnebago and fought it out there. But we *were* the producers, we weren't tokens. We were *there*."

After *Hustling*, Gallo and Kanin formed a production company but produced only one more film together, *Fun and Games*, starring Valerie Harper.[227] "We were very choosy," says Kanin. "We were offered other properties, but we thought they were not good for women or not good for us. We didn't make them."[228]

I Had to Build My Own Name

Dorothea Petrie also started to work in long-form drama, movies for television, in the late 1970s. Unlike Gallo, Petrie had no credentials as a producer. She had been an actress in New York, casting director for the *Theater Guild* and the *U.S. Steel Hour*, and an agent with the prestigious Lucy Kroll Agency. Her husband, Daniel, was an award-winning television and feature director working in the United States and abroad. Dorothea and their four children always accompanied him.

"No matter where we traveled, I always kept my hand in. In London, I read for a theatrical producer and recommended productions on Broadway that I felt could be transferred to London and vice versa. *The Man in the Glass Booth* was one. And I read for my husband, suggested scripts and casting ideas, and squeezed in a little time for me."

At a school conference in the early 1970s, Petrie was asked, "What do you do?" She replied, "I take care of the family, I do a little of this and that." "But what do *you* do?" the counselor repeated. "My husband, Dan," says Petrie, "heard this exchange. The women's movement was just gathering steam and we were both living in the Ice Age. It never occurred to Dan to help me get ready for a party or tend to the children or home matters. It never occurred to me to ask, either. It was very hard to learn to do that. The way I was raised, men were the breadwinners and women took care of the home. But Dan listened and understood what the school counselor was asking when she said, 'But what do *you* do?' Dan encouraged me and became my big support when I did strike out for myself."[229]

In 1973, Petrie's mother sent a newspaper clipping from her hometown in Iowa about a man, Ben Pippert, who had arrived there on an orphan train in 1894. That clipping launched Dorothea's long career as a producer. In the autumn of 1973, Petrie took her mother to a centennial celebration in the little town of Dysart, Iowa.

"My mother described how as a little girl she'd go down to the station and watch the trains come in, loaded with orphaned and abandoned children from the streets of New York City. The children lined up and people from the town and outlying farms would choose a child and take them home. I thought, 'What a wonderful story!' When I returned to

Los Angeles, I went to the UCLA research library but they had nothing on the orphan train. I went to the history department; no one had ever heard of the orphan train. I flew back to Iowa. Ben Pippert still had the tag he'd worn on his little coat, which had his real name on it, Benjamin Morris. The reverse side listed the rules for placing children, and in small print at the bottom the name of the Children's Aid Society, New York. That's where I began.

"One of the things I was most anxious about," says Petrie, "was not coming in on Dan's coattails. I had to build my own name and reputation. We never considered that he would direct *Orphan Train*. However, I knew I couldn't just walk in with my idea about an orphan train and say, 'I want to produce this story.' I had to have something to offer. I wrote a treatment and gave it to Marcia Nasatir, who was an agent with Ziegler Ross. I told her I'd like to make a film about this story and coproduce it. She was most encouraging."

The research for *Orphan Train* took several years, and by that time Nasatir had taken an executive position at United Artists. Through her, Petrie met with Joe Wizan, and *Orphan Train* was optioned as a feature for Steve McQueen and Ali McGraw. The picture was put in turnaround when the real-life romance between McQueen and McGraw split up. Petrie bought the project back and took it to Marian Rees and Roger Gimbel at EMI/Tomorrow Entertainment. Having written it from a man's point of view for McQueen, Petrie changed the story to focus on a woman protangonist. "The story takes place in 1854," she says. "My mother was a very independent Victorian lady. She was the model for the character who helps to transport the children across the country."

Though Petrie had planned to have an experienced coproducer by her side, Roger Gimbel said, "You produce it!" She did, surrounding herself with overqualified people, she says, like Jan Scott, the award-winning production designer in television. "We crawled over every period train in the U.S.!" Petrie says.[230]

The three-hour special aired on CBS in December 1979 and swept the night; it was one of the highest-rated three-hour productions ever. Petrie won the Writers Guild Award for Best Original Story for Television, and Millard Lampell won for Best Teleplay. Jan Scott won Best Designer as well. It was the first of Petrie's eighteen television movies to date.[231]

"I admired Marcia Nasatir for being such a trailblazer for women in our business. She was often salty and had nerve," says Petrie. "I was brought up in a different way; I worked hard not to be a threat to any gentleman in the room. I'm fortunate to be able to turn down material I do not feel passionate about. My 'office' is that desk there in the kitchen. That's the way I've always worked. My assistant has a real office down the hall. We set up an outside office when we go into production."[232]

The desk, painted white, about four feet wide by two feet deep, hugs the window wall. It is covered with papers, a plump daily appointment book, and to one side a little jar of pencils. It is not in an alcove or even a corner; it is a couple of steps away from the center counter. From this unassuming patch of territory, Petrie went on to produce award-winning films like *The Song of the Lark* (with Marian Rees), starring Alison Elliot, Max Schell, and Tony Goldwyn; *Crash Landing: The Rescue of Flight 232*, with Charlton Heston, Richard Thomas, and James Coburn; *The Perfect Tribute*, starring Jason Robards and Lukas Haas; and *Foxfire* (also with Rees), starring Hume Cronyn and Jessica Tandy.

Orphan Train also began Marian Rees's production career. Rees loved the project since Petrie had brought it to Tomorrow Entertainment. She became the executive producer in charge of the special. "It was," says Rees, "the only time I got a credit at Tomorrow."[233] In a year, she would start her own production company. Rees and Petrie would win Emmys and produce television movies together, off and on, for the next twenty years.

By 1979, media commentators were trying to describe the shape of the decade they'd all just lived through, but few commented about the social and legal forces that had made the entry of numbers of women possible. Women's reactions to their "new" lives varied, but despite problems or obstacles, they all agreed on the joy of work.

"It's the challenge of doing an end run," Marian Rees says. "It's getting an idea that isn't mainstream or current or even accepted on the air."[234]

"It's really wonderful to think that we all grew up in a certain kind of generation," Debra Hill says, "where women were supposed to do one thing, be wives, mothers, secretaries, nurses, mainly, and a whole lot of us simultaneously went, 'No.' It was like spontaneous combustion."[235]

Whether they worked for "a minute and a half" or established long careers, women had hit the beach.

6

YOU DON'T MEET BORING PEOPLE IN THIS BUSINESS

The crowd of newcomers, ushered in by the women's movement and the new federal statutes, raised their sights to become agents, writers, and producers. Some women, however, like Ethel Winant, had had substantial careers in television for years. They were dubbed "grande dames" or "legends" in the 1970s, not only for their professional merits but for their visibility—there were so few of them.

I Was Never a Victim

Anne Nelson has been with CBS for fifty-seven years. She doesn't mince words. "The girls are never going to get in the old boys' club," she says. "I don't care what you say. And you know what? I'm not sure we want to be in it. Because who needs that? We can do it without them."[236] Nelson was made director of business affairs at CBS in 1959, then senior director. In 1999, she was promoted to vice president, business affairs.

When she began at CBS, the network was an "old school" collection of gentlemen in three-piece suits under the watchful eye of William Paley. Nelson has been called a virtual institution at CBS—and no chronicle of television in any decade is complete without her. She is dressed for business in manner and apparel, wears her mink when she feels like it, and is warm, friendly, and feisty.

"I was in CBS radio and television from '45 to '52," she says. "I booked *The Ed Wynn Show*, the first TV show on the coaxial cable, west to east, and *Burns and Allen*; made the original radio deal on *Gunsmoke*, the deals for the TV pilot of *I Love Lucy*. Television was new territory. Nobody knew what they were doing, so how could they tell me I wasn't doing it right? It all worked out okay. Sure, I was passed over as vice president of business affairs in 1950. They just told me they couldn't let a woman handle the department. In 1952, when the division split, guess what? The boys got the television division and I got the radio division. But I didn't feel left out. I thought, 'Oh, well, what else is new?' I was used to that.

"You have to keep all this in context," she says. "At the time, the vice president in charge of the West Coast was *the* vice president. It wasn't a matter of being passed over as a vice president, it was a matter of getting a job to run the department. Vice presidents have proliferated only because it was a way to make it look like they were doing something for the women.

"I was promoted, finally, to director of business affairs for the radio division in 1955—the same year I had my twins—because I said to them, 'I've trained three guys and I'm not going to do that again. If you can't do something for me now, I'm leaving.' They put me in charge of the business affairs department until 1959, when they moved me over to television.

"Don't construe the fact that I was not promoted negatively or in a downtrodden way because there's nothing constructive about being downtrodden. I never was a victim in the sense that people talk about victims now. I did my best at all times, I tried to get promotions, and sometimes I did and sometimes I didn't. On several occasions they did create jobs with new titles so they could get me a little more money. Because I demanded it. They were listening. Donald W. Thornburgh, who was head of CBS out here, was a very great gentleman, old school. Like Mr. Paley, none of us ever called him Don; it was always Mr. Thornburgh. He'd listen to me and I'd see him trying to keep from laughing as I made my presentation because he rarely had some kid walking in his office, especially a female kid, telling him what she thought he ought to do. Every time I made a presentation, he did something about it."

Nelson was married, raised three children, loved her job, and looked forward every morning to getting up, walking her dogs, and going to work. "You don't meet boring people in this business," she says. As anyone might suspect, she is not "a big women's libber," but she promoted her secretaries, most of whom went on to have substantial careers. "I don't like generalizations," she says. "I've lived a long time in a basically black neighborhood in Los Angeles, a neighborhood of highly educated, decent people. If a black does something wrong, all blacks have done it wrong. If a woman does something wrong, all women have done something wrong. If a white man does something wrong—what an idiot! He was having a bad day. Why should anyone even categorize women as a group like race—that's what we're trying *not* to do. That's what bothers me about the women's movement. I don't like to be categorized as a woman. I like to be categorized as a competent person."

For most of her life Nelson has been the "first" or the only one. It started in junior high school in South Pasadena in the 1930s, when she wanted to take wood shop. Her mother had to go to the principal to get her into the all-boy class. In high school she wanted to take mechanical drawing and was finally allowed in the class by order of the superintendent of schools—but only if she took a desk in the corner facing the wall so that she didn't bother the boys during class.

"At least there was some loyalty at CBS. I mean both ways. Oh yeah, CBS had a farm system. Bill Paley trained his people. All those guys who got to the top worked their way up from usher or junior salesman. Bob Wood, Jim Aubrey, all those guys who became president of the network had really been trained. Nobody trained me and nobody moved me around. I just got thrown into the work of business affairs when the guys wanted to go play golf. Luckily, I succeeded. They took our work, they were happy to use it, and [they didn't] give us much credit. I got more credit than most.

"Let's face it, the boys take care of each other," she says. "If I'd been a guy, I'd have been a president of the division and then out with a golden parachute. But many of the guys," she adds with real warmth, "were wonderful to me."[237]

Nelson is still at her desk today, but the executive lineup is a little different: The president of CBS Entertainment is Nancy Tellem.[238]

Women Weren't That Important

"I tried to quit once," says Ruth Engelhardt. "I was an attorney in business affairs at William Morris, handling ABC shows. They kept changing attorneys and every time we had a contract, they'd cut and paste the worst things in contracts, and I'd spend hours training those ABC attorneys. I gave six months' notice after I'd trained yet another one. About three weeks before I was to depart, Larry Auerbach, who was the head of television then, said, 'God, Ruth, we can't lose you. You'd make a terrific agent.'

"So I became an agent. I hated it. It was a different philosophy, and it made me uncomfortable. I say what's on my mind but as an agent, you can't always do that with talent. I was used to being one of the best at what I did. I was not the best agent. I went back to business affairs. I was born to do it."[239]

Ruth Engelhardt began as a legal secretary at the William Morris Agency in 1947. The firm had two attorneys, Ann Rosenthal, lead attorney, and Sam Sacks. Engelhardt did the agency's act and band contracts, took dictation, worked nights. "I just did everything," she says. "It was like every other office. Women weren't that important. The agency was very paternalistic towards women.

"In '49, when television broke," Engelhardt says, "we expanded. In 1952, my assistant and I shared an office with a new attorney. He made a crack about Franklin D. Roosevelt being 'the great white father.' I looked at him and thought, 'God, I'm so much smarter than you are, but they'll never give me the chance until I'm an attorney.' I went to law school two nights a week for six years."

Engelhardt was promoted to a business affairs agent. "Phil Weltman, the agent at the office who covered CBS, backed me up one hundred percent," she says. There was no pressure on her to finish law school, but she'd always wanted to be a lawyer. She graduated in 1958 and passed the bar the first time. "I worked with Danny Thomas on all his shows, on *The Dick Van Dyke Show*, on *Andy Griffith* and *I Spy*. I became quite an expert even though I don't think I ever got paid what the guys did. It took me so long to build up, but I did get stock in the company and I did become head of the department for television.

"There's no question that being a woman held me back. At every stockholders' meeting," she recalls, "I'd get up and ask, 'When is a woman going to be on the board of directors?' They were going to put me on the board of directors, but by then I was over sixty-five. However, the firm has been very good to me even though it was very much the old boys' club."[240]

Engelhardt believes that her sister, Sylvia Hirsch, who was an agent with William Morris, should have been head of the literary department. That did not happen. In an article, Hirsch said, "There was a time when I wanted to be head of that department, but I was told by one of the executives that even though I was qualified, he didn't want to subject me to meeting with the executives from the various studios who would use questionable language. As if I hadn't heard it before."[241]

While a number of other women left the firm, Engelhardt stayed. "Joan Hyler was a terrific agent," she says, "and she wasn't the only woman who left—Toni Howard left, and others. They all went to ICM [International Creative Management], where they were paid more and got better positions. That was when William Morris finally started changing. But there was a time when it was terribly aggravating. They kept on bringing in men! At least it's different today. I don't think being a woman or a man stands in your way anymore."

The work was always exciting, and Engelhardt loved it. She remembers when they signed Ricardo Montalban. "He was absolutely gorgeous," she recalls energetically. "Ann [Rosenthal] had an appointment away from the office and asked me to meet with him and get him to sign all the agency contracts. In those days, we women wore the cashmere sweater and the fake strands of pearls. I'm at my desk, he's signing, I'm looking at him and twisting my pearls. The damn thing broke. Pearls go all over the office. He drops to his hands and knees and starts picking up my pearls. I'll never forget it as long as I live, him crawling around on his knees trying to find all those pearls.

"I accepted a lot of things I shouldn't have, like less money," says Engelhardt. "But with all its faults, I love William Morris. There are two kinds of agencies: the MCA school, which put everyone in competition, and the William Morris school—we're one team; everyone helps each other. William Morris really was a family organization, and yeah, it's true I had to fight the guys because they were paternalistic. When I needed them, they were here, but I don't blame Joan Hyler. Maybe I should have left."[242]

Engelhardt did not. She's still there, still working.

You Can't Be a Producer

Another woman who has weathered many storms is Meta Rosenberg. Now in her eighties, the peppery Rosenberg was an agent for about fifteen years until the end of the 1940s. "I hired Raymond Chandler to work with Billie Wilder on *Double Indemmity* and I asked him to inscribe a book to me. He wrote, 'Dear Meta, you remind me of nobody's mother.'" Despite this, Rosenberg adopted a daughter and says that from 1950 to 1959 she stayed at home with her.[243] If you could stay home, that was the decade to do it—the studio and network blacklists had arrived, and the House Un-American Activities Committee was holding new rounds of hearings in Hollywood. Survivors from that era have strong feelings about Meta Rosenberg, both for and against.[244]

Rosenberg returned to being an agent around 1960. "In the late 1960s, one of my clients, Jim Garner, suggested I come with him as a producer; he was forming his own company, Cherokee." She did. In 1971, she produced *Skin Game* for Warner Bros., starring Garner and Lou Gossett Jr. In 1974, with Stephen Cannell, she produced the long-running, intensely popular series *The Rockford Files*. By then, Rosenberg was one of the most powerful women working in television. She says she'd wanted to be a producer since the 1940s when she began working as a story editor. "I went to the head of the studio and said, 'I want to be a producer.' He looked at me and said, 'You can't be a producer. You have no idea how difficult it is for me to explain to the New York office what you're doing here at all.' "[245]

You Haven't Produced, That's Why

The new form in the 1970s, movies for television, offered a few established women the possibility to produce—if they had enough grit. One executive who took advantage of this in the late 1970s (many more would do so in the 1980s) was Renée Valente, a vice president of casting at Columbia Television, where she'd worked for a dozen years. In 1976, she says she was just trying to get through another season. "Tits and ass had hit television," she says. "I wanted to produce. In New York, I'd worked for David Susskind, who taught us to look for quality . . . I'd been able to do [casting] until T&A arrived.[246]

"I went to John Mitchell, head of Columbia television division, and bless his heart, that man liked working with women." Mitchell did not want Valente to leave casting, but she told him, " 'If you don't do it for me, I'm going to go someplace else. Where else will you get two for one? If I'm developing and it works, don't you think I'm going to think of wonderful actors?' So, in 1977, I became senior vice president of movies and miniseries." Among others, she produced *Contract on Cherry Street* in 1977, starring Frank Sinatra; a disagreement over credits caused her to quit Columbia and strike off on her own, as an independent producer.[247] Twenty years later, she's still producing.

Lila Garrett was a sitcom writer with Bernie Kahn in the 1960s for shows such as *Bewitched*. "I was a hot writer and my feeling was that they [executives] would recognize that if you really mean it, there's no arguing with you. And I really meant it."[248] Garrett wanted to produce what she wrote, and she was just ahead of the wave of women writers who would soon begin. She finally won the battle to produce her script, *The Girl Who Couldn't Lose* in 1975. She went back into battle to produce a script she wrote (with George Kirgo), and to direct it, *Terraces* (1977), making her one of the first, if not *the* first woman to write, produce and direct her own material on TV. A short-lived comedy series followed, *Baby, I'm Back*, in 1978; then in 1983, she produced *The Other Woman* (from a script she wrote with Ann Meara).

Another writer, Joanna Lee, was banging on the same door. Lee had started as a starlet in the Ed Wood movie *Plan 9 from Outer Space*, a credit which she'd denied for years. "I said it was some other Joanna

Lee, not me." Lee had written prolifically since the 1960s. When she received a copy of a revised script, the version the network deemed ready to air, she usually threw it across the room. "They were always changing my work." Like most writers, she wanted to have much more control over what she had written.[249]

By 1973, Lee felt stymied. She wanted to produce. "No one, no one, no one, no one would give me the chance," she says.

"You haven't produced, that's why," they told her.

"Neither has Abe, Joe, or Michael," she argued. "They hadn't produced before and they're doing it."

"Well, what can I tell you? I'm sorry. Until you produce, you can't produce."

"'All right,' I said, 'I get it.'" She had an idea for a film and went doggedly ahead with it—*Pocket Filled with Dreams*.

"I wrote, produced, directed, and starred in it," Lee says. "I sold my house to pay off the film's debts. That movie wasn't perfect . . . but when it was finished, I got to start producing and directing."[250]

Not all women working in film or television then wanted to produce, they just wanted to expand their opportunities.

The 'We've-Got-Our-Requisite-Gender-Fulfillment-Here'

Unable to get out of her secretarial slot at William Morris, Joan Hyler moved to IFA, which soon changed into ICM, and she became an agent. "ICM was the first place," says Hyler, "where I didn't feel any kind of gender problem." Meryl Streep, Faye Dunaway, and Andy Warhol became clients. Then she moved back to William Morris, which was catching up with the concept that women could actually function as agents.

In agency lingo, it was Woody Allen-Francis Coppola-Marty Scorsese time, the late '70s. "Everybody wanted to have one woman," says Hyler. "It was a great confluence of timing, ideas, and the women's movement . . . I break this into three periods. The first, the birth of women as a force in business, about '72 to '82, then the rise of women to corporate leadership, '80 to '95. The last or current generation goes from about '95 on as women assumed power in major roles in corporations, like Amy Pascal [now chair, Columbia Pictures] and Laura Ziskin [president, Fox 2000, now an independent producer]. It's much more egalitarian today."

Hyler feels women over forty have a hard time sharing power and are much more anxious about losing what they've struggled so hard to achieve than women in their thirties coming into the business now.

"There's a real generational difference," Hyler says. "Women under forty seem gender-blind in a very profound way. They're used to being mentored [by women], they're the younger sisters and daughters of the revolution, they just assume a certain ease with each other, and they share power more than women who competed with each other in the '70s and '80s.

"The women I grew up with in the agency business had only a few crumbs available, and most of those crumbs, once seized, were hidden and eaten in secret . . . because it all might disappear tomorrow." And sometimes it did. Women had reason to look over their shoulders dubiously at other women, and Hyler thinks this is why the first generation of women did not enjoy each other's successes. Success for other women might mean—and often did mean—less room for everyone else.

"The mentality of 'we've-got-our-requisite-gender-fulfillment-here' lasted until very recently." Also, Hyler recalls that it wasn't just men; the few women inside the walls were saying, "I'm sorry, there's only room for me." Sue Mengers at ICM was one. "She was a force, representing huge stars like Barbra Streisand, Ali McGraw and Candace Bergen."

In 1986, Mengers (author Peter Biskind called her "the last of the great gunfighters"[251]) quit ICM, took a couple of years off, and was then persuaded to head up the motion picture department at William Morris, where Hyler was a vice president.

"The agency gave a big dinner dance to celebrate seventy-five years of William Morris history," Hyler remembers. "Sue hosted a predance party to which she invited none of the women at William Morris, even though by that time, there were several very strong women like Toni Howard, Lisa Shapiro, Elaine Goldsmith. Ruth Engelhardt had been with Morris for years. A picture taken of Sue that evening shows her sitting in a chair in her living room surrounded by the men at William Morris. The queen bee. It was the late '80s and some women had real power—Sue Mengers was one; Dawn Steel, president of Columbia, was another. Sherry Lansing was about to go to Paramount, but she's a great exception because though she has power, it's not in her personality to be exclusive."

The queen bee mentality lingered on in the 1990s. "That's probably ontological when you're birthing a new culture," says Hyler, "and that culture is decidedly not your gender. The few women who get through do not share power. Sue and Dawn could share it with other women, but the minute any other woman got to their level, believe me, the gates shut. 'I'm sorry, there's only room for me.'

"Yes," she says, "there's still prejudice; yes, there's sexual harassment; yes, women are rarely partners in firms . . . [or] at the upper echelons of CAA, though you do at ICM, like Nancy Josephson and Toni Howard. By and large, there's a tremendous generation gap from the women that the first generation of women who worked so hard, all of us, and fought so valiantly. It is almost like the first generation of any new culture, like the first generation of immigrants who came here. A bit xenophobic. After the first blush of success, xenophobia sets in and it's us versus them."

Joan Hyler was the first woman to rise through the ranks at William Morris to the level of senior vice president. "When I realized that no matter what I did I'd never be on the board of directors, which was my dream, it broke my heart. One hundred years after its founding, William Morris still has no women in its inner circle. You have to know when to leave the room," she says.[252] Today Hyler has her own management firm.

If I'd Been a Man, They Would Not Have Been as Angry

Dolores Robinson got her job when she was in Los Angeles with her two small children, staying with a friend, Cleavon Little, whose agent, Maggie Henderson, thought Robinson might make "a good agent." "It was around 1974 and I hadn't a clue what she was talking about, but I needed a job, so Maggie hired me as her assistant and receptionist in her office, the Henderson Hogan Agency, which is still in existence."[253]

For most of her career, Robinson says she had no role models and no mentors; she sort of felt her way along. "If you leave yourself open and you just kind of flow with your life, it just sort of works out." By the late '70s, she was an agent. "I had this wonderful client, an actor, who had just done a little project called *Roots*, a program nobody had yet seen. LeVar Burton became my first client."

Robinson never thought she'd be an agent but rather a teacher, one of the only avenues open to her. "In those days, a black woman did not grow up thinking, 'I want to work in film and television' or 'I want to be a personal manager and producer.' That just evolved."

She wasn't just the only woman in the room. "How about the only black in the room? How about the only black in the restaurant? How about the only black at the party? My attitude was and is that I really like people and I understood the way the world was—and is." One night in the 1980s, she went to a gathering of young black women who were starting out in the industry. "I remember walking in that room and looking around and seeing all those women of color who were in the business whom I had never met. It was really, really, really wonderful. Half of them said, 'My name is so and so, and I got into this business because I read about Dolores Robinson or Suzanne De Passe.' The fact that I did what I did early on made me a role model, and I didn't realize that I was becoming one."

Robinson looks at a client's career as the spokes on a wheel. The center is the client. One spoke is business manager and another spoke is lawyer, another is publicity, another is the agent, then makeup and wardrobe. "Somebody has to make that wheel go around smoothly," says Robinson. "I'm that person. Once the deal is made, my involvement widens between myself and my client to all these other spokes on the wheel. My goal is nothing except the betterment of my client's career. I don't have to compromise . . . I'm not owned by a studio or by anybody."

A few years ago, one of her current clients was a bodyguard. "No one wanted this actor. He had no agent. I knew he was a great talent. Just a few months ago, Steven Spielberg told him, 'Tell the people handling your career to pick very carefully because you're going to have a very important career. I saw your movie. I cried four times, my wife cried six.' Michael looked at him and said, 'Mr. Spielberg, I'm over six feet tall, I weigh three hundred and ten pounds, I'm black, and I'm bald. How selective can I be?' A little reality dose. Michael Clarke Duncan. In 2000, he was nominated for an Oscar, Best Supporting Actor, for his role in *The Green Mile*. I love finding people like that. I found Rosie Perez in my son's dance club and shepherded her career up to an Academy Award nomination. That's pure delight to me."

Being a woman and a black woman helped and hindered. For a long time, all black actors came to her because she was the only black manager. Now there are others. "I was so busy surviving the black thing that I didn't have much time to consider the woman thing. I think women do help other women more than ever. My strongest relationships in the business are with women. I learned that instead of competing we can help each other."

Robinson formed her management company for talent in the late 1970s (now Dolores Robinson Entertainment). "Everyone has hard times," she says. Sometimes harder for women who run their own companies. "If a woman is strong and tough in business, if she has a 'winning attitude' like the men, she's called a bitch," says Robinson. "In the 1980s, some people were really furious with me. If I'd been a man, they would not have been as angry. One client of mine made up his mind he wanted to leave [his agent]. I backed his decision. He was busy directing a film so I called his agency and said he'd decided to go with another agent who was his friend. The whole agency turned against me. They declared war against me: 'Clients she has in this company have to make up their minds—stay with her or come with us.' A friend of mine, a lawyer who represented two of the clients, called somebody in the agency. 'Don't do this,' he told them. 'Those clients are going to stay with Dolores and you're not going to look good.' It was sort of like an elephant fighting a flea. I was threatening to them, and I should not have been."

Robinson links their reaction to her call that her client was changing agents to an attitude or a belief system that says, "Women should not behave like that. And, beneath that, there's a deeper conviction or assumption that a *black* woman should not make that kind of decision. If you've only seen black women cleaning your houses or caring for your children, a deep belief inside you is jarred if she contests you and then wins. Something is way off kilter. If a white man had made the same decision, would that agency's reaction have been so strong? I don't think people realize racism is involved, but it's very deeply carved into our society. It just creeps in and most people don't even know that it's there. I've seen it happen. If racism has affected me, it's in small ways like that, but it's never really gotten in the way."

Robinson grew up in a little town called Penllyn, outside Philadelphia. "We were very, very poor. My parents didn't graduate from high school. I was the first in my family to graduate from college. My mother was a survivor," says Robinson. "She cleaned people's houses. She took me to work with her every day and I'd clean the upstairs, she'd clean the downstairs . . . two houses a day. I learned pretty early that you had to work hard. It's never left me. I survived my mother, too, who was a very strict disciplinarian . . . She really believed in a heavy hand with the beatings. I didn't come out of that an angry person. I came out of it a determined person. My determination went like this: I am never going to treat my children like that. I'm only going to love them.

"I never lived in a house with running water until I went to college. We had a pump in the backyard and an outhouse. That same pump is now in my yard in Beverly Hills. It recycles water into my koi pond. I look out there every day and I feel so lucky. Every day I look at the water running through that pond. I've come a long way, baby."[254]

"Lunch Is on Her," He Said

Like so many women in agencies, even Sue Mengers, Michele Wallerstein started as a secretary, "typing and typing and typing. I was at the International Famous Agency, now International Creative Management, ICM. I'd been raised to be a wife and mother, and to be taken care of as if I wasn't capable of doing them myself. That attitude was hard for me to lose," says Wallerstein. "I heard that a job existed that combined the written word with the business of movies and television. It was called 'literary agent' and I was enthralled. I asked my boss at IFA if I could become a literary agent. However, since I was female, I was turned down. I then went to work for a wonderful agent, Lew Weitzman, and eventually told him I wanted to become a literary agent.

"He replied, 'I'm already planning to bring in a woman.' Case closed. The concept of having two women agents working for him was out of the question," says Wallerstein. "He was going to hire Sylvia Hirsch, who'd been an agent at William Morris Agency for years, a real pioneer... When she was promoted to an agent, they wouldn't give her an office at the agency, so she worked in the hall at a secretary's desk. Sylvia was vital, very capable, and a good friend of Lew's."[255]

Wallerstein got a job as an agent at the Contemporary Korman Agency. "It is one thing to say you want something," she says, "and another thing to get it. I was terrified of getting my dream." She was so green that when she took one of her first meetings with a producer on the MGM lot, after discussing the project, she said to him, "Is the meeting over now?" He laughed. "Yes, Michele, you did fine." Her humor, as well as theirs, always saved her. "When I was a little girl in Los Angeles, I played office, not house. A lady in an office with books. It was *beshert*, it was fate." She started her own literary agency in 1980.

"There was so much I didn't know," she says, "such as the hierarchy in a meeting or football and baseball expressions—real drawbacks. The hardest thing to learn was how to take credit and how to play the man's game. I'd stop and think, How would a man handle this? I tried to think like a man but behave like a woman. I was careful to be an agent first and a woman eighth. Most of the guys didn't help women. For years I felt they just wanted us to go away.

"But here's the upside. The first man I invited to a business lunch was Steven Bochco," says Wallerstein. "He was at Universal doing *Rockford Files*. This was just before *Hill Street Blues*. In those days, women didn't pick up the check. When the check came, the waitress handed it to Bochco. He handed it to me. 'Lunch is on her,' he said. I was so proud. I felt so good. What a guy. He accepted me on an equal footing."[256]

Many of the women in this chapter were not part of the younger group streaming through the opening doors of the mid-1970s, but they did have talent, stamina, confidence, humor, or the brute ability to work hard, which helped them. Joan Hyler sums it up: "I didn't know any better . . . I had a kind of reckless fearlessness . . . I didn't know what my place was. . . ."[257] On whatever level, in the 1950s or the 1970s, their inability to accept what had always been made them visible. And that helped everyone.

7

I DON'T KNOW ANY WOMEN—GETTING ORGANIZED

Until the 1970s, few women had positions at work that allowed them to hire. No "girls network" of any kind existed. Women might know of other women in the industry, but most were working "in a sea of men." Finding other women for support and information at work had become essential.

Lillian Gallo, producer, was in a position to help. She knew the professional strength of women because she'd seen it. Just out of college, she'd competed to be chosen one of fifty women students to serve in the U.S. Marine Corps, which was building a nucleus of women officers who could train others rapidly in case of emergency. "My family was, shall we say, disappointed when I applied," says Gallo. "In those days, you didn't want to see your daughter in the Marines. One of my relatives said that 'only camp followers went into the service.' "[258]

Gallo was assigned to the Pentagon in Washington, D.C., where the assistant secretary of defense had started an advisory group of top women to advise the services on how to attract more women. "Those women, like the dean of Vassar and Mrs. Nelson Rockefeller, had an impact on me," says Gallo. "I traveled with the committee to the bases and met other high-ranking women in and out of the military. Because of that experience, it never occurred to me that women couldn't go into any field that interested them."

Later, when Gallo was working at 20th Century Fox, she realized how few women worked above the clerical level. She was the only woman on the executive staff of ten. "Most men were not the enemy," she says. "They just didn't know who the women were that they could hire. Judith Rosener wrote that woman power had been the best-kept secret, and if men wanted to improve their bottom line, hiring women was the strategy.[259] That stuck with me. A whole section of the labor force appeared in the 1970s, a great resource that men had never thought of using before."

One day, Gallo got a call from an executive at another studio. He had a job for a person who would work directly for him. "Lillian, I'll consider a woman, but I don't know any." She sent him two candidates. "He called back to tell me that one of the women I'd sent over was by far the best for the job. 'But I can't hire her,' he said. 'I had to go with a guy.'

"Why?" Gallo asked.

"Lillian, she was just too beautiful!" the executive responded. "It would give me trouble in my marriage because whenever I came home late, my wife would be suspicious."

"That was the first time I'd heard that," says Gallo, "but not the last."[260] It was going to be challenging.

Getting Organized, Making Connections

Some women arriving in Los Angeles had already joined other women in a group purpose—making things better, engaging in the joy of the struggle.

In these rambunctious times, Paula Weinstein was just beginning her career, first as an executive, later as a producer.

"One of my earliest recollections," Weinstein says, "is of my mother [producer Hannah Weinstein], working to stop the Rosenberg execution.[261] We went to a demonstration. I was a child, but I was thinking that I could march and I would save them. Later, we were watching television, which showed a card at the time of their execution. It said it took ten volts to kill Julius and fifteen to kill Ethel. That was my first feminist moment: 'It took more to kill a woman than a man. How could that be?' My mother taught me early about the joy in the struggle. She didn't say it wasn't important to succeed—it was—but she said whether you win or lose, you still have to do it anyway. There is deep joy in engaging in the struggle, deep joy in it. I wasn't brought up to be goal-oriented when it came to what I loved or cared about."[262]

Lucy Fisher, who in the 1990s would become cochair of Columbia-TriStar Motion Picture Group, summarized her own experience: "I graduated from Harvard wearing a red armband with a red fist inside the woman's symbol. I was totally in the midst of all that."[263]

Diana Gould was a college student in the late 1960s in New York, when university life in that city was a noisy mix of war protests, recreational drugs, civil rights, and women's rights. "We had a sit-in at the offices of the *Ladies Home Journal*," says Gould, "and one of our demands was to get *LHJ* to put out a supplement on women's rights and issues—the kind they didn't print—which we did. Susan Brownmiller, Sally Kempton, Marlene Sanders, other women in media, and I wrote it.[264] I was very young. I assumed I only had my twenties to have *my* life. Then I'd get married and have children and *my* life would be over; it would belong to others. The women's movement gave me back my life."[265]

When Paula Weinstein heard about the first draft of the women's platform for the SDS (Students for a Democratic Society) in 1967, her reaction was, "Why do we need a women's platform?" Then she realized most of the women in the movement were still doing the secretarial work, the mimeographing. "I had come in handling the publicity," says Weinstein, "and talking to the press for our demonstrations. Women in the SDS were saying, 'Isn't it terrible? When we come in to do work in the office to organize the Pentagon demonstration, we're told to go sort the mail.' The guys were doing strategizing. How did that happen? It was the first moment I realized that if it was happening in this activist world where we're supposed to care about equality and freedom, it was happening anywhere. Time for a change.[266]

The women from New York had already been trained, their perceptions honed. They brought the change with them.

How Do We Get into the Men's Room and Come Out with a Deal?

A marriage between the politics of work and the need to organize began in Los Angeles when the WGA and SAG women's committees formed in 1971 and 1972. The Women's Steering Committee of the Directors Guild began forming in 1979.[267]

"When I came to Hollywood," says Diana Gould, "I found nothing like the awareness of women's issues that I'd known in New York. That's why I started the Women's Committee at the Writers Guild. We needed it."[268]

Kathleen Nolan led the effort to form the Women's Committee at the Screen Actors Guild. Among its goals were: "Erase ways women are stereotyped on and off the screen . . . work for equal opportunity for employment, regardless of sex . . . Accepting the fact that the media has done much to shape the image of the American female, it is our responsibility to assist in reshaping it toward more reality . . ." The group strove to "end the era of film that deceives other women who watch movies, television and commercials, and who are tired of trying to be these uninteresting and ridiculous 'on screen' types."[269]

In March of 1973, the publisher of the *Hollywood Reporter*, Tichi Wilkerson-Miles, wrote a note to her columnist, Sue Cameron, "I think we have to start a group to help women . . . You call your friends, I'll call mine, we'll have a brown bag lunch in my office next week." Stormy days lay ahead. The formation of the guilds' women's committees were models of order compared to the start of Women in Film.

Tichi Wilkerson-Miles had been the publisher of the *Hollywood Reporter* since the death of her husband in 1963. "If Tichi told you something," says Sue Cameron, "it happened. She never went behind your back."[270] Wilkerson-Miles, respected by the Hollywood community, is reticent and soft-spoken. Legend has it that her father, a contractor, fell in love instantly with her mother, but he didn't speak Spanish and she didn't speak English. It hardly mattered. They were married, and their daughter, Tichi, grew up in central Los Angeles in the working-class suburb of Inglewood. She married "Wild Bill" Wilkerson, publisher of the *Hollywood Reporter*, when she was eighteen. By 1973, she had become one of the most powerful women in Hollywood, known for her contributions to educational causes and women's concerns. According to many who know her well, her philosophy has always been "Give back."[271]

As a woman and a publisher in the 1960s, she once said she felt "alone and isolated. I had no one to talk to and I was sick of being patronized."[272] That, as much as any statement, describes the feelings of many women at the time, even the privileged, the professional, and the famous.

"It is very hard to grasp now, but there was absolutely no place for women to meet," Nancy Malone says, "to talk about our ambitions or about improving our working lives. We had no center and no connections. We knew there were one or two women cinematographers or lighting designers, but we didn't know where they were or how to reach them. When Sue Cameron called me about a meeting, I sprang at it."

At that first brown-bag meeting of nine women, they decided they first had to locate other women in the business. "The guys were helping each other," Malone says. "We all saw how the guys went into the men's room and came out with a deal. How do we find a way to move up without using the men's room? We decided to contact the women with professional profiles whom we personally knew and tell them a group was forming and ask them to bring another woman with credits to the next meeting."[273]

The women who attended the first meetings remember making a commitment even though they didn't know how to get it started or what was going to happen.[274] They compiled a directory of women in film later in 1973, a few photocopied pages of about a hundred women. It was the only source in the industry that showed where women worked and in which areas. A novel idea, it had never been done before.

According to Cameron, the embryonic organization would be "a small group of powerful women in the business who—if a studio was developing a project offensive to women—could pick up a phone and reach a studio production head. We wanted the organization to be a closed, hard-to-get-into lobbying group on behalf of women.

"By the second open meeting," Cameron says, "word had spread that a group was forming. At least fifty women were waiting in the lobby of the *Hollywood Reporter*. Tichi opened the meeting. 'A common experience binds us,' she said. 'If we get together, we can help each other.' "[275]

Barbara Boyle, about to become CEO of Roger Corman's New World Pictures, was at the meeting. "Until this organization, there were so few women in my professional life," she says. "Only four other women were in law school with me at UCLA. I was amazed to find that terrific women were working in the industry, because my whole world had been men. It was incredible to hear Renée Valente and Nancy Malone, two highly visible women at that time, describe their experiences and the kind of organization they envisioned forming. At that meeting, women were hollering and debating passionately."[276] Patricia Barry, a well-known actress in *Guiding Light* and *Days of Our Lives* and a frequent series guest star, remembers that "women just stood up and said, 'They won't let me through the door.' It was so desperate. There's really no way to describe today how dire it was then. That first group of women really fought hard. I don't think it was unlike the women who fought for the vote."[277]

It is impossible to communicate how isolated women felt at that time. Over and over in interviews for this book, women who met at guild committees, or at the nascent Women in Film meetings, described how wonderful and *weird* it was to talk with *women* about their work. Those conversations had almost never happened before. "It was wild to talk with women about the business we were all in," says Barbara Boyle. "I'll always be grateful to Women in Film for that. Tichi made it clear that some of the older women—I'd worked in the business since 1960 and she meant me—had an obligation to contribute what we knew."[278]

"In effect," Cameron says, "we had control of this group for about three weeks. This particular meeting was really explosive. Word of mouth was very powerful, and some women just invited themselves and were extremely vocal. They called us on the carpet. 'You're being elitist!' they yelled at us. 'It has to be open to everyone! You have to support *all* women!' We got into a big fight. I didn't believe, and neither did

Nancy Malone, that any woman with one credit should be able to get into Women in Film. We thought it should be difficult, that a member should have five years of credits or a major job title. No one was taking notes; we didn't have a board with bylaws. We were having loud, disorganized, philosophical arguments about what an organization for women in the entertainment industry would be or could be or should be. That night, it was mob rule. The women in that room were very angry. They felt disenfranchised, and they had been, they were! Some of us with a lot of experience argued fiercely that an elite group of professionals was the better way to go. I certainly did. We were outvoted."[279]

Wilkerson-Miles was named president of the newly minted Women in Film organization, and Cameron was vice president for a two-year term. They tried to shape the structure of the organization by placing well-known executives, producers, and writers on the board.[280]

Gloria Goldsmith, a writer, a single mother with two children, moved from New York to Los Angeles around the end of 1973. She was invited to a meeting at the *Hollywood Reporter*.

"I couldn't imagine what it was going to be," she says, "but most of the women who were visible, like Lillian Gallo and the attorney Norma Zarky, were there. A period of real excitement began and a sense of increasing empowerment that we felt then and later. We discussed problems women had in the industry, like access. We shared information—which jobs were open, which staffs were open to hiring women, which men were famous for hitting on women, particularly on writers. None of us knew how widespread sexual harassment was until later. Women were afraid to say anything."[281]

Women learned they shared many of the same problems at work, especially the newly named but old and familiar "sexual harassment." Of course, women did speak about it privately but never before openly—too many women had been fired for doing just that. One highly placed elderly executive at a studio was notorious for exposing himself to secretaries, "but when one of them complained, she was terminated," says an executive in a position to know.[282] Another well-known executive was known for hiring "bimbos" to work with him. An executive at a studio, and her husband, used to call those women "vice presidents of executive happiness."[283]

A television producer says, "At one of these Women in Film meetings, I was telling two or three other women, producers and writers, what had happened to me the week before which had upset me greatly. A man had come in to pitch me, a reputable guy, and at the end of the meeting he asked me to dinner. Very nicely, I declined. 'I don't date the people who pitch me. I don't think it's appropriate.' He went crazy. 'You have no right to do that!' he yelled. I couldn't get him out of my office. 'I'm not leaving until you say yes!' I gave my secretary the secret buzz, and she came in saying I had to get to another meeting 'right now.' At this Women in Film meeting, I'm asking the other women if I'd done anything to make this guy go crazy. They all cracked up. 'That happens all the time,' they said. All their stories came out about who had pulled it on them. That gave me real comfort because I'd thought I hadn't been professional enough with his guy, hadn't done this, hadn't done that." After a moment, she adds dryly, "Well, it's well known we cause the rapes."[284] Without the new organizations, women would not have known the extent of sexual aggression in the workplace or management's widespread lethargic attitudes toward it.

In an industry where change is the constant, Women in Film and the guilds' committees provided staunch business relationships and sometimes long-term friendships. The board of Women in Film began presenting programs of speakers from the industry, where members could hear directly from networks or production companies. That had never happened before either.

In June of 1973, Tichi Wilkerson-Miles ran a politic but straightforward front-page editorial in the *Hollywood Reporter* introducing Women in Film to the entertainment industry and stating that Hollywood was more prejudiced against women than anyone would admit. "Now is the time to solidify and verify our reputation as an equal opportunity industry by opening the doors wider to an ever increasing group of talented female filmmakers . . . They do need a chance to be seen and heard."

"Naturally, I got involved in Women in Film," says Goldsmith, "even though many of my male friends in the business said, 'Why are you wasting your time with all those women?' "[285]

Other women found contacts in the new organizations that jumpstarted their careers. Loraine Despres arrived in 1975 with no connections at all to the industry.

"I was a single mother in New Orleans," says Despres, "dreaming about Hollywood, but everybody told me, 'It's impossible, you'll never survive out there.' I'd graduated from drama school at Northwestern. Then I got scared and married an engineer. I had to leave him. I had to get back the courage to follow my dream."[286] Despres wrote nonfiction and industrial films. She was able to join Women in Film, which was sponsoring a series of informal meetings with producers, where she met the producers of *Family* and *Love Boat*. "I was turning out spec scripts," she says, "all dreadful because I didn't have a clue how to do it. I pitched ideas to the *Family* producers, Carol Evan McKeand and her husband, Nigel. They turned me down but said they had been thinking about one of my earlier pitches, a story about child molestation. This was before it was a hot subject. They said the executive producer, Aaron Spelling, thought the idea could be promoted, but that the whole thing turned his stomach. I said, 'Why don't we turn it around, and we make this a story about a man who is falsely accused of child molesting?' That was my first sale in television. I joined the Writers Guild. After that, I worked every year—*Dallas, Dynasty, The Waltons, Knots Landing,* and *The Lazarus Syndrome,* a medical drama in 1979."[287]

By 1977, the Women in Film directory had grown from a few stapled pages to a small printed booklet that some executives kept visible on their desks in case someone asked them to "recommend a woman." Some said at the time that they could not think of doing business without it.

To make the change in the business noticed—that women were there to stay—and to raise money, the board of Women in Film, led by president Barbara Boyle, hosted its first Crystal Awards luncheon in 1977 at the Sportsmen's Lodge in Studio City.[288]

Women giving other women awards was a real departure, and it met with some amusement. Of course, awards celebrations are endemic in Hollywood, but except for performers, women did not feature largely in editing, writing, producing, or directing tributes. Honoring just women for a body of work and for their "contributions to the industry" was unheard of. The awardees that first year were Lucille Ball, Nancy Malone, screenwriter Eleanor Perry, and Norma Zarky, the first woman to head the Beverly Hills Bar Association.

The board of Women in Film was extremely nervous. Would members pay thirty-five bucks to see four women win an untested, unknown award? Would important executives come? Would any ranking women come? Would *anyone* come?

"The place was jammed," says a member. The dining area was so crowded, women were leaning against the walls and standing beside tables. Bonny Dore, a producer, recalls, "They were so nervous. When it turned out to be a huge success, of course, all that was erased. When you remind them of what they said, they go, 'I didn't say that, did I?' I call it success amnesia."[289]

Of course, the women jamming the aisles at the Crystal Awards luncheon were, for the most part, not execs. Studios and networks sent their secretaries—who else would be interested in a program whose awardees were women? There were so few women executives that for the next decade much of the dais was filled with men. Men's work and women's work were still rigidly segregated, and the value of women in the industry in 1977 and well into the 1980s was not even marginally perceived.

Women who attended the 1977 event recall "Lucy up on the stage, drinking scotch, the funniest person in the blinking room and telling the crowd, 'This is real encouraging.' "[290] They recall the startling size of the crowd and what it was like just being in a room full of women to honor other women. The event gave them permission to speak up about what it was like to be a woman "in the business," who helped them, the best times in their work, the worst times. The Crystals are much larger today, but it is still safe for awardees to say what's on their mind or in their hearts: Fay Kanin in 1980, Verna Fields in 1981, Margaret Booth in 1983, Suzanne De Passe in 1988, Dawn Steel in 1989, Lily Tomlin in 1992. Marilyn Bergman in 1986 gave a hilarious and finely crafted acceptance speech composed of dictionary definitions of men and women; in 1981, Jane Fonda spoke of being on sets and looking at the crew and seeing only men; now she saw women, too. A secretary could and did walk out of those rooms and say to herself, "She did it, I can do it."

"It's sad that so much talent was ignored for so long," says Marcy Kelly, who arrived in Hollywood from Washington DC in the early 1980s, recruited by Paul Newman to head a new media-related nonprofit organization. "I didn't know a single person in town." By the 1980s, the organization was presenting workshops of all kinds. It was one way newcomers could learn about the industry from people in the industry. "They were wonderful," says Kelly. "I recall the pride I felt when a woman in a top position was on a panel . . . because very few women were in positions of power at that time and access was rare."[291]

In 1982, the Crystals honored Cicely Tyson. For her acceptance speech she delivered the speech Sojourner Truth made in 1851 to the Akron, Ohio, women's rights convention. The Ohio gathering was in chaos, disrupted by clergymen shouting down feminist speakers. Many did not want to hear Truth, a former slave and domestic worker who was active in abolitionist and women's movements, fearing the news-papers would mix the women's cause with that of abolition. But the chair of that convention said, "Sojourner Truth will speak."

"That man over there says that women need to be helped into car-riages and lifted over ditches, and to have the best place everywhere. Nobody ever helps me into carriages . . . And ain't I a woman?" Tyson's moving rendition of Sojourner Truth's words rang out on many levels to the audience in the Beverly Hilton Hotel. "I have ploughed and planted and gathered into barns and no man could head me. And ain't I a woman? . . . If the first woman God ever made was strong enough to turn the world upside down all alone, these women together ought to be able to get it right side up again! And now they is asking to do it, the men better let them."[292]

Power in Numbers

Women's groups sprang up all over town—consciousness-raising groups with a career twist. One woman started a group after she'd conceived and developed a sitcom and heard her husband take solo credit for it in a network meeting.

In the 1980s, the Hollywood Women's Political Committee was formed with purposes much larger than members' personal or even professional lives. The HWPC, a riposte to President Reagan's 1980s, raised funds for liberal political organizations and for mainly Democratic candidates. It began modestly in 1984.

"Basically, I am invited to a dinner," says Julia Phillips, "to get some women in the [entertainment] business upset that the California chapter of NOW is about to go under because of insufficient funds." The amount needed was about $2,000. Phillips thought that was easy and said so. "In Hollywood, the guys have their poker games and their big political contributions. 'We'll do a brunch,' I tell them. 'Invite fifty heavy-hitter women.' Why not buy entree into the Democratic Party? Guys like Lew Wasserman and Jeff Wald had been doing it for years."[293]

Phillips hosted the well-attended brunch. Marilyn Bergman, Oscar-winning songwriter (*The Way We Were*) and the first woman to preside over the ASCAP board; Anthea Sylbert, now a producer; Barbara Corday, who was now president of Columbia Pictures Television; and others came. Contributions totalled four thousand dollars. The next day, Phillips received a call from Paula Weinstein. She'd heard about the brunch and thought they should organize. A meeting was held, and the nonprofit Hollywood Political Coalition (later reorganized into the Hollywood Women's Political Committee) was born. Paula Weinstein and Julia Phillips became the unofficial heads of the steering committee that guided the HWPC. Ideologically, the group was liberal.[294]

"The Hollywood Women's Political Committee," says Paula Weinstein, "was the first group I'd been in in Los Angeles that was a feminist group. I was acting on the Movement all the way through until we dissolved the committee in 1998. I saw the power of being role models for younger women as a place for them to go."[295]

The Democratic Party, drawn to the money and the honey of Hollywood, approached the group, which started a chain of fund-raising events for presidential candidate Mondale and his running mate, Geraldine Ferraro. The heart of the group remained the same—Phillips, Bergman, Weinstein, and Sylbert. Millions of dollars were raised, one of the most exclusive events being an evening with Barbra Streisand in her home, singing. Members of the HWPC were "players" at a certain level; they were also concerned about issues such as nuclear waste, the environment, equal rights, justice—all the issues the Reagan administration was busy shoveling under the national rug. HWPC also had the distinction of proving that women could raise big money for national issues, and that Washington had to reckon with women in the Hollywood industry.

In 1998, the HWPC disbanded. The consensus among members was that they supported the need for campaign finance reform, yet as a PAC raising "soft money," they were part of the problem generating the need for reform. Therefore, the most honest solution was to disband and put their individual energies into the finance reform movement. Others thought the HWPC had become too aligned with financial transfusions straight to the Democratic Party. "Most," Corday says, "wanted to support issues, not candidates."[296]

■   ■   ■

An entirely different kind of group, still meeting today, is a monthly luncheon organized in 1978 by Nancy Hutson Perlman and Loreen Arbus.

"There were some senior women in the business," says Perlman, "but at the end of the 1970s there were a bunch of new kids like Claire Townsend and Paula Weinstein. If there were ten guys profiled, only about two women were on panels, in magazines, whatever. [Loreen and I] saw all these great new young women who never got a chance to interact with one another. We wanted to find a way to give women a chance to do that."[297]

Women could be working on the same lot or at the same network but they almost never met. If a woman was head of business affairs at a television production company on the Paramount lot, she rarely met an editor of a feature film on that same lot. "I could barely find a second woman to sponsor my membership to Women in Film," says Perlman. That's how hard it was to meet women regularly at that time. "You had to know women to get into Women in Film," she says, "and few of us did. So Loreen and I started the lunch."[298]

The lunch introduced women in the business to each other. Refreshingly, it had no bylaws, no membership fees, no elections, no fundraisers. You went to lunch and heard who was doing what where and how it might fit into your career scheme or not.

"There were always women who said, after a luncheon, 'Gosh, I've never found women to be supportive, but this is really great,'" says

Loreen Arbus who, after years as an executive at ABC and cable television, became an independent producer in 1987. "The lunch makes connections that cannot be made for women in any other way." Those connections were and are its most valuable service.

The lunch also had its amusing moments. "Women don't eat dessert in public," Arbus says. "It just doesn't happen. At one lunch, Fay Kanin, a writer and producer of so many wonderful shows, put up her hand and said, 'Isn't there dessert?' In front of everyone. I called for the waiter. He ran down the selection for her. 'Do you have any kind of cake?' she asks.

"He says, 'Yeah, chocolate cake.'

"'That would be good.'

"The room is kind of quiet. We don't see anything like this very often," says Arbus. "The waiter brings the chocolate cake, and we're all looking at her. Gosh, she's going to eat it all? We're staring. She looks up and says as only Fay can, 'It's my birthday.' And she ate it all."[299]

"Not too long ago, around 1999," Perlman recalls, "Loreen called me after having gone to one of those awards dinners. The dais was twenty men and one woman. She compiled a list and sent it to Chuck Fries, a successful producer who was the awards chairman, with a note: 'Maybe you don't know them, but here are a lot of women for your dais.' To his credit, he has added a few more."[300]

Women do clock prominent people on a dais. It's a public measure of status. "When you go to the Hollywood Television and Radio Society luncheons," says Judith Merians, an attorney and business affairs executive for many years, "and you see the entire dais is men, I wonder why isn't anybody conscious of this? There is something incredibly wrong here because no one's running in the aisles screaming. How about dais after dais of all white people, maybe one black person? Are the only people in America white except one black person? Isn't there something wrong with that? Why isn't anyone crying out against it? It's still going on!"[301]

President Is Not a Job for a Woman

In the summer of 1975, Kathleen Nolan ran for president of the Screen Actors Guild, an exceedingly competitive office. She ran on an independent ticket (the nominating committee refused to nominate her) in a vitriolic campaign with five men. When she announced her candidacy, Charlton Heston, a strong supporter of hers on the board, told her that "president is not a job for a woman."[302]

Nolan, an actress since the age of five, was known for television roles in series such as *The Real McCoys*. She had been serving on the Screen Actors Guild board as first vice president, the first woman ever to hold that position. The depiction of women in film and television was among the many issues that concerned her.

As the guild's first vice president, she had been working out of the president's office at SAG for two years. "I had already purchased for myself a big serpentine rolltop desk," she recalls, "which I had installed. My modus operandi was different—I put the desk in the corner and a couch and chairs in the center so people could sit down and talk to each other as equals, not talk to somebody sitting behind a desk. The president, John Gavin, was six foot three, and when you sat in the chair in front of his desk, you sank down and looked up at John looming over you."

When she ran for the presidency, one campaign attack was "Where did the rolltop desk come from?" Another: "She's made seventeen trips to Washington, and three trips to the White House. Who paid for her gowns and who paid for her hair?"

"I borrowed the clothes," says Nolan. "I was working on tax reform for the motion picture industry, which required a lot of trips to Washington and a lot of lobbying on behalf of SAG and the industry. Lew Wasserman, who headed Universal Studios, told me to get what I needed from the wardrobe department at Universal. I could not have afforded the kind of clothes needed for the work. Nobody asked where John Gavin's suit came from when he testified at the U.S. Senate."[303]

On election night, when members of SAG were huddled in a room counting the ballots, a woman left the tally room, drifted past Nolan in the lobby, and whispered, "It's a landslide." The next morning, the headline in both the trades was "Nolan Wins by a Landslide." She was the first woman to take the reins of SAG.

Nolan's remarkable victory raised the public stature of women, drew women together in a different way, and signaled distant possibilities: Could a woman win an election at the macho Directors Guild?[304] Could a woman become president of the board of the Academy of Motion Pictures Arts and Sciences?[305]

Nolan served two full terms as president of SAG. Since then, Patty Duke and, in 2001, Melissa Gilbert have been elected president of the Screen Actors Guild. (Duke served half a term.) The Writers Guild elected Mary McCall Jr. president for two separate terms, and, as noted, Victoria Riskin in 2001.[306]

The rambunctious and visible Nolan inspired women who were joining together all over the industry. Demands were the order of the day. In just five short years women had come from nowhere to somewhere.

They might not have been able to tell anyone just where they were, but it was better than where they had been.

■ ■ ■

One event measured the changing spirit of the times. The *Ladies Home Journal* televised its "Woman of the Year" awards on April 19, 1975. For the third year in a row it honored "a special breed of heroine: American women who, through their own achievements, inspire other women to new heights."[307] Among its honorees that year were Lady Bird Johnson, Lillian Hellman, Joan Ganz Cooney, Congresswoman Barbara Jordan, Sylvia Porter, and Helen Thomas, chief of United Press International's White House bureau. The *Journal* also honored women writers that year, noting their new influence in television.

Charlotte Brown was writing and producing *Rhoda*, the hit spin-off from the still-running, Emmy-winning *Mary Tyler Moore Show*. "I was flying first-class to New York," says Brown, "with Linda Bloodworth and Mary Kay Place, writing partners, who were getting this award with Treva Silverman and me." Place and Bloodworth (later Bloodworth-Thomason) were best known for an Emmy-nominated *M*A*S*H* episode entitled "Hot Lips and Empty Arms."[308]

"In New York," Brown recalls, "the four of us spent the entire day locked in the Ed Sullivan Theater with Helen Hayes, a presenter, Lillian Hellman, Barbara Walters, a presenter, Barbara Jordan, and other extremely important women. It was incredibly exciting. I remember we were all in one big dressing room, getting ready for the awards program, arranging our gowns, fixing our hair. The decibel level was unbelievable. I felt such a sense of camaraderie among the women there. Barbara Jordan was sitting in a chair, her dress draped over her arm, calmly waiting for the hubbub to subside with the most incredible poise. There were almost no events like it in those days, women honoring women. We'd been interviewed earlier, which was broadcast prime time with film clips of the shows we'd written. That's when we knew we weren't just working there at our typewriters. We were part of something new and exciting.

"The most thrilling moment for me," Brown says, "was meeting Lillian Hellman. She was this crusty lady, but I went up to her and blubbered inanely, 'Oh, Miss Hellman, it's such an honor to meet you . . . I've read everything you've ever written. I'm a writer but you're an *author*—'

" 'Oh, honey,' she said, 'it's all words.' "[309]

8

I WAS SUPPOSED TO BE HEDDA HOPPER

By the late 1970s, even though women held only a small percentage of the available jobs, it was stylish to hire them, especially in television. The presence of women was certainly not seen as a "reentry" of producers, directors, or executives, since almost no one yet realized that women had held numerous positions in the silent-film days. As Anthony Slide was uncovering the research for his book, *Early Women Directors*, every school in America taught film students about August and Louis Lumière, who shot their first footage in 1895, *Workers Leaving the Lumière Factory*, and Georges Méliès, who made short films in Paris from 1896 to about 1904. In 1896, a few months before Méliès, Alice Guy Blaché filmed *La Fée aux Choux* (*The Cabbage Fairy*). No schools taught about Blaché as "the screen's first woman director," or about the studio she built in 1912, the first built by a woman, or about the hundreds of films she made.[310] What good it would have done to know this in the 1970s is difficult to say now. Knowing it gives some perspective, and sharpens their reentry exertions to direct, photograph, and produce in the last thirty years.

Movies in the Late 1970s, Rougher Terrain

As directors or cinematographers, women were scarcely considered and almost never hired. "In the 1970s," one of the first studio vice presidents, Nessa Hyams, told the *Los Angeles Times*, "the attitude was 'We'll let her do it [direct], and she'll fail, and we won't let her do it again.' "[311] But they were a tough bunch. They willed their way in. The American Film Institute started its Women's Directing Workshop with Anne Bancroft, Lee Grant, Maya Angelou. Early member Lynne Littman says, "We were like the wild beasties."[312]

Dede Allen, editing films since 1958, says, "I never cut a picture for a woman director ... There never were a lot of women directors. The challenges were and are that you have to be twice as good as everybody else and you have to know twice as much, but I never thought of it that way. I just worked hard." Allen had wanted to be a film director. Her grandfather, who didn't believe in movies at all, introduced her to playwright and film director Elliott Nugent, who told her to "get in the cutting room" if she wanted to direct.

"I had a hell of a hard time getting in," says Allen.[313] Columbia Pictures hired Allen and Faith Hubley[314] as the studio's first two women messengers. It took Allen eighteen years to "get into the cutting room." She never directed.

"At film school [in the late 1960s] all the boys were going to be directors, and I was supposed to be Hedda Hopper," says screenwriter Diana Gould. "It never occurred to me to be a director because there were no women directors. There were no models for who I wanted to be. And very few women writers. If I were in film school now I'd have a completely different sense of my career. I think it's wonderful that I am able to write, but I would not have limited myself to being a writer. Sexism then was so pervasive, you can't even describe it as 'a problem.'" But Gould didn't feel she would be limited. She says she'd heard "We want a woman to write this" a lot.

"As I got older, I began to see that the limitations were more on me creatively, and that permission had to be given by men ... what seemed stirring to me, they felt was strident. Every writer, male and female, has his or her own set of sorrows and resentments, things they wanted to do but couldn't do. In many many ways, I feel privileged. Being a woman didn't prevent me from being a writer; I feel fortunate that I was able to do something that, even when everything else was closed, writing was always available."[315]

By 1979, Julie Corman had produced seven low-budget features for New World Pictures, the company she and her husband, Roger Corman, owned. She wanted to use women directors. The problem was finding them. Corman drove to the American Film Institute in Hollywood, which had launched its directing program for women.

"It was separate from the main one, for the men," says Julie Corman, "a little side thing they had developed, given the times. In one day, I looked at all the films the women had made there, maybe ten. When I finished, I was very wrung out. Looking at student films is my thing. I do it a lot. From a student film you can tell how the director works with actors and sets up shots. I had a feeling at the end of that day that I couldn't shake. I realized I was used to looking at films from the distance of a man's point of view. In those women's films that distance was taken away. They were close to the bone, to the emotion. That was years ago, but I've never forgotten leaving that screening room with that feeling."[316]

Which women in the United States were actually directing in the late 1970s? Besides the women in this chapter—Lynne Littman, Barbara Kopple, Martha Coolidge, Karen Arthur—Joan Micklin Silver had written and directed *Hester Street* (1975), *Between the Lines* (1977), and *Head Over Heels* (1979); Joan Darling directed her first feature, *First Love* (1977), and television episodes like *Taxi* in 1978; Lee Grant was preparing to deliver her first feature, *Tell Me a Riddle* (1980); Claudia Weill directed *Girlfriends* and *It's My Turn*; Nell Cox was directing television. Randa Haines was beginning to direct episodes of *Knots Landing*. Like many new directors of the time, Haines had already directed two dramatic movies for the Public Broadcasting System, which gave other women opportunities to make hour-long films or documentaries because a woman on the set as a director became tremendously visible. "When I started directing," Nancy Malone says, "and still to this day, I don't direct for me. I direct for twenty women in back of me—if I fuck up, they don't work."[317]

You Don't Have to Hire Her, Just Fuck Her

When Karen Arthur was in summer stock, she and a friend, Michael Gleason,[318] used to drink red wine and dream about going to Hollywood. She'd be a big actress and he'd be a big writer.

In the theater, Arthur had acted, choreographed, and directed before she took off for the West Coast. Hollywood, she realized, was not a stage town; it was a film town. "I went to UCLA and took one of those six-week courses, made a little sixteen-millimeter film, and I fell beyond deeply in love with film," says Arthur. "One of the strongest movements on stage is on the diagonal, and it's also true of camera movement or action in a film. I realized if I took the stage and stood it up, it became a film screen. Everything I had learned as a dancer and stage director applied to my work as a film director. It was very, very exciting."[319]

Arthur grew up in Florida, raised by her divorced mother, an interior designer. As a young woman, she got an internship with producer-director Arthur Penn (*Alice's Restaurant, Bonnie and Clyde, The Portrait*). "Wonderful man. Deep talent," says Arthur. "I learned so much from him. His focus puller was a young guy, John Bailey, who was married to Carol Littleton—she was cutting commercials.[320] I went to Johnny and said, 'I'm going to be a director and you're going to be my D.P. and Carol's going to be my editor.' I had this play called *Legacy*, written by Joan Hotchkis,[321] and they said, 'Okay,' and I started raising money, which I managed to do, and we made this movie. It was eighty-eight minutes long. It began to get a little attention from the festival circuit. I remember calling my mother and saying, 'Mom, I got this chance to go to a film festival circuit. They want me to show my film.' "

Arthur's mother told her she must go. But the festival was in Switzerland. "I did not have the money to get there, but my dear mother, who had never borrowed anything in her entire life, called me back that day and said, 'I've been to the bank and borrowed the money and you and I are going to Switzerland.'

"We did! We took *Legacy* to about fifteen film festivals all over Europe. It was nominated for awards and won the special prize at the Locarno International Film Festival. It was perceived in Europe as a political film, because it was accusatory of social behavior and the dinner-party mentality of a well-off woman who doesn't know what to do with her life, 'where have I put my crystal goblets' kind of thing."

Arthur came back to California and trotted *Legacy* around as proof she could direct and produce. "The response I got," she says, "was like, 'This is an art film and you're a girl.' They sort of patted me on the head."

Undeterred, Arthur began raising money for her second film, *The Mafu Cage*, and working at Universal in the camera department as a loader/clapper. She found out her old friend from summer stock, Michael Gleason, was working on the lot on the miniseries *Rich Man, Poor Man*. She took him a copy of her film and asked if he could get her some directing work on the show.

Gleason agreed to go to bat for Arthur. He went to an executive and strongly recommended her as a director for an episode.

"You don't have to hire her," the executive said, laughing, "just fuck her."

"No, you don't understand," Gleason said, according to Arthur. "I don't want to fuck her. I want her to be hired. She's talented. I'll stake my job on it."[322]

Gleason got her an assignment. Through it, she joined the DGA in 1976—becoming one of the first women admitted as a television or feature director since Ida Lupino in 1950.

"The guys—gaffers, grips, best boys—used to come on the stage while I was working," Arthur recalls, "look around, and say, 'Whoa, we hear a chick's directing and we gotta see this.' "

As a new director, Arthur says she had few problems. "If I couldn't speak millimeter language, I could certainly tell a cameraman what I wanted. Being a choreographer, I always had a way with camera movement. I made it a point to get on the camera the first day of the job and wheel those wheels around and move actors so that everybody in the crew could see that I knew what I was doing. It was really important in the '70s to show you could do that stuff.

"My only problem came the first morning I showed up for *Rich Man, Poor Man*. As soon as I walked in, the A.D. said to me, 'We're going to be doing scene thirty-two to start.'

" 'Yes, I know.'

" 'So I knew you'd want to get rid of this wall and I had them pull it so you can put your camera over there.' "

Arthur saw this as "The Test." "I waited a moment and then said, 'You're the A.D., right, the assistant director?'

" 'Yeah.'

" 'I'm the director, right?'

" 'Right.'

" 'So you don't pull walls. I'll tell you when I want a wall pulled. Now you put it back.'

" 'But that's going to take an hour.'

" 'Don't worry about it,' I said. 'The actors are in the same wardrobe for scene thirty-seven as they are for scene thirty-two. We'll move over to the dining room and do scene thirty-seven. By that time you'll have the wall back.'

"Rather contrite, he got the construction guys and the painters and put back the wall. I went over to the dining room set and did scene thirty-seven.

"When we came back to do thirty-two, I said, 'Okay, now you can pull the wall.'

"Other than that," says Arthur, "I really had no problems. I read everything I could about things like Elemat cranes or a type of Fischer dolly or a stint dolly. Some days, I'd sit with the dolly grip. What dolly grip doesn't want to sit with a pretty girl who can talk his language? He'd tell me more than I ever wanted to know or could ever use. By the time I did *Rich Man, Poor Man* I knew their jobs, their vernacular, and when they said, 'I can't do that,' I'd say, 'Yeah you can. We'll just pull it off of here, put it on a hard hat, and try it that way.' They'd go, 'Whoa, yeah, okay.' "

After making *The Mafu Cage* (1978), Arthur didn't direct another feature until *Lady Beware* in 1987. She developed it for six years "because of dear Verna Fields at Universal and dear Ned Tannen, who gave me a development deal."[323] While pushing *Lady Beware* forward, she worked as a television director on *Hart to Hart*, *Remington Steel*, and the television movie *The Rape of Richard Beck*.

Gender Discrimination Is Everywhere and All the Time

While Arthur was making *Legacy*, about the upper-class woman going stir crazy, Martha Coolidge was in New York making *Not a Pretty Picture*, a story based on Coolidge's own date rape, a subject that had not been done.

"When I stepped offstage and started directing plays," Coolidge says, "it was like coming home. It was what I was born to do." Until that moment, Coolidge had thought of herself as a performer; she even sang semiprofessionally at coffeehouses. "I didn't know of any women directors. If I'd thought about it at all, I would have figured being a director was impossible."[324]

Coolidge made several award-winning short films in New York, then worked for a year in Montreal, where she wrote and directed shows, made costumes, produced, and edited. "One day, an executive told me, 'We don't have women directors in Canada. If you want to be a director you really should go back to New York.'"

She did. She worked in commercials on props, as an editor, and as a script girl. A producer told her, "Whatever you do when you're applying for a job, don't tell them you want to be a director. Just put your eyelashes on, have your nails manicured, and tell them you really want to be an assistant."

A rocky but vigorous start. She applied to the graduate program of New York University's School of Cinema. She says that Haig Manoogian, head of the NYU film program and Marty Scorsese's mentor, told her, "You can't be a director because you're a woman. There are no women directors. You can't name five women directors in the world." Coolidge could only name Agnes Varda. "There were a few others," says Coolidge, "but no school taught us about women directors." NYU admitted her anyway.

"I was totally dumbfounded by what Haig said to me, but I didn't even think about it," says Coolidge. "I wore blinders. If I'd thought about it I could never have gone anywhere. Now I'm older, I have a career, and I *can* think about it. The attitudes about women directors was and is really severe."

She became a founding member, with Ed Lynch and Ed Emshwiller, of the Association of Independent Video, which grew exponentially and helped create the New York film community. Coolidge raised the money to do her own films—*David Off and On, Old-Fashioned Women, Not a Pretty Picture*—from family, friends, and people she worked with in the labs. "It probably didn't hurt to be cute, either." The budget for *Not a Pretty Picture* was $46,500. All this sounds easy, but each stage in making an independent short or feature is a mountain in, say, the Cascade Range—get the money, make the movie, finish post, get the distribution. For women, think Alps.

"Gender, being a woman, affects everything. It's universal. It's like the color of one's skin," Coolidge says. "Gender . . . even involves the way people speak to you. It isn't negative all the time. It's just that . . . you're a woman."[325]

Coolidge was going to have six rocky years, from 1977 to 1983. Then a script that became *Valley Girls* appeared out of nowhere, and she ran with it.

What Life Is Really All About

Until 1976, only four women had won or shared the Oscar for a documentary short or documentary feature: Nancy Hamilton for the documentary feature *Helen Keller in Her Story* (1956); Martina and Charles Huguenot Van Der Linden for their documentary short *This Tiny World* (1973); Sarah Kernochan and Howard Smith, for the documentary feature *Marjoe* (1973); Claire Wilbur and Robin Lehman for the documentary short *The End of the Game* (1976).

In 1977, at the 49th Academy Awards, two women each took home an Oscar for documentaries: Barbara Kopple won the documentary feature for *Harlan County, U.S.A.*,[326] and Lynne Littman won the documentary short for *Number Our Days*.

Kopple, one of the most prolific nonfiction and fiction filmmakers in the country, says that making *Harlan County* taught her "what life and death were all about."[327]

In the early 1970s, Kopple had been reading newspaper reports about events in the coal fields of West Virginia and Kentucky. "There was a movement in the coal fields that was going to change the face of labor, and from it emerged union members. Its leaders [Arnold Miller, Mike Trabovich, and Harry Patrick] had no experience, but they had a movement called Miners for Democracy. And they won. I wanted to see if they were going to keep their promises and organize the unorganized.

Harlan County was the first place they decided to move into, so I went in, too."

Her film documents the coal miners' strike against the Brookside Mine of the Eastover Mining Company in Kentucky, which had refused to sign a contract with the miners when they joined the United Mine Workers of America. Kopple filmed the strike by getting a $12,000 loan from Tom Brandon, who was with the Film and Photo League, a distributor of films in the 1930s.

"Being a woman didn't hinder me; it totally helped . . . because in the very beginning nobody trusted us at all. Harlan County was a tough place. My own crew got a little nervous about being there because on the first day a guy named Ray Widener was shot and taken off to the hospital. That's when my crew and I knew people were very serious there. But the next day, Ray was riding around in his car with a big sign saying, '38's AIN'T SHIT.'

"The women didn't trust us either," Kopple says. "They gave us phony names like Martha Washington or Florence Nightingale. We never knew who we were actually speaking to. That all changed. My crew and I were driving down Pine Mountain in a rainstorm on a very narrow road that had no guardrails. Another car zoomed next to us, pushed us off the road, and our car went over, upside down. We pulled ourselves out and walked three miles with all our gear back to the picket line. I think that's when the women, who were extremely important in the strike, knew they could trust us. They opened up their homes and their lives. We became part of the community."

The strike went on for a year; the violence, desperation, and determination escalated. The experiences Kopple recounts in Harlan County are totally outside the life of a producer-director in Hollywood. They remind us how tough filmmakers can be.

"About five five o'clock one morning," Kopple says, "we were filming on the picket lines when the strike breakers decided to open up with semiautomatic carbine machine guns. They fired and it lit up the mountainside. Everybody was screaming. The head gun thug for Eastover drove past us in his car, broke through the lines, and pointed his gun at my head. You can hear me screaming on the sound track, 'Don't shoot!' His car went across the bridge and then came back. By then, I wasn't really scared anymore, but I felt that since I'd brought my crew there, I was responsible. I walked forward and the company goons got the cameraperson, Hart Perry, and they were kicking me, but my Nagra tape recorder protected me and then I started swinging my microphone.

"I knew people with guns were up in the woods. People with guns were everywhere because by then all the miners had guns and all the strike breakers had guns," Kopple says. "At one point, you could hear the safety catches of the guns clicking off, and I could feel these strange juices in my mouth. I thought, *This is just going to be a massacre.* The women broke the standoff by starting to sing, 'We Shall Not Be Moved.' It was a terrifying moment in a terrifying morning.[328]

"When we were making that film, I called home right after that and told my mother that we were 'machine-gunned this morning.' She said something like, 'I forbid you to stay there another minute. You come right home.' I told her I was only kidding. 'Don't you ever tease me like that again,' she said.

"For me, it made me really happy when *Harlan County* won the Academy Award and the coal miners and their wives came from eastern Kentucky to see that and be part of it."

Kopple raised the ante for every filmmaker. Being a woman, she says, did not and does not change her experiences. She doesn't pay much attention to it. "I'm a filmmaker."[329]

Movies Teach Us How to Behave

Lynne Littman wanted to be an actress. The summer before she was to leave for the London Academy of Music and Dramatic Arts, where she'd been accepted, she was working in New York at a submarginal job for a producer, bringing his Rolodex up to date. One day, he and his partner were scrutinizing the Players' Directory. One of them said, "We'll take *her* to dinner tonight." Littman thought, *I'll never get picked.* "I called LAMDA, and canceled. I wasn't going to be an actress and be exposed to that kind of shit. I was going to be the one to do the picking. That changed my life."[330]

She stayed in New York and worked in public television, where she met two women producers, Ofra Bikel and Barbara Gordon.[331] She says, "Only because I'd met them did I know women could be in charge of their own projects. They were actually making documentaries!"

A chance meeting with Agnes Varda in New York changed everything again. "I spoke fluent French and I came to Los Angeles to work as her assistant on a feature film Varda was making, *Lion's Love* [1969]. She'd been in L.A. with her husband, Jacques Demy, who was making a feature for Columbia. Varda had nothing to do in Los Angeles, so why not make a movie?"

Varda was one of the very few women in the world directing features. "She was a miracle, a genius, brilliant and difficult," says Littman. "She makes films the way painters make paintings."[332] Littman worked for Varda for six months.

From 1971 to 1977, she worked as a producer, reporter, and director, making a film a week at KCET, L.A.'s public television station. There Littman formed a body of nonfiction work for which she won four Emmys, a Columbia/Dupont Journalism Award, and an Oscar.

"Being a woman doesn't hold me back," Littman told the *Los Angeles Times* in 1973, "it's the patterns I learned from being a woman all my life that held me back. When men come into an organization they get a sense of the politics of the place, where the power is and how the structure is arranged. I came in, found my own niche and decorated it. I didn't want to know how anything was being run as long as I was given a budget for my shows. This is the female mentality: 'give me my little space and don't make me worry about how the place runs.'"[333]

Around 1975, she heard anthropologist Barbara Meyerhoff speak at the Women's Writers building in Los Angeles, describing her fieldwork among aging Jewish women in Venice, California. Littman went up to her afterward and said, "You are talking about my grandparents. Let's make a movie."*Number Our Days* was completed in 1976.

"I brought the film to the academy basically in a brown paper bag," says Littman, "just making the deadline [for Oscar submissions] by running over there, snatching the forms, filling them out at the desk. Nothing about it was premeditated. Today kids gear their films to categories and are quite sophisticated.

"Once I was nominated for the Oscar, I prepared a little speech. I bought a floor-length gown of plum-colored silk crepe, sleeveless with a scoop neck. I wore a big silver necklace. The Oscars were held at the Dorothy Chandler Pavilion. The best part of that evening, other than winning, was the ladies' room. The stage lights around the floor-to-ceiling mirrors gave off a beautiful pink and amber light. Liv Ullmann stood in this glow, wearing a pink satin chemiselike dress. She was combing her daughter's strawberry-blond hair in the mirror. I thought I'd stumbled into a Bergman movie," says Littman. "It was a magical moment. That whole night was the best playing-out of a fantasy that I will probably experience because I was completely uncynical about it. I loved the film I'd made, I loved the old people, I loved Barbara [Meyerhoff], I was thin, and I was about to marry the man I loved [Taylor Hackford] . . . I had to have some kind of career security before I could consider getting married."[334]

Lillian Hellman presented the Oscar to her. "She called me John Littman. I was stunned that she was the one to hand me the award. I had her picture up on the wall, that ad of her in a Black glama mink from the *New York Times*, which I'd framed and carried around with me for years. It's on my wall right now. I never wore that plum-colored outfit since."

The next morning, after the Oscars, at six A.M., Littman was trolling the aisles of a supermarket in the Silverlake district of L.A. buying cakes for everybody at the office.

"Why was I there?" says Littman. "Because I learned a lesson from the movies. In *The Red Shoes* (1948), I admired Victoria Page's [played by Moira Shearer] humility and discipline. So I'm in the supermarket carrying my Oscar in a shopping bag because Moira Shearer was back at the ballet barre at six A.M. after her greatest success. I was supposed to get up and do normal stuff after a triumph. Movies taught us how to behave."[335]

Don't Con Me with a Lot of Technical Terms

The only road steeper than directing for women is director of photography (DP)—true in the late 1970s, true now. The route goes like this: a person may start as a member of the camera or light crew, move up to gaffer (head electrician), then to camera operator, then to director of photography. These union positions are rigidly controlled, and it's extremely difficult for men to attain them without the help of strong mentors or inside connections, like dads or uncles. The number of women who have been cinematographers on feature films would fit in a lunch booth.

Brianne Murphy speaks sweetly and calmly. "When women began to executive-produce their own films or start their own production companies, as Jane Fonda, Barbra Streisand, Goldie Hawn, and Sally Field did, I have to say they felt safer with their fathers than with their sisters," Murphy recalls. "That was understandable—their professional lives were at stake, too. Back then it was catch-twenty-two: you wanted women to do well because if they messed up, they messed up for everybody. But if they did well, it was an exception."

An example is *Like Mom, Like Me* (1978). "I'm sure it was a battle to get me on as cinematographer," says Murphy. "I knew Nancy [Malone, the producer] had a hard time getting an okay for me. But once we started shooting, everyone pulled together so nicely. It was a very compact family. Nancy was wonderful on that. I'd never seen a producer come on the set and talk to the crew members personally. She knew something about each of them and that was important, considering what I was trying to do—keep them enthusiastic about each shot."[336]

Like Mom, Like Me was written by Nancy Lynn Schwartz,[337] adapted from the book by her mother, Sheila Schwartz. It starred Linda Lavin, Kristy McNichol, and Patrick O'Neal. In the script, a family is torn apart when the father, a teacher, runs off with a student, leaving his wife and young daughter to cope with his loss. They renew their own relationship as mother and daughter, and then the father returns.

"I wanted Brianne Murphy to shoot it, but she'd never done a movie of the week," says Malone. An executive at CBS reviewed Malone's crew list and asked, "Who's this Murphy, what's he done?"

"I told him she'd done an afternoon special for me, *Five Finger Discount*, and she'd won an Emmy for it. 'I want her to shoot this.'

" 'No, no, she can't do this,' he said.

" 'Why?'

" 'We want Kevin or Mike—they'd be good, use one of them.' He pushed across a list of men who had many MOW credits.

" 'I owe this to Brianne Murphy,' I said. 'It's a moral thing. She needs to get into the next level.' I really felt that way. I was on the board of Women in Film and I felt this is what I needed to do. Otherwise, I was a charlatan.

"I fought this exec. He wouldn't give in. I brought five heads of departments up to his office. 'These are the people I want to work with.' I put all my cards on the table. Finally, I got it."

The director, not the producer, is supposed to pick the DP, but Malone felt so strongly about hiring Murphy for the project that she gave her director no choice in the matter. "Now I'm a director," says Malone. "I'd have killed a producer who did that to me!

"*Like Mom, Like Me* got a forty-share. It was the third highest rated movie that year," she says. "I went to sell another show like it and they said *Like Mom* was a fluke. Fluke? To get a forty-share? Fifty million people watched that show. I don't know how they define fluke. But they wouldn't do another 'soft' project."[338]

In 1978, Anne Bancroft, who played the unforgettable Mrs. Robinson in *The Graduate* (1967), had just starred in *The Turning Point* with Shirley MacLaine. Her next film, in 1980, was *Elephant Man*. Between these two, she directed *Fatso* (released in 1980). Bancroft, on her first directing work, hired a woman as her DP. Murphy went from *Like Mom, Like Me* to *Fatso*.

"She told me," Murphy says, "that she knew what she wanted to get but didn't know how to say it or who to say it to. I was sitting in her office and she came right out and said, 'I can tell you and you're not going to con me with a lot of technical terms.' I think she was reluctant, too, to tell men what to do." Moreover, Bancroft wasn't just directing; she wrote the script and was costarring with Dom DeLuise. The story was about Dominick DiNapoli, who has an eating disorder; he meets a girl and must decide between his appetites—the girl or the food.

Murphy recalls that as she and Bancroft were talking, Bancroft's husband, Mel Brooks, walked in. His new company, BrooksFilms, was producing *Fatso*.

"Hi. You're the lady cameraman, huh?" he said.

"Yes, sir," Murphy replied.

"You know all about film?"

"Yeah."

"And about lights?"

"Yeah."

"Do you know about those new lights, they have funny letters?"

"The HMIs?"

"Yeah."

"I know about those."

"Well, hope you like my wife."

As the filming began, Murphy felt Bancroft was not getting the backing she should have from Brooks or the studio. "The other thing was that I was never allowed to go to dailies," says Murphy. "Nobody went to dailies except Anne and Mel, so I'd see the film at the lab before I came to work in the morning. Usually at dailies, the DP goes with the director and the director tells the DP what she likes and doesn't like. The editor usually goes, too. But in this case only Mel went with Anne. I guess he told her what he liked. Word had gotten around that he was very controlling.

"But on the set everybody loved Anne and we had a wonderful camaraderie. Around four or five in the afternoon, Mel would come to pick her up. We never knew when he'd arrive, and it seemed to be at his convenience rather than hers because whenever he did appear, she'd start wanting to complete a shot. One day, he came on the set, not introduced to anyone and not saying hello to anyone, just standing there, letting Anne know he was ready. We were in the middle of a shot, the camera is rolling, the actors are playing the scene. Mel goes over to the video assist to look at it and in the middle of the shot he says, 'Cut, cut, that's no good, that won't work, cut it.'

"My camera operator, Bob Lavar, a big man, took his eye away from the camera, looked down at Mel, looked over at me, and said, 'Who the fuck is that little guy?' All hell broke loose. Very upset, Anne picked up her stuff and left. It was a wrap. Everybody was proud of Bob for saying what he'd said, telling Mel off for cutting her shot. That's unheard-of behavior. No one ever says 'Cut' except the director. Ever.

"The next day, I came in to the set and we're all lit and ready to go. No Anne. After an hour or so, the assistant director came to me and said, 'Bri, Anne wants to see you in her dressing room.' I went in. Her eyes were all red and she said that she'd been crying all night. 'This is just terrible what happened yesterday,' she said, 'and I hate to tell you this, but Mel says you have to fire Bob, the operator.'

" 'What on earth for?'

" 'Mel says he's potentially dangerous.'

"I'd worked with Bob for about six years," says Murphy. "I knew him and his family, and he was as potentially dangerous as I was. 'No, Anne,' I said, 'Bob paid you a very high compliment. He doesn't care who comes in. No one is going to call cut to his director's shot. Finally, he had to turn the camera off because everyone ran into the set and you were upset and no one would want that on film.'

" 'So he was protecting me?'

" 'Absolutely. He said something very brave, because Mel's recognizable and, you know, powerful.'

"Anne said she'd be out in half an hour. I went back to the set. Two hours later, the AD came by. 'Anne wants you in the dressing room.' I guess Mel had gotten to her," Murphy says. "She and I went through it again. I said I wouldn't fire the operator, there was no reason to, and he should get a medal. It was a standoff. We got no shots all day. The following day we all went back to the set. Bob said, 'Bri, if you want me to quit I will, because maybe what I said was out of line.'

" 'No, you did a wonderful thing. Get back to work.' After a while, we all got back to work.

"Anne Bancroft is a very talented person. I always thought she could have been a great director."[339]

■ ■ ■

By the late 1970s, the new young directors like Scorsese, Lucas, and Spielberg who had broken through the gates in the late 1960s were delivering wonderful, often fresh films, which also rained profits.

The standard of motion picture success in the force field that women were trying to get into had just shot to astronomical heights. It was easier for the industry to see women as producers, compared to directors. But not that much easier.

I Tried to Address Women's Equality

In 1977, Barbra Streisand won an Oscar for "Evergreen," the theme song she wrote for the first movie she executive-produced, *A Star Is Born*. By producing and starring in a motion picture, Streisand had done what no women had done since the early 1900s, when Lois Weber and others directed, sometimes wrote, and starred in their films. Seven years after her first production, Streisand would be directing.

Streisand had formed her own production company, Barwood; *A Star Is Born* was a Barwood/Jon Peters production.[340] Peters was a full partner in the production. For both of them, it was a "make or break" proposition.[341] Streisand brought years of film experience in front of the camera; Peters had almost none, but they were a team. For a while they were a good one, but this was a Streisand production from start to finish. She had final cut.

"I made an agreement with Frank [Pierson]," Streisand says, "that he would collaborate with me. He has full credit as director, but I staged a lot of that movie."[342]

The new version of *A Star Is Born* was set in the rock music world. Kris Kristofferson played John Norman Howard; Streisand played Esther Hoffman, whose fame eclipses that of her mentor.[343] The reviews were lukewarm, but Streisand's updated, rock music rendition of *Star* was popular and brought in about $90 million domestically at a time when ticket prices were about $3.50.

"It's not a perfect film," Streisand says, "but I tried to address women's equality, such as when Esther, wearing a man's suit, proposes to John Norman—'I want to marry you,' she says. 'No, you don't,' he replies. 'Yes, I do.'" For the film, Streisand had a song written, "Woman in the Moon," to express the equity or the power of women. "After they are married," Streisand says, "Esther doesn't change her name to his, though she adds his name to hers, things like that. She says, 'Why would I change my name?'" The film, like many of Streisand's, is seeded with culture spikes, pointing up the rocky, often ambivalent nature of men's relationships with women. At the first concert Esther attends with John Howard at a raceway, men pat her on the butt and treat her as an adornment, a groupie. At their wedding, "obey" is cut from the ceremony.

"In Japan, at the opening for the film," Streisand says, "I looked out at the press conference—two hundred forty-seven men and three women. I spoke about role reversals, about women standing up for themselves, having their own identities, not just becoming somebody's wife, as Esther is not just Mrs. John Norman Howard at the end. Everyone in that room looked at me with blank faces. That was culture shock. But in a way, isn't that what movies are all about? Maybe people don't like changes. They get used to artists appearing in the same kind of roles or doing what they're known for, just as people were used to me then being only a singer and performer. That also says a lot about how women are viewed in our culture, especially actresses who want to direct films are viewed as frivolous, not financially responsible. So in different ways, we're knocking against a lot of glass walls, not just glass ceilings."

Streisand says she was not thinking about directing *A Star Is Born*. In another way, however, she'd always been thinking about it. For instance, Streisand describes a scene in her earlier film, *The Way We Were* (1973)[344] in which Katie (Streisand) is very upset—her husband, Hubbell (Robert Redford), has left her.

"I always believed in serving the director's vision. I would always do it to the best of my ability," says Streisand. But that didn't mean she didn't have opinions. "Sydney Pollack, the director, who I love, wanted me to slowly close the typewriter and slowly take out Hubbell's clothes and put them in a suitcase, do everything slowly, then call Hubbell on the telephone. Arthur Laurents [*West Side Story, Anastasia, Gypsy*] had written a wonderful speech for me about Hubbell being my best friend, and that as my best friend I needed him to come over. In this case, my instinct differed from Sydney's. 'Why wouldn't I do it really fast and furious and angry?' I asked him. 'Slam the typewriter shut, pull out his clothes, slam the suitcase, take his shaving cream and dump it in the garbage, and *then* cut to a quiet scene sitting in a chair where I'm about to break down in tears and ask him to come over because he's my best friend.' Sydney didn't agree, and so we did it all slowly. Each person has his or her own vision," she adds. "There's no right or wrong."

Streisand participated in a documentary that covered, among other issues, she says, some political aspects of *The Way We Were*. She felt some scenes in Arthur Laurents's script that had political overtones were cut from the final film unnecessarily. "One scene," says Streisand, "explained that someone informed on Katie and accused her of being a Communist. She knows Hubbell would have lost his job in Hollywood if they'd stayed married. The whole front part of that scene is cut when Katie, having been informed on, says, 'It's amazing how decisions are forced on you willy-nilly.' A viewer might ask, 'What decisions?' Well, the decision to split up. Their breakup wasn't just about Hubbell schtupping another girl, it was about the *political* atmosphere of the times, the betrayals that occurred then, *and* the essential difference between the two characters. Hubbell belonged in Hollywood, Katie did not. She knows this and it's her decision to end the relationship with him. She is not a victim. In fact, she's the strong one.

"Don't get me wrong, I love this picture. I had a wonderful time making it. It works with or without these extra scenes, but I prefer the additional political element.

"In that movie," Streisand says, "I got a glimpse of how hard it was for me, creatively, to not have any control over my work."[345]

I Had to Give Up Fear

The bracing, cheeky films made in the 1970s certainly inspired women with or without visibility or even credits to reach for the work they dreamed of doing—even when their upbringing may not have prepared them in any useful way to do it.

One of those was Gale Anne Hurd, who was soon to produce *The Terminator* and dozens of other films. Her classmates wrote messages in her high school yearbook that added up to the same thought: "You're one of the nicest, sweetest people in the school. Don't ever change."

"That's the way I was—nice and sweet and everyone stepped on me," Hurd recalls. "I was a doormat. I was the person you called at midnight when you needed something done and you didn't want to give that person credit for it. I never demanded the credit. I had to give up fear— all the fears, fear of success, fear of doing everything differently from the way I'd been taught."

Hurd is not a doormat. She says what she means, gently, courteously. Her manner is poised, graceful, and a trifle retiring.

Hurd started working at New World Pictures as Roger Corman's assistant, a kind of secretary and publicity assistant. By late 1979, she was coproducing her first film for him, *Smokey Bites the Dust*. She had a three-day mix scheduled.

"I've come to trust my instincts," says Hurd. "If I have a bad feeling about something, I'm generally right, and that instinct had saved me numerous times. With *Smokey*, I was concerned that the sound effects editor wasn't going to deliver all the effects we needed for the mix. The day before, I went down to his shop and sure enough, he was nowhere near ready because he'd accepted a better gig on another film which paid more money. Though I was incapable of standing up for myself, I could always stand up for the film and for what was right.

" 'That's unacceptable!' I said. 'We've scheduled a three-day dub and you'd damn well better be ready.'

"To dub that fast, in three days, the best way was to mix in reel order. The next day, we put up the picture for the first reel, but the sound effects editor hadn't shown up. We're paying for this time at the mix, so we went ahead and mixed the dialogue and the music. I didn't see Roger arrive, but he was standing at the back of the dark room when the sound effects editor finally arrived.

" 'You're late!' I said. 'The clock's ticking and where have you been? Do you know how much money you're costing us? Do you know creatively what you've cost us? You can't do this!' Then I just moved on very quickly. 'How are we going to solve this?' I asked him.

" 'We can't do anything today,' he said. 'It's not ready—'

" 'How about the effects for reel one?'

" 'Ah, no, can't do it.'

" 'Reel two?'

" 'Nope, that's not ready either.'

" 'We have ten reels. Which ones can we do?'

"Finally we salvaged the day. Later, Roger said, 'Calm down, Gale, it's only a movie.'

"That shocked the hell out of me," she says. "*Only a movie?*

" 'I really appreciated how you handled it,' he went on, 'your commitment, loyalty, and your problem solving.' That's when I started to lose some of my fears."[346]

The next movie Hurd produced was going to create a sensation. It was called *The Terminator*.

What Language Is This?

Debra Hill seems optimistic and direct, in charge and cheery. "I was in that first generation of women who didn't go to college to look for a husband. My college was protesting—Vietnam, minority rights, women's rights. I thought if I worked really hard at a career instead of a family and marriage, maybe I could succeed. My mom was frightened for me. She wanted me to be a teacher or a nurse, but I wanted the movies."[347]

After working in commercials in San Francisco, she came to Los Angeles in 1975 with a few contacts. One of them was Larry Buchanan, famous for low-budget movies for American International Pictures (*Mars Needs Women*). He was directing *Goodbye, Norma Jean* on a $100,000 budget.

"I had no idea what to do, but I was willing to work for very little pay. I faked my way in, made them believe I could do the script supervisor job. I'd worked on commercials and had carried the script supervisor's notes from the set to the editor. As I walked along, I'd peeked at them: 'Take one, CU? What language is this?' That was the sum total of my script supervising experience."

Script supervisor is one of the few areas in film where women have flourished, and it's one of the best ways to learn how movies are made. "You're standing next to the camera all the time," says Hill, "talking with the director: 'We're putting a thirty-five-millimeter lens on, moving camera from right to left, and the actor is speaking in this direction.' It's a great vantage point because you're between the director and the camera and the actors, even though the phrase 'script girl' tended to downplay its value."

Hill worked on numerous independent productions before joining IATSE (International Alliance of Theatrical Stage Employees). But Hill constantly told her coworkers, "I want to produce, I want to produce." Todd Hallowell, now an executive producer, was then an art director. "Around 1976," says Hill, "we were in the back of the camera truck, and I said, 'I'm going to write and produce movies.' Todd told me later that when he heard that, he thought, 'Dream on, little girl.'" Hill knew she could do it, even though there were almost no women producers. It was (and is) extremely difficult to move up from script supervisor to producer.

"I knew the key for women was to write a screenplay because I could put 'D. Hill' on it and no one would know if I was David or Debra. I had no realistic ambitions to be a director. In those days, Joan Tewkesbury and Joan Darling were the only women directing that I knew, and they were perceived as 'women directors,' not big directors of sweeping male movies which sell in big theaters." Hill did not want to make "women's movies." Like many girls, she grew up watching *The Beast With Five Fingers*, *The Creeping Toes*, and *The Mummy*.

In 1976, she was script supervisor and assistant editor on *Assault on Precinct 13*, John Carpenter's second movie. She went with him to show it at the London Film Festival, where they met Moustapha Akkad, whose most recent production had been *The Messenger* with Irene Pappas and Anthony Quinn.

"Akkad loved *Assault on Precinct 13*," says Hill. "He wanted John to direct *The Babysitter Murderers*. There was no script, just a concept. John and I decided to collaborate: we'd cowrite the script, he'd direct it, and I'd produce it." They renamed the movie *Halloween*. It starred Jamie Lee Curtis and Donald Pleasance.

"While I was making *Halloween*, I felt like the little train that just goes and goes. So many obstacles are thrown against you, man or woman," says Hill. "The biggest challenge on *Halloween* was also the biggest blessing: we had very little money. We relied on ourselves to work out the problems. You can't just throw money at problems. You need a very good script *before* you start shooting because you can't 'fix it in the mix.' John and I worked for free—everything had to be about putting the money on the screen. It's still about that. A second challenge for me was learning that, as a producer, my job was not being with the film crew, because a producer also had a day job—making sure the picture is on schedule, doing cost reports, checking the budget, talking to the studio about marketing, release dates, publicity. When the shooting crew gets up at five o'clock in the afternoon for a night shoot, I was going to dailies, then going out to the set and shooting all night. I had to learn to separate myself from the action, which I'd always been a part of. That was one of my biggest challenges—leaving the set.

"By making a horror picture, then *The Fog* and *Escape from New York*," Hill says, "I wanted to set an example. Whether we create the story or are handed it, women don't have to be pigeonholed into one type of movie."[348]

Halloween was produced in 1978 for $360,000, a minuscule budget even then. It grossed $55 million.[349]

Not a lot of films have female protagonists, but two opened the decade: *Diary of a Mad Housewife* and *Klute*. The wife and the whore. In *Diary*, a long-suffering wife-servant (Carrie Snodgress) is married to an egotistical, vindictive man (played by Richard Benjamin).[350] *Klute* reveals the disintegrating spiral of a prostitute at the call-girl end of the business through Jane Fonda's Oscar-winning performance. A few films in the 1970s had female protagonists—*Alice Doesn't Live Here Anymore* and *Alien* come to mind. Two other films dealt with aspects of women's real lives—characters who were wives and, let's say, women of easy virtue, but also heroines: *The Lady in Red* and *Norma Rae*. *Lady in Red* was a low-budget picture that got little press and no awards; *Norma Rae* had a bigger budget, won awards, got lots of press. Both were stories about what women endure, what they can accomplish; both were produced by women.

By 1979, Julie Corman had made seven low-budget features and had produced three children. "I passionately believed in *Lady in Red*, the Dillinger story told through Polly Franklin, the 'lady in red' character," she says, "and I believed in the political and moral issues at the center of the story. It's low-budget, about nine hundred thousand dollars. It looks a little quaint, more than twenty years later, but it still works."

It was written by John Sayles, a new screenwriter (later, *Lone Star*, *Passion Fish*, *The Secret of Roan Inish*) and designed by Jac McAnelly, a new production designer (*Flicks, A Summer to Remember*). The music was by a new composer, James Horner (*The Mask of Zorro, Deep Impact, Apollo 13, Titanic*). The cameraman was Daniel Lacambre, the director Louis Teague. "We also cast fresh, spunky Pamela Sue Martin as Polly, the 'lady in red,'" says Corman, "and some old pros like Robert Conrad as Dillinger, Louise Fletcher as the madam, Robert Hogan, Christopher Lloyd, and Dick Miller. It was a terrific combination of talents."[351]

The story takes place in the 1930s. Polly, an abused farm girl, runs away to the city and works in a garment factory, where the manager molests the girls, causing the death of one. Polly becomes a dance-hall girl, is thrown in jail, then released, and becomes a prostitute so she can protect her friend in prison by bribing a sadistic woman guard. *The Lady in Red* is about women's lives at the bottom of society where they have no protectors.

John Sayles's only other script had been that rousing favorite, *Piranha*, in 1978 for Roger Corman. "I hired John," says Julie Corman, "to develop the characters and explore social issues in *Lady in Red*—feminism, communism, racism, the haves versus the have-nots. There's that fine line between hitting the issues too hard and losing the audience, or just glancing over issues haphazardly. Sayles handled the balance brilliantly, and he really built people in the film. When Pamela Sue Martin faces crucial decisions, we're right with her wondering what's she going to do."

Julie Corman hadn't seen *The Lady in Red* for years. Reviewing it recently brought back memories about the cast and crew and how much she herself believed in the film. "I've produced films with bigger budgets but they don't have the same level of enthusiasm," she says. "I miss that enthusiasm. Maybe it wasn't about high or low budgets at all. Maybe it was just a special time in my life and the thrill of making a film that stood on its own merits. That's what was special about making *The Lady in Red*."[352]

Norma Rae had bigger stars but it was also about wealth and poverty, exploitation and prejudice, fear and courage. Produced by Tamara Asseyev and Alexandra Rose,[353] it was nominated for a Best Picture Oscar; the writers, husband-and-wife team Harriet Frank Jr. and Irving Ravetch, were nominated for Best Screenplay. Sally Field won the Oscar for her role as Norma Rae.

The movie is about a southern textile worker, a single mother, who reluctantly then wholeheartedly joins the efforts of a New York union rep (played by Ron Liebman) to unionize her mill. In risking all, she gains all. Sally Field was known the world over as the flying nun ("lame-brained sexual stereotyping," as Roger Ebert characterized it), a hard role to shake. Norma Rae liberated Field from the nun and from television.[354]

"I was heading Roger Corman's distribution," says Alexandra Rose. "Roger picked up one of Tamara's films and that's how I met her. I had found an article in the *New York Times* about Crystal Lee Jordan, on whose life the *Norma Rae* story was based, but I knew I couldn't do anything with it because I was working with Roger and the times were wrong for that kind of movie. When I decided to be a producer, Tamara was looking for a partner, too, and we teamed up. *Rocky* came out, which made me think we could sell the 'Crystal Lee Jordan' idea. *Rocky* was important in film history because it was the first film made outside the studio system, a negative pick up, without studio money that had been a giant success."[355]

"Norma Rae said she wanted to make it better for her kids," says Asseyev. "That really appealed to us."[356] Rose says, "At a dinner for Betty Friedan [much later], Betty told me, '*Norma Rae* is a watershed film. Did you have any idea when making it that it would be a historic moment for women?' I said, 'No, I just knew when I read that article in the *Times*, in my mind I saw that woman when she knew she'd be going to jail and she'd have to tell her children who their real fathers were because they'd be hearing things about her. My heart went out to her. That's how it started for me."[357]

Asseyev decided Martin Ritt would be the right director.[358] "When Tamara and I walked into a meeting with him," Rose recalls, "he said to his secretary, 'Who are those two actresses?' That wasn't so bad because in a meeting at Columbia Pictures, we met an executive, who stammered, 'These women are the *p-p*-p-p of the project.' He couldn't say the word 'producers' and apply it to women."[359] According to Asseyev, Ritt told them that if they got Harriet Frank Jr. and Irving Ravetch to write it, he'd read the script.[360]

Harriet Frank Jr. and Irving Ravetch, her writing partner and husband, have been writing together for fifty-five years. "The idea is this," says Frank, "collaborating without ego, writing with your husband who is very much with you on everything. It's the two of you against the world." They worked often with director Martin Ritt—*Hud, Hombre, Murphy's Romance.* "He was wonderful with writers," says Frank, "he was defensive of writers. We were a formidable group, a kind of magic trio. I felt very secure flanked by these two guys. Marty was a writer's director all the way, businesslike, not temperamental, but also a fighter with a marvelous sense of humor.[361]

"I had never met Tamara or Alexandra," says Frank, "but I was very interested in the subject they presented. For instance, Tamara was a good producer, too, stalwart, not overpowering. She valued writers and she was lots of fun. They both were...It was so tough for women producers in the business then. Now people realize that women are extremely competent, that they relate to the money and to the craft. Back then, feature film production was a male field."[362]

The Ravetches signed on. "It was a joy to see the script come alive," says Harriet Frank, "a joy to work with my husband. It has always been a seamless collaboration."[363]

In those days, Asseyev says she and Alexandra read all the great scripts, saw every film. When the Ravetches turned in the draft of *Norma Rae*, "I knew it was the best script I'd ever read," says Assayev. "It presented a human condition in a situation that most people in America weren't familiar with and didn't particularly want to know about."[364] In the end, the union worker, Reuben, and Norma Rae did not fall in love, or, as Frank says, "they did not ride off into the sunset," which one reviewer, Roger Ebert, applauded. "We're sort of set up for [it]," Ebert wrote, "but they don't; the movie is steadfast in its determination to show Norma Rae growing because of her own thought and will, not under the influence of yet another sexual liaison. That's what makes the movie so special."[365]

"The first scene we saw in dailies," Asseyev remembers, "was of Norma Rae in the mill when she pulls her mother off the line and takes her into the doctor's office. 'My mama can't hear, this doesn't happen to my mama.' Everyone in the room knew it was a great performance."[366]

It was not easy to find the actress to play Norma Rae, and both Asseyev and Rose say, "practically every female star in Hollywood turned it down."

"We had a hard time getting a mill to shoot in because *Norma Rae* was based on a true story that took place in the J. P. Stevens Company, which was already in litigation with its workers, the primary one being Crystal Lee Jordan, whom we renamed Norma Rae because she wanted to be anonymous." Barbara Kopple had already approached Jordan to make a documentary about her struggle in the mill but Jordan chose Asseyev. "The J. P. Stevens case," says Asseyev, "was starting its long trek to the U.S. Supreme Court. Naturally, they didn't want us to shoot in any of their mills, and they made sure that we could not find a mill to shoot in."[367] The production ended up in a privately owned, fully-operating mill in Alabama.

"I was delighted by Sally's professionalism," says Harriet Frank, "by her energy and by the fact that she was a human being. Just forget movie stars. She had two children, she had to go home and run her household. In that era, women made common cause. We let our hair down and we were all girls together. Sally had a passion for the material, I had a passion for the material and so did my husband because at that point the J. P. Stevens Company was drawing a line in the sand.

"When we went into the mill to look at the location," says Harriet Frank, "it was tense. They weren't thrilled with the idea of people coming in from Hollywood to make a movie about unions in the South. The working conditions were appalling. You cannot believe what we saw and heard. We couldn't believe how people survived in that atmosphere. Then suddenly there's this ballsy woman who says she's going to get the union in there. She was at risk. Her economic life, such as it was, could be utterly swept away. But that woman stood up and said, 'This far and no more.' That was dazzling. More than dazzling. It was spectacular."[368]

Norma Rae was released more than twenty years ago when Asseyev and Rose were in their late-twenties and mid-thirties. After it screened in the Palais in Cannes, Asseyev says, "they put a spotlight on Sally Field and Marty Ritt. The audience stood up, applauding and cheering. And it kept on and on. Sally started to cry, Hank Ravetch started to cry, and I cried because we realized we'd made a good film that Americans and Europeans related to. That was one of the most extraordinary moments of my career."[369]

Rose says that *Norma Rae* (and a picture she produced in 1999, *The Other Sister*) are a true expression of who she is as a person. "They both show an aspect of women that won't be said 'No' to, won't be suppressed, and will tell the truth above all else. They . . . don't play the game, they live life equally, honestly. At very few times does anyone—even characters in movies—get the chance to be unagended. Important then, important now. Women have to keep examining and testing and saying, 'No, this isn't the way it should be.' Women do do this and women don't have anything to lose because we're already oppressed."[370]

Norma Rae was nominated for Best Picture, the first time two women producers had been nominated in that category without male partners. "And to be nominated for a film that was about a woman—it was so thrilling," says Asseyev. "These things are so rare."[371]

Oscar nominations often translate into greater opportunities. David Begelman, who had moved from Columbia to MGM, put Asseyev and Rose under contract at MGM in 1980. They were there for three years and never made a film, though a couple came close.

"Our inability to get something mounted at MGM had more to do with our sensibilities, the kinds of films we wanted to produce," says Asseyev. "For some reason, Hollywood has never recognized that women make up half the population and an audience of women is out there, waiting. Finally, I couldn't make features on the political, social, or human subjects that interested me. That's what eventually got me into television. The networks recognized that an audience of women existed. That audience reflected my sensibilities, politically, socially, humanly. Television was a boy's club where they'd play golf and make deals on the course, but television was also very open to me as a woman, and to women."[372]

Harriet Frank Jr. thinks American women need to get a break in American films. "Great European films address women. I'm a fan of American women who are very high achievers, but films have a shallow view of American women and we rarely see their complexity. Combine that with the age factor: actresses are cut off from careers so early, studio heads, directors and producers are terribly young. A new generation of movie makers today are into blowing things up. They don't necessarily relate to the human condition so it's no surprise that women drawn from real life don't show up on the screen. But the Women's Movement," she says, "made women a factor to reckon with.[373]

Certainly as the new decade opened, women could not be ignored or denied. "It seemed reasonable to expect," says Nancy Hutson Perlman, "that we women would get a decade like the one that brought us *Star Wars, Close Encounters of the Third Kind, Chinatown, Five Easy Pieces, The Sting,* and *Blazing Saddles.* Given the times, it was not unnatural to believe that stage would be the 1980s."[374]

Many women had that expectation. Opportunities increased, but the decade would be no less stormy.

$\mathscr{S}$ECURING THE PERIMETER: THE 1980s

"To shield or make secure from capture, destruction and hostile interference."
—WEBSTER'S THIRD NEW INTERNATIONAL
DICTIONARY

11

"We wanted to keep the gains coming," says one woman, an executive, "and it wasn't easy." But others say, "In the 1980s, the men backed us."

The decade was a whirl of corporate takeovers, colorization squabbles, and money—lots of money. Sherry Lansing took over 20th Century Fox Productions, and Ronald Reagan, a former president of the Screen Actors Guild, took over the country. MTV premiered, Pac Man and *E.T.* arrived, and Zsa Zsa Gabor went on trial for striking a Beverly Hills cop. Compact discs forever changed the music industry. Family values took on political muscle (as opposition to "a woman's right to choose" grew) and brought back family movies. The networks, celebrating the boom in miniseries that began with *Roots,* and shows like *Dallas* and *Dynasty*, began losing ground as the audience fractured—home video and myriad choices on cable, HBO, A&E, Showtime, and ESPN. No one seemed able to get a handle on it. The new forms offered outlets for documentaries, movies, talk shows, and news as never before. Studios joined the rush to home video, cable, and new technologies they once feared. By 1983, *Raiders of the Lost Ark* sold 500,000 videocassettes and made $20 million in rental revenue. By the end of the '80s, the networks began to look old-fashioned, out of touch.

Piece by piece, MGM was dismembered and "put down," a corporate fate in the 1980s. The studio was owned, controlled, or cannibalized by Ted Turner, Lorimar Telepictures, Warner Bros., and Sony/Columbia Pictures. All around that beleaguered studio, the business of making movies changed dramatically. Coca-Cola took over Columbia Pictures. Oilman Marvin Davis purchased 20th Century Fox in 1981. A series of dizzying mergers folded movie studios, television networks, magazine companies, and publishers into huge media conglomerates. Ted Turner snapped up the MGM library for an estimated $1.25 to $1.5 billion. Colorization of black-and-white movies like *The Maltese Falcon* sparked loud protests; Turner cracked that he had the right to color any film from the MGM library because he owned it. Kirk Kerkorian, left with MGM's withering production arm, took over United Artists in 1981 and renamed the company MGM-UA Communications in 1986. Media baron Rupert Murdoch took control of 20th Century Fox in 1985. Television networks scrambled to merge in 1986—ABC with Cap Cities, and NBC parent company RCA with General Electric in the biggest non-oil merger in American business history. Viacom acquired a stake in Showtime/The Movie Channel, purchased MTV, and took over Paramount Studios. Columbia Pictures and Tri-Star merged into Columbia Pictures Entertainment, still part of the Coke machine. In 1989, the biggest entertainment merger of all went through—Time Inc. and Warner Communications. (In January 2000, AOL took over Time Warner.) Box office and the bottom line reigned. "Greed is good," as Gordon Gekko (Michael Douglas) said in *Wall Street* (1987).

Splits and breakups went global. Moderate Mikhail Gorbachev, secretary general of the Soviet Communist Party, presided over the collapse of the Soviet Bloc in 1989; democratic candidates rose to power in Poland and Czechoslovakia, and Romania's dictator Nicolae Ceausescu was toppled. We saw it all. By 1989 the Cable News Network (CNN) was available in nearly every country in the world twenty-four hours a day.

Independent television producers gained by supplying 28^1/$_2$ hours of weekly programming, compared to 22^1/$_2$ for majors. In 1985, Robert Redford started the Sundance Film Festival. Independent films that year included *Stranger Than Paradise, Falcon and the Snowman, Mrs. Soffel*. The festival's significance was measured in 1989 when the low-budget Audience Award winner *sex, lies and videotape*, produced for $500,000 and debuted by the festival, was a critical and commercial smash.

In 1989, Dawn Steel was still the only woman running a studio. Television still offered more opportunities for women to create long-running shows like *Cagney & Lacey, The Golden Girls,* and *Dynasty*. Few women were directing films, but a few scored some hits. Barbra Streisand directed *Yentl* in 1983, Penny Marshall directed *Big* in 1988, and Amy Heckerling directed *Look Who's Talking* in 1989, which took in $100 million. Few women were producing films, and almost no African-Americans, Hispanics, or Asians. Lili Fini Zanuck became the second woman (after Julia Phillips) to take home an Oscar for Best Picture—*Driving Miss Daisy* (with her husband, Richard Zanuck).

The decade solidified women's positions as a visible and permanent part of the entertainment industry. But it did not bring them what they'd expected at the end of the '70s—parity.

9

YES, SIR, GIVING WAY TO YES, MA'AM

The sound of a crack in the glass ceiling opened the decade of the 1980s when Sherry Lansing became president of 20th Century Fox Productions, the first woman to hold that post at a major company.[1] Fox had enjoyed a distinguished history, run by Darryl F. Zanuck and Joseph M. Schenck from the 1930s to the 1960s. It produced important and controversial films like *Gentleman's Agreement* (1947) and *Pinky* (1949). In the early 1960s, *Cleopatra* buried the studio in a sea of red ink, but *The Sound of Music, Hello, Dolly!* and *Doctor Doolittle* pulled it back. In the 1970s, Fox delivered *Patton, The French Connection, The Towering Inferno,* and, just three years before Lansing arrived, *Star Wars.*

In the 1970s, Fox had had imaginative, energetic leadership from president Alan Ladd Jr. and Paula Weinstein, a very young senior VP of production. But they left in 1979. Fox needed an energy infusion. To some that looked like Sherry Lansing; to others, her post looked like window dressing.

On January 2, 1980, when Lansing drove on the 20th Century Fox lot, she wasn't thinking about historical precedents. "I was just overwhelmed by the amount of work I had to do *that day,*" says Lansing. "People said to me, 'You're the first woman to do this!' but I was thinking, 'I have to do the work now, that's all I've got to do.' Women who succeed just put their heads down and do the work. Of course, they realize they are among the first, but at the time they just start in on the work. I cared desperately about the movies we made and I just turned my focus completely to those movies and the people making them."[2]

Lansing had all the credentials—she'd been story editor and executive story editor at MGM; vice president of creative affairs, vice president of production, senior vice president of production at Columbia. President of production was the logical next step; it just hadn't been offered to a woman before.

"I remember that after my marriage ended," Sherry Lansing says, "I went into therapy to understand what had gone wrong. Therapy is such an interesting process. I was a vice president at Columbia Pictures, which, at the time, was in the midst of selecting the head of production. My therapist said, 'Do you think you could get the job?'

" 'No,' I said, 'a woman could never get that job.'

" 'Why?'

"Why? I was at a loss to explain it. I didn't know. His question really made me think. I began campaigning for the job. I didn't get it, but I started to think that reaching for that kind of position was a possibility. A few months later, I did get the job—at Fox." It was, she believes, a combination of her own belief in herself and external factors. The world was changing, attitudes were changing, and the industry was more receptive to a woman getting a top job. Lansing is right, though; as other women in the 1980s found out for themselves, having the dream is crucial to the act of winning the prize. In a way, being able to dream of producing or directing or heading a studio sets a path to the goal. Lansing's own belief in herself was decisive. "Also, I just worked hard," she says. "That's a big factor anywhere and it was one reason I got that job." Everyone who knows Lansing speaks of her dedication to the work, of returning all her phone calls, of her cheerfulness and grace.

"I really believe the movie business is ahead of other businesses by being gender blind," Lansing says. "I'm not saying we're there yet; we're not. But when women head motion picture studios, you have to say that business is gender blind."[3]

"The world press descended on the doorstep," Susan Merzbach recalls, "when Sherry became president of Fox Productions. The most incredible brouhaha. It's very hard to imagine now what that meant then."[4]

At MGM in the 1970s, Lansing had promoted Susan Merzbach to executive story editor. Merzbach moved with Lansing to Columbia and then to Fox as vice president of creative affairs. Lansing also brought in Claire Townsend,[5] a talented executive from MGM, as a vice president of production, and other women. Merzbach says, "Suddenly, in many [Fox] meetings, there were more women than men. Even when Bob Cort, head of publicity, and David Madden came in later, we still had a heavy concentration of women.

"It's hard to recall details of those days exactly because Sherry's ascension was so huge it sort of overshadowed everything else," Merzbach says. "I do remember saying to people in meetings, 'Gee, it's wonderful to have all these women around.' It felt truly different. Rather wonderful."[6]

9 to 5 and *Star Wars: The Empire Strikes Back* were about to be released, both put into the pipeline the previous year by Alan Ladd Jr. and Paula Weinstein. Lucy Fisher had been with them, too. When Ladd left to form his own company, Weinstein went with him. Fisher stayed on as a production executive.

Working at Fox was exhilarating, according to Merzbach, but also grew difficult.[7] Lansing was running into roadblocks. The CEO and chair was Dennis Stanfill. Alan Hirshfield, the new chief operating officer of the motion picture division, had hired Lansing, a skillful slice of the publicity cake; Norman Levy, formerly the king of distribution at Columbia, now emperor of distribution at Fox, was aggressive and ambitious. In 1981, Marvin Davis, oil caliph, bought 20th Century Fox;[8] Hirschfield survived, CEO Stanfill did not. Lansing was caught in a net of strong egos and opposing forces. Moreover, Davis called her "doll-face," which quickly got around. Although Lansing's position may have given heart to every woman in town, it was far from a perfect fit, which had nothing to do with Lansing's competence and everything to do with the politics of power.[9]

The studio's high-profile board of directors included Henry Kissinger and Princess Grace of Monaco. "When a board meeting was held on the lot, security was really tight," says Merzbach. "One day, I drove into my parking space marked 'Merzbach.' A studio guard appeared beside me, hooked a thumb at the 'Merzbach' sign, and said, 'Do you work for him?'

" 'No,' I said, 'I am him.'

"Some things hadn't changed," she says.[10]

Even so, 1980 was a heady time and full of optimism. Everywhere it was perceived that though women had nothing like equal status, they were definitely on their way up. "The atmosphere was much better than today," says Lili Fini Zanuck. She believes that widespread knowledge of the pervasive inequality actually worked to women's advantage in the 1980s. "The need for changes was being brought to everybody's attention. When the DGA statistics came out [in 1980] showing that only a tiny percentage of the DGA women members were working,[11] all of a sudden the reality that women were taking such a backseat was so clear, so out there, that in fact it became a good climate for women. Men were very open to helping you. It was a good time."[12]

The industry responded, changes were being made, women were promoted. In 1981, Suzanne De Passe became president of Motown Productions, the first African-American woman to head a major entertainment company; Paula Weinstein became president of the motion picture division at United Artists; in 1982, Barbara Boyle became senior VP of production for Orion, and Lucy Fisher became vice president of production at Warner Bros. In 1984, Barbara Corday moved from ABC to become the first woman president of Columbia Pictures Television, and the remarkable and controversial Dawn Steel, whom Dan Melnick nicknamed "The Tank," rolled on to become Paramount's production chief, then capping her career in 1987 as the first woman to be named president of Columbia Pictures. These women, plus Rosilyn Heller, Marcia Nasatir, Dede Allen, and Verna Fields, and a few others in television (Ethel Winant, Renée Valente), constitute the first group of women in the film industry. But think of it: six or eight years before, in the 1970s, Lansing had been a story editor; Paula Weinstein, a reader, then an agent; Lucy Fisher, a reader; Marcia Nasatir, an agent. Their swift pace seemed to predict even bigger changes. Creatively, for producers and performers, writers, directors, and other women in sound or picture editing, everyone expected the decade to improve their position conspicuously.

"Sherry Lansing headed motion pictures at Fox and Andrea Baynes headed television production," says attorney Melanie Cook. "I have a picture of them which made a big splash because a woman was heading film and a woman headed television. The caption said Sherry had been a schoolteacher. I'd only been a lawyer for about a year and I remember laughing about this with a friend. 'Oh, my God, we can do this!' we said. We were so impressed by it. It was empowering."[13]

Goldie Hawn's timing was perfect. In the fall of 1980, Hawn's first production, *Private Benjamin*, was released. She produced it with Nancy Meyers and her husband, Charles Shyer, and Harvey Miller.

"Friends who know her say much of her philosophy was embodied in the woman she played in *Private Benjamin*," James Ryan wrote in the *New York Times*. "She played Judy Benjamin, a pampered Jewish princess who joins the Army and discovers that she does not need to rely on men."[14]

Hawn had wanted to produce long before 1980. When Nancy Meyers approached her with a story idea called "Private Benjamin," Hawn told her to write it and she would produce it. It would be Meyers's first produced screenplay.[15] Hawn would star. Hawn formed a production company, K.M.A. She did not expect her first production to be a hard sell—but it was. She went from studio to studio in 1978, dogged. And she was pregnant. But performers could only control their destinies by producing. This is particularly true of actresses, whose onscreen career span is decidedly shorter than actors'.

Finally, Warner Bros. signed on in June 1979, and Hawn began a year-long development process. *Private Benjamin* was praised by critics and had made about $50 million by Christmas of 1980. It seemed an unlikely venture for Goldie Hawn. But Hawn was more than the flighty young woman who had entertained the world for so long. She was brash and entrepreneurial. Around this time, she met Anthea Sylbert, who became a good friend. "We need each other's support," Hawn said, "It gets lonely when you're out there doing a big job all alone. Most of us [women] in the industry were still pretty much underground, and we needed connections. We needed to exchange ideas and information."[16]

She Shot J. R.

On television, *Dallas* was the show everyone watched on CBS Friday night, particularly the last show of the 1979–80 season when someone shot J. R. Ewing. Who wrote that episode? A woman. "I thought I ought to work on *Dallas*," Loraine Despres says, "because, damn it, I came from the South. And it was a 'soft' show and I knew it would consider a woman writer." Through a Women in Film program she met the executive producer, Len Katzman. Despres began writing episodes; several months later she was outlining the episode "Who Shot J. R.?"

"No one was prepared for the sensation that episode caused," Despres says. "That summer the universe wanted to know who'd shot J. R. I wasn't allowed to tell anybody. One guy, a lawyer, asked me to tell him, then I could mortgage my house, he'd fly to London, make the bet for me, and I'd make a fortune. I said no. He was very, very annoyed. Someone at the gym asked me, and I wondered if he was going to beat me up to find out who shot J. R. I thought, If he hits me, I'll tell him. Instead he offered me twenty thousand dollars because if I told him he was going to lay it off in Vegas. I told him no, I couldn't tell."[17] The show created a frenzy, even, it was reported, in Russia. Everyone had to wait until November 21, 1980, when the world found out that J. R.'s mistress, Kristin, played by Mary Crosby, had pulled the trigger. That episode was seen by more people than any program in the history of television up to that time.

In the midst of the *Dallas* fever, *Variety* presented a reality check for Hollywood. The Women's Committee of the Directors Guild wanted a woman be hired to direct at least one of every thirteen TV episodes. From 1950 to 1980, it reported, 7,332 films had been made by major companies—and only fourteen were directed by women. About 65,500 hours of prime-time drama had been produced and aired since 1949—115 hours were directed by women. Both figures meant women directed 0.2 percent of the work.[18] Everyone knew that the number of women directors was small, but no one believed it was that minuscule. At the end of the year, *Variety* ran twin front-page articles, "Women Make Mark in the Pic Business" and "More TV Exex Suite Seats for Femmes." All true. Both articles included lists of women who were executives at the networks, studios, and large production entities, followed by a shorter list of women who were independent producers.[19]

The power line in Hollywood is drawn between the people who can "green-light" a picture—say "Yes, we will make this movie!"—and the hordes of developers and vice presidents who can only say, "Let me get back to you" or "No." Though cracked, the glass ceiling was firmly in place. A closer glance at the lists in *Variety* revealed that almost no woman could say "Yes." The women listed were below the boomlet of the woman-as-vice-president.

However, it was beginning, the natural outgrowth of the 1970s' sharp complaints, and the landscape looked bright.

■   ■   ■

The inaugural tone of the 1980s had been set a year earlier when Fay Kanin was elected president of the prestigious Academy of Motion Picture Arts and Sciences, best known for its Oscar Awards.

"Here's a picture," Kanin said in 1999, holding out a framed photograph. "Talk about being a woman alone, look at this—all these men and Fay. Those are all the past academy presidents who are still alive. I say the best way to guarantee a long life is to be an ex-president of the academy." In the photo, surrounded by men, Kanin looks friendly, assured. "There they all are with me in the middle. All men. I like men. Some women don't like men really, just as some men don't like women. I think it's more that way than women not liking men. But I like men and I like being with them. I also love women and I'm always thrilled when a woman gets elected to the academy board. I find that terrific. But there aren't many.

"I suppose it surprised people when the board elected me president for a one-year term. I think people felt it was a good step up for women."[20] She was reelected to four terms.

Kanin had just finished writing and producing *Friendly Fire* (1979), a Vietnam War drama starring Carol Burnett. Kanin didn't write or produce anything else until *Heartsounds* in 1984.[21]

"I must say I didn't miss the writing one bit," she says. "In fact, I like serving on boards and plan to do more of it." She had served on the Writers Guild board as vice president, as treasurer, and in other guild positions for years. "The WGA board got a little bit fractious in the 1990s, maybe even before that," Kanin says. "There were lots of fights which I didn't like. The academy board was always so polite and genteel compared to the guild. Writers are fighters."[22]

■   ■   ■

The times were full of propitious moves. For instance, when Suzanne De Passe became the president of Motown Productions, the television and film unit of Motown, she took the company to real prominence on the shoulders of many music-related television shows—*Happy Endings, Lonesome Dove, Class Act, Buffalo Girls, Streets of Laredo, Dead Man's Walk,* and the miniseries *The Temptations,* about the legendary Motown group. She's still producing today, a thirty-year career that started in 1968 when she was booking bands for clubs. In 1972, she got an Oscar nomination for her script, *Lady Sings the Blues.* De Passe, a phenomenon, is beginning to be credited with being the first Motown executive to audition and see the potential of the Jackson 5. Like many women, her style is said to be open, nurturing; her interest has been content, not cash. It's a risky way to live and survive.[23]

The year before Suzanne De Passe took over Motown Productions, Anthea Sylbert moved to United Artists as vice president of production. United Artists was in trouble. The ballyhooed release of *Heaven's Gate,* a western directed by Michael Cimino, who had won the Best Director Oscar in 1978 for *The Deer Hunter,* had been set for December 24, 1979, but was delayed. The summer of 1980, the studio's January-to-June reports were disappointing—*Carny, Fame,* and *Roadie* had sunk without a trace. But the executives at UA were confident that *Raging Bull* and *Heaven's Gate* would deliver.[24]

"At these big meetings," Sylbert recalls, "there were only two women in the room, the story editor and myself. Then word got around that Paula Weinstein was coming to UA as president of the motion picture division." Weinstein was a "baby mogul," who had some heat. The UA promotion put her on the same level as Sherry Lansing at Fox—but United Artists was not as stable as Fox. Everyone told Sylbert, "You're not going to be able to stay and work with her. You'll rip each other's hair out." Everyone told Weinstein, "You're going to have to get rid of that Anthea Sylbert. You're both too opinionated and you'll scratch each other's eyes out."

"Mark Rosenberg," Sylbert says, "was the only one who got it right. 'Are you joking?' he said. 'You're going to be the best of friends.' He knew both of us."[25] In about two years, Rosenberg would become president of production at Warner Bros.[26]

"At that period, women competed with each other," Sylbert says. "It's like the pie. If the pie is small, who is going to get the pie? Until the pie got bigger or until women could get some sense in their heads, we tended not to encourage or help each other. Many women didn't think of competing with the guys. They only competed with other women. I never went out of my way to do one or the other. It never occurred to me that I couldn't work with women, but I have to admit neither did I seek it out."[27]

"I think there is a female sensibility," Paula Weinstein says, "in terms of some of the work. The very presence of women is important because when enough women are in the room, the tenor of the discussion changes from 'who's the boss' to some version of the process."[28]

When Alan Ladd Jr. created the Ladd Company, Weinstein moved with him, collaborating on *Body Heat* and other films. Her next jump was to United Artists.[29] The month before she arrived, David Begelman had been moved out of MGM (or kicked upstairs or slipped sideways, depending on your point of view), to become chairman of United Artists. A year later, he was fired, and Freddie Fields, who had been running MGM, became president of MGM-UA Production.[30] Highly visible executives, usually male, shuffle or leap from one studio to another in the natural course of the business, but these were particularly jumpy times at MGM/United Artists.

Paula Weinstein grew up in Europe. During the McCarthy blacklist years, her mother, Hannah Weinstein, had decamped with her three daughters to Paris, then to England, where eventually she produced made-for-television movies and TV series, turning out some 435 of them, including *Robin Hood*, *Escapade*, *The Adventures of Sir Lancelot*, and *The Buccaneer*. She also formed her own production company, Sapphire Films, and employed blacklisted American writers who could no longer work in the States because of HUAC and the cowardice of the entertainment industry during those terrible years.

Hannah Weinstein returned to New York in 1963 and formed Third World Cinema with actors Ossie Davis, Diana Sands, James Earl Jones, and Brock Peters. In addition to producing films, like *Claudine*, starring Diahann Carroll and James Earl Jones,[31] Third World Cinema set its sights on the discriminatory practices of the film unions, getting them to admit two hundred people, primarily African-Americans.[32] "More than half—twenty-eight of the thirty-seven members of the crew—were black or Puerto Rican," said Hannah Weinstein, "and most of them came from our Third World training program."[33] Hannah Weinstein, one of the very few women producers of that period, is revered for her fighting spirit and high ideals.

"My mother influenced me hugely," says Paula Weinstein. "I saw what it was like to be a producer. I swore I'd never be in the movie business. I saw her being strong, meeting with writers and directors, and running her own studio. She was a single parent, a divorced woman, and I feared that no man would ever love her. I used to think, 'Why does she have to be so cross? Didn't she like the script? Can't she be nice to him?' I saw her be very successful and then suddenly very unsuccessful. I saw her survive it all. I was sure I would never be a producer. But, here I am."

Early in her career, Paula Weinstein wanted the safety of a studio life compared to the rocky insecurity she'd had as a producer's daughter. "But studios," she says, "are paternalistic by their very nature, and corporate. I rebelled. Being female didn't hurt, but it held me back from believing I fully belonged. I didn't feel part of a club." She was, however, part of the younger, radical-liberal antiwar film crowd around Jane Fonda and Tom Hayden. "I met Jane Fonda around some political demonstrations." When Weinstein came to Los Angeles, she started to read scripts for her. "Then Mike Medavoy, an agent at IFA [International Famous Agency], hired me as a reader." IFA was soon to merge with Creative Management Associates to form the powerhouse agency International Creative Management (ICM). A few months later, Medavoy left to head production at United Artists; Weinstein became an agent with Fonda's and Medavoy's support. "And then," she says, "I'm in it . . . [but] I didn't feel inside that world. That derived from a multitude of things— my femaleness, my politics, my love of the people who create movies as opposed to the people who finance them. As a studio executive later, I was diligent about not mistaking myself for the filmmaker."

Weinstein traveled from reader to agent to head production at United Artists in about eight years. "When ambition hit, and the possibility of success," she says, "when you're young you are foolish enough to believe in the title and the job and think those things *are* you. I think I put off marriage and children because I was too involved in my work. My work sustained me . . . Until recently my big high had been, first, organizing a demonstration and working against the war or working for civil rights, and later, making a movie. Those are moments when you believe in something greater than yourself. Now my biggest high is my daughter."[34]

Already in the soup at United Artists, Anthea Sylbert says she couldn't believe she'd traded the "safe, secure dominion"[35] of Warner Bros. for United Artists just before *Heaven's Gate* finally hit the nation's screens—only to be swiftly withdrawn for "re-editing."[36] Michael Cimino's $36-to-$40 million movie had to earn three times its production costs to make dollar one in profit. As one historian wrote, "This brought on the customary pronouncements from on high that something had to be done about costs . . . Hollywood no longer knows what a reasonable budget is."[37] Studios had survived titanic flops before, but UA was already shaky. "Then MGM bought UA, which generated changes about every other week," says Sylbert.[38]

Into this maelstrom strode Barbra Streisand, who had been searching for a studio harbor for her film, *Yentl*, which she had adapted for the screen from the story by Isaac Bashevis Singer (ultimately cowriting with Jack Rosenthal). Streisand planned to star, produce, and direct. No other woman had managed that since the silent-film days, nor had most powerful and popular male stars.[39] Given women's uneasy new place in the industry firmament, Streisand's directing goal came early, as had Goldie Hawn's initiative to produce *Private Benjamin* in 1980. But Hawn's movie was not as controversial as *Yentl*, was not a musical; Hawn had producing partners—Nancy Meyers, Charles Shyer, and Harvey Miller—and Hawn was not directing. Many warned Streisand that she was crazy to try, at forty, to play an eighteen-year-old masquerading as a boy. But Streisand saw Yentl as a twenty-eight-year-old spinster. She seized the reins and plunged forward.

"We had been turned down by almost every major studio until we came to UA," Streisand says. "We turned in the *Yentl* budget to United Artists on the day [Vincent Canby's] *New York Times* review of *Heaven's Gate* came out, which changed the movie business."[40] Media dislike, even hatred, for *Gate* was palpable and spread a pall over the industry. The industry was doing a course correction; big budget movies were out, at least for a while. (In her search for a studio, Orion had told Streisand directly, "There are no big budgets anymore." The point was moot— Orion didn't have the money, certainly not for an untried woman director. "We were cut from thirteen million dollars to ten million," says Streisand. "That was a horrible day.")

United Artists was beset. "It seemed like every time we had a green light to go ahead, the studio administration changed!" Streisand says. "I became obsessed. Obsessions are not easily accepted coming from a woman."[41]

Yentl had taken years to ripen.

In 1961, Freddie Fields and David Begelman had started a talent agency called Creative Management Associates (later International Creative Management, ICM). In 1968, Fields hatched an idea called First Artists Production Company so that Paul Newman, Sidney Poitier, and Barbra Streisand could choose and control—produce or direct—their own films.

David Begelman had been Streisand's agent when she was sent the

Isaac Bashevis Singer short story from which the film of *Yentl* was developed. "I loved the piece," says Streisand. "I sent it to David with a note: 'This is my next film.' David said, 'You've got to be crazy! You can't do this kind of movie about a girl studying the Talmud.'" Valentine Sherry, the producer, wanted Ivan Passer to direct. Streisand had seen Passer's work (*Loves of a Blonde, Crime and Passion, Silver Bears*) and thought well of it. "But Passer thought I was too old for the part," Streisand says. "I was twenty-five at the time. But I said, 'Oh, well, okay.' I wasn't even thinking of directing it. I wanted to act in it. But somehow, I just couldn't give up on it. Valentine Sherry died. I asked others to direct it. As the years wore on, I began to think I'd really like to direct it myself. I had the film in my head but I was frightened by the prospect. Could I handle it? I was very frightened."

The film forged links for her. One was theatrical and literary. She has said she didn't discover literature and classical music until she was sixteen because it was never read or played in her home. "I used to spend hours at the Forty-second Street library reading Ibsen, Shakespeare, and Dante. I read all the plays Eleonora Duse had appeared in.[42] She was a hero to me. Her acting was so simple. Then I read the plays that were written for Sarah Bernhardt. Bernhardt played boys' roles (young Napoleon in *L'Aiglon* and Hamlet in *Hamlet*)." All these memories danced in her head, and among them was a great actress playing "boys" in great plays.

More than that, the connection to her father made *Yentl* live for her. "My father taught at Elmira Reformatory. He was an assistant superintendent of schools there. I'd read one of his theses about how to teach English to prisoners and juvenile delinquents. Something in that particular thesis spoke to me. [In a way], I felt we were living parallel lives, that we had a lot of connections, that we were a lot alike. I wanted to dedicate this film to my father, and, as I said at the end of it, to all our fathers.

"The only picture I have with my father is one with my arm around his tombstone." The tombstone next to his had the name "Anshel" carved on it. At the time Streisand was developing *Yentl*, she took it as a sign— Anshel is the name Yentl takes when she disguises herself as a boy in order to be permitted to study the Talmud.

"I had a lot at stake. It was very emotional for me to recreate the father I never had. But I bit the bullet," Streisand says. She was going to direct.

In the wake of *Heaven's Gate*, and with Streisand as a first-time director, United Artists insisted upon a completion bond. A completion bond is a form of motion picture insurance from a private company that guarantees to pay any amount over budget the producer spends on the film. A completion bond is not unusual.

"Then, when everything is *finally* in place, war breaks out in Poland!" Streisand says. "But having survived the bloodshed of the negotiations with the studio, an armed battle only seventy-five miles from our locations [in Poland] seemed like no problem..."[43]

Anthea Sylbert remembers the "production meetings, the 'will-we-won't-we' do *Yentl*," and thinking that "the woman's going to sing, and that alone is probably worth it." She says, "Everyone in Hollywood who is Jewish thought [*Yentl*] was too Jewish...I think they felt it was like the old lunatic group had green-lit it to begin with but no one wanted to confront Barbra because she is such a big star. At this particular meeting, the proposed budget was only like eleven million—it seemed like a bargain. I was a very strong supporter of the film, and then, when we acquired it, all this turmoil started at the studio. Andy Albeck was out and Norbert Auerback replaced him [as president and chief operating officer of UA],[44] then we woke up one morning and MGM had acquired us, and then Steven [Bach] was out..." says Sylbert. "Then we were in London for a preproduction meeting, trying to cut the script down—it was very long—and Barbra would agree to a cut, and as I was marking my script she'd say, 'Remember the draft where I said this line?' We had cut something that she wanted back. I was wanting to strangle her and was about to leap across the coffee table to grab her neck—and she starts singing! Which reminded me why we were doing this in the first place. I thought she did a wonderful job with *Yentl*."[45]

Streisand also shot in England, where she says she "never felt any discrimination [from them] because I was a woman. Why? Because they have a queen and had a woman prime minister! They're used to females with power. They felt it was their professional obligation to give me what I needed. I always asked the crew when we were discussing a scene, 'Is what I'm asking too complicated? Would you like me to simplify it?'

"'No, no, we want to give you your vision.'"

Directing *Yentl* was "a glorious experience," she says. And, even though she was fiercely nervous the first day she walked on the sound stage, "...directing came easily to me. I don't understand when people ask, 'How do you direct and act?' I just think it's one less person to direct, one less person to talk to, one less person to negotiate with.

"We went one percent over the ten percent contingency in the budget," Streisand says. "It was not very much. I wonder if those complaints would have been made with a male director of equal professional experience. I don't think so, or certainly not about a first-time director, which

I was—a first-time director, a woman, an actress . . . and, by the way, a Jew."[46]

The press was relentless, picking up stories, true or false, no matter how minor, about cost overages and delays.

"It had to be made for a price," says Weinstein, who was then heading motion picture production, which meant she supervised *Yentl* and the other films in production, like *WarGames.* "Barbra had been working on it for years. David Begelman, the incoming president of MGM, had agreed to make it. But there was a lot of turmoil over at UA, so there were great restrictions on how much money she had to spend. But she did it. It was her directorial debut. Even though there was a lot of pressure on her, she withstood it quite extraordinarily.

"For instance, if just *hours* as opposed to days slipped by, they were all over her, and they were coming to me, wanting me to be all over her about it. They'd say to me 'What are we doing? How did we get into this? Make her do it for less!' Literally, if they got a report that the shoot that day started an hour late, I'd get a call from somebody, 'Wait, wait, wait! She's slipped an hour.' It was very, very hard. But it was worth fighting for. Her talent was obvious, I saw her commitment, she was really building a city and recreating a world. Her desire to make it great despite extremely difficult conditions paid off. It was a hard journey, hardest most of all for Barbra, but she did it bravely and brilliantly."[47]

"The struggle strengthened me, motivated me, inspired me," Streisand says. "*Yentl*'s passion was fired by my own passion, by the passion I had to sustain in the face of all the people who told me that making this film would be impossible. I felt grateful to finally be in control of my own work . . ."[48]

Not until the Equal Rights Amendment battles in the early 1970s did Streisand begin to glimpse the power of the women's movement. "I'd said to someone, 'What do you mean? This debate about women making the same amount of money for the same job?' It just seemed so crazy to me. As a singer I was never discriminated against as a woman. But that caused me to start thinking about it, and I realized that directing was a man's domain. It was shocking." Ten years later, she saw *Yentl* as a symbol. "Yes, it was a story about another time and place, but it symbolized many of these same issues."

Those who said *Yentl* couldn't be made or shouldn't be made had also stated that audiences outside New York or Los Angeles wouldn't be interested. "But as it turned out," Streisand says, "the New York Jewish audience was the weakest the picture had. Texas and Taiwan were stronger than Brooklyn. It broke records in unexpected places like Finland and Norway. It grossed over four times its cost, and the sound track album is triple platinum."[49]

"Some of the reviews and public reaction were good, of course," says Weinstein, "but some of the press . . . was not good. She had produced, directed, written, and starred in a single movie, which hadn't been done by a woman for eighty years. It was amazing, and she was so committed to getting the script right, collaborating with the Bergmans[50] on their songs, and with composer Michel Legrand. There was no area that she wasn't deeply entrenched in. No one sees that kind of commitment very often. I've felt very committed to her."[51]

The first review Streisand remembers seeing of *Yentl* was a piece that aired after Geraldo Rivera's interview with her. "The woman who did it actually had a TV cooking show and was now a critic," Streisand recalls. "I'll never forget her opening line: 'Well, I liked it but I didn't love it.' That review never dealt with the [central] idea of this movie being a celebration of women. Overall, I was surprised by the petty, superficial quality of the criticism, even technical criticism, that didn't deal with the theme of the movie. One woman reviewer talked about my yarmulka . . . my 'designer yarmulkas.' But I researched material for this film for years, and all costumes were either the real thing from the period or based on pictures of Polish Jews at the turn of the century. I used real Jews from the synagogue, I didn't use extras to play the people in the synagogue. I needed real Jews who didn't have to learn how to daven [to pray]."[52]

Streisand had been anxious for women to review the film but was shocked that the "harshest, most vitriolic" reviews came from women.[53] It made her begin to think about the way women perceive other women's success and failure. Were women envious if other women succeeded? Did they feel "diminished"? Did they feel "enormous pressure to prove they're equal to men" and therefore dealt "more harshly with members of their own sex"? Had women been "raised . . . to compete for men," and did they bring that "same mentality of competition . . . to other women's achievements"?[54] "When I think about it now," says Streisand, "actually they were reviewing *me*."[55]

Pauline Kael wrote that the movie seemed "distinctively feminine," citing some scenes that "are simply different from scenes conceived and directed by men."[56]

Stanley Kauffmann, not a fan of Streisand's films, liked *Yentl*, and found that for him "[Streisand] has gained control, in the literal and basically relevant senses. Her open declaration that she needs to run her own show indicates only that, at her own level, she has recognized what, for instance, Chaplin recognized: she cannot let anyone intervene between her and the audience."[57]

"She wasn't treated well in most of the press," actress producer Jane Alexander says. "... Barbra lets people know what she thinks and in a boys' world ... that can be hard. She's trying to buck those guys all the time."[58]

Liv Ullmann, best known for her roles in Ingmar Bergman's films, now a director, said that she had heard "so many horrible things" about *Yentl* that when she finally saw the movie, she couldn't believe it. "If a man had made it they would have said this is genius, and if not that, she's almost there. A wonderful first directing debut. I was so overwhelmed. Right now, as I'm talking about it, I'm seeing this face of hers as the boy. It is of beauty. A movie like that could not have been made by a man. Certainly if a man had made something like it, people in the industry would have said, 'Oh, my God, look what we have found! Look at this new director!' They would all have held that director in high regard."[59]

Women in positions of real power, what power meant and how they handled it, was going to be one of the contests of the 1980s and 1990s.

CHUTES AND LADDERS—EXECUTIVE GAMES IN THE

10

CHUTES AND LADDERS—EXECUTIVE GAMES IN THE 1980s

In the young children's board game Chutes and Ladders, if your dice throw lands you on a ladder, you move rapidly forward; on a chute, you move quickly back.

This chapter is all about executives in the 1980s, many of whom were adults trying to climb career ladders. The first generation of women (whose careers began in the 1960s and 1970s) were breaking new ground. Their visibility worked for and against them. Whose advice do you ask if you, at forty-five, suddenly become a senior vice president? You're supposed to know. But before the early 1980s these positions had rarely been offered to women. Their working experiences held some unexpected surprises.

These executives worked primarily with older men, many of whom were still uncomfortable with women in senior positions. The women were politically underprepared as they took on higher executive positions. Though many men showed women the corporate ropes, one man's corporate rope did not make a woman's corporate ladder.

The second, slightly younger group of women matriculating in the 1980s did not meet the same resistance (see Chapter 11). Unlike their older sisters, they could actually see women as executives and producers. For instance, Marcia Nasatir and Barbara Boyle became role models for executive Lucy Fisher and producer Gale Anne Hurd. This turning point started in the 1980s. These two groups had very different corporate lives. It took about ten years before women as a group began to understand the dance.

Generally, women competed with each other because openings for them were still limited. Every studio, network, or emerging new cable operation seemed to have one woman—*its woman*, the 1980s version of the Queen Bee syndrome. In a way, Queen Bee-ism worked for everyone: the women who got in felt special and *were* special; for men, it kept crowds of women out. Queen Bee is still around today. If a company has a few women delivering "the woman's point of view," why get more?

Through the 1980s, the widening stream of women at work does not seem to have been seen as a threat. Their value was beginning to be appreciated, they were organized and usually cheerful, they didn't talk about equality so much, and they worked harder for less money. But they were new to the executive game.

Naturally, I Wondered What I Was Doing Wrong

Orion Pictures had been formed dramatically by Arthur Krim, Robert Benjamin, Eric Pleskow, Michael Medavoy, and Bill Bernstein when they left United Artists in 1978 after disputes with the parent company, TransAmerica. Krim, as the saying goes, *was* United Artists, and when he decamped, he and his top management took with them the support of much of the creative community. Marcia Nasatir, who had been a VP at United since 1974, did not leave with them. She was hoping to fill Medavoy's vacant seat at UA, but that was not to be, and Nasatir says she never discovered the reason. She did finally join Orion, but not for long.

In 1982, Barbara Boyle became senior VP of production at Orion. During her four years there, she put into production or acquired films such as *Platoon, Amadeus, F/X,* and *Eight Men Out*. One of the first was *Desperately Seeking Susan*. "I championed that film and Orion made it against all odds," Boyle says energetically. The principals were women: director Susan Seidelman (*Smithereens*), producers Midge Sanford and Sara Pillsbury (*River's Edge*), writer Leora Barish (*The Breakers*). The stars were Madonna, in her first feature film role, and Rosanna Arquette, who had performed in many films.

"I could not get that project moving," Boyle says. "Mike [Medavoy, Orion's executive VP of production] said, 'You love this project? Go see Arthur Krim.' I took the red-eye to New York and was waiting at his office at nine-fifteen the next morning."

Boyle told Krim she had come to talk to him about *Desperately Seeking Susan*.

"You like it?" he asked.

"I like it a lot," she replied. "How often have I come to talk about a project?"

"Well, hardly at all," Krim said. "Can you make it for five million?"

"I'll make it for whatever you give me."

"You've got it." Boyle turned around and flew home.[60]

Orion's marketing people wanted to test *Desperately Seeking Susan* in Atlanta. Boyle knew that was the wrong place. She wanted to test it in Boston. "A university town. This is a smart movie."

On Friday, "I traipsed from L.A. to Atlanta with Midge Sanford and Sarah Pillsbury, Susan Seidelman, and all of marketing and distribution," says Boyle. "We do a preview sneak. The numbers are terrible. I tell everyone, 'Of course they're terrible. This is not a southern-girl movie.' "

Full of confidence, Boyle went to Boston on Saturday to screen it. The numbers were worse.

"By this time," says Boyle, "nobody's talking to me, except the director, Susan. We recut a little, then tested it once more in L.A. It did marginally better. No one had any hope for it. Then—surprise!—it opened to great reviews and great numbers!"

Boyle had years of experience as an entertainment lawyer, as a CEO of New World Pictures, but Orion was different. Boyle had little "corporate" experience.

"I was used to getting incredible support," says Boyle, "but at Orion that kind of support decreased and then suddenly changed. I didn't recognize the feeling of the change. At Orion, I saw that women were treated differently, about credit for achievement and salary, in terms of— it's a cliché—just being outside the club. I had never experienced that. Naturally, I wondered what I was doing wrong. I didn't realize that doing my job wasn't enough, that I had to be smarter politically, to not, as a woman, generously give away my credit to others instead of saying, 'Wait, I did that project.'

"I also needed to plan my steps up the ladder. I didn't do that. I should have stepped back, thought about heading production at Orion, thought about the kinds of movies they made, hired a publicist, and planned who among my counterparts I should talk to. Second, I should have made sure the guys I reported to at Orion knew exactly what I was doing.

"I did not know how to play the game and I didn't learn fast enough. In the mid-1980s, I didn't even know who to ask for advice. Moreover, in corporate life, you must know the rules. You can't play baseball if you don't know there are four bases and a pitcher. I didn't know that my position as senior VP automatically entitled me to get copied on memos from other departments, travel first class, hold private screenings, hire this writer, fire that director. The guys who had my kind of background knew those things by osmosis; they were in the club, they'd seen other men in action. Osmosis presumes you're standing *next* to someone who sends waves of knowledge to you. The guys sending the information were of a different generation, different sex, different everything.

"I had pieces of information because I'd been in a section of the film business for years, but I didn't have a clue about being an executive for Orion. I didn't know what I didn't know. Some of those facts that I did *not* know are taken for granted—by a title, by a position, by, well, by guys. By the '80s, we began to see some rules, an entitlement rule, a contract rule, a let's-be-smart-about-the-next-job rule, the let's-take-credit-wherever-we-can rule. I wish I'd seen those patterns earlier." In 1986, Orion fired Boyle.

"I was told some of the reasons I was fired had nothing to do with me," says Boyle. "Being fired made me realize how nonpolitical I'd been. It's like that line in *The Natural*—'I didn't see it coming.' Back then, a lot of us didn't have political savvy. When Eric Pleskow told me I was out, I said, 'I understand you're trying to save your company,' as opposed to, 'You son of a bitch, you know I'm not the reason for this, you are.' The second thing I said was, 'What about my people?' "[61]

The Higher I Got, the More Gender Issues I Had to Deal With

Many women began their careers as egalitarian producers at educational television stations that made up the network called the Public Broadcasting Service, or PBS. When they became execs with PBS or with commercial networks, they expected the work would change but did not expect that the responses to them as professionals would also change.

"Production was a great place for women in the PBS system," Phylis Geller says. "Partly because commercialism didn't drive it. It wasn't about power and money. It was about its own mission as a cultural institution."

In the 1970s, Geller was an associate producer at the New York PBS station WNET, working on the drama series *Theater in America*, which adapted regional theater productions into television shows.

"I had no sense that a woman couldn't be trusted with big decisions because they couldn't handle money or weren't tough enough," says Geller. "Joan Ganz Cooney, one of the great pioneers, created *Sesame Street*; women were senior producers, though not presidents or vice presidents—those were all men. Many women started with David Susskind and crossed over to public television as producers, already accomplished by the time I came along."[62]

At Smith College, Geller says she was taught women could do anything. By 1980, having produced programs for PBS series like *The Amer-*

ican Short Story and *Great Performances*, she joined KCET/Los Angeles, one of the top four stations in the system, as senior vice president of national programs—drama, the arts, history, and science. She built and managed national and international productions.

"Being an executive is *different*," Geller says. "The higher I got in management, the more gender issues I had to deal with. At lower levels, people who do a good job are valued; at higher levels the risk is bigger, of course, because more power and authority are at stake. I've seen women at higher levels continue to think that if they're good at the job they'll be rewarded. Not necessarily so. It is a horrendous lesson to learn."

In Geller's experience, most men seemed to know that another game besides work must be played. "Women kept organizing the tasks to be done," says Geller. "They didn't feel above performing any work. I have found that men let things fall through the cracks because they're more focused on relationships and on positioning themselves than on the task details. There are individual exceptions but I've seen it played out so many times. Both attitudes or processes are valuable, but how odd that it breaks down on gender lines. I never expected that.

"Men are so much better at taking credit for what they do," Geller says. "Some women do it well; I was terrible at it. I told myself it didn't matter, that my satisfaction was knowing I did a good job. That's total crap. I wanted credit as much as the next person, but I didn't know how to take it."

Geller realized some women made themselves visible and got acknowledgment by behaving deferentially with male colleagues. "They call it managing up," she says, "a corporate dynamic that has to be learned—a way to manage people above them and still accomplish what they need to without seeming to be managing anyone. Middle management means one manages people above and below."

"The corporate structure," says Geller, "just goes on, or someone moves in to fill a vacuum because they're always standing by to fill a hole. An executive, a man, called me into his office one day, closed the door, and asked me to join him in a scheme to sabotage another member of our manager 'team,' who was also a man. He'd worked it out, believed I felt competitive with the other executive, and was sure I'd love his idea. 'Not interested,' I said. I'm hardly thin-skinned, but this was so blatant it left me shaking.

"There's a lot of talk about team playing," Geller says, "but the structure of business is hierarchical. As an executive, I long to experience a truly undivided team approach on a daily basis, and I was in it for twenty-five years."[63]

Mother Deaf

"I remember a cartoon in the *New Yorker*," says Geller. "A number of men and one woman are at a boardroom conference table. One man says, 'Well, Barbara, I'm sure that was a wonderful presentation, but of course, since I am a man and you're a woman, I didn't understand a word of it.'

"I'm soft spoken. I have to be more strategic and louder to be heard and understood," says Geller. "I'm a good manager, collaborative, clear thinking. I cannot tell you how many times in high-level meetings, I'll say something that isn't heard or heard incorrectly. Didn't I frame it correctly or is it that at a certain level women just aren't heard?"[64]

"Either the men turn off the sound of the woman, or they're accustomed to responding to the man's voice, or women are actually not heard," says Laura Ziskin, a film producer, former president of Fox 2000, now president of Ziskin Productions. "I used to find it hard that I could say something, not be heard, and I'd think, 'Okay, I'm just going to say it six times until somebody hears me.' That was a disadvantage in a subtle kind of way. I don't find it particularly better today. I genuinely believe it's about timbre. The range of our voice does not command a room as a man's does."[65]

"How many times have we said the one thing that turns the meeting in the right direction," says Judith James, film and stage producer, "a man restates it, and five minutes later they are harking back to his restatement, congratulating him on turning the meeting around? Hundreds, thousands, millions of times . . . It's like they feel better when they hear it from men, that now it has been given import. I have great hopes that guys who need to restate everything in a meeting will get comfortable enough to hear a female voice deliver a comment that turns the meeting around."[66]

Almost everyone interviewed for this book had some comment about not being heard. Here's the back channel: A young story editor at one of the studios in the 1960s, working on a hit show, was called into the president's office. The chief informed him that he'd hired a woman writer, somewhat of an anomaly then. "Can you deal with that?" he asked the story editor. "Have you worked with a woman before?" The story editor said he had. "Well, you'll have to take all that crap. Can you handle that?"

The story editor felt that even though the woman had already been hired, the studio head was warning him about the kind of tensions women brought to the workplace, tensions that usually stayed at home. "I can handle it," the story editor said staunchly. "I have a mother and a sister and they talked a lot, too, but I learned how to just go on reading the sports pages while they chattered on. I sorta tuned it all out. It doesn't bother me."[67]

At the HBO think tank sessions, there were four women and thirty men. Ilene Kahn Power, a new vice president, watched the dynamics. "A woman would come up with an idea and the men wouldn't listen. It's like that saying, 'mother deaf'—kids don't listen to their mother's voices. When a guy came up with the same idea a few minutes later, I'd watch the men embrace it. We women had to figure out another way to be heard in smaller groups. Ultimately, my ideas were heard because I learned how to deal with each administration. It was a question of thrust and parry, when do you thrust, when parry, when to push."[68]

"Of course, when you're the president they have to listen to you," Ziskin adds.[69]

The Few Women Who Knew How to Play the Game Were Not Telling the Others

In Los Angeles, Johnna Levine was ABC's director (then VP) of business affairs for movies and miniseries just after the miniseries *Roots* burst into the entertainment scene like a cannonade. Overnight, miniseries were the networks' hot ticket to high ratings.

"Suddenly I had the business affairs responsibility for movies and miniseries," says Levine. "ABC was the king of miniseries. Everyone in the business was trying to figure out the pricing of what was a gargantuan movie. There was no precedent to go on. I improvised," she says. "I constructed numbers out of my hat."[70]

While she dealt with the miniseries maelstrom at ABC, a more basic corporate way of functioning waited in ambush.

"I did not operate in ways that drew attention to myself," says Levine, "and I did not complain about difficulties or complications. I handled them! That was a mistake. When I had a document that showed something had gone well or went wrong, I'd explain it to *one* superior. Others didn't know why I'd done something a particular way.

She recalls a delicate deal that had to be made to avoid the possibility of infringement of FCC regulations. ABC could not appear to be hogging distribution rights on house-produced shows. "I made what had to be called a very bad deal financially," says Levine, "but I was under direct orders to do it to meet FCC regs so that it *not* benefit us financially. When I sent out that deal memo, comments came back from executives, 'Whatever possessed you to make this imbecilic deal? We could have

Screenwriter Diana Gould (*I Love You, Goodbye; For My Daughter's Honor*) created the WGA Women's Committee in 1971. SAG's committee began in 1972, the DGA Women's Steering Committe in 1979. *(Photo by David Stoltz)*

Television writer Joyce Perry (*Quincy, The Waltons, Mannix, Laramie, Ironside*) was the member of WGA's Women's Committee who spilled the beans to the *Hollywood Reporter*. *(Photo by Bob Lopez)*

Ethel Winant with former CBS President Robert Dennis Wood at the moment in 1973 she was named—surprise!—vice president at the Affiliates meeting. *(From Ethel Winant's private collection)*

Brianne Murphy, ASC, was the first woman to get into the cameraman's union, 1973. She won an Academy Award for the Mitchell Camera Car, 1982. *(From the priavte collection of her sister, Gillian Murphy)*

Joan Darling, one of the first women directors of the 1970s, directs Louise Lasser on the set of *Mary Hartman, Mary Hartman*, a Tandem production, in 1974. *(From Joan Darling's private collection)*

Rosilyn Heller was one of the first female vice presidents in 1974, at Columbia Pictures. She later became a film producer (*Ice Castles, The Beans of Egypt*). *(Photo taken by family friend)*

Marcia Nasatir, a 1974 vice
president, Orion Pictures.
The "jungle producer" of
Hamburger Hill (1987) on
location in the Philippines.
(Photo by Dylan McDermott)

Women who survived the
1960s–1970s moved around
until they found their niche.
Nancy Malone, actress,
became a producer, a vice
president of Fox Television
in 1975, and a director from
the 1980s on. Here she's on
the set of *Star Trek: Voyager*.
(Photo by Kate-Leslie Hay)

Julie Corman in the editing
bay, c. 1979. Maybe she's
looking at *The Lady in Red?*
(Photo by Sharon Kirkpatrick)

Tamara Asseyev, film and television producer. Photo taken in 1979, at the time of *Norma Rae* (co-produced by Alexandra Rose). *(From Asseyev's private collection)*

Lillian Gallo, a producer with ABC in the 1970s. Here she's at Leeds Castle in England, making *Princess Daisy* (1983). *(From Gallo's private collection)*

Barbara Corday, at ABC as vice president, comedy development, c. 1980. *Cagney & Lacey*, which she and Barbara Avedon had created, didn't go on the air as a series until 1982. *(Photo by Jean Hoelscher)*

Karen Arthur, a film and television director since 1974, was an early episodic director of *Cagney & Lacey.* This photo was taken at the time she directed *The Disappearance of Christina* (1993). *(From Arthur's private collection)*

Anne Nelson, the legend. Fifty-five years at CBS. Today, she's vice president, business affairs, CBS Entertainment. *(CBS Photo)*

Barbara Kopple, producer/director, in the union battlefield of *Harlan County, U.S.A.* (1976). She has won many awards, including two Oscars and three DGA awards for Outstanding Directorial Achievement.

(Photo by Robert Gumbert)

Fay Kanin, writer/producer, first woman president of the Motion Picture Academy, 1979 to 1983. At her desk at home, with her Emmy for *Friendly Fire* in the background. *(Photo by Marlene Callahan Wallace)*

Barbra Streisand, director, *Yentl*, 1983, MGM/UA Entertainment Co. *(Photo courtesy of MGM CLIP + STILL)*

Anthea Sylbert, from costume designer (*Chinatown*) to executive (Warner Bros., United Artists) to producer of many films. Here she is on location for *Wildcats* (1986). *(Photo from Sylbert's private collection)*

In 1980, Sherry Lansing was the first woman to become president of production (at 20th Century Fox). In the 1990s, she became chairman, motion picture group, Paramount Pictures. *(Photo Sam Jones)*

Melanie Cook, attorney, partner, Bloom, Hergott, Cook, Diemer and Klein, with her children on the set of *Sleepy Hollow* (1999). *(Photo taken by family member)*

Director Lynne Littman on the set of *Testament* (1983) with performer Jane Alexander. *(Photo by Melinda Sue Gordon)*

Phylis Geller in the1980s when she was senior vice president, national productions, KCET-LA. Today, she's president of Norman Star Media in Washington, D.C. *(Photo by Mitzi Trumbo)*

Billie Beasley Jenkins, after being vice president of the Leonard Goldberg Company, c. 1990, in the maze at 20th Century Fox Studios. *(Photo by Sammy Davis Photography.com)*

Nikki Rocco, up from a clerk to president of Universal Studio Distribution, the first woman to run the division.
(Photo by Blake Little)

Helene Hahn couldn't get into the college she wanted because of the quota on women. Today, she's co-chief operating officer, DreamWorks. *(TMCopyright DreamWorks L.L.C.)*

Stage and film performer Jane Alexander produced *Square Dance* (1987). Here she is on the set with director Daniel Petrie. *(Zade Rosenthal)*

Donna Smith started as a file clerk. Here, she's the producer with production manager James Brubaker on location with *K-9* in 1989. *(Photo copyright 2001 by Universal City Studios, Inc. Courtesy of Universal Studios Publishing Rights, a Division of Universal Studios Licensing, Inc. All rights reserved.)*

National Geographic writer/producer Miriam Birch on location in China with the star of *Save the Pandas* (1982). *(Photo by David Clark)*

Dolores Robinson started as an agent. She is now a personal manager with her own company, Robinson Entertainment. *(Photo from Robinson's personal collection.)*

After producing the Oscar-winning *Driving Miss Daisy* in 1989, Lili Fini Zanuck directs *Rush* (1991). Left, cameraman Don Reddy. *(Courtesy of MGM CLIP+STILL)*

Sara Risher, chairman, New Line Productions. Working with New Line Cinema since 1974, she has developed and produced over 50 films. In the 1990s she started New Line's in-house production banner, ChickFlicks.
(Photo courtesy of NewLine Cinema)

Laura Ziskin was president of Fox
2000 in the 1990s, then went back to
producing with her own Ziskin
Productions (*Dinner with Friends,
Pretty Woman, What About Bob?*).
(Photo by Sayeed Adyani)

Winifred White Neisser, senior vice
president for television movies and
miniseries, Columbia TriStar.
(Photo courtesy of Columbia TriStar Television)

Janis Diamond,
writer/producer, multiple
media, live action, television
interactive CD-ROM—from
Bull to *Peter and the Wolf.*
(Photo by Craig T. Mathew)

Jude Weng, writer
(*Survival*) and director
of a short (*Steel*).
(Photo by Joan Hankammer)

Dina Lipton, production designer on
The Muse (1999). *(Photo by Sam Emerson)*

Grace Liu, assistant director, DGA, with background artist Suren Dua on a Las
Vegas location shoot. *(Photo by Gabriel Echeverria)*

Stuntwoman Leslie Hoffman going out a window. *(From Hoffman's private collection)*

Amy Halpern, gaffer, director of photography, IA 728. *(A self-portrait from her private collection)*

Chief Lighting Technician Andrea Sachs on the set of *Comedy Central*, c. 1999. *(Photo by Tom Houghton)*

Judith James, producer, *Having Our Say: The Delaney Sisters' First 100 Years* (1999), on location with producer Camille Cosby and writer Emily Mann. *(Photo by Adger W. Cowans)*

made a fortune on it.' When some of them came to me directly, I said, 'The FCC regulations have to be obeyed.' But what about the *other* people who saw the deal memo? They thought I'd shafted ABC. 'She's the one who gave away the store.' I didn't protect myself at all. That episode left a blot on my reputation for canny dealing. I had this female thing—and it is female, believe me—that it's immodest to talk business in most situations or to boast about how you handled something. I wasn't yelling 'Look at what I'm doing!' You have to do that."[71]

Why Didn't You Say So Before?

Christine Foster was, from 1977 to 1981, VP of movies and miniseries at Columbia Pictures Television; Andrea Baynes was a vice president in charge of television series. It was unusual then to have two women VPs at a studio in these two major areas. Foster had attended Immaculate Heart, had been taught by nuns, and had entered the convent; she'd seen women professors and doctors. "When men worked with nuns, they didn't look at them as sex objects," Foster says. "Nuns were sort of neuter. When I started working in the business, everyone knew I'd been a nun. I went about my work just as I had done when I was a nun."[72]

Before she went to Columbia, Foster had worked at the Wolper Organization as director of development and production. She knew she wasn't really well informed about corporate life, but she'd gotten along fairly well. At Columbia, when the vice president of movies and miniseries quit, Foster went to her boss and asked, "What are my chances of getting that job?"

He said, "Questionable."

Foster called her mother, a canny woman who had worked in a bank. When her husband had come home from the office every night, Foster's mother had questioned him. "You walked into the meeting," she'd said, "and what happened, step by step? Don't leave out the body language." Foster says she listened carefully.

Foster's mother suggested she start making some calls. In about two weeks, Foster had a job offer from none other than Alan Shane at Warner Bros. to come in as director of movies for TV and then in six months, vice president. She went to her boss at Columbia, told him about the offer, and said, taking her mother's advice, "What would you do if you were in my shoes?"

"Christine," he said, "what do you want?"

"I want to be vice president of movies and miniseries."

"Why didn't you say so before!?"

"I didn't say I wanted to do it, I can do it, I know how to do it," Foster says. "I said, 'What are my chances?' Mealymouthed! If you want something, say exactly what you want."[73]

The First Woman President of a Division of Coca-Cola in 100 Years

Barbara Corday had no trouble knowing how to ask for what she wanted. The writer who became cocreator of *Cagney & Lacey* was vice president of comedy at ABC. In 1982, she left to start her own production company, Can't Sing, Can't Dance Productions, with an overall deal at Columbia Pictures Television. Two years later, in 1984, she was asked to take over the entire television division of the studio, which she ran until 1988. She was the first woman president of Columbia Television, or any studio's television division.

At ABC, Corday had worked closely with women, particularly Marcy Carsey, and years before with her writing partner, Barbara Avedon. Slowly, at Columbia, she began to realize that she was the only woman "at this table." It took her a while to focus on it, but "it was a constant and it went on for years."[74]

"Coca-Cola owned Columbia," says Corday, "and although I had a lot of women working under me, there were no women in any positions like mine or over me. Coca-Cola gave me a dinner in Atlanta when I became president of the division. The chairman of Coca-Cola, a dynamic, interesting man, announced how happy he was that I was the first woman president of a division of Coca-Cola in a hundred years. He had no clue that was not a great announcement. Of course, from some points of view it was, but I didn't think it so." In 1984, women were not heading steel, coal, oil, finance, or the auto industry either.

"At financial meetings, planning sessions, and management retreats, it was sixteen men and me—because there were sixteen division heads and me. The first management retreat I went to was at the Woodstock Inn in Vermont. We arrived on Sunday afternoon because Coke always started their meetings on Sunday, which I thought was antifamily. We had to drop whatever we were doing and fly or drive to the retreat by late Sunday afternoon. At this management meeting, we had the little premeeting and our dinner on Sunday night. What did they do after dinner on Monday? They rolled in a big-screen television for the football game. That was the planned entertainment for the executives. Nobody thought there was anything the slightest bit odd about that.

"I debated whether to hang around and be one of the guys or go back to my room and read a book. I knew it would be nothing but drinking and football. I went back to my room. I didn't make a big deal about it, but I had no interest *as an executive* in watching football and drinking." However, "hanging around" watching football is one way to exchange a lot of business information.

Though more women were in meetings, ". . . many, many, many, many, many more men held the highest positions—the CEO and the corporate top spots. Very few women were in those jobs. Still work to be done."[75]

I Dared to Contradict Mumblefuck

Mary Ledding, last seen liberating the old MGM gym, was a senior vice president of business affairs in 1980.

David Begelman had been brought in to "save" the MGM studio. One of the best lessons Begelman taught Ledding was you cannot ever use the word *fair*. "Life is not fair, so you can't use fair. He brought a spirit of cordiality and southern manners to MGM. He never raised his voice. He taught me a great style. When new chiefs start, they make a huge example of a few people. He did that with a VP of creative affairs, grilled her unmercifully in front of everybody. It's a ritual; once they've made an example of someone, then everyone else is in a fear mode. I worked with him fairly often. He ran the studio like an agency, holding Wednesday morning production meetings. At the end of every meeting, he'd ask, 'Anybody have any good gossip?' This town runs on gossip. It's an agenda item. Gossip is a business asset."[76]

In 1989, Ledding, mother of two, beginning protracted divorce proceedings, left MGM and moved to Warner Bros. as deputy general counsel. "Some of the business affairs guys were from New York, and talked real fast. One of them dubbed this lingo 'mumblefuck.' Talking mumblefuck is a style of dealing. You talk so fast, you don't give whoever's on the other side a chance to contradict, and it's all said in a knowing tone so that the opponent can't say, 'Wait a minute.'

"I lost my job at Warner Bros.," Ledding recalls, "because I dared to contradict mumblefuck. An exec was talking about the pricing of a half-hour videocassette deal. I said, 'Wait a minute, that doesn't make sense. Your numbers are wrong because a half-hour videocassette costs less than a two-hour cassette.' There was like this big silence. As soon as this exec was promoted, I was fired. I was right, though, and he knew I was right. But I *contradicted* mumblefuck.

"Now, translate that to another situation. When I was a young lawyer I was negotiating against a senior lawyer who was representing a producer on a deal. We came to a point that we—the studio—didn't want to give. I started to talk without pause. It was like my mouth was talking but not my brain, and I just kept talking. When I stopped, I thought, 'Now he's going to give it to me and say that is the biggest crock of shit I've ever heard.' The man didn't say a word.

"Some guys, generally lawyers or business types, use mumblefuck. If you dare ask a question or interrupt, it means you are calling them on it, challenging their knowledge—and yours—because the effect on the listener is 'Hey, if I question him, I'm going to look stupid.' So you let it slide. Everyone wants to save face. It's a new version of a gentleman's agreement: I won't call you on it if you don't call me on it even if I don't know what I'm talking about. That's the essence of mumblefuck.

"Women want to be sure of their ground before they state their position. That's why women do more homework. Guys don't have to. They use mumblefuck instead. You don't have to prep for mumblefuck." In Ledding's experience no man has contradicted a mumblefuck presentation.

"In the 1980s we were striving to be treated equally," Ledding says. "Marcia Nasatir once said, 'I like to think that women do it better than men.' You have to take this in context," Ledding goes on. "At that time, it was a revolutionary thought. We were struggling just to be treated equally, but Marcia had a clearer view. Women work harder, do the homework more efficiently, strive for consensus and harmony. For all those reasons, women do it better than men.

"Women *do* work differently than men."

Ledding is currently senior VP legal affairs at Universal. "Have women gotten ahead by adapting to men's work styles?" she asks. "Yes and no. Working in the world of men, you have to adapt to their styles; you can't work like women. But Universal has a huge day care center, is one of the best places for working women, and Stacey Snider is the chair of Universal Pictures. In production meetings, she talks about her daughters. I never heard David Begelman say that."[77]

I Was Reading the Files and Learning All About How to Sell Film

In motion picture studios, distribution takes the movie and sells it to theaters, the exhibitors. The Paramount Decree, a federal antitrust move in 1947, split off the studio-owned theaters from studio production. In any studio, the men who run distribution know the theater owners and the film buyers; it's a closely knit business group to which women had zero access—except as office managers or secretaries, sometimes administrative assistants. Nikki Rocco arrived in Hollywood in 1981 when the New York sales department of Universal Pictures relocated. She had worked at Universal for fourteen years, starting as a part-time statistical analyst.

"I was one of the clerks who counted box office receipts, not in cash, in reported dollars," says Rocco. "No computers. I calculated what each theater owed Universal. I was seventeen years old." Rocco had a way with numbers, she was a people-person, and her mother had taught her to be self-sufficient. "I was the little girl who knew box office from the night before. Lew Wasserman [who headed the studio] would call me into his office and I'd shake because I was so nervous. 'How did we do at such and such a theater last night, Nikki?' he'd say. I'd give him the numbers."[78]

Rocco was to have a steep climb over rough terrain to gain her complete success. She knew the language, she knew the corporate business, she was savvy and smart, but she hit the wall most women meet in one way or another. It defeats many, but Rocco bested it and outlasted it.

In distribution, she had no mentors, so she decided to learn the business on her own. "When I worked in New York, I volunteered to stay late and do the filing for the executive offices. The other women there loved the idea. I was reading the files and learning all about how to sell film. I paid attention to every aspect of the business. I was self-taught."

By the 1980s, Rocco knew she would have a career. She wanted to be the first woman to control distribution. In 1984, Frank Price was chairman of the motion picture group and Marvin Antonowsky was head of marketing. "Marvin tapped me for information about film performance and patterns of release," says Rocco. "I was thirty-one and I had put in a lot of years doing menial tasks, but Marvin recognized I had ability and he became my mentor." She got her VP stripes in distribution during the Price regime.

Unlike women who started later, Rocco saw no women vice presidents. "In the 1980s? Forget it. Maybe head of publicity or casting, but not in the motion picture group. Now we have many, but in the 1980s everything was run by men."

Before Antonowsky's encouragement, it was hard to move up in the ranks in distribution. The "old-timers" were still running the business and they had "little use for females," says Rocco. "They couldn't conduct themselves on a day-to-day basis with a woman in the room. I handled it by shutting out a lot. Their foul language didn't bother me—I came from New York City. Most people at this company treated me with great respect."

One did not. He was "a true chauvinist, in my opinion," she says. "One day in the late 1980s, I heard him on the phone joking about offering my services as sexual favors to an exhibitor. He didn't realize how loud he was speaking. It's not fair for anybody to joke about something like that. I married at twenty-one and I'm still married to the same man, a very solid marriage.

"Later, comments were made by others when I relocated to Hollywood like, 'Who's she sleeping with to get the job?' I ignored it. I didn't let it interfere with my work. I tried not to bring those comments home. I didn't talk about it. But when I heard what was said to an exhibitor, I was looking at a situation like harassment. I needed advice. The counsel I got was that it was a lose-lose situation for me. I loved my work, my career was on the upswing, but if I started a lawsuit, I'd lose.

"I let it go. I developed bleeding ulcers. I could not discuss this problem with my husband for fear he'd go ballistic. I didn't tell my mother because she would have said, 'How do you stand that? Quit!' I didn't want to quit. I had friends at work and one colleague was very supportive, a good listener. I confided in him. He tried to coach me. He and his wife are still our best friends. He said, 'Just come to my office and blow off steam.' "

It got worse because the exhibitor [the chauvinist] had been speaking with on the phone repeated what he'd heard to others. Then she joined an old friend from Universal in New York for dinner and she told him what the man had been saying about her. "I no longer kept it a secret," says Rocco. "I didn't feel I needed to. When I got back from New York, I heard this bad guy had been saying I was sleeping with the man I'd just had dinner with. I went into his office, shut the door, and said, 'How dare you make these comments about me? Have you no respect for me or my marriage?'

"He didn't say anything. He turned red in the face. He must have heard that I was very angry about what he'd been saying about me and that I had told people about it. His harassment sort of stopped. But I worked for about eight years despising this guy.

"Every woman has had some of that on the job. This man was so different from all the other guys. He was the one bad apple. Those are good odds. I focused on what was important in my life. That's how I dealt with it."[79]

By 1990, she was named senior vice president of distribution and marketing. The experiences waiting for her were typical of those of some women executives in the business who, having survived the 1980s, reaped rewards in the 1990s.

■   ■   ■

The decade of the 1980s was not a walk in the park. Some women lost their way in the corporate forest, not having been prepared for the jobs with even minimal experience. Others threatened to sue, and some did.

I Almost Fainted When I Saw I Was Listed as His Secretary

"We thought it would be okay to go for the work we wanted to do," says Billie Jenkins, "but the guys didn't see it that way."

Starting as a secretary, Jenkins had worked for the hugely successful Leonard Goldberg Company and the Spelling-Goldberg Company for many years. By 1986, she was a vice president when Leonard Goldberg became president and chief operating officer of 20th Century Fox.

"Leonard Goldberg was interested in social issues," says Jenkins. "He did *WarGames*, *Something About Amelia*, and he made *SpaceCamp* to show kids that they could be astronauts. That's where he and Aaron Spelling differed. Aaron was a happy guy who tended to make the same TV shows over and over, just changing the people."[80] The Spelling-Goldberg company was immensely profitable—it created *Hart to Hart*, *Fantasy Island*, *Starsky & Hutch*, *Charlie's Angels*.

Leonard Goldberg took Jenkins with him to Fox. Even though she attended his meetings there, she still ran his production company based at Paramount, where it had a television series on the air, *The Cavanaughs*. Usually, when people move to a studio, they go in with the same or higher position. "I wanted to keep my vice presidency," Jenkins says. "I'd had it for over a year." Jenkins says she asked Goldberg and he said, "Yes, I'll take care of it. Give me six months."

" 'Why does it take six months?' I asked. 'Most of the people who know me assume I'll be there as a VP.' He didn't really answer me.

"A few months go by, I'm going to the meetings at Fox, I'm handling administration and other affairs for his company as well. A copy of Leonard's contract comes into the office and I almost fainted when I saw that I was listed as his secretary. 'What does *this* mean?' I asked him. He said it was a mistake. I was flabbergasted. He's the president and COO of Fox. Why would there be any question about who he made a vice president? And Barry Diller [who had become chief at Fox] knew me. I had a good reputation. I was devastated because both Leonard and I knew he could make me a vice president. My husband said, 'Are you sure this isn't going on because you're black?' I refused to believe it. 'No, it just can't be.' "[81]

Jenkins's family moved to Los Angeles in 1948. "There was no real housing for black people, so we stayed in one room of a big mansion on Sugar Hill, an area where prominent black entertainers lived. A few months later, we moved to a housing project in Watts." In 1955, her family moved to the west side, the white part of Los Angeles. Her father was an engineer working with the first space program; her mother worked for the post office. Jenkins went to the highly rated Louis Pasteur Junior High School. "Twenty-six hundred white kids and twenty-five black kids," she says.

Once, she recalls, a teacher held his whole class after school, waiting for Billie to appear to walk home with a friend. When she did, he insisted she say, "Hey, Beulah!" because he thought she sounded just like Butterfly McQueen. "Your class," she replied, "is going to stay here a long time because I won't say it."[82] After graduating and attending Santa Monica College, Jenkins began working in the entertainment industry as a secretary.

"My husband was right, I guess," says Jenkins. "When Leonard said six months, I contacted an attorney who suggested I keep a journal. Finally I had to admit they wouldn't promote me. There'd never been a black female vice president at Fox. There had been a few black men, one being Ashley Boone, a president in marketing. An executive told me I should be proud to be administrative assistant to the president of a major company. I told him I'd worked eighteen years with Leonard, I'd been a vice president, and why didn't I qualify now?

"There was never an answer. I quit both jobs I had with Leonard in late 1987. Fox made me director of administration in studio operations, overseeing seven departments. The senior vice president of studio operations came from a merchandising background, knew nothing, really, about movies, and had never worked on a studio lot. Joel Silver, the producer, talked the senior vice president of studio operations, my boss, into letting him shoot *Die Hard* at the Fox Plaza when that building was eighty-five percent occupied. He could have had out-of-state buildings that were empty, but Joel didn't want to leave town. He told my boss that he'd save seven hundred fifty thousand dollars in the budget if he could shoot in the Fox Plaza. The guy fell for it. Joel moves in with the crew and commences to trash the building. My first responsibility was to get over there and get it under control.

"I knew Joel, and he was a pistol. On this day, everyone was on the thirty-third floor setting off all kinds of explosives. When I show up, he says, 'Oh, Billie, I'm glad to see you. These son of a bitches are telling me they don't want me to shoot film now.'

"I said, 'Joel, I'm here to tell you that you can't do it.'

"He excuses himself, goes over to the director, John McTierman, and suddenly all hell breaks loose. Boom! Silver comes back to me. 'Billie, I had to get the shot.' I wondered what I'd gotten myself into," Jenkins says, "but I managed to calm some of it down."

In 1990, the motion picture division at Fox recruited Jenkins to develop a new department. She was made director of production services and resources. "They told me that I hadn't been put on track to be a VP. At that time, I was seeing career counselors who suggested that to be promoted it might help if I had a higher visibility in the film community. I became active in Women in Film [elected President in 1991] I also created programs at the American Film Institute. Fox kept saying fine, do the job on the director level for another year and we'll make you vice president."

But they didn't. As she was moved around, her offices got smaller, she felt marginalized and isolated, and no one replied to her memos about the department's work. After two years of no feedback from anyone about the new department she was developing, she wrote a report to a senior vice president. Her office was now in what had once been the stables at Fox. "I knew they wanted me to just go away," she says, "but I was determined to stay and I needed the job." During this period, she never spoke about her difficulties at Fox. "I was so shocked and hurt by it all," she says. "It was my problem, no one could do anything about it, so why burden them? I did confide in an executive I knew, Steve Mills,[83] and he suggested I talk to Barry Diller, who always supported people he'd worked with in the early days. Barry Diller helped me. When no one would answer my memos, he got them answered."

Diller left Fox in February 1992. That day, Jenkins's attorney called her: "You'll be next." On April 1, she was given three months to depart.

"A long time ago, a friend of my family told me that I would be fine as long as I didn't stop doing windows," says Jenkins. "I was terribly upset by his remark, and it took me a long time to understand what he meant. As long as I was quietly doing my servitude, I'd be fine. I started being visible and continued to want my VP stripes, and showed that I could really do all the work they threw at me, then they really got upset—because I had stopped doing windows."[84]

Jenkins finally brought suit for racial discrimination. It was resolved, the terms confidential.

Who Will Hire You? You'll Be Older, You'll Skew Their Pension Fund

Judith Merians, thirty-four, the mother of two small children, lived in the Valley and cooked gourmet meals. When she told her husband she was thinking about law school, he said it would ruin their marriage. He didn't want her to do it. "The words hit me like bullets," she says with characteristic drama. "He was saying, 'I don't want you to do what you need to do, I want you to do what I need.' I was devastated."[85]

She told a friend, an attorney, about her desire. " 'Who will hire you?' he said to me. 'Nobody. You'll be older, you'll skew their pension fund, you're never going to be hired.' " She went to law school anyway, in the San Fernando Valley near Los Angeles where she could attend part-time. She felt overwhelmed by the task. A friend who was a medical resident said, "When I started medical school, all I could think of was how to do Monday. When I finished Monday I thought, how do I do Tuesday? And then four years were up. Just do Monday."

Good advice. Very disciplined, she went to school in the morning and spent the afternoons in the law library. She was home by 4:30, made and served dinner, and helped the kids. "I had a housekeeper. I never in four years opened a schoolbook in my home because I had to prove to my husband that my home came first."

The first year, she made the dean's list and Law Review and got the American Jurisprudence Award. She graduated cum laude, passed the bar the first time, and got a job as a program attorney for ABC.

Merians loved the work, even though other women warned her one executive often hired women he wanted to sleep with. "He came on to me after I was hired. It was easy to say I'm married and have kids except *he* was married and *he* had kids." When a new executive arrived, she went into his office to introduce herself. She recalls, "He said, 'Sit down, tell me something about yourself. Are you married?'

" 'Yes, I have two children.'

" 'Do you fool around?'

"He'd just walked into the building that week! What's going on here?" She told the exec that she hoped they could be friends and have a good working relationship.

"They had a sense of entitlement," she says, "I'm entitled to sexually approach this person and even humiliate her. One of the first deals I made, the agent suggested we meet for lunch, and then he hit on me. I was astounded. I wasn't uninformed, but I didn't want to lift my skirt on the job. I know women who did it and got ahead. It was definitely one way to get a mentor. But it's a minefield out there; one reason I love being older is that I can run the minefield now. Older is better. I feel sorry for women who don't come in armor. In a way, they've been disarmored because they've been led to believe it's going to be equal. *We* were never led to believe that, so we got armor.

"Anyway, I got the message that I wasn't meaningful in the company; I was just a toy. I bought three books, *Games Mother Never Taught You*; *On Women and Power* by Jane Trahey, one of the best books of its kind; and *The Corporate Personality*. I realized I was in the Army and I didn't know how it operated."

Merians moved to Paramount Pictures as a director of business affairs, in the merchandising division. Richard Weston, vice president of merchandising, hired her. "He wanted to make deals and he needed someone to handle everything else as a merchandising attorney. My marriage was ending and I wanted a career. I staffed, fired, put systems in place, organized, did international business—became, in short, an executive."[86]

In 1978, Dawn Steel arrived at Paramount. "My job," Steel wrote, "was to help market movies and television series by developing products and promoting them."[87] Frank Mancuso was head of marketing and distribution. In six months, Steel was promoted to vice president of merchandising and licensing for Paramount's television and feature properties.

"I admired Dawn," says Merians. "She was smart, took on a whole new career, and succeeded. She was admirable in so many ways. Dawn was very nice to me outside the job. It's only when you worked for her that it was awful. She'd throw your door open and come in shouting orders. She was a take-no-prisoners kind of boss. The men loved her. She was a guy's kind of woman. She could be just as down and dirty as they were, and still sexy, and they were comfortable with her. She once said to me in the ladies' room, 'Women used to sleep their way to the top. Now they give it away. We should go back to the old way and at least get something for it.' "[88]

Dawn Steel had one of the most remarkable careers in the business of entertainment. She was slightly ahead of the wave of entering women, and took a lot of punishment. She also doled out plenty. But she was a mentor to both men and women. Teaching was a reason she said she wrote her book, *They Can Kill You But They Can't Eat You*.

"[I was] demanding and an absolute perfectionist to work for ... But do you think Jeffrey [Katzenberg, now one of the founders of DreamWorks] is any different ...?"[89] In 1987, when she became the first woman to be president of a studio, Columbia Pictures, she said, "A woman in that job is a lightning rod for criticism and judgment and I got my share."[90] On another occasion, when asked about getting along with female employees, Steel said, "I think that women will take abuse from men bosses and resent the mildest criticism from a woman."[91]

Steel liked being around the guys, wanted to be one of them, then got sick of it when she realized she'd never be one.[92] But that was later.

At Paramount, Steel was in charge of merchandising the first *Star Trek* movie. Already in production, it looked like an unmitigated disaster, wildly overbudget, thanks to special effects—"the black hole of film-making," as Steel called it.[93] Steel's challenge was to merchandise the movie, to convince manufacturers to "feature the *Star Trek* logos, themes, and characters on their products. But there was no film to show them . . . [The production] was a runaway freight train."[94]

Many people at Paramount were engrossed in *Star Trek*, the movie and the hassles. Copyright problems stemming from the television series were Merians's part of the runaway train.

"Some of the original episodes had gone out without copyright notice," Merians recalls, "and we're mounting this big campaign but very much afraid the Trekkies and the pirates were going to interfere with it, sleazy merchandise, all that. We're having heavyweight brainstorming meetings about how to protect the trademarks—Jeffrey Katzenberg, Dick Zimbert, who headed up the feature division, people from Gulf and Western—and I'm sitting there thinking, 'Hummm.' I researched who the pirates were, what all the lawsuits were, where we prevailed, where we didn't, and put it all together for the next big meeting."

At that meeting, the consensus was to give the program for protection of trademark and copyright over to the patent and trademark counsel of Gulf & Western, Paramount's parent company.

"I, being exactly a year and a half in the business, the least important person in the room," says Merians, "stood up and said that I didn't agree with any of them and started giving out my folders. I was too green to know this was inappropriate. Dick Zimbert, who liked me, said, 'Judith, wait a minute, just give me one and I'll read it tonight.' He called me the next day. 'I think you're right. I'm putting you in charge. Report to me every single week.' Out of ignorance came opportunity. I had the only standing appointment on the lot with the head of this film division. That's when I began to learn how to work with high-powered people. I learned he had three minutes for me, I went in with a list of questions that needed direction or blessing, I'd go down the list, he'd answer questions, and I was out of there. But I had those minutes with him every week." At one point, she said she wasn't getting paid enough ($30,000). The next week, her salary was $40,000. "I was a complete novice," says Merians, "but I learned at Paramount.

"I also learned to take the credit. I found some lost money and I was in some other lawyer's office telling him about it. He got on the phone, called New York accounting, says we've uncovered some lost money, and he proceeds to take credit for it right in front of me. The call was on speaker phone so I said, 'Jim, I researched this and found the money.' That's the corporate setting."[95]

Star Trek dealt Dawn Steel higher cards when she masterminded a *Star Trek* stage show for an audience of toy and merchandising tie-in manufacturers. She had no movie but she had the stars. And she had herself. She was "beamed" onto the stage with lasers, ". . . snapped into a running dialogue with a Hal-like computer . . . and zap, there was Leonard Nimoy, zap, William Shatner . . ."[96] Quite a show. Studio president Michael Eisner suggested she finish up *Star Trek* and then he'd make her vice president of production of features. Don Simpson, head of production, told her it was his idea. By 1980, as a production vice president, her startling climb began.

Merians had run into roadblocks in her department. She moved from Paramount to business and legal affairs at ABC Motion Pictures as a director, then vice president. Chris Warshaw, head of business affairs, had hired her into the company that would make, among other films, *Silkwood* (1983) and *Prizzi's Honor* (1985). In 1986, about three years before Mary Ledding arrived, Merians was at Warner Bros.

A few months after she'd started, one of the execs asked her into a screening room to see a film for legal reasons. "We're alone, it's dark, and I had my little pad and I'm taking notes at a table. He starts rubbing my back. Not mildly. I thought, I am here three months and this is happening. In his office, I'd sit at the table and he'd be in an easy chair and he'd want me to stand in front of him. I guess he wanted my crotch at his nose level? 'No, I'm perfectly comfortable where I am,' I said. I let it go. When he asked about my surgery, I told him I had limited movement in my knee, couldn't kneel. He said, 'We know what you can't do now.' When I came back from an exhausting business trip to Europe, he said, 'I know what you did to make you so tired.'

"That was it. 'Listen, I understand what you're saying, don't go on with it,' I said. He kept on. I said, 'I told you to stop.' He didn't talk to me for six months."[97]

When Merians left a few months later, she thought she'd never work again. She had a job offer the next day.

11

MORE LADDERS THAN CHUTES—THE NEWCOMERS

Younger women were starting careers in many areas of the business, but cable was the new, lower-case alternative route into television. Predictions, guesses, hunches declared it would proliferate program choices, create a new age for viewers, producers, directors, writers. In some ways, it was all true—cable broadened the production and distribution of fiction and particularly nonfiction programs. Few realized how rapidly the new arenas would grow.

Kay Koplovitz is called, accurately, a cable industry pioneer. She was the CEO of the USA Networks, the cable channel she built from 1977 into the nation's highest rated and first advertiser-supported basic cable channel. She was the first woman to negotiate the national cable rights to major league sports. In 1980, she transformed the sports-based network into a general entertainment network with series and high-profile theatrical movie packages. By 1989, USA became the first basic cable network, as compared to a pay-cable channel, to feature original movies.

A premed student in the 1960s, Koplovitz heard about new developments in satellite transmission in communications. She was so intrigued she switched her major, and after college (Phi Beta Kappa, University of Wisconsin, master's from Michigan State University), she joined Comsat, the first international satellite communications company, and then, in 1977, launched USA Networks. Koplovitz is one of the very few women ever to break the glass ceiling in the cable TV industry.[98] She was the first female network president in television history. She is hardy, tough, and utterly determined. "I'm an entrepreneur," she said, "and have built this company through a thousand different regimes."[99]

New industries often welcome women. The silent-movie era certainly did, and in the early 1980s, cable television, an industry searching for form and future, opened up, too. It was a frenzied period of start-ups and mergers, of wins and losses that resembled a land grab or a gold rush.

I Didn't Know Why Anyone Would Want to Work in Cable

"There's a big difference between the 1970s and now," says Sheila Nevins. "The same problems but a big difference. Because we have women who have made the past, who can protect you if they choose to."[100]

Sheila Nevins, whose documentary and family productions with Home Box Office have won numerous Oscars and Emmys, was born on the Lower East Side of New York City. "My father worked in the post office," she says, "and my mother was a college graduate, a communist, a liberal who did anything she could to make money for us—research, lab assistant, running a laundromat, furnishing rooming houses. I really didn't want to grow up. I spent most of my childhood at the Museum of Natural History because I was obsessed with dinosaurs. I knew the name of every one at that time." A documentary producer in the making. "I tried to see if I could make enough lines to trace back five million years to the time when they lived. I never got there. Today, 'dinosaur' means extinct. But I thought they were the most important things that ever happened because they weren't imaginary creations, they'd been real and then they vanished. That fascinated me."[101]

Documentary filmmakers present stories about real events and try to figure out what the past has to do with the present. The past has many uses—it reveals life's diversity, ephemerality, and continuity, from which we may draw appreciation or contempt or wonder, and thereby learn from them.

Among the first documentaries Nevins saw were Albert and David Maysles' films, *Gimme Shelter* and *Grey Gardens*, and Barbara Kopple's *Harlan County, U.S.A.* "If you listen to real people," Nevins once said, "the resonance and dialogue is way above anything that anyone could recreate . . . They were more gripping to me than any drama I'd ever read. The best stories are the real ones and the best people to tell them are the ones who experienced them."[102]

In the late 1970s, Nevins was working at CBS for Don Hewitt on the news magazine *Who's Who* when a friend called to ask if she knew anyone who would like to work in cable.

"I'd seen a cooking show and a few dirty things on cable," she says, "but I didn't know why anyone would want to work in it. They wanted someone to run documentaries. I didn't know what that meant. I was intrigued because it was new. I went to the library and read about cable and realized it was movies uninterrupted, no advertising, that you had to wire a whole country, and maybe it would grow. So I called back and said I'd be interested in the job but only if it was for thirteen weeks. I didn't want to join a company. I worked for thirteen weeks, and then I worked for thirteen more..." That was in 1979. Today, Nevins is executive vice president of original programming.

"It was like being on the back of Eli Whitney's cotton gin," says Nevins. "It was going to change the nature of *television*, not just technology. I had come from a network where everybody was older than I, and suddenly I was in this place where everybody was younger—I was in my thirties, they were in their twenties. My background had been theater ... so I didn't want anyone to interrupt the storytelling unless you chose it. I also liked the idea that people would pay for it. That was like the theater, buying a ticket to television instead of getting it free.

"When HBO told me that I was a director of documentaries I thought I was going to direct documentaries, which would be good because I could join the Directors Guild and then I'd get benefits. Michael Fuchs [who became president of HBO] was the director of programming, Frank Biondi was director of operations—we all started at the same level, scrambling around, and I figured we'd all do the same thing. I didn't know a corporation had a hierarchical scheme. After I was there a few months, I began to see the structure and discovered this was like the Army. There were five-star generals; you started as a private and worked your way up."

At HBO, Nevins was surrounded by men, just as she had been at the Yale School of Drama. "All these men and I were in this thing called cable," she says. "My ambition wasn't to break into their world. My ambition was to be able to control a film or an idea. I had been a directing major at Yale so I was used to being around a lot of men and doing what they did. I didn't think of it as prejudicial. I accepted it, but I questioned my own aggressiveness because my grandmother told me that if I wanted to be a nurse I'd find a husband. When I got married the first time, and he told me that I had to take his shirts to the laundry and I couldn't work evenings or weekends, I thought that was appropriate."

Unlike theater, television offered regular daytime employment. But her marriage ended about eighteen months later. "I was on a remote, filming a television piece on the Job Corps," she says. "I had been gone for five days and when I came back there were five coffee cups and five shirts waiting for me to clean. As I washed out the cups, I felt there was something wrong, because I'd been working day and night on the shoot. 'Hey, wait a second, this isn't fair, he's earning more than I am.' But none of that felt unjust until I opened my little pay envelope one day and found my check was stuck to someone else's check. 'Holy shit,' I thought, 'he does what I do, he has the same title, and he's earning so much more than I am.' He was earning about three times more."

Of all the programs she has developed for HBO, *The Broadcast Tapes of Dr. Peter* left a lasting impression.

"I never met Dr. Peter, a physician in Vancouver who was dying of AIDS," Nevins says. "He had a radio show over a two-and-a-half-year period during his illness, and the tapes were sent to us. His broadcasts had galvanized a rather homophobic community. I just fell in love with him from those tapes. That show gave me the pure television experience. In other words, I didn't know anything about him except the person I met on the tube. Discovering courage or evil, insanity, sexuality, or whatever through people on television is the most fascinating aspect of it. Meeting these people means that we're not alone in our sadness or our heroism or our misery. You can trade life experiences with others through television."

Needless to say, Nevins loves her work with a passion. She feels in some ways that she gave up her life to her work, or at least gave up living the way "other people" live it. "I have a son and I may not have been a particularly good mother. I was always distracted by my work. You can only love passionately one thing at a time, and the people around me suffered the consequences of my passion. When something I've worked on is on television, you get invited into people's homes and you can still be under the covers. It's even more exciting than theater, and I think that's what hooked me into TV: it allowed me to entertain with ideas, to be social through my work. I can shut my door and still be outside. Fundamentally, reality is always more interesting to me than fiction, because real people are the most courageous, the most devious, the most evil. And I don't know why you have to create these when you can find them ... at the foot of your bed."[103]

HBO Was Like the Wild West

Ilene Kahn Power was an independent producer of nonfiction films made by the company she and her husband owned, but she had no corporate experience. In 1981, she became VP of development for Freyda Rothstein—an independent producer of films including *In Broad*

Daylight, Love and Lies, and *Something in Common*—which led directly to Power's career with HBO.

"I was so isolated," Power says. "I joined Women in Film and met Loreen Arbus—we were both wearing platform shoes, so it was about 1979 or 1980—and Gloria Goldsmith." Power was a young mother with two small children. She and her husband had given up their production company, had mortgaged their home, and her husband had decided to write full-time. One of them had to get a job.

"Women in Film was my artery to what was going on in the town," says Power. When a friend of hers decided to become a single mother, "a really new thing then," Power wrote a story about it, pitched it to Jane Rosenthal, a young executive at CBS, and sold it. "I had a network commitment to a script without an umbrella company. Gloria Goldsmith told me Freyda was looking for a development head, that she wanted a guy, but Gloria told her to hire a woman. I met with Freyda. I had no idea what salary to ask for. I said thirty-five thousand, thinking I'd price myself out of the ballpark as a reader. 'I'll pay you forty thousand,' Freyda said. I realized I had undervalued myself (she had sixty thousand in her budget). She became, among others, my mentor."[104]

In the early 1980s, Home Box Office created a made-for-television movie division.[105] Through another Women in Film connection, Barbara Boyle at Orion made a persuasive call for Power, who got an interview with Michael Fuchs. Power had never worked for a big corporation. Her only credentials were her corporate films and her service on the board of Women in Film. She made the most of both.

"No one knew what a cable movie was," says Power. "It was somewhere between a feature film and a television movie. Michael Fuchs had just hired Jane Deknatel from NBC; he wanted a second in command of the new movie division. He hired me on the spot. Michael wanted fresh programmers who 'didn't come from the cookie cutter,' as he said, 'who were not afraid to do things.' He set no limits.

"What an odyssey! I was there for ten incredible years. We had to build a story department from the ground up, which was dumped in my lap while Jane got the division launched. Jane was a tall woman, tall enough to look directly into the eyes of the guys. There are certain unspoken things that can be communicated when you're as tall as most of the guys . . . otherwise you're a terrier." Power is short, but her height is the only short thing about her.

"Cable films were sort of a joke then," she says, "and we got warmed-over scripts. Michael told us, 'Don't be afraid to fail. Take the high road.

Don't think because you're cable that you can take the low road. Stretch yourself.' "

Power was among the very few at HBO who had children. "Almost everyone there was a man, and in the movie division, it was just Jane and me. After Jane hired Barbara Title, we agreed the next hire would be a man." Surprisingly, the man hired was offered more money and a title. Power was shocked. "We were all going to do the same work! It was the first sense I had of a betrayal. I'd heard about it but had never experienced it—women aligning with men, saying in effect, 'I don't want to be a member of a club that would have *me* as a member.'

"I also realized that I'd believed I'd get rewarded because I did the work well. That was not going to happen. There were other agendas here. I had to be smarter and stand up for myself. It was an epiphany, a real turning point. Barbara and I spoke up, told them what the new guy was making, and pressed them to give us the same title, vice president. We got it."

At HBO they made it up as they went along, refined, failed, and took on political subjects unheard-of for television. "We never worried about watering things down," says Power. "It was very competitive, amazingly exciting, and there were no elders around. I made sixty films over the ten years I was there through four administrations."

The casualty was her marriage. She was trying to divide her time between her family, her painting (she had an MFA in art and had been a painter), and her work. The work took over, and she allowed it.

"The children turned out great but I missed things about their growing up that I'll never get back," she says. "I was running the house with two children. My husband was a writer; he'd always pushed me to direct and produce, he'd allowed me to empower myself, and then, lucky me, suddenly I'm flying all over the world, making movies. He was proud of me on one level but he didn't want to be Mr. Ilene on another. We unraveled like a piece of fabric."

In the early 1980s, being a mom was still something you didn't talk about a lot, but that was changing, too, because these were the 1980s, "when women could have it all." The price was punishment.

"People still remember my kids in soccer gear coming up to the forty-first floor of the building in Century City," says Power. "I'd have to cajole friends to drop off my kids after school because my husband was in the middle of his writing day and didn't pick them up. I'd hide Adam in one of the empty offices, or I'd bribe them both to go to the mall—so few people at HBO had children! I was trying to do everything. I felt torn apart, inadequate as a mother and inadequate as an executive. I know women feel this all the time; they don't have enough time to be a mother but if they are a full-time mother they wonder, 'What have I done to myself?' We made it through somehow."

About a year into her work at HBO, Power met producer Hannah Weinstein at the Women in Film Crystal Awards. Weinstein was getting a Crystal Award. Power approached her. "God, Hannah," she said, "I'm so pleased to meet you. You have three incredible daughters, how did you work and be a parent?"

"I only have one piece of advice for you," Weinstein said. "Listen to your children and they'll tell you what they need. But listen, listen right."

Sherry Lansing was another woman Power looked to as a role model. Lansing was producing in partnership with Stanley Jaffe. "A couple of Sherry's movies hadn't done well," says Power. "This was just before *Fatal Attraction*. She had an unmitigated belief in her product. I was a buyer and I could smell it when people didn't have conviction or a dedication to what they were pitching. She had real belief in it. I loved her positivism. It was infectious. You felt she'd push it through the goal posts, and that's what it's all about."[106]

In 1989, the Berlin Wall crumbled. By 1991, the old Soviet empire was collapsing. Power was in Russia on her first independent production, *Stalin*, starring Robert Duvall. She would return with an award-winning film.

■ ■ ■

Here's the difference between the 1970s and the 1980s: After a year of being a "good scout secretary" at William Morris, Joan Hyler saw that they were not going to promote her. "In the 1970s, they had no women in their training department. A lot of men started as secretaries—they were called assistants—and I watched them zoom right past me. I was aghast. They were very patriarchal, very male, the Harvard of agencies. Why change? Women, homosexuals, African-Americans had slipped under the radar at William Morris, which at the time was being poached by the just-formed Creative Artists Agency."[107]

"I was never held back because I was a woman," says Iris Grossman. "One, when I started in the 1980s at ICM, everything was turning around for women. The training program opened up [to us]. More important, I wouldn't have been able to do what I do today if it hadn't been for all the women who came before me and struggled to open those doors. I never had to push hard. By the time I came along, women were part of the business. Second, agenting is all about your client list. ICM was women-friendly. They didn't care if you were a man or a woman. The question was—who are you representing?"[108]

Why Don't You Get a Secretarial Job?

"The first week I was working at ICM as a secretary in 1981," Iris Grossman says, "I get on the elevator with a little old man wearing a golf jacket and this little hat. I pressed the button for my floor and I say, 'Sir, what floor would you like?'

" 'Oh, darling, we're going to the same floor.'

"I hear the voice, I recognize it, I turn around.

" 'Hi,' he says. 'I'm Larry Olivier.'

"Who wouldn't like to work in a place like that? I was young and I couldn't wait to get to the office to see who I was going to meet."[109]

Grossman came from New York, where, at age twenty-three, she started her own theater company, The Public Players. In two years, she produced twelve off-off-Broadway showcases, but she really wanted to be a playwright. She arrived in Hollywood with a friend, knowing no one else. Someone suggested she get a secretarial job at the ICM agency. Personnel there sent her to a young agent, Dan Petrie Jr.[110]

"Dan's office was a mess," Grossman recalls. "When I told him I'd get his coffee and straighten up his office, he hired me. I didn't know it then but Dan didn't want to be an agent. When he closed his office door, he was writing *Beverly Hills Cop*, which he sold to Paramount, and the next thing you know he's a big writing star."

The talent agent in the office next door, Michael Black, represented Fred Astaire, Tommy Lee Jones, and Paul Schrader. When his secretary left, he asked Grossman to work for him.

"He trained me to be an agent in a generous, entertaining, intelligent way. To this day, because of him, I know how to negotiate deals and how to keep track of the changes—in different color pens. He'd start a deal off in black. Then the deal would change and he'd go to red or green or orange."

Sue Mengers worked down the hall. "I used to hear Sue calling a studio executive," Grossman says, "and putting together a picture on the phone. 'So Gene Hackman,' Mengers would be shouting, 'and Sidney Lumet are going to do this piece by blah, I'll have my business affairs call you.' Click. She was funny, eccentric, brassy, she had great style, and she was tough. Some people were terrified of her, but I liked her."

At the time, Grossman was stuck as a secretary; ICM had no formal training program. "The boys were in quasi-training," she says. "They'd work on a secretarial desk that was designated 'preagent training.' The reason women weren't allowed to be in the mail room, a great training ground, was that 'the film cans were too heavy for us to carry.' That's what they said." Barry Diller, Michael Eisner, and David Geffen all worked in the William Morris mailroom, and probably did carry a few film cans, but mailroom workers usually rolled carts loaded with mail.

"Then I met Sylvia Gold," Grossman says. Everything changed. On a day in 1983, Sylvia stopped at Grossman's secretarial desk and looked at her. 'You're an agent, kid,' she said. 'Better be good.' She took Grossman into the television department and for the next ten years guided Grossman's career.

Grossman was good at getting people jobs ("I could get the dead a job"), but she was not good at signing actors. "I was frightened, and fear holds you back." She began to feel burnt out as an agent. "When a friend told me he was going to Turner Network Television, TNT, 'Would you like to be head of casting?' he asked me. I took it."

Turner Broadcasting System is a subsidiary of Time Warner, a major producer of news and entertainment around the world and leading procurer of programming for the basic cable industry.

"Now I was convincing them this actor is right for that role with that director," says Grossman. "The transition was easy, but the job was bigger. I was uneasy in another way, because all of a sudden all the information I got as an agent, which bombards you—what every studio is doing and what everybody else is doing all over town—I didn't hear." But she was talking to agents all over the town and began to realize she'd been a really good agent.

"I was blessed I had a woman and a man who were real mentors," says Grossman. "They weren't doing it consciously, like, 'Oh, now I'm mentoring Iris.' They did see that I was thirsty for knowledge, that I enjoyed what they did and what I was doing.

"I don't know why women still don't help other women enough," Grossman says. "Maybe they think that by helping others they are somehow diminishing their own power. That's not how it works." At Turner, Grossman worked for a woman, Julie Weitz, the executive vice president of programming. "She has children and she encouraged me to adopt."[111]

A single mother with a son whose boss encourages her to take him to Friday morning classes? It's a preview of the 1990s.

Ohhhh, Who Are All These Women?

The first job Cheryl Boone Isaacs got in the industry was as a staff publicist on *Close Encounters of the Third Kind*. Her older brother, Ashley Boone, was head of marketing at 20th Century Fox, then embroiled in *Star Wars*.

"When I was little, I wanted to be a musical comedy star," Isaacs says. "But my relatives said, 'Oh yeah, what part are you going to play? You're not as pretty as Lena Horne, and you can't sing as good as Ella [Fitzgerald].' The standards of those who did achieve were so high. Our family was from Massachusetts, very middle class. The goal was to get the kids in *college*, to achieve academically, not be a performer. So I put it in the back of my head because Ashley, my brother, was doing so well, and there aren't many doors open for more of us. Two from one family? Forget it. What's sad about this was that I wasn't depressed; it was just the way it was. You accepted it and moved on.

"When I told my brother I wanted to get a job in the film industry, he said, 'It's not going to be easy at all.' I came down to Los Angeles, met people, but there were no jobs. Ashley made no calls for me. We had a pact—I could pick his brain about different positions or directions, but I didn't want him to get me a job. I'm thankful to this day that I did it that way—for me and for him. Then someone suggested Columbia because they were gearing up for this humungous movie!" So began Isaacs's career in publicity and marketing.

"There were always women around, especially later at Paramount. Suzanne De Passe was president of Motown. Claire Townsend, Lucy Fisher, Sherry Lansing were at Fox," says Isaacs. "Margaret Loesch was a senior vice president at Columbia Pictures and later at Fox, a high-ranking woman in distribution, which was an old-guy world. Paula Weinstein was at Warner Bros. (Later, I worked on *Ghost*, which Lisa Weinstein produced.) I was just starting out, but I knew who they were and what they did and I watched them."[112]

Isaacs rarely met other minorities, men or women. She says it was "slightly lonely but that was the way it was."

In the early '80s, Isaacs joined Melvin Simon Productions, a big independent production company. In five years she became vice president of worldwide advertising and publicity, working on pictures like *The Stuntman*, *Love at First Sight*, and *My Bodyguard*. Her boss, Jonas Rosenfield, had headed marketing at Columbia and 20th Century Fox. "I was fortunate. I had a one-on-one with a real leader in the field, like a crash course for a Ph.D.," she says. In the mid-1980s, she got a call from Bob Dingilian, head of marketing under her brother, Ashley Boone, at the Ladd Company.

"How would you like to come over and work with me at Ladd?"

"Does Ashley know?" she asked. Ashley was head of Ladd's marketing and distribution.

"Of course he does. You know I have to ask him first."

"I talked to Ashley later that night," Isaacs says. " 'Oh yeah, Bob and

Laddie [Alan Ladd Jr.] came in and asked me, "Are you an equal opportunity employer?"

" 'Of course I am. What are you talking about?'

" 'Good,' Laddie said, 'Bob wants to hire Cheryl.' "

Isaacs went to the Ladd Company as director of advertising and publicity for *The Right Stuff, Police Academy,* and *Once Upon a Time in
America.*

When she joined Paramount in 1986 as senior VP of publicity (then
executive VP of worldwide publicity, orchestrating campaigns like *Forrest Gump*), Isaacs began working with some of the most powerful women
in the industry.

"Dawn Steel was president of production," says Isaacs, "Lucie Salhany
headed television, Deborah Rosen was doing corporate publicity, Buffy
Shutt was president of marketing—all these women! I was lucky. If I'd
started just a little earlier, I wouldn't have had that experience. I really
liked and had great respect for Dawn. She wasn't difficult. She was decisive. You asked a question, you got an answer."

To Isaacs, Steel's position said that the industry was "all about the
product, what you do with it. It wasn't about gender." In 1992, Sherry
Lansing became chair of Paramount's Motion Picture Group.

Isaacs had worked with women since she started. In 1997, she moved
to New Line Cinema as president of theatrical marketing.

"I knew that women had to work harder," says Isaacs. "That was
instilled in me growing up. But to make it anywhere, I had to be twice
as good. Being an African-American woman didn't hold me back exactly.
I can't really put my finger on it. I've done well. I guess if I'd been a
white female I would have moved faster, and if I'd been a white male I
would have moved twice as fast." At Paramount for thirteen years, Isaacs
felt it took her an unusually long time just to be made head of the
department. "People were brought in who had the same experience I did
and I wondered why that was happening. Also, women did not help
women as much as they do now. I think we're more confident since
we've been allowed access to bigger and better jobs.

"Women have a tendency to give everybody else the power. I did that,
but you know what? When I stopped handing off my power, when I
kept it, my work was easier and communication was much better."

Being a vice president or a senior vice president *and* an African-
American woman was part of the built-in challenge. "Quite often," says
Isaacs, "I felt when I walked into a meeting, that unless people there
knew me, the initial reaction was going to be, 'Oh, my goodness.' I would
feel it and I could see it in their faces, a kind of astonishment . . . What
does this mean? I was starting from less than zero. It was like a mini-

thought in my head. I knew I wasn't less than zero. I knew what I could do. But when I saw their faces for those few seconds, the thought would come into my head . . . it wasn't even like a thought . . . sort of a little blip that I was aware of, and then I just went to the work at hand.

"For instance, at Paramount, we acquired a movie," says Isaacs. "I knew the gentleman in charge of it. At the time, there were a number of women in marketing. When we all walked in the room, I felt the men going, 'Ohhhh, who are all these women?' Someone pointed out that I was going to be their day-to-day person on the picture. I could see their brains going cha, cha, cha . . . The movie went on to be incredibly successful, we all became real good friends, and I became the point person on every movie they worked on after that because I did the job. I wasn't going to sit around moaning, 'Oh, I know you don't think I can do this.' Who cares? *I* know I can.

"You wonder when is this [division of the races] going to be over? It's not over. It's not. It's better now, but it's still not great. For instance, I still look around and it's like, where are all the minority execs? More people of color have executive jobs, but they're not in the front. They're still not in the front."[113]

It's Called Mentoring

While Isaacs was a staff publicist at Columbia, Lucy Fisher was looking for work. "Paula Weinstein was a big vice president at Warner Bros.," Fisher recalls, "and I was a little nothing when I went in to see her." Warner Bros. didn't have anything for Fisher, but Weinstein said she'd keep her in mind.

Fisher took a story editor position at MGM in 1978, the studio few wanted to be with—it was in the final stages of dismemberment. "I cried. I kept myself up all night before I started the job, crying," says Fisher. "The next day, as my friends helped me move my few little boxes into my office, the girl who was leaving turned to me and said, 'This is a real dead end.' Great."[114]

A few months later, Weinstein called. She'd moved to Fox as senior VP of production, and she had an opening. Fisher had only been at MGM for six months.

"I felt bad about quitting, because despite its problems," says Fisher, "MGM had been very nice to me and had promoted me. I'd helped buy the scripts of *Fame* and *One from the Heart.* I talked to the head of MGM, Frank Rosenfelt. 'I feel embarrassed, but Fox has offered me a job, vice president of creative affairs.' Fox was a hot studio. 'What should I do?'

I asked him. He gave me a big hug. 'I'm proud of you,' he said. 'Don't be an idiot. Good luck!' "

At Fox, Weinstein introduced Fisher to Gareth Wigan, a producer in the early 1970s who had gone back into the studio system, and Alan Ladd Jr., then president of the studio.

"Paula was a creative wunderkind," says Fisher. "She was unbelievably kind and protective of me. That was around 1979, the Fox heyday—*Star Wars* and films about women like *Norma Rae, Turning Point, Julia.* It was paradise, and Ladd was an inspired leader. Filmmakers really wanted to be at that studio. All the movies cost under eleven million, including *Star Wars.* It was a very creative team.

"My first week there they were trying to find a director for *9 to 5.* I didn't know anything but Paula and Ladd called me out of my dailies. 'We need to talk to you,' Paula said. 'Mike Nichols is maybe interested in doing *9 to 5,* and we want to know what you think.'

" 'What *I* think? It would be the greatest!' They were pretending to delay making a decision until they included me. That was so incredible, then or now. Paula and Laddie made it a community team. In most studios now, everybody backbites. Imagine asking someone during their first week on the job, 'Would Mike Nichols be a good idea?' That's how I learned, because they included me even though I was at the bottom level of being able to make a contribution. They invested the time and the energy to teach me.

"Six months later," says Fisher, "the entire top echelon of that wonderful studio quit. 'Come with us,' they said to me. I was tempted, but I felt I still had never seen a movie through. I had never been anyplace long enough to actually accomplish anything." She stayed at Fox for two and a half years.

As it turned out, staying behind worked to Fisher's advantage. "People who would never have called me," she says, "talked to me, a low-ranking VP, because I was the only one still there. Often, I went home, moaning, 'I don't know what I'm doing,' and my boyfriend would say, 'You're not an earthquake victim.' It was trial by fire but very good because I was thrown in to make decisions and learn from my mistakes. Believe me, I made so many."

Francis Coppola had just finished *Apocalypse Now.* He asked Fisher to head up his new enterprise, Zoetrope Studios, which she did, but in a year it folded. Marc Canton, now a heavyweight production executive at Warner Bros., called. When she'd been a reader for Marcia Nasatir at United Artists, she had worked with Mark Canton. Canton was soon to be president of production. He asked Fisher to come to Warner Bros. She also had an offer from Columbia.

"After I decided on Warner Bros., I had second thoughts," says Fisher. "I was in New York when I began thinking that Warner Bros. was going to be too square after Zoetrope—I'd never meet people like Jean Luc Godard on the Warner Bros. lot. I kind of freaked out. I called Mark. 'I decided I'm not coming. It isn't right for me.'

" 'Where are you?'

" 'I'm in the lobby of a theater. I'm watching *Sophisticated Ladies.*'

" 'Do you really think that's a good place to make a life choice? Don't you think you should wait until tomorrow instead of deciding right in the middle of a Broadway show?'

" 'I guess I'll think about it tomorrow,' I told him. I'll always be grateful to him. Tomorrow came and Warners seemed like a good idea."[115] She stayed for 14½ years.

Attaining That Balance

Helene Hahn arrived in the entertainment industry in 1975, straight from her graduation from Loyola Law School. "In 1976 or 1977, we formed a group of women entertainment lawyers to support each other," says Hahn, "from that network of women who worked together at ABC and then at Paramount." At Paramount, Hahn was a staff attorney, then director of business affairs, vice president in 1981, and senior vice president in 1983. She moved to Disney in 1984 with Michael Eisner, Jeffrey Katzenberg, and Frank Wells—all from Paramount. At Disney, she headed business and legal affairs, probably the first woman to do that for a major studio. She is known for hiring and supporting women, which she says Jeffrey Katzenberg encouraged when she went to Disney.

"We started a program to train both female and minority writers, to increase their admittance, and executives," Hahn says. "It was a corporate goal and something that I enjoyed doing. I've been involved both at Disney and now at DreamWorks in our internship programs, a really gratifying part about the job, helping somebody get started on their career. I remember the people who helped me."[116]

Something else happened at Disney. "When you are part of a movie that changes the way people think or perceive things, that's what's great about being in this business," Hahn says. "At Disney, we were involved in animation and screening old, classic movies, then talked about them. In the initial movies, the women were passive, waiting for their prince to come. I think it came from Jeffrey, who had twins, a boy and girl, watching them grow up together—it became a real motivation for us to make sure the girls in our pictures didn't have passive roles. That was one of the things about *Beauty and the Beast*—she didn't pick the good-looking guy and she liked to read books. We were conscious of how we were projecting images. Girls and women today see themselves differently than when I was growing up."

At Disney, Hahn supervised business affairs for the theatrical groups (Disney, Touchstone, Hollywood Pictures, and Animation) including negotiations for all talent, cofinancing, acquisitions, and distribution agreements—millions and millions of dollars. She also oversaw administration, labor relations, and minority recruitment for the studio and spearheaded the hiring, training, and promotion of women to a variety of executive and managerial positions throughout the company. That was a real step because prior to her arrival, the studio had few if any female executives in any division.

"The first person I hired at Disney as my number two was Robin Russell, with whom I'd worked at Paramount. The second was Bernadine Brandeis. Robin was in charge of legal and Bernadine was in charge of business affairs. So immediately, there were three of us." The next two people she hired were Alan Myerson and Art Frazier.

Being a woman didn't hinder Hahn's career, though she didn't get into the college of her choice because at the time they had a quota on the number of women they admitted. Being a woman did help her get into Loyola Law School.

"I found that sort of balance throughout my career, something withdrawn, something given. People were willing to hire women lawyers, because when I started in the industry corporations particularly needed to hire women, and even some of the law firms. It was harder to get promoted when I started. No one was quite ready to make a woman head of a department in the business area. Some people I worked with, like Jeffrey Katzenberg, really like working with women. With him it was all about performance, not about gender. Others were less comfortable.

"Many women, Barbara Boyle being one," Hahn says, "have said women have to work harder. Nobody works harder than Jeffrey. I think women work *differently* and have different priorities, different attitudes. In certain jobs it's a strength and in other jobs it's not. Some of the male qualities propel you to success quicker, we've seen that, but I think it's individual. In business affairs and legal, I think women have a different style of negotiation." Because there weren't many women when she started, being female was in some ways an advantage because people were not used to a different negotiation style. "It gave you a leg up, because it wasn't the normal reaction they expected." Like what? "I can't give away all my secrets," she says with a rippling laugh, "but I think there are some gender-specific approaches to problem solving, and business affairs is very much about compromising, seeking solutions, and trying to make a deal work for everybody."

In 1994, with Jeffrey Katzenberg, she moved into a newly created studio, DreamWorks, founded by Steven Spielberg, Katzenberg, and David Geffen. "There's a world of difference between Disney and DreamWorks," says Hahn. "It's not nearly as corporate. It's much smaller, much more about individual passions for projects as opposed to putting out a slate of pictures.

"I think a lot of the stereotypes women have struggled against are gone." Hahn landed in a work atmosphere that was supportive, not combative. The advice Hahn gives women is to find the right people "that you click with. No matter how good you are at your job, if you're not with the right people who will see those strengths and appreciate you, leave. If you have the right people around you, who have confidence in you, people you enjoy working with, it's worth putting in the time—and it does take time. As frustrated as I was for all those early years, when the good times started, they were worth waiting for. I was working for people I thought were the best in the business, which enabled me to find this balance."[117] Today, Hahn is co-chief operating officer of DreamWorks.

■   ■   ■

Many people remember when the meetings in the 1980s began to change. Barbara Corday was executive vice president of prime-time programs for CBS Television from 1988 to 1990. "There were three women and two men in the room," she recalls. "The women were talking about the project we were there to talk about, and the men were talking about their new babies."[118] At another conference with two producers, a writer, and a studio executive, someone looked around and exclaimed, "My God, we're *all* women!"

"It was amazing enough to make us all aware of it and want to note it," says Corday.[119]

Women producers and writers taking meetings with women execs, from development all the way to senior vice presidents or presidents of production, witnessed a sea change that became routine because in the 1990s, younger women stopped noticing who was in the room.

Before leaving corporate triumphs and corporate angst, let's pause a moment with Anthea Sylbert, former costume designer, now vice president of production at United Artists. In 1984 she was about to make a big professional change.

Why Don't We Start Our Own Company?

MGM and United Artists had joined in an uneasy, arranged, corporate marriage (MGM/UA). The executive lineup, masterminded by MGM owner Kirk Kerkorian, created dissention and travail. David Begelman had been made president of MGM to bring the dying studio back to life (by 1982 he was out). Begelman had brought in his old friend and former agency partner, Freddie Fields, to run production at MGM, and had called on Paula Weinstein to head production at UA. *WarGames* (1983) was about to begin shooting. The story deals with a young man (Matthew Broderick) who cracks into a top-secret military computer linked to the U.S. nuclear arsenal and innocently starts a countdown to World War III.

"I was in a meeting with Freddie Fields," says Anthea Sylbert, "who headed MGM production, and Paula headed UA production. MGM and UA were supposed to be separate but equal, but it began to be clear that maybe we weren't so separate and maybe not so equal. Freddie wanted to see the *WarGames* set. I took him in, pointing out where the NORAD screens were going to be when they went up. 'What's going to be up there?' he asked.

" 'The screens.'

" 'You know what would be interesting? Build little walkways and things in perspective so it has depth.'

" 'Depth? What depth? That's the end of the building. The screens are there.'

" 'No, you build it like—'

" 'Wait a minute. You want us to build these walkways in perspective and then what? Hire midgets to walk on them? You won't be able to see the midgets anyway because the screens are going there.'

"Freddie gave in when the screens went up," Sylbert says, "and saw no way anyone could build what he wanted. One week into shooting, he was looking at dailies. He thought that Marty Brest, who had developed and supervised the film's design and had been shooting for a week, had to be replaced. Freddie felt his footage was not interesting." The producer of the film was Lisa Weinstein, Paula Weinstein's sister. Fields was ambitious; Paula Weinstein was in his way. The *WarGames* director became a casualty. "Paula fought the good fight," says Sylbert. "She tried to save Marty's job, but the powers that be came down on Freddie's side." Brest was out. Lisa Weinstein soon joined him.

"So now we're replacing a director," says Sylbert. "Freddie asked me to see a movie made by somebody he thought was very talented, a kind of horror, killer movie. I like those movies, but this one was not good. I came away from seeing it and thought I must be losing my mind."

Sylbert called Fields and told him that the horror director was out of the question. "You can't replace a director like Marty Brest with somebody who is a no-talent."

She recalls that Field said she had no right to say that; she didn't even know the director in question. She countered, "I don't need to know him. I just saw the work."

"Paula had given the script to several other directors," says Sylbert, "among them John Badham, who, by the way, finally did direct it. [Later] we were having a meeting with our English and German financial partners when Paula and I started to talk about the directors we were considering for *WarGames*. Freddie brings up this no-talent guy again. I thought we'd settled all that. Paula and I were taking it to other directors. So I said, 'What are you talking about, Freddie?'

" 'Shut your fucking mouth or I'm going to shut it for you,' Freddie says to me in front of all those people.

"I rose from my chair like a volcano. 'Let me say something to you. I have had fights with the best of them. I *love* a good fight. But not even a disgruntled lover has ever spoken to me that way. So I tell you what— I'm leaving this meeting altogether.' I went out the door and down the hall. Paula was running after me, saying, 'No, no, you can't leave me here.'

" 'I will not stay in a room with that man.'

"I went off to lunch," Sylbert says. "When I came back I found a really ugly bouquet of flowers on my desk and a note: *'Rudeness is not my suit.'* Freddie had left out the word 'strong.' *'I wish to explain.'* I took a new pad and wrote: *'Thank you for the flowers, I await your explanation.'* Some time later, Paula came into my office. 'Freddie says that the reason he said that,' Paula began, 'was that he was only trying to position the other investors so they'd put more money into the movie.'

" 'If that was the case,' I said, 'he should have let us in on it. I don't see this as a valid explanation. I don't want to stay here anymore.' I gathered my little pencils and called Barry Hirsch, my lawyer. 'I'm leaving.'

" 'Are you a crazy woman?'

" 'I refuse. I just refuse. I'm out of here.'

"He kept trying to tell me that they were going to fire us all anyway in a minute," says Sylbert, "and if we just relaxed, we'd get some money out of it. 'Just stay there and wait to be fired.' Freddie probably did want me to quit," Sylbert says, "and I fell right into his hands. But I didn't care, partly because the lunch I'd had was with Goldie Hawn. I was in a tirade. Goldie said, 'I don't know why you stay there anyway. Why don't we have our own company?'

"I couldn't believe my incredible good fortune. I leaned across the table, kissed her, and said, 'Yes. Yes. Yes!' And we did. We moved right into producing *Swing Shift*."[120]

12

WOMEN MAKE GOOD PRODUCERS—MOVIES

"Ah," she thought, "*this* is what I wanted to do." Anthea Sylbert had moved to the other side of the desk. She was not supervising productions for a studio; she was a producer in her own right.

"Goldie and I formed our company in 1984," Sylbert says. "*Swing Shift* was our first credit, though we didn't take credit because a producer [Jerry Bick] had already been attached."[121] Starring Goldie Hawn, Kurt Russell, Christine Lahti, and Ed Harris, *Swing Shift* is about two friends (Lahti and Hawn) who work in an aircraft factory during World War II, have relationship problems, suffer betrayals, but at the end are even better friends. Roger Ebert wrote, "This may be the first buddy movie about women."[122] The original story, by several uncredited people such as Buck Henry, Robert Towne, and Nancy Dowd (as Rob Morton), held promise. Jonathan Demme, who had few credits at this point, most with Roger Corman and New World Pictures, was directing.[123] The production was not a picnic. Hawn did not like Demme's original cut (more like, it was said, an ensemble movie than a star movie). She convinced Warner Bros. to let her do another cut, the one seen today. Sylbert has commented diplomatically that Hawn disagreed with the focus Demme had brought to the cut.

That same year, 1984, Hawn and Sylbert were also working on *Protocol*, their first official project for the Hawn/Sylbert Movie Company. The comedy was about a cocktail waitress who winds up working for the State Department after she accidentally foils the assassination of an Arab official. Buck Henry wrote the script.

After *Protocol*, Sylbert produced eight other films with Goldie Hawn, among them *Wildcats* (1986), directed by Michael Ritchie, and *Overboard* (1987), coproduced with Alexandra Rose (the coproducer of *Norma Rae*).[124]

As an executive and as a producer, Sylbert feels now that the material that attracted her had a lot to do with being a woman. "If the material didn't directly deal with the challenges women confronted, which it mostly did in *Swing Shift* or *Yentl*," she says, "it had to do with the humanity of a situation. For instance, I adored *Greystoke*, the script Robert Towne never finished. It was so wonderful it could make you cry. Much of it had to do with the relationship between Tarzan and his ape mother, an emotional bond I responded to, that I understood. In that sense, the choices I've made absolutely have to do with being a woman."[125]

■ ■ ■

The business was shifting under everyone's feet—cable television, VCRs, computerization, MTV, pay TV—only the basic need for the story seemed to remain, both courted and neglected.

In the 1980s, "first generation" executives, such as Anthea Sylbert, Marcia Nasatir, Sherry Lansing, or Rosilyn Heller, were emerging from skirmishes with various studios or networks, or they were being isolated in their corporate posts until they either quit or were forced out. What was a former senior vice president or president to do? They produce! And so did younger women with very little experience. And they were good at it.

Columbia executive Rosilyn Heller had already produced *Ice Castles* for the studio before she began producing with Guber-Peters and Warner Bros. briefly in the 1980s, and then independently (*That Girl*, *American Heart*, and *The Beans of Egypt, Maine*). Sherry Lansing produced with Stanley Jaffe the immensely popular thriller-slasher *Fatal Attraction* in 1987 (seen by some as the 1980s response to the wildly feminist 1970s). In 1988, they made their own response to the woman-as-stalker—*The Accused*, woman-as-victim, starring Jodie Foster. Kathleen Kennedy began a remarkable producing career in 1982 with *E.T. the Extra-Terrestrial*, and went right on producing movies all through the 1980s, some with her husband, Frank Marshall, most for or with Steven Spielberg: *Twilight Zone—the Movie*, *Gremlins*, *Indiana Jones and the Temple of Doom*, *Empire of the Sun*, *The Color Purple*. Lynda Obst and Debra Hill partnered to make *Adventures in Babysitting* and *Heartbreak Hotel* before doing *The Fisher King* in 1991. Lauren Shuler made *Ladyhawke* and *St. Elmo's Fire* in 1985, and *Pretty in Pink* in 1986. With Sally Field's company, Fogwood, Laura Ziskin produced *Murphy's Romance*, *No Way Out*, *The Rescue*, *D.O.A.*, and *Everybody's All-American*. Nancy Meyers produced *Irreconcilable Differences* in 1984, and *Baby Boom* in 1987. Polly Platt produced *Say Anything . . .*, *War of the Roses*, *I'll Do Anything*, and *Broad-*

cast News. Well connected in Hollywood or not, women on every level were starting to produce in numbers in film, in television, and in the "Wild West" of cable. And *that* was new.

Women Read, Men Do

"That's why I was hired," Marcia Nasatir says, referring to her work as an agent and as a story executive at United Artists, "and that's why women traditionally have been hired—because we knew how to read." In the 1980s, Nasatir was not with United Artists or Orion; she was senior VP at 20th Century Fox, then president of Carson Productions.[126] Soon she, too, would be an independent producer. While she was with Carson Productions, Nasatir was trying to sell *The Big Chill,* whose final ascension to celluloid has long been associated with her. *The Big Chill* is about a group of 1960s students, now in their thirties, who gather for their friend's funeral over a long weekend. It is talky; it has no car chases or murders. Roger Ebert called it "The Son of the Return of the Secaucus Seven," and yet it rings true—life after the 1960s.[127]

"It had already been turned down seventeen times. By every major studio," Nasatir says. "Seventeen! I thought then and think now that the men who made the decisions at the studios hadn't read the material. They either got a reader's report or they didn't think it would appeal to audiences because it was talky. Someone told me 'too many people talking and it's not funny.' I thought it was hysterically funny. Most of the people who turned it down were young. The writer, Lawrence Kasdan, was probably thirty-five, and the people working the studios were thirty-five to forty. I was in my late fifties."

Nasatir thinks it's all about reading. "These people could not read or didn't read or didn't want to read or didn't want to believe there was room in the market for a different kind of story, which is proven—there is!"

For years, Nasatir says, she's heard stories about women discovering what worked for them in crunch situations.

"My offering on that subject is what happened on *The Big Chill,*" she says. As usual, Nasatir's solution, however temporary, ran counter to almost everyone else's game. "I was in Frank Price's office at Columbia. They had read or said they'd read the script, but they were still dilly-dallying around a marketing report that stated that no one would be interested in seeing the movie. In this meeting, Larry Kasdan was selling the movie hard all over again. I'd been a studio executive, I'd sat in the Frank Price, Guy McElwaine, Marvin Antonowsky, Wendy Margolis chairs, and I'd had people come to sell their projects to me. I thought the dance around this script in that office at that time was just rotten. It was humiliating because Larry was being forced to sell all over again a script they'd already read. I was thinking, if they didn't want to make the movie, then don't make it. But don't make people humiliate themselves. I still feel emotional about that moment. It hurt me.

"I started to cry. Tears came down my cheeks. Not only shouldn't you cry, you should have something to back it up with. My backup was that we [Carson] had a 'put' arrangement with Columbia. That's a very male term—it comes from 'put it to them.' 'Put' arrangements mean that they had to make the film at a certain budget—in this case, eight million. I had another argument for them: Larry was going to be an important director. You've got to give people a logical reason to do something beyond bullying them. And you have to give them an emotional reason as well.

"So, the tears are rolling down my cheeks and Frank Price says, 'I don't think anybody has cried in an office since Louis B. Mayer died. And it was Mayer who was crying.' "[128]

The Big Chill was finally produced in 1983 and went on to be nominated for Best Picture (Michael Shamberg), Supporting Actress (Glenn Close), and Screenplay (Barbara Benedek and Kasdan, who was also the director).

An Old Boys' Network Run by Younger and Younger Boys

One first-time producer was a respected stage and screen actress, Jane Alexander. The system in Hollywood was smaller than it is now, but it was and is built on relationships formed during work on many different levels. Though well known and well liked, Jane Alexander developed and wanted to produce scripts, but in the 1980s, they languished in "development hell"—not even making it to production limbo. She did produce *Calamity Jane* for CBS (1984), *Square Dance* (1987) with coexecutive producers Charles Haid and Daniel Petrie, and *A Marriage: Georgia O'Keeffe and Alfred Stieglitz* (1991) for PBS's American Playhouse.

Alexander, a Broadway stage and film star, did expect to be taken seriously as a producer. "We just couldn't get them to the guys who green-lighted. We got stopped at the lower levels," says Alexander. "It was very, very frustrating. I loved talking to Lynda Obst, who has a kind of verve and enthusiasm for it. She gets frustrated, but she doesn't give up. I remember the day she [and Debra Hill] got *The Fisher King* done. I don't know how long they'd worked on it, probably years. Lynda had always had this little thing—she'd tell me about *Fisher King*, what a wonderful story it was, that nobody'd done it yet, and then she'd say, 'But don't worry, they will!' She knew that if you just hang in there and keep squeaking that wheel, it would get oiled.

"That's the way I felt about an absolutely brilliant film I had, *Jaguar*—someday it will be done. My experiences [trying to get it done] were very negative, frustrating, and I always felt I was in a boy's world. I never was greeted with any enthusiasm. I'd see guys backslapping other guys. I felt it was an old boy network run by younger and younger boys. And all white. A really closed shop."[129]

"Jane Alexander produced one of the first independent movies that went to Sundance, *Square Dance*," says Alexander's agent, Joan Hyler. "Dan Petrie directed it; Rob Lowe, Jason Robards, and Jane starred in it. It is about a teenage girl [Winona Ryder] coming of age in Texas. The difficulty of getting just one movie made in the mid-'80s that was about a woman and starred women was like winning ten Academy Awards. It's got to be measured against the odds. It is especially hard after it's made, because you've got to start all over again. But that's the business. Everybody does it. It was just harder for women."[130]

By the end of the decade, Alexander felt the struggle was impossible, and she left that particular battlefield. "I decided that I couldn't market a script because I wasn't part of the system they'd developed in Hollywood. That's the way I looked at it. I longed for more women in it. I longed for them." There were a few, more than before, but not nearly enough.

"I felt as long as the banks are controlled by men," says Jane Alexander, "the country's economic system, and the corporate power is in the hands of men, there weren't going to be a lot of stories told by women—yet. The stories I wanted to tell were often about women, but not always—*Jaguar* was about a very macho guy. I wanted to see a woman's studio that had women bankers behind it. But the system was excruciating. It's a little bit like Congress. [Wyoming senator] Al Simpson said a great thing when he left the Senate. A newspaper reporter asked him: 'What do you wish you had known then when you came into the Senate at the beginning of your terms that you know now?' Al said, 'That it takes twenty years to pass a bill.'

"That's the way I feel about the producing business," Alexander says. "Life is too short."[131] In 1993, the four-time Oscar nominee was off to head the National Endowment for the Arts.

I Used Every Ploy I Could Think of Except Flirting or Crying

"I wouldn't be here today," Gale Anne Hurd says, "if I'd started my career running up against all the obstacles other women faced in the male-dominated world that Hollywood was in the 1970s." Only in retrospect did she realize that Roger Corman's universe, where she'd worked in marketing and a sort of producer trainee, imposed no limits on what women could do in films. She learned how different it was in the industry when she started trying to get made a script she and James Cameron had written around 1980. The script was called *The Terminator*.

People made it clear to her that the film was too complicated or too action-oriented to be produced by a woman. But Hurd was convinced it would be a great movie for her to produce and Cameron to direct. At that time, Cameron, a production designer, had one small directing credit, *Piranha II: The Spawning*, a rare Corman box office failure.

"Some actors turned down the film," Hurd says, "because Jim was attached as the director. Buyers approached Jim as the director provided he got rid of me as producer. I trusted him and he trusted me. We held out and were able to do it essentially on our own terms. I thought if I just persevered I'd get the movie made. My idealism and my naiveté carried me through at least two years of trying to get it together and keep it together. If I'd known then what I know now, some twenty-three pictures later, I'm not sure that I would have persevered."[132]

She used every ploy she could think of—except flirting or crying. She desperately wanted to meet Barry Plumley at Hemdale Film Corporation.[133]

"Of course, he wouldn't return my phone calls—practically no one would." Hurd found out through a mutual friend that he was selling a desk, and she needed one. She thought if she said she was interested in buying his desk, he'd return her phone call, which he did. She didn't mention that she was going to bring the forty-eight-page, single-spaced treatment under her arm.

The desk was in storage in Hollywood, and it was exactly what she was looking for.

"We struck up a conversation, and as I handed over the check for about a hundred dollars under my limit, I handed him my treatment. 'I'd really appreciate it if you'd read this. I think it's perfect for Hemdale.' He seemed kind of startled. I was amazed when he called me the next day. 'I love this,' he said."

One of the first people Hurd had approached about the movie had been Barbara Boyle, whom she'd known since the Corman days. As Hurd was hawking the script around, Boyle was moving into Orion. "Barbara talked Mike Medavoy into reading the script," Hurd says, "talked him into meeting with Jim and me."[134]

"It was wonderful to work with Gale and Jim," Boyle says, "though in those days Jim was pretty inarticulate. Everything he had to say, he'd kind of draw. I remember when we were going to talk to Medavoy about *Terminator*, I said, 'Now listen, you have to pitch this to him,' so he came in with drawings that covered a wall. It was his vision of the movie—and Mike got it. The fact that he saw the movie so clearly is something you wish most directors could do.

"For me, the big surprise was [Orion cofounder] Arthur Krim's first reaction. 'You're turning my company into an exploitation company like Roger Corman's! You're ruining my company. This is the company that brought the world *Cuckoo's Nest*.' Well, what do you say to that? I just replied that I liked the movie."

The Hemdale financing came in and *The Terminator* got rolling. "In terms of the production, Gale and Donna Smith ran it," says Boyle. "It was a nonunion show, shot downtown in Los Angeles. Gale was a complete pro, even though this was her first major movie production."[135]

It's the Sci-fi One!

That movie was a turning point not only for Hurd but for Donna Smith, too.

Smith had only been working in L.A. since 1979, and had few credits as a production coordinator and manager. That Christmas she and her husband, Gordon, were on a flight to Florida to visit his father.

"I had three different movies offered me," Smith says, remembering them gleefully, "and I took the scripts with me on the plane. 'Honey, one of these scripts is sci-fi—that's the one I'm *not* going to do.' I read the scripts. 'Honey, I know which one I'm going to do. The script is brilliant.'

" 'Which one is that?'

" 'It's the sci-fi one! *The Terminator*.' "[136]

Hurd, a brand-new producer, was hiring women—Smith as the production manager, Melanie Cook as the production attorney, Betsy Magruder as the first assistant director, and Hillary Wright as the costume designer.

"Gale's first movie," recalls attorney Melanie Cook, "none of us really knew what we were doing, but we were all doing it well and really hard. It was a real bonding experience."

Cook, a new lawyer, was not yet in entertainment law. She comes from a family of passionate debaters, at the dinner table or over croquet. She had worked as a cocktail waitress after graduating from UCLA as a dance major. Her father, a judge, suggested she go to law school. She got her law degree from UCLA. Today, she sees the new girls' network "as a group of people who have grown up with each other in the business, have a certain level of trust, and that's really the key . . . There were so many women working on *Terminator*. It was novel then. Now it's more like, 'This good thing happened to my girlfriend, she got a job.' Back then it was, 'My God, it's a woman!' You don't have the same reaction anymore."[137]

"Hemdale insisted that a man be brought in as executive in charge of production to keep an eye on me," Hurd says, "even though he did absolutely nothing."[138] Barbara Boyle at Orion did not impose anyone on her. "Hemdale was scared," Boyle says, "and why wouldn't they be? The director didn't talk much, he drew pictures; the producer's only credit was as an associate on *Smokey Bites the Dust*. No one at Orion had confidence in the movie. But I think that a good executive can recognize talent, and I had no doubt that Gale could produce and Jim could direct. I knew they would pull it off."[139]

"Now, everybody in town knew of that *Terminator* script," Smith recalls, "because it had been all around. Everybody knew that it had a woman as producer who cowrote the script with some guy with no credits called Jim Cameron and that he came with the package as the director—that's why it hadn't been picked up. That's always dicey. When the crews in town asked, 'Who's the production manager on that movie?' the answer came back, 'They've got some broad on it.' And it was, like, dismissed. I was the 'some broad.' After *Terminator* was released, my credit in town became 'Get me the broad that did *Terminator*!' That's when I started working steadily."

Smith thought the work of production manager is like planning how to construct a building, but in other ways, she says, "it's like a war." On *Terminator*, the crew called Smith "the Sergeant Major." "Watch out!" they'd say, "Sergeant Major's coming." Smith got the army moving in the right direction. "It was like constantly choreographing troop movements," says Smith, "who goes where, when and why. Movies get made in prep—before the movie is filmed. If you really prep you're going to be okay during the shoot. Every day you lose on prep is going to make for a tougher shoot later. Prep is awesomely valuable. Poorly prepared directors never value prep much."[140] Hurd and Cameron did.

"The reviews were sensational for that kind of movie," recalls Barbara Boyle. "In *Terminator* there's a club called Technoir in a scene. Gale and Jim were so smart, they were sure the picture was going to get attention, and they wanted it to have a genre type of its own. So after the movie was done, when they were asked during interviews to describe the movie, Jim said, 'It's a technoir.'

"Jim had scripted *Aliens*, the second feature in that series," says Boyle, "but he wasn't attached to direct. He and Gale asked me to show clips of *Terminator* to Fox to prove that he could really direct, which of course I did. Orion was of course anxious to work with them again. This is a bitter memory for me. Jim and Gale and I were having lunch in New York with Eric Pleskow and Bill Bernstein of Orion. Gale did all the talking, of course. She wanted Orion to take out a full-page ad congratulating them with the success of *The Terminator*, which would help them put the final nail into the Fox deal for which they were still negotiating. Eric said absolutely not, those ads are outrageous, don't mean anything, and he wouldn't do it. The result—Jim and Gale did not do *Terminator 2* for Orion."[141]

But the Fox deal for *Aliens* was made, Cameron was signed as director, and since none of the former *Alien* producers (David Giles, Walter Hill, Gordon Carroll) were available, Hurd and Cameron fought the usual battles and she became the producer of *Aliens*.

"Being a woman has shaped my work in a couple of ways," Hurd says. "Creatively, I wanted to have the women characters in my films not be just girlfriends or victims." In sci-fi action movies, very few strong women came along until Sigourney Weaver's Ripley character in *Alien*. "Second, I realized that I had to be stronger, better prepared, and less emotional than anyone would expect so that I wouldn't be judged as, or dismissed as, a female.

"I saw the way men interacted—they were tough and firm and if they were emotional they weren't crying or apologizing. I also saw that a lot of men weren't prepared. But because they were men, because they knew the lingo and were part of the boys' club, they could get away with not being prepared. I realized very early that a woman could not. I felt that was true of Barbara Boyle, Donna Smith, and the first AD, Betsy Magruder, on *The Terminator*. Even the women who had already made huge inroads in the business by the time I met them had pretty much adopted the same approach. I missed the worst of it, but the old attitudes were still blatant in the 1980s when I produced *The Terminator* and especially *Aliens*."

The Terminator had not yet been released in England, where they were scheduled to shoot *Aliens*. When she was interviewing for her English crew, Hurd recalls some of the department heads said, "How can a little girl like you expect to produce a big movie like this? Who's *really* producing this film?"

"I felt I had entered *The Wizard of Oz*," says Hurd. "'I'm producing this film,' I told them. 'Why don't you check with the guys at the studio?' One man flatly said, 'I won't take orders from a woman, I won't report to you.' I stood up. 'Thank you for coming in. Clearly we won't be collaborating on this movie.'

"They were shocked. Many of them called Tim Hampton, head of Fox in the UK, and said, 'Okay, Tim, who's really producing this film? I just had a meeting with this vile girl who said she was the producer. Will you put her in her place?'

"'No, I won't. She's producing the movie,' Tim said.

"By that time, Jim and I were married," Hurd says. "Some people called Tim and said things like, 'I know she's the director's wife, but can't you bring in someone to really produce the movie?' Tim Hampton could have sold me down the river a dozen times. He could have called Fox in Los Angeles and said, 'You got to get rid of this woman, give her credit but get her off the production.' He did not. Tim backed me up. He was a staunch ally.

"I went through more being a woman on *Aliens* than on any other movie. The film technicians saw Jim and me as two young, know-nothing Yanks, which drove Jim up the wall because he's Canadian. We were treated with no respect.

"I already had a reputation of being ruthless because I'd insisted the first director of photography be fired. Jim didn't like firing people. The DP was very respected, very good, but not the right DP for the movie and this director. Jim would say to him, 'I want the scene front lit here . . .' The DP would say, 'Well, governor, you'll get what I give you.' It was incredibly frustrating, we were falling behind schedule, so I fired him."

Her tough reputation grew.

"We replaced him with a man who'd never been a director of photography on a major film before (Adrian Biddle), though he had extensive work in commercials," says Hurd. "We paid him basically a flat rate, which my production supervisor was incredibly upset about—the DP's camera operator was making more than he was. In England, you can't have the 'governor' making less money than the camera operators.

"'I don't care what people think,' I said, 'I'm not giving him any more money. We made a deal and if he didn't want it he shouldn't have agreed to it. Has he complained?'

" 'No, but it isn't right.'

" 'Yes, it is right. He's getting an incredible opportunity. He'll have a current feature film, which is what he wants, and that's fair.'

"I was called tough and unfair," says Hurd, "but I had a budget to worry about, and the DP was given a big break."[142]

The crew mutiny occurred when she fired the AD. "The first assistant director, an aspiring director, felt he should be directing the film. We were falling behind and the AD was blaming it on Jim. 'Jim doesn't know what he wants.' Anyone who has ever met Jim knows he knows exactly what he wants and how to get it. The AD was a lot older than we were and he wanted to see Jim fail. So we decided to fire him."

The crew and cast stopped work and threatened to walk off the picture.

"We were in a very difficult position. I looked at the situation as incredible disloyalty to a director. I was able to turn it around. To this day, I don't know how I did it. I hate to speak in public, but I got up in front of the crew and said, 'If you want to save the AD's job, we have to make up the time we've lost. We have to bring this movie in on schedule and on budget. As producer, it's been my responsibility to make sure that all the departments are informed about what's going on, what's ahead of us. Maybe my door hasn't been open enough for people to complain about something and I take full responsibility. The studio has said the AD is the person responsible for making sure we make our day, and now that we're falling behind, we were told, you have to get rid of the AD. If we all do better, we won't have to fire him.'

"People really got behind the movie, supported the AD, and the AD got behind the director, and it turned around. I never lost my temper. I felt that if I responded emotionally, I'd never be taken seriously. The few times I let emotions take over were times I regretted. Now, people say I'm cold and unfeeling, but I do keep my business life and personal life separate. Other people may not have to.[143]

"I did lose my temper when Jim and I were doing the European publicity tour for *Aliens* in 1986. We were in Frankfurt, Germany, having a cursory interview with an Austrian journalist who was writing a feature article about the film, about us, and about Sigourney Weaver. When it was over, he turned off his recorder and said, 'I just want you to know that personally, although I'm not a film reviewer, I think the premise of this movie is outrageous. The idea that a woman would be fighting this monster when the man was disabled! Crazy! Any woman would be cowering and crying in the corner while the man saved her ass.' He said a lot more than that in a very hostile and threatening manner.

"I completely lost it. I leaped across the table, jumped right on his chair, knocked it over. I was going to strangle him. 'I have women relatives in the Israeli army,' I shouted. 'You should talk to them about women who can handle very dangerous situations, basically in combat!' "[144]

■ ■ ■

Three years before she met Gale Anne Hurd, Donna Smith and her husband, Gordon, had moved to Los Angeles not knowing anyone.

"We had eleven dollars, so I signed with a temp agency, which sent me on an interview," says Smith. "The guy looked at my resume and said, 'So you know how to do this Shakespeare shit, but what else can you do?'

" 'Shakespeare shit?' I was so insulted. 'I know I don't want to work with you.' I was really offended."[145]

Smith's first job had been a "basket girl"—mail delivery at the Pillsbury Company, where only women took the mail around to the departments. Each woman was assigned a floor; Smith's was the executive suites. A few years later, she met her husband at the Guthrie Theater in Minneapolis, where he was the stage manager and she worked as assistant to the director, Sir Tyrone Guthrie. In 1977, Gordon asked her if she wanted to move to New York or California. "Let's go to California. I don't like the snow." After "Shakespeare shit," Smith began to understand the antitheater tone of Hollywood. She got a job filing, which she felt was "a little beneath" her, but it was only for two weeks.

"On the second day, I look up from my filing, and my God—there's Rocky! What's Rocky doing here? I'd seen the movie, I didn't know the actor's name, he was just Rocky to me. I'm a Minneapolis girl and Rocky was walking by. Two days later, I'm filing and Travis Bickle comes walking in. What's *he* doing here? Robert De Niro, of course. I'd seen *Taxi Driver*. I asked Lupe, the secretary, 'What kind of a company is this?'

" 'We do movies.' It was Chartoff-Winkler, the production company that made the original *Rocky*.

"Lupe was the production coordinator for a production manager, Jim Brubaker, who is about this tall and mean as a snake. 'You!' he'd bark. 'Come in here! Do this! Do that!' Personally, I thought he was pretty amusing. After I'd been there about a week, he said, 'Lupe, come in for this meeting and you get in here too.' He was talking to me. I get my paper and pencil, go in there, and write down every word. It was really foreign turf. He kept talking about Sly. 'Rocky II is already filmed but Sly wants a new ending.' I thought that was the silliest thing I'd ever heard. 'We have to reshoot the ending. We need to get three thousand extras, we need to get the Sports Arena again, we need to get all the principals back, it's going to be a month's work, this is Donna Smith, she'll be the production coordinator . . .' "

Smith quit writing. She just sat there. Afterwards, she went over to him. "Mr. Brubaker? I think you made a mistake."

"I don't think I did. I've been watching you. I think you can do it, and if you don't think you can, I'll get somebody else."

"No, no, chill. I can do it."

"I don't know what made him think I could do it," Smith says. "Maybe my smart mouth. The week I'd been there, he'd walk by me and snarl 'Filing . . .' and I'd say, kind of lippy, 'You got something better for me to do?' "

The next day she was taking notes as they planned the Rocky II re-shoots. A guy came up to her and said, "Toots, what emulsion are we using?" Smith did not have a clue. "I'll get back to you on that," she said. She didn't even know what the word "shoot" meant, let alone "emul-sion," but she felt she could figure things out—this is where we are, we want to do this, we need this many people, it will cost this much money, we have to be there, we'll do this, and then we'll get over there. "I'm good at that. I knew that from working at the Guthrie. I also knew I'd seen that word emulsion. I called the drugstore, asked about the emulsion on film, finally found Kodak in the yellow pages, called them, and said, 'I'm the production coordinator on Rocky II reshoots. Do you know what emulsion we're using?' "

The next time she saw the guy who called her "toots," she gave him the emulsion number and told him not to call her "toots" again. " 'Hey,' I thought, 'I can do this. It's all about reasoning!'

"Brubaker, Rocky II production manager, was built like a bulldog and yapped at me a lot," says Smith. " 'We've got to do this, we've got to do that.' He was a pro. When we finished shooting, I was sitting in the Sports Arena, and I realized I'd never had so much fun. I'd never been on a set before or seen the camera setup but I had nailed whatever Brubaker gave me to do."

She started taking files home at night. Her husband, Gordon, was helpful. He was beginning to get some television work directing Circus of the Stars. She'd show him a production report or a call sheet, learned the difference, figured out cost reports and what terms like "best boy," "key grip," and "turnaround" meant. She started to realize there were unions—IATSE, DGA, SAG, WGA—and what initials meant. "Everybody talked in initials. 'Get that blah-blah from the WGA.'" She learned the guilds had rules. She called them, got the rule books, and learned them from beginning to end. "Brubaker was kind of surprised on *Rocky II* when I quoted a union rule to him that affected our reshoot." At the end of *Rocky II* reshoots, he said, "Hey, kid, you're okay. I want you to do my next movie with me."

"You've got a whole movie lined up?" she said, astonished.

"Yeah. *Raging Bull.*"

"I was on that for a real long time," says Smith. "First, we shot all the fight scenes in Los Angeles, which was why 'Travis Bickle' had been in the office. Scorsese was always around, too, and I thought he was kind of a nut case. I didn't know who he was. He'd talk so fast. I'd never heard anyone talk that fast. No matter what he needed or wanted, I'd learned enough on *Rocky II* to pull it off.

"Every meeting was men and me. I've always called it that—men and me—and it's still true today. Not as much, but it's still mainly men and me. I always was candid and I never had a rough time. If anyone gave me an award, I'd thank all men—except for Gale Anne Hurd, there were no women around, and it breaks my heart."[146]

Smith's desk faced Brubaker's in the same office. "I liked that style," she says, "because we could hear the conversations. He'd be on the phone, 'I'll take care of X and Y,' and I'd go, 'Got it! X and Y!' It was wonderful. But we also pushed each other's buttons a lot."

One day he said to her, "You think you know everything? Think you can wear my pants?"

"Yeah," she replied. "I think I could. You're short."

"You think you're so goddamned smart," he said.

"'I am smart,' I told him. 'I'm helping you with a shitload of your work now.' He just laughed at me. Then he stood up and unzipped. The production assistants were all looking. I stood up. It was like two gunfighters. 'You think you can wear them?' he said.

"'Yeah.' But I was thinking, 'Oh jeez, I don't know where this is going.'

"He took off his bell-bottom trousers and threw them at me. I unzipped, took off my trousers. We're standing there in our underwear. The production assistants were yelling, 'Get the camera, get the camera!' There were a lot of people on that shoot.

"Now, you know and I know that girls can always wear men's pants. Men cannot wear girls' pants. I put on his pants. 'Gee, they're still warm,' I said. 'Big in the waist, I expected that. Perfect length. Thank you very much indeed.'

"'Give me my pants back.'

" 'No.'

" 'Give me my fucking pants back.'

" 'No. I'm wearing the pants now. If you can put these on, do it. Otherwise you look pretty stupid standing there in your underwear. I've got work to do.' I sat down and kept on working.

" 'Get me a teamster in here now!' he yelled. It really was wonderful.

"A teamster came in. 'Jeez, boss, you don't have any pants on.'

" 'Shut the fuck up,' Brubaker said. 'Go out and buy me some Chemin de Fer.' He's taking money out of his wallet and the teamster's laughing, looking at me.

"That's when Brubaker and I bonded in a real affectionate way. The next day he had to have the last word. I came to work and on my desk were thirty pair of trousers. He went right through his closet, took everything out, put them all on my desk. To this day I wear what I call my Saturday clothes, my Bru britches, all bell-bottoms. I had never known anyone like him before."

All through the 1980s, Smith worked as a production manager, all nonunion films or television miniseries, including *I'm Dancing As Fast As I Can*, *Little Gloria*, and *Reckless*. David Nicksay, a production manager who worked with Edgar Scherick and Scott Rudin, asked her to coordinate *Reckless* and put her in charge of the production. "The job became a 'line producer'—a new tag, new title," she says. "Whose ass is on the line? It's the line producer!"[147]

13

GETTING ON THE YELLOW BRICK ROAD—
PRODUCING FOR TELEVISION

"Women can do everything a man can do," producer Patricia Finnegan says, "but a man can't do everything a woman can."[148] In the 1980s, television continued to be more of a home for women than motion pictures, and some shows defined the decade: *Cagney & Lacey, L.A. Law, Dynasty, Dallas, China Beach.*

Dynasty (1981–89) was created and produced by Esther and Richard Shapiro (and Aaron Spelling, his first venture into prime-time soaps). Like *Dallas*, it was about another oil-rich family whose concerns and ideals matched the 1980s perfectly in greed and superficiality. The show hired women writers and directors, among the latter Gwen Arner, Gabrielle Beaumont, Lorraine Senna Ferrara, and Nancy Malone, who directed the one-hundredth episode. It was Malone's first paying job as a director. "Enormous pressure," she recalls, sighing. "It was luck, timing, and Esther Shapiro, my godmother, and the producer, Elaine Rich. My assignment was, 'If you fly with this, you'll be hired again, and if you fail you may not be hired anywhere.' I had a wonderful cameraman, Michel Hugo. He was charming and helpful and we ate dinners and laughed and screamed and he helped me through it."[149]

Marcy Carsey left ABC to start the Carsey-Werner Company with Tom Werner—television, motion pictures, animation, and syndication. In 1984, Carsey-Werner had *The Cosby Show* on the air, *Roseanne* in 1988, *Grace Under Fire* in 1993, and *Cybill* in 1995. Linda Bloodworth-Thomason, a writer since the 1970s on shows like *M*A*S*H*, created *Designing Women* in 1986 (it ran until 1992); Diane English created *Murphy Brown* with Candace Bergen; Susan Harris sent forth *The Golden Girls* from 1985 to 1992, a show aimed at (primarily) women of any age, whose viewers rivaled, in loyalty, those of *Cagney & Lacey*. Harris's third show in the 1980s was *Empty Nest*. With talent, tenacity, and good timing, they and other women rode the opportunity wave breaking for women in the 1980s.

The television producers who follow brought us *Grace Under Fire, A Different World, The Baxters, Cosby, Home Improvement, Roseanne, Thunder Alley, Soul Man, China Beach, Cagney & Lacey,* and movies and miniseries, *Love is Never Silent, Declaration Day, Kane and Abel, Eleanor, First Lady of the World, Heartsounds, Quicksand, This Child Is Mine, Dark Holiday,* and *Circle of Violence: A Family Drama.*

I Resorted to Prayer

The survival rate for entrepreneurial, financially at-risk, independent producers has always been low. TV dramas or movies with socially significant themes have an even lower rate.

In the 1970s, Marian Rees headed development for Roger Gimbel at Tomorrow Enterprises in the 1970s, successfully selling ideas to the networks, and producing, in effect but without credit, Dorothea Petrie's *Orphan Train.* Rees moved to Nicholl, Ross and West, a production company of writers (*The Jeffersons*), set up their feature division, and produced *Angel Dusted* with Petrie (Jean Stapleton, Helen Hunt) and *The Marva Collins Story* (Cicely Tyson). When Don Nicholl died, the partnership fell apart.

Out of work and at a crossroads in 1980, Rees went to friends for advice—John Mitchell, then president of the TV Academy; Bob Wood, president of Metromedia, who had been president of CBS when Tandem was doing *All in the Family;* and her attorney, Dixon Dean.

"I had gone through all of the tribulations and the excitement of working for other people—Tandem, Tomorrow Entertainment, Tomorrow Enterprises, NRW," says Rees, "but I had had no equity in those companies and no contract. That came partly from my own culture and the culture of the business at the time. One, I didn't think I needed a contract; it was a handshake and we'll-take-care-of-you kind of thing. But they didn't. I had to ask Tandem for severance pay. I don't think I would have had to do that if I'd been a man. Two, I would have made sure I had a contract; it would have been expected. Three, at the time I didn't have aggressive ambitions." Rees says that Marcy Carsey at Tomorrow Entertainment amazed her. "Marcy knew exactly what she wanted to do. For instance, when the Equal Opportunity Act was passed or amended in 1974, Marcy told me, 'Now they have to hire me.' She knew what it meant. She went to ABC. I think her goal was to be president of ABC. That was the possibility the Act offered. It changed laws."

Rees was not as confident or as brash as Carsey, and did not have a powerful husband or male partner, as many successful women in the business do. Nor was she young—she was in her late forties. If not now, when? "I told my lawyer, Dixon, that I wanted to start my own company," says Rees. "Some friends thought I was just absolutely crazy . . ." Dixon pointed to her ability to sell ideas—twenty-two shows to CBS for Tomorrow Enterprises, and all of them got made. Dixon supported her.

"I mortgaged my house, my insurance, my car—everything," Rees says. The only thing she had ready to sell was a script from NRW that hadn't been produced, a semiautobiographical story about beauty queens called *Miss All-American Beauty*. She wanted to do an off-center take on it.

"The papers were drawn up. Lou Horowitz, now a major broker in the industry, was there with Dixon. They made me read everything, wanting me to know exactly what I was doing. I did. I was prepared to lose it all. Because that's what it meant."[150]

Here's the risk: Most of the entities that sell to networks and cable are studios or major production companies, such as, in the 1980s, Tandem, MTM, Lorimar. The producer and the network agree to a license fee, the up-front funds from the network to produce the show. In the early 1980s, that was up to $2.5 million for a ninety-minute show. The sum covers the budget, essentially. "The trick is to avoid a deficit. Pull it off, and you've got a film the network has paid for, but to which [the producer] owns all foreign rights and all domestic syndication rights"— the fabled "back end," which makes it possible for some producers to "deficit finance" their films, "putting up additional money of their own on top of the network license fee" to hire a better cast to make the film more valuable to world buyers.[151]

"I incorporated as Marian Rees Associates and took offices on Radford Avenue in Studio City," says Rees. "Ann [Hopkins], a story editor at Tomorrow, and my assistant, Maggie [Nedder], came with me, and Maggie's sister, Kate Forte, who'd come in one Christmas to wrap presents and stayed. Kate's now head of Oprah Winfrey's production company, Harpo Films.

"I had a strange confidence that if I could just get *Miss All-American Beauty* made it would be all right," says Rees. "But the network resisted. They had entrenched ideas about whom they would do business with. I had no studio or other production company to support me. Steve Mills was the head of the network. Peter Frankovich, an executive at CBS with whom I had worked, liked *American Beauty*. They were nice guys, but it got back to me that I had to put up a bond of a hundred thousand dollars more than business affairs had asked. I said okay. I just kept saying okay, okay, and still nothing came out of business affairs.

"One day Peter took me to lunch. 'Marian, they're just not going to order a picture from a woman whose company has no more than what you're offering.'

"'That's all I have,' I said, '*and* my ability to make a picture.'

"'I know that, but they're not going to do it. For them it's a risk they won't take.'

"'I'm not going to give up, Peter, so go back and tell them that that's not good enough.'

"It was simply not acceptable," Rees says. "If you take that, then you capitulate, you accept that as the way it is. That was not compatible with who I am as a person. Also, I was angry. Anger doesn't solve the problem, but it can motivate. Life isn't fair but you still have to set the terms on which you're going to live it. In that sense, you make your own destiny. I just couldn't think of giving up. That wasn't a good enough reason. Giving up wasn't going to change my gender, or change the rules. If I gave up, nothing would change."

But CBS wasn't budging. No order to start the film came out of business affairs, even though she'd agreed to all their terms.

"I resorted to prayer," says Rees. "It was Christmastime. I was sitting at my window in my new office on Radford. I could see the CBS administrative building across the way, and I meditated on them changing their mind."

On December 23, Steve Mills called her. "Marian, go make your goddamn picture."[152]

Miss All-American Beauty, starring Diane Ladd and Cloris Leachman, came in on schedule and $60,000 under budget. *Miss All-American Beauty* aired in December 1982. Rees's next production was *Between Friends*, starring Elizabeth Taylor and Carol Burnett.[153] Through the 1980s and 1990s, MRA made twenty-six pictures. *Love Is Never Silent* (1985) was produced with Dorothea Petrie; it was written by Darlene Craviotto. It was the story of a young woman (Mare Winningham) torn between her duties to her deaf parents and her desire to make her own way in a hearing world. They used deaf actors to play the leads, portraying the parents; CBS was reluctant, but finally approved. It won two Emmys—Outstanding Drama and Best Director (Joe Sargent)—and the Christopher Award, and appeared in film festivals all over the world.[154]

Society expected women to marry and have children and serve the community, an ethic particularly strong in Iowa, where Rees grew up.

"That expectation was unspoken and pervasive," says Rees. "I was the first woman in our family to go on to college. The year between high school and college, I worked for a businessman in town, one of the pillars of the community. I taught his kids to swim and kept the books in his business. I mentioned to him that I was saving my money to go to the university.

" 'You can't do that,' he said. 'No daughter of mine will ever go to college.'

"He was absolutely serious. 'If you were my daughter, you would not plan on that, nor would I give you my permission.'

"I knew I didn't have to have his permission, but I had always known 'the attitude.' That was what was unspoken. He was more honest than other people, and his girls did not go to college. But I liked school. I liked the sense of ideas being so powerful . . . positive or negative. Some were repugnant, like my first encounter with racism. Didn't have any of that in my family or my church.

"I audited courses at the university. One guest lecturer was Dr. Howard Thurman, a renowned theologian. I had two jobs, one at the dorm and one as a waitress. We lived in Quonset huts. There wasn't enough housing. I'd come home from my shift and sit on the stoop of this Quonset hut in the early evening. It was my first time away from home. I was so homesick, I'd sit and cry and cry before anybody came back. I began to notice a man taking a stroll. It was Dr. Thurman. His black face tilted up, he clenched a pipe between his teeth, and we began to acknowledge that he was walking and I was sitting. Sometime later I mentioned my awe of this man, what his lectures had brought to my life, and I learned that he had to take a trolley twenty-five miles outside Iowa City to Cedar Rapids to get his hair cut because he was black. In that instant, the world changed for me. It affected me and it's affected all my work."[155]

Women Are Seen as Less Threatening

Patricia Finnegan began producing after she'd raised four children. She formed a production company with her husband, William, in the mid-1970s with two employees, Patricia and Bill. She had "kept her hand in," but had not produced before. Bill had been working professionally for years on series like *Dr. Kildaire* and *Hawaii Five-O* as second assistant, then first, then production manager, then producer. "He didn't come out of nowhere like I did," says Patricia. "When we began this company, I was suspect because I was a woman, the wife of a veteran producer.

The attitude was, 'She's just tagging along.' It was obvious. I knew it was there, I knew I had to prove myself. I made no excuses, I just charged forward.

"I didn't just walk in as a partner-producer. I started typing and answering the phone and sending out proposals," Finnegan says. "When we got our first movie, *Big Hawaii*, I worked as a production coordinator, then as an associate producer on *Danger in Paradise*. I worked my way from the ground up until I felt I knew what I was doing, as opposed to pretending. I never felt I had to prove my ability to Bill. He's unique among men. He doesn't feel competitive toward his wife or toward women in general."[156] Their partnership works, she says, because they are totally separate—she does movies for television, and he does films. One of her first was *The Ordeal of Patty Hearst*.

"I felt being a woman helped me because women are seen as less threatening. When a man knows he's going to deal with a woman, he relaxes. The competition isn't there. Bill has a strong personality; he's tougher than I am. I'm a peacemaker. He will say, 'Absolutely not, no way, and dah, dah, dah.' I tend to see ways to work it out."

Finnegan says her most difficult production was a miniseries in France, *King of the Olympics*, financed by RAI in Italy, SFP in France (the French nationally owned studios), and Frank Agrama, representing Harmony Gold Productions in the U.S. "It was a can of worms like you couldn't believe, with everybody sneaking around undermining everybody else." Crew work rules and habits are different in different countries. They shot in France with French crews. "I felt the head of the SFP hated American film people," says Finnegan, "particularly women in positions of power. Instead of being a help to me, I found him a total hindrance, continually trying to set me against the director and the director against me. He'd say to me, 'Oh, sorry, I'm French. You Americans are the only people who know how to make movies.' The director, Lee Phillips, an American, was very good. I had x number of days to do the job and I just plowed ahead."

Finnegan produced and executive-produced about twenty-nine movies for television in the 1980s and 1990s; five were miniseries. During those years, she began to see that women handle production problems differently than men.

"A woman goes around a production and looks for where trouble might erupt," says Finnegan. "Maybe the set decorator and the production designer can't get along. As a woman, assuming both those positions are men, I may try to make peace by listening to both sides. Women tend to be nurturing. We listen to problems as opposed to saying, 'Go do your job.' Most people just want someone to listen to them. Of course, all good producers, men and women, do what's necessary to get the film finished. But women, I've found, do something more. Another producer I know was on location with a very difficult star and went to the gym with her every day. The producer had no time at all to go to the gym, but she recognized that she had to do whatever kept the production moving. I think men have a problem with that. What they might see as demeaning to their position, a woman doesn't; she'll just do it to get the job done.

"I had an actress who was on a shoot for one day but she had an important part. We'd paid for a certain house for that day. The woman got the flu. It was ten in the morning and I was the one taking a tray with tea and toast to her dressing room, encouraging her to get through it. 'I know you can do it. Drink your tea and eat your toast and you'll be okay.' The poor thing was terribly sick but we got through the day and she was very good. I don't think a man would walk into a trailer with a tray of tea and toast for a day player. If she had not been able to go on, it would cost a day's work. What was I going to do? I didn't have the location for another day, if she couldn't get through that day. That's an advantage women have. Their ego does not get in the way. I've done it and seen it over and over again, and heard stories just like it from other female producers. Also, we can say things to a DP or a director that might sound insulting if they came from a man. It's true a woman can do everything a man can do, but a man can't do everything a woman can do."

In the 1980s, barriers against women were being dismantled, a wall falling from its own weight, others coming apart slowly, stone by stone. "Those barriers," says Finnegan, "are still coming down. It's not yet equal. There is still resistance to handing over a twenty-million-dollar miniseries to a woman."[157]

Talk About Glass Ceilings, We Hadn't Gotten Past the Floorboards Yet

Gayle Maffeo also describes herself as a peacemaker. "That's the way I grew up. It's my challenge to try to keep everybody happy and on an even keel to get the job done," she says. That got harder in 1988 when she was one of the producers for *Roseanne*, a show so hot it was like producing *Platoon*, the aggressively funny, blue-collar family-war sitcom.

"We just knew *Roseanne* was going to be a success," says Maffeo. "It was terribly exciting. Looking back, I tended to have in my work some challenging relationships with women. Because I like to keep the peace—I really enjoyed Nell Carter on *Gimme a Break!* It was a difficult time for her and we had to spend some time working things out. But I never had much trouble because I was always willing to step back. It wasn't my spotlight. *Roseanne*—that was a challenge every step of the way, the physical production and the personalities. Roseanne and I are two people who would not necessarily meet or associate with each other socially. We did not have easy communication. I'm proud we got it launched and on the air. Everything in this business is done with partners in one way or another. This partnership did not work. I made it through the first thirteen episodes and then I left to work with Matt Williams [the show's creator]."[158]

The next year, she began an eight-year run as producer of an entirely different kind of show, *Home Improvement.* Its creators were Matt Williams, David McFadden, and Carmen Finestra.

Like Patricia Finnegan, Maffeo has a charming, down-to-earth style. You want to start talking about your relatives or endangered species or the "terrible twos"—just about anything.

Maffeo started as a secretary at CBS in New York in the 1960s. "My first question to them was, 'Can I produce your TV shows?' They said, 'Can you type and take shorthand?' " She ended up in the secretarial pool in the programming department. Her boss was a woman. "She set an example for me in a negative way because she was so terrified that anyone would know her personally. She wanted power and respect. I couldn't call her by her first name. She had me typing until all hours because I had to make sure there were absolutely no mistakes in her correspondence. I used to cry over my typewriter, sobbing 'This isn't what I got into this business for.' I decided that I never wanted anyone to feel negative about working with a woman. I sure wanted it to be a level playing field. I feel sorry for her now."

Maffeo moved up to script supervisor, worked on *The Perry Como Show,* and met her husband, Neil, an associate director at ABC. They moved to California; she had children in the 1970s and tried to be a Woodland Hills housewife. "I'd disappear for six weeks and do script supervising on a show and then come back. I still wanted to be a producer." A friend asked her to associate-produce a half-hour pilot—*A New Kind of Family*, starring Eileen Brennan, produced by Jane Eisner and Margie Gordon.

"We had the support of two powerful men in the industry, their husbands, Michael Eisner and producer Larry Gordon," Maffeo says. "But those two women *were* producing their show, though nobody believed that and no one gave them credit for it. When the *L.A. Times Calendar* reporter came out to do an article, everybody got really excited, but the article slammed them, stating the only reason they were having any success was due to their powerful husbands." Women have used their husbands' contacts and friends for access, but after getting the opening shot, they have to deliver the goods.

"This was 1979, 1980," says Maffeo. "Talk about glass ceilings—we hadn't gotten past the floorboards yet. Later, I also discovered I wasn't being paid as much as the guys for the same job. You see, most women in our industry didn't know one another. We were isolated. We had no way to network, no support system."

After *A New Kind of Family*, which lasted one season, Maffeo produced all through the 1980s—*Mary* for MTM with Mary Tyler Moore, *Head of the Class* for Warner Bros.—and became the executive in charge of production for the much-praised *Buffalo Bill*, starring Dabney Coleman. Then came *Roseanne* and *Home Improvement*. "After the run of every show, I asked myself, did we see something real? Did the show make a difference?

"*Roseanne* was about a blue-collar worker in a dysfunctional family," says Maffeo. "*Home Improvement* was based on the men's movement. It was a functional family, and the issues we dealt with went from vasectomies to children's health to realistic drug problems. We tried out new technology, including high-definition television. For a videotaped audience show, we did numerous locations off the stage, outside the studio, which hadn't been done in situation comedy. We also used different types of camera techniques."

In the 1970s, Maffeo never "tooted her own horn" because it made her uncomfortable. She sees that as inherently female. "We always stood back. Today, we have many options. We are the only ones who can restrict our destiny.

"My daughter wants a career in entertainment, and she's worked on the set, physically pushing and pulling. She can wield a hammer and a drill better than many of the guys, negotiate talent deals, and intelligently evaluate scripts. She'll move through her career differently. *We* definitely had to fight for it. We were not entitled. Our challenge was always this: were we going to become malelike when we fought for it, or were we going to maintain our femininity? As time went on, sometimes it became an advantage to be a woman. Nothing stands in my daughter's way. I only leashed myself. Many of us didn't realize we had so many choices."[159]

• • ▪

In the early 1980s, AfterSchool Specials on television became a province, some said ghetto, for women producers. They were low-budget productions for young television audiences, shot in 16mm, and made on tight schedules.

I Don't Have to Do All Those Things I Was Taught to Do

"Not many women came out of motion pictures or thirty-five millimeter shoots," says Joanne Curley-Kerner. "Most came out of television . . . Those specials taught me everything because there was no money and we were dealing with kids and animals. It's a tough way to shoot, but you got the essentials down."[160]

Show business can be dangerous work. "We worked with everything from rattlesnakes to cougars to horses," Kerner says. "The scariest time was *Charlie and the Great Balloon Chase*. We were working with a balloon every day. They fly early in the morning or early evening when there's no wind. Actor Jack Albertson was in the basket with a pilot who was down out of sight. We had wires attached to the basket. The balloon was going up slowly, slowly, slowly, and suddenly I heard somebody say 'Oh, shit.' A wire had snapped. The next second, the other wire snapped, and there goes Jack in Pasadena, just going up. Thank God the pilot was in there. After a real nail-biter struggle, they landed in the middle of a thoroughbred pasture."

Kerner came from Connecticut, where, she says, she was brought up to belong to the country club, marry the doctor, and have five kids. She graduated from high school in 1959. "My parents wouldn't let me go to college, that was the thinking then, and it made me rebel. Okay, I'm not going to get married and have five kids and live in Connecticut. I'm going to have a career. I had no idea that I would end up in Hollywood, producing."

She got a job in New York as a secretary for an advertising firm. "I remember sitting in my cubbyhole, underlining *The Feminine Mystique*," Kerner says. "It just totally changed my life. I quit the Junior League. I became a Democrat. I started wearing blue jeans. I moved down to the Village. I can still see myself in that cubicle saying, 'I don't have to do all those things I was taught to do.' We remember so few moments that clearly. It was an absolute defining moment for me."

In another part of New York City, Sybil Niden Goldrich had just arrived home from the hospital with her new baby.

"I had bought a book called *The Feminine Mystique*. I have one little child, just two, crawling around the floor, and a brand new infant laying on the bed with me as I read *The Feminine Mystique*, and I could not stop crying. Jimmy, my husband, walked in and says, 'What's the matter?' I said, 'Did you know that I had *rights*?' And he said, 'Of course I did.' I said, 'Then why didn't you tell me?' That book changed my life. I knew that being a mother was going to be my life, but I was going to always have film, too. I had to. It was a real necessity for me. The first chance I could I went back to school."[161]

In the late 1960s, Kerner worked as an advertising copywriter "because women were writers then, not producers." She came to Los Angeles with a friend, Fran Sears, who was producing a commercial, stayed, started her own copywriting business, but disliked it because she was "a people person." She forced herself to write in her tiny office every day. Her friend in New York returned to film another spot.

"It was for Meow Mix, and I had to convince Tiffany's to stay open because they had a bowl we wanted to use. I convinced them. Solving problems with different kinds of people was such fun that I sold my typewriter." In a month, through Sears and Danny Wilson Productions in New York, she began producing the new television fare, AfterSchool Specials.

"If the crews know that *you* know what you're doing, they're fabulous," she says. "We had a crew that we used for these AfterSchool Specials, the nicest guys. One time we were in Kern County on the Kern River, and we were shooting a little Indian boy in a canoe going, God help us, down the rapids. All the grips and everybody got poison ivy from pulling cable. I had calamine lotion and stuff flown up from L.A., and they dropped trou, all the guys, and Frannie and I just sprayed them. It was beyond male-female. These guys were really in pain."

By the 1980s, Kerner, around forty, was married to Bruce Kerner, a producer, and had two very young children. "I felt I had to get into sitcoms or soaps because the mom really can't travel," she says. "That reality certainly shaped my career." At the time, however, she'd only worked on low-budget AfterSchool Specials. Her husband told her he'd heard Paramount needed someone who knew children's shows. When the sitcom *Webster* had to go on location to a park in the San Fernando Valley, Kerner saw it as an opportunity that fit her new needs as a working mother. She had to start all over again at a lower production level and move up. Never mind; she took the job as an associate production executive to handle that particular episode. The experience was an eye-opener.

"For an AfterSchool Special, we had one five-ton and two vans. On this thing, I had thirteen five-tons, I had teamsters, but no petty cash to bribe the gardeners. 'What are you going to do with the mow-blow-and-go guys?' I kept asking. I had to use my own money to bribe people to help us out." That show led to another, *Mr. President*, also on the Paramount lot. She signed on as associate producer, then took over as supervising producer. Then she was fired.

"I think that exec fired me because I'd tell him what something would really cost and he didn't want to hear it. Costs are pretty finite. He'd say, 'How much is that going to cost?' I'd tell him, like eight thousand five hundred and twelve dollars. He'd scream and yell."[162]

Kerner says being fired was "wonderful" because a new sitcom, *A Different World*, was looking for a producer. Ann Beattes, the head writer, got her an interview with the producers—Tom Werner, Marcy Carsey, and Caryn Mandabach. Kerner had never produced a sitcom. It was quite a different proposition.

"Basically the bottom line is to keep it all going smoothly, compared to 'you have this much money and in six months it's over.' On a sitcom, you never know whether it's going to be over or not. It took me a while to realize that the budget wasn't the most important thing; the family of the show was. So I stumbled a bit, but Tom and Marcy were great." *A Different World* (1987–93), a spin-off of *The Cosby Show*, starring Lisa Bonet, was produced by Yvette Lee Bowser for Carsey-Werner. Neema Barnette, Debbie Allen, and Ellen Falcon were among the women who directed episodes, though most of the directors were men.

Kerner moved to *Grace Under Fire*, then to *Cosby*, both for the Carsey-Werner Company—all because she wanted to spend more time at home with her children. "A while ago," says Kerner, "I told my daughter, who is fourteen, 'Maybe after *Cosby*, I'll retire and do my garden.' She said, 'Mom, Mom, you can't do that! What will I tell people you do?' Jeez, I thought, a stay-at-home mother is a kind of disgrace. How could I even *think* about doing that? It was hysterical."[163]

What a resounding change in the business in the 1980s for women like Kerner. They made no secret they were also raising small children. From the days of young development execs hiding pictures of their kids, children were out of the closet.

You Can Have It All But You Can't Have It All at the Same Time

"Along the yellow brick road," says writer-producer Georgia Jeffries, "it was women who read and responded to my material. But at that time, very few women were in positions of authority, so the women I met would take me as far as they could. Ultimately, a man would decide to hire me or approve the material or send me to the final level, the end of the yellow brick road, which led to the wizard behind the curtains. The wizard was always a man, too. It was impossible to enter the inner sanctum of success without the male stamp of approval. But for all the wizards, you have to open the curtain yourself, and you did that by the kind of work you were creating."[164]

That analogy works for both men and women dealing with the illusion of the business. "We walk into it with such dreams," says Jefferies, "immature illusions about how fast we'll move or even how business is conducted, and we learn along the way.

"The best lesson I learned was that you have no control," Jeffries says. "You only have the power to say no to work that you know will not reflect your strongest character and talent. No matter how many projects you want to do, or how many people you want to work with, you don't have control. You *do* know what you want to be associated with and you know what you don't want to be associated with. The essence of 'power' is discernment. Know what you want and what you're willing to risk to get it."

Jeffries was writing spec scripts and articles for *American Film*. She was married (her husband, Michael, worked for his family-run company) and had two small children when she got her first staff position on *Cagney & Lacey* in 1984. The route to it went like this: an independent producer, Richard Hellman, was making a CBS movie-of-the-week starring Jaclyn Smith. He'd read an article about sexual harassment in the armed forces. Through a mutual friend, ICM agent trainee Charlotte Flynn, he met with Jeffries to ask if she thought there was a screenplay in it. "Instantly, I knew there was," she says. The script she wrote was called *Nobody's Fool*.[165] It was never made but it led to the wizard, Barney Rosenzweig, producer of *Cagney & Lacey*.

In 1983, Jeffries was producing the Women in Film Crystal Awards program, which had become a big event. Phil Fehrle, vice president of Tomorrow Entertainment, Jeffries's guest at the Crystals, told her he'd just met a talented young BBC producer, Nikki Marvin, and asked if Georgia could help her.

"I met with Nikki, who has since gone on to produce *The Shawshank Redemption*," says Jeffries. "I introduced her to three people I knew, set up lunches for her, but—no job offer. Meanwhile, through her own connections she got a job as executive assistant to Barney Rosenzweig. She told me 'Barney would love your work,' so I sent him *Nobody's Fool*. Months passed, no word. Nikki went on to a new job. In May 1984, I get a call from my agent. Barney had read my script and he wanted me to do an episode.

"Lisa Seidman (later a writer for *Knot's Landing*), was the secretary who took Nikki's place with Barney. Lisa had found my 'lost' script on a slush pile, read it, gave it to Barney, and said 'This woman should be on staff.' I have so many links in the chain, primarily female, but there were important men along the way, including Phil Fehrle, who believed in the power of female networking, and Barney, the wizard himself. Only he had the power to hire me for that show. When I first went on staff for *Cagney & Lacey*, I worked primarily with men—ironic, considering the show."

During Jeffries's second year on *Cagney & Lacey*, the show won the Emmy for Best Drama Series, Sharon Gless won her first Emmy, and Jeffries was nominated for writing as well as producing the show. "The third season I was there was our strongest creatively; we brought in writer-producers Shelley List and Jonathan Estrin, and we had a great staff that year, half male and half female." When Jeffries won her first Writers Guild award for a *Cagney & Lacey* script ("An Unusual Occurrence"), she thanked Barbara Corday and Barbara Avedon, the cocreators of the show, the actors, and Rosenzweig. "I said, 'His ego is exceeded only by his talent.' Barney loved it. A former producer of the show," Jeffries says, "had warned me Barney was 'evil.' Clearly, he intimidated some staff members. I think he sometimes abused his power, but I worked with many people who abused their power. In fact every project and series I've worked on, men and women have abused power. There's a fine line between talent and tyranny we all have to be careful not to cross.

"I once told Barney that the characters of *Cagney & Lacey* were the best part of him. He personally identified with those characters and passionately wanted outstanding work for the show. In a sense, I think he became a 'feminist' because of his fierce commitment to these fictional female heroines, and he did empower a lot of women in front of and behind the camera. In that sense, Barney was totally committed to equal opportunity. He tolerated female challenges to his authority from a benevolent paternalistic viewpoint. Males were not given that leeway. By the time I left the show, I felt Barney and I shared a hard-earned mutual respect. We learned to serve each other's work in a way that transcended gender, and for that I'll always be grateful."[166]

Women all over town were eager to be associated with the few women who were visible then, like Marcy Carsey and Diane English and Linda Bloodworth-Thomason. "There were so few," says Jeffries, "but the most

visible women often weren't that interested in joining women's organizations—they were too busy moving up the traditional hierarchical route
internally, which meant they dealt exclusively with the men in power.
They didn't necessarily take time to broaden their net and bring in other
women with them. But some did. Marcy Gross and Ann Weston, the
producers [*A Place for Annie, Invisible Child*], hired me for my first network rewrite. Loreen Arbus, one of my first supporters, was a vice president at ABC who encouraged producer Viva Knight to option my
treatment, which got me into the Writers Guild. Women like those were
not stars but well-known professionals who took risks. It didn't serve
their careers to reach out to unknown women like me, but they had a
commitment to something larger, they knew they were dealing internally with all the struggles being women, and they wanted to support
other women. They knew that only more women in the workplace would
make things better. They were astutely taking a longer view."

Jeffries was told that she was the first mother hired on *Cagney & Lacey*.
Barbara Corday, the cocreator, was a mother, but didn't have toddlers
as Jefferies did, and anyway, Corday was head of Columbia Television
and not actively involved in the day-to-day running of the show. Tyne
Daly was a mother, but she was the star.

"Steve Brown, a producer then, considered a mother who was a writer-
producer as kind of unique," says Jeffries. "He thought I could bring
extra elements of real-life experience to the character of Lacey, which
was absolutely true. Tyne Daly often asked me to write 'mother
speeches' for her character.

"One agent, whom I'd known as an executive, submitted a script from
one of her writers. We hired the writer. The agent asked me to lunch.
I said, 'I'm glad we're working together now, but I never felt I had much
support from you before.'

"She said, 'You're right, and I'll tell you the truth. When I met you,
I didn't think you'd be particularly important in the business because,
number one, you were blond.' I wasn't blond. I think I had highlights.
'Number two, you lived in the Valley, and you were a housewife.' I was
a mother and I had two young children, and even though I was working
as a journalist, she saw Valley and children and pegged me as a housewife. 'Number three, you were older.' I was twenty-eight.

"I was incredulous. She'd adopted the worst male prejudices of the
business. That's an example how in the mid-1980s women felt—they
had to outmale the men to get ahead. They had to be tougher, meaner,
more demanding, less compassionate, because any perceived weakness
could destroy their careers."

Though being a woman was an advantage on that show, it took her longer to reach the heftier salaries offered to men. The breakthrough was in 1989, when she had a choice between being a supervising producer on *China Beach* or *L.A. Law*. Either show meant even longer hours away from her children. She took *China Beach*, the other big dramatic show about women in the 1980s.

"It differed stylistically from *Cagney & Lacey*," says Jeffries. "We could take more creative chances." As always, she brought her parenting skills with her.

"The nature of television and film is very much about allaying the anxiety of the powers that be," Jeffries says. "Everybody is terrified when they go into production. It's like mounting an army for battle. For executives and line producers, it's often about the bottom line; the actors are often fearful they'll look foolish. What best prepared me for being a producer—not a writer but a producer—was being a parent. I was constantly parenting the people I was dealing with, soothing, listening, comforting. On *Tin Wife*, a USA film starring Anne Archer, I was the sole executive producer. The first week of the shoot, the line producer was very upset with the director and pressures from the production company. I took him out for a long walk and talk. By the time we came back, he was calmer. It turned the energy around for the rest of the shoot. He and I were aligned. The point is, I used my parenting skills. It's a female talent, and as females we're taught to have radar, to be hypersensitive to our environment. That always served me very well."

Jeffries's husband had resigned his position to be the primary parent for five years while she dealt with demanding series hours, first on *Cagney*, then on *China Beach*. She says, "My career became my third child. It needed nurturing and development. In the early 1980s, working on the first treatment which got me into the Writers Guild, I delivered my second script to my agent, Bernie Weintraub, and I was carrying my baby son with me, Patrick, who started drooling all over his expensive Oriental carpet. Fortunately, Bernie was a dad with a sense of humor, though he said I was the first client to deliver a script with a baby in tow. Many more women are still struggling to have both worlds. You can have it all, but you can't have it all at the same time. I believe that deep in my bones." By 1993, Jeffries needed more balance and gradually focused her career energies away from the all-consuming series schedules to cable movies so that, as an agent once told her, "You have a life."[167]

Not Making It Was Not an Option

Fern Field did not have children. She went where her interests led her, and in the 1980s, she was on a roll. She had started as a secretary to a producer of *Maude*, produced a documentary on employing the handicapped, produced the sitcom *The Baxters*, was the supervising executive on *Facts of Life*, then coproduced movies for television like *Eleanor, First Lady of the World* in 1982.

At Tandem Entertainment, Field worked with Virginia Carter, a vice president. "Virginia and I were a perfect combination," says Field, "because when she was crazed I was calm, and when I was calm she was crazed. If I wanted to direct, I said so. She said, 'Okay, direct.' Norman Lear would have said the same thing."[168] Famously, Carter had a large illustrated poster on the wall of her office: "A woman needs a man like a fish needs a bicycle."

Production was shifting away from Los Angeles to Canada, to Europe. Field, born in Italy of Russian parents, took the Embassy Television miniseries *Kane and Abel* to New York, Toronto, and France in 1984. It starred Peter Strauss and Sam Neill and was shot on location in fifteen weeks. She, too, describes it as a war.

"There was friction between the executive producers, the producers, and Buzz Kulik, the director, who was lovely until he started shooting and delightful as soon as he finished shooting. Buzz was used to the studio system—the director in the trenches with his armed camp versus the enemy studio. As soon as he started to roll camera, I became the enemy. I had never been cast in that role before. The director was the general, commanding the army, and I was a general, too," she says, "when I needed to be."

Field began as a coddled child raised in Europe. "My father was always served first at my home. He never carried a package. I was raised with the 'you need to be taken care of.' And I hated it. I have never let anybody take care of me, which is also a loss. I was a latchkey child—except who knew? We didn't have a name for it. My upbringing did not give me any confidence. I did not feel I could achieve my dreams.

"When I was in my thirties, I flew my mother from Italy to visit me in New York. She's looking at my little apartment and says, 'I never thought you could do it.' That was a turning point in my life, because from then on I didn't have to prove that I could take care of myself. I could accept help.

"My mother," Field says, "really believed that had she been a man born in this country she would have been president of the United States.

She felt handicapped being a woman. She always worked; she was successful and very smart. The legacy I got from my parents was that 'not
making it was not an option.' They had to leave Russia during the
Revolution, then they left Germany, then they left France, then they left
Italy—they were always starting from scratch and they were always
making it. The first time my mother went into business she arrived in
a brand-new country, rented a tiny store, put her fur coat in the window,
and became one of the top fur designers in Milan. So not making it was
not an option."[169]

Field says she was lucky to start out working with people like Norman
Lear and Virginia Carter. Other women were just as lucky, but some
were not. Helen Hayes is often quoted as saying, "The hardest years in
life are those between ten and seventy." Most women directors in the
next chapter would instantly agree.

14

A DIFFERENT TAKE ON THE SET

Since that November day in 1980 when the DGA Women's Steering Committee announced the shockingly minuscule number of women who were directing—0.2 percent in film and television since 1950—the number, by 1986, had shot up to a whopping 5 percent.[170]

"The kind of strength needed to direct has nothing to do with brute force," said Norman Lear, commenting in 1986 on the limited opportunities for women directors. "It has to do with strength of character. A deeper voice does not a director make."[171] Dawn Steel, still president of production at Paramount in 1986, said, "It's about talent, not lawsuits. I don't want to be in the position where I thought I got the job because I was a woman. No other woman wants to be in that position either."[172]

Michelle Manning said, when the first feature she directed, *Blue City*, bombed: "I'm not a war criminal. I don't think many directors' first films are perfect . . . You're under a microscope [as a woman director]. You suddenly become a media event for no good reason."[173]

In 1983, all the studios and most independent production companies had agreed to negotiate remedies to "alleged" discrimination against women and minorities in areas of production covered by the DGA.[174] The guild called for goals and timetables to establish minimum hiring levels, the "teeth" to make affirmative action plans work. Many welcomed the threat of a lawsuit to force producers to open interviews for directors to women. Nothing much came of these efforts, and in 1986 the Directors Guild dropped its threat of litigation. It was not about to sue the heavy hitters who hired their members. Very gradually, a few more women began directing. By 1992, a new DGA report showed that women worked 8 percent of the total 49,368 days worked by all directors in 1991; African-American directors worked 818 days, or 1.7 percent, of the total days worked.[175]

A year later, *Variety* reminded the industry: "Women Still Outside

TV's Top Ranks." Despite gains seven years into the decade by women in television, the industry remained "guilty of pervasive bias that keeps women from working at the top jobs" in top-rated television programs.[176] The National Committee on Working Women (NCWW) in Washington, D.C. had published a study, "Prime Time Power," citing the best and worst shows for women directors, producers, and writers. One of the worst was *Murder, She Wrote*, which had no women working in any of those capacities; some of the best were *L.A. Law, My Sister Sam,* and *Dynasty*.[177]

For women directors, the 1980s were much like the 1970s. Maybe a little less hostile.

I Gave Up My Career as a Script Supervisor!

"The first couple of days I directed, I was thinking, 'Why did I want to do this? This is insane,'" Randa Haines recalls. The drama for public television was a kind of "road show" about Elizabeth Cady Stanton and Susan B. Anthony campaigning through Kansas in the 1860s for women's suffrage. *Under the Sky* had no budget and no two scenes in the same place. "We were shooting 'Kansas' in Rhode Island in the middle of winter. We had to shoot a lot of low angles against the sky to try to avoid frozen lakes because it was supposed to be summer in Kansas. Ice crunched under our feet. I kept thinking. 'This is so hard! What am I doing here? I gave up my career as a script supervisor! I could have been perfectly happy.' About the third day, something clicked and I suddenly realized, 'Yes! I see why I wanted to do this.'

"Everything I'd ever been interested in, all the little projects I'd made in my room when I was a child, decorating, telling stories, reading, dancing, daydreaming, were suddenly useful to me. Every director comes with a different background, a different set of ingredients. As a child I was quiet and withdrawn; I observed and watched. On that shoot, I felt for the first time I had a creative outlet for all that stuff I'd seen and made. When I collapsed in my bed at night every cell in my body had been useful to me. That was the first time I'd felt that way. I was really proud when—even though we had this tiny budget, shooting in Rhode Island—a reviewer commented on the 'John Ford exteriors of the west.' Yes!"[178]

Haines directed a second show for PBS, *The Jilting of Grammy Weatherall*, part of the American Short Stories series. Then nothing, the drought. She didn't work for two years, though she was offered a couple of teen movies, "the only movies women were directing." Haines couldn't relate to them. "I didn't go to the proms, I didn't know how to make a movie about a prom. I gambled and turned things down that weren't right for me. It was a very scary time."

People who know Haines talk about the clear picture she has of what she wants to do, and she herself speaks about her perseverance and commitment, but during this period, "I'd wake up crying in the morning. I'd been crying in my sleep in despair," says Haines. "But I'd get up, make phone calls, go to meetings, do what I had to do to make my career happen. Yet I was in a kind of mourning when I thought about what I'd done to my life."

She was "making the rounds," showing her PBS film around town, when she met Paula Wagner, an agent at the time (now a producer, C/W Productions, *Mission Impossible I & II*). Wagner had seen Haines's film and liked it. "She told me she knew these really interesting guys doing this new TV show," says Haines. "At a party, she shoved me in a corner with a guy called Greg Hoblit. The new show he was working on, which hadn't aired yet, was called *Hill Street Blues*. Poor guy, it was so awkward, he had to talk to me. 'Yeah, yeah, I'll see your film,' he said. He and [Steven] Bochco both looked at it, and Bob Butler, who'd directed the pilot and created the whole look of *Hill Street Blues*. Bob said he thought what I'd done in the film was 'surefooted,' and I think he had a lot to do with them considering me, because the film I was showing around was the polar opposite to *Hill Street*.

"It was one of those unusual cases of people having the imagination to say if she was good at this, she might also be good at that," says Haines. "Usually, people say, 'We have a chicken in our film. You've never directed a chicken, so we don't know if you can really do it.' "

Hill Street Blues burst on television January 15, 1981, a new kind of police drama, shocking, sharp, sometimes funny, always human. Every episode started with roll call at seven A.M. and ended at night after a day of passion, insult, heartbreak, and fear in the decaying neighborhood of the precinct with its diverse characters inside and outside the station.

"It was the first episodic show I'd ever done," says Haines. But she had worked on crews as a script supervisor. They had been her family for seven years, she respected what they did, and, she says, "I knew their jokes."

"The style of *Hill Street Blues* was six pages of dialogue in one elaborate dolly shot," Haines says. "It was very complicated staging with characters walking in and out, combining different scenes into one long camera move around that great set. That was another first, for me—the resources, the equipment, the crew, the time, and the set all designed to be able to do something wonderful and complicated. I was so excited about making that first shot that I looked at the dolly grip, like 'Isn't this great?' Then I realized he did this every day. I'm just a captain who has jumped on for the week and next week some other guy will be in here going, 'Wow, isn't this great?' Episodic television is a train that keeps rolling."

A woman director on a hit show in 1981 was a true novelty. People were constantly coming up to Haines and saying, "I've never worked with a woman director before. This is really interesting, this is nice." At one point, the experienced script supervisor and Haines were in the ladies' room. The woman looked at Haines and said, "This is the first time I've ever been in the bathroom with the director."[179]

In 1983, Haines began shooting a movie for television, *Something About Amelia*. Deborah Aal, who headed development at the Leonard Goldberg Company (she would soon be president), had met Haines two years before. Aal had developed the *Amelia* story and was looking for a director. She thought of Haines even though Haines had never done a movie for television.

"My agent said, 'I'm sending this script to your house. It's about incest,'" Haines says. "I thought, God, it's going to be a sleazy exploitation. I didn't want to read it. I was standing in my kitchen making a cup of tea, looking at the first page. I never moved. I read the entire script standing in my kitchen. It was written by William Hanley, the kind of great writing where the characters are not saying what they mean. They're talking about the weather but really they're talking about something much more complex. It's all subtext. The Goldberg Company was nervous about the project, but somehow between Deborah Aal and my agent they took a leap of faith, convinced the network, and I got the job."[180]

Something About Amelia brought incest out of America's closet. At the time, the public did not perceive that incest was widespread or that it occurred at all levels of society.

The television movie was a critical hit and widely covered in the press. Billie Jenkins, a vice president at the Goldberg Company, said, "After it aired, we got hundreds of letters and calls, and everyone was talking about it at work or in restaurants. I don't think I talked to one person who hadn't heard of that kind of experience from some friend or relative, but they'd never spoken about it before. It was mind-boggling."[181]

Ned Tannen, head of Paramount, had an award-winning play that had been in and out of development for years with various scripts, stars, and directors. It was called *Children of a Lesser God*. *Something About Amelia* had received so much attention that Tannen wanted to talk with Haines.

"The play's subtleties resisted all efforts to translate it into film," says

Haines. "I hadn't seen Mark Medoff's play, so I read it and saw how it could be a movie. I met with Ned and by the time I drove away from the studio and stopped at the 7-Eleven to call my agent about the meeting, Ned had already talked to him. I was hired."

Children of a Lesser God was about a teacher at a school for the deaf and a young hearing-impaired woman, a janitor. It was an unusual story of life and love, starring Marlee Matlin and William Hurt. "We got so many letters from people saying 'I saw it with my wife and for the first time in years we talked about our relationship, and decided to recommit to each other,' or decided to break up, or make it work," says Haines. "Some letters said the movie made them think about deaf people. Very gratifying.

"The real joy of directing to me is getting an image in my head while I'm reading the script," says Haines. "It's an image that seems to capture the essence of a moment, a visual metaphor that shows an emotion or the meaning without dialogue. That's incredibly exciting. It's just some little germ that grows into an idea that the cameraman embraces, the designer embraces, and then there it is on the screen! And it works and the audience gets it. Thrilling. I think movies are like collective dreams."[182]

Different People Tell the Story They Know Because They Live It

"Being a woman and an African-American director, well, the industry didn't quite know how to deal with me," says Neema Barnette, "and I felt I had to show them we *are* qualified, that we *can* do this."[183]

In New York, after directing the first of many plays, *The Blue Journey* for Joseph Papp's Public Theater, Papp suggested she enroll in the Third World Cinema program, where she produced *To Be a Man*, which won an Emmy.

"I didn't know what it meant," says Barnette. "Coming from a poor background, it didn't really hit me." Someone suggested she apply for the AFI Directing Workshop for Women in Los Angeles, but others warned it was "celebrity oriented," that she'd never get in. "My attitude was what the hell, I'll apply." AFI admitted her. She made a film called *Sky Captain*, about an urban and suicidal Peter Pan from the Bronx, which producer Fern Field saw in rough cut, without music. Field was searching for an African-American director for an AfterSchool Special, *One More Hurdle—The Donna Cheek Story*.

"I was so new and untested," says Barnette. "I'd never worked with a crew before. The first day the cameraman comes over to me and says, 'Where do you want the camera?' I looked around and said, 'Put it over there and let me look at it and if I don't like it I'll tell you to move it.' If he can play it off, I can play it off. I knew I had a sense of drama and storytelling from all my directing work in the theater. I learned film as I went along and studied on my own. I studied and studied." *One More Hurdle* won an NAACP Image Award and was nominated for a Daytime Emmy.

The Silent Crime, a documentary on domestic violence that received four Emmy nominations, got Barnette into the Directors Guild. Barnette sat down to organize her career. "I didn't really know anybody in L.A., but since I came from theater I decided to start with sitcoms." *What's Happening Now* let her observe, and a black director, Tony Singletary, opened his book and showed her how the shots were composed.

"The assistant to the producer," Barnette recalls, "an African-American woman, sent my reel to the head of Columbia Television, who ordered the sitcom to give me an episode. This was around 1986. I didn't know what a novelty I was. I also didn't know I wasn't supposed to say anything about the script. When I observed the other directors, I didn't understand why they were sitting there if the script wasn't working. Coming from theater, you're the boss and you have to take the script to the lab. Not in television."

Columbia Television learned from the Directors Guild that no African-American woman had ever directed a sitcom before. The studio planned a press release. "About two weeks later," says Barnette, laughing, "they changed their minds. They didn't want to make a big deal out of it because African-American women directing sitcoms should be an everyday thing."[184]

Barnette's *Sky Captain* was admitted into the Whitney Museum's New American Filmmakers series. Roland Jaffey, director of the museum, showed a copy of it to David Puttnam, the new president of Columbia Pictures. Puttnam, a well-known British producer (*Midnight Express*, *Chariots of Fire*), was promising films of social merit and lower budgets. Putnam liked offbeat movies and independent filmmakers. He suggested Barnette expand her sixty-five-minute *Sky Captain* into a feature, gave her a development deal for a feature she wanted to make (*Listen for the Fig Tree*), and nominated her for one of the four coveted slots in his New Directors Program at Columbia—young, multiethnic filmmakers. "We got an office at the studio and a secretary," says Barnette. "I still didn't have a clue. I was just moving along." She was seen as a talented director, a woman of color who would open doors for other women.

Frank's Place starred Tim Reid. She was hired to direct an episode. It was an offbeat comedy with a collection of eccentric characters who worked in or ate at a New Orleans Creole restaurant. It lasted two seasons, 1987–88, on CBS.

"The first morning I arrived," says Barnette, "I went up to an assistant director to ask him a question. He glanced at me and said, 'Yeah, you're the extra playing a prostitute. When are you going to get dressed?'

" 'What do you mean, get dressed?' I thought, okay, the AD's assumed I'm playing a prostitute, what's next?

" 'Yeah, yeah,' he said, 'you're dressed, that's funny. You better get over to Wardrobe.'

"You should have seen how red his face turned when the producer introduced me a little later as the director. It wasn't his fault. Nothing he'd ever read, seen, heard, or experienced would have taught him that the director could possibly be a black woman."[185] Barnette had a two-to-one shooting ratio, which means she shot efficiently. They gave her another episode.

Meanwhile, David Puttnam's sojourn as president of Columbia Pictures, part of the Coca-Cola empire, was in trouble. He wasn't producing any blockbusters. Over at Paramount, Dawn Steel, president of production, was not having an easy time either, though for quite different reasons. She had married Charles Roven and by 1986 she was pregnant. "Everything changed with the pregnancy . . ." she wrote. "Maybe they [Frank Mancuso and Ned Tannen, who ran the studio] had changed beforehand and I wasn't aware of it . . . But they didn't like me anymore. Period."[186]

Steel's words have an eerie echo. A decade before, Rosilyn Heller had also felt a studio chill when she became, as she says, "the first pregnant vice president."[187] Heller hadn't been head of production but was one of the first women to attain a vice presidency in 1974, which, with Renée Valente's and Ethel Winant's, had set off a mini chain reaction of other vice presidencies for women.

"One of the things that was used against me [by executives]" says Heller, was " 'Oh, of course, Rosilyn is still a great executive, but ever since she had her child she's mellowed.' Believe me," she says, deepening her voice, "I have never mellowed. It was a strategy of undermining me . . . 'mellowed' meant I didn't have that edge anymore."[188]

Ten years later, in her last months at Paramount, Steel thought she was being paranoid. "I felt surrounded by people plotting against me," she said. "Probably because they were . . . the gossip intensified." On the day her daughter was born, Paramount announced that Gary Lucchesi would be executive vice president, reporting "directly to [Ned] Tannen, which was a signal to the industry and to me that effectively I was no longer president of production."[189] She was there but she wasn't there, a time-honored Hollywood limbo.

A few months later, David Puttnam was dismissed and Dawn Steel became the first woman to be president of Columbia Pictures. She reveled in it, and her position was seen as another great stride forward for women, though it wasn't greeted with the hosannahs celebrating Sherry Lansing's capture of president of production at Fox in 1980. Certainly, Lansing was better liked; the stories in and out of the industry about Dawn Steel were riveting, but not all were true. More important, seven years had elapsed between these two achievements. It could now be seen that though one woman attained high position, it might not affect the industry's attitude toward women, nor would it greatly increase job access for them, which was moving at its own pace.

"She was one of a kind, a force of nature," says Hollace Davids, a publicist at Columbia Pictures who witnessed the transition from David Puttnam to Dawn Steel. "Very few of the movies Puttnam put into production made money. I remember him saying about one of them, 'This is either going to be really big or this is going to be disastrous.' It was a disaster. But he did have the foresight to pick up Bernardo Bertolucci's *The Last Emperor*, which won nine Academy Awards in 1988. But by that time, Puttnam was out and Dawn Steel was in." Davids was a senior publicist during this rocky period for Columbia, just before the studio was bought by Sony. Many people were fired; on top of her own work, Davids inherited most of the special projects work when that director left, but was not given a new title or more money.

"The day before the Oscars," Davids says, "there was a lot of buzz about *Last Emperor*. I was at Dawn's house in the kitchen about two A.M. after a party, and Dawn and her husband Chuck and I are standing there when I bring up the fact that even though I'm only a coordinator, not a director, I deserve to be made vice president. Dawn says something like, 'You're right, you should be VP.' But I go on talking. Chuck is listening to me restate my case and he says, 'You have to learn to take yes for an answer.' I've never forgotten that. Dawn's intervention got me promoted to vice president. Dawn was brilliant, had quite the temper, loved filmmakers, was passionate about the work and clear about the importance of friendship. She was friends with Linda Obst, Debra Hill, and Nora Ephron. She supported their work and made movies with them. It was the start of a network in the 1980s."[190]

So when Steel became head of Columbia Pictures, the press hailed her, deservedly.[191]

In a modest trailer office on the Columbia lot, Neema Barnette and other filmmakers in Puttnam's New Directors Program were ecstatic when Steel became head of the studio. "It was thrilling!" says Barnette. "We composed a letter saying we're women and she's a woman and how great that she's president and we'd like to tell her about the projects we were working on. We got a letter back saying we had two months to clear out. I don't hold what she did against her because I know something about what she was up against."

Barnette was being courted. CAA's Michael Rosenfeld came by *Frank's Place* set. "The guy with him was Bill Haber, who said he'd seen the episode and wanted to represent me.

"I said, 'Who do you have who's black in the agency?'

" 'I have one girl right out of the mail room,' Haber said. 'You want somebody black, huh?'

" 'Yeah,' I said, because I was young and political and I didn't want to be in a slave camp. Haber put me with Donna Shabe and Michael Rosenfeld. I was so naïve that I still didn't know what was happening. I signed with them, did the second episode of *Frank's Place*, then Haber had a talk with me. 'You're black, you're a woman, we've got to plan your career. I want you to do an episode of *It's a Living*.' I did two."

Carsey-Werner asked Barnette to come in and talk to Mr. Cosby.

"Bill and I got along well, and they gave me a script to read," says Barnette. Jay Sandrich, an award-winning director who'd given Barnette advice about directing when she was doing *Frank's Place*, was also working on *The Cosby Show*. "Now, at Carsey-Werner," Barnette says, "Jay told me, 'I don't know why they gave you this script, Neema. This is so hard for you. We'll get you another episode.' I put my hand on his shoulder. 'That's okay, honey, I can handle it.' That was 'The Day the Spores Landed,' where all the men got pregnant, including Bill." She laughs. "Jay would have loved to take that off my hands." Barnette won the International Monitor Award for Best Director for that episode.

She signed a two-year pay-or-play contract to direct episodes of *Cosby* and episodes of *A Different World*, those Debbie Allen didn't want to direct. (Allen acted in, choreographed, and directed *Fame, Family Ties*, and many other shows.) "I still didn't really understand how hard it was to get directing work," Barnette admits. "That would come later." On the African-American shows she directed, she was "very image conscious," questioning the validity of some characters or the action scripts called for. Producers were not used to that.

"Bill's show was positive. He had integrity," says Barnette. "And Debbie Allen was a great influence. But I had a run-in with a producer there on a script for a show that called for putting a mop on some girl's head. I went to Marcy [Carsey] and told her I'd argued with the producer when the actress came to me crying that she didn't want to put the mop

on her head. Marcy said, 'Neema, you're talented but you're so rambunctious. [The producer] is the boss and you have to do what she
says.' It was an image battle," Barnette says, "but I realized that this is
their clan, this is how they do it. I went back to New York and directed
Bill's shows."[192]

Barnette found that women producers "understood the struggle [of
being a woman in the business] from their point of view," says Barnette,
"but they didn't really understand the kind of support women *directors*
needed, didn't realize how hard it was for us to get directing work, how
one negative comment, one failed show, can destroy us.[193] For her part
in this equation, Barnette didn't understand that once a show is a hit,
no one wants directors to make changes. "They just want them to go
with the flow," she says, "but I wasn't that kind of director." She wanted
to make image changes. "It limited me from doing a whole lot of shows
except for Bill Cosby's."[194]

Barnette's agent sent her a script, *Better Off Dead*, for Viacom and
Lifetime. Rosilyn Heller and Gloria Steinem were the executive producers. The story dealt with the relationship of two women, one black, one
white, one in prison, one a district attorney.

"Rosilyn was very personable," says Barnette. "She had her little
glasses perched on her nose, she spoke her mind. She had that mogulette
flavor. She knew how to control a room. I asked Rosilyn why she hired
me. 'I thought you'd be more fun.' "

The story involves big issues framed by the two main characters:
Mare Winningham played the white woman on death row; Tyra Ferrell
played the African-American DA who tries to save her.

"Around the third day of the shoot," says Barnette, "I began getting
calls from executives at Lifetime about the black female character, the
district attorney. They wanted her to be more animated. 'What do you
want,' I asked, 'more like Mrs. Jefferson?' "

Barnette began to understand the powerful mythic image of black
women in America. "The television execs were perpetuating the image
that they, in television, had created. I am a black woman and I was
trying to create a *real* image. It really came home to me around a scene
where Tyra, playing the district attorney, brought some greens home,
which her mother offered to cook. Tyra says, 'No, Ma, you relax and let
me do my thing.' I get a call from the women at Lifetime. 'Neema, she's
a district attorney, she wouldn't speak like that to her mother—"let me
do my thing." The executive kept wanting Tyra's character to be happier. I didn't want her, the black character, to be accommodating. I didn't
want a Pearl Bailey image, everybody lay your head on my breast, I'm
everybody's mammy. I wanted the two women to become friends

through their emotional experiences, because to Tyra, Mare Winningham's character [in prison] was dirty white trash. To Mare, Tyra was just a nigger. When you bond through that kind of relationship the bond can't be broken. In terms of these characters I knew what I was talking about, but no one believed me.

"For example, I directed *Scattered Dreams* (1993), which starred Tyne Daly and Gerald McRaney. It's about a poor Southern woman trying to get her kids back from the Florida foster-care system. Now, I knew zero about sharecropping," says Barnette. "Gerald McRaney showed me how to get a mule to go across the field. He was raised in the South and I have to go with what he's saying because it's his thing. So if I tell you Tyra wouldn't say this or that, believe me, I think I know."

Barnette now had a reputation as a "difficult" director. Despite that, she directed more films.

"At the Directors Guild Women's Committee," says Barnette, "we're all women directors and our journeys are similar, but in more ways they are different. Being black is a very difficult situation. I've worked mainly on white shows where they've never had a black on the set, let alone as a director. And we *are* dealing with the myth of a black woman versus reality. Many white executives don't think that we're capable of directing our own stories, or they don't want to deal with the changes that need to be made in those stories to develop true images. I don't know any black female director who isn't image conscious. We have so much to change in terms of black female images, just like the changes of white female images that began in the 1980s. Black women should direct shows about black women.

"For instance, in *Run for the Dream*, the Gail Devers story, which was a Showtime movie, I hired Paula Kelley to play Gail Devers's father's wife. An executive told me she thought she was too thin to be a preacher's wife. She also wondered why she was talking back to the preacher. 'They don't talk back to their husbands,' this executive said.

" 'Who told you that?' I asked her. 'Do you think the men run their churches? Their wives run the churches!'

"We all know our own world. Those execs only knew the media image of it. When you bring in a sense of truth, it kind of startles people," Barnette says. "African-Americans also have to lead double lives. I went to the New York City High School for the Performing Arts, and I'd come out of my subway at One Hundred Forty-fifth Street talking Shakespearian English. I *learned* to adapt."

Barnette grew up in Harlem. Her father, a trumpet player for Louis Armstrong's big band, died when she was fourteen. Her mother was a secretary to the president of City College's Alumni Association. It was a mixed marriage. "My mother continued to live in Harlem and raise her two children," says Barnette. "She instilled in me that I could do anything I want.

"Different people tell the story they know because they live it. One of the first films I developed at Columbia while Puttnam was there was *Listen for the Fig Tree*. An executive said to me, 'I don't get the point, Neema. All this blind girl does is go looking for her mother.' You had to have been raised in a Brooklyn ghetto by an alcoholic mother to understand that when it's midnight and it's snowing and your mother is out in the street in sandals, you have to go look for her. That *is* the story. If you don't know that journey," Barnette says, "you won't understand it. We need more black female executives. If there's no one in the room to counter what's being said, the voices of woman directors are not going to be heard and the images on screen won't change."[195]

Many writers, directors, and producers have said that a single voice in the room doesn't carry weight and isn't heard. "What really happens in the studios is the influence of one person and the influence of numbers," says Marcia Nasatir, who has been both executive and producer. "It's the reason women had no influence and now have some."[196] Whoever is in the room, male or female, black or white, will contribute or through timidity will not contribute to decisions about the kinds of movies to be made. In effect, they determine what the world will see. It is a profound process, which is often dealt with, Nasatir and others believe, in a bewildering or expedient way.

When Barnette directed an episode of *Hooperman*, actress Betty Thomas asked if she could observe. "I got to know her a little," says Barnette. "A few years later, CAA gave me *The Brady Bunch* script to read. I turned the movie down, not because I didn't think it was funny but I just didn't think I was familiar enough with that lifestyle to do it justice. It was right up Betty's alley and I suggested her. I see her years later, she's a big director, and I'm like, 'Go Betty!' "[197]

From Lying about Something, I Got the Dream I Wanted

"When I was observing," Betty Thomas says, "I wanted to stand up and say, 'Here, put the guy there, put the camera here, put a fifty on it, bring it back this way and you've got the fucking shot and it'll be funny.' That's how ready I felt. I mean, I couldn't wait."

Thomas had been playing Lucy Bates, who went from rookie to sergeant on *Hill Street Blues*. In the late 1980s, she strode into *Hill Street* creator Steven Bochco's office, told him she wanted to direct, and asked if she could observe on *L.A. Law* and Bochco's new show, *Hooperman*, starring John Ritter.

"Steven let me go to story meetings, to castings, hang out on the set and in the editing rooms for a year and a half, every day. That's how I got to be a director. I knew the development of every character, I knew what the editors and the DP hated and loved. I asked every question I could think of. It was the best training I could have had. I pretended it was a job. If the call was for seven A.M. the next day, I was there at seven A.M. Sometimes I was really bored, but I tried to use that time to learn things I didn't know. At the end of the year, 1988, I happened to be at one of these celebrity, silly bullshit tennis things, and Army Archerd sat down next to me at dinner, and he said, 'So, Betty, what are you doing since *Hill Street*?'

"I said, 'What am I doing?' Long pause. 'I'm directing.'

"He said, 'You are? I had no idea! What?'

" '*Hooperman*.' I made a snap decision and said it. The very next day it was in his column—'Betty Thomas will direct *Hooperman* this year, blah, blah, blah, John Ritter, old friend of blah, blah, blah.' I get a phone call, not from Bochco but from the coexecutive producer, Bob Goodwin, who went on to do *X-Files*. He says, 'So, Betty, I read in the paper—'

"I said, 'Wait, it was a dinner, I can explain, I was just talking—'

" 'Stop, stop,' he said. 'We're going to have you direct the Christmas show.'

" 'You're kidding.'

" 'No, Bochco and I were putting together a list of directors for this year and we were thinking that you should be on the list. You've been around here a year, you know everything about the show, and John Ritter's behind you.'

"I went, 'Holy shit.' From lying about something, I got the dream I wanted. Whatever happens after you get the dream, it's up to you. You either do it or you don't do it and they say, 'Hey, we gave her a shot, it didn't work, and good-bye.' But it turned out okay.

"The first hour I started directing I knew I was home," she says. "The first fifteen minutes! There's nothing like directing because ... it's like improvisation, on stage ... You're basically in front of a hundred and twenty guys in shorts who want to know what's going to happen next. 'What are you going to do next, Betty?' They really love it when something goes wrong. They all turn to you and go, '*Now* what are you going to do, Betty?'

"I say, 'You know what, let's try this.'

"In the last three years I've been able to say, 'Hold everything, guys, I've made a mistake here. I don't like this shot. It's not going to be right for the actor. I know we lit it and we're ready to do it, but I'm not doing it. Here's the shot I want to do.' Now I know you can do that, nobody dies, nothing bad happens, and you get the shot you want instead of living with what you set up and looking at the movie for the rest of your life and going, 'Why didn't I change that shot?' "

Betty Thomas was born in St. Louis, Missouri. As an art major at Ohio University, she took the one film class offered and decided Stan Brakhage, the exuberant experimental filmmaker, was her hero. She would make art films "with no dialogue, just music." In the late 1970s, in L.A., many women were forming networking groups, and she joined one.

"We had to keep notebooks, make five-year plans," she says. "Just last year I found my five-year plan, which I'd done in late 1978. It says, 'My five-year plan is that I will be directing a movie about dolphins, blah, blah, blah, and it's a comedy.' That meant that I was thinking back then about directing, which I hadn't remembered at all!

"I hate it that a woman director has never won the Academy Award. I want to win it. I want some women to win it so that it's done with, so that women have won it and we don't have to think about it anymore, we can go on with life."[198]

I Prayed It Was Not Some Porno Film

In 1981, as Randa Haines directed her first *Hill Street Blues* and Neema Barnette was shooting with Third World Cinema in New York, Martha Coolidge was living in a room over a friend's garage in Los Angeles. She had made *Not a Pretty Picture* and short films; she was trying to finish postproduction on a movie she'd directed in Canada, *City Girl*, which the producers, broke, had abandoned. Coolidge was not going to let it die. "Peter Bogdanovich saw it as a woman's picture that had been shot down," says Coolidge, "a metaphor that was not lost on me. He . . . gave me the money to finish shooting. I was editing . . . when his company went under."[199] At that low point she wondered what had come of all the years she'd been shooting movies.

"I went into a depression," says Coolidge. A friend and his partner asked her to dinner and told her they were financing a low-budget film. "I was jealous," Coolidge says. "Then he said, 'That's why we want to talk to you, because you're a woman and we'd like you to direct it.' He gave me a script titled *Valley Girl*. Neither one of these guys wanted to direct it. Why? It was about girls. I went home and prayed that it was decent and not some porno film."[200]

Coolidge thought *Valley Girl* was an unfocused Romeo and Juliet story. That was her way into the story. Moreover, she knew the music scene "backwards and forwards," she says, because "*City Girl* had been set in the music clubs of Toronto and the film I'd worked on for Coppola, *Photoplay*, was in the music clubs of L.A. I knew I could really really make this film called *Valley Girl*. I knew it could change my life. I knew it."[201]

The distribution execs didn't want her. "She's too much of an artist," one said. "We want an exploitation film."[202] But the producers, Wayne Crawford and Andrew Lane, prevailed.

"Finally, I was called to a meeting and was told, 'Okay, we're going to accept you but you've got to make a promise. You've got to show naked breasts four times in this picture. Do you have a problem with that?' "

"No," Coolidge said, "as long as I can do it in my way."

"Oh, we don't care how you do it," was the reply. "We just want to see them."

"That is a direct quote," says Coolidge. "That's exactly what was said."[203]

Coolidge prepped *Valley Girl* in a few weeks, helped rewrite the script and called in favors from contacts she'd made in Los Angeles from years of struggle.

"I called cinematographer Fred Elmes, whom I'd met at NYU, and my friend Mary Delia Javier, who worked as a set decorator on *Apocalypse Now*. She became the production designer. The entire art department budget including gas and wardrobe was three thousand dollars. We all put our wardrobe into the pile. The cast was the key. Even people I turned down became stars, like Eric Stoltz and Judd Nelson. Nicolas Cage, one of the leads, was the last person in. My friend, Michael Papali, put together a sound track that kicked butt. From beginning to end it was six months. It came out in April and was just huge."

The screening she remembers best was when she showed it to the distributors. "Two sleazy guys, two producers, and me," she says. "When it was over, they turned around and said, 'Jesus, it's a real movie.' It was made for three hundred twenty-five thousand dollars plus a hundred and fifty thousand in the sound track." The distributor took out billboards on Sunset Boulevard. But through the financial alchemy of low-budget pictures, "I never got paid more than my five-thousand-dollar fee."

After *Valley Girl*, Coolidge was hot. Paramount gave her an exclusive four-picture deal. She moved into Sylvester Stallone's offices on the lot. "They only offered me horrible teenage movies. I had my first dreadful studio union experience, *Joy of Sex* (1984), made for the television division.

"Once I get on a set, I go into a zone," Coolidge says. Every director speaks about the experience in different ways. "It's a state of mind that is extremely *in the moment.* The director attends to every detail of what's going on-camera because if it isn't there it never will be. You're creating *in that moment* what will be permanent, so you're utterly focused. It's very Zen. Unlike an actor who is living the moment, the director has to be aware of how every moment relates to the entire picture. So that a director is aware of what's in every take, what's not there, the arc of the character, how it relates to the scene shot before and after. I could not tell you what happened that day on the set. I'm living in the movie, not on the set. I'm solving problems on the set but my mind is in the movie with the actors, so I know if their emotional arcs are correct, if this take matches that take, even though we shot them two weeks apart. That's a Zen world to me, living in the fiction, totally aware, totally concentrated. The weird thing about being a director is you walk in and out of this state—you solve a problem on the set, but I do it with only part of my mind because my real focus is on the fiction moment with the actors in the scene, the past and future of all those moments. I love it. It's like a dance. It's like dancing."[204]

Surely Now I'll Be Able to Get a Job

Having made an independent feature, *The Mafu Cage*, in 1978 with an old friend, cinematographer John Bailey, and his wife, editor Carol Littleton, Karen Arthur was off to Cannes to show the film on the tenth anniversary of Directors' Fortnight. *Mafu Cage* starred Carol Kane and Lee Grant. "Suddenly people were pulling me up on stage," Arthur recalls, "and I was holding hands with, I realized, Truffaut, and standing in a line of film directors who'd hung on the curtains ten years before to demand the chance to show more directorial vision films, not just commercial films. That's how Directors' Fortnight was born. From that high, I came home thinking, 'Surely now, I'll be able to get a job.' And I could not."[205]

Finally, she went to an old friend, Duke Vincent, "a fabulous librettist," who was working on Aaron Spelling's television show, *Hart to Hart.*

"I had heard that Stefanie Powers was interested in finding some women directors for the series," says Arthur. "She is a great lady. Duke went to the producers and literally begged, then I met with Stefanie and Len Goldberg, and I think because Stefanie had been kicking up some ruckus and Duke . . . they decided to try me out." Arthur directed multiple episodes of that show, then *Remington Steel* and *Cagney & Lacey*, where she met her husband, Tom Newirth, a director of photography, and won an Emmy.

Then Orion gave her a movie-of-the-week, *Victims for Victims, The Theresa Saldana Story*, about the actress's brutal attack by a crazed fan, which led to her involvement in the victims' rights movement. Since 1984, she has directed television movies ("long form") or miniseries every year, a body of television work matched by few women directors, but only one other feature, *Lady Beware* (1987), which Leonard Maltin called a "feminist exploitation film."

"What has served me well over the years has been an unbridled optimism," says Arthur. "For me, the joy of work begins when I read the book or the screenplay and I get that tingling feeling, and I feel afraid. It's the fear of stepping up to the challenge that forces me to say, 'Yes.' It's like stage fright. I can feel the energy flowing. Once challenged, that's the joy. If you are inclined to dream, then you will want to see your dreamtime in a book or on a stage or in a film."[206]

Other women were directing in the 1980s. Stage and screen actress Lee Grant made a documentary, *The Wilmar 8* (about the women who led the longest bank strike in history), and television movies—*A Matter of Sex, Nobody's Child, No Place Like Home*—all based on true stories. In 1981, Barbara Kopple produced and directed *Keeping On*, a dramatic feature for PBS's American Playhouse series about a local textile mill in the South trying to unionize, then began working on *American Dream*, a feature-length documentary that would win her another Oscar in 1991. Kathryn Bigelow directed *Union City, The Loveless, Blue Steel*. Amy Heckerling made *Fast Times at Ridgemont High* in 1982 and *Look Who's Talking* in 1989. Penny Marshall, still performing in the 1980s, was also directing—*Jumpin' Jack Flash* (1986), *Big* (1988), *Awakenings* (1990). Joan Micklin Silver did *Crossing Delancey* in 1988. Penelope Spheeris produced, wrote, and directed *The Decline of Western Civilization* and *The Wild Side*, then directed *The Boys Next Door, Hollywood Vice Squad, Dudes*, and *The Decline of Western Civilization Part II: The Metal Years*.

Not all directors were shooting on sound stages.

"I've Got to Film These Pandas," I Cried

In 1982, writer-producer Miriam Birch was on an arduous assignment in China for a National Geographic Television Special, *Save the Panda*. It was not the first time she realized nobody in the world knew where she was exactly. "We're just here," she recalls thinking at that time, "we're doing what we're doing but nobody knows where that is."[207]

Birch had started out as an actress/singer, performing in many musical comedies on the stage, and freelancing by singing on ships. Then she got a job as a mermaid on a TV travel show produced by Bill Burrud Productions. Burrud hosted his own shows and asked her to write some of the on-camera narration on specials like *This Nation Israel*, which she also directed.

Finding work as a writer or director was more difficult then because nonfiction on network television was a limited menu except for Walt Disney and National Geographic. Linda Reaveley, a postproduction coordinator at National Geographic TV, told Birch they were looking for a writer on a show about the Namib Desert in West Africa.

"Linda was a feminist," says Birch. "I was not. I was just a single woman trying to make a living. I showed Linda my scripts. She removed my name from them and submitted them to the producers. She felt they'd be much more likely to give them a fair read if they didn't know a woman wrote them. The producers liked the scripts, didn't mind, once they found out, that I was a woman, and hired me. That was my break. I wrote *The Living Sands of Namib* (1978) which won the Dupont Columbia Award, and I was thrilled to be working for the Geographic Society Specials. It was the cream." Though a few women had been writer/producers for National Geographic, they were usually part of a husband-and-wife team. Chris Zurbach Wiser, working alone like Birch, was probably the first, coproducing/codirecting the NGS special *Search for the Great Apes* in 1974 and producing-directing *The Animals Nobody Loved* in 1975. As one paper wrote about her earlier work with NGS, "[Zurbach] joins ABC's Helen Secondari and NBC's Lucy Jarvis as TV's small band of lady documentary makers."[208]

Indeed, the number of "lady docs" was small, but increasing. In the late 1970s, the executive producers of the specials were in Pittsburgh and in Washington, DC, which meant that filmmakers on the road had a tremendous amount of responsibility and creative latitude. "It's not like going into a studio with a final script and it's up to you to make sure it gets on film," says Birch. "In documentaries you're creating every second because you decide where and what you're going to shoot and pick the people, the incidents, and the locations."

To make *The Living Treasures of Japan*, she worked with five men, all employees of WQED Pittsburgh Public Broadcasting. "Here comes a woman writer-producer from outside," Birch says, "who's going to tell *them* what to do? It was hard. I had to be totally, totally insistent. The first time I asked them to shoot, we were driving in Japan and I saw this unbelievable sky, streaked pink and blue and violet. One sequence was about a man who handmade and hand-dyed papers that looked just like that sky. 'Stop! We're going to film the sky.' The crew didn't want to stop. They looked at me like I was crazy, but they didn't have the whole show in their heads—I did. I had to absolutely insist. Finally, grudgingly, they shot it. It got easier, but I couldn't say it ever got easy."

Backstage at the Kabuki theater, where "all the actors are men, even old men playing beautiful young women, it's such a different world. I was thinking, 'If I'd stayed an actress I wouldn't be here.' It really opened doors to amazing people, members of the Imperial Family of Japan, top world scientists, and artists of all kinds."

After that special, Birch did all of the Geographic's art or cultural films, such as *Jerusalem Within These Walls*, and *Bali, Masterpiece of the Gods*. In 1986, she wrote and produced *A Day in the Life of America*— the largest one-day shoot in the history of television. She had twenty-three crews on fifty locations in one twenty-four-hour period.

The roughest of all was *Save the Panda* in China. Produced in association with the World Wildlife Fund with the world-class biologist and author George Schaller, Birch had a crew of two, a cameraman and a soundman.

"The base camp was at about six thousand feet. The hill-tribe people, who'd only seen two European women before, carried my equipment, books, and clothes. We climbed two thousand feet farther to eighty-three hundred feet and joined the camp where George Schaller was studying the pandas. It was snowing; it was freezing. We lived in tents. We kept the tent warm with little stoves. The base camp had no telephone, no electricity. We were there for two months.

"To make a call or handle any correspondence, I had to walk back down two thousand feet, and I'm not a Girl Scout. After the two-thousand-foot hike down the mountain, I got in a Jeep and was driven, by prearrangement, for four to six hours across the Szechuan plain to a hotel in Cheng Du. There, on a good day, I could make a call and reach the United States. Many weeks into the shoot, I discovered the film we thought had already been sent home was languishing in Beijing. It was rugged.

"You can't do anything in China without complete government permission and supervision at all times. You are there as the guest. I had all these permissions and a letter. At one of our two base camps in the mountains, the Chinese had a large enclosure for eight captive pandas that had been rescued or orphaned. This scientific station was way, way up in the mountains where the bamboo grows. Behind them, they'd built a huge enclosure of bamboo and other natural plants. I had written permission that the animals were to be let out of their cages so that we could film them against the background of bamboo and mountains. We weren't seeing any pandas in the wild. They're elusive, very cautious about people. To show something like pandas that looked normal, we had to show them in the enclosure. The people who gave me the permissions were not there in the mountains, and Dr. Schaller was at the other camp where they were studying pandas in the wild. I'm the only one there with the guy in charge of these pandas. He would not let them out of their cages. I guess he was afraid he'd lose his job. I kept showing him the letter of permission and repeating, 'Let the pandas out of their cages.' The man wouldn't budge. I started threatening him, 'If you don't let us film the pandas, I'm going to report back to your boss.' Of course his boss was a long way away in Beijing.

"I was so frustrated and angry, I felt tears welling up and I thought, 'Oh my God, don't cry, don't show your weakness.' There was that split second where I could cry or not cry. I thought, 'Hell, let it go.' I let the tears come brimming out of my eyes and turned into a sobbing female. 'I've got to film these pandas,' I cried.

"That turned the trick. Suddenly everything was possible, and the cages were opened. He let the pandas out."[209]

I Was Acutely Aware No Other Women Were Doing Sound Editing

It was as difficult for women to work in postproduction in the 1980s—even now—as in directing.

Witness, Top Gun, The Hunt for Red October, Terms of Endearment, The Accused, Flashdance, Days of Thunder were all hits made or released in the 1980s. All had numerous Oscar nominations or wins of one kind or another. Other films of note then were *The Accused*, Jaffe/Lansing, and *Flashdance*, resurrected by Dawn Steel, produced by Don Simpson, Jerry Bruckheimer, and Lynda Obst. All were directed and picture-edited by men.

However, they have in common the work of one woman, a sound editor, a rare position for a woman in the 1980s, and even today.

"For some bizarre reason," Cecelia Hall says, "after I saw *Bonnie and Clyde*, I knew I wanted to be a film editor. I was fourteen. I told Dede Allen that story years later. I just got this editing thing in my head. I also had a great role model, my mom, a single parent, self-employed, a custom dressmaker and designer. I always knew that I'd be able to earn a living, that women could do that."

Hall, like Verna Fields, came from St. Louis, Missouri. Hall was named after Saint Cecilia, the patron saint of music, but she can't carry a tune. She had no formal film training. From 1978 to 1992, Hall was a supervising sound editor at Paramount Studios.

Until the mid-1980s, sound editing did not have true creative status and nowhere near the public recognition it has today. "Sound design is very subjective," says Hall. "One of the best examples is *Raging Bull* (1980), directed by Martin Scorsese. He told Frank Warner, one of the premier sound designers, 'You will be my composer, you will create my sound design.' As a result, there's very little music in the picture, and what's there is very effective. That is a unique working relationship. The best sort of creative endeavors happen when all the people on a film feel they're making the same film. And it doesn't happen very often."

The supervising sound editor on a picture is responsible for the quality of all sound on the final sound track except for music. Hall supervised the sound editors' work and coordinated it with music editors and the mixers. "The mix," says Hall, "has to do with the world that's created by the sound track. It is an artistic endeavor."

She began working at Paramount in the late 1970s, twenty-six male sound editors and Hall.

"I got there at nine in the morning," she says, "and never went home before ten or eleven at night. I was acutely aware no other women were doing sound effects editing." Some of the men were very supportive. For instance, the first work she did with Don Simpson and Jerry Bruckheimer was as a sound editor on a little movie called *Flashdance* (1983). Hall's boss, Paul Haggar, who is currently executive VP of postproduction at Paramount, recommended Hall for it. "I had a great experience on *Flashdance*, working with Don and Jerry." Hall went on to *Beverly Hills Cop* the next year.

"About six months after *Beverly Hills Cop*," Hall says, "I ran into Jerry in the parking lot. Jerry always remembered everyone's name. 'Cece! I've got this movie I want you to do. You'll have a good time. Probably next year we'll be ready.'

" 'Okay, great, what's it about?'

" 'Jets.' "

Hall spent a lot of time in the '80s with Don and Jerry—*Top Gun, Beverly Hills Cop I & II, Days of Thunder*. "Billy Weber was the picture editor of *Top Gun*, and a very big supporter," says Hall. "Every guy in town wanted that sound job—it was a very big *guy* picture, the ultimate macho experience. Lucky me."[210] She smiles. She went to Miramar to record the jets, "to be there when they were taking off and landing. All that stuff you don't get to do when you're a little girl, and all the toys you don't get the play with."[211] She took a three-man recording team to Nellis Air Force Base in Las Vegas, a huge fighter plane base, and spent days recording the the Thunderbirds.

"I had no personal life," she says. From the late '70s to the late '80s, Hall felt a lot of guys were waiting for her to fail. By the time she finished *Top Gun*, "I felt they couldn't touch me. I can record the damn jets. I can live on the Air Force base and get the sounds," says Hall. "I had proven myself to them and, more important, to myself. The whole opening of *Top Gun* takes place on top of an aircraft carrier. You can't actually record anything there because the noise is deafening. You have to recreate them. Ninety-five percent of the *Top Gun* track was recreated. The film was released in Dolby Stereo, which brought the experience of being in a fighter plane or around them right into the theater."

Her work on *Top Gun* won her an Academy Award nomination for Best Sound Effects Editing, the first woman ever to be nominated in that category.

"I chose a field dominated by men and it hasn't changed much," Hall says. "I had something to prove to myself." Hall is known for hiring and promoting women, and when she had the opportunity to do so, she didn't hesitate. "But there were so few women editing sound or picture. Even now, there are a number of women in other areas of the business, but few doing these jobs in postproduction. The schedules are so short and the demands today are so heavy, women are too smart to edit," Hall says. "I'm kidding, of course, but it's very hard work, and why would women work seven days a week and make themselves crazy?"

The first big movie she worked was the first *Star Trek* (1979), directed by Robert Wise. Wise had been the picture editor on Orson Welles's *Citizen Kane.* "I was in awe," Hall says. "One day, he beckons. 'Come with me. A friend of mine is doing ADR in the next room, dubbing, looping.' We went in and there was Orson Welles sitting there, a shaker of vodka nearby, and he looked up and smiled. I was a girl from the Ozarks who had landed in Hollywood, and I had met my two gods."[212]

In 1987, Barbara Streisand's production, *Nuts*, was in post. Hall heard that Streisand said, "I want the woman who edited *Witness*." Teri Schwartz was the executive producer, Martin Ritt directed.

"I found Barbra really easy to work with as the producer," says Hall. "She was actively involved, very hands-on, and she worked hard. She had a clear, strong vision of what she wanted so nothing was confusing. That made my job easier. Sound effects can create important, significant, and subtle nuances in a scene. In *Nuts*, her character was in a kind of mental ward, which offered lots of fascinating sound backgrounds. I loved working with her and with her executive producer, Teri Schwartz.

"If anyone in the business has failed to receive the support they should have had, [who has] not had the career as a director she should have had, it's absolutely Barbra. Show me a first-time director's film that's better than *Yentl*. If Barbra had been a man she'd be a Spielberg."

In her own case, Hall thinks being a woman was sometimes a help when they worked in areas that were not threatening to men. "About ten years ago, I don't think directors were necessarily threatened by a good sound person. Maybe they thought it wasn't an artistic endeavor so there wasn't a lot of ego or competition involved. At that time, virtually no one knew what the hell we did. Women have a harder time when they are in direct conflict—writing, producing, directing, even performing. Where men are less threatened, less challenged by women, women can thrive. I was lucky because I'd chosen a craft not readily understood, and I was able to avoid that kind of direct conflict. I saw my responsibility as helping them arrive at their vision, but I was very opinionated and always ready to do battle if I disagreed creatively with the director."

She says she fought Peter Weir, the director of *Witness*, passionately. "Peter is a generous and creative soul," Hall says. "We had a couple of real battles but he made me understand—I was new to the work, comparatively—that it was my job to help him arrive at his vision. 'It's *my* movie,' he said to me. I never forgot."

Hall went from the air in *Top Gun* to big-time speed beneath the sea— *The Hunt for Red October*. Anyone who saw that film may not recall the music track but can probably remember the sound of the "ping" ("One ping only," says Sean Connery), or the change in the sound from inside a sub to outside on land.

"There is one moment," Hall recalls, "a tiny scene when they leave the U.S. ship and go out in the SRV, the little submersible submarine, crossing over to the big Russian sub, where they tap on the hull. That whole scene sounds exactly the way it should sound. Not important, not dramatic, but there's no false note, you believe where you are. That's something I try to stress when I teach this stuff: the single most important element to sound design is making your audience believe they're in that environment. That's hard to accomplish."[213] Hall won the Oscar for Best Sound Effects Editing for *Red October*.[214] Kay Rose had been awarded the first Oscar for sound effects in 1984, at the time a special award, for *The River*, starring Sissy Spacek and Mel Gibson.

Back on land, Hall was working another big-boy toy, the Simpson/

Bruckheimer movie that sent Hall to the racetracks—*Days of Thunder* (1990).

"By the early 1990s," Hall says, "I was completely burned out and my long relationship had pretty much ended. I'd come to Paramount for a year and stayed for fourteen. I was ready to quit or do something different. My boss said, 'No, no, no, you're not going anywhere.'" She began overseeing projects and became more involved in running the department. That November, Sherry Lansing became chairman of Paramount Pictures Motion Picture Group. "A woman is running the studio," says Hall, "and I work with several other women directly, like Michelle Manning, president of production. That's in 2000. In the 1980s, guys were doing those jobs." In 1996, Hall became a vice president, and in 1999, she was promoted to senior VP postproduction sound.

Hall says that sexism in her postproduction sound world persists—women are seen as dialogue editors or as ADR (automated dialogue replacement) supervisors who record dialogue in sync with the picture after filming is completed. It used to be called *looping.* "The guys draw the big-effects pictures. It's a big business now and very competitive," she says. "A large part of postproduction is the mix. Three or four women are in it now. Anna Behlmer is the only big-time feature mixer. Editors, production designers, gaffers, best boys, grips—few women."[215]

It is hard to describe how demanding these jobs in production, postproduction, or in the highest executive offices are. Sherry Lansing says, "I gave up time. You work and work and work and I gave up time to do other things . . . I don't regret it in any way, though there may come a time when I do."[216]

"I made a mistake," Hall says. "I woke up in 1990 and I had forgotten to have a life. I haven't paid a high price because I was a woman, but I paid a very high price because I didn't know how else to do the work. I forgot it was important to be happy. I'm Zen about it now. In those first years at Paramount, I just felt an awesome responsibility to never fail. I worked at night after the assistants were done building the tracks; I'd double-check to make sure everything was in the right place. I knew I was young and inexperienced. I was really anxious."

She had other reasons for her anxiety. "I was afraid because I was the only woman working there that if I failed, they'd never hire any other woman," Hall says. "I'd jinx it for everybody. Mostly, I didn't want to make a fool of myself. If there had been even a few other women working, I probably wouldn't have been as worried, but for women at that time, we were concerned about the women coming up. We were extremely conscious of our responsibility to set an example, to show everyone that women could do this work and do it well."[217]

■ ■ ■

All through the 1980s, women increased ground won in the 1970s, incrementally at times, but as one woman said, the difference in that single decade—the 1980s—was "night and day." Women who began working in the mid-1980s could easily find examples of other women to inspire them, which many could not find in the late 1970s. At the close of the 1980s, Lili Fini Zanuck and Richard Zanuck won the Academy Award for Best Picture—*Driving Miss Daisy.* Lili Zanuck was the second woman to win this Oscar, the first was Julia Phillips. Both women produced their pictures with their husbands.

In the '80s, Men Were Open to Hiring Women

Long before she dreamed of directing or producing, Lili Fini married a preeminent Hollywood film producer, the son of Darryl Zanuck, who had formed 20th Century Fox in 1933 with Joseph Schenck. Zanuck Sr. had had a great run—Oscars for *How Green Was My Valley, Gentleman's Agreement,* and *All About Eve;* nominations for pictures like *Alexander's Ragtime Band, Twelve O'Clock High;* and, as an independent producer, *The Longest Day.* He was a three-time winner of the Academy's Irving G. Thalberg Award.

Richard Zanuck produced his first picture, *Compulsion,* in 1959. He became executive vice president of production at Fox when his father, Darryl, was asked to save the studio from the financial ruin of the *Cleopatra* debacle. During that period, Fox sold its immense back lot and made *The Sound of Music, Butch Cassidy and the Sundance Kid,* and *The French Connection.* In 1972, Richard formed Zanuck-Brown Productions with his friend, David Brown, and produced *The Sting, Jaws, MacArthur, The Verdict, Cocoon,* and others.

Lili Fini Zanuck was born in Leominster, Massachusetts, was raised in Europe, attended college in northern Virginia, and began working as a research assistant at the World Bank. She married Richard Zanuck shortly after she came to Hollywood in 1977. She says she did not dream big dreams. In 1979, when her husband's partner, David Brown, pressed her to do some part-time research on *The Island,* she began a kind of internship, working as a production assistant on *Neighbors* (starring John Belushi and Dan Aykroyd) and on *The Verdict* (starring Paul Newman, directed by Sidney Lumet).

After two years, she began reaching out for new, nonmainstream sources of material for Zanuck-Brown, soliciting work from never-before-produced writers and little-known agents. This unconventional approach led her to a manuscript "about aliens and old people." It had an unlikely title, *Cocoon*. She personally saw through every stage of its development over a four-year struggle to get it made.

"There weren't that many women around in the early 1980s," says Zanuck. "When a woman got promoted, another woman would call me and say, 'She slept with so-and-so, that's how she got that.' A man never told me that. I think it was that there weren't that many of us. The atmosphere just wasn't that charitable. Our part of the pie was so small..." When Lili Zanuck began in 1979, Verna Fields had just been promoted to a vice presidency at Universal. Sherry Lansing was at Columbia, soon to go to Fox, where the Zanucks were working. "Being a woman in the 1980s was a help," says Lili Zanuck, "because people were saying, 'Gee, there's a real problem here, we've got to do something about this, and if she's good why not hire her?' We were all mentored by men, but as the 1980s wore on, I didn't find that when we were in strong positions that we were mentoring women. Maybe because we hadn't been mentored by women."[218]

In an interview, Zanuck said that Alan Ladd Jr. convinced her to take the credit for producing *Cocoon*. Getting credit was a fight. "And it came after the fact," she said. "I had already functioned on pictures before without credit... Producing never felt like the Peter Principle to me. It was more like I'd already done the work and was begging for recognition I'd already earned as opposed to something handed to me..."[219]

When she began working seriously, being the only woman in the room didn't affect her. "In those early days, it happened every day. The worst thing about being the only woman in the room is to realize that since you were there, alone, other women had not advanced to reach the table."

In 1988, the Zanucks formed their own company. Its first film was *Driving Miss Daisy*, starring Jessica Tandy, Morgan Freeman, and Dan Aykroyd, and directed by Bruce Beresford. It was an unlikely film, and another film about old people.

"The assumption is that if I'd been Richard Zanuck, it would have been easy. Let me tell you, it would have been just as difficult to get *that* film off the ground if I'd been a man. My husband had had nothing but success, and we could not get that movie going. It was just plain hard, period. My husband was embarrassed at a certain point; he said, 'You know what? You're making a fool of us. Nobody's going to make this movie.' I don't care about being embarrassed. I fought very hard to get it made."[220]

Every studio turned it down; every independent turned it down.

"Then private syndicates started turning it down, all the little groups that want to invest some money. Australian money turned it down, Canadian money turned it down, I started networking with anybody who ever said they wanted to invest. I even went to some people who invest in theater in New York." She sat in her office with a headphone trying to make the deal to get the financing every day. She had the script, she had Tandy, she only wanted seven and a half million. "I left no stone unturned. It was a combination of fortitude mixed with desperation."[221]

After *Driving Miss Daisy*, Zanuck turned to directing—*Rush* in 1991, and *From Earth to the Moon* in 1998. *Rush*, set in Texas in 1973, took some heat over whether a drug-addicted narcotics agent was a great role model for women. But Zanuck says, "These little local Texas police departments would take women and put them undercover so the department wouldn't have to be embarrassed by having uniformed policewomen in their police stations." Of the heroine, she says, "She's the only character who ever recognizes what happens . . . Both lead characters become addicted . . . but when she finds him in trouble, she has to nurse him. I felt that's what happens to us as women. We do our job plus this female thing . . . In the film, after a party, one character comments, 'Some party!' and she says, 'Yeah, and look who's left doing the dishes.' Even when we're equal partners—and that character was his equal partner—we are left doing the dishes."[222]

She says she's been told by men that when a woman is directing, the macho territorial domain of the shoot decreases. "It's not 'This is my set, you work for me,' it's more democratic than that, actors tell me. If I say to an actor, 'That's a very attractive thing you do when you blah blah,' I think he believes me as a woman. There's a comfort level.[223]

"Another thing that happens is that women can quickly get put into a female niche, personal stories about women. They don't really see us doing things that have to do with wars and hardware. The opposite doesn't happen to men. Nobody says *Driving Miss Daisy* should have been directed by a woman. Opening up the minds of people in terms of what would interest us or what we could do well is one of the most important things we have to do. We have to develop material like that so that it's our material, it's our *Apocalypse Now*." If women do not develop their own material that cuts across expectations, they are dependent upon the studios and producers who have developed it and who will select producers or directors along traditional lines.

"Even when a movie wins an Oscar," says Zanuck, "that doesn't mean it's going to be any easier the following year for those filmmakers or for that type of movie. [With] *Driving Miss Daisy*, it was 'that's old people, blah, blah, and it worked,' and they go, 'that was just a one-off

situation.' Women aren't getting big action pictures. Most of us are stuck
in the low-budget world. Nobody's giving us hundred-million-dollar
movies, though Mimi Leder's *Deep Impact* might be one of the bigger
budgets. The worst thing now, for both men and women, is that there's
not a lot of forgiveness. If an established director has a couple flops in
a row, somebody would rather take a chance with a commercial director
who has never made a movie. You can read in the trades every day a
director on a picture you've never heard of who did, like, the Budweiser
commercial on the Super Bowl, and now he's got this hundred-million-
dollar feature. And that's very common."[224]

The ability to dream is all. She says that her imagination was stunted
or stymied. First she was a "gopher, then in development, then maybe
an associate producer. I didn't have the gumption, believe it or not, to
think that big until I'd already earned [the credit]." She needed to see
other women producing and directing before she could dream. The
dream precedes the act. "That's what I didn't have," she says. "That's
what my generation didn't have."[225] She feels that her dreams could have
had a lot more focus.

"Being a woman today is a hindrance," Zanuck says. "It's not a receptive atmosphere. It's a lot of lip service. At least in the 1980s, you had
guilty feelings about women not being hired, so you had an effort. Now,
because you can see a number of women in the industry and X number
of women in positions of power, it's like, it isn't a problem anymore. It
is a problem, because fewer women directors are being hired today than
they were ten years ago. Men are still mentoring women, but they are
also there for each other. I don't know that we are."[226]

The 1990s brought the perception that "everything's equal now."
Terms like "hiring practices" and "job equality" were boring and tacky.
"Feminism" was really out. For women, the chances to work as producers and executives widened; those jobs used all women's skills from
organizing to nurturing. By the early 1990s, just over the horizon, the
Internet beckoned, a brand-new territory, new media in another Wild
West. By virtue of being a new enterprise, would it be as good to women
as the Hollywood decade between 1910 to 1920 had, when movies were
new? Would the 1990s in other areas of the industry redeem the 1980s?

$\mathscr{B}$REAKTHROUGH: THE 1990S

"A thrust that penetrates and carries beyond a defensive or reinforcing line . . . a sensational advance."
—WEBSTER'S THIRD NEW INTERNATIONAL
DICTIONARY

III

When the Olympic Games began in the seventh century B.C., Greek women were not permitted to take part or even to watch. If they were caught, penalties were stiff. One hundred years ago, in 1900, women were allowed to participate in certain Olympic competitions. In September 2000, at the opening ceremony of the games in Sydney, Australia, the torch was passed from one Olympic champ to another, all women: Dawn Fraser, Shane Gould, Shirley Strickland de la Hunty. Debbie Flintoff-King ran through a pathway of the women athletes and passed the torch to the 400-meter world champion, Australia's Cathy Freeman, who lit the flame. The triumph of women athletes at Sydney 2000 holds a long lens at the distances all women have run.

The troubled 1990s saw breakups—the Soviet empire continued to crumble—and connections—to unlimited, instant information on levels never available before, to the personal lives of the celebrated or notorious, to other cultures and countries. Cable television and the Internet brought the diversity of the planet, a global grab bag, into the home. Everything was in public view. News and entertainment merged. News events were like long-running miniseries: the rockets flaring in the desert skies in 1991, kickoff to the Gulf War ("a live trade fair for military hardware"); the all-white, all-male Senate Judiciary Committee grilling Anita Hill during its confirmation hearings for Clarence Thomas, Supreme Court nominee; the writhing scandal of the popular first baby-boomer president, culminating with his impeachment by the House of Representatives; the white van cruising lugubriously along deserted Los Angeles freeways to O. J.'s arrest, trial, acquittal. Shorter shows: Susan McDougal in shackles; Heidi Fleiss's threats to reveal the Hollywood names in her black book; Dolly standing in her pen for photographers, clone of her mom; students fleeing Columbine High School after two classmates went on a shooting spree. The teenage killers hoped (from a videotape they left behind) that their last act would be chronicled in a movie.

Artists funded by the National Endowment for the Arts had to present their work for review and, if it was judged "obscene," had to return their grants. Female boxing became a fad. Abortion clinics were under fire. One in nine college women were date-raped in the U.S., sixteen women an hour.[1]

In this conservative and expansive decade, DVD, short for digital video disc or digital versatile disc, arrived—better images, better sound, a herald of a complete overhaul of film production, distribution, and exhibition. The Internet, hatched by the Department of Defense in 1958, was a fact of life; and in 1994, the Web was growing at a rate of 341,634 percent. A movie got up to 70 percent of its revenue overseas. *Notting Hill* earned $116 million in domestic and $238 in foreign distribution, and even the lambasted flop *Striptease* in 1996 racked up $80.2 million around the world. Sex and violence sold big here and bigger there. One critic said, "The whole world may have to change before the picture for women in Hollywood gets brighter."[2] The 1990s belief in a big women's audience for film (as existed for television) ran into blocks because a domestic audience alone was no longer a reason to make a movie. "The grosser the movie the bigger the gross."[3]

Madeleine Albright became the first woman secretary of state, and in 1992, a record forty-six women ran for Congress. California elected two women senators. In Hollywood, no one would ever say again, "I don't know any women." By 2000, three women were chairing studios—Stacey Snider, Universal Pictures; Amy Pascal, Columbia Pictures; and Sherry Lansing, Paramount Pictures. Nina Jacobson was cochair with Todd Garner of Disney's Motion Picture Group, Buena Vista. Kathy Nelson was president of Theatrical Music. In just fifteen years, women filled middle management and expected to be vice presidents; stuffed toys came to the office and men started talking knowledgeably about their children's schools. Lucie Salhany headed television network Fox Broadcasting (in 1995, she became chair of the new United Paramount Network); Geraldine Laybourne founded Oxygen Media in 1998; Nikki Rocco became the first president of distribution, Universal Pictures; Ann Sweeny became president of the Disney Channel/ABC Cable Networks; and Jamie Tarses became the first woman to be named president of an entertainment division of a big-three network, ABC Entertainment. In the industry and beyond, the 1990s were a breakthrough for women on almost every level.

By 1999, it was widely believed that the women's movement had done its work and had died happy.

The real story was this: the handful of women producers, writers, and executives in the 1970s had increased to many, but women had not come close to genuine equality in entertainment. All over America, working women were an acknowledged fact, but the same old cultural restrictions were working right along with them. Of the 70 million new jobs in the country, about 43 million went to women, 28 million to men. Secretarial jobs were still women's jobs (98.6 percent); only 30 percent of the managers and administrators were women. Most women were cashiers, registered nurses, sales workers, waitresses, and receptionists.[4] In 1973, a woman earned about fifty-six cents to a man's dollar, $14,268 to $25,194 annually. Twenty-seven years later, she earned about seventy-five cents to his dollar ($15,866 to $21,684).[5] In Hollywood, the Writers Guild kept surveying its members: women and minorities started at $30,000 and climbed to $48,000; white males started at $50,000 and climbed to $61,000.[6]

But everywhere, the talk was about "how equal it is now," and comparatively, it *was* better. In Hollywood, women were visible and influential, but the ultimate power in the Hollywood business of truth and fantasy was not theirs yet. The movies streaming forth to the world were still primarily men's stories for men. However, more women's stories and viewpoints now had a chance to find their place in the market. It seemed clear that future changes would depend on the women themselves.

15

THE SUIT WITH LEGS

In 1973, CBS astonished Ethel Winant by giving her a vice presidency at an affiliates meeting. By the 1990s, for women a vice presidency was not an unnegotiated surprise or grudging reward. It was an expected step up the career ladder.

The differences between the 1970s and the 1990s are so startling that women just beginning their careers in the '90s are amazed to hear how few women were producing in the 1970s. Most of the old pitfalls or inequities savvy women learned to deal with are not even recognized by younger women whose only career context is the 1990s.

In 1991, Women in Film issued a rare study on executive employment in film and television. It surveyed 1,124 women execs in twenty companies, from director to president. Three hundred seventy-eight women held these positions, 34 percent. Women had made significant strides, mainly into middle management. However, they were virtually invisible at the top executive spots.[7] Three women were presidents, at Paramount TV, Columbia Pictures, and Fox Broadcasting. Forty-five men held the job title of president.[8]

The numbers revealed the still uneven playing field. In the study, women compared their progress to that of men who entered at the same time, same level, who invariably received more promotions. The report attributed this to the natural bias that favors men in male-dominated companies, informal social business opportunities (often centered around sports) that tended to favor men, women's family responsibilities, and, finally, the fact that some women removed themselves from the race to the top when they saw the price men pay to reach those positions.[9]

"Having a baby is not seen as a smart career move. You're perceived differently—as if you're no longer serious about your career," one woman said. "Women around here [at a network] become pregnant, have babies, and then they disappear. It's like some mysterious illness has claimed them all. The women are good, the company has invested in them; but there's no flexibility after they've had kids."[10]

Commenting in the *Los Angeles Times* on the study, Barbara Boyle strongly recommended having children and a career: "Motherhood definitely put a damper on our life when the visibility you should be seeking to get you on the road to the top is curtailed . . . I went to one of the ten best law schools in the country [UCLA] and actually had a professor say, 'You're taking up someone else's spot. You're just going to have babies.' I said, 'Of course I'm going to have babies. Don't men become fathers and also become lawyers?' " Boyle was married for almost thirty-seven years, has two grown sons, and would put her relationship with them next to that of any mother who stayed home. "I don't think my children have suffered . . . Motherhood did not deprive me of a career . . ."

What troubled Boyle in 1991 was that she saw the number of women working in film increasing in general, but not in power positions. She didn't see the woman who would be the Barry Diller of the future. "We get so far, then something happens. Do we not want it? Are we prevented from getting the top spot? I can only say we should not avoid the joys or the limitations of being a woman just as we cannot avoid the joys or the limitations of being a particular, individual person."[11]

Other women quoted anonymously in the Women in Film survey wondered "how many of the hurdles to top positions are innate and how many exist only from habit . . . if women could reorganize executive jobs so that they included time for other areas of life." *There's* an original concept with legs.

Most women in the survey were hopeful about the future, claiming that "as women in the industry are perceived to reflect the vital link to female viewers and audiences, their voices will more forcefully be heard . . ." An executive predicted that the end of the decade would see virtual parity between women and men in most industry jobs. That survey has not been done. Most of the women surveyed said progress as "too slow—glacial."[12]

In the offices, progress to many did not feel "glacial"; women seemed to be well represented, although mainly at certain levels where their access was no longer disputed.

"Our business is way ahead of others," said Sherry Lansing in 1999. "I participate in a lot of women's forums in different fields and [that access for women is] just not true in other businesses. It will eventually be true. We have women executives at every studio. Three are running these studios. When Stacey Snider was made chair of Universal, it was not the front page of the *New York Times* as it was when I made president [of production] of Fox, which only showed how prejudiced we were then. [Snider's promotion] was reported properly in the business section—as if it's now okay. That doesn't mean there are enough women cameramen or enough women directors, but there will be."[13]

Younger women's experiences in the 1990s differ from those who started in the 1980s. The mommy track got serious. Everyone's talking about their kids. But being a mother still put many women at a disadvantage. Women and some single dads find ways to make parenting and work coexist. The power of numbers begins to be acknowledged. Having more than one woman at the conference table who share a sympathy or an interest in the material being considered is heartening and can be crucial. Men are still the major mentors of women, but more women are mentoring other women. Is there a girls' club? Is it different? The boys' club, after all, is not just a support network—it's information, protection in battle, recreation after battle. Did women by the end of the century feel they have this kind of support from other women?

This chapter mainly covers a few executives who began their careers in the mid-1980s. The following chapters include women who made the most of long careers in various ways in the 1990s.

I Always Worked with Women

Amy Pascal's story is classic. She began as a secretary in the early 1980s, became vice president of production at 20th Century Fox in 1986, moved to Columbia Pictures as executive VP production, became president of Columbia Pictures in 1996, and by 1999 she was chairman. It's a story that, for women, could not have happened until the 1990s.

"I've had an unfair advantage because I always worked with women," says Pascal. "They were very important to my career. When I worked for Tony Garnett, whose Kestral Films had an independent deal at Warner Bros., Lucy Fisher was our executive. She was a very significant woman in the business, and very important to me. Soon after, I worked for Dawn Steel, who was my mentor. So I've always worked with a lot of women."[14]

Pascal says she didn't feel like a typical movie business person in the 1980s. "Tony Garnett taught me that writers are the most important people. I paid attention to them when it wasn't quite as fashionable. And I continue to. We treat writers very seriously at Sony [Sony bought Columbia Pictures in 1989]. I've always known they were the foundation of movies. That's probably what has helped me the most—I made relationships early on with a lot of writers who were unknown, and because of that I got some very good scripts."[15] In 1999, Pascal struck a precedent-setting deal with screenwriters whose work had reached high earning levels. The arrangement, for the very first time, guaranteed these screenwriters a percentage of gross receipts of the movies they wrote. For many years, such agreements had been given only to select directors, actors, and producers.[16]

For years Pascal has supported the idea that teenage girls form a large untapped movie market. "I don't know if I thought they were a great market, but I certainly liked them the best," says Pascal. "Perhaps my own taste was like a teenage girl. It probably still is."[17]

Most movies are still told from boys' or men's point of view—their adventures, conflicts, goals, fears, or triumphs. In 1998, Women in Film gave actress Meryl Streep (*Out of Africa*, *Silkwood*) a Crystal Award. During her speech to the assembled industry folk, Streep noted the recently released list of the 100 best movies of the 20th century by the American Film Institute: "All but four are driven by male protagonists," she said. "*Snow White*, *The Wizard of Oz*, *All About Eve*, *The Sound of Music*. How many girls contributed to this vote?" she asked the audience. "Who voted?" She pointed out the paucity of roles for "aging women like me, which does let me stay home more with my kids ... But how about putting our stories on the screen instead of showing twenty-year-old women marrying sixty-year-old men?"[18]

"Unfortunately," says Pascal, "it's still true that both boys and girls will go to movies about boys, but boys will not go to movies about girls. So before those movies could be really successful, we had to wait until there was a large enough female audience who would go to the movies by themselves. More girls have earning power today and more girls assert their interest in what they want to see."

Many executive women in the 1990s feel the same way. Sara Risher, chair of New Line Productions, says: "Women are half the population. I feel that if [the marketing people] can't make a success out of that kind of movie, then someone's marketing it wrong. They often say, 'I can't sell those movies.' Well, learn. We've got to reach women, they're out there, they watch movies."[19] Risher started the ChickFlicks division of New Line in 1999.

One of the movies Pascal worked on, although she wasn't there for its final stages, was the 1994 version of *Little Women*, starring Winona Ryder. It was produced by Denise DiNovi, written by Robin Swicord, directed by Gillian Armstrong. It was a worldwide hit and earned three Oscar nominations.

"Robin Swicord and I dreamed of doing it years before," says Pascal. "I sensed [the story] would connect with a contemporary audience of primarily women in the way it always had. But [at the studio] many did not. They were wrong, because that movie has worked so many times. It's one of those stories you can keep making. *Pygmalion* is another."

Pascal always wanted to have a career. Her academic family had no connections to the entertainment community, but they instilled their daughter with the value and enjoyment of work. At UCLA, she majored in a field far from the entertainment industry—international relations, specifically Chinese foreign policy.

"I didn't think about being a studio executive," she says. "Scott Rudin talked me into it. He forced me to take a job as a studio executive at Fox. But I think women make very good executives and managers because it uses so many of our nurturing skills. It's also about compromise and it's about not leaving your fingerprints because it doesn't need to be about you. That's what makes a good executive. Being a woman was my greatest advantage because [in the 1980s] it made me different than other people who wanted the same job. Now so much has changed and other women are doing the kind of job I'm doing, like Stacey Snider. That is so great. I can't imagine why magazines still do women's issues—it's hardly that we're lonely out here.

"But I know it was very different for women in the 1970s. I am so lucky because of the women who came before me—Dawn Steel, Lucy Fisher, Sherry Lansing, Paula Weinstein—all these women were not only already doing the work but willing to help me and many others. When I was starting out, it wasn't fashionable to be a female director." But Pascal got to know directors Penny Marshall (*Riding in Cars with Boys*), Betty Thomas (*28 Days*), and Diane Keaton (*Hanging Up*, which was produced by Nora Ephron, who wrote and directed *Sleepless in Seattle*)—all Columbia releases.

Pascal saw the 1980s as an opportunity for women just as other women look back on it as a training ground, even though, as Pascal and others say, "Women have to work a little harder to get to the same place. The current statistics of women at work in the industry are so embarrassing. You know what's important? Movies, television, and books give people role models, some good, some bad, but these forms of communication are all about people connecting to and learning from other people."[20]

A Different Kind of Woman Was Coming into the Industry

Unlike Amy Pascal, Amy Baer grew up in the entertainment industry (her father is Tom Bosley, best known as Mr. Cunningham on *Happy Days* and Father Frank Dowling on *Father Dowling Mysteries*). She fled to Georgetown University in Washington, DC because she "needed to get out of Los Angeles in order to come back here," she says. "I needed to clear the cobwebs." She was not sure she wanted anything to do with the movie business.

She went to work for Creative Artists Agency as the late Jay Maloney's assistant in December 1988. After a while she realized she didn't want to be an agent, but through Maloney she got to know Stacey Snider, who was with Peter Guber and Jon Peters at the Guber-Peters Entertainment Company. Snider offered her a job as a story editor in 1990. Baer helped develop *Single White Female* (1992) and *Jumanji* (1995). "Stacey was very young, twenty-eight, when I went to work with her," Baer says, "just five years older than I. She was promoted very quickly, and was president of production at TriStar when she was thirty-one."[21]

At that time, as Baer looked around, she did not see a lot of women in production. "But many of the women I worked with at CAA were agents—Paula Wagner, Rosalie Swedlin—or became agents—Karin Sage, Beth Swofford—young women on desks like myself. The rest were men. There weren't *that* many women," says Baer, "but a different kind of woman was coming into the industry. They didn't feel as obsessively driven about their careers; they were getting married and having families sooner rather than later.

"Stacey was my mentor. She hired me, promoted me, was a major force in my career and still is. Lucy Fisher came to Sony in '96 [as vice-chair, Columbia TriStar Motion Picture Group]. She was amazing, particularly as a role model for working women with children. When I was five or six months pregnant, she came into my office and said, 'This is how you do it. This is how you're going to feel when you go on maternity leave. And this is how you're going to feel when you come back from maternity leave.' She was so honest and forthright. She demystified it all."

In Baer's career so far, being a woman has both helped and hindered her "a little."

"Statistically, there are always more men than women who apply for the jobs that come up," she says. "Being a woman helped me because it is beneficial having a woman's perspective in a room that's usually more male-oriented than female. Where it doesn't help is that women in this business don't tend to network the way the men do. The men have an unspoken club, an older definite club [that works] for the guys. They will go away on a river-rafting trip. Women don't get together in the same way. Women don't just hang out. Women have to find different ways to forge relationships with agents and executives and talent because we don't go off and do those 'boy club' trips. I don't know why women don't do that. Maybe we don't feel as safe with other women in the way guys do around other guys. They never talk about it, but the guys seem to have an implicit 'I'll scratch your back, you scratch mine' among each other in this business. That isn't quite there for women." Another theory is that women are too busy with husbands, homes, children, and their careers to go river-rafting.

"I've been in a studio for most of my career," Baer says, "and I know for example that it's always beneficial to have one guy, an executive, who can do the party circuit. It's never said, 'Oh, we need a girl to do the party circuit and hang out with the talent.' There are women who are incredibly good at managing talent, but it's just different, there's a different assumption. That's why I say it doesn't help if you're a woman who'd like to build those kinds of relationships. We have to do it in a different way."

Even so, Baer and her contemporaries can always call on women in the business for advice or information. "But we don't have that club thing. Maybe there's none because there are fewer opportunities for women, compared to men, many fewer women in the ranks compared to men. Maybe that makes women nervous about helping each other. Maybe they feel they'll undermine their own chances [for the one or two or three spots opening up]."

Baer would be hard-pressed to cite any example of a woman blatantly paid less than a man "simply because she's a woman. It may exist at the top levels where a woman who becomes head of production might get paid less than a man, but I'd be shocked if that's still the case."

In 1996, Baer became executive vice president of production for Columbia Pictures. She developed and managed the productions of *My Best Friend's Wedding* (1997), which grossed over $275 million worldwide; *The Mask of Zorro* (1998); and the children's classic *Madeline* (1998).

"I try to make doing business easy. I try to be honest and I try to be nice. If I believe in a project, I'll fight to the death for it. And I try to be a really good listener. It's a karma thing for me—I feel it's always going to come around. For instance, I believed in *Zorro*. We had so many starts and stops, there were so many directors, the movie got stuck in a studio regime change, Mark Canton had just left and John Calley was coming in, and no one was sure why we were making the movie. They were trying to sell off half the rights. The movie got green-lit because we already had so much money in it that they figured, what the hell, we might as well go for it. I was pregnant during preproduction and production and it was difficult. At the same time, it ended up being a really good movie, and successful!"

At Baer's all-girl high school, her women's studies teacher was active in the women's movement, in NOW, in the efforts to ratify the Equal Rights Amendment. "I didn't worry about being taken seriously or about being prevented from doing certain work because I was a woman. I'm sure that women five years behind me may have had a very different experience. Stacey Snider says she was lucky because she worked for men like Peter Guber and Jon Peters, who were incredibly supportive of women before it was in vogue. Amy Pascal worked for Dawn Steel, and I'm sure it was different for Dawn, who had to scratch and claw to get ahead."

The only time Baer felt being female might work against her was at the very beginning when she was looking for a job and still not sure what she wanted to do. People suggested she be a secretary. "I was scared that being someone's secretary meant I'd be that for the rest of my life. I didn't realize that the position had really changed because what used to be a career secretary has become the entry-level position across the business, the job men and women have before they move on to the next job."

The main influence Baer's mother had on her was the importance of having "something in your life, a craft, a work, that fulfills you." Her mother, a professional dancer with a theatrical background in New York, died when Baer was a child. "She didn't get married until she was thirty; she was thirty-four when I was born. When we moved to Los Angeles, she was older and there weren't as many opportunities for dancers here. Essentially, she stopped working. She was incredibly frustrated. I think about this a lot when the guilt of being a working mother sometimes sets in. That's a dilemma my friends and I go through every day. It is better to be fulfilled than to just be around. My mother would have been so much happier had she been working and doing her thing while being a mother. She was sort of modern in her own way without really knowing it, because she craved a life for herself. One of the reasons I admire Lucy [Fisher] so much is that she had three kids and still did her job. Many people still say, 'Oh well, now that you have a kid you can't possibly be a studio person anymore.' Why not?"[22]

He Could Not Compute that I Could Be a Lawyer

Debra Martin Chase began working at Columbia in 1989 in motion picture legal affairs as an attorney. "We were sort of the transition generation," says Chase, "between the pioneers, those women who came in in the early 1980s as assistants, and my generation of women, who solidified the base compared to actually creating the base."[23]

Chase studied law and practiced for a few years as a corporate lawyer. She was not only the only woman, she was an African-American woman and young, twenty-five, when she joined her first law firm. In one case, the firm represented a minister who was testifying on behalf of the community.

"I was in my blue suit," says Chase, "sitting next to one of the partners during the hearing, taking notes, doing the associate role. After we'd been there about a week, a man came over to me and said, 'It's so nice they let the reverend's wife sit there with the lawyers.' I'm looking at this guy and that's when you know how deep racism and sexism go. He could not compute that I could be a lawyer. So rather than cast aside his assumptions, because all the evidence pointed him in that direction, he went to a totally illogical place to explain my presence there."

When Chase became involved in Michael Dukakis's presidential campaign in 1988 and later in the administration of New York City's Mayor David Dinkins, she met people from the entertainment business.

"I decided to go for my dream," she says, "applied for and got a job at Columbia Pictures. Frank Price was the new chairman. I sat next to him at a luncheon and we hit it off. One of the projects he'd brought with him was a book set at Harvard, *Professor Romeo*, about a man who was sleeping with his students and gets his comeuppance. I was doing the legal deal on it at the studio. 'If you have a chance to read the book,' Price said to me, 'I'd be interested to hear your thoughts on it.' That weekend I locked myself in, I read the book like three times, took notes, called him Monday morning. 'I had some free time over the weekend and took a look at the book. I'd love to come talk to you about it.'"

Chase became Price's executive assistant. "Basically, I went with him to all his meetings, kind of issue-spotted and made sure nothing fell through the cracks. Most important, he wanted me to learn. I'd ask, 'Why did you make this decision? Why are you marketing this that way?' It was invaluable."

At the end of that year, Price left the studio and Mark Canton arrived. Chase, with a two-year contract, was now on the executive staff as director of creative affairs. "In retrospect, I had the feeling I was the lone Democrat in a Republican White House. I was making my peace with it when one Monday I was walking across the lot to the commissary and ran into Denzel Washington. I'd never met him before but a little voice in my head said, 'Go talk to him.' I introduced myself, explained I was at Columbia. He had a deal at TriStar. 'Let's get together tomorrow and talk about some projects,' he said. I didn't know that he'd split with his manager that weekend and was on his way to meet some friends about someone to run his company. At lunch, they told him, 'We know the perfect person for you.' They named me.

" 'That's unbelievable,' he said. 'I just met her twenty minutes ago.' "

Chase ran his company for three and a half years. "At that time, 1992," says Chase, "women were in the studios' pipeline, midlevel/senior executives, but they still stood out. I got to Columbia at the tail end of Dawn Steel's reign. She'd brought Amy Pascal up through the ranks. Dawn was very important, but the employment of women was still an issue, so to speak, because there were miles to cover, though no one ever said, 'What are *you* doing here? How can you ever expect to be X or Y?' I didn't have to grapple with 'We can't promote you because you're going to go off and a have a baby.' That time was behind us."

At Denzel Washington's Mundy Lane Entertainment, Chase was senior vice president. She and Washington coproduced *Hank Aaron: Chasing the Dream*, which won a Peabody for Best Cable Documentary and was nominated for an Oscar and an Emmy. She executive-produced *Courage Under Fire* and coproduced *The Preacher's Wife*. Next, *The Pelican Brief*, adapted from John Grisham's best-seller. The issue became: how would an interracial love story play?

"It was a big casting issue," Chase says. "Warner Bros. was very nervous casting Denzel in it even though the two characters in that film didn't have any physical contact. Julia Roberts put her foot down and said either Denzel's in by tomorrow or I'm out. I can still remember the day when you hardly saw a black person on screen who was not playing 'a black person.' So, yes, we've come some distance on that one. We still have a ways to go."

Chase viewed being a woman and being black in the same way. She thinks that by the time she began working in entertainment either could be an advantage. "If you were good at what you did, you were different— as a woman, as a black woman—from everybody else. Certainly, you voiced different thoughts. Once people had confidence in you, being African-American and being a woman both became assets." But a black woman in entertainment, as in most fields, has to make it over the initial hurdles. "When you walk in the door and they look at you, whatever preconceived notions they have [show]. I figure the onus is on you to overcome them. Once you get past that and begin talking about the project or whatever, it's fine. I won't say there's no discrimination—I think it's in the air, it's still in the air, it's institutional, but not debilitatingly so."

Next, Chase became executive VP of BrownHouse Productions and producing partner of its president, Whitney Houston. Her first production there was *Rodgers & Hammerstein's Cinderella*, starring Brandy, Houston, and Whoopi Goldberg (for Disney/ABC 1997). It got seven Emmy nominations, including Outstanding Variety, Musical or Comedy Special. Chase remembers being really tested during the production.

"We all truly believed in it and we had a vision of it. It was different and difficult because of the casting and because it was a musical. [No one] was certain the time was ripe for it. We felt we were breaking the mold and it was really hard. I was constantly saying, 'I believe in my vision, it will work.' It had been developed at CBS but they got cold feet as the budget started to escalate. We took it to Disney, and to their credit they never blinked an eye. 'We're Disney and this is Cinderella, and this works.' They really never questioned the multiracial concept of the casting. But everybody else did. As we were trying to cast, people would say, 'But I'm a white woman and how is it going to look for me to have a black child?' It was not only a very expensive two-hour movie, it was a musical and so it was r-i-s-k-y. One night, about ten o'clock, after another crisis meeting at William Morris, our agent's assistant said, 'Why is this so hard? Why are we meeting resistance every step of the way?' It dawned on me at that moment. Because it hadn't been done before. By definition that's difficult—it was a multiethnic Cinderella. Now, it's 'of course!' A good friend of mine, whose judgment I trust, said, 'I don't think this is going to work. I can't visualize it.' You have to listen to that. I put the phone down and took a breath and said, 'I see it and I'm going to go with that.'"

After years of poor decisions and overspending, reassessment was inevitable for studios and producers. "The studios became divisions of larger corporate entities," Chase says, "and the bottom line is more important than ever. As the studios decide how to allocate their money, they're more interested in the return. They are looking for the big special-effects movies compared to an inspiration story that will touch people's hearts. It's much harder to get that kind of movie made. But I get up in the morning feeling that I'm making a contribution, and that motivates me a lot."[24]

The Women Already There Made It Easier for Me

In 1995, Winifred White Neisser moved from NBC to Columbia TriStar as senior VP, movies for television and miniseries. "I explained to Helen Verno, the executive VP who hired me, that I had a husband and two children. Lucy Fisher, who was vice chair of the feature division, always made time for her family and is very vocal about it. She and the women like her made it easier for me."[25]

Ten years before at NBC, Neisser had not paid much attention to working mothers. When she became pregnant, she realized most of them had left. She called one and asked her why she'd left. The answer: managing career and motherhood had been too overwhelming. "I also noticed when I left NBC that men were starting to say, 'You know what? I need to leave every Thursday afternoon to coach my kid's soccer team.' "[26]

Neisser has had a long and consistent career. She came from Madison, Wisconsin, to NBC in Los Angeles in the early 1980s as a general management trainee in variety and comedy programs. After graduating from college and getting her master's degree, she'd taught school for two years in Puerto Rico. "It was something of an adjustment in a quite different culture," Neisser says, "but moving to Los Angeles and working in television was an even more difficult adjustment. I'd sit in a meeting at NBC and when it ended everyone would, like, nod their heads and go back to their offices. I'd been listening carefully but I didn't know what they'd decided. *What are they going to do now?* Sometimes I thought I knew what was going on, but then somebody would have drinks or play golf with someone else and the next morning it was completely different. Wherever they did it, it was someplace off screen. It was bewildering."

At that time, Neisser was the only woman in the comedy and variety department at NBC, and the only minority person. "There were other black executives in the company," she says, "a couple in programming, one in daytime, one in children's, and business affairs executives as well. I think there were more then than there are now because affirmative action was stronger. It was a hopeful time in many ways. By now I would have expected to see African-American, Hispanic, and Asian executives at the networks and their production companies. I don't really. That has not improved in the way I imagined."

In 1981, Ethel Winant was in charge of miniseries at NBC. "The higher you got in the company, the fewer women there were," Neisser recalls. "That was very clear. But Ethel was a force to be reckoned with, and she was very encouraging to me. I remember she said, 'I'm going to tell you something right now. When you come to work here you can't ever be afraid to lose your job.' That made no sense to me at the time, and seemed to be part of the whole cultural thing [in television] I didn't understand. People didn't always say what they meant but everybody seemed to think that was okay. Another thing that struck me as odd in those early days was people sort of got fired but that didn't seem to be any kind of problem."[27]

When she was at NBC, a department head left for reasons she did not understand. The executives were called together. Afterwards, Neisser walked into the hall, where she saw an African-American woman who worked as an administrator in business affairs. "She wanted to know what had happened in the meeting. I told her that he was leaving to go into independent production, that he wants to be a producer, and that everybody clapped. 'You are so naive,' she said. 'He's been fired. You watch, they'll throw him a party and then you're going to read in the trades that he's got another job where he's making more money than he did here.' She was right," Neisser says. "Those things were foreign to me."[28]

Neisser's father was a dentist, her mother a bacteriologist. She learned that if you worked hard you'd be rewarded. "The entertainment industry was not that logical," she says. "I was fascinated by it and a little frightened by it. I had a wonderful mentor, my boss Saul Ilson, in charge of variety and comedy."[29]

At NBC, Neisser became director of children's programming; then vice president, family programming; director of motion pictures for television in 1989; and vice president of movies and miniseries in 1992. Among many programs, she supervised the Danielle Steel "franchise" of movies for television.

Racism and sexism still exist, but they are difficult to deal with today because they're usually not overt. "Out here you won't find many men telling a racist joke," Neisser says. "They certainly won't do it around me. But they will tell sexist jokes and make sexist comments all the time. My boss, Helen Verno, and I were in a meeting with a group of men a couple years ago. One of them kept saying, 'Well, we can't make this deal because it would require spreading our legs.' There were four other executive men in the room who were on higher levels than Helen and I were. Nobody said anything. Comments like that happen all the time."

Neisser brought a project with an Asian protagonist to a meeting. "Without even thinking, the executive said, 'We can't do that. It's about Asians. Who's going to be in it?' This executive was an intelligent person, someone I liked. I said, 'Wait a minute. Do you hear what you're saying?' There's a sort of double standard at work here. Mainly, Hollywood is a liberal, progressive, caring community, but it has a perception that audiences won't accept stories about people of color or movies and series that star people of color. If it's a well-written story and the performances are sharp, people will come. America is not out there turning off the television sets because they see black or Asian faces. America is diverse! But television, which could really be a leader, is falling behind. Television is culturally timid. Television can make a difference," Neisser states. "Television has the power to bring all kinds of messages and it can make us feel good about ourselves, too. That's what attracted me to it from the very beginning."[30]

There's No Yes Involved in No

Alyss Dixson is a smart, handsome woman with an open, unpretentious manner. She arrived in Hollywood in the mid-1990s. She doesn't have a sense that women have been in the industry for a short time. "But I do have a sense that just a few years ago it used to be very different," she says. "I'd like to believe that I'd be here if there had been no civil rights or women's movement. It's hard to tell. There are landmark women who made it possible for me to be here."

Dixson was born in Portland, Oregon, got a scholarship to Yale in 1990, and majored in comparative literature and linguistic anthropology. When she graduated, "I was set to work at ESPN as an associate producer-director for the satellite feed to Latin America, all the soccer games, because I spoke Spanish and Portuguese, but I got into Columbia University film school."

In Hollywood in 1996, she interned at New Line Cinema. "I love Sara Risher [chair of New Line]. She will not take any shit off of anybody," says Dixson, who spent a year and a half there, worked as an assistant and "floater," then on *Money Talks*, a New Line release. She got to know the director, Brett Ratner, whose action films (*Rush Hour, Double Take*) have been very profitable. She moved to his company, Rat Entertainment, supervising production and development of all projects. "It was hard after *Rush Hour* hit, three-page phone sheets and I'm so green, I don't know what's going on, trying to return all these phone calls. Brett was great. Most of the time, I was the only girl. On the shoots, except for costume designer, hair and makeup, everyone was a guy. They're telling off-color jokes, and I'm like, 'Hey, you guys, I'm still here. This is not amusing.' One guy is going, 'Yeah, this is sexist. You guys should stop.' They're all going, 'Oh, you are so PC.' Another guy says, 'You know I love you.' I'm like, 'Yeah, that's like child abuse. If I kick my kid in the head, I can still love him, but that doesn't mean he should take me kicking him in the head.'

"I've been in meetings [before moving to Paramont], I'd ask a question, and they'd try to pass it off like I'm ignorant or naive or female or something. 'Oh, she doesn't know what she's talking about,' or 'It'll be okay.' I just want them to answer the question, don't yes-ma'am me. 'Oh yeah, don't worry about that, honey.' I heard that all the time like I'm getting all in a tither over nothing. Women don't tend to tell me not to worry. It's a certain age range of guys who came up in the '70s and the '80s and saw that business was done a certain way. But there's a group of women who came up with them who sort of ducked by being very girly . . . about every little thing. Or women who are constantly on the defensive.

"I know it's better now than it was [for women]; I've heard stories from older women, horrible stories, but they made it. Now others can aspire to any position. I don't feel any brakes."

Dixson feels the problem today is that women of her age still have to contend with sexism on a day-to-day basis. "What's heartbreaking is that women are perpetuating it. A woman came to me and said, 'Oh, I'm glad you spoke to that guy.' I'm like, 'He wouldn't have harassed my ass if you'd said something to him.' Like, if you'd put a stopper in that door, it would not have opened again. I find that a lot of women—to me they're girls—they're afraid to speak up. I think they've been brainwashed. Black people could have been victimized forever. My father is a retired defense attorney who grew up in Watts, he's black, and my mom's an office manager for an environmental planning company within the Sierra Club. She's Japanese. I learned if you say no, that's it, there's no yes involved in no.

"It's about a certain level of programming. Once you learn to accept those things, it gets like normal, like violence in the media. If you see people shot dead on television every day it becomes acceptable. When I left Oregon I had never seen blood in the television news. I'd just gotten to Yale and I'm watching the news and they showed all this blood at a murder scene. Blood everywhere. I almost threw up. My parents kind of sheltered us. And in Oregon in general you're very sheltered. I believe that if you hear somebody calling that woman a cunt, you start to get programmed and then it becomes acceptable. But some women are either unaware of the law or they've heard this stuff so much it's like seeing blood on television—it just doesn't mean anything."

Dixson says she always wanted to make films, since childhood. It's her dream. She thinks that in terms of numbers everything is equal now, but not in terms of power. She has hopes for a girls' club, but so far in her experience it's not as strong. "The girls turn on you so fast. We had a great group of girls who used to meet once a month for little cheesy brunches and we'd talk about different jobs. What seems to happen with guys is that they make time to go out for beer with other guys, talk about who knows who and you should meet so and so, let me hook you up. The girls tended to drop off the group as soon as they got a boyfriend. All of a sudden they couldn't fit in the time anymore.

"I want to get to certain levels, put movies together. Being a woman is more of a challenge than an obstacle. I don't think that there's a glass ceiling for me or for a lot of women. I've always reached the goals I set for myself."[31]

16

DON'T EVER TAKE IT PERSONALLY

Being older in a younger market: Women who started in the 1960s or 1970s are hitting the Hollywood ageism wall. "There's no business except our business where experience is considered a negative," says Sherry Lansing. "It's true. It used to be called wisdom. Now it's called old."[32] All women and many men find that age in this business is against them. Women who struggled, achieved, and opened doors, the women we cheered, must recreate themselves, sustain themselves, or be shut out. But, as Betty Thomas says, "If you make the money for them, there's no such thing as any 'ism.' If you don't make the money, every ism in the world counts."[33]

Some remarkable women executives, like Lansing, sidestepped the trap of Hollywood's youth fantasy with long careers in the studios and in the volatile arena of new media.

It's the 1990s! Put Strong Women in Strong Films!

In 1999, Sara Risher, chairman of productions, New Line Cinema created ChickFlicks, a division of New Line. It is based on the proposition that since women are now bringing their own money to the marketplace and making buying decisions, they are more likely to select movies that relate in some way to their own lives.

"Films directed toward men," says Risher, "which have a component women will like, such as strong women characters or emotional stories like *The Sixth Sense*, seem to work best. Or women's stories that have something for men like *Double Jeopardy* or *Shakespeare in Love*. I thought *City of Angels* with Meg Ryan and Nicolas Cage was a chick flick. My goal now is to concentrate on those movies because no one else is. The business still seems to think they're a fluke. In *Double Jeopardy*, they added the Tommy Lee Jones character because they didn't think anyone would see a movie of a woman [Ashley Judd] trying to get her kid back.

"For ChickFlicks, we're doing a feature version of [the Fred Mac-Murray sitcom] *My Three Sons*. I consider it a chick flick because it's emotional and funny, and it's about a man trying to learn how to mother his children. Men don't really know how to relate to each other. They have to learn. The father in this case is a successful provider, and after his wife dies, he thinks providing is all he needs to do. But he learns he must be an emotional center for his family as well. That's what single mothers have always done. I was one and I did both. As a woman, I also have a different style of managing. I see the differences every day. Women are nurturing. I give booster conversations all day—'You can do this!' and 'Good job!' Male managerial situations are more exclusive. They work on their own to prove they can do a task, they don't share information in the same way, and they're much more competitive."[34]

Risher has worked with New Line her entire career, starting in 1974 in New York, where she managed all filmmaking activities including development, physical, and postproduction. She says she did not know any other women in the New York film business; there were few in her own company, which mainly acquired films for its various divisions. "It was a difficult area to work in," says Risher, "because the men were old-timers."

After moving to Los Angeles and setting up New Line, West Coast, she became president of production in 1987. "I felt like an outsider here—I was forty, a single mother with my son, I wasn't part of the L.A. club, and I don't think it was gender as much as it was age and not being from here."

The first ten years in Los Angeles were financially rocky for New Line. "We didn't have much money," says Risher. "Our movies were very low budget. I was trying to put packages together, come up with ideas, get scripts written, and find new directors when we couldn't pay enough. But we did it." Risher has supervised the development and production of over fifty movies. The hits made them—the *Nightmare on Elm Street* movies and the film she acquired, *Teenage Mutant Ninja Turtles*. Risher had one mentor, New Line Cinema President and COO Robert Shaye. "Bob was a kind of person who turned things over and said, 'Do this. Learn on the job.' He's very good about entrusting power to people he trusts, male or female. And New Line here has been quite open to women," she says, "because we've tried to do offbeat, original material. We've had a number of female executives, and the career situation for women is easier now, but there are definitely still problems. There are so few women directors."

Ultimately, she was replaced as president of production by twenty-seven-year-old, self-styled "bad boy" Michael De Luca. "The perfect choice!" she says without a trace of sarcasm. She moved up to chairman of production. "Mike's expertise is half that he's a man, half that he likes comic books, action, and rough, edgy movies. Both characteristics have a lot to do with success in Hollywood."

The problems on the contemporary scene for women in entertainment are: "It's more age over sex, being a mother over being a development executive, and the boys' club," she says.

"There definitely is a boys' club. There's a strong female network now, too, but I can't call it an exclusive club like the boys' club. Women are inclusive. You get together and talk about what can you do *together*. The men are out there with the other guys, hustling. They're not going to include anyone else, certainly not women. That's why I think we don't have many women directors. The boys' club undermines that position because women don't get the same opportunities to learn. They make one mistake and they don't get another job, whereas men seem to get job after job after job even if they do terrible work."

Showing strong women whose active lives influence society is a must to women like Risher. "If we don't show those in film often enough they won't be recognized in society. That's why I want to show how women really are today—incredibly strong, active, and productive. But they're not shown *as that* in film. It will be easier as women grow up to be like the role models they saw in films. Look at the films of the '40s—strong, powerful, wonderful women, and then they disappeared. We have to get those kinds of films back."[35]

I Don't Shake Hands with Women

"A young man once asked me, 'How do you do everything? You travel all the time, you have children, you have a husband.'

"I said, 'I can do this because my husband is proud of what I do, and he's so supportive.'

" 'A man would never say "I can do this because my wife is so supportive." A man says he does this because he's so good at it.'

"I thought about that a long time," says Marion Edwards, "because men don't work with the social pressure. Women have to maintain a nurturing parental role in the midst of building a successful career.

We're a society in the middle of a deep change, and we have very different expectations for men and women."[36]

International television syndication is a specialty in the business. Edwards started when she was young and the field was young. They grew up together.

"We try to make sure that everyone on the planet has a chance to see as much American television programming as possible," she says, succinctly. She has been executive vice president for 20th Century Fox International Television since 1994. In its simplest form, international television licenses all the films and television programs produced by a particular studio (such as Fox's *X-Files*) to other television outlets in over 200 countries in a wide variety of dubbed and subtitled versions. At Universal in the 1970s, Edwards worked for the head of the division in an administrative capacity.

"Nobody knew anything about international television," Edwards says. "It was such a small, sedate business. We went to many international networks and tried to get them to buy episodes or films made at Universal to broadcast. In those days, a film was in a theater and a program was on television. No video business, no pay television, no cable. The network license fee to producers paid for the production of a show. Selling the same show internationally was icing on the cake, additional revenue. That business has really changed. The cost of producing an hour of television now far exceeds the license fee paid by the network. Consequently, the revenue from international offsets the deficit finance. It's become crucial to the financial health of production companies."

Most international television used to be state-owned networks, like the BBC. Governments auctioned certain frequencies, which large commercial enterprises bought. The result: new channels. All European countries now have commercial television broadcasting, which has created a livelier and more lucrative marketplace. In the 1990s, digital television took off in Europe, creating even more channels.

"Television is the last frontier of entertainment because that medium will finally converge with the Internet and the computer. That's almost overwhelming in terms of entertainment and information," says Edwards, "and this isn't going to happen in movies or video. We've always thought that television is the little sister to the mighty theatrical film business, but television is going to drive how people spend almost all of their entertainment time."

When Edwards started, many women worked in senior positions in Europe at various networks, mainly because World War II had decimated a generation of young men. However, there were no senior women in Africa, Asia, or Latin America.

"I was young and impressionable," she says. "I never thought of myself as being defined as a woman, but other people labeled you that way. It was a slap in the face to be suddenly reminded that someone saw me 'just' as a woman. In the late '70s, someone from Australian television said to me, 'I don't shake hands with women.' Clients from Latin America said to me, 'We've never dealt with a woman before. We're grateful to find someone who'll make a decision, and here you are making decisions. But you're a woman, it's great.'"

Bob Bramson trained Edwards in the international business. "He was fair, ethical in all business dealings. Working together for a long time made him a little hesitant to send me off on business trips alone. He really didn't want to put a nice young lady in a position where something might go wrong."

When Bramson retired in 1988, Edwards went to MGM/UA Telecommunications to become a vice president. "It was a wild ride," Edwards says. "The company slid into being for sale and then 'We're sold,' and 'No, we're not,' 'Yes, we are,' and back to being for sale again." It was wild in other ways. International TV syndication was a guys' field in the 1980s and 1990s. "Even now, I'm in meetings where I'm the only woman in the room.

"I was married and had children. One male executive said to me, 'If you wanted to have a career, you should have been sterilized.'"

When she returned from having her second child, she was told just before a staff meeting to stay outside and answer phones. "I was the vice president of the division," says Edwards. "That's one of those times when [being female] slaps you in the face. First, I had to prove that I was a serious person who wanted a serious career. Then I got married and had to prove that I was *still* a serious person who *still* wanted a career. I had my first child and I had to prove that I was *still* a serious person who wanted a career. After the birth of my second child, I said, 'That's it, I'm not going to prove myself again.' When you start out, women have to do it, maybe everyone has to prove they're serious. But how many times do we have to re-prove ourselves?"

She was proving herself all through the 1980s, not the 1970s or 1960s. "I hope now that preconceived notions about women only taking jobs until they get married has changed, because that's definitely what every man I worked for thought—'Okay, you're good, but you'll get married and then you'll quit.' In the '80s, being a mother was career-threatening. Part of the reason I agreed to re-prove myself repeatedly was it was do it or leave. Finding another job at the same level with an infant seemed worse than the embarrassment of proving myself yet again as a serious executive."

She found the support at 20th Century Fox. "Bill Mechanic and Mark [Kaner] give us an opportunity not to be a man or a woman but to be a human being in the workplace. I've been more articulate, too, about what's important to me. I realized I was leaving home at six-thirty in the morning, getting back at nine at night. I was traveling all the time. In a flash of insight, it occurred to me that if anybody had said how much money would it take to own my life, I'd say my life's not for sale. But I had given it for free. We ourselves give them twenty-four-hour-a-day access, we don't draw any lines, and it drives you crazy. I wasn't seeing my children and I was exhausted. I needed to clarify where the lines were in my life and what I needed to continue to do this job. When I said those things, the answer was very surprising—in essence [they said] that they'd do whatever I wanted, and what changes did I want to make? I was an idiot," says Edwards. "I could have done that earlier. What always got me through was laughing with people or making them laugh, or myself."

Edwards says her mother had a great sense of humor, had a career, gave it up, and then picked it up again after her children were born. "My mother came from a farm in Utah. She said her dad told her, 'Be somebody yourself because if you marry as soon as you get out of school, you'll be somebody's daughter or somebody's wife. Be somebody yourself.' She told me that when I was a little girl, so even though I was not in a generation of girls who were encouraged to have careers, I learned that I should be somebody—individually, just me—not somebody's wife or somebody's daughter."[37]

Women Are the Most Underserved Audience in Cable TV

Geraldine Laybourne, chair and CEO, founded Oxygen Media in May 1998 with her husband, Kit, to produce branded content for the Internet, TV and other media, focusing on women's and children's markets. "Traditional media," said Laybourne at the time, "have missed the boat with the modern woman. There is nothing that serves women the way ESPN serves men and Nick serves kids. We want to create a brand on both television and the Internet that brings humor and playfulness and a voice that makes a woman say 'You really understand me.' "[38]

Laybourne has remarkable influence. She is an executive star and one of the most powerful and well-liked women in American business. As a teacher, she was an early advocate of media education. Her reputation as a pioneer came from her innovative television programming for children with Nickelodeon. She took over the management of the network in 1984, was named president in 1989 and vice chair of MTV Networks in 1993.[39] She created and built the Nickelodeon brand and launched Nick at Nite in 1985, the prime-time sitcom lineup that became the top-rated, twenty-four-hour cable programming service, winning many awards. She expanded the brand by distributing it around the world, creating the Nickelodeon movie, toy, and publishing divisions.

In 1996, she became president of Disney/ABC Cable Networks, supervising Disney Channel and ABC's interests in Lifetime, A&E Network, the History Channel, and E! Entertainment Television. She played a major role in the creation and management of ABC's Saturday morning children's programming. In 1998, Laybourne left Disney.

Laybourne *is* Oxygen. Its mission, she says, is "a media revolution by women and kids." Oxygen struggles for convergency, trying to reach women both as a new cable network for women (7 to 10 million so far) and as a presence on the Internet with extensive Web sites. In September 1998, she made a deal with AOL, which sold three of its women-oriented services to Oxygen—Electra, Moms Online, and Thrive, a health issue service. The deal was widely seen as testament to the growing importance of women to online marketers. According to AOL "about 51 percent of its 13 million users [at that time] are women—up from 16 percent in 1994."[40]

Powerful programming partners joined forces for the cable TV network: Marcy Carsey, Caryn Mandabach, Tom Werner (Casey-Werner-Mandabach), and Oprah Winfrey. Winfrey committed her company, Harpo Productions; Carsey-Werner-Mandabach is the chief programmer for the new network. Significant funding came from America Online and Paul Allen, Microsoft cofounder.[41]

"Cable TV's top-rated shows are wrestling, football, and *Rugrats*," *Variety* noted. Laybourne, citing her famous line about women being "the most underserved audience in cable TV," also states that she hopes the cable industry will see Oxygen as "a solution for them. They need to do a better job programming to women because women control 70 percent of consumer spending."[42]

Laybourne and Oxygen Media anticipate the convergence of TV and the Internet, but its coverage on nationwide cable networks is still lower than the much older Lifetime Channel. On the Web, Oxygen has plenty of competition, but the question persists: What do women want? Web sites aimed at women abound and many more have bloomed since Oxygen was founded. But the Web is an integral part of Laybourne's Oxygen concept, just as color is to a painting. Through the Web, Oxygen is trying to identify topics that appeal to women. They seem to be discovering old news, that women in the aggregate want information about kids and parenting, shopping and hard news, makeup, health, education, and—a boost for any Web site—horoscopes.

Oxygen, whose influence cannot yet be predicted, acquired a staff of "veteran girl zinesters with lots of Web savvy," Janelle Brown wrote for Salon.com, "...and purchased indie webzines like Girls On Film and BreakUp Girl. Younger women were optimistic that the cable channel and Web sites would start developing content with an edgier, hipper sensibility than Women.com or iVillage. But two years later, Oxygen.com has let its acquisitions languish, and rather than developing any unique properties for its Web site, Oxygen.com now consists of a haphazard group of sites including two dedicated to Oprah, one to 'keeping it simple,' another to 'thinking like a girl.' "[43]

Lifetime and Oxygen Media/Oxygen.com take a lot of heat, but they are both in the game, however *that's* defined, and the fact that two major cable channels and innumerable Web sites exist just for women is a harbinger.

In the late 1990s, it was believed the new media would offer women many new and higher-paying jobs as the octopuslike growth of television, cable, pay TV, and other media grew phenomenally. "There's nothing comparable to the Internet, where the number of options are virtually infinite," says Winnie Wechsler, who has been building and operating major Web sites since 1995. She began her career in cable television. "Like television," she adds, "the Internet is fundamentally a commercial medium, but unlike television, anyone can have their own 'channel.' "[44]

Do new media (and cyber business within it) hold more promise than traditional entertainment media for women? Is it wide open, y'all come? Women are found in almost all areas, though their numbers at the top—ownership, corporate CEO positions, venture capital—are thin.

Mariana Danilovic, CEO of Digital Media X, believes that many women are attracted to these situations because they have to deal with the glass ceiling and promotion issues in traditional media, which lead them to look at the new media companies as an opportunity to fully explore their potential.

"When we went to raise money for our fund," says Danilovic, "we made trips to the East Coast and Silicon Valley and talked to investors in Los Angeles. We did not meet with any women on those trips. In most cases, women are restricted from gaining access to running companies, and it probably stems from the fact that women are not in charge of capital sources overall. Very few women are managing six-hundred-million-dollar-plus funds." Danilovic runs "a small fund," which puts seed-stage money and management into companies. As women gain access to capital, she feels most of the glass ceilings will simply crumble. "Women need access to financial capital to be successful in building the human capital piece," she says, "but that's beginning to happen."[45]

"Many venture capitalists are anxious to recruit qualified women as CEOs of new Internet businesses," says Winnie Wechsler, "although currently the percentage of women holding those jobs is extremely low. The Internet business is really a part of the computer technology industry, which, notoriously, has had very few women in senior management positions."

Wechsler spent years with Disney, where she became senior vice president of Buena Vista Internet Group (now Walt Disney Internet Group). In early 1999, she moved from the category of children's entertainment to children's education on the Web when she became executive VP and general manager of Internet and broadband services of Lightspan, Inc.

"I've worked in areas that are personally interesting to me, such as creating entertainment and education content for kids and families. For better or worse, many more women work in companies that focus on developing Internet products and services for families and children than you might find in other types of Internet publishing. I don't know the exact statistics, but women still tend to gravitate to marketing, sales, content, or business development [more so] than to technology or engineering jobs."

Does being a woman help or hinder their work in new media?

"I don't think being a woman has helped me," says Winnie Wechsler, "but I don't think it has hindered me, either. I like to believe that it all sort of evens out. Generally, to succeed, women have to work harder than men and spend more effort to prove themselves. That's probably a loaded statement, but I believe that."[46]

Wechsler started at The Disney Channel in October 1985 just after John Cooke joined the company as president and set up plans to relaunch the cable network. In about eighteen months she was promoted from manager to vice president. She worked with many women as peers, she recalls, but none as bosses. As a company, Disney wasn't known for having many women in senior management, but Wechsler found her bosses very supportive of her work, including running aspects of the Disney Channel domestically and finding ways to launch it internationally.

In late 1994, she was part of the team that recommended the company create a new division, Disney Online, to establish a strong, centralized presence for Disney in the emerging on-line world. When it was approved and the division formed in mid-1995, she helped launch, manage, and run Disney.com, which initially included Disney Store on-line, Family.com, about twenty-five domestic Web sites, and ten internationally based Web sites. In essence, Wechsler's work took her from television to on-line in 1995. Four years later, she went from building on-line entertainment destinations for families to education sites when she joined Lightspan, a small education software company.

"By its nature, the Internet provides multitasks and multiple choices or inputs, but it is being managed and developed primarily by guys," says Jane White, director of the International Children's Digital Library. She has wide experience in media programs for the Internet. "A few women are in high positions," she says, "like Cathy Wilson at Viacom, a real leader, Geraldine Laybourne with Oxygen, but it's hard to think of others."

In many ways, the structure of new media business follows traditional lines. Men and women work in different areas: men in engineering, technology, animation, programming, venture capital, and financing. "The worker bees are the producers who make it happen," says White. "[They're] the ones who knit it together, and I use that verb, 'knit,' deliberately because that's the function we do. There are a lot of women producers and women in marketing at the midlevel area—the higher marketing levels are mainly men."[47]

The changes in new media come so fast that patterns and people are as hard to fix as quicksilver. One permanent player, Red Burns, a legend—teacher, outspoken critic, and innovator—says, "What's interesting about [this new media] is that there are more women who are engaged in this pursuit. Women by nature are highly collaborative. They are not competitive. And I think this is a collaborative medium, and so I am expecting a lot of interesting stuff to come from women. If women would stop thinking about busting through barriers and would just start to imagine things . . . I think the barriers would be busted automatically."[48]

By 1990, Beth Kennedy had already created and managed business plans for an interactive division at Universal for four years. She left the studio for the new media world, fearing she was going to miss the boat. "It took me a while to realize the dock hadn't even been built."[49] Her goal then was to show how a body of material could be created for distribution across all media. She wanted particularly to create interactive programming for women. In 1994, Kennedy became a creator and producer of on-line entertainment on AOL, designing and providing content for *The Daily Fix* and managing *Keyword Complaint.* She also consulted for other companies who were beginning to watch the on-line world "with interest and doubt," including Microsoft, Jenny Craig, and Sony. Kennedy was the creator and executive producer-showrunner for

CyberJustice, The World Where Everyone Gets What They Deserve, and for ChillOUT, a unique multiplayer game, for nearly five years.

In 1996, Kennedy and her husband were in Houston, Texas. "This is the weekend before the Kennedy Center's Imagination Celebration. We're the 'honored' guest. We've been showcasing *CyberJustice* and AOL's on-line technology in the Dallas/Fort Worth schools for a week. The following weekend, we were doing a special event for seven hundred fifty deaf and hearing-impaired junior high and high school students from all over Texas. A reporter comes over to take our photograph and interview the creators. He talks only to Michael, who, bless his heart, keeps directing him to me by saying, 'I don't understand this technology at all. You'll have to talk to Beth.'

"Women are still more harshly criticized for failings," Kennedy goes on. "The press and the hallway gossip never seems to be as hard on a man. They don't slam the guys' clothes or hair."[50]

Dawn Steel wrote in her book: "From Jeffrey [Katzenberg, at Paramount], who was a brilliant executive even then, I learned what I called the 'Jeffrey Katzenberg Theory of Getting Things Done,' which is this: *If they throw you out the front door you go in the back door, and if they throw you out the back door you go in the window, and if they throw you out the window you go in the basement. And you don't ever take it personally.*"[51]

"That's my mantra—do it anyway," says Kennedy. "I'll listen to all the excuses of why a woman can't do this or have that, I understand why the men in charge may not want to do it, I understand it's a difficult decision, but women are going to do it anyway. Now let's figure out how."[52]

I Want to Run the Division

The glass ceiling didn't break, Nikki Rocco says; it just got another crack on February 4, 1996, when she became, as *Variety* headlined it, "U Setting a President—Rocco Becomes First Femme as Distribution Head."

"None of that would have happened," Rocco says, "if I hadn't had the support of many men at Universal for many years. Brian Grazer [producer, *Apollo 13, A Beautiful Mind*] took me to lunch one day in the early 1990s, and asked me what I wanted to do with my life. I said, 'I want to run the division . . . I guess I want to be the first woman to have the control.' "[53]

In the 1970s, a woman would not have dreamed of running a studio division. In the 1980s "a woman might head publicity," she says, "but the guys controlled divisions." By the 1990s, a woman like Rocco could say the dream out loud and it would be taken seriously. Universal was a good spot for women in the 1990s and still is.[54] "If I'd been a man," says Rocco, "I probably would have had the position years earlier. The industry didn't [and still doesn't] take women too seriously in distribution."

Rocco brought a new approach to the work when she was made senior VP of distribution and marketing in 1992. "Establishing relationships with the filmmakers," says Rocco. "I see distribution and the people who run it as a service for the filmmaker because every film is some filmmaker's child. All through the '90s I worked extremely hard to establish relationships with filmmakers. I wanted to be the one they called (and still do) at five o'clock on a Saturday morning when their film opens that weekend. It was a major strategy of mine—to nurture filmmakers."

Cape Fear, released in 1991, was produced by Barbara DeFina and Kathleen Kennedy, edited by Thelma Schoonmaker, and directed by Martin Scorsese. It was a remake of the 1962 movie starring Gregory Peck and Robert Mitchum about a whacked-out ex-con who sets out to terrorize the family of the attorney who put him in prison.

"I was not running the division," says Rocco. "I was a new senior VP when [MCA president] Sid Sheinberg invited me to a screening in New York and afterwards to join him with Marty [Scorsese] and Michael Ovitz to discuss how to release the film. I was thrilled. Ovitz leaned across the table and asked me how I'd release the film.

" 'Around this time,' I said, 'early November before Thanksgiving to get the word out, to launch it . . .' That release strategy turned out to be what we did. My plan did not sit well with the man running the division at the time; he was unhappy I'd been invited to the screening. But I knew it was a turning point in my career."

Six years later, another turning point. "On a Friday afternoon in 1996, I was told to attend a meeting Monday morning with my boss, the chief financial officer, and the head of the motion picture group. 'What should I prepare for?' I asked.

" 'No,' I was told, 'you don't need anything.'

" 'Uh-oh,' I thought, 'I don't need anything.' What the hell was going on?"

Monday morning she appeared at the meeting in the office of Casey Silver, the president of production. Silver told her that the current president of distribution had chosen to be a consultant for the company, and that she would be named his successor. "I was so surprised," says Rocco.

"It wasn't that I couldn't do it, wasn't that I didn't expect it or hadn't worked for it—I had. It was just that it was happening."

Being head of a division is a completely different perspective. "Four months later, *The Nutty Professor* [1996] was on our slate," says Rocco. "When and how are we going to release it? It's one of the most vital elements of the distribution business. I worked closely with Brian Grazer [the producer] on it. I called the shots about how to sell the film, and I was very much involved in the release date of the film."[55] It was her first triumph as the new president of the division when it grossed over $100 million.

12 Monkeys was another tense release. An eccentric, toxic, Bruce Willis time-travel movie directed by Terry Gilliam, it was a remake of Chris Marker's *La Jetée*, written by David and Janet Peoples. "*Jumanji* for adults," *Time* magazine called it.[56]

"An exhibitor called me," says Rocco, "and told me he'd heard that I was 'pioneering' this movie's release date. 'What are you,' he says to me quote unquote, 'fucking out of your mind? With that playdate you're going to get killed!'

" 'No,' I said. 'I think it's a brilliant strategy.' We released it on January 5th, which was unheard of in those days, to go the week after Christmas. Another triumph. Sometimes," Rocco says, airily, "I remind this exhibitor of what he said to me—'being fucking out of my mind' and 'being killed.' "[57] She's had failures, too, and they can be cutting. What disturbs Rocco now is that she doesn't see any women being groomed in her position at other studios. Distribution is still a man's domain.

Do Not Invest Your Ego in This

Donna Smith also parlayed her skills into the nineties. She's the woman production manager Jim Brubaker discovered in 1979 at a filing cabinet in the Chartoff-Winkler office. By 1986, she was "queen of non-union production," and had become a highly bondable producer.

"Somewhere along the line," says Smith, "I wrote myself a one-liner, 'Do not invest your ego in this.' I still have that in my wallet. Hollywood is egos and personalities. I have Midwest values. I'm a Minnesota girl."[58]

Smith didn't go to college and never trained for a career. Her family lived paycheck to paycheck and couldn't afford to send five kids to college. Smith went to night schools as an adult. "As a child, I think I learned my people-handling skills abstractly. My father worked for the

Social Security Administration, and his job moved him almost every year. I went to nine schools and instead of resenting the move, I'd wonder what the kids would be like in the new school. I looked at each change as a new challenge. I transferred that attitude to work and always applied my 'do not invest your ego' principle."

In the mid-1980s, Smith left production to become VP and chief operating officer of Entertainment Completions International, a motion picture completion bond company. She learned the world of international banking as it applied to filmmaking. Independent productions must have a bank loan or private financing, which necessitates a completion bond for each film. That bond guarantees that the film will be completed and delivered.

"At the time, the studios didn't need completion bonds for their movies because they were self-bonded," says Smith, "which means they put more money into a movie if or when needed to enhance it." Smith drew on her knowledge of producers, production managers and all the other people who make up a production plus her experience working with budgets, locations, and crews to determine which productions were good risks.

"The Gordon boys, Chuck and Larry—I love them dearly. They were producing *Field of Dreams* [1989] when Universal green-lit another movie for them, *K-9*," says Smith. "They called me. 'You've got to quit that chickenshit job and do this *K-9* movie for us.'" Smith laughed, but she did miss production. She resigned from the bond company and became executive producer of *K-9*. Smith had finished on time and on budget when Casey Silver, president of production at Universal Pictures, the studio releasing *K-9*, asked her to come in for a meeting.

"White-knuckled, I drive to Universal," says Smith, "thinking something must have gone wrong with *K-9*. I go into a meeting with all the hot shots—Tom Pollock, who chaired the Motion Picture Group then; incoming president of production Casey Silver, and Sean Daniels, the outgoing president of production. 'We want you to head up production for us.'" Heading physical production for the studio? Smith hesitated. She was back as a filmmaker now; wearing pantyhose in the Black Tower, the executive high-rise on the Universal lot, wasn't her idea of filmmaking.[59]

"When I told my attorney, Tom Hansen, about the offer, he said that Hollywood had never in its ninety years of existence had a woman head of physical production in any studio—ever. Oh, wow, I thought. That really gave me pause. I mean, feel the pressure! I remember telling him, 'Then I've got to do this one for the girls. Let's make the deal!' "[60]

Smith became senior vice president of production and postproduction for Universal Pictures. She expected to stay two years; she stayed seven,

1989 to 1996, working on over 150 movies, such as *Schindler's List*, *Jurassic Park*, *Babe*, *Casino*, *12 Monkeys*, *Fried Green Tomatoes*, *Back to the Future II* and *III*, *Do the Right Thing*, *Waterworld*, and *Apollo 13*.

"Going in, I didn't know the studio stuff," says Smith. "I reported directly to Casey [Silver], Casey reported to Tom Pollock, and Pollock reported to Sid Sheinberg and Lew Wasserman. That was the food chain. Casey was aces and not afraid to work with a woman. I really could handle the job because I knew how to make movies. I think Casey and Pollock liked that they'd had the courage to hire a woman as head of production." But, as in her earlier work, "it was still men and me," says Smith.[61]

When You're President, They Have to Listen to You

"I see being a woman today as an advantage," says spritely Laura Ziskin, head of Ziskin Productions, former president of Fox 2000. Like Smith, Ziskin started in production.

"In those early days . . . we women were more willing to do the shit work," says Ziskin. One of her first jobs was as an assistant to Jon Peters and Barbra Streisand on *A Star Is Born*. "Women were more willing to be secretaries. I felt if you wanted to know what was going on . . . the secretaries knew everything and it was a great way to learn the business, whereas the men [wouldn't do it]. Now the guys have caught up with us. Lynda Obst had this great line, 'Are the boys the new girls?' Because more young men today will take assistant positions."[62]

Up to the late '80s, secretaries were not called assistants and the job was not usually a training ground. The new role of secretary/assistant was one of the major changes in the business in the 1990s.

Ziskin graduated from the USC School of Cinema. After *A Star Is Born* and *Eyes of Laura Mars*, she partnered with Sally Field (Fogwood Films) and produced *Murphy's Romance* and *No Way Out*, which starred Kevin Costner, then a newcomer, and Gene Hackman. She formed an association with Kaleidoscope Films and Ian Sander, and produced *D.O.A.* and *Everybody's All American*.

"Men have defined our working environment, as they do in most businesses," says Ziskin. "I hate to use words like 'disadvantage,' but there is some kind of difference being a woman in those [working] kinds of situations. I always like to say men have created the world in their image and somehow we end up trying to fit ourselves in it. And then we subtly change it. I think that's what goes on. As a producer I might want to make movies for women, but when I started producing independently my first audience was men. Marketing sold to men. As a consequence, the studios or executives sometimes didn't see things the way I saw them. Ultimately, I sold everything [I made], though some films were hard."

Ziskin also thinks it was hard to get other women to champion pictures that were different and difficult. "I'm suggesting it's not necessarily a disadvantage to be a woman. Rather it's the kind of disadvantage one expects if you're in a minority. For example, if you're in a roomful of men and you're the only woman, is that a disadvantage? Maybe." But being in a room full of men happens less frequently in the 1990s. "It's changed so dramatically," she says. "Women named Sherry, Amy, Stacey, and Elizabeth are presidents of divisions, studios, companies . . . but there are no woman owners, no female counterparts to John Malone or Rupert Murdoch or Ted Turner or Gerald Levin. I personally think that's about lifestyle choices. I could be wrong."

But women's peak career-building years coincide with childbearing years. "That is a big [career] difference in . . . any male-dominated endeavor," says Ziskin, who moved out of production into an executive job because she had a child and needed steadier working hours. "There are only so many hours in a day, and no matter what men say about how they devote themselves to their family, it's different from being pregnant for almost a year, giving birth, being a mommy, and taking on all those responsibilities for the next, what, eighteen years."

Ziskin had a producing deal at Disney when Jeffrey Katzenberg ran the studio. "He always has a lot of women around because he knows women work harder for less money," Ziskin says. "I think it's true that inequity still exists. You have to fight like mad and you have to not accept less. One of the problems is that you start lower, you go up the pay scale slower, and so you're playing a lot of catch-up. I think that business still puts more value on men than on women. I don't know why that is. In terms of pay, maybe they still think a woman doesn't need [as much]. Maybe women don't measure their success by the money they make as men do. A woman might feel that even though she's not making X amount, she has pretty much what she wants. Men are in the . . . I call it the dick-measuring business. It's just part of their makeup. How much you're paid is a dick measurement. But I find that women tend to say 'Am I being paid fairly for the work I'm doing?' Maybe I'm wrong, but I think for men it's about the number. They fight harder for higher numbers."

Ziskin fought against salary inequities because as a producer—*What About Bob?*, *The Doctor* (directed by Randa Haines), and the hits *Pretty*

Woman, To Die For, As Good As It Gets—"I felt grossly underpaid compared to the men," she says. "It became a really big issue with me. I had to push really hard."[63]

Then, when she had an opportunity to be an executive, at first she didn't want the job. "Lynda Obst has a funny thing in her book about me. Because I didn't want the job, they kept throwing more money at me. That's one way to get more money."[64]

Women executives she noticed when she started were Rosilyn Heller and Marcia Nasatir. "I heard of only one producer, Hannah Weinstein. I was working for producers and I knew I wanted to do what they were doing, but I wasn't consciously thinking I didn't know any women producers. I never thought I couldn't do it because I was a woman, but I remember looking around and thinking, 'Oh, my God, there's nobody doing this.' Then I got pregnant and thought, 'There's nobody doing this who has children. Help.' "

She doesn't remember any women as mentors either, but says Barbra Streisand was a tremendous influence on her.

"She was a perfectionist. I just sent her a note around her special award this year [2000] at the Golden Globes, which touched me. I wrote her truthfully that for years after I'd worked for her, I'd be doing something and I'd wonder, 'If I were doing this for Barbra, would this be good enough? Would this withstand that scrutiny?' That kind of check was great for me, because I'm not a perfectionist, even though I want to make things as good as they can be. In another way, I am a perfectionist because I'm aware that I'll never attain perfection. I'm a realistic perfectionist. Barbra has standards. The other big influence she had on me was I got to see a woman with a lot of power in the profession who had to put up with a lot of things because she was a woman. She was alone, and so was Jane Fonda."

Today Ziskin feels women are influencing movies more than ever before. "Some executives and producers wonder about the quality and constancy of that influence," she says. "Historically, the movie business is a testosterone-driven business. The greater number of women with decision-making power means that maybe we can work an estrogen-driven business. I think women have an extraordinarily unique opportunity, but unfortunately, women are still co-opted by men, and most of the marketing of movies to women is done by men who don't necessarily know how. Why should they? They only have demographics and statistics to guide them . . . Ironically, when I started out, everyone said I had to make movies for eighteen-year-old boys, which of course I didn't know how to do and didn't do. But today, we make movies for eighteen-year-old boys and eighteen-year-old girls. Thanks to Amy Pascal, *Little Women* showed Columbia that an audience of young women existed, that young women would go to the movies on their own or with their friends."

Ziskin believes that pictures like *Little Women*, Lisa Weinstein's *Ghost* (1990), and her own *Pretty Woman* (1990) began to wake up the slumbering giants of marketing. "Hello! Women are an audience!" she says. "Every time one of those movies works, they say, 'What a surprise!' The new movie's success shocks them. Gee, the movie worked, and I guess women are an audience."[65]

Yes, and here to stay. The presence of women in the executive ranks in the 1990s made it visible. The executives who hold the keys to the fate of many creative folk are changing the industry on certain levels, but not as much as we once thought.

"Someone was asking me the other day," says Sherry Lansing, "that since there are more women today, did I think there will be more women's films? I said, 'Yes,' but now I'm not sure. I mentioned that of course we're doing movies that appeal to us about subjects we like, movies maybe with women heroines. Then I remembered, whoa, Barbara Stanwyck and Joan Crawford were working at a time when there were no women executives or heads of studios, and yet those years turned out some great women's roles and films. I'd like to think that the presence of all these women today has made a difference. In our studio [Paramount] we've done *First Wives Club, Double Jeopardy, Clueless,* but then I think back to that heyday when there were no women, except as performers. You'd . . . think that with women running companies they'd be drawn to certain types of material which men might not be drawn to, as well as making films like *Terminator*, which was produced by a woman."[66]

The jury is still out. But the promise is there.

17

HIRING A WOMAN (WRITER) IS THE HIP THING TO DO

Women writers, directors, and producers believed the increasing number of women executives in the 1990s made it more possible for them to work. Though attitudes about women were undoubtedly changing, some thought the changes were just cosmetic. Even so, if the 1990s were nothing else, they were fluid. As former restrictions melted, women writers sometimes produced and directed, and it was much easier to move from film to television and back again. Certainly, on many levels, except for some union jobs, most positions were open to women, though all were problematic in various ways as the women in this chapter and the next describe.

The Good News and the Bad News for Women in 2000

"This experience of mine," says writer-producer Georgia Jeffries (*China Beach, Cagney & Lacey*) "is about women in the '90s and about illusion and reality in this business.

"In June of '99, my agent called me about a hit television drama, let's say *Drama Y*. The star was one of the most difficult in the business. *Drama Y* was looking for a female coexecutive producer.

"'Why are you calling me?' I asked.

"'Because the coexecutive producer knows you,' my agent said, 'and he wants to talk.'

"I'd never seen the show. All I knew was what I'd heard about the star. I watched an episode and knew there was no way I could be involved in the series. I told my agent that I'd personally call the producer.

"'I hope your agent told you what I told her to tell you,' he said to me.

" 'You mean, about [Star] being terrible to women?'

" 'Yes.'

" 'She did tell me that, but I thought she might be extrapolating. Those were your words verbatim?'

" 'I insisted your agent be truthful with you about it.'

" 'If he's terrible to women,' I said, 'why on earth would you want a female coexecutive producer on the show?'

" 'Number one, I love your work. You know the character he plays has several ex-wives. [Star] thinks we need a woman on staff to bring out the more sensitive, 'relationship' aspect of his character.'

"I just laughed. We both did. The producer did good-quality work. He was kind of apologetic that the star's infamous reputation had put him in this awkward situation. To me, this whole conversation summed up 'women in the '90s.' Here's an actor who has a reputation of being an asshole to women, yet his producer will hire a woman writer-producer because it's the fashionable thing to do. They're trying to expand the demographics for the show and they want to help his *character*'s reputation with the female audience. Yet he, the actor, and his *personal* character exemplify his objectionable attitudes toward women. Look at the irony of it! The star wants to be perceived as a sensitive guy who would try to develop that side of this character as an actor, and it was a complete lie."[67]

The perception of women as window-dressing was persistent. It takes generations for deeply ingrained attitudes to change. Why are we surprised that they haven't vanished in twenty years? The changes in the early '80s were cosmetic. Real changes didn't start until the 1990s.

"I was lucky," says Jeffries. "If I'd been trying to work ten years before that curve, I would have had a much, much, *much* tougher time. At least they were developing serious female-led drama after I left *Cagney & Lacey* in the mid-1980s, which is why I had the opportunity to write several different female-driven drama pilots in that decade. Unfortunately, none were ordered to series. In *produced* series, male leads still predominate." To some extent, this is changing—*Judging Amy, Family Law, Crossing Jordan.* "It's the same with features. When female-led pictures began breaking in the 1990s, they were called exceptions. How many exceptions do we need before it's not an exception? It's still the reason they develop so few, proportionately. *Drama Y* simultaneously reflects the good news and the bad news for women in 2000."[68]

In 1987, women were writing about 7 percent of major feature films in America. In 1999, that figure had climbed to just 13 percent; in 2000, 14 percent (14 percent of all writers working on the top 250 American films produced, 13 percent of the top 100 films; in television, it's 27 percent). Therefore, currently, about 86 percent of these films had no women writers.[69] In 1999, women were still writing mostly romantic dramas (36 percent), and romantic comedies (32 percent); they wrote only 13 percent of animated features, 7 percent of horror, 6 percent of action films, and no sci-fi.[70]

The Only Woman in the Room in the '90s Is a Man

Josann McGibbon was working as a receptionist for a small literary agency in Los Angeles, Brandson and Rogers, when Sara Parriott came in looking for a job. McGibbon hired her as her replacement. McGibbon herself became an agent.

McGibbon says, "I didn't like it, but it was a good education." Parriott had no secretarial skills, but McGibbon hired her because they had such a good time together. "Sara would type stuff up and I retyped it before the agents saw it. But she answered phones beautifully." On reflection, working at the agency "was a pretty good job because I got my first husband and Sara, my lifelong writing partner, there."

McGibbon grew up in New York and Europe. Her father was in advertising and marketing research, "but every now and then he'd quit his job . . . so we could go to Europe for two years," she says. "My mom was a high school math teacher." McGibbon majored in playwriting at UCLA but, being in Los Angeles, figured she'd better aim for television writing.

Parriott grew up in Finley, Ohio. "My mother wouldn't let me go to college in Ohio because she didn't want me to become pregnant and live in Finley," she says. Parriott graduated from the Rhode Island School of Design and worked as a textile designer. But she didn't like it. She started writing humor books and got them published. Her brother, Jim, a television producer and director, told her to "come over to television. It's a good way to make a living."[71]

McGibbon and Parriott wrote their first spec script in 1985 and got their first assignment a year later—*Worth Winning*. Starring Mark Harmon as a playboy, the story was about a bet that he could get engaged to three different women in three months. It was made into a movie almost immediately.

"That's really cool!" they thought. "You write a script and they make it."

Women helped all along the way. On another script, *The Favor*, an executive at Fox, Sara Colleton, and Wendy Dozoretz at A&M Films had read the script earlier and remembered it. McGibbon and Parriott insisted that Dozoretz get an associate producer credit. "We sort of bullied her boss into giving it to her," McGibbon says. "She told us later that if we hadn't done that she would never have gotten it."

The Favor came about this way: "Josann had this old boyfriend," Parriott recalls. "I was single then, and one day she found out I was going to a high school reunion near Columbus, Ohio, where he lived. She joked, 'Go look him up for me, and while you're at it sleep with him, because I never did.' That was like the stupidest thing, but we made a funny, 'what if' story that our agent, Dan Ostroff, sold. It got made and was on AMC last night. Lauren Shuler Donner produced it with us. Donna Dubrow was the exec." Harley Jane Kozak played the married woman, Elizabeth McGovern the friend, Bill Pullman the husband, and Brad Pitt the old boyfriend. "Women loved it because it included the married *woman*'s sexual fantasies. Men said, 'If she's happily married I don't buy that's ever going to happen, those fantasies.' Women shrugged and said, 'Yeah, good point.' You know, some people you can't help. I guess no married man ever had any fantasies," she says drolly.

That script got them "a lot of meetings." It was filmed in the fall of 1990 but didn't come out until '94, one of the films, they say, that got "stuck when Orion went bankrupt. The good news was that Brad Pitt became a star in between."

Parriott and McGibbon write romantic comedies—chick flicks. In their experience, "the only woman in the room in the 1990s" is a man with eight powerful women.

"We got in trouble one day," says McGibbon, "because we pitched to the woman in the meeting, not to the guy. She's a very powerful producer, and we knew he was the other producer, but we're used to thinking the women hold the keys. We'd been told if she wants you, you've got the job. No one mentioned him. Afterward, we heard how hurt he was. Everyone else in the meeting loved the idea of the film, but he was a stickler. In these meetings when someone asks difficult questions they're really saying 'I'm not happy.' He was asking questions like that. It took two months to gather this whole group of people together again. We faced him this time, pitched it to him, and he was delightful. We were very contrite. We felt bad about making the mistake the first time around."

Parriott and McGibbon have written two movies for Sandra Bullock's production company, Fortis Films, *Exactly 3:30* and *The List*, both produced by Sara Pillsbury and Midge Sanford (*Desperately Seeking Susan*). "There's usually a guy at those meetings, so we'll look at him and say, 'What's the man's opinion about that?' It's like, okay, we'll talk to you now."

Their agent, Ostroff, who was just starting out as they were, was extremely supportive. "We were so fortunate," they say, "because when we jumped in, some women were moving into positions of power, and they were doing women's stories.

"Sara and I," says McGibbon, "write the kind of movies people expect women to be good at. It's much harder for women who write action. We do relationship movies and character pieces and battle of the sexes. I think in that respect being women helped us."

Historically, men have the final are-we-making-the-movie-or-not power. "Even though more women are in that position now," says Parriott, "the guys still have that power. But we've never had any feeling from a guy saying, 'Screw it, they're women, let's not make their movie, it won't sell.' "

Runaway Bride began its trek to the screen ten years ago when Bill Horberg (*The Talented Mr. Ripley*), an executive at Paramount, and David Madden, the producer, both big fans of 1930s screwball romantic comedies, began playing with the idea of the archetype of the "runaway bride." They knew of McGibbon-Parriott's work and asked them what they could do with the idea of a runaway bride and a reporter. Parriott and McGibbon came up with a story and were hired.

"Geena Davis and Harrison Ford were set to star in it about a year and a half after we wrote it," says Parriott. "Maybe five different directors were attached . . . and it kind of went south. Different stars were attached, like Sandra Bullock. It was always about to get made and it was always falling through the cracks, but it was good for our career because everyone knew about the script. Our agent was always sending it out. At every meeting, people would ask, 'What's happening with *Runaway Bride?*' We didn't believe it when our agent told us that Julia Roberts and Richard Gere were doing it. We didn't even tell our husbands. We thought they'd just say, 'Uh-huh, that's really exciting, honey. What's for dinner?' Finally, my mother read about it in *People* magazine, so we believed it."

"Writing scripts," says McGibbon, "is the most amazing career. Imagine being able to support a family and be home with your kids full-time. I started working when my kids were in nursery school, and Sara and I worked around my kids' school hours."

"We have made choices," says Parriott. They have been asked to do TV pilots, but they want flexible hours because Parriott is "hard into parenting young children. When we were producers on *The Favor*," she says, "we alternated weeks going to Portland, Oregon, where it was shot. That's been great in our partnership too, how often we can split the tasks."

"Remember that commercial of a woman on the tennis court and she says, 'I'm cleaning my oven'?" says McGibbon. "Easy-Off is doing it while she's playing tennis. I'm with my kids and I'm writing my screenplay because Sara's home typing away." They have been asked to direct, too, but they've decided not to—right now. "I couldn't possibly make every creative decision alone," says McGibbon. "To work at our best, we need each other's minds. It's kind of wild how we collaborate. We say one mind, two bodies."

Parriott and McGibbon rode the crest of the wave of new women, coming into the business during the late 1980s. "We might have been a novelty as a team," says Parriott, "but we weren't breaking down the door. We were flying in at a cool time while it was fresh to see new writers: 'Wow, we have women writers here!' Our hats are off to the women who did that for us ten years earlier, most of all to women in the studios and producers who broke down the doors. [In the 1990s] all of a sudden we were meeting with women in solid positions who were choosing material and looking around for writers that they'd feel comfortable with."

"Let's talk about the effect we have on the men in those meetings," says McGibbon. "Two attractives make one gorgeous." She explains, "I'm brunette and Sara's blond, and we're both tall and thin and we walk in and there's often a sort of 'Oh, ho, two cute girls walking in the room and they're both looking and smiling at me.' We're not flirtatious but we're lively and funny. The underlying message, I think, is this: 'If I've got to be in a room with somebody for six months to get this movie up and running, would they be fun?' "

"It's a little different when we're in the room with women," says Parriott, "and in five minutes we're talking about boyfriends and husbands. With men there's a little more male/female energy bouncing around. No matter who we're with, Josann and I make each other laugh, and I think people have fun in a room with us."

"We pick jobs [for] quality of life," says McGibbon. "It's six months to a year of your life; do we want to see their faces and get their notes? People like to work with people they like. Of course, that used to be going on just between the guys. Now it's different."[72]

We're Moms, Wives, Daughters, Sisters, Producers, Writers

"I'm not a female writer; I'm a writer who happens to be a woman," Janis Diamond says. "I learned that when I was on staff. The production company was having a bad time and cut back everybody's salary. I found out they cut me back more than anybody else. Was that because I was a girl? I went to the executive producer and said, 'For some reason, you think I'm a girl and I don't need as much money. If only the bank would give me a lower interest rate on my mortgage. Would you want your daughter to be treated this way?' Now I can't believe I did this.

"That's when I realized I'm a writer. What's the difference if I'm a girl or a boy or a dog or a cat? I'm a writer, and my gender shouldn't impact anything. Maybe we all rely on the basic belief that everyone instinctively knows the difference between right and wrong. You have to choose your fights wisely. What did I get from this experience? Know when to yell and when to be quiet, trust yourself, and when all else fails go into your office, shut the door, and write your way out of it. Your ultimate revenge. Ultimately, you just write your way out of it."[73]

Diamond writes and produces for series television, live action, interactive CD-ROM, and animated series from *Law & Order* to *Where in the World Is Carmen Sandiego?*

"I like going back and forth between interactive and live action," she says. "It's funny—if you're in animation they don't really want you to do live action. In interactive you need sharp dialogue, you've got to get to the point—short, sweet. It's a different set of skills, which I think helps my live action [linear programming]. In interactive, even in gaming, you need a beginning, middle, and end, a story so my linear writing skills help gaming and interactive. That's why I was brought in ten years ago on my first interactive, *Mystic Midway*. At first I wasn't hired because they didn't really believe they needed a creative writer. They called me back when they were under the gun—it wasn't working. They needed a story and dialogue."

Around 1992, she did *Girls Club*, which was about "who was going to win the date." The idea was to play it with a group of friends. At the time, there was no interactive programming for girls. "There's still not enough," Diamond says. "Dating is really just about relationships. We all have them—sister, brother, husband, lover. That's what I loved about *Girls Club*. It was gaming with stories. As a player, you could find out about yourself and your choices, picking your soul mate, even girlfriends. I knew nothing about the new media world. All those words like *icon* seemed so foreign. Now *e-commerce* just rolls off your lips. It was a great learning curve for me. Basically, I was just applying my writing skills, characters, drama, comedy, conflict resolution, making it entertaining."

Diamond was on a mommy track and the sole supporter of her family. She got up at five A.M., worked, dealt with her son, worked at night. "The mommy track," she says, "is the sidebar track. You're running on a different loop. When you get back into the game and you want back on staff, you're almost put at the back of the line. In the '80s, I was still working full-time at studios. When the nanny didn't show up and I had a meeting, I'd take him with me. I remember going to the studio to see some editing. I plopped him in a guy's lap, and he looked at me. I said, 'You have kids, don't you? Hold him for a second. He's sleeping.' I guess ignorance is bliss, but I just didn't know what else to do. What would they have me do, leave him alone in the closet? Slowly, I saw more kids show up on the days schools were out; spring break was always the horror. We were in our offices with our kids and a lot of toys.

"The generation before us told us, if you get married, have children, then divorce or whatever, you can always go out and work," says Diamond. "Did anyone try this out before we did it? I can tell you it was hell. What was everyone thinking? I remember saying to my mother the other day, 'No one tried it out. They just said you can have it all. Well, what does that mean?' I see women having kids now and I think, 'Oh, just take off, raise your kids, and then go back.' But if they do, they'll have to start all over again. Okay, you do it. Women will take any job to get back in line because there comes a point where your kids are ready to be on their own. You want your life back."[74]

Day-care facilities weren't established as part of a studio or network until the early 1990s. Gary David Goldberg at Paramount and Lucy Fisher at Warner Bros. created the first templates, which, as more women started working, others copied.

"All of us who have child care at studios now can thank Gary David Goldberg because he was the first," says Lucy Fisher. "He did it at Paramount, even though it was on a small scale. He deserves to be lionized." Fisher explains that the *Family Ties* creator/executive producer made the child-care issue a sticking point when he was in negotiations with Paramount to renew his contract. "The studio wanted to sign him up again. He said the studio needed to make a real day-care center, not just give him a crib [on the set]. He said it had to be at least for ten or twenty kids. Paramount did it because they wanted him to stay on the show. Others asked for a plane or for a boat, but he asked for that. The model we made at Warner was larger—we built a whole set of buildings for a hundred kids."[75]

In 1987, Lucy Fisher asked Warner Bros. for a four-day week when she had her first child; then she had a second, and a third. When her third child was about a year old, she says, "I just couldn't hack it anymore. I went in and said, 'Please reduce my salary. I want to work three days a week. I know it's not what you want, but I'll get all the work done, I promise. I feel like I'm letting down my kids, I'm letting down my job, I can't do it all, please reduce my salary and let me change my schedule again.'

"Bob Daly said no. I begged him, probably much to his surprise. 'Okay,' he said, 'I'll let you work a three-day week but only if you extend your contract by a year.' He was a prince. He knew I'd continue working as hard as I already did."

It took five years to build the day-care center. Fisher calls it "a miracle of biology over bureaucracy. There were two people from human resources, wonderful women, Adrienne Gary and Sharon Feldman, who made it happen." Fisher started working on it when she was pregnant with her first child. By the time they cut the ribbon, she had three children, and the eldest was too old for it.

"Others have followed suit," she says. "When Peter Guber came to Sony, basically he copied the Warner model. Sony has a fabulous child-care center."[76]

Almost everyone says that raising children gives you a fuller set of skills. "You get a lot of seasoning," says Janis Diamond. "You learn to problem-solve. If there's a glitch in production, you say, let's find an answer. The first time your child has a one-hundred-and-five-degree fever, you get scared. The second time and the third, you go into action. You learn what you really need to do is act. Those skills are priceless."[77]

Diamond was a scholarship student at Temple in Philadelphia, a constitutional history major on her way to law school, when she took a job in a small TV station to write, produce, and direct all the on-air promotion. When she graduated, she moved to California and UCLA Law School. She realized that though she loved the law and had grown up in a family of lawyers, she couldn't think of anything more boring than to practice it. She started to write for *Law & Order*.

"It's divided into two halves, the police investigating the case and then the law, the trial. What's fascinating is the twist in law in the last half. I could come up with oddball twists. The first one I did was 'Seed.' When I came up with the twist for it, I called the producers and said, 'Promise you'll still think I'm a nice person because my idea is so disgusting.' They went, 'Oh, yeah.' The story was about a family whose daughter was very ill with a disease like leukemia. As parents, they couldn't donate bone marrow, so they decided to have another child who could be a donor and save their first child's life. Back then, this concept was new. In the story, the couple has the second child, but genetically it doesn't match at all to the first child. Why? Because the clinic infertility doctor had used his own, not the father's, sperm. His line, 'God doesn't make babies, Mr. McCoy, I do,' showed what an egomaniac psycho he was."

On most of her writing jobs, Diamond has been the only woman. "In the beginning on *Law & Order*, I was almost the only woman, but there are more now on staff. My best buds in the industry are guys, writers.

"I'm married," says Diamond. "I'm taking care of our children [and] our parents. We're moms, we're wives, daughters, stepdaughters, sisters, sisters-in-law. In our society, we are expected to take care of everybody. The difference is that my husband is also a father and a producer but he's not looking at whether we have enough milk for tomorrow morning, or if the watering system broke down.

"That's part of the whole story about women, not just in our industry but everywhere," she adds, "though maybe more in this industry because we tend to wear more hats. An attorney is an attorney, but you're also writer-producer, you're writer show-runner, flipping into interactive or the new media that uses the same and different skill sets."

Peter and the Wolf started as an interactive CD-ROM, turned into an Emmy-winning television program,[78] then a feature overseas. Diamond wrote a book for it, which became a stage show, and then a one-hour piece with Kirstie Alley and Lloyd Bridges. "Those productions were all about 'how good can we make it?' That's rare. No egos. *Peter and the Wolf* was for ABC Television, and European money really made it happen."

Sergei Prokofiev had set the old folk story to music. Though Peter's grandfather warns him not to go into the woods, Peter crosses the meadow and enters the woods when a wolf devours his duck. Armed with nothing except his wits, Peter snares the wolf.

" 'Boys like Peter are not afraid of wolves,' " quotes Diamond. "That line drew me into that project. The line permitted me to lengthen and reinvent Prokofiev's musical folktale for today.

"Maybe that's what trying to make it in this business is all about, that '*people* like Peter are not afraid of wolves.' When we can reach for what we need to do, deep down, inside each of us is a creative person. We must do it, it's part of us, so we do it no matter what. Chuck Jones, who did all the animation, asked me, 'What is it?' I said, 'People like Peter are not afraid of wolves. That's the heart of Prokofiev's piece, in the music and the story.' All the courage and tenacity women need are set out in that one line."[79]

It's a Myth That You Can Have It All

Cynthia Cidre's parents came from Cuba when she was nine. She was raised in Miami. In 1979, she was one of eleven winners of a writing contest sponsored by Columbia Pictures. Cidre and the other winners were brought to Hollywood to be in the Columbia Pictures Writers Workshop to write feature film scripts at the WGA's minimum rate. Columbia bought five of the scripts that were written, Cidre's among them.

"I was paid ten thousand dollars," Cidre says, "more money than I'd ever seen. There were six men and five women in the program, including one Native American, and I was the only Latino. I was twenty-one years old and used to living on the cheap—we were immigrants in Miami—so ten thousand dollars went a long way."[80]

"There were not a lot of Latinos writing," she says. "I was treated as though I was some exotic thing. I had a lot of people to my house for Cuban food—people just invited themselves over, studio presidents and others, which felt a little weird. I didn't realize they didn't know that many Cubans."

She remembers the visible women who were around and particularly a young exec, Lauren Shuler. "I walked into her office one day—she'd been a camerawoman for a network and she wanted to be a producer—and I saw *Little Havana* on her desk. 'I wrote that,' I said. We talked for about three hours. But in the early 1980s, there weren't many women."

Cidre says she had only one bad experience, when she volunteered to do an adaptation of a novel owned by the company, which had been written by a major author. "I volunteered because somebody else had done a version that the author hated. I was friendly with the secretary in the producer's office. I had read it and I said, 'I can do this.' I locked myself in a room for eight days and wrote it. I was young then. Now it takes me a year to write a script. The author liked my script, and we became friends. There were several directors attached to the movie at various times, but one was a problem. He just didn't like women. He said right up front, 'I don't think she should be the writer because what does she know? The story's about a man, it's about Vegas.' The producer, God bless him, because I'd volunteered to do the script, felt he owed me something, and said, 'She's going to be the writer.' I went to New York but I had to write through a friend, a guy, an older writer. He and I met for breakfast every morning, we'd talk about the script, and then he'd call the director and tell him how it was progressing. He pretended to be cowriting the script. I wrote it. When the director treated me like an idiot, I went out and I got books on how to write, which I'd basically done on instinct. Instinct is iffy. You can't count on it. You have to know what you're doing. Structure in screenwriting is everything, and structure is like math. Building a script is like constructing a building—you know where the girders and the beams go, then you put on the stucco, but the girders better hold up the building. That director did me a favor because I still rely on what I learned from all that reading I did just to prove to him I wasn't an idiot."

Cidre wrote for television—*I Saw What You Did* in 1988 and *Killing in a Small Town*, which she coproduced in 1990. Her first feature film was *In Country*, a Vietnam War picture starring Bruce Willis. "I think I got that job because I fed Cuban food to Mark Rosenberg, who was president of Warner Bros. I'd met Paula Weinstein; I didn't know she was married to Mark Rosenberg. They were in love with Cuba, and asked me, 'Can you make us some Cuban food?' "[81]

Cidre married the Columbia business affairs executive who administered the Writers Program, J. David Marks. They have one child. "It's a myth that you can have it all," she says. "I'm convinced it's a big lie that puts women under a lot of stress. I took a year off, I nursed him, and then it was time to go back to work or give up the career that I'd spent twenty years putting together. It was very hard. I'm a workaholic and I used to work until six o'clock. Now I work until four, and when I'm finished making dinner, feeding the baby, feeding my husband, and feeding myself, I'm passed out on the kitchen floor. My work habits had to change. Then Denise DiNovi talked me into adapting the book called *The Cutout*. She has two kids, and she said, 'I will make this easy for you. I'm going to get everybody in my office to help you, and we're going to organize everything.' They really did that." Very '90s.

Her first film script, *Little Havana*, was finally made in 1991 as *Fires Within* with Jimmy Smits and Greta Scacchi. "In the first eight years or so, being Cuban helped me because . . . anything remotely Hispanic came my way, even though I said I know nothing about Colombia or Mexico or Costa Rica. My calling card was the script of *Little Havana*." When it was finally filmed, it bore no resemblance to the Cuban experience as Cidre knew it. "Afterward, I used to have a dream that I'd win the lottery and could reshoot the whole movie!"[82] Every writer's dream.

This Business Is Not About How Good the Screenplay Is

In 1984, when Robin Swicord came to Los Angeles from New York, where she had written plays like *Last Days at the Dixie Girl Cafe* and *Criminal Minds*, she met the cadre of women working in development.

"That sort of D-girl job was filled by highly educated and intelligent women who had a great story sense. They weren't setting some kind of example for me, because I didn't want to be an executive, but I felt upon meeting them that there were other intelligent, ambitious women here."[83]

Swicord was doing draft after draft of her first screenplay. She said to a friend, "Gee, if I can ever get this screenplay right..." He pulled the door slightly closed and said, "This business is not about how good the script is."

"I was naive," she says. "Another thing I noticed right away was that the dress code out here was very different for men and women. Men can go to meetings wearing T-shirts, blue jeans, and sneakers, but if a woman goes to a meeting dressed like that she's too casual. Women have to be more dressed up at meetings to be taken seriously. It's clear that men are offered different kinds of movies. There aren't that many women on the Hollywood A-list of writers. The women on that list are not offered the Elmore Leonard novels; they're offered movies about dogs and horses and mermaids and genies coming out of bottles. Men are offered movies with male or female protagonists. Women tend to be offered movies with female protagonists. It's very limiting.

"The first four screenplays I wrote did not have female protagonists (one was called *Stock Cars for Christ*). I like to write female protagonists and I want to see more movies made in which women are driving the car. You don't want to feel that your gender automatically sets you into a separate camp where you're allowed to earn a living by writing only certain kinds of movies for certain audiences." Swicord thinks that is the reality in the 1990s. In the 1980s, it was not as true—Swicord was offered scripting on movies with male protagonists.

"Around ten years ago, I began being offered movies with women in them," she says. "Female screenwriters all say the same thing to me. 'It's a girl...? Hey, I'm your writer.'"

In the 1990s, "chick flicks" finally had their day. Swicord wrote one of the biggest, *Little Women* (1994).

"Amy Pascal [then President of Columbia Pictures] and I tried to get that film made for about twelve years," says Swicord. "The 1980s were wrong for it—they were making little teen comedies, not what they called costume dramas. I thought, naively, it was a no-brainer, just a great story with castable parts. Women were always complaining about not having good roles; I thought we'd get it made right away. No. But by the 1990s, *Little Women* was possible."

Even so, Swicord, as writer and coproducer, had to make the marketing pitch at Columbia. "I was fortunate; Sid Ganis was in charge of marketing and he had four daughters. He understood our argument, which was that a large, multigenerational audience of women liked to go to the movies together. Even though the studio viewed *Little Women* as a movie that wouldn't cross over to other markets, we felt the existing market for it was big enough to warrant their investment in the movie. It took a lot of convincing. Sid Ganis was convinced, but many there were not. It took a lot of people—Amy Pascal and Lisa Henson and others—to get it going. There were many obstacles; they even took the money away from us while we were shooting. And yet we prevailed," she says. "*Little Women* made money and was one of the studio's two big Christmas movies [with *Legends of the Fall* by writer Susan Shilliday].

"After that, people stopped talking quite so much about movies aimed at female audiences being flukes, which is what they always said if you mentioned *Beaches* or *Steel Magnolias*. *Little Women* broke down a barrier. Some of it was the press, because the director, Gillian Armstrong, producer Denise DiNovi, and I talked in the press about this intra movie-business perception that women don't go to the movies. My point was they made up half the audience for *Lethal Weapon II*. Now that the audience has been identified, just as they've identified the teen market once again, now instead of saying 'Great, that's a wonderful script, this could be a wonderful movie,' let's say 'Let's make it,' because we know the audience is there. Okay, once that phase has been acknowledged, now begins the pandering machinery. 'That audience is there, we're going to give them this movie, we know they're going to like it because they like to cry and they like to see pretty clothes.'

"It's discouraging. The projects offered to you are not *Little Women*. They're something that's designed to get that dollar out of that woman's pocketbook . . . I keep thinking there's going to be some kind of breakthrough about quality of work. Again, my supreme naïveté. Maybe one day it'll be about the quality of work."

Hit movies earn hundreds of millions of dollars for studios; producers, directors, and actors can receive gross points (a piece of the gross revenues in addition to their fee), but not writers. However, in the groundbreaking deal orchestrated by the Writers Guild, Sony/Columbia Pictures (the studio that released *Little Women*) agreed to award screenwriters whose work had reached high earning levels gross points.

"Once you get over the thrill of being paid money for your script and having a dental and medical plan, you begin to focus on getting your movies made the way you intended them to be made," says Swicord. "At the Writers Guild a group got together to talk about strategies to improve the writer's situation. That group decided to go on a man-of-La-Mancha mission, tilting at studios to get gross points for writers. In return, we'd offer them spec scripts and a guaranteed number of screenplays, and other things."

Swicord's husband, Nicholas Kazan, was on the WGA committee-of-five who contacted every studio. Only one was willing to talk about the proposition, Amy Pascal at Columbia. A deal was struck, the old taboo broken.[84]

In 1993, Swicord directed a short film, *The Red Coat*, her first foray into directing.[85]

Swicord says she has encountered backlash even in today's atmosphere. "Women who've struggled so hard to erase differences in opportunities between men and women get angry when you say those differences still exist. But it's not equal. We can't pretend it is. I look at the ballot lists from WGA that come out every year that list all the feature films made, and I find only a few women writers. For years. Yet my husband, also a writer, gets one feature after another. I can't deny that." Women find it even more difficult to get work below the line, a budget term that's been used for decades. Performers, producers, writers, directors, sometimes the DP are above the line on budget sheets; members of the crew—gaffer, grip, script supervisor—are below. "For instance, there are very few women DPs. First ADs have a hard time moving up to director, and women in general in those jobs below the line have a hard time getting employment."[86]

My Biggest Supporters Are Men

Founded in the early 1970s, the AFI Directing Workshop for Women is still operating—there are new classes each year, and the alumnae list is lengthy. Lynne Littman referred to her class in the '70s as "the wild beasties." In contrast, Jude Weng, 1998 AFI alum, thought some of her classmates were too timid, focusing on making documentaries about women. "I support that kind of work," says Weng, "but I wanted to get to the mainstream world, to direct comedy-action features. They kind of poo-pooed me, except one who wanted to do commercial TV. Some of the older women in the group were almost militant about women getting to the top. I believe in it, but I'm not militant about it. Or maybe, since they were older, they've tried to get into the commercial world and didn't get it, so it's an easier route into documentaries."

In January 2000, Weng was writing for the biggest "reality" show on television, *Survivor*.

"I was hired as a 'challenge' writer," she says. "I wrote some spec challenges, they liked my ideas, and I wasn't afraid to say I'd never done anything like it before or to say 'I'm going to work really hard for you.' And I did, believe me."[87]

The show pitted contestants against each other in a "survival" contest of favorites and factions. It was one of many "reality TV" shows (MTV's *The Real World*; CBS's *Big Brother*), which James Wolcott labeled "the new voyeurism ... professional high-tech mass entertainment."[88]

Weng says, "I created the competitions for food and luxury items and some of the games like the rescue mission and distress signal. It was hard. The games had to be fair for men and women and also for the age range, twenty-two to seventy-six, a balance of intelligence and the physical. We actually had to prototype every game developed, so when we got our crew together in the *Survivor* office, we'd go out and test the games.

"Everyone asks, 'So what do you write on a reality show?' They needed a head writer to go to the island, write for the host, and write out everything the network, CBS, needed to know. For example, in episode one, how many minutes will be devoted to reality, how many minutes will be devoted to the challenges and a 'tribal council.' They asked me to write up a mock script. But that show was reality."

The *Survivor* show was set in the middle of the jungle. "About twenty feet away from the council area, they'd built a little house to do live editing. Of course, all the shooting was live. We don't reshoot. So we're in this tiny, tiny room," says Weng, "and there's, like, twenty people stacked in it, producers, and field producers, and it's all men except one female field producer and me." In the production offices, she says, the other women were two working audio and the women on the production staff. "They were very pretty. When I walked into the production office I was, like, wow, these women are gorgeous, like Charlie's Angels. Then I realized they were office decoration, easy for the producers to push around.

"After *Survivor*, I'll never sweat the small shit again," says Weng. "Number one, we're working on a remote island off Borneo. Two, the technical difficulties. When the printers broke down, that was bad. Guess what? I'm writing by hand. It was like being a war correspondent. I was writing for the host, an omnipotent character, and I had to know everything that's going on—the story lines that are developing, the relationships, how people are going to be voting, what they're eating, how they're feeling. We had to get into their heads, so it was like a big psychological mind-fuck."[89]

Weng is twenty-six, "young and hungry," which is why she gets jobs, she says. She was born in Taiwan, her parents divorced when she was four, and her father raised her and her sisters in San Francisco.

"It's a rather unusual childhood," she says. "My father was a Special Forces agent in the Taiwanese Army. His specialty was training female assassins. I was six years old when he taught me to use a gun and a knife . . . showed me how to be fearless, basically. That's always stayed with me. And even though my father is kind of misogynistic by nature, because that's what the military breeds in men, he also said, 'You will never ever take any shit from anybody.' My two sisters and I are all extremely independent.

"It's really because of my dad that I'm doing this work. He's a story-teller and an artist at heart. When I got my scholarship at AFI, he came to visit and I showed him around campus. As we were leaving, he said something so sad and striking. 'You know, if I'd had a choice I would have been a painter and a writer, but all I knew how to do was kill.' Him saying that just stopped me."

She had worked as an assistant at New Line Cinema in the sound-track department for two years. Then she was admitted to AFI, finished a short film, made another, *Steel*, in 1998—on film, not video (she talked Panavision into loaning her a camera package). She got a sample di-recting reel together. Nancy Jacoby at Travel Channel saw it and hired her to do some thirty-second spots—Weng's first paying job. From that she got a music video and was then hired to write *Survivor*. That's how it's done in the late '90s when you are in your twenties.

"The women in the '70s and '80s," she says, "they really paved the way for women of my generation. However, my biggest supporters are men. The women aren't as available—they're working! The guys, for whatever reason, seem to feel some type of guilt, maybe because their wives or daughters want to go into the business, too. The guys who've hired me are sympathetic."

Weng takes meetings to pitch her ideas and sees the industry from a different vantage point than someone who's been in it for ten years. Most of the people she pitches to are men. "I pitched to one man who was clipping his toenails throughout. I pitched a woman at a studio, a very nice woman, who was late for our meeting and showed up barefoot."

Weng says that being a woman has "absolutely" helped her. "There aren't that many women around, and there aren't many doing action *and* comedy, and there aren't that many Asians. All the things I don't want to pigeonhole me are helping me. Jerry Bruckheimer Films is a super manly place. Can't get more testosterone-driven than that. I was early for a meeting, sitting in the outer office in a big leather coat. I have short hair and my back was turned. Jonathan Lipman came out, 'Where's this Jude? Is he late?' He'd only read my scripts and just assumed I was a guy. I turned around and he was astounded. A woman, and Asian. We actually had a very long meeting."

Martha Coolidge, an AFI graduate, spoke to Weng's class. "She was awesome. But she bummed me out at the end. She said that if you're a woman and a minority, you're double fucked. That's true, but if you believe that, then you might as well give up. I take advantage of the fact that I'm Asian and a woman. Walking into a roomful of guys, if you're able to bring up the words 'blow job' in the first five minutes, they'll relax. 'I can talk about anything with this woman.' I use my humor and my dirty mouth. My friends joke, 'Jude will never have to sleep her way up.' No one has to," Weng says firmly.

Weng, from her early-days view of the industry, thinks there's "enough pie around for everyone. If there aren't enough, go make your own."[90]

18

THIS IS WHAT MEN DO

Directors of photography (DPs), production designers, unit production managers (UPMs), first or second assistant directors (ADs), gaffers (key electricians), grips, sound, and costume or script supervisors form the crews on motion pictures—"below the line." Traditionally, most of these union positions were filled by men. Few feature films with female crews have been made. Nancy Schreiber, a director of photography with many credits, worked as a gaffer in New York in 1973 on an all-woman feature, *The Waiting Room*; her cogaffer was Celeste Gainey. "Shortly afterwards, Schreiber went to China to work on Shirley MacLaine's first documentary, and continued to work as DP mainly on all-women crews, in addition to gaffing and camera assisting on mixed crews, often as the one female in the electrical department."[91] In the wild and woolly 1970s, teams of women shot mainly documentaries, moving into features or movies for television, if they survived, in the 1980s and 1990s, such as Claudia Weill, a director (*Face of a Stranger*, 1991) with Tyne Daly and Gena Rowlands. As director of photography, Schreiber shot *The Celluloid Closet*, *Girl in the Cadillac*, and *Your Friends & Neighbors*.

In 1987, according to surveys, women cinematographers were at 0 percent of their field. Women were working; they just weren't on the radar screen of top motion pictures. In 1999, women cinematographers had moved to 3 percent, in 2000 back to 2 percent.[92] Since the day in 1973 when Brianne Murphy attended her first union meeting and saw her union brothers part like the Red Sea in total silence when she entered the hall, other women have made it, but not many. Tami Reiker was the director of photography on *The Love Letter* and *Girl* in 1999; before that, *High Art*, *Far Harbor*, *Alchemy*, and *Little Women in Transit*. Reiker often works with women writers and directors.[93] Ellen Kuras shot *Blow* and *Bamboozled* in 2000; *Summer of Sam*, *The Mod Squad*, and *Just the Ticket* in 1999. Carolyn Chen started as assistant camera in 1987, then worked second unit assignments and camera operator (*Frank and Jesse* in 1994) to director of photography on *Culture* in 1998.[94]

The position of production designer is slightly easier for women to attain, but not much.

How Old Are You, Honey?

In 1989, Dina Lipton, a twenty-eight-year-old art director with a few years of experience (*General Hospital, Days of Our Lives*) walked into a producer's office to apply for the production designer job on a new soap opera, *Generations.*

"The producer was sitting behind a huge desk," Lipton says. "I've got my portfolio and resume, I'm young, I'm a woman, and I had to convince him that I was the right person for his show. I sit down across from him, thinking that he's going to ask me where I went to school and what's my experience. No. His first question was, 'How old are you, honey?'

"I was really surprised, and I'm wondering how to respond to that. I said, 'Well, how old are you?'

"If I'd been a man, there's no way he would have asked that. Anyway, he hired me, my first production design job, but I've never forgotten. It still happens to me because people look at my resume and then I go in for the interview and they say, 'Wow, how could you have done all that stuff?' "

Lipton was raised in New York until her family moved to Hollywood (her dad was a vice president at United Artists Records). She worked in summer theater, building scenery, graduated from North Carolina School of the Arts (the only university in the country with an undergraduate program in set design), and moved to New York in 1984 to work for a man who designed television commercials. "In '86 I was steered toward soap operas," Lipton says.[95] She was art director on *General Hospital* for about two and a half years, doing five hours of television a week, designing new sets every day. She spent the rest of the decade on another soap, *Days of Our Lives.*

Production designers design the entire look of the film, inside and out. They are "architects, painters, builders." They take the film from a concept or a script into "a visual conception . . . they actualize the environment."[96] For instance, production designer Polly Platt (see Chapter 3) convinced her husband, director Peter Bogdanovich, to move *Paper Moon* from the South into Kansas, because Kansas, flat and bare, had the look of the Depression.[97]

"The competition between men and women production designers," Lipton says, "is fascinating. Besides our ability to design, and our credits, here's one thing we do differently: When women go in for an interview, we have to give serious thought to what we're going to wear because we're probably going to meet a bunch of men. Now, keep in mind that production design is weird. We deal mainly with carpenters and wood and saws and painters and technical things. I'm five-four, look young, they see me and I know they're thinking, 'How's she going to be able to do that?' Other women have said the same. Some women producers feel threatened by women and don't really want to hire them. I also have to weigh the image I'm portraying. Some male production designers I know have grown their hair long and have goatees to look more 'artsy.' It's worked. They get more jobs. I haven't figured out how to grow a goatee.

"On some interviews I know who I'm up against for the job, and I'm thinking, 'I have better credits than that guy, so I'm not worried about him.' But he gets the job. I go back wondering, what's that all about? Did I wear the wrong clothes, what did I do? Do men go back thinking that? I don't know. I've tried to analyze it and then friends snap, 'Oh, that director never hires women.' Nothing I can do about that, because a director and a production designer have to click, not just on a creative level but as people.

"Bottom line for an interview is," says Lipton, "you have to consider how men react to women. When I interview with a woman, it's totally different, a whole different feel, not necessarily camaraderie, sometimes more like competition. Unfortunately, women tend not to hire women, which I don't understand." As an art director, Lipton has worked with only one woman director, Jessie Nelson, on the Whoopi Goldberg film *Corrina, Corrina* (1994). "Jeannine Claudia Oppewall was the production designer," Lipton says. "She taught me a lot.[98]

"In my very first set design class in college, the teacher said, 'If you're in this business for money you should leave. If you think this is going to be fun and games, you should leave.' He goes down a list and then he says, 'Oh, by the way, if you're a woman, multiply all that by two because it's going to be that much harder for you.'" Women were and are expected to be costume designers, which they are, far outnumbering men in that field.

In Lipton's class of twenty-five people, ten were women. Out of that group, Lipton was the only woman who graduated in 1984. "But I could never do anything else with my life," she says. "I love it."

In 1998, Albert Brooks hired Lipton as the production designer on his film *The Muse*. "Albert was a great collaborator," Lipton says. "It wasn't just scenery to him; it was about telling the story and allowing the scenery to help tell the story. Many directors or producers do not have the same respect for designers that they do for cinematographers, but you are both telling the story visually and you need each other. Albert really understands that. When looking for locations, directors often want their cinematographer there with the production designer, which is kind of a pain for us because a production designer wants to set the visual look. Then the cinematographer comes in and figures out with the director and production designer how to shoot that look. Often the cinematographer becomes the director's sidekick and the production designer becomes a forgotten child.

"Albert and I were going to look for locations, and I asked him if he wanted the cinematographer to come along. Albert said, 'No. You and I, Dina, decide what the movie looks like and he'll shoot it and that's how it works.' I appreciated his respect for my job. It doesn't happen that often."

Lipton worked as an art director on *Mr. Holland's Opus* (1995, directed by Stephen Herek). The producer, Judith James, gave Lipton a chance to production-design her next film, *Trigger Happy* (aka *Mad Dog Time*, 1996).

"Judy understands what it means to help other women," Lipton says, "but being a woman has hindered my career and it's definitely easier for men. It goes back to a perception that hammers and nails are boys' things. Art directors, who are sort of the production designers' assistants, are more often women. When I joined the union in 1986, there weren't that many women production designers who run crews, are responsible for a lot of money, sometimes millions, deal with construction, paint, set dressing, props, oversee costume design, everything that's visual about the film. I think the attitude of many producers about a women designer is that 'I'm not going to give my wife the checkbook.' Younger men are absolutely more open, not nearly as gender biased as the old guys."

Rapper Ice Cube was putting his film, *The Players Club* (1998), together when Lipton interviewed for it. "Here I am this young, white, Jewish girl going in to meet Ice Cube," Lipton says, "and I know I'm never going to get this job. He didn't see any of that. He looked at my work! Imagine that! How refreshing." She also did *Next Friday* (2000) with him.

Lipton is married to a producer she met while working on *Mr. Holland's Opus.* She was the art director; he was the production manager. She has three stepchildren, aged eight, thirteen, and fifteen.

"I want to have a child, but I often wonder how'll I deal with it? We go to work at seven in the morning and rarely come home before eight at night. That's not a normal life. When we're not working it's fabulous because you can take off two months... For *Here On Earth* I was working eighteen, nineteen hours a day. How do people do this and have children? Do men think about how they're going to handle their jobs *and* their kids? We have to think about everything, not just kids, but if there's food in the refrigerator, the laundry, or who's going to walk the dog. I don't want my dog locked up all day. If I feel guilty about my dog, how am I going to feel about my child? I know my husband thinks about the kids, but he doesn't think about all the other things that women stress over."

When Lipton began working, she thought she was going to design scenery and never thought about being a "woman" in that line of work until she heard comments like "Why are you doing this? This is what men do," as one producer said to her.

"Wow," I thought, "did I make a mistake? Should I have gone into hair and makeup?" Her grandfather owned a lumber company, and she remembers the smell of fresh lumber and the look of moldings or handrails. "I worked there. I love wood and nails. I may be a girl, but, hey, I love it."

Filming *The Muse* with Albert Brooks took place in the middle of a hot summer. It was a low-budget film. They were shooting in a warehouse in Sylmar, a suburb of Los Angeles. Sometimes, Lipton thinks, women are just seen as the main provider, no matter what their job, and sometimes it's funny.

"Albert wasn't thrilled with the site," says Lipton, "and kept saying, 'Just make sure we have enough air-conditioning.' I had nothing to do with maintaining air-conditioning, but I kept reminding the production manager, producers, and first AD about it. We had four sets erected in that warehouse. The first day, I'm miles away at another location building with my crew when Albert calls me from the warehouse. He's very upset. 'Dina, it's so hot in here! Do you remember that scene in *Broadcast News* when I was sweating? That was real, Dina, that was really me!' I'm wondering why he's calling *me?* Then he says, 'Dina, I can't be funny in Sylmar.' I'm trying to choke back my laughter because he was really mad and he wanted me to fix the problem, but that was *funny!* Albert is funny even when he is being very serious. I realized that he was calling me because he knew that I would take care of him. When I called the producers, they said, 'We've got three air conditioners in there, and everybody's freezing, wearing parkas, except him!'"[99]

Women Cannot Make a Mistake

The technical motion picture unions, under the powerful umbrella of IATSE (International Alliance of Theatrical Stage Employees) are male-dominated.[100]

"I was wearing blinders," says Andrea Sachs, a chief lighting technician who came to Los Angeles from New York in 1990. "It never occurred to me that someone would say no because I was a woman. When I walked into those interviews, I felt I was a contender—always. But it is daunting when you walk into an interview, they're all men, and they make it clear they're not sure you can do your job."[101]

Sachs majored in theater lighting at college. "That experience was harder than any professional work I've ever had," says Sachs. "The guy teaching lighting design hated women. There were only about twelve of us in the whole senior class. On a lot of levels, this professor was excellent and I learned there's no excuse for failure and no excuse for doing a half-ass job. He told me in my first year, 'I am not going to let you graduate. I don't care what you do.' It was a real tough road. I'd spend weeks preparing a project, turn it in, and he'd lose it. He'd say, 'You need to hand this project in,' I'd say, 'But I gave it to you.' He'd say, 'You never did. You have to redo it.' The attrition rate was very high. I was the only senior left in my class. The college had given me an internship in New York at an industrial film and video production house. When I finished that, the lighting professor grilled me during an oral exam before the theatre department. He asked questions that I wouldn't have known had I been in film for five years—electrical stuff I had not been exposed to at all. On the basis of that, I was told my internship was bust. It felt so unfair."

Three months before she was to graduate, she went back to New York and began lighting off-off-Broadway plays, then some low-budget features. She got into NABET, the National Association of Broadcast Employees and Technicians, in 1979.

"Light is incredibly beautiful," Sachs says. "There are no rules. Aesthetically, [working the light] is a personal choice. When I was about four, I remember sitting under my mother's ironing board watching the particles of dust in the light. I remember that so clearly. Lighting is mystical. A tone or angle of light, its color, evokes specific emotions from people. When you're doing a movie, consistency in the lighting affects the mood. For example, in the beginning of *Elizabeth*, the 1999 feature, the light was very cold, the environment sterile, uninviting, dangerous. As the movie progressed, the light warmed up. It really invoked a mood carried through the whole picture."

Sachs has a reputation for expecting a lot from her crews. "Some guys are uncomfortable with that," she says, "but we're well paid, and when I'm giving a hundred and ten percent, I expect whoever's working with me to do the same. I'm not a slave driver, but I am tough."

The gaffer, or CLT (chief lighting technician), works hand-in-hand with the director of photography and the key grip to establish the mood and the look of the film—the way it will be illuminated. The CLT heads his or her department, overseeing the crew and safety procedures.

When Sachs was lighting the feature *Nowhere to Run* in San Francisco, she was not allowed to hire the people she wanted.

"The union was sending people they wanted," says Sachs. "It was a closed shop there, not working from the union rolls. It was infuriating because I knew guys there who were good, but the union's sending me guys from their opera house who had no film experience. I brought a best boy with me who was afraid to tangle with the union, so I was really on my own. The first day we were shooting, I find out the son of one of the union people was to be my generator operator.

"We were shooting a scene before we got into principal photography with some little kids running through a barn. I was with the grips and all we had out was a grifflon, a tough plastic material held in a frame on a stand. It was a bright sunny day, but the wind gusted up. The little kids were at the base of the grifflon when it started to come down. I jumped on one side, the key grip jumped on the other, and a few others came to help. This generator operator said to me, 'I'm going to bring you up on charges. You're touching equipment that's not electrical.'

" 'You know what?' I said. 'You're fired. I don't want a guy like you on my crew.' I started a war. Every guy the union sent me was the most inexperienced knuckle-dragger. First, they hated that I was a woman. Second, that I came from L.A. And then the woman from L.A. fires this guy—I absolutely stepped into a very nasty swell. When we were wrapping, the crew destroyed some equipment, cut our cable, broke HMI bulbs, and tossed equipment all over the place.

"There's hard stuff to go through. Guys will not respect you unless you show that you are tough, but you can't be a nightmare either. Walk softly, carry a big stick. Men won't respect a woman who's a shrew. They respect you if you do your job, if you're consistent and strong."

The electrical department on a film has a substantial budget. Being a CLT involves a lot of decision making—which gear is to be used, for how long and where, the manpower, and who gets hired. "That's my job," says Sachs. "I choose who will work on my crew, and every week I get about fifteen phone calls from guys who need work."

She credits a number of DPs who have been good to work with, like John Schwartzen and Peter Menzies. "The only time I got a job *because* I was a woman was for a Tampax commercial.

"Being a woman made it harder, but it never prevented me from having a career," says Sachs. "I've worked steadily. But the next step up is DP, and being a woman has inhibited that to some extent. It's a lot easier for men to move up the ladder than it is for women. Women cannot make a mistake. I learned in college that if a woman makes a mistake it stays with you for a really long time. Men have shorter memories of mistakes other men make. A guy can do something horrendous on the set and it seems to just go away in a year. If I did something like that, it might never go away. There's so few women doing this work, our profile is so high, we cannot make errors. You're really in trouble if you do."

But overall Sachs says that being a woman CLT is easier now. People are not surprised when she walks on set. "Women producers seemed less comfortable with me as a gaffer than they are with men," she says. "They question me closely when I put in an order for gear, but they seemed to think it was good I was there. When it came to the job, they weren't quite sure if I could or couldn't do it. It's less like that now. At least, I get a little camaraderie from them, though I don't think women fall into that as much as men. They don't travel in packs like men do. Women are lone wolves."[102]

In her work as a gaffer and lighting cameraman, Amy Halpern would agree and disagree. "Being a woman prevented me, period," she says. "Not from performing the work, but *getting* the work. A sense of humor is essential, because the humiliation of not being hired, having less continuity in employment, and dealing with people who are still surprised to see you there...that's constant. The two [HBO] pictures I just worked on, Nastassia Kinski, who's been around the block, was astonished to see me on the set. Why should someone of her sophistication be surprised to see [a woman gaffer]? That can wear on you. Ironically, I think women are highly qualified to gaff. Who else is raised to pay attention to how space feels, or the arrangement of things in a room? We're trained from our mother's knee. Being a woman *has* helped me in terms of crew work. Crews are supposed to work together seamlessly, as one entity. Women are hardwired to assist in an egoless manner— it's part of our biology, which helps exactly and directly."[103]

In 1998, Andrea Sachs was working a low-budget film out of town. "A girl shows up to work that day as an electrician, one of my juicers.

I'd never met her before. She's wearing fabric sneakers, which would be hellish if something came down on her foot. We were working in really rough terrain and she was wearing Keds! She had huge hoop earrings, a fresh manicure, long nails, and a lot of makeup. I pulled her aside. 'I'm going to talk to you as a friend,' I said. 'Take the earrings out of your ears, get yourself a proper pair of shoes, and wear something that a man's going to respect if you're working next to him. If you're working with me and throw a bunch of cable over your shoulder and pull that earring through your earlobe, you're going to be in the hospital. Protect yourself.'

"I was embarrassed for her and for the women in my union," says Sachs. "Appearing like that chips away at the gains we've made."[104]

What? And Leave All This? No!

"Stuntwomen have been around as long as stuntmen," says Leslie Hoffman, stunt coordinator and stuntwoman. "Lillian Gish was a stunt-woman the minute she got on the ice floe." That was for *Way Down East* (1920), and Gish was proud she never used a double or a stand-in. "Ever since films have rolled, women have been taking chances doing their own stunts. There's more work for men—even the word 'stunt' has macho mystique—but women who are skilled and lucky can make a living in this industry."[105]

Hoffman, the daughter of a pharmacist from quiet Saranac Lake in upstate New York, has done hundreds of different kinds of stunts. "Most stunts are pratfalls, which is being able to fall down without hurting yourself." In *Police Story*, she was pushed out of a car; in *Charlie's Angels* she did a stair fall; on *Love Boat*, she took a seventy-eight-foot fall off the ship. On *Remington Steele*, she was a regular double for series costar Doris Roberts. "When I got stunt jobs early on I'd call my mother and say, 'I'm going to be doing a fight scene on such and such, or I'm going to be jumping off the Love Boat into the water.' She said, 'Leslie, tell you what. Why don't you call me *after* you do these stunts?' "

Hoffman did the motorcycle sidecar jump in Steven Spielberg's ill-fated *1941*. "It was supposed to be a motorized sidecar," she says, "which jumped off a ramp. I was doubling for Wendie Jo Sperber, who played Maxine. [I was] sitting on top of the car; a stuntman was sitting in the car. It was supposed to hit the ramp and jump into the back of a truck. We tried it several times, but they had to restart the car each time because it stalled out. We finally zoomed down the ramp, but it stalled again and hit the back end of the truck. I shot off the top of the sidecar and slid onto the back of the egg truck. Had we hit the truck any lower, I would have collided with the back end of the truck. *That* was a real scary time."

She says the best time was working with Dennis Madalone, who co-ordinated *Star Trek: The Next Generation, Deep Space Nine*, and *Voyager*. She was one of his assistant coordinators, covering production meetings and being on the set as the stunt coordinator. "Dennis doesn't look at me as a stuntwoman, he sees me as a person who can break down a script, go to production meetings, or be on a set setting up stunts."

Usually, the career progression is this: stunt person, stunt coordinator, second unit director. Once you get your second unit director card, you can go off with a crew and film stunts for a movie. Most coordinators are men, Hoffman says, because the industry doesn't see women as capable of coordinating.

"Habit," she says. "They've always used the same coordinator, and why switch? But at some point somebody gave that stuntman a break. One of the most important jobs of a stunt coordinator is to make sure the set is safe. When I talk to people about women coordinating, and they say no, I point out that in a way stunt coordination is what a mother does—she makes sure that her child doesn't fall down and hurt itself. Why not a stuntwoman as coordinator? Another reason women are almost never used as stunt coordinators is that people think women can't rig stunts on cars or they don't have mechanical knowledge, which is untrue."

Stunt coordinators create routines, fights, falls, and car work for stunt people. They also show actors how to fight safely without hurting each other. "A director may say to the stunt coordinator, 'I need a five-punch fight routine. This actor has to be in this position when the fight is over.' A coordinator doesn't just show up on the set the day of the stunt," says Hoffman. "They break down the script, give a budget to the production company, set up the right equipment on the set, and create the sequence."

Hoffman was the first stuntwoman elected to the board of directors of the Screen Actors Guild in Los Angeles, the American Federation of Television and Radio Artists (AFTRA) national board, and the Los Angeles AFTRA board. Currently she is chairwoman of the Women in Film Stuntwomen's Committee. "I've attended many meetings at the women's committees of the guilds and various women's professional organizations. I've always received a sympathetic ear, but I've walked away with no gains for stuntwomen. At two different meetings, women have announced to the room that they would not hire a woman as a stunt coordinator. I wish those women could hear themselves. Sadly, not one of the unions or women's organizations has helped instrumentally to make changes for stuntwomen or stunt coordinators.

"Some stuntmen honestly believe that no woman is capable of certain stunts, or they just trust their buddy. He may use a new, young man to do a stunt, even though he doesn't know whether the guy can do it or not. If he's saying 'I'm not going to give this job to a woman because she might hurt herself,' he honestly believes that and he'll never give her the chance."

Hoffman has been doing stunt work since the 1970s. She lectures on safety to various unions, film organizations, and universities. "I also do student projects for the American Film Institute and USC," she says. "No one's told these kids that women can't be coordinators, so I get calls from the students, male and female, to coordinate their projects."[106]

Hoffman worked on the first *Nightmare on Elm Street.* The shoot was in an abandoned high school. As she walked in, she saw a slime trail down the hallway. Another low-budget horror film.

"They were filming the scene with the body bag," she recalls. "The girl was all bloody and she had to be dragged off, so they tied a wire to the body bag and slid it off camera. Then they put my hair in these ponytails and gave me a striped sweater to wear. Wes Craven came up to me: 'Okay, you're the hall monitor. After she knocks you down I want you to say "Where's your pass?" '

"Nancy [the heroine, played by Heather Langenkamp] comes running down the hallway," Hoffman recalls, "bumps into me, and knocks me to the floor. One take. That's another thing about being a stunt person: are you known for doing a stunt in one take? In a low budget, there's no money for retakes unless absolutely necessary."

Hoffman was outfitted with razorlike claws on her hands. Craven told her, "I want you to say, 'Hey, Nancy, no running in the hallway,' and then do a sinister laugh."

"That show became the *Nightmare on Elm Street* classic. I was the only woman who played Freddy Krueger," says Hoffman. "Everyone wants to be remembered for being in a special movie. I didn't expect mine to be a horror cult classic.

"The worst thing a woman or a man can do on a stunt job is take a job they can't do. Everyone's standing around and if the woman can't fall or drive the tractor, they have to replace her immediately, which is almost impossible. That stops the production flat and perpetuates the myth that stuntwomen can't do certain stunts. I saw that once on a stunt that involved climbing a gym rope. The woman just assumed she'd be strong enough to pull herself up. She could not do it. Unfortunately, they put a wig on a man and he did the stunt. I would have turned that job down because I know I don't have that upper-body strength. I can hang and do a high fall, but I can't climb up a rope."

"In *Laverne & Shirley*, we did a pyramid, about ten of us climbing up on each other's shoulders," Hoffman says. "That's just hiring the right people, putting the routine together. A choreographer hires dancers capable of dancing. A stunt coordinator sets up the situation and gets the right people to do it."

Hoffman says that today only a few women are stunt-coordinating television shows. "On those sitcoms that have a full-time stunt coordinator," she says, "how difficult can the stunts be? If you don't trust a stuntwoman to do *Indiana Jones*, at least consider her for a sitcom. You're not firing someone out of a cannon on a sitcom every week.

"This is a business you love and hate. People have said to me, 'You got complaints? Why don't you get out of the business and do something else?'

" 'What?' I say. 'And leave all this? No!'

"If I could live my life over again," says Hoffman, "I'd still be a stunt-woman."[107]

Once in a While You'll See a Lone Woman Grip

Just coming into the industry in 1996, Grace Liu started out as a script coordinator on the Don Johnson TV series, *Nash Bridges*—a production office position, working on script changes. "At the time," she says, "I was sort of cutting-edge when it came to computers. The executive producer, a techno freak, loved his gadgets, but had no idea how to work them. His male assistant had no clue either. So I'd show them how to work it. That producer took me with him on his next film, *Kull The Conqueror*." She worked as an assistant to the director, John Nicolella, shooting five months in Slovakia—fifty-six men and three women, the wardrobe woman, a production assistant, and Liu.[108]

Born and raised in San Jose, California, Liu majored in English at the University of California, Berkeley. Her father is a nuclear engineer, her mother a homemaker. "I knew I wanted to work in the movies when I saw *Star Wars*," says Liu. "My generation was just blown away by it. I was twelve. I knew nothing about movies. My family came to the States from Hong Kong in the '60s. I don't know if they went to movies over there, but to this day they have not seen a movie in a theater here."

She graduated from college, still wanting to work in film but not knowing how to break in. "It was unacceptable in my family for me to work in films. My mom kept saying, 'Girls don't make movies.' It was

partly cultural, because in Hong Kong or China women who made movies were associated with prostitutes. I just did it, but it took a heavy
psychological toll on me. If I'd been a boy it would have been more
acceptable, but in traditional Chinese families parental control is very
strong, regardless of gender."

She came to Hollywood in 1996. "I started in the production office. It
was very hard to get a position on-set because people tend to think
women belong in the office. I bluffed my way onto a set job on *Red
Corner*, the Richard Gere movie set in China. They wanted a production
assistant who spoke Chinese. I spoke Cantonese; they wanted Mandarin.
Most of the producers were Caucasians, and I figured they'll never know,
right? One had a Chinese last name. I memorized a few lines of Mandarin. In the interview, this Chinese AD said, 'So you speak Chinese?' I
said, in Mandarin, 'Of course I do.' I said a few other things to him. 'Oh
great, you're hired.' That job was quite stressful. I had to convert my
dialect to theirs. They'd come up to me on the set and say, 'Your Chinese
is so bad,' and I'm, like, 'Yes, but can you understand what I'm saying?'
They said, 'Yeah.' At least it got me out of those offices."

After *Red Corner, Kull the Conqueror*, and *Splitsville*, she worked as a
set production assistant, then entered and passed the rigorous Directors
Guild exams for the trainee positions assigned to every production. At
first they assigned her to television—*Party of Five, ER*, and *Buffy the
Vampire Slayer*.

"The crews are still predominantly male," she says. "The women are
in hair, makeup, and wardrobe. There are a lot more women assistant
directors now. It's sort of the female route to go. *Red Corner* had a
woman producer. The UPMs [unit production managers], camera and
electrical, grips, directors, and the first ADs are mainly men. Predominantly, women are producers and second ADs. Once in a while you'll
see a lone woman in the grip or camera department. That's so rare, it's
great when you see that. I worked with a female DP on *C.S.I.*, a Touchstone pilot [now a series], and I'd never seen that before."[109]

Liu was still a set production assistant on the Robert De Niro feature
15 Minutes. She's soft-spoken, about five feet tall. One of her tasks was
to keep the crew quiet when a scene was being rehearsed or when the
cameras were rolling.

"It's stereotypical that the grips are the loudest department," she says.
"They're big, brawny, hardworking, tough-drinking guys. They've got
Playboy posters in their trucks. So I'm trying to keep these guys quiet
outside, saying, 'Shh,' like I was leaking air. This big guy comes up to
me and says, 'What are you—springing a leak?' He pulls out some tape.
'You want me to plug that leak? Let me put some tape on that.' I look

at this guy, then slap my butt, and say, 'Yeah, right here, baby.' He goes, 'Whoa, sister, you're okay.' From that day on he helped me keep the other guys quiet."

Being an AD is all about people skills and organizing. It requires flexibility. Liu thinks being female actually helps her on a crew because women "can wear so many different personas to get what they want, in the best sense," she says, "to get the production moving and motivate people. It's like real life—you can be aggressive, but you can be sweet and girly, too."

Today, most young women in production work have experienced some degree of sexual harassment. "It's mainly crews and producers trying to pick up extras," Liu says. "I'm certain that the casting couch exists still. Sets are sexually charged places. I don't have a problem with that. In fact, it makes things kind of interesting. But there are some producers who, even though they're young, they're old school in the sense that they're going to try to get some from any female crew member—*if* the woman lets them. But then, really," she laughs, "what's a woman to do? You sort of try to joke it off. As a DGA trainee, we've had all these seminars on sexual harassment, but when it comes right down to it, you're not going to say anything because you'll get a reputation for making trouble. Or for not being fun. You kind of toss it off. I worked with one producer who was just horrible in that sense. He made constant comments, really unmentionable. You toss it off. That's all you can do."

When Liu became a full-fledged AD in 2001, she had more protection from her guild status, she says, because she's never seen a producer harass a female AD. "They pick on the lowlier ones," she says, "the vulnerable ones, the extras, the production assistants."

One thing Liu has noticed over the five years she's been almost con- tinuously on sets is that when a woman makes a mistake it's more serious than a man's mistake. "I was working on a show for a TV series," she says, "and we'd had a series of big-name male directors. One episode was directed by a woman. To be honest, she was a little slow. She took her time. It was unspoken, but you could feel the vibe. The guys were think- ing, 'This woman, she doesn't know what she's doing.' We've had guys who were equally slow. We've had guys who were inept as directors. But the vibe that day was, she's a woman and therefore she doesn't know what she's doing. It was entirely unspoken, but it was there."

Assistant directors coach actors on dialogue, see every frame that's shot, and work with or serve the director every day. In the late 1990s, there were more women than men in Liu's DGA trainee class—three men out of fifteen. When Liu met the twenty-two-member class of 2000, five were men. One of the goals of the training program is to recruit and train women and minorities, which it seems to be accomplishing.

"I haven't decided whether this was just being a trainee or whether it's being a woman," says Liu, "but I'm beginning to think this happens partly because I'm a woman. In my work as a DGA trainee, I had the feeling that trainees were expected to smile, be nice, act as if we didn't know what we were doing, and run everything by our supervisors. I've talked to other trainees about it. They think it's gender. I'm not sure. I don't have to bloody smile all the time if I don't feel like it. People never say to guys, 'Hey, smile.' Guys say that to women all the time, like we're supposed to be little cheerleaders. It makes me feel 'wifey.' Smile and support your husband, the director.

"I think I get along better with guys," says Liu. "The women I met as a trainee and as a PA were not very supportive. My advisors and unofficial mentors are men. The ADs I keep in touch with who help me find my next job are men. The worst experience I had was with an AD team of mainly women—the first AD was a man, the second and third were women. We had major personality clashes. It's bad to say this, but it was just too, too female. I wasn't used to working with all these women. I think because they were women they put me, another woman, on a tougher standard."

Liu and other women her age who work in production start to wonder where their personal lives are. "I'm beginning to think about family. There's no way I could have a family if I were a director. Some women have done it, I don't know how. I've never worked with a female AD who had a child. My God, I only know one female AD who is married."

Liu thinks being Chinese helps her. "I never feel that I'm Asian or a minority when I'm on a film crew, but it's useful when we're shooting in Chinatown or working with an all-black cast. The fact that I'm Asian and technically a minority puts me, in a funny way, on their side. I can't put my finger on it. It's like this invisible line between white and anybody nonwhite, so the black guys are calling me 'sister.'

"Everything is not equal for women," she says, "though in some positions it is, like being an AD. The buzz is that women make better ADs than men, but I think that's a bad stereotype, arising from an AD being like a wife. ADs organize the life of the director, support him in every way so he can make that picture. I think that's why people think women make better ADs. It's still very difficult for women to break into the technical positions . . . It's harder for women to break in—period."[110]

19

MAKING THE WHOLE FRAME IN THE '90s

At a meeting in 1999 at the Directors Guild, actress-director Debbie Allen moderated a panel of women directors. She introduced the evening by saying, "A woman in 1895 had a great idea of making a film into a story. . . . In 1912, she directed a movie called *In the Year 2000* about a time when women would rule the world!"[111]

Not yet. Though American productions drove the entertainment business, if not the art, in the 1990s, producing became as global as the business itself. In the late 1990s, women as producers compared to directors or writers became the single largest new group in both television and film. Directing was still a hard row—even for famous performers—but by the late 1990s, women would think nothing of aspiring to writing, producing, or directing, inside or outside the Hollywood entertainment fort. Young women might train in music videos, then write, direct, or produce a feature maybe as an independent, maybe as a cable movie.

The women in this chapter produced and/or directed all over the world, from North Carolina to China. Some came to the effort late in their careers, some in midcareer; one is just beginning.

I Didn't Want to Be Part of the Picture, I Wanted to Make the Whole Frame

After nearly forty years as an honored international performer (*Cries and Whispers, The Emigrants, Scenes from a Marriage*), Liv Ullmann began directing almost by accident.

In 1990, she was asked to adapt a novel to a script for a planned Danish film, *Sofie* (1992). She says she thought the request strange; she was not a screenwriter. When she finished, the producers asked her to

No ...

direct it, even stranger. "I didn't quite believe it was true until they said it again in a press conference."[112]

Ullmann had no idea what kind of director she'd be, but found the proposition exciting. Her many years as a stage and screen actress had taught her more about directing than she knew and in ways she had not recognized until she began.

"I realized that I didn't want, and hadn't wanted, to be just a part of a picture," says Ullmann. "I wanted to make the whole frame. The framework has always been important to me. As I got older, I hadn't realized why I felt more and more inadequate as an actress. When I began directing, I knew. I had never been part of making the framework—I had always been in somebody else's frame, and the older I got, the less I liked their frame. It didn't give me enough room."

She knew she was a novice director. She came on the set well prepared. "After the first week. I knew I'd never felt so fulfilled," says Ullmann. "I was most worried about my plans for the actors, but that worry vanished. I took such pleasure seeing what they gave the scene, not from what I had prepared for them. As an actress, I've worked with good and bad directors, I saw what not to say or do, how not to kill an actor's fantasy. When I was acting, I never liked talking about being an actor, but from the director's point of view, I realized how wonderfully creative actors are. The director should just be there, give them earth to plant their ideas, and watch them grow."

Her difficulties came from the rest of the team—the line producers, technicians, crew. "There I was, a middle-aged woman, which is not so good, an actress, not so good, and a neophyte, not so good. Getting their respect was very tough."

She had two difficult weeks with the cinematographer. "He wanted to quit because I said where I wanted the cameras to be and he didn't believe I'd thought it out. We had a terrible meeting." But he stayed on and by the end of shooting, Ullmann says they had a wonderful working relationship. "He realized I knew what I wanted and why I wanted it."[113] He also shot her film *Faithless* (2000).[114]

Looking back on those early days, she now thinks her problems with the cinematographer were her fault. Though she clearly described the shots she wanted, she also tried to play "the little woman, running around giving them coffee," Ullmann says, "asking them if there was anything I could do for them so they'd like me more. That did not work. That is not how you get respect."

The second film she directed was *Kristin Lavransdatter* (1995), which she also scripted, adapting the classic novel by Sigrid Undset. For it, she feels she went too far the other way; she was too tough. "With my third, *Private Confessions* (1996), I found my voice," Ullmann says. "I didn't have to play a subordinate role or a tough role. I just trusted myself and my woman's voice."

On the set, Ullmann thinks a woman director changes the atmosphere. "We are less controlling. We know what we want, but we're not afraid to listen to others with different opinions. We don't lose our craft or dignity by allowing others to be part of it. I find it makes the work more efficient, too—there are fewer commandos, fewer secrets, fewer grudges. I've also found that women don't dress up what we want to say in technical terms just to make it sound good. I can say 'I'd like the camera to float as it moves from this person to that person.' I don't think a man would say that. That may just be my way of expressing it."

Ullmann dislikes speaking in generalities but says she's found in her experience that some male actors she's directed are less afraid of exposing their souls to a woman than to a man.

"Offstage, in private life, if men confess their innermost feelings at all, very often it will be with a woman because men don't seem to have the language to do it between them. If, as a director, you can make that bridge to an actor, you can allow him to do the same in his role in the film."

However, Ullmann and another actress worked with a woman director on a film in the 1980s. "It made us both sad because we felt this director was doing what you shouldn't do as a woman. She was controlling, she had everything written out beforehand, she didn't listen to us and allowed no discussion. She was more difficult to work with than many male directors I've worked with. Now, I think she was probably very afraid. Very afraid."

Liv Ullmann wrote and directed a segment, which she'd long forgotten, called "Parting" in a Canadian movie composed of different episodes, *Love* (1982). Annette Cohen, Nancy Dowd, Mai Zetterling, and Ullmann directed segments of the script. Dowd, Ullmann, Zetterling, Joni Mitchell, Edna O'Brien, and Gael Greene each wrote a section. It was produced by Renée Perlmutter.

"I've worked with two women producers," says Ullmann, "both wonderful. Ingmar Bergman scripted *Private Confessions* [1996]. 'Listen,' the producer, Ingrid Dahlberg, said to me, 'if you have any trouble, if he comes on the set, if you have any problem, call me, because you're the director. Everything you do is your decision, not his.' He kept away. He gave me the script, and then I didn't see him again until the editing. But you never know, because he likes to control. I'm working with another woman producer on *Faithless*, who is very supportive. For instance, the men who produced *Kristin* were not team players. They didn't work hard enough to supervise it, but when they realized someone else was doing the work, then they wanted to run the production. Women work much harder."

Ullmann is glad to see other women directing films around the world. "Martha Coolidge's film *Rambling Rose* could only have been made by a woman," says Ullmann. "It looked like a European woman had done it, particularly in the details and the pace—that wonderfully slow pace, as if we had time to explore what was happening in this family."

Ullmann sees improvement in the position of European women who want to produce or direct, but their problems mirror those of women in the U.S. "In Norway," she says, "we have five or six women directors, fewer in Sweden and Denmark. Even today it's tough for us. Only about two of us in Norway are working with any regularity." It's the stone wall of ageism. "Over a certain age, it's so much tougher and women don't get hired," Ullmann says. "The only reason I'm working in Denmark and Sweden is that I have been an actress and am still a name. Age is against women. The producers are younger. They want to work with the people they know, who are mostly men. If they wanted to work with a woman they'd find one they knew, no matter how little experience she might have.

"I do not understand why men who are not that talented get to do one film after another. They always get new chances. It's not like that for women."

Her film *Kristin Lavransdatter*, which she wrote and directed, is an example. Adapted from the classic Norwegian trilogy of the same name by Sigrid Undset, the film was a box office smash.

"It made history," Ullmann says, "the biggest audience response of any movie made in Norway. I have not had one offer to direct another movie in Norway. From other places, yes; from Norway, no." Despite its great success and good reviews, Ullmann found that the film was not publicly discussed by men—directors, producers, critics, or film experts—when they were interviewed about film or wrote about it.

"Publicly, the film community that drives public opinion and knowledge of films did not talk about *Kristin*. I think that happens to Barbra Streisand, too, and other women directors. Privately, I got wonderful letters from other women about my films. The men stick together and women don't. Maybe [it's harder for us] because we don't have enough women heading up production or studios or distribution. We will just have to continue to support each other."[115]

You Mean It Could Have Been Like This?

Barbra Streisand would agree with Ullmann. A producer since 1976 (*A Star Is Born*), a director since 1983 (*Yentl*), Streisand's production company, Barwood Films, has produced features, movies for television, and documentaries of an amazing variety.

In 1990, as Ullmann was scripting *Sofie,* not realizing she would direct it, Barbra Streisand was producing and directing *The Prince of Tides,* which was shot during the spring and summer of 1990, released in 1991.[116] Streisand has produced, directed, and acted in her films. Ullmann, so far, has directed and written; she is not acting in or producing them at the same time.

The Prince of Tides, the best-selling novel by Pat Conroy, is about a South Carolina family, the Wingos, whose children grow up suppressing the memory of a violent event in their childhood. Tom Wingo (played by Nick Nolte), ostensibly to help his depressed, suicidal sister, goes to her psychiatrist, Dr. Lowenstein (played by Streisand).

Streisand had shot *Yentl* partially in England and had nothing but praise for her crews and their response to her. "I was shocked when I made *Prince of Tides* in America," she says. "Finally, I said to the cameraman, 'Do you have any problem with me being a woman ⌈director⌉?'

" 'Absolutely not,' he said. But when we started to shoot and I'd ask, 'Can we do this shot this way?' he would say, 'No, you can't do that.' Everything I asked for he'd say 'No.'

"I called my cameraman in London, David Watkins. 'Why is he saying no?' I asked him. 'I'm used to the way you and I worked—I'd describe a shot and you wouldn't have a problem. What is this?' He didn't know. In England, if I said I wanted to shoot a scene all in one shot, that's what we did. I'm used to being in the theater, I'm used to long takes. I don't like little bits. I like the actor to have a scene to play. The camera has to accommodate the actor. But on *Prince of Tides,* I realized something else was happening. There was a boys' club."

Many women directors (but not all) recite contests with their cameramen or directors of photography. Maybe it's a rite of passage. Off the record, one cameraman said, "They don't know what they want or they're dithering around trying to figure out the setup, or they change their minds. It's frustrating."

In one scene in *The Prince of Tides,* Tom Wingo shows Dr. Lowenstein a film of his younger brother. "We'd done his closeup and were on me for my shot across his profile," Streisand says. She had a video monitor at her feet that showed the scene being shot. Before she spoke her line, she looked at the video to check the shot. "I realized he was saying the wrong lines and I could see his mouth moving in the shot, which meant it would not cut with his closeup. I said to Nick, 'You know you're saying the wrong words, and [in the shot] we can see your mouth because you're in profile.'

"He said, 'I didn't think you saw my mouth.'

"I asked one of the cameraman's assistants, 'Don't you see his mouth in this shot?'

"The guy said, 'No, I can't see his mouth.'

"I walked over to him and said, 'On the video, I can see his mouth clearly. Why aren't you telling him the truth?'

"He shrugged and muttered, 'The boys' club.'

"I couldn't quite believe it," Streisand says, "but that's what happened. That's American misogynism."

Toward the end of the shoot, he had to leave for another job and was replaced. "The new operator was a terrific guy who'd worked for Woody Allen," says Streisand. "The whole thing changed. 'Ah,' I thought, 'you mean it could have been like this?' When I'd describe a shot to the new man, he'd say, 'Oh, sure.'

"At the end of a take," Streisand says, "I'd look at him and he'd go thumbs up or say, 'Maybe you want to look at it.' He was kind, truthful, had no cynicism, didn't disparage or belittle.

"I don't care if women or men are running the camera," she says. "I want them to be kind people who want to get the job done well. I can't say I'd rather work with women. I like working with men because there's a dynamic between men and women. I want to work with the best people."[117]

In 1996, Streisand directed *The Mirror Has Two Faces.* Barwood Films, with Streisand as executive producer, also made television movies such as *Serving in Silence: The Margarethe Cammermeyer Story*, with Glenn Close. Documentaries from the company include *Rescuers: Stories of Courage: Two Women* in 1997, *The First Women of Film* (2000), outlining early women working in film from 1903 to 1925. The company produced *City at Peace* (1998), an amazing and controversial documentary about teenagers in Washington, DC, a film by two independent filmmakers who had been turned down everywhere, and found a home at Barwood.[118]

"Mom, When Are You Going to Get Another Job?"

Mimi Leder began directing television in the late 1980s after six years as a script supervisor. "Before that, I was at Los Angeles City College," she says. "In the '80s, it became possible to direct, even though there still were many obstacles. The women's movement made it possible. Women found their voices and men were listening, wonderful men, like Greg Hoblit and Steven Bochco—they gave me my first directing job on *L.A. Law*."[119]

Her father, Paul Leder, a low-budget filmmaker with a mile of credits (*I Dismember Mama, Marigold Man*) trained her.

"I did every possible thing," says Leder. "He dragged me to Korea when I was twenty-four and said, 'Okay, you're the script supervisor, the first AD, and the second unit cinematographer. Teach the Korean crews how to load this Mitchell (we were shooting in three-D). My brother, a writer, was the soundman. We did what we were told, had a great time, and made a very funny film. My father had a very powerful influence on me. He was quite the feminist and really encouraged me to pursue anything I wanted. He wrote a thirty-minute short film for me to direct, *Short Order Dreams*. He gave me seventeen thousand dollars. My brother gave me ten thousand. I showed that film to Greg Hoblit and Steven Bochco and they hired me. And after that, John Sacret Young hired me for *China Beach*, and then John Wells for *ER*."

Leder became an outstanding television director, winning two Emmys and three nominations from the DGA. In the 1990s, "Steven Spielberg saw some of my *ER* dailies," she says. "He hired me to direct *Peacemaker*. I asked him, 'Why are you offering me this? I don't do action, I do character work.' He said, 'You direct action every day on television better than most.' He really fought for me, and I know he had to put his belief on the line because *Peacemaker*, released in 1997, was their [DreamWorks'] first movie. It was a truly exciting experience, maybe I should say an exciting ride. I'm [still] on it and riding hard."

The Peacemaker was a big action thriller—train sequences, helicopters, car crashes, chases, explosions—"exhilarating," says Leder. It was shot in Slovakia, Macedonia, and New York City. Though she had ten years of experience directing television, she had no feature experience per se, and no effects experience. But she'd shot with her father in Korea, and he'd said to her, "Teach them how to load this Mitchell camera." She'd done it. "I figured out how to do it," she says. "With *Peacemaker*, I didn't know how to do any effects. I'd done a fire here or there, people running out of buildings on fire, but nothing that had to do with visual effects. I learned on the job. The script also has a long train sequence. I was, like, 'Oh, God, I don't know anything about trains.' All right, I read books on trains, looked at every piece of film I could find on trains, trains moving from side angles or from front angles, and really evaluated what looked best. I went down to train yards in Europe. I just immersed myself completely in trains. I ended up appreciating the massive machine and really finding the romance in them."

Though it's easier now, it's still hard for any director to go from TV to features; directing styles and techniques are different and there's so much more money at stake. Leder thinks Spielberg saw something in her work that others had not seen or wouldn't see. "He has great instincts," she says. "A lot of people are way too competitive. We all need a great supporter in our lives and in our careers."

Before the happy occurrence with Steven Spielberg, even though Leder was a top television director, she found it very hard to get a shot at directing a feature.

"For example, I'd won an Emmy for directing and one for producing," Leder says.[120] "I told my agent I'd like to meet with people at HBO. I loved their movies and wanted to be a part of that. (These people are no longer there.) The person at HBO refused to meet with me. I was just a TV director. Later, after I'd made *Peacemaker*, he came up and introduced himself.

" 'Hello,' I said. 'Yes, I'm Mimi Leder, the one you wouldn't even meet with.' The words just came tumbling out of my mouth. But his behavior had been quite rude. I thought I'd forgotten it, but obviously, I hadn't. You know," she says, laughing lightly, "a woman scorned."

Working with actors, setting a shot, creating the scene: "It's like dancing, setting a very long steadicam shot. It's also like being an investigative reporter. I like to get right in there and evaluate what is the truth." She, like Martha Coolidge, compares the chaos, grind, and exhilaration of directing to dancing.

No other work in film or television is as demanding, and what's "truly difficult" is being a director *and* a mother *and* a wife. "It's so hard to find a balance between those three roles," says Leder. "But you just do it. I took a year off after *Deep Impact*. A few months ago my daughter said, 'Mom, what are you doing here? When are you going to get another job? When's your next movie? You should go back to work.'

"Once you do an action movie, you get sent all these action scripts, but I did character work for ten years in television before I started making movies. Now I'm getting character work in movies, too, and I hope I can do a whole bunch of everything."

Deep Impact (1998) was a character-driven action adventure story about a meteor colliding with Earth.[121] "The producers really wanted thousands of people on the beach," says Leder, "when Jenny, played by Téa Leoni, meets her father [Maximilian Schell] and reconciles with him, and dies with him. I was going for a kind of *On the Beach*, end-of-the-world flavor, isolated, desolate. I'm proud of that scene, particularly of the moments before it when she goes to see her father. I think it was an emotionally truthful moment between the two of them on that beach.

I fought passionately. I used my words and my heart to put across what I really truly believed would be the best scene possible."

Leder has not yet worked with any women cinematographers, but she is looking at their reels. "What shocks me are the current statistics about women directors," she says.[122] "If there are more women executives in charge, maybe more women will be hired. Primarily, I've been hired by men who have done the good deed, but it wasn't based on gender. The more women can practice any art form, the better they'll be at what they do."[123] Experience is everything.

Being a Woman Is Kind of Helpful

"My first film, *Xiu Xiu*, it was like lightning, it was a madness," says Joan Chen. "It was something I had to do. It's about my generation, it is my connection to China and Chinese history. Without making that film, bringing a closure, I wouldn't be able to start my American existence. I had lived here so many years that I had an urgency to do it. Many good friends told me it was impossible, that I was not a lesser person if I quit. But I couldn't, I couldn't. I had to do it."[124]

Joan Chen, whose parents were doctors, was born in Shanghai, China, and selected for the Actors' Training Program by the Shanghai Film Studio in 1975. Audiences first saw her in *Youth*, directed by the veteran director Xie Jin. Her second film, *The Little Flower*, won her the Best Actress award in China in 1980. She left China for America in 1981, studied filmmaking, and graduated with honors from California State University, Northridge. *Tai-Pan*, *Twin Peaks*, *The Last Emperor*, and many more roles followed. But Chen was not entirely comfortable with acting.

"I fell into it. I never had the ambition of being an actress. John Gielgud said that acting is shameful and glorious . . . Shame exposing yourself and glorious forgetting yourself. It's so very true. But shame and glory make me uneasy."[125]

Chen produced, directed, and cowrote *Xiu Xiu: The Sent-Down Girl*. It is about a Chinese teenage girl, innocent, corrupted, and betrayed, who personifies the millions of Chinese youth swept from the cities during the Cultural Revolution and forced to relocate in the country. Chen lived through that period and was not "sent down," but it was all she and her friends talked about—how to keep from becoming one of the unfortunate ones. After adapting it from a friend's novella (Yan Geling), Chen went back home and filmed the story in a remote region of China near the Tibetan border, 13,000 feet high, with a crew of sixty, shooting without the permission of the government, shooting on the run.

"Every day we worked we worried that our equipment would be confiscated and that the film negative would never get out of China," she says.[126] She says she never saw dailies; the video machine broke down. She took all the shot film with her when she left and had it processed in San Francisco.

"It's not just another Cultural Revolution movie," Chen said for the *Los Angeles Times*. "This was as important to my generation and my people as the Holocaust is to the world. Why did Oliver Stone make three Vietnam pictures? Why do people still make World War II movies?"[127]

Chen says filming was grueling, the hardest in her life. "Everyone worked so hard. I have chosen to work with women if I can. In *Xiu Xiu*, even the people who raised the money [a million dollars] were women. The writer, the editor, the line producer—they were all women. I feel a certain affinity with women, although there are great men in the crews like my DP and my production designer. But I tend to seek out more women. Before I made *Xiu Xiu*, I was never part of the job market. I'd wait for my agent to call; I went on an audition for an acting job. Once I was doing *Xiu Xiu*, I realized the women working with me worked harder, they weren't as strict about overtime, and when they spoke about it, it was apologetically. The New York crew for *Autumn in New York*, men as well as women, worked hard. There were a few women on the crew, not in the most key positions; they were so helpful. They were not very . . . territorial."

Chen's second film, compared to her first, was "a job opportunity that I couldn't possibly turn down." A Lakeshore/MGM production, it stars Richard Gere and Winona Ryder. "I'm grateful for the chance," she says. "Not many people would offer a big-budget picture to a newcomer—a woman as well as a minority woman." Inexperienced as a director, and knowing it, she was conscious of the studio's careful supervision throughout the production. "Before I started *Autumn*, I wondered how the New York crew, which to me would be a pretty macho crew, would accept me. But they were perfect."

She had been thinking about directing years before she created *Xiu Xiu*. "As an actress, I always loved the dynamics on the movie set, I loved the crews, I didn't stay in my trailer. When I began directing, it didn't feel like a big change. I knew I needed to be the person who is nurturing, mothering, protecting. It felt natural."[128]

When Chen arrived in New York, she learned in her first auditions as an actress that "I didn't look Chinese enough, and I was the only Chinese there. I was trying so hard to look like a white woman."[129]

She thinks we badly need a different approach to storytelling. "Minority women have this freshness. They bring something we are hungry for, something different from the formula," says Chen. "I've always viewed being female and Asian as an asset because I grew up in China. When I came here, it was such a struggle to have myself exploited in the right way. Just allow me to contribute, allow me to tell a story my way because at least it's different, it's unique. But in the pursuit of numbers, the pursuit of popularity, there is no singularity. It's astounding how we don't utilize a unique perspective. And it is difficult to explain. Certain things can be explained and communicated about a story, but many are intangible, unsayable. It's hard to explain in words. Where you don't have the freedom to do what you know is true in a story, you lose your perspective, you lose your uniqueness. So much money is spent making a film, the stakes are so high, that they don't allow you the freedom."

The work has joy, the work has pain. "It's the intensity you find only in your most intense first love," says Chen. "The intensity of the pain, the intensity of the joy. It can be so much fun and it can be crushing at the same time. It's character building. If you are directing, you're responsible for it. It's the same thrill of gambling."[130]

On That Set We Knew We Had Made Another Country

"My mother," says Judith James, "thought I'd be a great actress so I went to summer stock to act, found that acting sucked (too naked for me), but I discovered the technical side of stage craft." By age seventeen she knew she wanted to be a producer. At eighteen, she applied as a stage manager to a dance festival. They told her they didn't hire women for that job. She wrote them a letter listing the reasons a woman should be able to stage-manage. She got the job. "I was the stage manager there for three years while working very hard in the civil rights movement. Back in the '60s, we were shaping ourselves for the women's movement."[131]

She produced her first play off Broadway at the age of twenty-one. In 1969, after mounting eleven socially conscious plays (such as *Cages* by Lewis John Carlino, and Martin Duberman's *In White America*), James came to Los Angeles, a city embroiled in busing battles and school desegregation. She was a single mother; her son was six years old; she was pro-busing and anti–magnet schools. She became chairperson of the local school council, the areawide council, the citywide community council, and finally a superior court commissioner on the monitoring committee for the desegregation case that had ignited Los Angeles. She also ran for the school board.

By the early 1980s, James needed to get back to what she knew. She became codirector of the Mark Taper Forum's department of film and television with Elizabeth Daley.[132] She met Richard Dreyfuss at the Forum, they began to option material together and produced the television special for ABC on the U.S. Constitution, *Funny, You Don't Look 200* (with Dreyfuss, John Gielgud, Whoopi Goldberg, and many others) for the bicentennial of the Constitution. "When the guys at ABC looked at it," James says, "just before it went on the air opposite Monday night football, they said, 'Why didn't you tell us this was so good?' Welcome to television," she summarizes dryly. Dreyfuss and James have been producing partners ever since.

"I'm shocked at both the interior and exterior wrenching of this industry which deeply affects women. The exterior is the 'E' ride, the rollercoaster, the horror action movie, versus the interior about us human beings, which makes the movie that will open your eyes, bring you new emotions. That's in disfavor. Those movies don't make the big bucks. I think women are trapped in the middle of that crunch."

Women's rhetoric in the 1970s was effective then, James feels, but it also "made the guys dig in their heels. By the '90s, I felt men were saying, 'Hey, wait a minute, we didn't mean that you'd still be here.' We are still here," she says, "but the kinds of shows we care about are not in fashion." That is a tough place for creative people to be in.

James feels two truths about women and the industry today need to be restated: one is the right to make a living in it; the other is the right to communicate.

"People who are attracted to this work," she says, "have something to communicate, and we as women have come a distance to get the right to make a living as something more than secretaries. But how many of us have reached the point of being able to *communicate* what we as women or we as quirky individuals want to communicate? If we're going to do more than just make a living in this industry, we have to find a way to communicate our own myths and stories *and* find a way to make our stories make money."

She feels the problem never was men, but maleness. "However, when we talk like that in mixed company, there's an immediate discomfort and an assumption that if you talk like that you must be a lesbian or hate men. It could not be further from the truth, but it's certainly driven the topic from the top of the list of socially permissible discussions."

Women don't seem to feel the women's movement is dead so much as they feel it is past. Attitudes and actions change rapidly, but issues women might have raised at a dinner table in the 1970s when they heard distressing or demeaning references, they may or may not respond to in the 1990s.

"We have to pick our battles," says James. "When you're trying to get through the working day, you have to decide if you're going to listen to the joke or the metaphor or the 'truth' that is so male-oriented you could take it as an insult. Or you say to yourself, 'Maybe this is a chance to remind them that fifty percent of the people in the world are women.' Or you say, 'Hey, I'm going to let that one go. I'm just going to get through this day.'

"Younger women working today don't always realize what they have to do to keep the mechanism of change going. We can slip back if they don't keep working at the change and making some choices. Get through the day, yes, but make some choices. Push a little bit when you can. Once a week would be good. That's picking the battles. Frankly, I don't care if they don't know what came before. I care that they keep their eyes open today."

James often finds herself the only woman in the room, but not when she and Camille Cosby produced *Having Our Say: The Delany Sisters' First 100 Years* (1999), a two-hour television movie for CBS. It starred Diahann Carroll, Ruby Dee, and Amy Madigan. Lynne Littman directed. Emily Mann wrote both the play (produced by Cosby and James) and the film script, based on the book by Sarah and A. Elizabeth Delany with Amy Hill Hearth. They had a film set full of women.

"It was wonderful," says James, "not because we were happy *not* to have men. Men were working with us. It was just nice to have a group of women in those positions on that show. We had a comfort level with each other where no one said, 'Oh, there she goes being touchy-feely,' or any of the statements that often come up with men around women." Sometimes James talks out loud about a problem. "I'm not waiting for a guy to say, 'Look, you should do this.' I just need to throw a thought out there, hear people's thoughts on it—not their answer to the problem, but their thoughts on it. I get annoyed when the guys assume I don't know what I'm doing or just doubt it. For instance, I really know contracts and budgets—but men don't believe that and neither do a lot of women . . . Sometimes I feel we've dragged from the last decade old signposts, found out they weren't signposts anymore, but delayed discarding them."

On the set of *Having Our Say*, James felt the women didn't have to couch judiciously a demand or a thought. "We just had a different management style. The guys showed us pictures of their babies instead of talking about the Rams. The crew in Charlotte, North Carolina, brought their wives and children to the set, which wasn't *un*usual but wasn't *usual.*"

James does not want to overstate her experiences. In any career over the years, one works in certain expected ways, and then suddenly you see another way. For instance, on the production of *Mr. Holland's Opus* (1995), the crew was mainly men, as well as the director and the writer, but the subject matter, about the human heart and human interactions, spoke to everyone on the film. It is, she thinks, the kind of film that often women bring to the industry.

"*Opus* is about music and art and loving our children," says James, "giving them the best step forward, and about a deaf child. That's not the movie's log line, but those issues lodge deep inside the movie. We had the happiest crew. It was the first movie I've been on where the whole crew read the script, right down to the second and third grips. Several crew members had a deaf person in the family. They brought them to the set for the first time. The signers we had for the deaf actors translated for kids what a gaffer did. No one felt they were imposing by bringing a child to the set. It had nothing to do with male-female. It was human."[133]

The crew on *Having Our Say* was about half male, half female, with a male DP, a male UPM (unit production manager), a male first AD.

"Judy and Camille, the producers, were like the mama lions," recalls Lynne Littman, the director. "They kept the 'note-givers' away. They allowed the creative process to keep on going. That production was a different experience. It was not mysterious, it was thrilling! Every woman should have some taste of this, and it had nothing to do with not adoring men. I got a glimpse of the kind of entitlement that's been a male experience [as they film] throughout the world. Experiencing that, it's heady stuff."

As a director, the only time she felt anything comparable was when she first directed at the American Film Institute Women's Directing Program. "I stood on a table giving orders and people actually did what I asked. I remember it so clearly because I couldn't believe it. Women are not raised to be in charge of anything except a classroom or the children. I was out in the professional working world in a room full of adults. Even though I'd been brought up with alternatives and educated in rebel training grounds—music and art and Sarah Lawrence were no obedience schools—that first directing experience at AFI was unforgettable."[134]

"We laughed so much on *Having Our Say*," James says. "Once in a while, we'd hear that slightly derisive tone from a guy saying, 'Well,

356 Women Who Run the Show

make up your mind.' We'd make a joke of it and he'd laugh and we'd all laugh." Part of the joy was the shorthand. "It's just easier when you're talking to a woman," says James. "Men have shorthand, too, which makes it easier for them to work together. Having a lot of women on the set in control of the work made communication faster for us. In a way, I guess it's the numbers. Guys have controlled their sets for decades."

James produced *Having Our Say* on Broadway, where about half her crew had been women; the general manager was a man. "A good balance that worked well," says James, "and felt good. People have a good time when they share the same language."[135]

"What an unbelievable feeling to be on that set," Littman says. "We were all stunned by how unfamiliar it was to be in charge. I'm not talking about as a director. To be in charge *as a group*. It must be the way Jews felt when they first went to Israel and they gave their name Shapiro or Siegel with no second thought of 'They'll know I'm Jewish.' The world is sexist and the film world is sexist. Sexism resides on an unconscious level in us. But on that set . . . we knew that we had made another country . . . we were not explaining ourselves. We didn't have to translate. We were the creative team. It wasn't the network's, it wasn't the production entity's. It was ours."[136]

Lynne Littman was last seen in Chapter 8, carrying her Oscar around in a paper bag at a Silverlake market.

In 1984, she directed *Testament*, starring Jane Alexander, "I was too young to know how extraordinary the experience was. I was happily married, had two beautiful boys, and I left that cocoon to direct *Testament*, which was like a series of sequential fallings in love for me. It was an incredibly female experience. First I fell in love with the writer, then with the cinematographer, then with the editor. The process of directing is like sequentially giving your heart and taking theirs. Each exchange is a little different. But it feels to me like you're making and exchanging babies, giving them back and forth—the writer gives you a baby, you take it and you give it away through the actors. The cinematographer takes it from you and makes it into something else. If it works, it's a wonderful creation, and it worked all the way through *Testament*. There wasn't a dead moment. I didn't know any of that then. I was young. That's what youth is."[137]

The film was about a small town just before and after a nuclear attack. "We were in the bliss of making the film work. You just have to have the courage. We all go through stages of bravery. I think people respond to courage, to belief. We hunger for people who care about anything. My hardest task is finding material I care about."

After *Testament*, her famous divorce "really knocked the stuffings out of me." She made one documentary, *In Her Own Time*, about Barbara Myerhoff, who was dying. "...I stopped working. I dropped out," says Littman. She was part of the Women's Steering Committee at the Directors Guild. "I raised my two children, who took my intestines out the door with them every morning. Hard as it is, making a movie was easy after that."

Her comeback was more of a normal female director's experience than what had happened to her in the 1970s and early 1980s, because public ovations for *Testament* and her Oscar "bumped" her over most of the obstacles.

"My early successes and the Oscar had been erased by time," says Littman. "I had more difficulty. Some people told me they'd heard rumors I'd been institutionalized. 'What happened to Lynne? No one trashes that kind of career. She's got to be crazy.' " Littman's hiatus was so long it shocked her friends, and "it was shocking to me when I woke up." She hadn't worked in ten years, but her absence gave her insight and some wisdom. "You recognize abuse. When you're young, you're resilient, you don't know anything, you think this is the way it is, you keep going. I really did not meet any discrimination until I started back the mid-1990s."

After her return, one of her jobs became "the ultimate nightmare" with a producer on shoot. "I came away saying I understood the Holocaust," she groans. "I understood terror. The same thing has happened to other women repeatedly, but not to me. It's the kind of terror where the producer of the movie, which was about women, tyrannized and bad-mouthed the actors and the director, probably most directors he'd worked with ... [His] abuse of me was personal and vile, and I don't think the way he treated me was in any way unusual. I felt I was treated like a hired prostitute. Forget aspirin. Take arsenic."

Then, in 1999, two films she directed aired on television the same night: *Having Our Say* on CBS and *Freak City* on Showtime.[138] She'd been attached to *Freak City* for nine years as the producer "dragged it around until we got it made." She had almost finished editing it when James called about directing *Having Our Say*.

"I'd look around that set and see Judy and Camille, the writer, Emily Mann, Ruby [Dee], and Diahann Carroll," says Littman, "and one of my oldest friends, Rita Riggs, who was doing the costumes, and I know it seemed amazing to us that all of us were there. We were not only women, we were *older* women working with a bunch of terrific guys. I thought, *What is happening here?* No drugs, no extramarital affairs on that set, no tantrums, no insults, no power plays. We took care of each other. We made number signals. Someone would say, 'Ten.' That was the signal for me to stop biting my nails," says Littman. "Four was your breath smells. Three was stop pulling on your chin. Five, you have too much rouge on. Maybe guys have used that stuff on their sets or maybe they don't care about it. See, we were making the show but still worrying about whether our hair looked good. What was really wonderful was that we could admit it."[139]

■ ■ ■

By the late 1990s, the press regularly covered women directors and producers: Lauren Shuler Donner (*You've Got Mail*, *Bulworth*, *X-Men*); Stacey Sher (who produced *Erin Brockovich* with Danny DeVito); producer-director Rachel Talalay (*Hairspray*, *The Borrowers*, a director of *Ally McBeal*); Stephanie Austin (*Terminator 2* coproducer, *The Long Kiss Goodnight*, *True Lies*); Christine Vachon's (with partner Pam Koffler) Killer Films, turning out Kimberly Peirce's *Boys Don't Cry*, Mary Harron's *I Shot Andy Warhol*, and other films like *Velvet Goldmine*. Some young directors say they've never encountered any problems. "I don't think sexism is the operative force for or against me," Kimberly Peirce says.[140]

Impressively, women are turning out a variety of work for motion pictures and television. But you wonder how much has really changed when director Allison Anders moans in print that she is "sick of the boy-wonder myth. Where's the girl-wonder myth?"[141] Maggie Renzi, partner of John Sayles and producer of *Girlfight*, said, "There were so few [women] when John and I started. But you look a little deeper and I really don't think anything's any different."[142] Others feel that it will be easier when women start making commercial films that show profits.

In September 2000 director Allison Anders brought about seventy-five women together in Santa Barbara for a Women Filmmakers Summit. "Motivated in part by the political activism of the NAACP, they were determined to attack what many of them saw as rampant sexism at every level of the industry."[143] Anders has directed independent films—*Sugar Town*, *Grace of My Heart*, and *Gas Food Lodging*—and the television movie, *Things Behind the Sun*, a story based on her own rape. A major issue at the conference was that male directors "make a film that bombs and they turn around and get a huge studio deal . . . When our movies don't [succeed], we don't get a chance to make a second movie." One woman assistant to a powerful producer said, off the record, "Not one of them will talk about this . . . They don't hire women, and

they just don't see it as a problem, and they never will." As writer/
director Nancy Savoca said at the same meeting, "You suffer rejection
and you think, 'Wow, I must really suck.' Then you get into a group
and you realize it's about something bigger than you. As a group, women
filmmakers have been quiet for a long time."[144] So true.

EPILOGUE

How Far Is Far?

We forget history so fast in this country. "Like water on a hot side-walk," says writer Dianne Dixon. "It evaporates before it's recorded."[145] Occasionally, something happens that makes us aware of past and present at the same time.

"Around 1994, in Los Angeles, a group of young women, story editors working on the index for the first year of *Friends*," says writer-producer Charlotte Brown, "decided to host a cocktail party because they felt they had no way to network with other women in television. Everyone was working on their [separate] shows. The party was held in a private club on a Saturday afternoon. They sent out beautiful invitations, using names of any woman they saw listed on the credits of shows on television at that time.

"It wasn't my favorite thing to do on a Saturday afternoon but I went. It was a depressing yet uplifting experience. Some other old vets like me were there, but most of the women were very young, self-confident beyond belief. There was no formal program, just about a hundred and fifty women talking and walking around.

"At one point, I was looking at the room and couldn't help but think—I know it's corny—that though they didn't know the older women, with-out us these younger women wouldn't be here today. That was a self-pitying moment, but I did feel that way. Seeing how cocky they were, I thought, 'Oh, girls, enjoy every minute of it because it's going to go by so fast, and I hope you play the game well.'

"I remember having those thoughts and at the same time having a real sense of the stream of history, which we aren't often aware of, where you find yourself truly in the present moment while looking back with a certain understanding, which stays with you."[146]

How strange and wonderful to be twenty years older in a room full of women working in your field and realize that when you were their age you couldn't have put ten women in the room.

How much of this remarkable change is real, how much is window dressing? How far is far? Opinions vary.

"Here it is, the start of a new millennium," says Anne Nelson, the CBS executive who began her career in the 1940s, "and I see male secretaries running around with the Xeroxes, taking them to the girls—the women—instead of the other way around. It is quite staggering. I used to be the only woman at every meeting I was ever in. Now I see the women outnumbering the men. I don't wonder the men are in a certain backlash mode. That's part of the problem now. White guys feel threatened by minorities coming in, but you know what? Those who are coming in . . . impress me greatly."[147]

"In the early 1980s," says literary agent Michele Wallerstein, "men just wanted to get rid of us. Yesterday I had a breakfast meeting with two women producers. When I started in the business, none of us would have been women. That tells you how hard it was before."[148]

"Incredible inequality between women and men still exists today at some deep levels," says producer Gale Anne Hurd. "Every time a high-profile movie directed by a woman fails, it affects all women, and anytime it succeeds, she's still a special case."[149]

To young women who were toddlers in the 1970s and are just starting their careers now, "It seems about equal now—in terms of numbers, not in terms of power."[150]

Martha Lauzen, whose statistical studies about women in the industry have shocked and enlightened, admitted that "changing Hollywood is going to be like turning around a battleship."[151] Many women in the 1980s expected parity by 2000. Forget it.

The 1980s told women they "could have it all." The 1990s said, "Let's examine that."

"I wonder where we're going," says Mary Ledding, "because the new message is you can't have it all and you don't need it. We do have to make choices. If I had stopped my career, raised my kids, and then came back, I would not have had the same career. At times, it was crazy and very difficult. Who got that idea that you can have it all? Sit down to a buffet, you can't eat it all. I was so lucky to have wonderful child-rearing help. The assumption that kids are only going to get the best if you're the one giving it to them is hugely egotistical. I don't do my own dentistry."[152]

"Certainly there are more women in the room now, and outwardly, the attitude about them changed," says Barbara Corday. "Women in those jobs became much more accepted [in the 1990s] . . . What did not change was the backroom politics . . ."[153]

Buried in the turmoil of thirty years is the almost unchanged structure of the entertainment enterprise, still run along models built by men for their social or professional tastes, attitudes, and needs. "Do men run the world? Yes. Get over it," says Lydia Woodward, executive producer of *ER*.[154]

In the 1980s, women tried to fit in, and some succeeded by being "little men," as one woman says caustically. From another: "A lot of women have taken on the coloration of men. It's sort of like the hostage thing where the prisoners take on qualities of the guards. Some are more like men in their attitudes . . . that old adage—if you can't beat them, join them."[155]

"To be successful, young women today need to take initiative, throw ego out the door, and do whatever it takes," says Iris Grossman, an agent with ICM. "But if you think you're supposed to be a man when you get successful, that's crap. You have to be who you are. The most successful women are true to themselves. And believe me, it takes inner strength."[156]

"I can understand why a lot of the women I know who are ambitious and are working," says Anthea Sylbert, "tend to deny their inner child more than the men I know, who let their child romp around all the time. Maybe we feel that if people think we're silly they won't take us seriously."[157]

Women who were mentored by men learned how the business worked but could not, they discovered, emulate their male mentors and get the same results.

"When I left MTM," says Charlotte Brown, a writer-producer on *Rhoda*, "and went out into the real world, it was a real eye-opener. This was in the 1980s and I wasn't prepared. My role models had been men like Jim Brooks and Allan Burns at MTM. I was directing pilots for a period, and when I was in doubt, I'd ask myself, what would Jim and Allan do? At network meetings, my MO, based on what they did, was to protect the material and 'stand up for what you believe in.' That did not work. I got a reputation as a difficult woman. I didn't scream or do anything outrageous. I did what Jim and Allan did. If a woman stands up for principles, she's a ball buster; if a man does that, gosh, he's admired. [The difference] was blatant and clear. Had there been, perhaps, women role models for me, they might have warned me, uh-uh, don't go there. What Jim and Allan could say flat out, I had to find a different way . . . I had to soften, go around."[158]

"I was sticking up for some story point," Ann Marcus says, "when a male executive said, 'Boy, I wouldn't like to be a son of yours.' I have never forgotten that. I was protecting the material, speaking out."[159]

But today there's a great sense that "we're girls and we're glad." Differences between the way men and women work are beginning to be valued. Ironically, what held women back professionally in the 1980s increases their currency today—like being a parent and having the skills that come with it. "If you have one child you are multitasking," as Lynne Littman says.[160] Parenting skills count in producing and directing—soothing, keeping things going, scolding, organizing.

Thirty years have taught us some things. Contrary to a once-popular myth, many women *are* team players. Women see problems or situations differently because their experiences and their status as women are different. Men and women communicate differently and bring different viewpoints to the process.

"A linguistic study around 1996 examined the way men and women talk—different languages," says Lynne Littman. "If guys are hiring a director and have a choice of going with someone who speaks their language or with someone who makes them ask, 'What *is* she talking about? What's she *doing*?' which director would you go with?"[161]

"The worst experience I ever had [as a writer] was when nothing I was trying to communicate was understood," says Treva Silverman. "I was working with an executive producer on another show and I'd love to say he wasn't talented and smart and therefore he didn't understand me. He was very talented and very smart, but just in a different way . . . It was awful because he just didn't know what the hell I was writing . . . or talking about. And I couldn't make it better because if you don't like asparagus, you don't like it—good or mediocre, you just don't like it."[162]

"The politics of life are the politics of life," says Jane White. "Who's going to give up things or change easily? I adore men, but it would be nice to have a real dialogue. Maybe we screwed up in the '70s, freaked the guys out, had no real dialogue with them. Maybe we should have said, 'Isn't it just a miracle that we're on this planet and let's figure out a great way to communicate.' I can't do my work without guys and they can't do it without us. We want them to recognize the need to communicate, but they aren't doing it. They're not apt to give up power, which is money, to a new group that they don't know how to talk to."[163]

One person can make a difference. When that person is a woman, it's a different difference. It's the ultimate reason film and television need the influence and point of view of women—those media affect the emotions and behavior of people all over the world.

Marcia Nasatir was a vice president in 1974 at United Artists. *Coming Home*, in 1978, starred Jane Fonda and Jon Voight. Both stars won

Oscars, as did the screenwriters. Hailed by critics, the film was nominated for Best Picture.

"I had real reasons for thinking the picture would be a success," Nasatir says. "Waldo Salt and Robert C. Jones wrote the script, based on a story by Nancy Dowd; Jerome Hellman wanted to produce it, and Hal Ashby to direct it—great guys. Jerry Hellman had made *Midnight Cowboy* in 1969, also from a Waldo Salt script, and it was a feat to get it made. So here's Jerry Hellman bringing us *Coming Home* in 1976 at a time when, in movies, the Vietnam War was box-office death. I wanted to do it because I thought the audience would be involved in how a paralyzed man copes, what his life is about, how it affects everyone around him and the woman who loves him.

"So finally we got *Coming Home* made and we screen it for the New York distribution and sales guys. Vietnam wasn't mentioned in the movie, not a word. After the screening, we have a meeting. I can still see us in Mike Medavoy's office, these twelve men and me. One of the guys, head of distribution, said, 'The picture isn't going to make twenty-five cents.' Other guys chimed in and there was a lot of 'No one wants to see a picture about Vietnam.' That's all they saw in it.

"Eric Pleskow, head of United Artists, was in New York. Mike [Medavoy, head of production] had to tell him advertising, publicity, sales, and distribution all had a very negative reaction. The picture was on its way to the graveyard and I felt awful. For some reason, I had to go to San Francisco, and I remember walking into the hotel room, putting down my suitcase, turning on the television, and there's *Midnight Cowboy*. I called Mike and said, 'I'm looking at Jon Voight and Dustin Hoffman in *Midnight Cowboy*. If UA can make that kind of picture an Oscar winner, they can make *Coming Home*, too.'

" 'You've got to call Eric and tell him,' Mike said.

"I called him. 'Eric, I'm looking at *Midnight Cowboy*. Now, if you can sell *Midnight Cowboy*, you can sell *Coming Home*.'

"Incredibly, that's what we did.

"What really happens in the studios," says Nasatir, "is the influence of one person *and* the influence of numbers. It's the reason women had no influence and now have some. Each person in a meeting makes a contribution. Lindsay Doran, a former president of United Artists,[164] once said, 'You can make a difference if you're standing there, even if it's saying "Feel better, it's going to be okay." ' Each contribution creates an incremental step toward change. If women are going to make any difference, we have to believe in what we're doing and *stand up for it*. What concerns me most is that there are many cowards in the business.

"There is no one thing in this equation of change we're all in," Nasatir says. "It's usually not about men or women; it's not about *one* but *each* person in the group who make the decisions about which movies we will see—that's what makes the real difference."[165]

I am beginning to have a new respect for the simple power of numbers. Yes, one woman can make a difference, but something else happens when a lot of women are in the room or on a set—the process of producing the world's stories and the communication of them change.

Judith James and Lynne Littman speak rapturously of making "another country" on the set of *Having Our Say: The Delany Sisters' First 100 Years.* So does producer Marian Rees about her production of *Ruby Bridges,* which aired in January 1998. "It was not an intentional gathering of all these women," Rees says of the director, the producer, the executive producer, the writer, the composer, the associate editor, and the executives at Disney. "I was standing on the set one day and thought, 'This is as good as it gets.' "[166] In the late 1990s, other women producers could say the same thing as more women wrote, produced, and directed shows like HBO's *If These Walls Could Talk* and *Sex and the City* and network shows like *Family Law* and *Judging Amy.* Shows like these deliver women's views on stories only women can really tell.[167]

"Women are more invested in the nuances of relationships. They like to know all the shades of feeling. What grabs them is different," said writer Ann Beckett. In *First Do No Harm,* Meryl Streep (also one of the producers), plays a woman who has "become a learned advocate in seeking treatment for her epileptic son while her truck-driver husband has hung back, feeling inadequate because he doesn't earn enough and doesn't know how to talk to doctors. At the start of rehearsals, Streep turned to Beckett and asked: 'Where do you think she is with him at this point?'

" 'Knows the truth that's emerged and plays wife looking to husband here to soften it,' Beckett answered. Streep nodded and proceeded to play the scene perfectly.

"Afterward, producer Jim Abrahams asked Beckett, 'What were you talking about? It was like you were talking in code . . .' Beckett tried to explain. Finally, she just said, 'I think it's a woman thing.' "[168]

It's the old "culture difference." Men have been writing about women for centuries, but it's still new today to get it from the source—women. Ann Kenney, the executive producer of the CBS drama *Family Law,* thinks "women writers have to contend not only with men's individual perceptions of women but with 'this huge body of existing work that depicts women. Women are like this and not like this. But who wrote those things?' "[169]

Lindsay Law once commented on these intrinsic differences: "[Women] dig deeper into themselves, both in what they bring to the project and the subject matter. Women seem to make things they care about as opposed to 'I can sell this.' "[170] Law gave many women their start at American Playhouse, PBS, and later at 20th Century Fox. Recently, he said that he'd had a difficult time convincing networks and studios to hire women, that selling an inexperienced female director to management was much harder than selling an inexperienced male. He wasn't talking about the 1980s; he was talking about the late 1990s.[171]

Women are speaking a different language; they're irritated by having to explain "endlessly" to men what seems obvious to them, and which the women in the room instantly know. Women in meetings all over town are explaining to men why a scene or female character will work as written or played.[172] Women read thrillers by and about men, they read action comic books, they crowd into *Die Hard* and *Lethal Weapon*. Women have observed men for centuries—what they do, how they think—because they have to. Men have not spent centuries analyzing why women do one thing instead of another—because they don't have to.

From 2000 On . . . What?

Ask women "what's next" now that they "have rights," and the conversation dives into discussion areas such as: "it seems equal but . . .", too few stories by women for women, choosing the right battles, and the different perspectives of women under thirty.

PERCEPTION VERSUS REALITY

Confusing truth and illusion is frame and fabric to Hollywood. One myth in the 1990s was "Everything's equal now." Many women who survived the skirmishes and succeeded became invested in the public sense of the win, the image that everything's equal now. They did not like older malcontents or younger firebrands to pick at their battle scars.

But let's review a few numbers. 1999 and 2000 statistics of women's employment in film and television are gloomy. Of the top 100 highest-grossing films in 2001 (the figures are not that different for the top 250 films, which were also studied): 17 percent of executive producers are women. Producers: 22 percent. Directors: 7 percent. Writers: 13 percent. Cinematographers: 2 percent. Editors: 13 percent.[173]

For television, overall women comprised 23 percent of all creators, executive producers, producers, directors, writers, editors, directors of photography.[174]

Our eyes and minds glaze over. What's it all mean, really? Try another angle. Imagine a film and television industry where 93 percent of the directors, 78 percent of producers, 87 percent of writers, 87 percent of editors, 98 percent of the cinematographers, 83 percent of the executive producers, 70 percent of the reviewers, 75 percent of the senior agents, and 97 percent of the CEOs of large corporations are women.[175]

In this imaginary situation, a director, a woman, comes on the set. It is an ordinary workday and most of the people she's working with are women: five out of seven of her producers, and both writers; the performers are about 30 percent men to 70 percent women because the script is about an adventure involving women; the few men lend local or romantic color. The crew is 90 percent women, the stunt coordinator is a woman, the production designer, the gaffer, the editor, the DP. The television studio that bought the movie is run by women; the execs in charge of the production are women.

In *this* picture most of the people working on the set speak the same language. Did the woman running sound make a mistake? She's having a bad day. Guess she'll fix it. Did the director take her time on that shot? She's an artist, she knows what she's doing.

This scenario could be seen as positive—parity and more achieved on screen and behind the scenes, a reflection of women's representation and more in the population, as men do now; it could be expanded for race and ethnicity. The scenario could also be viewed as having a negative result: nothing changes, the same movies are made, *Lethal Weapon 9*, *Matrix 4*. Or the industry as a whole becomes devalued—salaries decrease, status wanes—because women took over. But that seems unlikely. The ravenous world appetite for entertainment will probably grow as fast as cable channels and convergencies in new media.

This imaginary situation is only a way to grasp the current structure of the entertainment universe and women's influence in it as a group— not in terms of *women's* percentages, which are so familiar, but in terms of *men's* percentages. Reality.

SO WHOSE STORY ARE WE TELLING?

The "woman's slant" on a story has been knitted into the industry fabric for years, but today wanting it has politically correct cachet. It just makes sense on a variety of levels for a male executive to run a "woman's story" past the lead female exec.

Those stories are still cemented in that fragment of the south forty where women should write or direct women's pictures and shows. The question is, whose "women's stories"—men's or women's? They can be quite different, though at this point we don't really know because, as director Randa Haines pointed out, "Until women directors [and writers] can offer the public a much larger body of work, there is no answer to that question."[176] She said that in 1986, and it's still true today. Women are not often offered science fiction, westerns, or thrillers. The embedded view held by many men, and many women, too, is that action is still the guys' preserve. Why should women write or direct or produce *only* women's stories? Steven Spielberg said, "I think it's a terrible handicap when male producers only assign feminine subjects to women directors."[177] Men aren't limited, why should we be, women want to know.

"I hear these remarks on all sides," says Fay Kanin, "that there are certain subjects women can't write. Nobody ever told me that. If anyone had said to me, 'You can't write a man because you are not a man,' I'd say, 'I write a man in a way a woman writes a man.' That's very important. I don't think we should just have men write men."[178]

"I think being a woman has influenced my career in terms of storytelling," says producer Paula Weinstein. "Part of this is trusting one's instincts, that emotional and instinctual intelligence, once accepted and appreciated and allowed to flourish, is great. I've learned how to trust that and not go to the more male head side, particularly in making movies and telling stories. Does my instinct tell me this is true, do I believe it, and is it something I want to see?"[179]

We are startled by the mosaic of old and new contests today: Many women want to see more strong movies made by women, an unfulfilled market that producer Lynda Obst has been talking and writing about for years. "We need strong stories, the way boy movies have," she's said. "I'd love to find a film with a strong premise that isn't as sexist as *Fatal Attraction* but that taps into a girl myth as powerfully as that movie tapped into a boy myth."[180]

Director Joan Micklin Silver: "Men have been directing childbirth scenes for years."[181]

"But do women support women-made movies?" wonders Phylis Geller. "One of the new strategies must address the political imperative of promotion. I spoke once to a national women's leadership group, women in business, education, government. They admitted they were not aware when a film is directed by a woman but if they knew, they'd make the effort to see it. We all got excited about a potentially huge network of women's groups who would spread the word (so much simpler now with the Internet) that such-and-such a film deserved the support of women."[182]

"Whose story is being told and who is telling it?" is a real challenge of the next decade.[183] Its political and creative dimensions have stepped out of the shadows only because a lot more women work in film and television.

GETTING THROUGH THE DAY

Numbers don't tell everything, even though statistics about women in film and television draw deep, persistent inequities. One person's reality is not necessarily another's. Some women feel they are still dealing with '90s leftovers, such as the "don't-worry-your-pretty-little-head-about-it-dear." Women use different methods to get through the day.

"A couple years ago," says Judith James, "TNT wanted to do a two-hour special about women in power in Hollywood. I wanted to do a segment with women's faces darkened out and their voices altered, telling how they got through the day. One woman in a high position might get through with 'Daddy, may I . . . ?' Others might use sexual innuendo. I thought we'd also do interviews on the street, asking other women how they get through their day. We could be funny and sophisticated about it. I wanted to do that special because we should grow up—these things are in our world and we have to deal with them.

"It scared the shit out of TNT. 'That's not appropriate, we're in responsible positions, we don't think like that.' Even friends told me, 'I've never found that [in my work].' It may not be a male world now, but it is a male-*constructed* world, and I think some women still get scared. They are protecting their image and their hard-won gains."[184]

WHICH BATTLES DO I FIGHT TODAY?

Issues for women may be subtler, but some are still bald. When "bad things" happen in production or in meetings or when sexist (rarely racist) jokes are told or when "We can't just spread our legs for them" is used to describe a business deal, no matter how long a woman has been in the business, it comes down to choosing the battle. It comes down to speaking up.

"Just a few days ago at Universal," says Donna Smith in 2001, "I'm sitting in a meeting and a male executive said, 'Not enough titties.' I looked at him and said, 'You are out of line.'

" 'Oh, c'mon, Donna, you know . . .'

" 'Yes, I know, and I'm calling you out on that comment.' "[185]

Speaking up can be costly. If there are five guys and one other woman in the room who can fire you in a heartbeat, you think twice. Other women say that ten years ago they didn't say anything in certain situations. Now, they say they've changed but men have not. "They are still patronizing us," says a producer with pages of credits. "They're saying in effect, 'We're so glad that you're so creative and you got this project going. Now the guys will take over.' It's like, respect, guys, a little respect. When we really make an issue of it, they go, 'Yes, you're so right,' and then start patronizing us all over again. What I'm hoping is that each time we speak up it will raise their consciousness for the next time. You have to speak up. You have to nip it in the bud."[186]

Sexism or sexual harassment is often called "a dead issue" today, but sexism to some is not sexism to all. It depends on age, position, or power. "In meetings," Dixson says, "there are off-color jokes. I don't mind that within the context of the story—it's make-believe. But I don't need to hear in conversation or in an elevator that somebody's assistant 'looks really fuckable.' "

Recalling another incident, she says, "We're right in the middle of the studio, we're just leaving a pitch meeting, the studio exec is to my right, this other producer, his partner, is to my left, we just sold this pitch, and this guy grabs my ass. I slapped him. He tried to laugh it off but it wasn't funny. This is the year 2000. That man called my boss and tried to make a joke out of it, but my boss was very supportive of me."[187]

"I was on a plane recently," says one woman who is about fifty, "when I heard the CEO of my company say about me to the president, 'Now, is [she] coming to this?' Not only am I the executive vice president of the company, but I put all the elements together for this project; I negotiated and closed the deal to create the program we were flying in to finalize. On the plane, the president of the company was flabbergasted at his CEO's comment. I mention this because it represents an inability to understand the importance of today's subtleties. Here I am, playing this rather important role, and this guy—if he can't put me here and can't put me there, he can't comprehend just what I do or its significance. If you called him up right now and asked how valuable I am, he'd say I play a phenomenal role. This was like a little misspeak but it indicates what happens, a small but poignant example.

"I've been lucky to work with some of the strongest men around. I've been acknowledged and I've been validated. I've been asked to take on more and more responsibility. I've learned a lot from these guys. When a little misspeak like that occurs, your eyes sort of roll back, and it's like, 'Yeahhhh.' It doesn't stop me or any other woman, but you know oppression in a subtle quiet way, and you wince.

"That's what girls and women go through all our lives. This little wincing. It's a reminder, keep your guard up, keep being out there, stay in their face, claim your credits, or you will sink."[188]

YOUNGER WOMEN, AN ENTIRELY DIFFERENT VIEW
It's a whole new generation without the history many in this book experienced.

"I think we have a generation of young women who are rather complacent," says Debra Hill, writer-producer-director. "A friend of mine

graduated from Berkeley, got in the right sorority, got the right husband, had two kids, and suddenly said, 'There must be more.' She ended
up getting divorced, working her way through KNXT and on and on,
Good Morning, America, she's a major news producer who has won a lot
of awards. Her daughter went to Brown and then went on to journalism
school. My friend, her mother, said to her, 'Why do you want a master's
in journalism?'

"Her daughter said, 'I can always be a news producer.'

" 'What do you mean by that?'

" 'It's a good fallback position.'

"In one generation," says Hill, "an entirely different perspective."[189]

Younger women did not live the struggle of the first group. They see
many women in the business, even though they admit they work mostly
with men. What's the big deal? They're making their films; being a
woman doesn't seem to be an issue; no one's ever held them back.

And yet...."Women are rarely aggressive about their salaries or
about what's in store for them," says Sheila Nevins. "I've worked with
women in their twenties. I push them ahead; they are not self-
motivated. Men always ask me for more. Women are still intimidated.
They're grateful for raises and bonuses; men expect them. Still. Some
guy once wanted to know my five-year plan for him, and I told him my
five-year plan was that he wouldn't be here. No woman has ever asked
me for a plan. Never. If I can get a raise for a woman, she's so thankful.
Men don't thank you. They deserve it. For all the changes that have
occurred, there's a distinct difference still, and it's mainly in expectation. Oddly, women can be competitive, aggressive, and ambitious, but
they feel less entitlement than men. I don't know why that is. I prefer
working with women. I feel a sisterhood with the struggles of women.
I like working with men, too, but there's a distinct difference. There *is*
a difference."[190]

"Women were starting to move in and up in the 1970s," says attorney
Judith Merians, "because it was already dangerous to say 'my policy is
against women.' But young women today are not well equipped to understand the signals or fight the battle because they don't know that it's
this battle and not *that* battle.

"Young women expect that they can have everything they work for.
I think that's nice. Some are very smart, know how to align themselves
and consciously build a career. Most think that they'll work hard and
be recognized. They're not smart enough to know that there's something
primal going on. I don't put men down for being chauvinistic. There's
something natural in that, so ingrained that I can't believe that it's an
accident. I've had a lot of young women, age twenty to thirty, on my

staffs. They're wide-eyed when I tell them how to deal with a man in the workplace. They don't know that they're talking to somebody who has to beat his chest. If he has to beat his chest and you want to win your point, you don't take his hand off his chest; you make him scratch his nose so he has to take his hands off his chest. He'll think he did it and you didn't make him do it. I made them deal directly with the difficult bosses because I thought that was part of their training. Be in a room with somebody you're afraid of and learn to survive. It's not taught anywhere, so where the hell are they supposed to learn this?

"When I left one executive position for a variety of reasons, I wanted them to make me an offer of severance. I deserved it. I never brought up the term 'severance.' Number one, don't talk to the madman, talk to somebody whose mind works like a cash register. To him it will be just, 'What's the number? And what's the other number if I don't do this?' And it worked.

"Young women today feel that they should have great opportunities, and are ready to feel equal to any man. But since they don't realize there's a hidden agenda, they're going into battle without a rifle. They've never been in battle, so why would they know there is a battlefield? Of course there's a battlefield. It's not the same one we were on; it's greener, there are more opportunities, and for the most part talent will out, especially if you're willing to take chances. Women get some great opportunities that were not available even ten years ago, but for the most part, our chances are not the same as any guy's. At least young women don't have ghosts running around in the attic. I'm happy they don't feel they have to say thanks to anybody."[191]

It's human nature not to appreciate what the generation before you achieves, but in all these interviews, no woman of the beachhead generation has said, "Damn it, they should be grateful to us." Not one. Rather, the women who have a sense that things weren't great before they started working in the 1980s say, "Thank God they were there and I didn't have to push those doors down. I just walked through."[192]

"I'm grateful to the women who opened doors," says commercial director-producer Leslie Smith. "Otherwise, I could not have graduated as a DP without resistance. I really felt I could do whatever I wanted to do. I say thank you everybody for making me feel safe enough to move forward. I left the Women in Film luncheon last year [1999] and went home and cried. It hit me so hard when Amy Heckerling said that about being a young girl and her dad saying, 'You can't be a director. Show me in the newspaper where there are any female directors.' I went through the paper that night and, gee, there are so few. It just shouldn't be that way."[193]

"There is deep joy engaging in the struggle, deep joy in it," says Paula Weinstein.[194]

Weinstein is president of Spring Creek Pictures. In 1999, it partnered with HBO to make *Iron-Jawed Angels*, a movie for television about the suffragists in 1917 who were arrested for picketing the White House. Georgia Jeffries wrote the script. "The suffragists were sent to prison, where they went on a hunger strike to demand their civil rights," she says. "They wouldn't take no for an answer. These militant women just kept showing up. Women who last in our business say, 'I'm worthy of being seen and heard. This film is worthy. I refuse to take no for an answer.' You just keep showing up."[195]

Anthea Sylbert describes a five-year battle to get *Something to Talk About* made, which she produced with Paula Weinstein, Goldie Hawn, and William S. Beasley. It starred Julia Roberts and Dennis Quaid. "I used to say when we started that project that I was a tall blonde who turned into this short, gray-haired woman. That's one thing that's true about a lot of movies. They get done because someone wouldn't give up."[196]

"Perseverance is everything. I'm opinionated, and I know that helped me believe in my own convictions," says producer-director Joan Chen.[197] "You owe it to yourself to . . . live deliberately, to suck the marrow out of the bone."[198]

One part of the new challenges is the extent to which women help other women, which they are and are not doing.

"I started working in the business in '79," says Lili Zanuck, "and almost all of us who came up at that time had men who mentored us. But when we got ahead, I didn't find we were hiring women. Maybe because we hadn't been mentored by women. Now it's 2000, my friends are successful, and I call their office and a guy answers the phone. I'm thinking, 'God, at least we could hire each other as assistants because that's still a real learning opportunity.' That's the *least* we can do.

"This is a time when we have the illusion of women succeeding because some women are in positions of power," she says, "but the numbers of the DGA and the WGA are awful. That means that women are not hiring women. Women I know in positions of power—you don't see women directors on their slates! They are not hiring women. I don't know if we end up respecting men more or do [these executives] think that since they can't direct that other women can't either but men can do everything. I don't know what that's about."[199]

"Whatever it is, the boys' club seems to stick together," one woman says, as if speaking about an obscure but powerful tribe on the unexplored upper reaches of a river she's heard a lot about.[200] Another pointed out that women study applicants' resumes with a microscope and don't recommend anyone until they're absolutely sure, but men recommend other men much more easily. Women may be tougher on themselves and on other women, but fundamentally they don't have the same kind of support network they can count on. It's a numbers game; numbers count in a primal way. Experienced or just starting out, if you have a broad-based, industrywide brotherhood that comprises 75 percent to 90 percent of the people in that industry, mistakes or misjudgments are not as crucial compared to being in a group that comprises only 10 percent to 25 percent.

"The guys take care of themselves," another says. "A woman gets fired from a high-profile job; her little silver parachute plops and crashes. They do not have the same golden parachutes. It's ding-dong-the-witch-is-dead. A guy gets fired from those jobs and the mind-set is that he needs to be taken care of and set up, and I think that's still pervasive today."[201]

Others see the proposition differently. "I see a new girls' network as a group of people who have grown up with each other in the business," says Melanie Cook, "who have a certain level of trust. I did not grow up with the more senior men in the business as I have with Stacey [Snider] and Amy [Pascal], so I'm not sure that [a girls' or boys' club] is completely a function of gender as much as it is age."[202]

But, as Anne Nelson says, "I'm not sure we want to be in the boys' club, because who needs that?"[203]

The Next Frontier, and the Next, and the Next

"I don't think there's been a woman's movement for at least a decade," says Mary Ledding. "Is that dangerous?"[204]

No one seems to know what post-feminism means but we are definitely in it. Scholars have defined it as "arbitrary cultural constrictions favoring those men in power."[205] But even the term, post-feminism, points to struggles that are won and they're over. Feminism has been around a long time, since the days of the French Revolution, then in America in the 1840s, then the suffrage movement in the early 1900s, then in the 1960s, modern feminism from Betty Friedan, and yet it's clear that "women are coming to see the essentially repetitive nature" of the struggle.[206] It's also clear that "not all women are equally oppressed," which might be one signpost for the future.[207] Historian Rosalind Miles blames Hollywood for much of the mythology once and still perpetuated about women and men. Film, television and commercials, "pseudomodern

industries, the mass media, lead us . . . backward into the future," she
writes, and now "we can recognize the new arena in which the next
stage for freedom and equality of women will be fought out."[208] Now,
there's an argument for women's presence in the industry, for their viewpoints in history, for the right to define themselves on big and little
screens.

No one denies clusters of big changes have occurred. "Now, no one
notices a woman film producer because there are so many," says Alexandra Rose, co-producer of *Norma Rae.* "Betty Friedan said to me, speaking of those who began working in the late 1970s or early 1980s, 'Your
generation was the only one that had any fun. My generation got so
beaten up being in the trenches of feminism that we're exhausted and
angry. You're the first telephone line person, the first film producer, first
commercial airline pilot, first firefighter, first policewoman. Every other
woman that comes after you will be like the men, one of the crowd.' And
she was right, I did have fun. I enjoyed everything I did. Then she said,
'You are lucky.' They were warriors, they never got what they fought
for. They fought for us but didn't themselves receive the benefits. They
took all the slings and arrows for us."[209]

Big political gains like those in the 1970s are followed by slower shifts
in attitude. These changes probably won't have the mass support (or
boosts from the "guilt trip") of earlier decades but the fact remains that
"the women's rights movement became the first in history to have been
planned and executed by women."[210] Wider, deeper changes or wake-up
calls now will have to come from women.

It seems certain that the influence of women in film and television
will gradually increase as they and others realize their value in the art
and enterprise of global entertainment. As limited as some things still
seem for some women, the outline of their influence can now be seen—
because they made themselves part of the picture in the last thirty
years.

Fay Kanin says, "Movies are the people's art form . . . They are in
every part of life, more important than books, more important than anything I can think of."[211]

"Our entertainment business is the last, pure American export," Nancy
Hutson Perlman says. "It's the most influential business in the world
because it's in every part of the globe . . . and we are deciding the quality
and subject matter of the images . . .

"Creativity is the foundation of entertainment. Women are uniquely
geared to foster it and appreciate it . . . Creativity always comes from the
bottom . . . I am sure the statistics [about women in film and television]
are accurate, but they are sending the wrong message. Entertainment

has never been a group effort. It is individual pieces of creativity that rise or are by accident left alone in a vacuum and all of a sudden there it is! Women should not be discouraged about success. If they are, they're discouraged about the wrong thing. They need to focus on the work and stop worrying about a statistical profile. It's like that wonderful line from Ira Levin's play, *Death Trap.* 'I've written a screenplay so good that not even a gifted director can hurt it.' Women need to be more in touch with their femaleness instead of whether or not the system employed 15 percent fewer women last year. Play to your strength. Don't protect your territory. The minute you start that, you've already lost. Open up . . . support other women because the only criterion for genuine success is whether or not you can pass it on."[212]

"In 1999," says Jane Alexander, "I gave the commencement address at Smith College, which is the oldest and largest women's college in the country and the fifth largest endowed college in America.

"I found myself giving a rather radical speech. The kids loved it. I felt safe, too, because the graduates, student body and many of the teachers were women. When I finished and sat down, the male provost next to me didn't say a word. About fifteen minutes went by and then, with a red face, he whispered, 'Well, *that* was a pretty radical commencement address.' What I'd said was that I had been around a long time, in film, on the stage, in politics, and I felt that incontrovertibly women should be running the world.

"But until we have some kind of massive change at the very top, there's going to be a lot of lip service paid. The good thing is, I think there are more women moving into the economic structure in the United States. They're starting low, but in another generation I think they'll start taking over."[213]

"Women have an extraordinarily unique opportunity," says Laura Ziskin. "Men have built the cities, made and defined the culture, interpreted the world. At no time in recorded history have women been culture-makers. Movies are arguably the most influential, important medium in the world. They have a tremendous cultural impact. Because women are now making movies, then women's ideas, philosophy, point of view will seep into that culture. And that's never happened in history. Ever, ever, ever. We can't even see the impact of that yet."[214]

AUTHOR'S NOTE

This book is based on more than 125 interviews conducted mainly in Los Angeles, in person and by telephone. I have also used secondary materials—books, magazine and newspaper articles, and some unpublished studies—to fix events by date, and to augment facts related in the interviews. But the thrust of the book relies on the candor and the memory of those interviewed, their sense of their own experiences, their point of view; their accounts are both factual and subjective, a cousin, perhaps, of the oral history. When accounts differed with others, I have noted it, but generally recollections did not differ much where they interconnected. Some of the women, and men, interviewed, did not want their remarks on the record, or asked that a portion of their remarks be kept confidential; therefore, some comments are noted as "anonymous." Most interviews were done entirely on the record.

ENDNOTES

Introduction

1. Dawn Steel died of a brain tumor in December 1997. She wrote *They Can Kill You But They Can't Eat You* (Pocket Books 1993).
2. Lois Weber formed her own production company in 1917. In 1923 she returned to Universal, where she directed films off and on through the 1920s. The president of Universal, Carl Laemmle, with whom she worked closely, said of her: "I would trust Miss Weber with any sum of money that she needed to make any picture that she wanted to make. I would be sure that she would bring it back. She knows the Motion Picture business as few people do and can drive herself as hard as anyone I have ever known." Anthony Slide, *The Silent Feminists: America's First Woman Directors* (Lanham, MD: Scarecrow Press, 1996).
3. The following year Cary Beauchamp's excellent biography of Frances Marion, *Without Lying Down* (New York: Scribners, 1997), was published.
4. Between 1932 and 1985, eight other women writers shared awards *with* partners (1933, 1938, 1942, 1946, 1950, 1955, 1978, 1985). After Jhabvala won her solo award in 1986, Callie Khouri won in 1991 for *Thelma and Louise*, Jhabvala again in 1992 for *Howard's End*, Jane Campion in 1993 for *The Piano*, and in 1995 Emma Thompson won for her adaptation of *Sense and Sensibility*. Screenwriting and editing are often cited as disciplines "friendly to women." Of the sixty-six Oscars given since 1934 for editing, eleven were awarded to women—the last one in 1987 for *The Last Emperor*.
5. These interviews include: Pamela Brockie, Christine Foster, D. C. Fontana, Lila Garrett, Sybil Niden Goldrich, Gloria Goldsmith, Max Goldenson, Joanna Lee, Ann Marcus, Judith Merians, Kathleen Nolan, Dolores Robinson, Jean Rouverol, Linda Seger, Leslie Smith, Renée Valente, Kac Young.
6. Gayle Maffeo, interview by author, 10 January 2000.
7. Barbara Boyle, interview by author, 4 March 1999.
8. In addition to the autobiographical sources cited elsewhere in this book, other sources on contemporary women's experiences in film and television as a group include: Denise D. and William T. Bielby, "Women and Men in Film, Gender Inequality Among Writers in a Culture Industry," *Gender & Society*, vol. 10, no. 3 (June 1996). This study cites a number of reasons for these inequities,

among them, "The overwhelming majority of those who make decisions about matching creative talent to commercial project are men." The Bielbys also cite the "empty field" phenomenon originally described in a study by Gaye Tuchman, *Edging Women Out: Victorian Novelists, Publishers, and Social Change* (New Haven, CT: Yale University Press, 1989).

9. "A Personal Report from Ms.," Ms., July 1972, Volume 1, Issue 1.
10. "Letters," Editorial note, Ms., July 1972.

I. Beachhead: The 1970s

1. I DON'T WANT TO WATCH, I WANT TO PLAY

11. "Bitch, bitch, bitch . . . support her two children." Joyce Perry, interview by author, 14 February 1999. Perry is a television writer (*Laramie, Mannix, The Young and the Restless*, and many others). In 1982, she was elected to the board of the WGA.

12. "She was from New York . . . feminist." Noreen Stone, interview by author, 4 February 1998, 5 April 1999. Stone wrote features, movies for television, dramatic episodes, and has produced TV pilots and documentaries. "I was the third chair of the committee," says Stone. "One year I served with Sue Grafton, then with Jean Rouverol."

13. "When the networks . . . assumed to be men." Jean Rouverol, interview by author, 5 February 1998. Rouverol is author of *Refugees from Hollywood* (Albuquerque, NM: University of New Mexico Press, 2000), *Writing for the Soaps* (Cincinnati, OH: Writers Digest Books, 1984), and screenwriter of *Face in the Rain; The First Time; So Young, So Bad*. She was blacklisted with her husband, Hugo Butler.

14. "I was working for Gene Roddenberry . . . a woman wrote it." D. C. Fontana, interview by author, 22 July 1999. Fontana was story editor on the original *Star Trek* series, *Fantastic Journey*, and *Logan's Run*; associate producer on *Star Trek: The Next Generation*; writer on *The Streets of San Francisco, Then Came Bronson* (nominated for WGA Award), *Prince Valiant, Babylon 5*, and many others. She was awarded the Writers Guild Morgan Cox Award for service to the guild, and was twice elected to the board of directors.

15. "Sometimes, you got in . . . very much, actually." Fontana, interview.
16. "How do we convince . . . discriminated against?" *WGA Journal* (June 1989), 20.
17. "So very isolated . . . not good enough." Perry, interview.
18. "I was a widow . . . rapport and respect." Rouverol, interview.
19. "An ongoing committee skirmish . . . free Scandia lunch." Shelly Burdach, interview by author, 19 November 2000. Burdach was the source for Viking Club activities. He has no memory of women WGA members being excluded from a free lunch. However, he says, "what probably happened is that unless women were escorted by a member of the Viking Club, she would probably not get a lunch." Burdach took his female staff to lunch after they donated blood. He says the group was fundamentally a way to do some good in the community, such as the blood drive and providing toys at Christmas. The Scandia exclusion was one of the first actions of the WGA Women's Committee. Sources: "Council Actions," *WGA Newsletter* (January 1972), 3, and transcript of Diana Gould,

#46, recorded 22 August 1978, 8: "... Women [WGA members] were excluded from Scandia to donate blood."

20. "What is it ... get lunch, too?" References to the exclusion appear in the *WGAw News,* including Diana Gould, "Women Writers" (June 1972), 16–17. In Gould's update on the "Viking Club Blood donation barrier," she wrote, "[W]e have finally received the first letter from Jerry D. Lewis which does not say in a postscript, 'Sorry GIRLS, we'll take your blood but you can't eat at the lunch counter.' Excluding women members from a Guild function is no different from exluding Jewish or Black members, and just as atrocious." The wrangle over the blood donations and lunch went on for months.

21. "I'd probably had ... get some statistics!" Perry, interview. Cochairs Stone and Rouverol agree that at a meeting in 1972 or early 1973, Perry came up with the idea of a survey.

22. "That's confidential ... financial information in them." Perry, interview.

23. John Furia, interview by author, 19 October 1999. Furia is a writer (*Hotel, Kung-Fu, The Singing Nun*), and producer.

24. "Howard was always ... with our survey." Stone, interview. Screenwriter Howard Rodman penned the Paul Newman racing movie *Winning, Coogan's Bluff* with Clint Eastwood, and others.

25. "We got lucky ... check the records." Gloria Goldsmith, interview, 30 December 1997. Goldsmith was a Rockefeller grant winner, and New Dramatist (which to playwrights is what MacArthur grants are to other artists).

26. "It felt like ... what we were finding." Perry, interview.

27. "The numbers were mind-boggling." Stone, interview.

28. "I remember sitting ... weren't good enough." Perry, interview.

29. "We had copies ... the statistics." Stone, interview; confirmed by Rouverol, interview. Rouverol provided author with the one extant copy of the committee's first statistics.

30. "The women's movement ... other eight positions?" Sue Cameron, interview by author, 11 December 1997.

31. Perry had not given the survey ... "You'll never work here!" Perry, interview.

32. "That survey was an explosion ... on which project." Cameron, interview.

33. "Quinn Martin ... a man's game." Bill Greely, "Women State TV Writing Bias," *WGAw News* (December 12, 1973). First published in *Variety* (November 1973).

34. "Have you ever communicated ... prime time television shows." Will Tusher, *Hollywood Reporter* (April 15 1974).

35. See Susan Brownmiller, *In Our Time* (New York: Random House, 1999), for a complete account of the social and legal battles in New York at the time. See also Judith Marlane, *Women in Television News Revisited* (University of Texas Press, 1999).

36. "I'm really not sure ... the women's movement." Ethel Winant, interview by author, 18 January 1999.

37. "I don't think [CBS] ... a little more money." Winant, interview.

38. "I didn't want to come ... and laughed about it." Renée Valente, interview by author, 28 December 1998. Valente remained at Columbia until 1979. She became an independent producer of television movies, miniseries, and features, including *Poker Alice, Love Thy Neighbor, Valley of the Dolls.*

39. In late 1972 "... male violence are sick." Mary Murphy and Cheryl Bentsen,

"Fighting to Enter the 'White Male Club,'" part 1 in "Women in Hollywood," *Los Angeles Times*, 14 August 1973.

40. "Alcoholics love alcohol . . . feeding the habit." Murphy and Bentsen, "Can Females Become More Than Just Faces?" part 2 in "Women in Hollywood," *Los Angeles Times*, 15 August 1973.

41. "Break down barriers . . . strong roles." Murphy and Bentsen, "Can Females Become More Than Just Faces?"

42. "Dino's the real ding-a-ling . . . short since." Murphy and Bentsen, "White Male Club."

43. "This is what it was . . . making cookies or something?" Brianne Murphy, interview by author, 8 December 1999.

44. "the largest social movement . . . in the world." Rosalyn Baxandall and Linda Gordon. "Second-Wave Soundings," *The Nation* (3 July 2000).

45. "first in history . . . executed by women." Rosalind Miles, *Who Cooked the Last Supper? The Women's History of the World.* (New York: Three Rivers Press, 1988, 2001). 234.

46. "everyone was a vice president." Winant, interview.

47. "Tomorrow Entertainment was a lovely company." Fay Kanin, interview by author, 25 May 1999.

48. "It was one of the first . . . unusual for its time." Diana Gould, interview by author, 14 May 1999. Gould's film and television credits include *Jenny, Sharing the Secret,* and *For My Daughter's Honor.* She was a producer/writer on *Dynasty, Kay O'Brien,* and *Berrenger's.*

49. "Knowing those writers . . . victimized by it." Gould, interview.

50. "When I moved from New York . . . of making a mistake." Marcy Carsey, interview by author, 3 June 1999. Carsey is owner/executive producer of the Carsey-Werner Co. (*3rd Rock from the Sun, Cosby, That '70s Show*).

51. "trashy, awful dialogue . . . don't complain." Nancy Malone, interviews by author, 26 November 1997 and 16 December 1997.

52. "He said to Malone . . . learn how to produce. Malone, interview.

53. "She couldn't see . . . I will never know why." Malone, interview.

54. Tandem Entertainment was founded by Norman Lear and Bud Yorkin. Its productions include *All in the Family, Maude, Sanford & Son,* and *Mary Hartman, Mary Hartman.*

55. "Tandem, the production company . . . television became history." Marian Rees, interviews by author, 7 December and 14 December 1998. Rees is an Emmy award–winning independent television producer. Her credits include *Miss Rose White, Between Friends* (one of HBO's first movies dealing with women, Rees says, written by Shelley List), and many others.

56. Marian Rees says, "I gave the article to Fay's agent, Sylvia Hirsch, who sent it on to Fay." Rees, interview.

57. "I don't remember . . . just right for that movie." Kanin interview. Kanin was a reader in 1939, then a writer on her own and later with her husband Michael Kanin—*My Pal Gus, Teacher's Pet,* and other features. Later, Kanin wrote on her own, television movies like *Hustling* and *Friendly Fire,* which she also produced.

58. "You'll get in over . . . I got in." Murphy, interview. Murphy, ASC, served on the American Society of Cinematographers executive board, 1983–85. Her cred-

its as cinematographer include *Little House on the Prairie, Secrets of the Bermuda Triangle, Fatso,* and *Like Mom, Like Me.*

59. "He gets up to me ... hang in there." Murphy interview.

60. "If you're working ... never meet a woman grip." Amy Halpern, interview by author, 10 January 2001. Halpern was finally inducted into IA 728, the International Alliance of Theatrical, Stage Employees, Motion Picture Technicians, on July 28, 2001. She teaches motion picture photography at California State University in Los Angeles and has been DP on *The Muse* and *The Last Hunt,* and gaffer on *Molly and Gina, Guests of the Astoria Hotel,* and Julie Dash's *Illusions.*

61. "Brianne told me ... her name was Brian." Halpern, interview.

62. "Just about every night ... Does your car have tires?" Murphy, interview.

2. WE DON'T WANT ANYTHING ITSY-POO

63. In 1973, *Cannon, Columbo,* and *Kojak* had no women writers, according to the WGA survey; *The Waltons* was written by 37 1/2 men and 2 1/2 women: and *The Streets of San Francisco* by 43 men and 1 woman.

64. In 1973, *All in the Family* was written by 69 men, 4 women; *M*A*S*H* by 37 men, 1 woman; *Mary Tyler Moore* by 50 men, 25 women, *Sanford & Son* by 49 men, no women; and *Maude* by 30 men, 7 women.

65. "But I didn't relate ... pair with him." Lily Tomlin, interview by author, 20 January 1998.

66. The title of the sketch was "Juke and Opal." Tomlin, interview.

67. "three-hundred-sixty-thousand-dollar jerk-off." Tomlin's show was not a low-budget show, but obviously, budgets for shows were much lower in 1973 than they are today.

68. "Jane wrote a piece ... air it but they finally did." Tomlin, interview.

69. Outstanding Comedy/Variety (Irene Pinn, executive producer; Herb Sargent, Jerry McPhie, producers; star Lily Tomlin) and Best Writing to Tomlin, Jane Wagner, and others. Tomlin has written, produced, and starred in, and Jane Wagner has written and produced, other Emmy-winning or-nominated specials, such as *Appearing Nitely,* executive-produced for HBO by Wagner and Tomlin; Wagner was the principal writer. *Edith Ann's Christmas: Just Say Noel* was executive-produced by Wagner-Tomlin; it won a Peabody.

70. Dramas featuring a woman began in 1974 with *Police Woman,* starring Angie Dickinson. *Cagney & Lacey* did not start its long run until 1982.

71. "Our idea for *Maude* ... have an abortion." Irma Kalish, interview by author, 20 July 1999. A television writer-producer, she partnered with her husband, Austin Kalish on *All in the Family, Maude, Carter Country, My Three Sons, Good Times, Good Heavens, F Troop,* and many more. She also produced, on her own, *Facts of Life* and *227,* and was the executive producer of *Carter Country* and *Good Times.* Kalish served as president of Women in Film from 1986 to 1987.

72. Susan Harris created the controversial *Soap* (1977–81) and its spinoff, *Benson* (1979–86), *Hail to the Chief* (1985), *Golden Girls* (1985–91), *Empty Nest* (1988–95), *Good and Evil* (1991).

73. "We went over there ... acknowledged presence in it." Kalish, interview.

74. "the curse of ... need good writers." Gail Parent, interview by author, 23 October 2000. Parent was coexecutive producer of *The Golden Girls,* producer of

Tracy Takes On! She authored four books. She was nominated for 17 Emmys, "and even won a couple," she says.

75. "first copy 'boy' with a D-cup." Ann Marcus, interview by author, 7 October 1999. Marcus wrote sitcoms in the 1960s (*Lassie*, *The Hathaways*), was a staff writer on *Peyton Place* and *The Debbie Reynolds Show*, and was head writer for *Love Is a Many-Splendored Thing*. She cocreated *Forever Fernwood*, *All That Glitters*, and *Julie Farr*, *M.D.* Marcus has served on the steering committee of the Caucus of Writers, Producers, Directors, and served six terms on the board of directors of the Writers Guild of America.

76. "Lear had gone through . . . lied through my teeth." Marcus, interview.

77. "One was a hilarious . . . something like that." Marcus, interview. See also Ann Marcus, *Whistling Girl* (Los Angeles, CA: Mulholland Pacific Publishing, 1999).

78. "But it was a different time . . . it was such fun." Marcus, interview.

79. "I was probably the only . . . and Joan Darling." Fern Field, interview by author, 23 June 1999. Field has written, directed, supervised, and/or produced documentaries, television sitcoms, movies, and miniseries. Her work has won the George Foster Peabody twice, the NAACP Image Award, seven Emmy nominations, and one Emmy award. Field was president of Women in Film from 1987 to 1988.

80. "I wanted it to go . . . as a television show." Joan Darling, interview by author, 8 January 2000. The blue-collar nighttime soap *Mary Hartman, Mary Hartman* was eventually syndicated and ran from 1976 to 1978, a huge hit. The writers, Ann Marcus, Jerry Adelman, and Daniel Gregory Brown, won an Emmy in 1976.

81. "Chuckles Bites the Dust" aired October 25, 1975.

82. "At last, I can earn . . . describing her life to me." Darling, interview. Actress-director Darling was nominated three times for an Emmy (she won a DGA Award and an Emmy in 1984 for *Mom's on Strike*). She has directed television shows, *Doc*, *Rhoda*, *Rich Man Poor Man*, *Amazing Stories*; she was the only woman to direct an episode of *Magnum, P.I.* She directs plays in New York and Los Angeles, and is a renowned teacher at the Sundance Institute.

83. Other popular shows headed by women prior to *The Mary Tyler Moore Show* and *Maude* were *I Love Lucy*; Eve Arden in *Our Miss Brooks*, the wisecracking English teacher at Madison High; *I Married Joan*, with Jim Backus as a judge who draws analogies from the cases before him to his wife's ditzy domestic activities; *Private Secretary*, starring Ann Sothern; and *Hazel*, starring Shirley Booth as a maid who runs the Baxter family. These series reflected some of the current perceptions of women, which were mined for comedy.

84. "The female characters . . . a big click." Valerie Harper, interview by author, 23 January 1998.

85. "We were at our wit's . . . nobody was right." Winant, interview.

86. "I told my secretary . . . I loved that show so." Winant, interview.

87. "I was at MTM . . . experiences only women have." Parent, interview.

88. "There were oceans of material . . . funny to boot!" Harper, interview.

89. "Episodic comedy . . . comedy writers." Charlotte Brown, interview by author, 30 January 1998. Brown became a writer/producer (*Rhoda*, *The Goodbye Girl*, *Between the Lines*), and also directed (*Cagney & Lacey*, *The Associates*, and other shows).

90. "I had no idea . . . fifteen hundred per script." Brown, interview.

91. "Jim Brooks and Allan Burns . . . absolutely wonderful time." Treva Silverman, interview by author, 14 October 1999. Silverman has written television features, plays and thirteen Off-Broadway children's musicals.

92. "I wasn't aware . . . idealistic place to be." Brown, interview.

3. SHE'S YOUNG, SHE'S PRETTY, AND—SHE'S A PRODUCER!

93. Bette Davis produced one film, *A Stolen Life*, in 1946. Michel Kraike produced *Night Plane from Chungking* (1942), *Criss Cross* (1949), *Bedtime for Bonzo*, starring Ronald Reagan, and other films. Dorothy Arzner directed throughout the 1920s until the early 1940s (*Get Your Man, Working Girls, Craig's Wife*). Marion Gering, Leigh Jason, and Ida Lupino also directed.

94. In the early 1970s: Nelly Kaplan directed *A Very Curious Girl* in 1969. Joan Collins and Jill Godmilow made *Antonia: A Portrait of the Woman* (1974), a feature-length documentary on Antonia Brica. Joan Tewkesbury was writing a screenplay for director Robert Altman, *Thieves Like Us*. Joan Micklin Silver had written the script of *Limbo* and was working on *Hester Street*, which she would also direct (1975). In 1973, Leigh Brackett, a feature film screenwriter for years, scripted *The Long Goodbye*. Jay Presson Allen had adapted and scripted *Travels with My Aunt* and *Cabaret* in 1972; in 1975, she would write *Funny Lady*. Gillian Armstrong produced and directed three short films (*My Brilliant Career* was not until 1979). Mai Zetterling was one of eight directors (including Arthur Penn and Milos Forman) on *Visions of Eight*, a documentary about the 1972 Olympics, which Dede Allen edited. Lina Wertmuller directed *Love and Anarchy* (1973), which brought her a lot of attention in the U.S. (*Seven Beauties* was released in 1979). Claudia Weill, a documentary filmmaker (*The Other Half of the Sky: A China Memoir*, which she directed, edited, and photographed, would appear in 1975). She was four years from producing and directing *Girlfriends*, a feature about the differences that arise between female friends when one chooses a career and the other chooses to be a homemaker.

95. A few male stars were producing, too: Warren Beatty produced *Bonnie and Clyde* (1967), *Shampoo* (1975), and directed *Heaven Can Wait* in 1978 (Elaine May cowrote with him). Sidney Poitier began directing in 1972—*Buck and the Preacher, Uptown Saturday Night, Stir Crazy*, and others—and produced *Free of Eden*. Clint Eastwood directed *Play Misty For Me* (1971) and *High Plains Drifter* (1972); he produced *Honkytonk Man* and *Foxfire* in 1982. Robert Redford directed *Ordinary People* in 1980 and started producing in 1981 (*The Solar Film*). Earlier, John Wayne had been producing pictures since the 1950s—*Ring of Fear* (1954), *Blood Alley* (1955), *The Alamo* (1960). James Cagney produced *The Gallant Hours* (1960) and directed *Short Cut to Hell* (1957). Richard Widmark produced *Time Limit* in 1957 and two other films in the 1960s.

96. "I was pregnant . . . made them hate me." Julia Phillips, interview by author, 19 December 1999. Phillips produced *Steelyard Blues, The Sting, Taxi Driver*, and *Close Encounters of the Third Kind*. She is the author of *You'll Never Eat Lunch in this Town Again* (New York: Random House, 1991) and *Driving Under the Affluence* (New York: HarperCollins, 1995). Julia Phillips died at age 57 on 1 January 2002.

97. "If you want a job that sucks . . . It's a terrible job." Julia Phillips, *E! True Hollywood Story*, 1999.

98. "Something to do . . . dick love story." Phillips, *You'll Never Eat Lunch*, 135.

99. "I inherited . . . call it now." Phillips, interview.

100. "gambler and embezzler . . . high rolling instincts." Phillips, *You'll Never Eat Lunch*, 122.

101. "They gave me . . . they got mad." Phillips, *E! True Hollywood Story*.

102. Begelman's hire of Hyams was reported in *Variety*, December 3, 1973. Hyams cast such films as *What's Up Doc?*, *The Exorcist*, and *Blazing Saddles*. In 1987, she directed *Leader of the Band*; in 1993, she produced *The Saint of Fort Washington*.

103. "Nessa (concert empresario . . .) in the middle." Phillips, *You'll Never Eat Lunch*, 135.

104. "Phillips decided to talk to Heller . . . *Fear of Flying*." Phillips, interview. Rosilyn Heller (interview by author, 5 November 1999), says that it was natural Phillips dealt with Hyams on *Fear of Flying*, since Phillips knew the author, Erica Jong. Heller also says that she and Hyams were not competing.

105. "To an extent . . . *Close Encounters*." Phillips, interview. Heller, interview.

106. "I didn't have any problem . . . why he hired us." Rosilyn Heller, interview.

107. "It had a 'down and dirty' . . . budget was bigger." Heller, interview.

108. "She paid a big price . . . medicated her pain." Howard Rosenman, *E! True Hollywood Story*, 1999.

109. Phillips, *You'll Never Eat Lunch*.

110. "It was crushing . . . hang with them." Phillips, interview.

111. "I was a young publicist . . . she was great." Cheryl Boone Isaacs, interview by author, 31 August 1999.

112. "No matter who's . . . producing is hard." Phillips, interview.

113. Spielberg has spoken often about Verna Fields. He acknowledged his debt to her, also, at the Mentor Awards program, hosted by Women in Film in 1999, describing the important roles women had had in his career and asserting that Field's editing was a signal reason for *Jaws'* phenomenal success.

114. The Motion Picture Editors Guild says it keeps no statistics on members regarding race or gender. Unofficially, they say about 30 to 35 percent of their 5700 members are women, a percentage that would include editors, assistant editors and sound and music editors.

115. "By 2000, the number of women editing . . . a decade before." Martha M. Lauzen, Ph.D., *The Celluloid Ceiling: Behind-the-Scenes Employment in the Top 250 Films of 2000* (San Diego: School of Communication, San Diego State University 2000). Women accounted for 19 percent of all editors working on the top 250 films.

116. "The figures for television . . . are almost the same." See Lauzen, *Where The Women Are . . . And Aren't: Study of On-Screen, Behind-the-Scenes Representation in 1999–2000 Prime Time Season* (San Diego: San Diego State University, September 2000).

117. "Editing has long been considered a woman's work, but it isn't." Dede Allen, interview by author, 9 February 2000. Her many credits as an editor include *Little Big Man*, *Slaughterhouse Five*, and *Reds*, which she also executive-produced.

118. "Viola Lawrence cut . . . her being included." *Hollywood Reporter*, "Special Issue: Women in Entertainment," 8 December 1992, cited by Douglas Eby in "A Few More Good Women," Rocamora.org/AOL.com.

119. See Slide, *The Silent Feminists*.

120. Verna Fields did edit *Studs Lonigan*, which was directed by Irving Lerner. Some of the other films she edited are *Cry of Battle, Medium Cool, American Graffiti, Paper Moon, Daisy Miller*, and *The Sugarland Express*.

121. "In my generation in the '50s . . . where it was really really hard." Allen, interview.

122. "I call myself . . . It was possible." Polly Platt, interview by author, 3 November 1999. Production designer on *Terms of Endearment*, executive producer on *Broadcast News* and *The War of the Roses*, producer on *The Witches of Eastwick, Say Anything . . .*, *I'll Do Anything*, and many more. In 1978, she wrote the screenplay for *Pretty Baby* (Louis Malle). Her first films with Bogdanovich were *Targets, The Last Picture Show, What's Up, Doc?* and *Paper Moon*.

123. "It's aberrant in a certain way . . . a lucky girl." Platt, interview.

124. "I could always recognize . . . seeing the space." Platt, interview.

125. "The loss of Peter . . . and that was wonderful." Platt, interview.

126. "It was like running a film school . . . just go do it." Julie Corman, interview by author, 20 October 1999. Corman is a veteran producer of twenty-nine films, including *Boxcar Bertha, Da*, and *The Lady in Red*.

127. "The guy at the studio . . . probably really smart." Boyle, interview. Boyle became executive vice president, New World Pictures, general counsel and chief operating officer in 1974.

128. "There were always women . . . gender blind." Boyle, interview.

129. "I don't think discrimination . . . getting the films made." Corman, interview.

130. "Roger wanted to make a deal . . . I never noticed." Boyle, interview.

131. "It was my first production . . . *there's no money*." Corman, interview.

132. "No one else would hire women . . . they all started with Roger." Boyle, interview. Teri Schwartz worked as assistant director and as a producer on Corman movies (*Eat My Dust!, The Bees*). She started her own rock video company, making videos for Barbra Streisand and Roger Daltry, among others, then in the late 1980s began producing films again (*Nuts, Beaches, Joe Versus the Volcano, Sister Act*).

133. "When I produced . . . sums it up." Tamara Asseyev, interview by author, 2 December 1999. Her extensive producing credits include *Norma Rae, I Wanna Hold Your Hand* (Robert Zemeckis's first film with Steven Spielberg), and television movies such as *After the Promise* and the four-hour miniseries *Beryl Markham: A Shadow on the Sun*.

134. "He'd come back from a science fiction . . . low-budget movies." Asseyev, interview. At New World, Asseyev also worked on *The St. Valentine's Day Massacre*, starring Jason Robards and George Segal; *The Devil's Angels*, starring John Cassavetes; *The Trip*, written by Jack Nicholson, starring Peter Fonda and Dennis Hopper; *The Pit and the Pendulum*, starring Vincent Price. She was the associate producer on *The Wild Racers* for Corman.

135. "I produced it . . . I'd worked for Corman only about a year." Asseyev, interview. *Paddy* was released in 1970.

136. "We called it *Paddy* . . . if you're a man or a woman." Asseyev, interview.

137. "Out of all my films . . . but for our children." Corman, interview.

138. "I remember . . . wonderful and arduous." Anonymous, interview by author.

4. THE START OF A WONDERFUL HEYDAY FOR WOMEN

139. "I just went in to Peter . . . had dared to ask before." Heller, interview. Heller began as creative affairs exec for Palomar/ABC Pictures, New York City. At Columbia Pictures (1973–81), she supervised such films as *Taxi Driver*, *Julia*, *Close Encounters of the Third Kind*, *Eyes of Laura Mars*, and *The China Syndrome*.

140. Lynda Obst, a film producer (*The Fisher King*, *Sleepless in Seattle*), wrote *Hello, He Lied*, a classic book about Hollywood (New York: Little Brown, 1996).

141. The Begelman scandal was documented by David McClintick is his book *Indecent Exposure* (New York: Dell, 1982): the head of Columbia Pictures (Begelman) deposited a check into his own bank account, a check intended for actor Cliff Robertson. Begelman was found out and suspended. His friends rallied around, got him reinstated, but finally he was forced to resign Columbia and was indicted on grand theft. His sentence was reduced to a misdemeanor. In an amazing comeback, a couple of years later, he became CEO of MGM, but was out after more misdeeds and a string of bad films. He committed suicide in 1995. Peter Guber joined Jon Peters to create an amazingly successful production company, Guber-Peters, and became in the 1990s the heads of Sony Pictures Entertainment. Their successes and excesses at Sony are well documented. Peter Bart called their adventures there "a failure of almost operatic proportions . . ." (*Who Killed Hollywood?* 1999, 79). Stanley Jaffe, a major film producer, left Columbia to join forces with Sherry Lansing in the 1980s, producing hits like *Fatal Attraction* and *The Accused*.

142. "When they made me vice president . . . wrestled from them." Heller, interview.

143. "That is why so many women quit." Marcia Nasatir, interview by author, 10 November 1998. Nasatir, an independent film producer today, came from New York publishing and became a literary agent at Ziegler, Ross, Tennant. She was one of the first women vice presidents of production, first at United Artists (*Rocky*, *One Flew Over the Cuckoo's Nest*, *Annie Hall*), then at Orion; she was later president of Carson Productions (*The Big Chill*).

144. "Mike! How are you? . . . he'd never been in a meeting with a woman." Nasatir, interview.

145. "She was like a god . . . Filmmakers loved her." Lucy Fisher, interview by author, 21 October 1999.

146. "She was very much a socialist . . . vice president." Nasatir, interview.

147. The move was announced by Eric Pleskow, president, and Mike Medavoy, vice president in charge of West Coast production, as reported in the *Hollywood Reporter*, 22 July 1974.

148. "And we began . . . would not have happened in New York." Nasatir, interview.

149. "I remember walking out . . . nothing to do with us!" Paula Weinstein, interview by author, 3 June 1999. Weinstein is a producer with Spring Creek Productions (*Fearless*, *Analyze This*, *Citizen Cohn*, *The List*).

150. "When Jack Haley Jr . . . a short film." Malone interview. The film was *Merlene of the Movies*, in which Malone had cast her friend, Gloria Stuart (now widely known for her survivor role in *Titanic*).

151. "They said they'd heard . . . I was producing." Malone, interview.

152. "I was excited, challenged . . . selling my heart out." Malone, interview.

153. "I'll never forget it . . . weren't supplied with dates." Malone, interview. Malone moved into directing television in the mid-1980s—*Dynasty*, *The Colbys*, *Cagney & Lacey*, *The Brady Bunch*, *Melrose Place*, and many more.

154. "A lot of the networking . . . in twenty minutes, dear." "Ethel Winant, Finding

Opportunities: From Pioneer to New Frontier," *Reel News*, Women in Film 1, no. 7 (November 1991).

155. "I belong to the generation . . . and go into business." Beth Kennedy, interview by author, 3 March 1998. Kennedy was an executive at Universal Studios/ MCA from 1975 to 1990 as director of information systems, VP management consulting (MCA, Inc.), VP administration (Universal Studios), senior VP business development and administration. Today, she is CEO of the Kaisen-Heron Group, a convergent media development and production company.

156. "Kennedy was twenty-four . . . out of his check." Kennedy, interview.

157. "They didn't like it . . . her performance review." Kennedy, interview.

158. "You know Joan's a lawyer . . . their perception of me." Kennedy, interview.

159. "there were so few women in management . . . not really marketing." Willette Klausner, interview by author, 29 July 1998. Klausner was director, then VP, marketing and marketing research at MCA, Inc. (1975–81). Today, she produces and develops stage productions (*Fully Committed, Kat and the Kings, Three Mo' Tenors*).

160. At Universal, as at other studios, a few women became vice president: Joannie Robbins was VP of finance and the first woman to be a corporate VP; Verna Fields became a VP in postproduction in the mid-1970s; and others like Bobbi Fisher, senior VP of domestic TV syndication. At Universal, Klausner, Phyllis Grann (VP in publishing), and Beth Kennedy were the only female VPs at management meetings. "One hundred men and us," Kennedy recalls.

161. Lucy Fisher became a senior production executive at Warner Bros. in 1982.

162. "I found out *after* I left . . . their language to me again." Klausner, interview.

163. "My father wanted me to . . . the myths I grew up on." Anthea Sylbert, interview by author, 9 March 1999. Sylbert is an Oscar-nominated costume designer (*Chinatown* and *Julia*). She was VP of production, Warner Bros., 1978; executive VP production, United Artists, 1980; then independent producer heading her own company with Goldie Hawn (*Swing Shift, Protocol, Overboard, Something to Talk About*).

164. "*Chinatown* was thrilling . . . I lost that one." Sylbert, interview.

165. Sylbert designed costumes for Elaine May's films *A New Leaf* and *The Heartbreak Kid*, and for Nichol's *Carnal Knowledge* and *The Fortune*.

166. "I liked working with people . . . I was in charge of." Sylbert, interview.

167. The last of the big MGM-type musicals were about to be released—*The Boyfriend*, with Twiggy, and *Travels with My Aunt*, with Maggie Smith.

168. In the 1930s, Irving Thalberg transformed the newly formed MGM, overseeing virtually all productions and maintaining a high-standard balance between commerce and art—*Grand Hotel, The Broadway Melody, A Night at the Opera, The Hunchback of Notre Dame*. He died at the age of thirty-seven in 1936.

169. "I had access to every piece . . . my great joy." Susan Merzbach, interview by author, 2 November 1998. Merzbach was story editor at MGM, then moved to Columbia Pictures in 1978 as executive story editor and to 20th Century Fox as VP creative affairs in 1980.

170. Samuel Marx was a famous 1930s story editor who acquired classic material like *The Thin Man* and *Grand Hotel*.

171. Margaret Booth was presented an Honorary Oscar in 1977 for "exceptional contribution to the art of film editing."

172. "I was efficient and organized . . . ever heard of D-girl." Donie Nelson, interview

by author, 25 August 1999. Nelson began as a secretary, then became assistant story editor, then story editor at MGM.

173. "As Carl's secretary . . . somebody's nephew for your job." Nelson, interview.

174. "Carl had told personnel . . . nephew out of Harvard." Nelson, interview.

175. "I was her first hire . . . might be changing." Mary Ledding, interview by author, 26 November 1999. In her eight years at MGM, Ledding was director of television business affairs, assistant to the VP of motion picture business affairs, then senior VP. She became VP business affairs for Act III Television, a division of Norman Lear's entertainment and communications corporation, then deputy general counsel for Warner Bros. She was president of Women in Film in 1983.

176. "I started off in TV business affairs . . . shooting on one stage." Ledding, interview.

177. "We had one male file clerk . . . full name to my work." Merzbach, interview.

178. "Bennett was trying valiantly . . . instead of down—on us." Nelson, interview.

179. "This was just a year after . . . to give me more." Sherry Lansing, interview by author, 2 November 1999. Lansing has had a long and distinguished career as an executive and as a producer. After MGM, she moved to Columbia Pictures, became senior vice president, then became the first woman president of production (at 20th Century Fox). She partnered with Stanley Jaffe in 1983, produced *Fatal Attraction*, among other films, then formed her own production company, Lansing Productions (*Indecent Proposal*). In 1992, she became chairman of the Motion Picture Group of Paramount Pictures.

180. "We had no template . . . I can relate to that." Merzbach, interview.

181. "It was like a country club . . . a Hollywood studio was like." Ally Acker, *Reel Women, Pioneers of the Cinema* (New York: The Continuum Publishing Co., 1991). Frank, partnered with her husband, Irving Ravetch, wrote *Hud, Hombre*, and many other films.

182. "Ledding asked me . . . 'Beware, Women Present.' " Nelson, interview.

183. "It was our routine . . . Marcia Nasatir joined us." Nelson, interview.

184. "It was gorgeous . . . we were in their face about." Ledding, interview.

185. "Sherry had a more open approach . . . Carl to do that." Nelson, interview.

186. "Shortly after Sherry arrived . . . escaping to Holland in 1936." Merzbach, interview.

187. "nonambitious person . . . keep moving, preferably up." Nelson, interview.

188. "Nelson stumbled . . . is fire Susan." Merzbach, interview.

189. "Sherry gave me . . . how it really worked." Nelson, interview.

190. "Being a woman . . . protected me." Ledding, interview.

191. Nelson got her first screen credit, associate producer, at Christiana for *Like Normal People*. Today, Nelson is a career and marketing consultant for screenwriters in film and television. Merzbach has her own production company.

5. GET ME A WOMAN!

192. Leonard H. Goldenson with Marvin J. Wolf, "Other Recollections: Roy Huggins," *Beating the Odds*, (New York: Charles Scribner's Sons, 1991), 330–32.

193. "Working with Barry Diller . . . Diversity is good for all of us." Lillian Gallo, interview by author, 14 January 1998. Gallo is a television producer (*Hustling, Playmates, The Lookalike, The Lifeforce Experiment, Princess Daisy*). During her tenure as ABC's director of Movies of the Weekend, she produced twenty-two movies, including Steven Spielberg's *Duel*.

194. "I knew ABC was . . . had gray hair." Carsey, interview.

195. "One of the many jokes . . . Friday night." Carsey, quoted in Goldenson, *Beating the Odds*, 357.

196. "I learned that I loved . . . the right place to work." Carsey, interview.

197. "We ran a casual shop . . . everything was fine." Goldenson, *Beating the Odds*, 358.

198. "Very soon after . . . encouraged that." Carsey, interview. Carsey left ABC in 1980 and founded the Carsey-Werner Company with Tom Werner.

199. Their productions include *Bob and Ray—The Two and Only; Big Fish, Little Fish; Goldilocks;* and *Flanders & Swann.*

200. "the lowest of the low . . ." Johnna Levine, interview by author, 23 January 1998.

201. "I hate legalese . . . ABC's grudging recognition." Levine, interview.

202. "He flew me to . . . back to L.A." Sue Cameron, interview by author, 21 April 2000.

203. "For the next year . . . remember asking him [why]." Cameron, interview 11 December 1997.

204. "The day I arrived . . . a job on ability." Cameron, interview, 21 April 2000.

205. "I had little to do . . . in the meeting." Cameron, interview, 11 December 1997.

206. "I still had a lot . . . I hate it here." Cameron, interview.

207. Today, Sue Cameron edits the magazine for the Jonathon Club in L.A. She has published two novels and is working on a third.

208. "At the ABC flagship . . . 'high-level' positions." Bonny Dore, interview by author, 22 January 1999. Dore went on to produce television movies and miniseries, *Reason for Living: The Jill Ireland Story*, and *Glory! Glory!* She is a former president of Women in Film and a member of the Caucus of Producers, Writers & Directors.

209. "For many many years . . . position was fierce." Dore, interview.

210. "In retrospect . . . in the work force." Loreen Arbus, interview by author, 24 April 1998. Arbus rose through the executive ranks at ABC from story analyst to program exec to executive producer of variety specials, movies, late night and early morning programming before her move to Showtime as VP original programming in the 1980s.

211. "Women at the networks . . . was willing to pay." Arbus, interview.

212. Several women recalled similar moments, the triumph of getting companies to post job openings internally before going outside or filling them inside. Producer Phylis Geller cited that a women's group at WNET staged a sit-in in the office of the head of personnel in 1970.

213. "This made it possible . . . take care of everyone's feelings." Arbus, interview.

214. For example, Paula and Lisa Weinstein, daughters of Hannah Weinstein, followed their *mother* into film production. TV performer-producer Marlo Thomas is the daughter of Danny Thomas. Alan Ladd Jr., "Laddie," a respected executive producer. Nora Ephron, screenwriter (*Silkwood, When Harry Met Sally, Sleepless in Seattle*, among others) and director, coscripted *This Is My Life* (1992) with her sister Delia. The Ephrons' parents were screenwriters with a long history in the business.

215. "We're going to do a story . . . Get Linda, get Mary . . . !" Silverman, interview.

216. "for a minute and a half." Brown, interview.

217. Renamed *Sons and Daughters*, the show aired in 1974, starring Gary Frank and Glynnis O'Connor.

218. "Barbara was one of the earliest . . . And we all knew it." Barbara Corday, interview by author, 22 September 1999.

219. "Barbara and I pitched . . . 'we'll wait.'" Corday, interview.

220. Some CBS execs thought *Cagney & Lacey* was too harsh, too women's lib, not feminine enough. "Bra burners," one was quoted as saying. In the movie for television, the stars were Tyne Daly and Loretta Swit. In the original TV series, Daly costarred with Meg Foster, who was later replaced by Sharon Gless. In the 1982–83 season, the series was marginal, and in 1983 it was canceled. Letters flooded CBS, demanding the show be put back on the air. The network brought it back in the spring of 1984, running ads, "You Want Them! You've Got Them!" See Tim Brooks and Earle Marsh, *The Complete Directory to Prime Time Network and Cable TV Shows*, 6th ed. (New York: Ballantine Books, 1995).

221. "he and I took it to CBS . . . a network executive.'" Corday, interview.

222. "I loved doing that job . . . point it out—a lot." Corday, interview.

223. "Being a girl from Springfield . . . be right for *Hustling*." Gallo, interview. *Hustling* (1975) was produced by Filmways Pictures and Lillian Gallo Productions for ABC.

224. "Lillian was a producer . . . it's you two!" Fay Kanin, interview.

225. "I'd seen the girls . . . He did." Kanin, interview.

226. Gail Sheehy took Kanin . . . she was wonderful." Kanin, interview.

227. After *Hustling*, Kanin produced and wrote *Friendly Fire* and *Heartsounds*. Gallo produced *Princess Daisy*, a four-hour miniseries based on Judith Krantz's bestseller, and *The Lookalike*, starring Melissa Gilbert and Diane Ladd.

238. "They'd see us standing there . . . We didn't make them." Kanin, interview.

229. "No matter where we traveled . . . strike out for myself." Dorothea Petrie, interview by author, 15 December 1998.

230. "My mother described . . . period train in the U.S.!" Petrie, interview.

231. Dorothea Petrie produced many television films, including the Emmy-winning *Love Is Never Silent* (with Marian Rees) and *Caroline?* She also wrote a novel based on the orphan train saga in America with James Magnuson, which was published by Dial Press.

232. "I admired Marcia . . . we go into production." Petrie, interview.

233. "It was the only . . . credit at Tomorrow." Rees, interview, 7 December 1998.

234. "It's the challenge . . . on the air." Rees, interview.

235. "It's really wonderful . . . combustion." Debra Hill, interview by author, 7 January 1998.

6. YOU DON'T MEET BORING PEOPLE IN THIS BUSINESS

236. "The girls are never . . . do it without them." Anne Nelson, interview by author, 26 February 1998. Nelson joined CBS as an assistant director in sales services. When Leslie Moonves, president and CEO. promoted her to vice president business affairs, he said, "Anne is the soul of CBS." Her career spans radio days, the Golden Age of Television, and now HDTV.

237. "I was in CBS radio . . . were wonderful to me." Nelson, interview.

238. Nancy Tellem spent a decade as senior business affairs executive for Warner Bros. and CBS before gaining her current position in 1998. She is credited with engendering a strong collaborative spirit at CBS. Other women at the network include Nina Tassler, senior VP of drama; Maria Crenna, executive VP CBS Productions; and Sunta Izzicupo, senior VP of movies and miniseries.

239. "I tried to quit once . . . born to do it." Ruth Engelhardt, interview by author, 19 January 2000. Engelhardt, formerly senior VP business affairs, William Morris Agency, is now a consultant to the company.
240. "I just did everything . . . old boys' club." Engelhardt, interview.
241. Kathleen O'Steen, "Pioneer Woman," *Emmy*, October 1996.
242. "Hyler was a terrific agent . . . Maybe I should have left." Engelhardt, interview.
243. Meta Rosenberg, interview by author, 20 August 1999.
244. Rosenberg testified to the House Un-American Activities Committee in 1951. According to author Victor S. Navasky, Rosenberg and television writer Richard Collins tried to limit the damage of their testimony by naming people in the party who 1) were dead, 2) had already been called to testify, or 3) had left the party years before. According to Navasky, it was this third group that caused so much damage, because the individuals named were then pressured to reveal more names to the committee. The contagion spread. Collins says he and Rosenberg did not foresee the committee dealing so harshly with these individuals. Navasky, *Naming Names* (Harmondsworth, Middlesex, England: Penguin Books, 1981), 228–30, 283–4, 319.
245. "In the late 1960s . . . doing here at all." Rosenberg, interview.
246. "Tits and ass had hit television . . . until T&A arrived." Renée Valente, interview by author, 20 May 1998.
247. "I went to John Mitchell . . . as an independent producer." Valente, interview. Valente produced many TV movies, such as *Love Thy Neighbor*, *Valley of the Dolls*, *Masquerade*, and the eight-hour miniseries *Blind Ambition*. She was the first woman elected president of the Producers Guild of America. She began as a secretary and assistant story editor with David Susskind's Talent Associates.
248. "I was a hot . . . no arguing with you." Lila Garrett, interview by author, 3 March, 1999.
249. "I said it was . . . changing my work." Joanna Lee, interview by author, 26 October 1998. Lee was first a sitcom writer (*My Three Sons*, *I Dream of Jeannie*), then writer/producer/director (*Children of Divorce*, 1980.) Her autobiography, *A Difficult Woman in Hollywood*, was published by Vantage Press, 1999.
250. "No one, no one . . . start producing and directing." Lee, interview.
251. Peter Biskind, "When Sue Was Queen," *Vanity Fair*, April 2000. Biskind is the author of *Easy Riders Raging Bulls*, (New York: Simon and Schuster, 1998).
252. "ICM was the first place . . . leave the room." Joan Hyler, interview by author, 3 November 1999.
253. "It was around 1974 . . . still in existence." Dolores Robinson, interview by author, 10 August 1999.
254. "If you leave yourself open . . . a long way, baby." Robinson, interview.
255. ". . . typing and typing . . . good friend of Lew's." Michele Wallerstein, interview by author, 11 March 1999.
256. "It is one thing . . . on an equal footing." Wallerstein, interview.
257. "I didn't know any better . . . what my place was." Hyler, interview.

7. I DON'T KNOW ANY WOMEN — GETTING ORGANIZED
258. "My family was . . . into the service." Gallo, interview.
259. Judith Rosener, *America's Competitive Secret* (Oxford, UK: Oxford University Press, 1995).
260. "Those women . . . but not the last." Gallo, interview.

261. Julius and Ethel Rosenberg were executed as spies in 1953.

262. "One of my earliest . . . loved or cared about." Weinstein, interview.

263. "I graduated from Harvard . . . midst of all that." Fisher, interview.

264. The sit-in at the *Ladies Home Journal* lasted for hours and caused a media stir. For a full account see Susan Brownmiller's book *In Our Time—Memoir of a Revolution* (New York: Dial Press, 1999).

265. "We had a sit-in . . . gave me back my life." Gould, interview.

266. "Why do we need . . . Time for a change." Weinstein, interview. In the 1980s, Weinstein would be one of the founders of the Hollywood Women's Political Caucus.

267. The Women's Steering Committee of the Directors Guild was formally organized in 1986 by Susan Bay, Nell Cox, Joelle Dobrow, Dolores Ferraro, Victoria Hochberg, and Lynne Littman.

268. "When I came to Hollywood . . . We needed it." Gould, interview.

269. "Erase ways women . . . ridiculous 'on-screen' types." "SAG-WGA Joint Women's Committee Goals," from the archives of Kathleen Nolan, former president of the Screen Actors Guild.

270. "I think we have to . . . never went behind your back.' " Cameron, interview, 11 December 1997.

271. Wilkerson-Miles (Kassel) contributed over many years to Los Amigos del Pueblo; was named Madrina de Los Angeles for humanitarian work and preservation of Olivera Street; established a community center and educational program for Olivera Street; created a scholarship program with the Women's Press Club for students to finish their careers in film and journalism; started the Wilkerson Foundation to encourage young talent in motion picture and entertainment, providing scholarships to students at UCLA's School of Cinema; and created scholarships for children of Hispanic Command Officers Association, to further their education.

272. "alone and isolated . . . being patronized." Recalled by Kayla Garen, Wilkerson-Miles's longtime friend and associate, interview by author, 14 March 1999.

273. "It is very hard . . . to the next meeting." Malone, interview.

274. For the first meeting of Women in Film, Tichi Wilkerson-Miles called Marcia Borie (author and magazine writer), Zepha Bogert (publicity and public relations), Norma Zarky (entertainment attorney, first woman president of the Beverly Hills Bar Assn.), Georgianne Heller (president, Publicity West Company), and Francoise Ruddy (writer/associate producer). Sue Cameron invited Nancy Malone (actress/producer/director) and Portia Nelson (composer/lyricist/producer). "Those are the only original founders of WIF," says Sue Cameron, "and Georgianne Heller and Francoise Ruddy left after that first meeting. The rest of us decided to go ahead." Nancy Malone agrees with Cameron's recollection.

275. "a small group . . . can help each other." Cameron, interview.

276. "Until this organization . . . debating passionately." Boyle, interview.

277. "women just stood up . . . fought for the vote." Patricia Barry, interview by author, 15 March 1999. Barry, an actress in daytime drama, television movies, and series (*Marcus Welby, M.D., Alfred Hitchcock Presents, Twilight Zone, Columbo, Dallas, All My Children*), was president of Women in Film, 1993–94.

278. "It was wild . . . what we knew." Boyle, interview.

279. "In effect . . . We were outvoted." Cameron, interview. Women in Film's mem-

bership criteria soon became three years' minimum experience ın film or television as an executive, writer, producer, performer, editor, executive, or
director. Each new member had to have two current members as sponsors.

280. Within a few years, Women in Film had sister organizations in New York,
Washington, D.C., Atlanta, and Dallas, and had forged international ties.

281. "I couldn't imagine . . . afraid to say anything." Goldsmith, inteview. Goldsmith
is a television writer (*Confessions of a Dependent Woman, Right On, Martha, Single
Parent*) and playwright (*My Mother, My Daughters and Me, The Compensation
Factor*). President of Women in Film, 1978 to 1980.

282. "One highly placed . . . in a position to know." Anonymous, interview by author.

283. "Another well-known executive . . . vice presidents of executive happiness."
Anonymous, interview by author.

284. "At one of these Women in Film . . . cause the rapes." Anonymous, interview
by author.

285. "Naturally, I got involved . . . with all those women?" Goldsmith, interview.

286. "I was a single mother . . . follow my dream." Loraine Despres, interview by
author, 15 December 1999. Despres traded in television for books, *The Scandalous Summer of Sissy LeBlanc* (New York: William Morrow, 2001).

287. "I was turning out . . . *Knots Landing.*" Despres, interview.

288. Some thought the site, given its name, an odd choice—but it was available on
the right date at the right price.

289. "They were so nervous . . . success amnesia." Dore, interview. Dore served as
president of Women in Film, 1980–1981.

290. "Lucy up on the stage . . . is real encouraging.'" Dore, interview.

291. "It's sad . . . access was rare." Marcy Kelly, interview by author, 28 July 2000.
Kelly had produced public service campaigns and films for the federal government in Washington before moving to Hollywood. She was president of
Women in Film, 1990–91; she founded Mediascope in 1992. She is a veteran
in public policy and communications.

292. Carol Hymowitz, Michaele Weissman, *A History of Women in America* (New
York: Bantam Books, 1978).

293. "Basically, I am invited . . . been doing it for years." Phillips, *You'll Never Eat
Lunch*, 446.

294. Ibid.

295. "The Hollywood Women's . . . place for them to go." Weinstein, interview.

296. "Most wanted . . . not candidates." Corday, interview.

297. "There were some senior women . . . a chance to do that." Nancy Hutson Perlman, interview by author, 25 October 1999.

298. "I could barely find . . . started the lunch." Perlman, interview.

299. "There were always women . . . ate it all." Arbus, interview. Arbus was vice
president of original programming for Showtime. In 1982, she became the first
woman head of programming for a cable network: senior VP in charge of
program development, production, acquisition at Cable Health Network/Life-
time, where she helped launch the twenty-four-hour network. Later, she supervised program development and production for Viacom's network/first-run
syndication divisions.

300. "Not too long ago . . . added a few more." Perlman, interview.

301. "When you go to . . . It's still going on!" Judith Merians, interview by author,
4 December 1999.

302. "president is not a job for a woman." Kathleen Nolan, interview by author, 28 October 1999.

303. "I had already purchased . . . at the U.S. Senate." Nolan, interview.

304. Yes! Martha Coolidge became the first woman to head the DCA in March, 2002.

305. Yes! Fay Kanin became president of the Academy of Motion Picture Arts and Sciences in 1979. See Chapter 9.

306. McCall Jr. was president of the Writers Guild 1942–44 and 1951–52.

307. "a special breed of heroine . . . to new heights." *Ladies Home Journal* program announcement, April 19, 1975.

308. Bloodworth later created *Designing Women* and *Evening Shade*. Place played Loretta Haggers on *Mary Hartman, Mary Hartman*, and also wrote some wonderful sitcoms for MTM and *The Paul Sand Show*.

309. "I was flying first-class . . . it's all words." Brown, interview.

8. I WAS SUPPOSED TO BE HEDDA HOPPER

310. Anthony Slide, *Early Women Directors* (New York: DaCapo Press, 1984), 15.

311. "In the 1970s . . . won't let her do it again." Narea Mills, "Women Directors: Door Opens," *Los Angeles Times*, 19 November 1986. Hyams was VP West Coast production for Columbia Pictures in 1974.

312. Lynne Littman, interview by author, 6 October 1999.

313. "I never cut a picture . . . getting in." Allen, interview.

314. Writer/animator/producer Faith Hubley worked in partnership with her husband, John Hubley, cocreator of *Mr. Magoo* and many others.

315. "At film school . . . writing was always available." Gould, interview.

316. "It was separate . . . room with that feeling." Corman, interview.

317. "When I started directing . . . they don't work." Malone, interview.

318. Michael Gleason was writer/executive producer of *Rich Man, Poor Man*; co-creator/executive producer of *Remington Steele*; and writer on *Six Million Dollar Man*, *McCloud*, and others.

319. "I went to UCLA . . . very exciting." Karen Arthur, interview by author, 22 September 1999. Arthur is a film and television director (*Charleston*, *Lady Beware*, *Cracked Up*, *Shadow of a Doubt*, *Against Their Will: Women in Prison*, *The Staircase*).

320. A few years later, Carol Littleton edited *Body Heat*, *E.T.*, and many others.

321. Hotchkis adapted her play *Legacy* to the screen with additional characters.

322. "Wonderful man . . . stake my job on it." Arthur, interview.

323. "The guys—gaffers . . . gave me a development deal." Arthur, interview.

324. When I stepped offstage . . . being a director was impossible." Martha Coolidge, interview by author, 16 November 1999. Coolidge's credits include *Old-Fashioned Woman* (1974), *Not a Pretty Picture* (1975), and *Valley Girl* (1983), among many others. She became president of the Director's Guild in 2002.

325. "One day, the head of the station . . . you're a woman." Coolidge, interview.

326. Kopple also won the L.A. Film Critics Special Award for *Harlan County, U.S.A.* The film was listed on the National Film Preservation Board in 1990 with such classics as *All About Eve* and *All's Quiet on the Western Front*.

327. "what life and death were all about." Barbara Kopple, interview by author, 13 October 1999.

328. "There was a movement in the coal fields . . . in a terrifying morning." Kopple,

interview. Kopple is a fiction and nonfiction producer/director and Oscar winner: *Keeping On, Century of Women, Fallen Champ: The Untold Story of Mike Tyson, My Generation*, and many more. She has also directed episodes of *Oz* and *Homicide: Life on the Street.* She has won numerous awards, including the Cannes Film Festival Critics Choice Award, the Grand Jury Prize at Sundance Film Festival, and awards from the Directors Guild of America.

329. "When we were making that film . . . I'm a filmmaker." Kopple, interview.

330. "Lynne Littman wanted to be . . . That changed my life." Littman, interview.

331. Both Bikel and Gordon were documentary producers at WNET. Gordon authored the book *I'm Dancing as Fast as I Can.*

332. "Only because I'd met them . . . painters make paintings." Littman, interview. Vanda's films include *Cleo 5à7, Loin de Vietnam, La Boneur* and *L'une Chant, l'autre pas.*

333. "Coming to Grips with Power," *Los Angeles Times*, 17 August 1973.

334. Several women in these pages spoke of "waiting to marry," or of giving themselves "permission" to marry only after they had established their careers.

335. "You are talking about . . . taught us how to behave." Littman, interview. Producer/director Littman has directed feature films and movies for television.

336. "When women began . . . enthusiastic about each shot." Murphy, interview. Brianne Murphy, ASC, was a founder of Behind the Lens, the first woman member of the American Society of Cinematographers, the first woman director of photography to belong to International Photographers, IATSE. Her credits as cinematographer include: *To Die to Sleep, Bermuda Triangle, Cheech & Chong's Nice Dreams, The Lawyers, Love and War, Heat of the Night, Breaking Away;* and as director, *Educated Heart, Blood Sabbath, Acapulco Heat, The Magic Tide.*

337. Nancy Lynn Schwartz authored *The Hollywood Writers' Wars* (New York: McGraw-Hill Book Co., 1982) which was completed by her mother, Sheila Schwartz.

338. "I wanted Brianne Murphy . . . do another 'soft' project." Malone, interview.

339. "She told me . . . could have been a great director." Murphy, interview.

340. Joan Didion, John Gregory Dunne, and Frank Pierson were credited with writing the screenplay, though, according to Nancy Griffin and Kim Masters in their book, *Hit and Run* (New York: Simon and Schuster, 1996), "in a protracted and tortuous preproduction period . . . fourteen screenwriters, three directors, and four musical collaborators worked on the production."

341. *A Star Is Born*, the first film Jon Peters actually produced, was followed by *Eyes of Laura Mars* and *Caddyshack.* Then he and Peter Guber formed their own company, Guber-Peters, in 1981 and produced dozens of films, including *The Witches of Eastwick, The Color Purple, Rain Man*, and *Batman.*

342. "I made an agreement . . . a lot of that movie." Barbra Streisand, interview by author, 4 August 1999.

343. In the 1954 version of *A Star Is Born*, James Mason played Norman Maine and Judy Garland played Esther Blodgett. The first version appeared in 1937 with Janet Gaynor and Fredric March.

344. Nominated for Best Picture at the 1974 Academy Awards, *The Way We Were* was edited by MGM's Margaret Booth; Marilyn Bergman wrote with her husband, Alan, the Oscar-winning lyrics to the Marvin Hamlisch music (he also won an Oscar). *The Way We Were* was produced by Ray Stark and directed by Sydney Pollack.

345. "It's not a perfect film...any control over my work." Streisand, interview. Streisand: director/producer/performer, *Yentl, Nuts, The Prince of Tides, The Mirror Has Two Faces.* She has also produced *The Long Island Incident; City at Peace; Rescuers: Stories of Courage: Two Women; Serving in Silence: The Margarethe Cammermeyer Story* (three Emmys and the Peabody); *What Makes a Family; Frankie & Hazel; Varian's War.* She is the first female composer to win an Academy Award ("Evergreen," from *A Star Is Born*).

346. "You're one of the nicest...some of my fears." Gale Anne Hurd, interview by author, 11 September 1998. Through her production companies, Pacific Western and Valhalla Motion Pictures, Hurd has produced many films, including *Aliens, Virus, Raising Cain, Safe Passage, Sugartime, The Abyss, Dante's Peak* and the award-winning *The Waterdance.* She is on the National Advisory Panel of the Institute for Research on Women & Gender and is a member of the Artists' Rights Foundation and the Producers Guild.

347. "I was in that first generation...I wanted the movies." Debra Hill, interview by author, 7 January 1998. Among her many productions are *The Fog, Escape from New York, Attack of the 50-foot Woman, Escape from L.A., Halloween II* and *Halloween III,* and *Crazy in Alabama.*

348. "I had no idea...into one type of movie." Hill, interview.

349. Hill, interview.

350. Carrie Snodgress won a Golden Globe for her performance; newcomer Frank Langella played the role of the lover. Eleanor and Frank Perry's best-known film is *David and Lisa.*

351. "I passionately believed...terrific combination of talents." Corman, interview 20 January 2000.

352. "I hired John...*Lady in Red.*" Corman, interview 20 October 1999. Julie Corman's films include *Moving Violations, The Last Resort, Nightfall, The Westing Game, Nowhere to Run,* and, through her own production company, Trinity Pictures, family films like *A Cry in the Wild.*

353. Alexandra Rose produced, with Tamara Asseyev, *I Wanna Hold Your Hand* and *Big Wednesday.* Her other film productions are *Nothing in Common, Overboard* (with Anthea Sylbert), *Quigley Down Under,* and with Garry Marshall, *East of Eden, Frankie and Johnnie, The Other Sister.*

354. Sally Field's remarkable career as a performer includes *Forrest Gump, Not Without My Daughter, Places in the Heart,* and *Absence of Malice.* She wrote, directed, and produced *The Christmas Tree* (1996), produced *A Woman of Independent Means* (1995), *Dying Young* (1991). She directed *From Earth to the Moon* (1998) and *Beautiful* (2000).

355. "I was heading...a giant success." Alexandra Rose, interview, 12 December 2000.

356. "Norma Rae said she wanted to make it better for her kids." Tamara Asseyev, interview by author, 2 December 1999.

357. "At a dinner for Betty Friedan...started for me." Rose, interview.

358. "...the right director." Asseyev, interview.

359. "When Tamara and I...and apply it to women." Rose, interview.

360. "...he'd read the script.'" Asseyev, interview. Asseyev's movies for television include *The Hijacking of the Achille Lauro* (3 Emmy Nominations). She became the youngest member of the Producers Guild of America, served on its Board of Directors, and is a founding member of the L.A. Museum of Contemporary Art.

361. "The idea is this . . . a marvelous sense of humor." Harriet Frank, Jr., interview by author, 27 February 2000. Frank, Jr. and Irving Ravetch have written many films, *The Sound and the Fury, House of Cards, Murphy's Romance, Stanley and Iris.*

362. "I had never met Tamara . . . was a male field." Frank, Jr., interview.

363. "It was a joy to see . . . seemless collaboration." Frank, Jr., interview.

364. "I knew it was the best script . . . want to know about." Asseyev, interview.

365. "We're sort of set up for it . . . the movie so special." Roger Ebert, *Microsoft Cinemania* review.

366. "The first scene . . . it was a great performance." Asseyev, interview.

367. "We had a hard time . . . a mill to shoot in." Asseyev, interview.

368. "I was delighted by Sallys' . . . It was spectacular." Frank, Jr., interview.

369. "they put a spotlight . . . moments of my career." Asseyev, interview.

370. "They both show . . . we're already oppressed." Rose, interview.

371. "And to be nominated . . . These things are so rare." Asseyev, interview.

372. "Our inability to get something . . . and to women." Asseyev, interview.

373. "Great European films . . . factor to reckon with." Frank, Jr., interview.

374. "It seemed reasonable to expect . . . would be the 1980s." Perlman, interview.

II: Securing the Perimeter—The 1980s

9. YES, SIR, GIVING WAY TO YES, MA´AM

1. Andrew J. Neff, "20th-Fox Gets a First Lady." *Variety,* 2 January 1980.

2. "I was just overwhelmed . . . people making them." Sherry Lansing, interview.

3. "I remember that after . . . business is gender blind." Lansing, interview.

4. "The world press . . . what that meant then." Merzbach, interview.

5. Claire Townsend was extremely well liked. Before she entered Princeton in 1970, the Townsend Group, her team, investigated abuses of the elderly in nursing homes under the aegis of Ralph Nader. In 1976, she was hired by Alan Ladd Jr. as West Coast story editor at Fox, and became one of the "baby moguls" with Paula Weinstein in the 1970s. In 1978, Townsend became VP of creative affairs, then went to UA as VP of production. In 1980, she went back to Fox as VP of production under Sherry Lansing. In 1982, she left Fox to get her law degree. She never returned to the business. She died at age forty-three of breast cancer.

6. "Suddenly, in many meetings . . . Rather wonderful." Merzbach, interview.

7. "Working at Fox . . . but also grew difficult." Merzbach, interview.

8. Marvin Davis wasn't in the film business for long. Four years later he sold 20th Century Fox to press baron Rupert Murdoch, who had just added Metromedia Television to his burgeoning empire. Metromedia was a chain of big-city independent television stations.

9. See Rachel Abramowitz, *Is That a Gun in Your Pocket,* for a detailed discussion of Sherry Lansing's career.

10. "When a board meeting . . . hadn't changed." Merzbach, interview.

11. On March 1, 1980, the newly formed DGA Women's Steering Committee presented a report to the National Board of the DGA that demonstrated the talents of women directors "were being under-utilized." Actually, their research showed

that since 1950, women members of the DGA did only about 0.2 percent of the work as directors of films or television shows. Summary of DGA Women's Steering Committee history, from the committee.

12. "The atmosphere was much better . . . a good time." Lili Fini Zanuck, interview by author, 9 May 2000.

13. "Sherry Lansing headed . . . It was empowering." Melanie Cook, interview by author, 15 February 2000. Cook is a partner in the law firm of Bloom, Hergott, Cook, Diemer, and Klein. Her practice includes representation of actors, actresses, writers, directors, and producers in feature films and television.

14. James Ryan, "Hawn in Her Golden Years: Forever Blond, Forever Smart," *New York Times*, 1 December 1996, Arts and Leisure section.

15. Since 1980, Nancy Meyers has produced and written *Father of the Bride, Baby Boom, I Love Trouble*; she has written *Irreconcilable Differences, Protocol, Once Upon a Crime* (the 1998 remake of *The Parent Trap*) and *What Women Want* (2000). She also directed the latter two films.

16. "We need each other's . . . ideas and information." Marc Shapiro, *Pure Goldie*, (New York: Birch Lane Press/Carol Publishing Group, 1998) 99.

17. "I thought I ought to . . . I couldn't tell." Despres, interview.

18. "From 1950 to to 1980 . . . .02 percent of the work." *Variety*, 20 June 1980.

19. "Women Make Mark in Pic Business," *Variety*, 13 November 1980.

20. Bette Davis served as president of the Academy from October to December 1941.

21. *Friendly Fire* won the Emmy for Outstanding Drama or Comedy Special in 1979 (Fay Kanin and Philip Barry, coproducers; Martin Starger, executive producer). Kanin was also nominated for Outstanding Writing. *Heartsounds* was produced by Fay Kanin and Fern Field; Norman Lear was the executive producer. The ABC Theater Presentation starring Mary Tyler Moore and James Garner was nominated for an Emmy in 1985.

22. "Here's a picture . . . Writers are fighters." Kanin, interview.

23. Johnnie L. Roberts, "Lady Sings the Blues," *Newsweek*, 1 November 1998.

24. "The studio's January-to-June reports . . . would deliver." *Variety*, 16 July 1980.

25. "At these big meetings . . . knew both of us." Sylbert, interview.

26. Reported in *Hollywood Reporter*, 26 July 1983. Rosenberg resigned in September 1985. In 1990, he and Paula Weinstein started Spring Creek Productions in a pact with Warner Bros.

27. "At that period . . . did I seek it out." Sylbert, interview.

28. "I think there is a female sensibility . . . of the process." Weinstein, interview.

29. Weinstein was VP of production at Warner Bros. 1976; senior VP of Worldwide production at Fox, 1978–79; moved to the Ladd Company in 1979 (*Body Heat*); moved to UA as president of film production (*War Games* and *Yentl*). In 1984, she started WW Productions with Gareth Wigan, then became executive consultant for MGM's worldwide division and kept on producing (*The Fabulous Baker Boys*).

30. *Variety*, 19 November 1982.

31. Diahann Carroll was nominated for an Oscar, James Earl Jones for a Golden Globe, and writers Tina and Lester Pine for a WGA award in 1974. *Claudine* was directed by the formerly blacklisted Jack Barry.

32. "Third World," *Los Angeles Times*, 18 July 1977.

33. "More than half . . . Third World training program." Hannah Weinstein, quoted in the *Hollywood Reporter*, 19 December 1974.

34. "My mother influenced me hugely . . . is my daughter." Paula Weinstein, interview.

35. "safe, secure dominion." Sylbert, interview.

36. See Steven Bach's *Final Cut* (New York: Newmarket Press, 1999) 362–65 for an account of reviewers' critical reactions before and after the "recut."

37. Thomas M. Pryor, *Daily Variety 48th Anniversary Issue.*

38. "Then MGM bought UA . . . every other week." Sylbert, interview.

39. See Slide, *The Silent Feminists*, p.xiii

40. Canby wrote, among other memorable lines, *"Heaven's Gate* is something quite rare in movies these days—an unqualified disaster." Bach, *Final Cut.*

41. "We had been turned down . . . coming from a woman." Streisand, interview.

42. Eleanora Duse (1859–1924), a great Italian actress, the only rival to French actress Sarah Bernhardt (1844–1923).

43. "I loved the piece . . . seemed like no problem." Streisand, interview.

44. After *Heaven's Gate*, Andy Albeck was made chairman of UA; Norbert Auerback became president and chief operating officer of UA.

45. "production meetings . . . a wonderful job with *Yentl*." Sylbert, interview, 9 February 2000.

46. "never felt any distrimination . . . by the way, a Jew." Streisand, interview.

47. "It had to be made for a price . . . bravely and brilliantly." Weinstein, interview.

48. "The struggle . . . control of my own work." Excerpted from Streisand's speech upon accepting the Crystal Award from Women in Film, 31 May 1984.

49. "I'd said to someone . . . triple platinum." Streisand, interview.

50. Songwriters Marilyn and Alan Bergman, close friends of Streisand, worked on *The Way We Were, A Star Is Born, Yentl,* and many other films.

51. "Some of the reviews . . . committed to her." Weinstein, interview.

53. "The woman who did it . . . how to daven [to pray]." Streisand, interview.

54. "harshest, most vitriolic." Streisand, interview.

54. "Were women envious . . . achievements?" Streisand, Crystal Awards, 1984.

55. Streisand, interview.

56. "distinctively feminine . . . directed by men." Pauline Kael, "The Current Cinema," *New Yorker*, 28 November 1983.

57. "[Streisand] has gained control . . . her and the audience." Stanley Kauffmann, "Streisand on the Roof," *New Republic*, 19 December 1983.

58. "She wasn't treated well . . . guys all the time." Jane Alexander, interview by author, 4 August 1999.

59. "so many horrible things . . . director in high regard." Liv Ullmann, interview by author, 31 July 1999.

1 0. CHUTES AND LADDERS

60. "I championed that film . . . and flew home." Boyle, interview.

61. "A university town . . . 'What about my people?' " Boyle, interview. After Orion, Boyle went to RKO Pictures as executive VP of production. From '88 to '92, she was president of Sovereign Pictures, her own company, then was a partner in Boyle Taylor Productions until 2000. She is now a partner with Gale Anne Hurd, Valhalla Productions. She served as president of the Independent Feature Project/West (IFP/W) and of Women in Film, 1977–78.

62. "Production was a great place . . . by the time I came along." Phylis Geller, interview by author, 8 January 1998.

63. "Being an executive . . . twenty-five years." Geller, interview. At WETA/Washington, D.C., where she produced *The Kennedy Center Presents* (a series of specials) and *In Performance at the White House;* supervised Ken Burns's documentaries with Florentine Films; and created the weekly series *In the Prime.* She was president of Women in Film, 1982–83.

64. "I remember a cartoon . . . just aren't heard?" Geller, interview.

65. "Either the men turn off . . . as a man's does." Laura Ziskin, interview by author, 31 January 2000. Ziskin was president of Fox 2000 (*The Thin Red Line, One Fine Day, Anywhere But Here*), 1994–2000.

66. "How many . . . turns the meeting around." Judith James, interview by author, 26 October 1999. Stage and film producer, Dreyfuss-James Productions, (*Mr. Holland's Opus, Quiz Show, Having Our Say*).

67. "A young story editor . . . doesn't bother me." Anonymous, interview by author.

68. "A woman would . . . when to push." Ilene Kahn Power, interview by author, 20 March 2000.

69. "Of course . . . have to listen to you." Ziskin, interview.

70. "Suddenly I had the business affairs . . . out of my hat." Levine, interview. Levine served as president of Women in Film, 1984–85.

71. "I did not operate . . . You have to do that." Levine, interview.

72. "When men worked with . . . when I was a nun." Christine Foster, interview by author, 18 January 2000. At Columbia, Foster developed *The Blue and the Gray, Fallen Angel, Dream Merchants.* At the Wolper Organization, she supervised staff and contact producers on network prime-time miniseries and movies—*Roots, Sandburg's Lincoln.*

73. "What are my chances . . . say exactly what you want." Foster, interview.

74. "at this table . . . it went on for years." Corday, interview. Corday was VP comedy at ABC, 1979–1982. She became president and CEO of Columbia Pictures Television in 1984. She cocreated the Emmy-nominated drama *American Dream.*

75. "Coca-Cola owned Columbia . . . work to be done." Corday, interview.

76. "Life is not fair . . . a business asset." Ledding, interview. Ledding was an eight-year veteran at MGM, serving finally as senior VP, motion picture business affairs. She was chair of the Los Angeles County Film Commission, 1987–89, and president of Women in Film, 1983–84.

77. "Some of the business . . . never heard David Begelman say that." Ledding, interview.

78. "I was one of the clerks . . . give him the numbers." Nikki Rocco, interview by author, 4 November 1999. Rocco joined Universal Pictures' sales department in 1967. She was promoted to assistant to the general sales manager in 1981, and vice president of distribution in 1984. Since February 1996, she has been president, Universal Pictures Distribution.

79. "When I worked in New York . . . how I dealt with it." Rocco, interview.

80. "We thought it would be okay . . . changing the people." Billie B. Jenkins, interview by author, 6 February 2000. Jenkins was an administrative assistant, then vice president of the Leonard Goldberg Company, directly involved in the production of pilots, series, features, and specials, including *Brian's Song, Charlie's Angels, Hart to Hart, Home Alone.* At 20th Century Fox, she was director of administration, where she directed seven departments in studio operations, and director of production services and resources. She was program coordinator

for the AFI Gary Hendler Minority Filmmakers Program and president of Women in Film, 1991–93.

81. "I wanted to keep my vice presidency . . . it just can't be.' " Jenkins, interview.

82. Jenkins's family moved ". . . because I won't say it." Jenkins, interview.

83. At the time, Steve Mills was president of Quintex Television Division.

84. "My husband was right. . . . I had stopped doing windows." Jenkins, interview.

85. "The words hit me like bullets . . . I was devastated." Merians, interview, 16 November 1999. Merians, currently senior VP, legal and business affairs, Regent Entertainment, was formerly senior VP, legal and business affairs, Saban Entertainment, Saban International.

86. "Who will hire you . . . became, in short, an executive." Merians, interview.

87. Dawn Steel, *They Can Kill You*, 105.

88. "I admired Dawn . . . get something for it." Merians, interview.

89. "[I was] demanding . . . is any different?" Hilary de Vries, "A Look Inside the Studio Gates," *Los Angeles Times*, 29 August 1993. Katzenberg was a vice president and assistant to Paramount's production chief, Don Simpson.

90. Ibid.

91. Douglas Eby, "Women of Talent—Power and Control," Rocamora.org/aol.com, 23 October 1997.

92. de Vries, "A Look Inside." See also Steel, *They Can Kill You*.

93. Steel, *They Can Kill You*, 109.

94. Ibid., 112.

95. "Some of the original episodes . . . That's the corporate setting." Merians, interview.

96. "snapped into a running dialogue . . . William Shatner . . ." Steel, *They Can Kill You*, 114.

97. "We're alone . . . for six months." Merians, interview.

11. MORE LADDERS THAN CHUTES

98. Sallie Hofmeister, "USA Networks CEO Kay Koplovitz Resigns," *Los Angeles Times*, 10 April 1998.

99. Ibid. In April 1998, the Seagram Co., coowner of USA, struck a deal with Barry Diller, selling him USA and its Sci-Fi Channel, a spin-off created in 1992 that reached 48 million homes in 1999 (USA reaches about 75 million). Koplovitz had to resign. Two years later, she created her own channel, Broadway Television Network, to offer Broadway shows to cable viewers.

100. "There's a big difference . . . protect you if they choose to." Sheila Nevins, interview by author, 3 November 2000. As an executive producer, Nevins has won more Oscars and Emmys than Walt Disney. She became executive vice president, original programming for HBO in 1999, responsible for overseeing the development and production of all documentaries and family programming for HBO and Cinemax and their multiple channels. Her programs include *King Gimp*, *The Personals*, *One Survivor Remembers*, *I Am a Promise*, and *Common Threads: Stories from the Quilt*.

101. "My father worked . . . That fascinated me." Nevins, interview.

102. "If you listen . . . ones who experienced them." Jenny Offill, Feed Special Issue, "Documentary: Sheila Nevins," (feedmag.com), 14 February 2000.

103. "I'd seen a cooking show . . . foot of your bed." Nevins, interview.

104. "I was so isolated . . . my mentor." Power, interview. At HBO, Power super-vised the development and production of over sixty films, including *The Jose-phine Baker Story, Murderers Among Us: The Simon Wiesenthal Story, Long Gone, Mandela;* as an independent producer, her films won Golden Globe awards and Emmys.
105. HBO aired one of the first made-for-cable films, *The Terry Fox Story,* in 1983.
106. "No one knew what a cable movie was . . . what it's all about." Power, interview.
107. "good scout secretary . . . just-formed CAA." Hyler, interview. Hyler became senior VP, William Morris Agency.
108. "I was never held back . . . who are you representing?" Iris Grossman, interview by author, 27 March 1998. Grossman was senior VP, talent and casting, Turner Network Television (TNT) and Turner Pictures (*George Wallace, The Man Who Captured Eichmann, The Hunchback of Notre Dame, Amelia Earhart: The Final Flight*) and president of Women in Film, 1996–2000.
109. "The first week . . . going to meet." Grossman, interview.
110. Dan Petrie Jr. screenwriter, producer, *Shoot to Kill, The Big Easy;* director, *Dead Silence, Framed;* a former president of WGA. He is Dorothea and Dan Petrie's son.
111. "Dan's office was a mess . . . encouraged me to adopt." Grossman, interviews.
112. "When I was little . . . and I watched them." Isaacs, interview.
113. "Slightly lonely . . . They're still not in the front." Isaacs, interview.
114. "Paula Weinstein was a big. . . . 'This is a real dead end.' Great." Fisher, inter-view.
115. "I felt bad . . . Warners seemed like a good idea." Fisher, interview. Fisher, as vice president and executive vice president, worked at Warners for fourteen years, developing and overseeing such films as *The Fugitive, The Bridges of Madison County, The Color Purple, Gremlins, Malcolm X, Empire of the Sun, Crossing Delancey, Stand and Deliver.* She pioneered the start of Warner Bros.' on-site child-care center. In 1996, she moved to Sony Pictures Entertainment as vice chair of Columbia TriStar Motion Picture Group.
116. "In 1976 or 1977 . . . the people who helped me." Helene Hahn, interview by author, 17 July 2000.
117. "When you are part of a movie . . . find this balance." Hahn, interview.
118. "There were three women . . . about their new babies." Barbara Corday, quoted in Nancy Mills, "Women Directors—Vive La Difference?" *Los Angeles Times,* 26 November 1986.
119. "My God, we're *all* women! . . . want to note it." Corday, interview.
120. "I was in a meeting with Freddie Fields . . . moved right into producing *Swing Shift.*" Sylbert, interview, 9 March 1999.

12. WOMEN MAKE GOOD PRODUCERS
121. "Ah," she thought . . . had already been attached." Sylbert, interview, 9 March 1999.
122. Roger Ebert, *Microsoft Cinemania* review.
123. Demme is better known for his later work, such as *The Silence of the Lambs,* for which he won an Oscar.
124. In the 1990s, Sylbert executive-produced *My Blue Heaven* (written by Nora Ephron), *Something to Talk About,* and *Truman,* and produced with her husband, Richard Romanus, *If You Believe* and *Giving Up the Ghost.*

125. "If the material . . . with being a woman." Sylbert, interview.

126. Carson Productions was the film arm of the Johnny Carson Corporation, which made a deal with Columbia pictures to produce feature films.

127. "Son of the Return of the Secaucus Seven" . . . Roger Ebert, review of *The Big Chill*, Microsoft *Cinemania*, 1996.

128. "That's why I was hired . . . Mayer who was crying." Nasatir, interview. More recently, Marcia Nasatir was the executive producer of *Vertical Limit* (Columbia Pictures, 2000).

129. "We just couldn't get them . . . a really closed shop." Alexander, interview. Alexander grew up in a suburb of Boston, understudied in *A Thousand Clowns*, and costarred in *The Great White Hope* on Broadway (for which she won a Tony). For the next twenty years, she appeared in numerous stage, film, and television productions.

130. "Jane Alexander produced one . . . harder for women." Hyler, interview.

131. "I decided that I couldn't . . . Life is too short." Alexander, interview. She chaired the National Endowment for the Arts, the first actor to hold a position usually assigned to administrators, from 1993 to 1997. She also organized "Art 21: Art Reaches into the 21st Century," a national conference on the arts, in 1994.

132. "I wouldn't be here . . . I would have persevered." Hurd, interview.

133. Hemdale produced, among other films, *Tommy* and *Platoon*.

134. "Of course, he wouldn't . . . meeting with Jim and me." Hurd, interview.

135. "It was wonderful to work with . . . her first major movie production." Boyle, interview, 18 January 2000.

136. "I had three different movies . . . *The Terminator*." Donna Smith, interview by author, 6 March 1999.

137. "Gale's first movie . . . the same reaction anymore." Cook, interview.

138. "Hemdale insisted that a man . . . did absolutely nothing." Hurd, interview.

139. "Hemdale was scared . . . would pull it off." Boyle, interview, 4 March 1998.

140. "Now, everybody in town . . . never value prep much." Smith, interview.

141. "The reviews were sensational . . . *Terminator II* for Orion." Boyle, interview, 18 January 2000.

142. "Being a woman has shaped . . . given a big break." Hurd, interview.

143. "The first assistant director . . . may not have to." Hurd, interview.

144. "I did lose my temper . . . basically in combat!" Hurd, interview.

145. "We had eleven dollars . . . I was really offended." Smith, interview. Smith has been a production coordinator on *Rocky II* reshoots, *Raging Bull*, *True Confessions*; production manager, *Soul Man*, *Reckless*, *The Terminator*; line producer, *Little Gloria* and *Mussolini*, miniseries, and many other films. In 1989 she became senior VP of production and postproduction, Universal Studios. Currently, she is president/CEO of Cinema Completions International.

146. "Let's go to California . . . it breaks my heart." Smith, interview.

147. "I liked that style . . . It's the line producer!" Smith, interview.

13. GETTING ON THE YELLOW BRICK ROAD — PRODUCING FOR TELEVISION

148. "Women can do . . . a woman can." Patricia Finnegan, interview by author, 7 October 1999.

149. "Enormous pressure . . . helped me through it." Malone, interview, 26 November 1997.

150. "I had gone through... that's what it meant." Rees, interview, 7 December 1998.

151. Marian Rees, as quoted by Michael Bygrave, "She Makes Films Her Way," *The Executive*, 1984.

152. "I incorporated as... your goddamn picture." Rees, interview.

153. Executive-produced by Marian Rees, and produced and written by Shelley List and Jonathan Estrin from List's novel, *Nobody Makes Me Cry*.

154. In addition to their Emmy for *Love Is Never Silent*, Rees and Petrie have received numerous other awards and nominations. Rees won an Emmy for *Miss Rose White* and a Peabody for *Foxfire*. Petrie won an Emmy for *Caroline?*

155. "That expectation was unspoken... affected all my work." Rees, interview. Rees was president of Women in Film, 1988–89. Recently, Rees and her partner, Anne Hopkins, created ALT Films with Steven Kulczycki (a senior VP of programming and station manager at KCET-LA) to produce and distribute films based on the work of American writers for Exxon/Mobil Masterpiece Theater's American Collection, including *The Song of the Lark*, Willa Cather; *Cora Unashamed*, Langston Hughes; *The Ponder Heart*, Eudora Welty; *A Death in the Family*, James Agee; and *Almost a Woman*, Esmeralda Santiago.

156. "He didn't come out of nowhere... toward women in general." Finnegan, interview. Finnegan has produced many films, including *Dark Holiday*, *Summergirl*, *Not My Kid*, and *This Child Is Mine*.

157. "I felt being a woman... miniseries to a woman." Finnegan, interview.

158. "That's the way I grew up... left to work with Matt Williams." Maffeo, interview. Maffeo produced *Home Improvement*, and was senior VP of television for Wind Dancer Production Group at the Disney Studios (*Buddies*, *Soul Man*, *Carol & Company*). She was also executive in charge of production on *Buffalo Bill*. Earlier in her career she worked as script supervisor on *The Sid Caesar Show* and for six years as Jack Benny's associate producer. Currently, she is president of Gold Star Productions.

159. "My first question to them was... we had so many choices." Maffeo, interview.

160. "Not many women came out of... got the essentials down." Joanne Curley-Kerner, interview by author, 23 March 1999. Kerner is a producer whose credits include *Webster*, *A Different World*, *Cosby*, *Grace Under Fire*. She began her career producing AfterSchool Specials, including *Pippi Longstocking*, *Are You My Mother*, *Little Vic*, *Hewitt's Just Different*, *Horrible Honchos*.

161. "I had bought... back to school." Sybil Niden Goldrich, interview by author, 5 September 1998. Goldrich did make it back to film school, but life took over. In the 1980s, after surgery for breast cancer, she founded the Command Trust Network, international silicon implant information center.

162. "We worked with everything... He'd scream and yell." Curley Kerner, interview.

134. "Basically the bottom line... It was hysterical." Curley Kerner, interview.

164. "Along the yellow brick road... work you were creating." Georgia Jeffries, interview by author, 14 March 2000. Multi-award-winning writer/producer: *Tin Wife*, *Confessions*, *Nobody's Fool*, *Fatal Memories*. Board of Trustees, Writers Guild Foundation.

165. Jeffries's script, *Nobody's Fool*, won the Gold Award for Best Screenplay at the Houston Film Festival, 1981.

166. "The best lesson I learned... always be grateful." Jeffries, interview.

167. "There were so few . . . You have a life." Jeffries, interview.
168. "Virginia and I were a perfect combination . . . have said the same thing." Field, interview. Producer writer director Field was also vice president of original programming for the USA Network and the Sci-Fi Channel.
169. "There was friction between . . . was not an option." Field, interview. In 1984, Field produced *Heartsounds* with Fay Kanin, starring James Garner and Mary Tyler Moore. It was nominated for an Emmy; it won the Peabody award, Field's second Peabody. Then she produced *Guilty of Innocence: The Lenell Geter Story*, and coproduced the five-hour NBC miniseries *The Fortunate Pilgrim*, starring Sophia Loren.

14. A DIFFERENT TAKE ON THE SET
170. Nancy Mills, "The Plight of Women Directors Improved—But Not Much," *Los Angeles Times Calendar*, 17 November 1986. In the first in a series of articles, Mills quoted Norman Lear and Dawn Steel, among others.
171. "The kind of strength . . . does not a director make." Ibid.
172. "It's about talent . . . be in that position either." Ibid.
173. "I'm not a war criminal . . . for no good reason." Nancy Mills, "Women Directors: Door Opens," *Los Angeles Times*, 19 November 1986. Michelle Manning is now president of production at Paramount.
174. David Robb, "DGA-Industry Minority Talks," *Variety*, 10 June 1983.
175. The 1992 DGA report, quoted in "Col, Barnette in 2-year pact," *Variety*, 22 April 1992.
176. "guilty of pervasive bias . . . at the top jobs." Dennis Wharton, "Washington-Based Group Says Despite Gains Females Remain Shut Out Of Most Exec Posts," *Variety*, 25 August 1987.
177. Sally Steenland, "Prime Time Power: Women Producers, Writers and Directors in TV." Reported in *Variety*, 25 August 1987.
178. "The first couple of days . . . exteriors of the west.' Yes!" Randa Haines, interview by author, 24 November 1999. Haines was nominated for an Emmy and a DGA Award for *Something About Amelia*.
179. "the only movies women were directing . . . bathroom with the director." Haines, interview.
180. "My agent said . . . and I got the job." Haines, interview. *Something About Amelia*, produced by Michelle Rappaport, won the Emmy in 1984 for Outstanding Drama/Comedy Special; William Hanley won the Emmy for writing. Haines was nominated for Best Directing.
181. "After it aired . . . mind-boggling." Jenkins, interview.
182. "The play's subtleties . . . like collective dreams." Haines, interview.
183. "Being a woman and . . . we *can* do this." Neema Barnette, interview by author, 14 February 2000. Barnette's directing credits include prime-time television— *Cosby, Hooperman, It's a Living, The Royal Family, A Different World, The Redd Foxx Show, Frank's Place, China Beach*, and the American Playhouse special *Zora Is My Name*, starring Ruby Dee.
184. "I didn't know what it meant . . . should be an everyday thing." Barnette, interview.
185. "We got an office at the studio . . . be a black woman." Barnette, interview.
186. "Everything changed with the pregnancy . . . didn't like me anymore. Period." Steel, *They Can Kill You*, 219.

187. "the first pregnant vice president." Heller, interview.

188. "One of the things . . . didn't have that edge anymore." Heller, interview.

189. "I felt surrounded . . . I was no longer president of production." Steel, *They Can Kill You*, 230–31.

190. "She was one of a kind . . . network in the 1980s." Hollace Davids, interview by author, 22 April 2000. Davids is currently senior VP, special projects, at Universal Pictures and president of Women in Film. She was associate producer of *Timothy Leary's Dead*.

191. See Abramowitz, *Is That a Gun in Your Pocket?* for a detailed account of Dawn Steel's career.

192. "It was thrilling . . . directed Bill's shows." Barnette, interview.

193. "one failed show can destroy us." On a related area of the business, see screenwriter William Goldman's article, "The Gray '90s," *Premiere*, November 1999. "No female star would have been given so many chances [citing Richard Gere's and Mel Gibson's film duds]." He cites Rene Russo in a string of 1990s hits. "In 1997, she finally gets to play the lead. *Buddy* didn't work. Guess what? No more vehicle parts. No breaks like Gere or Gibson got . . . You may know why there are so few female stars. Best I can come up with is simple: Guys run the Hollywood show. And guys don't really want women to be stars . . . Remember that movies began—really—as entertainment for illiterates."

194. "understood the struggle . . . except for Bill Cosby's." Barnette, interview. *Different Worlds, An Interracial Love Story*, an AfterSchool Special, brought her a DGA nomination.

195. "Rosilyn was very personable . . . the images on screen won't change." Barnette, interview.

196. "What really happens in the studios . . . and now have some." Nasatir, interview.

197. "I got to know her a little . . . Go, Betty!" Barnette, interview. Barnette serves on the executive board of the DGA African American Steering Committee, has been on the board of the Black Filmmakers Foundation since it began, and operates her own production company, Harlem Lite Productions.

198. "When I was observing . . . we can go on with life." Betty Thomas, interview by author, 8 September 1999. Thomas has directed motion pictures (*Private Parts, Only You*) and prime-time television episodes (*Hooperman; Doogie Howser, M.D.; Star Trek: The Next Generation; Dream On*). Her company, Tall Trees, with Leonard Goldberg and Flower Films, produced *Charlie's Angels* (2000), a Columbia Pictures release.

199. "Peter Bogdanovich saw it . . . His company went under." Coolidge, interview. Among the films Coolidge has directed are *Introducing Dorothy Dandridge, Out to Sea, Three Wishes, Crazy In Love, Real Genius*, and HBO's *If These Walls Could Talk 2*.

200. "I went into a depression . . . not some porno film." Coolidge, interview. Among the films Coolidge has directed are *Introducing Dorothy Dandridge, Out to Sea, Three Wishes, Crazy in Love, Real Genius*, and HBO's *If These Walls Could Talk 2*.

201. ". . . backwards and forwards . . . I knew it." Coolidge, interview.

202. "The execs didn't want her . . . want an exploitation film." Coolidge, interview.

203. "Finally, I was called to a meeting . . . That's exactly what was said." Coolidge, interview.

204. "I called cinematographer . . . It's like dancing." Coolidge, interview.

205. "Suddenly people were pulling me up on the stage . . . And I could not." Arthur, interview. In the 1980s and 1990s, Arthur directed primarily miniseries and movies for television.
206. "A fabulous libertist . . . on a stage or in a film." Arthur, interview.
207. "We're just here . . . nobody knows where that is." Miriam Birch, interview by author, 15 September 1999. Birch, a producer/writer/director, made many National Geographic Television Specials and is the recipient of Alfred A. Dupont-Columbia and Peabody Awards and a three-time Emmy nominee. Other credits include *California and the Dreamseekers* for A&E; films for the Cousteau Society, TLC, TBS, and Lufthansa; and published short stories.
208. "[Zurbach] joins . . . documentary makers." *The Oregonian*, 13 October 1970. Zurbach Wiser wrote and produced (and directed some segments of) *The Big Cats* (1970), and wrote, produced, and directed *Zoos of the World* (1970).
209. "Linda was a feminist . . . He let the pandas out." Birch, interview.
210. "For some bizarre reason . . . Lucky me." Cecelia Hall, interview by author, 1 November 1999.
211. "to be there when . . . toys you don't get to play with." Alexandra Brouwer and Thomas Lee Wright, *Working in Hollywood* (New York: Avon Books, 1990), 458.
212. "I had no personal life . . . I had met my two gods." Hall, interview.
213. "I want the woman who edited *Witness* . . . That's hard to accomplish." Hall, interview.
214. Gloria Borders won the Oscar in sound editing the year after Hall for *Terminator 2*.
215. "By the early 1990s . . . few women." Hall, interview. Under her guidance as supervising sound editor, Paramount was the first studio sound department to begin using digital editorial technology in 1991. That department has been involved in many award-winning sound tracks, including *Face/Off, Titanic, The General's Daughter, Double Jeopardy*, and *Mission Impossible II*. In 1984, she was the first woman elected president of the Motion Picture Sound Editors.
216. "I gave up time . . . a time when I do." Lansing, interview
217. "I made a mistake . . . and do it well." Hall, interview.
218. "about aliens and old people . . . hadn't been mentored by women." Zanuck, interview.
219. "And it came after the fact . . . something handed to me." Karen Lustgarten, "The Drive of Ms. Lili," *Reel News* (Women in Film publication), March 1992.
220. "In those early days . . . very hard to get it made." Zanuck, interview. *Driving Miss Daisy* won Best Picture, Best Actress, Best Screenplay, and Best Achievement in Makeup. The Producers Guild named the Zanucks Producers of the Year. It ranks, at over $100 million, as one of Warner Bros.' most profitable films ever.
221. "Then private syndicates started . . . fortitude mixed with desperation." Lustgarten, "The Drive of Ms. Lili."
222. "These little local . . . doing the dishes." Ibid.
223. "It's not 'This is my set . . . comfront level." Zanuck, interview.
224. "Another thing that happens . . . And that's very common." Zanuck, interview.
225. "gopher, then in development . . . my generation didn't have." Lustgarten, "The Drive of Ms. Lili."
226. "Being a woman today . . . I don't know that we are." Zanuck, interview. In 2000, Lili and Richard Zanuck produced the 72nd annual Oscar presentation. Laura Ziskin produced the 2002 awards.

III. Breakthrough—The 1990s

1. *The American Chronicle, Six Decades in American Life, 1920–1980* (New York: Athenium, 1987). Gordon, Lois and Alan.
2. Jan Wahl, quoted by Jeannine Yeomans in "Hey, Hollywood: What's Wrong with this Picture?" Womensenews.com, 19 September 2000.
3. Ibid.
4. U.S. Department of Labor, Women's Bureau, "20 Leading Occupations of Employed Women, 1999 Annual Averages," 1998–2000.
5. U.S. Department of Labor, Women's Bureau, "Women's Earnings as Percentage of Men's 1979–99," and "Annual Earnings Year-round Full-time Workers by Sex, in Current Real Dollars, 1951–98," ed. Michael Williams.
6. Writers Guild of America, "Overall Trends, Employment and Earnings, WGA Members, 1987–91," Figure 11, TV and Film writers.

15. THE SUIT WITH LEGS

7. Over half the director-level jobs were held by women; five of the twenty companies employed at least 30 percent women at the VP level; two companies, CBS and Viacom, had no women above senior exec level.
8. In 1991, Women in Film issued . . . men held the job title of president. Sally Steenland, *The Employment of Executive Women in Film and Television: 1991*, Published by Women in Film. 1,124 employees at 20 companies were surveyed. In film: Columbia Pictures, Paramount Pictures, TriStar, 20th Century Fox, Universal Pictures, Walt Disney Pictures, Warner Bros. Pictures. In TV: Columbia Pictures Television, Lorimar, New World Television, Paramount Television, 20th Century Fox Television, Universal Television, Viacom Television, Walt Disney Television, Warner Bros. Television, and the networks: ABC, CBS, NBC, Fox.
9. In the study, women compared . . . to reach those positions. Steenland, "Executive Women," 10.
10. "Having a baby . . . after they've had kids." Steenland, "Executive Women," 11.
11. "Motherhood definitely put a . . . particular, individual person." Barbara Boyle, Counterpunch, "Women, Motherhood and the Film Industry," *Los Angeles Times*, 26 August 1991.
12. "as women in the industry . . . too slow—glacial." Steenland, "Executive Women," 12.
13. "Our business is way ahead . . . but there will be." Lansing, interview.
14. "I've had an unfair advantage . . . a lot of women." Amy Pascal, interview by author, 29 October 1999. Pascal was VP production, 20th Century Fox, 1986–87; executive VP production, Columbia Pictures, 1987–94; president of production, Turner Pictures, 1994–96; then back to Columbia as president, remaining in that position when Columbia and TriStar merged operations; and chairman of Columbia Pictures, 1999. Films include *Black Hawk Down, Ali, Groundhog Day, Little Women, Charlie's Angels.*
15. "Tony Garnett taught me . . . some very good scripts." Pascal, interview.
16. See Chapter 17 for Robin Swicord's comments regarding this groundbreaking precedent.

17. "I don't know if I thought . . . It probably still is." Pascal, interview.
18. "All but four are driven . . . marrying sixty-year-old men?" Meryl Streep, acceptance speech, 23rd Annual Women in Film Crystal Awards, 19 June 1998. Among her many stellar roles, Streep also produced *First Do No Harm* for television in 1997. Gale Anne Hurd and Lucy Fisher were also honored at the Crystal Awards that year. Introducing Fisher, Jack Nicholson said, "She is the suit with legs."
19. "Women are half . . . they watch movies." Sara Risfer, interview by author, 18 February 2000.
20. "Unfortunately, it's still true . . . learning from other people." Pascal, interview.
21. "needed to get out of Los Angeles . . . when she was thirty-one." Amy Baer, interview by author, 24 February 2000. Baer graduated magna cum laude in English literature from Georgetown University. She was director of development, Guber-Peters Entertainment Company (*Jumanji, Single White Female*). Currently, she is executive vice president, Columbia Pictures.
22. "But many of the women . . . Why not?" Baer, interview.
23. "We were sort of the transition . . . creating the base." Debra Martin Chase, interview by author, 8 June 1999. Chase, an independent producer, served as executive VP of Whitney Houston's BrownHouse Productions, a Disney-based company, 1995–2000. She was previously senior VP of Mundy Lane Entertainment, Denzel Washington's TriStar Pictures–based production company, 1992–95 (*Devil in a Blue Dress, Hank Aaron: Chasing the Dream*); she executive-produced Fox 2000's *Courage Under Fire* and coproduced *The Preacher's Wife*. At Columbia Pictures (1989–92), as attorney in MP legal department, she worked for studio chair Frank Price as executive assistant.
24. "I was in my blue suit . . . that motivates me a lot." Chase, interview.
25. "I explained to Helen Verno . . . easier for me." Winifred Neisser, interview by author, 16 September 1999. Currently, Neisser is senior VP, movies for television and miniseries, Columbia TriStar Television. She began her career at NBC in comedy and variety, became a director of children's programming, then VP, family programming; director, motion pictures for television; then VP, movies and miniseries. She served on the board of overseers, Harvard University, and on the board of Women in Film. Among the projects she's supervised at Columbia TriStar are *Long Island Incident* (1998), Barbra Streisand's Barwood production of the story of Carolyn McCarthy, whose husband was murdered on a Long Island train; *The Crossing* for A&E; and the Judy Garland story, *Me and My Shadow*, produced by Lorna Luft.
26. "I also noticed when I left . . . my kid's soccer team.'" Neisser, interview.
27. "It was something of an adjustment . . . any kind of problem." Neisser, interview.
28. "She wanted to know . . . Those things were foreign to me." Neisser, interview.
29. "The entertainment industry was not . . . in charge of variety and comedy." Neisser, interview.
30. "Out here you won't find . . . from the very beginning." Neisser, interview.
31. "But I do have a sense . . . I set for myself." Alyss Dixson, interview by author, 17 July 2000. Dixson interned at New Line Cinema, worked on *Money Talks* as an assistant, then director of development; worked as head of development directing/producing for Rat Entertainment (*Double Take, Family Man, Rush Hour 1 & 2*). In 2000, she moved to Paramount as a VP of production.

16. DON'T EVER TAKE IT PERSONALLY

32. "There's no business except . . . it's called old." Lansing, interview.

33. "If you make the money . . . the world counts." Thomas, interview.

34. "Films directed toward men . . . they're much more competitive." Risher, interview. Risher is chairman of New Line Productions. She was also the executive producer of *In Love and War*, *Last Man Standing*, and many other films. As chair, she is in charge of the corporate overview of the production department and has most recently opened an in-house production banner, ChickFlicks.

35. "It was a difficult area . . . got to get those kinds of films back." Risher, interview.

36. "A young man . . . expectations for men and women." Marion Edwards, interview by author, 28 February 2000. Edwards was a vice president, MCA Universal International TV, vice president of MGM/UA Telecommunications, 1988–92, then moved to 20th Century Fox as executive VP, International Television.

37. "We try to make sure . . . or somebody's daughter." Edwards, interview.

38. "Traditional media . . . 'You really understand me.'" Saul Hansell, "The Media Business: Advertising," *New York Times*, 16 September 1998.

39. MTV started Nickelodeon; Viacom is the parent of Nickelodeon and MTV.

40. "a media revolution . . . up from 16 percent in 1994." Hansell, "The Media Business."

41. Bill Carter, "3 Women in TV Form Cable Channel for Women," *New York Times*, 24 November 1998.

42. "Cable TV's top-rated shows . . . 70 percent of consumer spending." Cynthia Littleton and Rich Katz, "Ox Set for Air," *Variety*, 25 November 1998.

43. "veteran grrl zinesters . . . 'thinking like a girl.'" Janelle Brown, "What Happened to the Women's Web?: They promised a revolution but all we got was horoscopes, diet tips and parenting advice." Salon.com, Technology, 25 August 2000.

44. "There's nothing comparable . . . can have their own 'channel.'" Winnie Wechsler, interview by author, 22 February 2000. Before becoming executive VP and general manager of Lightspan, Inc., Wechsler was a senior vice president with the Disney Channel, then senior vice president of the Disney Company's Buena Vista Internet Group. She was one of the founders of Disney Online, launched and managed Disney.com, and helped establish Disney's Internet prominence internationally.

45. "When we went to raise . . . that's beginning to happen." Mariana Danilovic, interview by author, 31 March 2000. Danilovic is CEO/President, Digital Media X LLC, which she founded in February 2000. The firm provides seed financing and venture services to digital media and convergence companies. Prior to founding DMX, Danilovic founded and managed the Digital Media Business incubator at KPMG LLP, the practice that successfully assisted the sale of the Well to the Salon. She has also headed business development for Mandalay Entertainment, Sony Pictures Entertainment, and 20th Century Fox International Television Group.

46. "Many venture capitalists are anxious . . . but I believe that." Wechsler, interview.

47. "By its nature, the Internet ... levels are mainly men." Jane White, interview by author, 2 February 2000. Formerly, White was director of educational services, ABC News; cofounder of ABC News InterActive; executive producer, Paramount Interactive; director of development, Viacom New Media.

48. "What's interesting about [this new media] ... would be busted automatically." Interview with Red Burns and Stefanie Syman, Live Feed, 11 March 1996. Burns founded the Alternate Media Center, 1971, and is currently chair of the interactive telecommunications program at the Tisch School of Arts of New York University.

49. "It took me a while ... hadn't even been built." Kennedy, interview, 15 September 1999. Beth B. Kennedy was at Universal Studios/MCA, 1975–90. She designed and installed MCA's first on-line computer systems and supervised the implementation of more than three hundred computer systems for MCA divisions. Later, she was CEO, Kaizen Heron Group, and a senior consultant in strategic planning and advanced technology.

50. "This is the weekend ... eyes or hair." Kennedy, interview.

51. "From Jeffrey [Katzenberg] ... And you don't ever take it personally." Steel, *They Can Kill You*, 126.

52. "That's my mantra ... Now let's figure out how." Kennedy, interview.

53. "None of that would have happened ... have the control.'" Rocco, interview.

54. "a woman might head ... and still is." Rocco, interview. "During Casey Silver's regime," Rocco adds, "Buffy Shutt and Kathy Jones ran marketing; Nadia Bronson, still with the company, runs international marketing and distribution operations; Mary Ledding runs legal affairs; Donna Smith ran physical production; Mary Parent, thirty-two, is executive VP of production; and Stacey Snider was copresident and is now chair."

55. "If I'd been a man ... release date of the film." Rocco, interview.

56. *Time*, 8 January 1996.

57. "An exhibitor called ... and 'being killed.'" Rocco, interview.

58. "queen of nonunion ... I'm a Minnesota girl." Smith, interview. Smith was senior VP of production and postproduction at Universal, 1989–96, the first woman to head physical production at a major movie studio.

59. "Smith didn't go to college ... her idea of filmmaking." Smith, interview.

60. "When I told my attorney ... Let's make the deal!'" Smith, interview. Carl Laemmle, president of Universal in 1912, hired Lois Weber and her husband, Phillips Smalley, to head production. Weber directed one short film a week. At that time, Universal had the largest group of women directors at one studio, about nine under contract. Most studios then had one or two. See Slide, *The Silent Feminists*, 33, 41.

61. "Going in ... pretty nifty." Smith, interview.

62. "I see being a woman ... will take assistant positions." Ziskin, interview. Partnered with Sally Field, Fogwood Films, she produced *Murphy's Romance*. Also produced *No Way Out*, *Spider-Man*, and was executive producer on *Pretty Woman*, *What About Bob?*, *The Doctor*, *Hero*, *Dinner with Friends*. President of Fox 2000 Pictures in 1994, a feature film division of 20th Century Fox.

63. "Men have defined our ... push really hard." Ziskin, interview.

64. See Obst, *Hello, He Lied*.

65. "I heard of only one ... I guess women are an audience." Ziskin, interview.

66. "Someone was asking me ... which was produced by a woman." Lansing, interview.

17: HIRING A WOMAN (WRITER) IS THE HIP THING TO DO

67. "This experience of mine ... it was a complete lie." Jeffries, interview, 18 March 2000.
68. "I was lucky ... bad news for women in 2000." Jeffries, interview.
69. Lauzen, *The Celluloid Ceiling*.
70. "In 1987, women were writing ... and no sci-fi." Lauzen, *The Real Story on Reel Women: Behind-the-Scenes Employment in the Top 250 Films of 1999* (San Diego: San Diego State University, June 2000). See also Lauzen's television study. *Where the Women Are ... and Aren't*.
71. "I didn't like it ... way to make a living there." Sara Parriott and Josann McGibbon, interview by author, 15 February 2000. McGibbon and Parriott are screenwriters of romantic comedies, including *Worth Winning*, *Runaway Bride*, and *The Favor*.
72. "That's really cool! ... Now it's different." Parriott and McGibbon, interview.
73. "I'm not a female writer ... your way out of it." Janis Diamond, interview by author, 15 March 2000. She has written and produced for multiple media, she was story editor for *Brimstone*, creator/writer/producer of the pilot *White Rabbit*, and coproducer/executive story editor/writer for TNT's first series, *Bull*.
74. "I like going back and forth ... You want your life back." Diamond, interview.
75. "All of us who ... building for a hundred kids." Fisher, interview.
76. "I just couldn't hack it ... fabulous child-care center." Fisher, interview.
77. "You get a lot of seasoning ... skills are priceless." Diamond, interview.
78. *Peter and the Wolf* won the Emmy for Outstanding Children's Program in 1996; the writers (Diamond and George Daugherty) were nominated for the Writers Guild Award.
79. "It's divided into two ... in that one line." Diamond, interview.
80. "I was paid ... ten thousand dollars went a long way." Cynthia Cidre, interview by author, March 22, 2000. Cidre is a screenwriter whose credits include *In Country*, *Fires Within*, and *The Mambo Kings*.
81. *In Country* was directed by Norman Jewison. Cidre says "... he didn't think a woman could write a Vietnam story. Eventually, Rosenberg hired Frank Pierson, who rewrote me. [But] I got credit." Cidre, interview.
82. "There were not a lot ... reshoot the whole movie!" Cidre, interview.
83. "That sort of D-girl ... ambitious women here." Robin Swicord, interview by author, 21 April 2000. In addition to credits such as *Little Women*, Swicord's feature script, *You Ruined My Life*, was made as a movie-of-the-week for Disney, *Shag* (with Bridget Fonda), and *Matilda* (with Nicholas Kazan).
84. Swicord and Kazan are to write an original comedy, *Loco for Lotto*, under the new "Sony Deal."
85. The grandmother was played by Teresa Wright, who starred in Alfred Hitchcock's *Shadow of a Doubt*, among many other films. Annabeth Gish played the granddaughter.
86. "Gee, if I can ever get this screenplay ... a hard time getting employment." Swicord, interview.

87. "I support that kind of work … believe me." Jude Weng, interview by author, 22 June 2000. Director/writer Weng joined the AFI Women's Directing Program in 1998, made a short film, *Apartment 8;* produced another short, *Steel; Storm Watch,* a spec for her AFI master's thesis; and *Breech,* a music video, also for AFI. She also did interstitial material for Discovery's Travel Channel, and music videos such as *Glowsticking* for Drunkmunky/Frangrant Records.
88. James Wolcott, "Now, Voyeur," *Vanity Fair,* September 2000.
89. "I created the competitions … psychological mind-fuck." Weng, interview. A follow-up series, *Survivor II,* set in the Australian outback, aired during the 2000–2001 season.
90. "young and hungry … go make your own." Weng, interview.

18: THIS IS WHAT MEN DO
91. "Shortly afterwards … in the electrical department." Alexis Krasilovsky, *Women Behind the Camera: Conversations with Camerawomen* (Westport, CT: Praeger Publishers, 1997), 158. The MacLaine documentary was an all-women team of four that included Joan Weidman and Claudia Weill.
92. Lauzen, *The Real Story on Reel Women.* 20.
93. Some of the women Reiker has worked with : Ingrid Rudefors, Adrienne Shelly, Barbara Heller, Maria Maggenti, Lisa Cholodenko, Suzanne Myers.
94. According to Lauzen's survey published in June 2001, women film editors are better off than directors, but not by much. They made gains from 13 percent in 1987 to 15 percent in 1997, but by 2000 women editors working on the top 250 films were 19 percent.
95. "The producer was sitting … toward soap operas. Dina Lipton, interview by author, 10 January 2000. Lipton's credits as production designer include the films *The Muse, Trigger Happy* (aka *Mad Dog Time*), *Here on Earth, The Assassination File;* and on TV, *Generations* and *Fresh Prince of Bel-Air.* As art director, *Mr. Holland's Opus; Corrina, Corrina; The Last Seduction.*
96. Brouwer and Wright, *Working in Hollywood,*
97. Platt, interview.
98. "The competition between men and women … She taught me a lot." Lipton, interview. Jeannine Claudia Oppewall was nominated for her work as production designer for *L.A. Confidential.* Her other credits include *Snow Falling on Cedars, Pleasantville, The Bridges of Madison County, The Vanishing, Music Box, The Big Easy.*
99. "In my very first … wearing parkas, except him!" Lipton, interview.
100. The International Alliance of Theatrical Stage Employees has affiliated 1000 local unions in North America, controlling and regulating set painters, property crafts, art directors, sound and lab, makeup, script supervisors, screen cartoonists, gaffers, grips, etc., even employees of film distribution and exhibition.
101. "I was wearing blinders … do your job." Andrea Sachs, interview by author, 16 July 1999. Sachs is a chief electrician technician (gaffer), IA 728 LA, IA 52 NY. Credits include *Nowhere to Run, White Sands, Higher Learning, The Beautician and the Beast,* and many national commercials.
102. "That experience was harder … lone wolves." Sachs, interview.
103. "Being a woman prevented … exactly and directly." Halpern, interview.
104. "A girl shows up … at the gains we've made." Sachs, interview.
105. "Stuntwomen have been around … living in this industry." Leslie Hoffman, in-

terview by author, 24 March 2000. Hoffman's credits as stunt coordinator include *Ophelia Learns to Swim* and *Everything Put Together;* and as stuntwoman, *Mystery Men, Mars, Scream 2, Alien Nation, Naked Gun,* and *Death Wish 3.*

106. "Most stunts are pratfalls . . . to coordinate their projects." Hoffman, interview. See *Burns, Falls and Crashes, Interviews with Movie Stunt Performers,* ed., David Jon Wiener. (Jefferson, NC: McFarland & Co., 1996).

107. "They were filming the scene with the body bag . . . I'd still be a stuntwoman." Hoffman, interview.

108. "At the time . . . *Kull the Conqueror.*" Grace Liu, interview by author, 25 June 2000. Liu has worked on *Martial Law, Rush Hour, Flubber,* and *15 Minutes.*

109. "I knew I wanted to work . . . I'd never seen that before." Liu, interview. *C.S.I.,* the series, is about the Las Vegas P.D. Crime Scene Investigation Bureau.

110. "It's stereotypical that the grips . . . harder for women to break in—period." Liu, interview.

19: MAKING THE WHOLE FRAME IN THE '90S

111. "A woman in 1895 . . . women would rule the world," Lisa Mitchell, "Four Decades of Women Directors: An Evening with Distinguished Directors," *DGA Magazine,* January 1999. The panelists were Lynne Littman, Neema Barnette, Nancy Malone, Mimi Leder, Kim Friedman, Lee Shallat Chemel, Randa Haines, Debbie Allen (moderator), Victoria Hochberg, and Betty Thomas. Sponsored by Women in Film and the DGA Women's Steering Committee.

112. Ullmann interview. Actress/director/author (*Changing, Choices,* and *Letter to My Grandchild,* a collection of letters from internationally known people to their grandchildren), Ullmann began directing in the 1990s: *Sofie, Kristin Lavransdatter, Private Confessions, Faithless* (the latter two scripted by Ingmar Bergman).

113. "I realize that I didn't want . . . why I wanted it." Ullman, interview.

114. *Faithless,* script by Ingmar Bergman, starring Lena Endre, Erland Josephson, Krister Henriksson, Thomas Hanzon.

115. "The little woman . . . continue to support each other." Ullmann, interview.

116. *The Prince of Tides* was written by Becky Johnston and Pat Conroy, based on Conroy's novel; it was produced by Barbra Streisand and Andrew Karsch. It was nominated for seven Oscars, including Best Picture but not Best Director. Many in the film community felt this was a major oversight.

117. "I was shocked . . . I want to work with the best people." Streisand, interview.

118. Barwood Films also made *The Long Island Incident* (the story of the shooting on the commuter train); *Varian's War,* about the rescue of artists from Nazi persecution in World War II; *Frankie & Hazel;* and *What Makes a Family.*

119. "Before that, I was at Los Angeles City College . . . directing job on *L.A. Law.*" Mimi Leder, interview by author, 8 October 1999. Leder directed *Deep Impact, The Peacemaker, Pay It Forward.* Her television credits include *ER, China Beach,* and numerous television films.

120. I did every possible thing . . . for producing." Leder, interview. Leder received four Emmy nominations for *China Beach,* three DGA nominations, won two Emmys for *ER,* received the American Film Institute Franklin J. Schaffner Award, and in 2000, the Crystal Award from Women in Film.

121. 1998 also saw the release of *Armageddon,* a movie about an asteroid "the size of Texas" shooting toward Earth. Produced by a number of people, among

them Jerry Bruckheimer and Gale Anne Hurd. Joan Bradshaw, Steven Spielberg, David Brown, and Richard Zanuck, among others, produced *Deep Impact*.

122. Directors, 1998, 8 percent; 1999, 4 percent; 2000, 7 percent. Lauzen, "The Celluloid Ceiling," p. 6, Executive Summary.

123. "I told my agent . . . the better they'll be at what they do." Leder, interview.

124. "My first film . . . I had to do it." Joan Chen, interview by author, 7 July 2000. Chen, the writer, director, and producer of *Xiu Xiu: The Sent-Down Girl*, also directed *Autumn in New York* (2000). She began as a performer—*Turtle Beach*, *Heaven & Earth*, and *Paper Angels*.

125. "I fell into it . . . glory make me uneasy." Chen, interview.

126. "Every day we worked . . . would never get out of China." Richard Corliss, "Show Business," *Time*, 5 April 1999, 62.

127. "It's not just another Cultural Revolution . . . make World War II movies?" Scarlet Cheng, "Applying the Hard Lessons," *Los Angeles Times*, 23 June 1999.

128. "Everyone worked so hard . . . It felt natural." Chen, interview.

129. "I didn't look Chinese enough . . . like a white woman." Corliss, "Show Business," 61.

130. "Minority women have this freshness . . . same thrill of gambling." Chen, interview.

131. "My mother . . . for the women's movement." Judith James, interview. Originally a New York theatrical producer of eleven award-winning off-Broadway plays, James was executive producer of *Kissinger and Nixon*, *Quiz Show*; and producer of *Mr. Holland's Opus*, *Prisoner of Honor*, and *Having Our Say: The Delany Sisters' First 100 Years* (the Broadway play and the television movie).

132. At the Mark Taper, Judith James produced, with Margot Winchester, *Brotherhood of Justice* for ABC and "Daniel and the Towers" for PBS's *Wonderworks*.

133. "When the guys at ABC . . . It was human." James, interview.

134. "Judy and Camille, the producers . . . at AFI was unforgettable." Littman, interview.

135. "We laughed so much . . . they share the same language." James, interview.

136. "What an unbelievable feeling . . . It was ours." Littman, interview. In 1993, Littman created the *Tribute to Women* that opened the 65th Academy Awards.

137. "I was too young to know . . . That's what youth is." Littman, interview. *Testament* was produced by Lynne Littman and Jonathan Bernstein; associate producer was Andrea Asimow. It starred Jane Alexander, William Devane, and Lukas Haas; Kevin Costner and Rebecca De Mornay played small parts. It was made for American Playhouse, Entertainment Events, Paramount Pictures distributed.

138. *Freak City* was produced by Sandy Stern. It was written by Jane Shepard and starred Samantha Mathis. Marlee Matlin, Jonathan Silverman, Natalie Cole, Peter Sarsgaard, and Estelle Parsons.

139. "We were in the bliss . . . was that we could admit it." Littman, interview.

140. "I don't think sexism . . . for or against me." Kimberly Peirce, quoted in Laurie Winer, "The Industry, Women on the Side," *Los Angeles Magazine*, September 2000.

141. Stephen Witty, "Female Directors Join Forces to Win," *San Diego Union Tribune*, 11 August 2000.

142. Maggie Renzi, quoted in Witty, "Female Directors."
143. "Motivated in part by . . . level of the industry." Winer, "Women on the Side."
144. "make a film that bombs . . . have been quiet for a long time." Ibid.

EPILOGUE: HOW FAR IS FAR?

145. Dianne Dixon, interview by author, 10 May 2000. Dixon is a television writer (*Designing Women, Nurses*). She also writes animation and children's programming.
146. Charlotte Brown, interview by author, 30 January 1998.
147. Nelson, interview.
148. Wallerstein, interview.
149. Hurd, interview.
150. Dixson, interview.
151. Jeannine Yeomans, *Women's enews.com*, 18 September 2000, quoting Martha L. Lauzen, Ph.D.
152. Ledding, interview.
153. Corday, interview.
154. Susan Littwin, "What Do Women Writers Want?" *Written By*, April 2000.
155. Anonymous, interview by author. Restated in other interviews and in the press in various ways. See Charles Piller, "Gender Gap Goes High Tech," *Los Angeles Times*, August 1998.
156. Grossman, interview.
157. Sylbert, interview.
158. Brown, interview.
159. Marcus, interview.
160. Littman, interview.
161. Littman, interview.
162. Silverman, interview.
163. White, interview.
164. Among Lindsay Doran's credits are *Sense and Sensibility, Pretty in Pink, Ghost*. Doran is now an independent producer (*Sabrina*).
165. "I had real reasons . . . that's what makes the real difference." Nasatir, interview.
166. Rees, interview.
167. Some of the directors on *Sex in the City* are Allison Anders, Victoria Hochberg, and Susan Seidelman. It is produced by Suzanne and Jennifer Todd. Colin Callender, president of HBO Films, was praised by the producers of *If These Walls Could Talk* at the 2000 Lucy Awards, Women in Film. *Judging Amy* is executive-produced by Barbara Hall, who is also the head writer, Ann Kenney is the co-executive producer of *Family Law*, Alison Cross is the writer/producer of *Philly*.
168. "Women are more invested . . . I think it's a woman thing." Littwin, "What Do Women Writers Want?" Ann Beckett (*The Broken Cord, First Do No Harm*) is a WGA Award winner.
169. Littwin, "What Do Women Writers Want?" 32.
170. Nancy Mills, "Women Directors: Door Opens."
171. Phylis Geller, interview by author, 21 August 2000, quoting from her conversation with Lindsay Law.
172. For hilarious and sad reading, see Susan Littwin, "A Show of Her Own" (about

Barbara Hall, executive producer/head writer of *Judging Amy*), *Written By*, April 2000, 25.

173. Lauzen, *The Real Story on Reel Women*, 22.

174. The figures for television: statistics by Lauzen, *Where the Women Are...and Aren't*, San Diego State University study, September 2001, are similar to those of film except producers fared better, 35%, and directors of photography came in at 0%.

175. The figures cited simply reverse Lauzen's statistics in the previous paragraph and from her entire studies of TV and motion pictures. For instance, overall in TV, men occupy 77 percent of all behind-the-scenes positions. Figures for CEOs of large corporations, agents, reviewers are estimated.

176. Haines, quoted by Nancy Mills, "Women Directors—Vive La Difference?"

177. Mills, "Women Directors—Vive la Difference?"

178. Kanin, interview.

179. Weinstein, interview.

180. Lynda Obst, quoted by Suzanna Andrews, "The Great Divide: The Sexes and the Box Office," *New York Times*, 23 May 1993.

181. Ibid.

182. Geller, interview.

183. See Andrews, "The Great Divide . . ." 15. For instance, in 1992, women bought 45 percent of the movie tickets nationally. "Women say [they want and don't get] sophisticated, character-based movies in which women have leading roles."

184. James, interview.

185. Smith, quoted from her remarks at the Arbus-Perlman monthly lunch, April 2001.

186. Anonymous, interview by author.

187. Dixson, interview.

188. "I was on a place recently . . . or you will sink." Anonymous, interview by author.

189. Hill, interview.

190. Nevins, interview.

191. Merians, interview.

192. Grossman, interview.

193. Leslie Smith, interview by author, 20 July 1999.

194. Weinstein, interview.

195. Jeffries, interview.

196. Sylbert, interview.

197. Chen, interview.

198. Richard Corliss, "Show Business," *Time*, 5 April 1999, 61.

199. Zanuck, interview.

200. Anonymous, interview by author.

201. Anonymous, interview by author.

202. Cook, interview.

203. Nelson, interview

204. Ledding, interview.

205. Goldstein, 39.

206. Miles, 277.

207. Miles, 282.

208. Miles, 284–86.
209. "Now, no one notices a woman producer . . . arrows for us." Rose, interview.
210. Rosalind Miles, *Who Cooked the Last Supper: The Women's History of the World* (New York: Three Rivers Press, 2001), 234.
211. Kanin, interview.
212. Perlman, interview.
213. Alexander, interview.
214. Ziskin, interview.

LIST OF WOMEN INTERVIEWED

Jane Alexander, performer, *Eleanor and Franklin: The White House Years, Playing for Time, Testament;* producer, *Calamity Jane, Square Dance, A Marriage: Georgia O'Keeffe and Alfred Stieglitz.* Formerly chairman of the National Endowment for the Arts. Author, *Command Performance: An Actress in the Theater of Politics.*

Dede Allen, ACE, editor, *Bonnie and Clyde, Serpico, The Hustler, Alice's Restaurant, Slap Shot, Dog Day Afternoon, Slaughterhouse-Five, Wonder Boys, John Q;* editor and producer, *Reds.* Nominated for two Oscars.

Loreen Arbus, president, Arbus Productions, *Case Closed, Crimes of Passion.* Former vice president of original programming for Showtime, senior VP in charge of program development, production, acquisition at Cable Health Network/Lifetime; supervised program development/production for Viacom's network/first-run syndication.

Karen Arthur, director, *Legacy, The Mafu Cage, The Jacksons: An American Dream, Crossings, The Rape of Richard Beck, The Song of the Lark, Pride and Prejudice, The Staircase;* episodes of *Hart to Hart, Remington Steele.*

Tamara Asseyev, producer, *Norma Rae, The Hijacking of the* Achille Lauro, *Murder by Moonlight, Penalty Phase, After the Promise, Beryl Markham: A Shadow on the Sun.*

Amy Baer, executive VP production, Columbia Pictures.

Neema Barnette, director, *The Silent Crime, One More Hurdle, Zora Is My Name!, Better Off Dead, Run for the Dream: The Gail Devers Story, Close to Danger, Spirit Lost;* TV series, *The Cosby Mysteries, Diagnosis Murder.*

Patricia Barry, performer, *Guiding Light, All My Children, Days of Our Lives;* many feature films, *The End of August, A Cry for Love;* TV guest appearances, *Murder She Wrote, Charlie's Angeles, Ironside.*

Miriam Birch, documentary filmmaker, one of the first women to write and produce National Geographic Society Specials, such as *The Soul of Spain, Voices of Leningrad, Save the Panda, The Living Treasures of Japan.*

Barbara Boyle, attorney, executive, and producer, *Phenomenon, Instinct, Mrs. Munck;* executive producer, *Bottle Rocket, Eight Men Out, The Hi-Line.*

Pam Brockie, senior VP, business affairs, ICM.

Charlotte Brown, writer/producer, *The Mary Tyler Moore Show, Rhoda, Valerie;* director, *The Tortellis, Goodbye Charlie, The Good News.*

Sue Cameron, columnist, *The Hollywood Reporter;* first woman VP, ABC daytime programming, 1975–78; novelist, *Honey Dust* (New York: Warner Books, 1993), *Love, Sex & Murder* (New York: Warner Books, 1996).

Marcy Carsey, Carsey-Werner Co., *Cosby, Third Rock from the Sun, Cybill, Roseanne, That '70s Show;* founder, The Oxygen Channel.

Debra Martin Chase, executive producer and producer, *Hank Aaron: Chasing the Dream, Courage under Fire, The Preacher's Wife, The Princess Diaries.*

Joan Chen, writer/producer/director, *Xiu-Xiu: The Sent Down Girl;* director, *Autumn in New York;* performer, *The Last Emperor, Tai-Pan, Turtle Beach, Twin Peaks, Heaven & Earth.*

Cynthia Cidre, screenwriter, *Little Havana, The Mambo Kings, In Country, I Saw What You Did;* writer/producer, *A Killing in a Small Town.*

Melanie Cook, attorney, partner at Bloom, Hergott, Cook, Diemer & Klein.

Martha Coolidge, director, *Rambling Rose, Valley Girl, Lost in Yonkers, Angie, Introducing Dorothy Dandridge, If These Walls Could Talk 2, Out to Sea, The Ponder Heart;* writer/producer/director, *Not a Pretty Picture.* In 2002, she became the first woman to be president of the DGA.

Barbara Corday, co-creator, co-writer, *Cagney & Lacey;* former executive VP, CBS; president/COO, Columbia Pictures Television; currently, chair, Motion Picture/TV Production, USC.

Julie Corman, producer, *The Lady in Red, Boxcar Bertha, Da, Nowhere to Run, A Cry in the Wild, Max Is Missing*; currently, chair, Graduate School of Film, Kanbar Institute, Tisch School of the Arts, New York University.

Joanne Curley-Kerner, television producer, *A Different World, Cosby, Grace Under Fire, Imagine That.*

Mariana Danilovic, CEO, Digital Media X LLC.

Joan Darling, director, *Mary Hartman, Mary Hartman, The Mary Tyler Moore Show, Amazing Stories, Hizzoner, Taxi, Rhoda, M*A*S*H*; performer, *Owen Marshall: Counselor at Law, The Defenders.*

Hollace Davids, senior VP special projects, Universal Pictures, Marketing.

Loraine Despres, television writer, *Dallas, Dynasty, Knots Landing, The Love Boat*; author, *The Scandalous Summer of Sissy LeBlanc.*

Janis Diamond, writer/producer, *Bull* (TNT's first series), *Brimstone, Law & Order*, also Movies of the Week, live action, interactive/CD-ROM, animation.

Alyss Dixson, VP, production, Paramount Studios; formerly head of feature development, Rat Entertainment.

Bonny Dore, producer, *The Sinking of the Rainbow Warrior, Reason for Living: The Jill Ireland Story, Glory, Glory!, Sins*; television series, *First Impressions.*

Marion Edwards, executive VP, Fox International TV.

Ruth Engelhardt, senior VP business affairs, William Morris Agency.

Fern Field, producer, TV miniseries, *Kane and Abel, The Fortunate Pilgrim*; films, *Eleanor, First Lady of the World, Heartsounds*; TV series, *The Baxters*; executive at Tandem Productions and USA Network.

Patricia Finnegan, producer, *The Choice; Dark Holiday; Quicksand: No Escape; Goodbye, Miss 4th of July; Keeping Secrets; A Father for Charlie; To Dance with Olivia; Black Widow Murders; Marked for Murder.*

Lucy Fisher, formerly vice chair, Columbia TriStar Motion Picture Group (*As Good As It Gets, My Best Friend's Wedding*). Currently, producer, Red Wagon Productions, *Girl Interrupted, Gladiator, Stuart Little.*

D. C. Fontana, screenwriter, *Star Trek: The Next Generation, Star Trek: Deep Space Nine, Babylon 5;* TV series, multiple episodes, *Star Trek, The Waltons, Bonanza, Then Came Bronson, Logan's Run.*

Chris Foster, literary agent, Shapiro Lichtman; formerly, senior VP Columbia Pictures Television.

Harriet Frank, Jr., screenwriter (with her husband, Irving Ravetch), *Norma Rae, Hud, The Reivers, Hombre, Murphy's Romance, Stanley & Iris;* writer-producer, *Conrack.*

Lillian Gallo, television producer, *Princess Daisy, Haunts of the Very Rich, What Are Best Friends For?, The Stranger Who Looks at Me.*

Lila Garrett, writer/producer, *The Girl Who Couldn't Lose, The Other Woman* (Emmy); writer/producer/director, *Terraces, Who Gets the Friends?*

Phylis Geller, formerly senior VP, cultural programming and new media, WETA; currently, president, Norman Star Media.

Gloria Goldsmith, writer, *Critical Path, The Secret Life of Kathy Mc-Cormick, Friday Dinner on Middleneck Road*, CBS Playhouse: "Terror Times Two," *MacMillan;* playwright, *Womanspeak.*

Diana Gould, writer, *I Love You, Goodbye; Jenny; For My Daughter's Honor;* miniseries, *I'll Take Manhattan, Two Women;* producer/writer, *Dynasty, Kay O'Brien, Berrenger's;* founder, WGA Women's Committee.

Iris Grossman, agent, ICM; formerly senior VP talent and casting, Turner Network Television.

Helene Hahn, co-chief operating officer, DreamWorks SKG.

Randa Haines, director, *Children of a Lesser God, Something About Amelia, Wrestling Ernest Hemingway, The Doctor;* television, *Alfred Hitchcock Presents, Hill Street Blues.*

Cecelia Hall, senior VP, postproduction sound; Oscar for sound on *The Hunt for Red October, Top Gun, Witness;* first woman president of the Motion Picture Sound Editors.

Amy Halpern, IA 728; director of photography, *Breaking the Maya Code, The Muse, Broken Bridges;* gaffer, *Killers Inside, Fatal Passion;* best boy/electrician, *Sioux City, Stand and Deliver;* director, *Falling Lessons.*

Valerie Harper, performer, four Emmys—*The Mary Tyler Moore Show, Rhoda, Valerie;* movies for television, *Strange Voices, The Execution, An Invasion of Privacy;* stage, *The Dragon and the Pearl, Death-Defying Acts.*

Rosilyn Heller, film producer, *Ice Castles; Who's That Girl?; The Killing of Randy Webster; American Heart; The Beans of Egypt, Maine;* one of the first women VPs, Columbia Pictures, 1974.

Debra Hill, writer/producer, *Halloween, Escape from L.A.;* producer, *The Fisher King, Crazy in Alabama, Attack of the 50 Ft. Woman, The Dead Zone;* television director, *Dream On, Monsters.*

Leslie Hoffman, stunt coordinator, *Ophelia Learns to Swim, Me and My Hormones;* stuntwoman, *Star Trek: Deep Space Nine, Star Trek: Voyager, Alien Nation, Naked Gun, The Love Boat, Charlie's Angels.*

Gale Anne Hurd, producer, *The Terminator* (also writer), *Aliens, The Waterdance, Alien Nation, The Abyss, Switchback, The Ghost and the Darkness, The Relic, Armageddon.*

Joan Hyler, Hyler Management; formerly senior VP, William Morris.

Cheryl Boone Isaacs, formerly president, theatrical marketing, New Line Cinema.

Judith James, theatrical and film producer, *Mr. Holland's Opus, Kissinger and Nixon, Brotherhood of Justice, Quiz Show, Prisoner of Honor, Having Our Say: The Delaney Sisters' First 100 Years.*

Georgia Jeffries, two-time WGA award–winning writer/producer, *Cagney & Lacey, China Beach;* also *Iron-Jawed Angels, Your Blues Ain't Like Mine.*

Billie Beasley Jenkins, VP, The Leonard Goldberg Co., director administration, studio operations; director, services and resources, Motion Picture Division, 20th Century Fox; president, Masala Productions.

Irma Kalish, writer (with her husband, Austin), *Maude, All in the Family, My Three Sons;* writer/producer, *227, The Facts of Life;* executive producer, *Carter Country, Good Times.*

Fay Kanin, writer, *Tell Me Where It Hurts;* writer/producer, *Friendly Fire, Hustling.* First woman president of the Academy of Motion Picture Arts and Sciences.

Marcy Kelly, founder of Mediascope, nonprofit media policy organization; partner in Night Hawk Productions.

Beth Kennedy, CEO Kaizen Heron Group; Internet pioneer; producer/creator/writer *CyberJustice* (AOL 1994–99); former senior VP studio operations, MCA/Universal; first woman executive on the backlot; Exec. Director, Entertainment Industry Affairs, City of Los Angeles ("Film Czar").

Willette Klausner, producer; president of Edgework Productions; VP, marketing and marketing research, Universal Pictures; the first black woman vice president (1970s) in that arena.

Barbara Kopple, Oscar-winning producer/director, *Harlan County, U.S.A., El Salvador: Another Vietnam, American Dream, Fallen Champ: The Untold Story of Mike Tyson, A Conversation with Gregory Peck, My Generation*; television, *Defending Our Daughters, Friends for Life: Living with AIDS.*

Sherry Lansing, chairman, the Motion Picture Group, Paramount (*Titanic, Forrest Gump, Braveheart, The First Wives Club, Angela's Ashes*); producer, *The Accused, Fatal Attraction.*

Martha M. Lauzen, Ph.D., Department of Communication, San Diego State University. Conducts annual studies (since 1995), on women's employment in the film and television industries, such as "The Celluloid Ceiling: Behind the Scenes Employment of Women in the Top 250 Films, 2000," and "Boxed In: Women On-Screen and Behind the Scenes in the 2000–2001 Prime-time Season."

Mary Ledding, formerly senior VP, motion pictures business affairs, MGM; currently, senior VP, legal affairs, Universal Pictures.

Mimi Leder, producer/director, *China Beach, ER*; director, feature films, *The Peacemaker, Deep Impact, Pay It Forward, Smoke and Mirrors.*

Joanna Lee, writer, TV series, *The Waltons* (Emmy), *The Governor and J.J., Julia*; writer/producer, *Mary Jane Harper Cried Last Night, Like Normal People, Mulligan's Stew*; writer/producer/director, *Children of Divorce.*

Johnna Levine, first woman VP, legal affairs, ABC (1975); VP business affairs, Warner Bros.

Dina Lipton, production designer, *The Muse, Here on Earth, Mad Dog Time, Next Friday, The New Guy*; art director, *Mr. Holland's Opus; Corrina, Corrina.*

Lynne Littman, director/producer, *Number Our Days, Testament, In Her Own Time*; director, *Having Our Say: The Delaney Sisters' First 100 Years, Freak City, Rescuers: Stories of Courage: Two Couples.*

Grace Liu, DGA Trainee, features, *The Sum of All Fears* (desert unit), *America's Sweethearts, Double Take*; television, *C.S.I, The Agency, ER, The West Wing*; director's assistant, *Kull the Conqueror.*

Gayle Maffeo, television producer, *Roseanne, Home Improvement, Thunder Alley, Soul Man;* currently, president, Gold Star Productions.

Nancy Malone, stage, film, television performer, *The Man Who Loved Cat Dancing, The Trial of the Catonsville Nine;* director, *Resurrection Blvd, Star Trek: Voyager, Beverly Hills 90210;* producer, *Like Mom, Like Me; There Were Times, Dear.* First woman VP of television, 20th Century Fox, 1975.

Ann Marcus, writer/producer, *Knots Landing, Falcon Crest;* a co-creator of *Mary Hartman, Mary Hartman, All That Glitters;* head writer, *General Hospital, Search for Tomorrow;* TV movies, *Women at West Point, Letters from Three Lovers.*

Josann McGibbon and Sara Parriott, screenwriters, *Worth Winning, Runaway Bride, The Favor, Exactly 3:30, The List.*

Judith Merians, formerly senior VP, legal and business affairs, Saban Entertainment and Saban International; currently senior VP, business and legal affairs, Regent Entertainment.

Susan Merzbach, VP, Jaffe/Lansing Productions; president, Sally Field's Fogwood Films, executive VP, Clavius Base; executive VP, Segue Productions.

Brianne Murphy, cinematographer; first woman admitted to the local cameraman's union, 1975; first woman member of ASC, 1983; Academy Award recipient (technical) for the Mitchell Camera Car, 1982.

Marcia Nasatir, producer, *The Big Chill, Ironweed, Hamburger Hill, A Match Made in Heaven, Vertical Limit;* first woman VP, United Artists, 1974 (*Rocky, One Flew Over the Cuckoo's Nest*).

Winifred White Neisser, senior VP, movies for television and miniseries, Columbia TriStar Domestic Television.

Anne Nelson, VP, business affairs, CBS Entertainment.

Donie Nelson, president, Career Strategies for Writers, and consultant to screenwriters.

Sheila Nevins, executive vice president, Original Programming, HBO; award-winning producer, *I Am a Promise, Educating Peter, Common Threads: Stories from the Quilt, You Don't Have to Die.*

Kathleen Nolan, performer, *The Real McCoys, Broadside* (TV series), *Steel Chariots, The Switch, The Immigrants.* First woman president of SAG (two terms) 1975–79.

Gail Parent, creator, *Babes; Mary Hartman, Mary Hartman*; television writer, *The Carol Burnett Show*; co-executive producer, *The Golden Girls*; producer, *Tracy Takes On*; screenwriter, *The Main Event, Cross My Heart*; author, *David Meyer Is a Mother.*

Amy Pascal, chair, Columbia Pictures (*Awakenings, A League of Their Own, Hanging Up, Ali, The End of the Affair*).

Nancy Hutson Perlman, Hutson Management, Inc.

Joyce Perry, television writer, *Mannix, Laramie, Ironside, Fantasy Island, Eight Is Enough, Room 222, Mickey Spillane's Mike Hammer, True Confessions, Monty Nash, The Waltons.*

Dorothea Petrie, television producer, *Love Is Never Silent, Caroline?, Captive Heart: The James Mink Story, Crash Landing: The Rescue of Flight 232, The Echo of Thunder, The Song of the Lark.*

Julia Phillips, producer. First woman to win the Oscar for Best Picture—*The Sting*. Also produced *Taxi Driver, Close Encounters of the Third Kind*; author, *You'll Never Eat Lunch in This Town Again, Driving Under the Affluence.*

Polly Platt, production designer, *The Last Picture Show; What's Up, Doc?; Terms of Endearment*; producer, *Broadcast News, Bottle Rocket, The War of the Roses*; screenwriter, *Pretty Baby, A Map of the World*; first woman admitted as production designer to Art Director's Guild, 1973.

Ilene Kahn Power, producer, *Gia, Stalin, Roswell, Fatherland, They Call Me Sirr, White Mile, Buffalo Soldiers.*

Marian Rees, producer, Marian Rees Associates, *Miss Rose White, Between Friends, Love Is Never Silent, In Pursuit of Honor, Decoration Day, Cora Unashamed, The Song of the Lark, Almost a Woman, A Death in the Family.*

Sara Risher, chairman, New Line Cinema Productions; executive producer, *Deep Blue, In Love and War, Last Man Standing.*

Dolores Robinson, personal manager, Robinson Entertainment.

Nikki Rocco, president, Universal Picture Distribution; first woman to head a studio distribution division.

Alexandra Rose, producer, *Norma Rae, I Wanna Hold Your Hand, Big Wednesday, Nothing in Common, Quigley Down Under, Frankie and Johnnie, The Other Sister.*

Meta Rosenberg, producer, TV series, *The Rockford Files*; films, *Skin Game, Scott Free, The New Maverick, Off the Minnesota Strip.*

Jean Rouverol, screenwriter, *So Young, So Bad; Face in the Rain;* TV writer, *Guiding Light, As the World Turns;* author, *Refugees from Hollywood, Writing for Daytime Drama.*

Andrea Sachs, chief lighting technician, *Nowhere to Run, Love Letter, White Sands,* second unit, *Deuce, Dunston Checks In, Last Action Hero, Higher Learning.*

Linda Seger, international script consultant; lecturer; author, *Making a Good Script Great, Creating Unforgettable Characters, From Script to Screen, When Women Call the Shots, Making a Good Writer Great, The Art of Adaptation.*

Treva Silverman, television writer, *The Monkees, Room 222, Taxi,* first woman executive on a comedy show, *The Mary Tyler Moore Show* (Emmy), television features (*Act One, Going All the Way, Nice Girl*) and plays (*Heart's Desire, Scandal*).

Donna Smith, President/CEO Cinema Completions International; at Universal, senior VP; first woman to head physical production for any major studio.

Leslie Smith, director-producer, national commercials.

Noreen Stone, screen and television writer, *Amy, Tricks of the Trade, The Paper Chase, Power's Play.*

Barbra Streisand, director/producer, *Yentl, The Prince of Tides, The Mirror Has Two Faces;* producer, *A Star Is Born, The Main Event, Nuts;* writer, *Yentl;* composer, "Evergreen" for *A Star Is Born,* "I Finally Found Someone" for *The Mirror Has Two Faces,* and the score of *Nuts.*

Robin Swicord, screenwriter, *Shag, You Ruined My Life;* writer/producer, *Little Women, Matilda, The Perez Family, Practical Magic.*

Anthea Sylbert, costume designer, *Julia, Chinatown* (Oscar nominee for both); producer, *Protocol, Something to Talk About,* Emmy-winning *Truman;* writer/producer, *If You Believe, Giving Up the Ghost.*

Betty Thomas, performer, *Hill Street Blues;* director, *The Late Shift, Doctor Doolittle, The Brady Bunch Movie, Can't Hardly Wait, 28 Days, I Spy;* executive producer, *Charlie's Angels.*

Lily Tomlin, multiple Emmy Award–winning performer, writer, producer, *Lily, Lily; Sold Out; The Search for Signs of Intelligent Life in the Universe;* three animated Edith Ann Specials, written by Janet Wagner, executive-produced by Wagner-Tomlin.

Liv Ullmann, performer, *Cries and Whispers, Scenes from a Marriage, Face to Face;* screenwriter/director, *Sofie;* director, *Private Confessions, Faithless;* author, *Changing;* editor, *Letter to My Grandchild.*

Renée Valente, producer, *Contract on Cherry Street, Blind Ambition, False Witness, Burning Passion: The Margaret Mitchell Story, A Storm in Summer;* one of the first women as VP, in casting, Columbia/Screen Gems, 1973.

Michele Wallerstein, literary agent, The Wallerstein Company.

Winnie Wechsler, Internet executive; formerly executive VP and general manager, Internet & Broadband Services, Lightspan, Inc.; formerly senior VP, Buena Vista Internet Group.

Paula Weinstein, president, Spring Creek Pictures; co-president with Barry Levinson, Baltimore Springcreek Pictures (*Fearless, Truman, The Cherokee Kid, Analyze This, The Perfect Storm*).

Jude Weng, writer, *Survivor, Boot Camp;* director, *Rock and Roll Mystery Tour,* VH1; lead director, *Rivals,* ABC; *24-hour Pass,* NBC.

Jane White, Internet executive; formerly, executive VP and executive producer, Protozoa (3-D performance animation for television and the Web).

Ethel Winant, producer, *George Wallace, All Fall Down;* one of the first women VPs, talent and casting, CBS and NBC.

Christine Zurbach Wiser, producer/director/writer, *Return with Honor,* award-winning feature documentary; *Prospecting for Planets,* and *Stardust: "The Astronomers,"* series, KCET-PBS, National Geographic Specials, *Search for the Great Apes, Zoos of the World.*

Kac Young, director/producer, television and cable, specials and series; currently, VP television production and development, Universal Studios Hollywood.

Lili Fini Zanuck, producer, *Cocoon, Driving Miss Daisy;* director, *Rush, From the Earth to the Moon;* first woman to co-produce the Academy Awards (in 2000); second woman to receive Best Picture Oscar.

Laura Ziskin, president, Fox 2000 (*Courage Under Fire, Soul Food, The Thin Red Line, Fight Club*); producer, *Pretty Woman, No Way Out, What About Bob?;* executive producer, *As Good As It Gets, Dinner with Friends, Fail Safe.* Produced the 74th Academy Awards, 2002.

BIBLIOGRAPHY

Abramowitz, Rachel. *Is That a Gun in Your Pocket?: Women's Experience of Power in Hollywood.* New York: Random House, 2000.

Acker, Ally. *Reel Women: Pioneers of the Cinema.* New York: The Continuum Publishing Co., 1991.

Auletta, Ken. *The Highwaymen.* New York: Harcourt Brace & Co., 1997.

Bach, Steven. *Final Cut: Art, Money, and Ego in the Making of* Heaven's Gate, *the Film That Sank United Artists.* New York: Newmarket Press edition, 1999. Also, New York: William Morrow, 1985 edition.

Bart, Peter. *Who Killed Hollywood?* Los Angeles: Renaissance Books, 1999.

Basinger, Jeanine. *A Woman's View: How Hollywood Spoke to Women, 1930–1960.* Uncorrected Proof. New York: Alfred A. Knopf, 1993.

Beauchamp, Cari. *Without Lying Down: Frances Marion and the Powerful Women of Early Hollywood.* New York: Scribner, 1997.

Biskind, Peter. *Easy Riders, Raging Bulls.* New York: Simon & Schuster, 1998.

Brooks, Tim, and Earle Marsh. *Complete Directory to Prime Time Network and Cable TV Shows,* 6th Ed. New York: Ballantine Books, 1995.

Brouwer, Alexandra, and Thomas Lee Wright. *Working in Hollywood.* New York: Avon Books, 1990.

Brownmiller, Susan. *In Our Time: Memoir of a Revolution.* New York: Dial Press, Random, 1999.

Brownstein, Ron. *The Power and the Glitter.* New York: Random House, 1990.

Estrich, Susan. *Sex and Power.* New York: Riverhead Books, 2000.

Francke, Lizzie. *Script Girls.* London: British Film Institute, 1994.

Friedan, Betty. *The Feminine Mystique.* New York: Dell Publishing Co., Laurel, 1984.

Goldenson, Leonard H., with Marvin J. Wolf. *Beating the Odds.* New York: Charles Scribner's Sons, 1991.

Goldstein, Joshua S. *War and Gender.* Cambridge, UK: Cambridge University Press, 2001.

Gordon, Lois and Alan. *American Chronicle: Six Decades in American Life, 1920–1980.* New York: Atheneum, 1987.

———. *American Chronicle: Year by Year Though the Twentieth Century.* New Haven, CT: Yale University Press, 1999.

Griffin, Nancy, and Kim Masters. *Hit and Run.* New York: Simon & Schuster, 1996.

Haskell, Molly. *From Reverence to Rape: The Treatment of Women in the Movies.* New York: Holt, Rinehart and Winston, 1973.

———. *Holding My Own in No Man's Land: Women and Men and Film and Feminists.* Oxford and New York: Oxford University Press, 1997.

Hymowitz, Carol, and Michaele Weissman. *A History of Women in America.* New York: Bantam Books, 1978.

Kandel, Thelma. *What Women Earn.* New York: The Linden Press/ Simon & Schuster, 1981.

Krasilnosky, Alexis. *Women Behind the Camera.* Westport, CT: Praeger Publishers, 1997.

Lee, Joanna. *A Difficult Woman in Hollywood.* New York: Vantage Press, 1999.

Marcus, Ann. *Whistling Girl.* Los Angeles, CA: Mulholland Pacific Publishing, 1999.

Marlane, Judith. *Women in Television News Revisited: Into the Twenty-First Century.* Austin, TX: University of Texas Press, 1999.

———. *Women in Television News.* New York: Columbia University Press, 1977.

McClintick, David. *Indecent Exposure: A True Story of Hollywood and Wall Street.* New York: William Morrow & Co., 1982.

McCreadie, Marsha. *The Women Who Write the Movies.* New York: Birch Lane Press, 1994.

Miles, Rosalind. *Who Cooked the Last Supper? The Women's History of the World.* New York: Three Rivers Press, 2001.

Obst, Lynda. *Hello, He Lied.* Boston: Little Brown and Company, 1996.

Phillips, Julia. *You'll Never Eat Lunch in This Town Again.* New York: Random House, 1991.

Powdermaker, Hortense. *Hollywood, the Dream Factory.* Boston: Little, Brown and Company, 1950.

Redding, Judith M., Victoria A. and Brownworth, *Film Fatales: Independent Women Directors.* Seattle, WA: Seal Press, 1997.

Rich, B. Ruby. *Chick Flicks: Theories and Memories of the Feminist Film Movement.* Durham, NC: Duke University Press, 1998.

Rosen, Marjorie. *Popcorn Venus: Women, Movies and the American Dream.* New York: Coward, McCann & Geoghegan, 1973.

Rosener, Judy B. *America's Competitive Secret: Utilizing Women as a Management Strategy.* Oxford, UK: Oxford University Press, 1995.

Seger, Linda. *When Women Call the Shots.* New York: Henry Holt, 1996.

Shapiro, Marc. *Pure Goldie.* New York: Birch Lane Press, Carol Publishing Group, 1998.

Slide, Anthony. *Early Women Directors.* New York: Da Capo Press, 1984.

———. *The Silent Feminists: America's First Women Directors.* Lanham, MD: Scarecrow Press, 1996.

Sorensen, Jeff. *Lily Tomlin: Woman of a Thousand Faces.* New York: St. Martin's Press, 1989.

Steel, Dawn. *They Can Kill You but They Can't Eat You.* New York: Pocket Books, 1993.

Underburger, Amy L., ed. *The St. James Women Filmmakers Encyclopedia: Women on the Other Side of the Camera.* Farmington Hills, MI: Visible Ink Press, 1999.

INDEX

Aal, Deborah, 245
ABC, 1, 14, 16, 18, 24, 58, 63, 80–
   91, 93, 101, 152, 158, 176,
   178, 186, 189, 203, 224, 225–
   26, 231, 238, 272, 285, 297,
   318, 424, 428, 432
Abrahams, Jim, 366
Abyss, The, 427
Academy of Motion Picture Arts
   and Sciences, 160, 427
Accidental Tourist, The, 45
Accused, The, 210, 261, 428
Act One, 431
actors
   women as, xi–xii, 3, 18, 32, 34–
      36, 62, 116, 123–24, 129, 140–
      42, 145, 239, 250–51, 253,
      254, 256, 257, 259, 310, 321,
      342–44, 350–51
Adam, 12, 8
Adams, Sam, 92
Adventures in Babysitting, 210
Adventures of Sir Lancelot, The,
   161
A&E, 151
African Queen, The, 60
African-Americans, 67–68, 109,
   157, 162, 183–84, 196, 198–
   201, 242, 246–53, 283–85,
   287, 289
After the Promise, 423
AfterSchool Special, 246
Agency, The, 428
agent(s)
   in the 70's, 29, 38, 42, 58, 92,
      101–3, 105–10, 163, 196
   in the 80's, 196–98, 211, 238,
      239, 244, 245
   in the 90's, 280, 309, 311, 362,
      363
Agrama, Frank, 229
Akkad, Moustapha, 144
Albeck, Andy, 166
Albertson, Jack, 233
Alchemy, 327
Alda, Alan, 25
Alexander, Jane, 169, 212–13, 356,
   377, 423
Alexander's Ragtime Band, 266

Alfred Hitchcock Presents, 426
Alfred Stieglitz, 212, 423
Ali, 430
Alice Doesn't Live Here Anymore,
   145
Alice's Restaurant, 46, 128, 423
Alien, 145, 217
Alien Nation, 427
Aliens, 217, 218, 219, 427
All About Eve, 266
All Fall Down, 432
All in the Family, 5–6, 24, 26–27,
   37, 225, 427
All Night Long, 45
All That Glitters, 32, 429
Allen, Debbie, 235, 250, 342
Allen, Dede, 3, 45, 46–47, 158,
   261, 423
Allen, Paul, 297
Allen, Woody, 45, 105, 347
Alley, Kirstie, 318
Allied Artists, 55
Ally McBeal, 358
Almost a Woman, 430
Amadeus, 171
Amazing Stories, 425
American Dream, 258, 428
American Film, 236
American Film Institute (AFI), 337
   Directors Workshop for Women
      of, xiv, 126, 323, 325, 326,
      355
American Graffiti, 19, 40, 44
American Heart, 210, 427
American International Pictures,
   52, 53, 143
American Short Story, The, 173–74
America's Sweethearts, 428
Amy, 431
Analyze This, 432
Anders, Allison, 358
Andy Griffith Show, The, 102
Angel Dusted, 225
Angela's Ashes, 428
Angelou, Maya, 16, 126
Angie, 424
Animals Nobody Loved, The, 259
Another Vietnam, 428
Antonowsky, Marvin, 181, 211

AOL (America On Line), 152, 297,
   300, 301
Apocalypse Now, 202, 256, 268
Arbus, Loreen, 87, 88–91, 122–23,
   194, 238, 423
Archer, Anne, 239
Archerd, Army, 254
Arkoff, Sam, 52
Armageddon, 427
Armen, M. (Margaret), 6
Armstrong, Gillian, 6, 322
Arner, Gwen, 224
Arquette, Rosanna, 171
Art Director's Guild, 49, 430
Art of Adaptation, The, 431
Arthur, Bea, 26, 29
Arthur, Karen, 45, 128–31, 257,
   423
As Good As It Gets, 307, 425, 432
As the World Turns, 431
ASC, 429
Ashley, Ted, 69–70
Asner, Ed, 81
Assault on Precinct 13, 144
Asseyev, Tamara, 54–55, 146–50,
   423
assistants, 3, 247, 305, 362
Association of Independent Video,
   132
Astaire, Fred, 70, 197
At Long Last Love, 50
Attack of the 50 Ft. Woman, 427
attorneys
   in the 70's, 51–52, 54, 55, 66, 72–
      73, 75, 79, 84–85, 101–2, 123,
      424
   in the 80's, 172, 179–80, 186,
      203, 204, 207, 225, 226
   in the 90's, 283–84, 372
Aubrey, Jim, 101
Auerbach, Larry, 101
Auerback, Norbert, 166
Austin, Stephanie, 358
*Autobiography of Miss Jane Pittman,
   The*, 2, 16, 39
Autumn in New York, 351, 424
Avedon, Barbara, 24, 91–93, 178,
   237
Avildsen, John, 61

Awakenings, 258, 430
Award(s), 123, 227, 247, 250, 259, 263
   Academy (Oscars), 31, 40, 43, 45, 121, 132, 134, 135–36, 145, 146, 160, 249, 255, 258, 264, 266, 268, 357, 365, 434
   Crystal, xiv, 120–21, 196, 236, 278
   Emmy, 20, 26, 34, 39, 62, 135, 227, 237, 258, 285, 348, 349
   Golden Globe, 307
   Palme d'Or, 43
   Peabody, 25
   Woman of the Year, 125
   Writers Guild, 97, 237
Aykroyd, Dan, 266, 267

Babes, 431
Baby Boom, 210
Baby, I'm Back, 104
Babylon 5, 425
Bach, Steven, 166
Bad News Bears, 50
Badham, John, 207
Baer, Amy, 280–82, 423
Baez, Joan, xiii
Bailey, John, 128–29, 257
Bali, 260
Ball, Lucille, 29, 119
Baltimore Springcreek Pictures, 432
Bamboozled, 327
Bancroft, Anne, 126, 137–39
Barish, Leora, 171
Barkley, Deanne, 16, 63, 82, 83, 94
Barnaby Jones, 8
Barnette, Neema, 235, 246–53, 249–50, 255, 423
Barney Miller, 83
Barry, Patricia, 116, 424
Baxters, The, 225, 240, 425
Baynes, Andrea, 177
Beans of Egypt, Maine, The, 210, 426
Beasley, William S., 374
Beast with Five Fingers, The, 144
Beattes, Ann, 235
Beatty, Warren, 15, 46–47, 70
Beaumont, Gabrielle, 224
Beauty and the Beast, 204
Beckett, 45
Beckett, Anne, 366
Begelman, David, 15, 42–43, 58, 149, 162, 164–65, 167, 179, 180, 206
Behlmer, Anna, 265
Belcher, Jim, 31
Belushi, John, 266
Ben Casey, 6
Beneath the Planet of the Apes, 45
Benedek, Barbara, 212
Benjamin, Richard, 145
Benjamin, Robert, 60, 171
Bennett, Carl, 71–72, 73–74, 77
Beowulf, 13
Beresford, Bruce, 267
Bergen, Candace, 106, 224
Bergman, Ingmar, 169
Bergman, Marilyn, 61, 120, 121, 168
Bernhardt, Sarah, 165
Bernstein, Bill, 171, 217
Berrenger's, 426
Bertolucci, Bernardo, 249
Beryl Markham: A Shadow on the Sun, 423
Better Off Dead, 251, 423

Betty White Show, The, 34
Between Friends, 227, 430
Between the Lines, 128
Beverly Hills 90210, 429
Beverly Hills Cop I & II, 197, 262
Bewitched, 104
Big, 152, 258
Big Chill, The, 45, 211–12, 429
Big Easy, The, 45
Big Hawaii, 229
Big Wednesday, 430
Bigelow, Kathryn, 258
Bikel, Ofra, 134
Bill, Tony, 40–42
Biondi, Frank, 192
Birch, Miriam, 258–60, 424
Birth of a Nation, The, 45
Black, Michael, 197
Black Widow Murders, 425
Blancé, Alice Guy, 126
Blazing Saddles, 150
Blind Ambition, 432
Blondell, Joan, 62
Bloodworth-Thomason, Linda, 24, 125, 237
Bloody Mama, 53
Blow, 327
Blue City, 242
Blue Steel, 258
Bluhdorn, Charlie, 81–82
Bob Newhart Show, The, 26, 34
Bochco, Steven, 15, 110, 244, 254, 348
Body Heat, 45, 162
Bogdanovich, Peter, 47, 48–50, 51, 54, 255, 328
Bonanza, 425
Bond, James, 60
Bonet, Lisa, 235
Bonnie and Clyde, 46, 128, 261, 423
Boone, Ashley, 184, 198, 199–200
Boot Camp, 432
Booth, James, 46
Booth, Margaret, 46, 70, 120
Borrowers, The, 358
Boston Strangeler, The, 45
Bottle Rocket, 424, 430
Bound for Glory, 60
Bowser, Yvette Lee, 235
Boxcar Bertha, 53–54, 425
"Boxed In: Women On-Screen and Behind the Scenes in the 2000–2001 Prime-time Season," 428
Boyle, Barbara, 51–52, 54, 55, 116, 119, 157, 170–73, 194, 204, 215, 216, 217, 276, 424
Boys Don't Cry, 358
Boys Next Door, The, 258
Brackett, Leigh, xi
Brady Bunch Movie, The, 253, 431
Brakhage, Stan, 255
Bramson, Bob, 295
Brandy, 285
Braveheart, 428
Breakers, The, 171
Breaking the Maya Code, 426
Brennan, Eileen, 231
Brest, Marty, 206–7
Brian Keith Show, The, 26–27
bribes, 87
Bridges, Lloyd, 81, 318
Brimstone, 425
Broadcast News, 210–11, 430
Broadcast Tapes of Dr. Peter, The, 193
Broadside, 429
Brockie, Pam, 424
Broderick, Matthew, 206

Broken Bridges, 426
Brooks, Albert, 329–30, 331
Brooks, James, 15, 34, 36, 37, 363
Brooks, Mel, 138–39
Brotherhood of Justice, 427
Brown, Charlotte, 35, 36, 39, 125, 361, 363, 424
Brown, David, 41, 266
Brownmiller, Susan, 13, 114
Brubaker, Jim, 220–21, 222, 223
Bruckheimer, Jerry, 261, 262, 264–65
Buccaneer, The, 161
Buchanan, Larry, 143
Buena Vista Internet Group, 432
Buffalo Bill, 232
Buffalo Soldiers, 430
Buffy the Vampire Slayer, 339
Bull, 425
Bullock, Sandra, 312
Bulworth, 358
Burnett, Carol, 160, 227
Burning Passion: The Margaret Mitchell Story, 432
Burns, Allan, 15, 34, 36, 37–38, 363
Burns and Allen, 99
Burns, Red, 300
Burton, LeVar, 107
business affairs, 100–101, 320. *See also* attorneys
Butch Cassidy and the Sundance Kid, 266
Butler, Bob, 244

CAA (Creative Artists Agency), 250, 253, 280
Cage, Nicolas, 256, 291
Cagney & Lacey, 92–93, 152, 178, 224, 225, 236–39, 258, 309, 424, 427
Calamity Jane, 212, 423
Calley, John, 69, 282
Cameron, James, 214–20
Cameron, Sue, 9–10, 86–88, 115–17, 424
Cannell, Stephen, 103
Can't Hardly Wait, 431
Canton, Mark, 60, 202, 203, 282, 283
Cape Fear, 302
Captive Heart: The James Mink Story, 430
Career Strategies for Writers, 429
Carey, 161
Carol Burnett Show, The, 2, 9, 28–29, 430
Caroline?, 430
Carpenter, John, 144–45
Carradine, David, 53
Carroll, Diahann, 162, 354, 357
Carroll, Gordon, 217
Carsey, Marcy, 16, 17–18, 81–83, 87, 88, 91, 93, 178, 224, 225–26, 235, 237, 250–51, 297, 424
Carsey-Werner Co., 93, 250, 297, 424
Carter Country, 427
Carter, Nell, 231
Carter, Virginia, 240, 241
Case Closed, 423
casting, 11, 35, 42, 104, 198, 254, 433
Cavanaughs, The, 183
CBS, 1, 11, 19, 24, 25, 29, 64, 80, 84, 86, 93, 99–101, 159, 191, 194, 205, 212, 225, 226–27,

231, 285, 324, 354, 362, 425, 429, 432
CBS Playhouse, 426
"Celluloid Ceiling, The: Behind the Scenes Employment of Women in the Top 250 Films, 2000," 428
Celluloid Closet, The, 327
Chandler, Raymond, 103
Changing, 432
Chaplin, Charlie, 60, 169
Chariots of Fire, 247
Charlie and the Great Balloon Chase, 233
Charlie's Angels, 93, 183, 335, 427, 431
Chase, Debra Martin, 283, 424
Chen, Carolyn, 327–28
Chen, Joan, 350–52, 374, 424
Cherokee Kid, The, 432
ChickFlicks, 278, 291–92
Children of a Lesser God, 245, 246, 426
Children of Divorce, 428
China Beach, 224, 225, 239, 309, 348, 427, 428
China Syndrome, The, 58, 79
Chinatown, 69, 150, 431
Choice, The, 425
Choose Me, 45
Cidre, Cynthia, 319–20, 424
Cimino, Michael, 161, 163
Cinema Completions International, 431
cinematographers, 21–22, 343, 346, 347, 356, 373. See also gaffers
    in the 70's, 20–23, 136–39, 323
    in the 80's, 218–19, 254, 256, 258
    in the 90's, 323, 327–28, 343
Circle of Violence: A Family Drama, 225
Circus of the Stars, 221
Citizen Kane, 263
City Girl, 255, 256
City of Angels, 291
City of Peace, 347
Claudine, 162
Clavius Base, 429
Clayburgh, Jill, 95
Cleopatra, 155, 266
Clockwork Orange, A, 13
Close Encounters of the Third Kind, 6, 42–44, 58, 150, 198, 430
Close, Glenn, 212
Close to Danger, 423
Clueless, 308
CNN (Cable News Network), 1, 152
Coates, Anne V., 45
Cocoon, 266, 267, 432
Coleman, Dabney, 232
Colleton, Sara, 311
Color of Money, The, 45
Color Purple, The, 210
Columbia Pictures, xii, 41, 42–43, 44, 57–58, 78, 79, 105, 149, 152, 155–56, 187, 199, 202, 210, 211, 212, 247, 249, 253, 267, 272, 277, 279, 281, 284, 308, 319, 320, 321–23, 423, 426, 431. See also Sony/ Columbia Pictures
Columbia Pictures Television, 104, 121, 158, 177, 178, 247, 248, 424, 426
Columbia TriStar, 59, 113, 280, 286, 425, 429
Columbia/ScreenGems, 12–13, 432

Columbo, 24
comedy, 363
    for the 70's, 24–40, 82, 91–93, 104, 125
    for the 80's, 286
Coming Home, 60, 364–65
Common Threads: Stories from the Quilt, 429
Compulsion, 266
Connery, Sean, 264
Conrack, 426
Contract on Cherry Street, 104, 432
Conversation with Gregory Peck, A, 428
Cook, Melanie, 158, 215, 216, 375, 424
Cooke, John, 299
Coolidge, Martha, 128, 255–57, 326, 345, 349, 424
Cooney, Joan Ganz, 173
Cooper, Jackie, 12
Coppola, Francis Ford, 56, 58, 105, 202, 256
Cora Unashamed, 430
Corday, Barbara, 24, 91–94, 121–22, 158, 178–79, 205, 237, 424
Corman, Julie, 51–56, 127–28, 145–46, 425
Corman, Roger, 15, 48, 51–56, 116, 127, 142–43, 146–47, 209, 214, 215
Corrina, Corrina, 329, 428
Corrington, Bill, 53
Corrington, Joyce, 53
Cort, Bob, 156
Cosby, Bill, 250, 251
Cosby Mysteries, The, 423
Cosby Show, The, 224, 225, 235, 250, 424, 428
Costner, Kevin, 305
costume designers, 45, 68, 205, 215
Counselor at Law, 32, 425
Courage Under Fire, 284, 424, 432
Cox, Nell, 128
Crash Landing: The Rescue of Flight 232, 98, 430
Craviotto, Darlene, 227
Crawford, Joan, 308
Crawford, Wayne, 256
Crazy in Alabama, 427
Creating Unforgettable Characters, 431
Creeping Toes, The, 144
Crenna, Richard, 25
Cries and Whispers, 40, 51, 342, 432
DeVito, Danny, 358
Crime and Passion, 165
Crimes Closed, 423
Critical Path, 426
Cronyn, Hume, 98
Crosby, Camille, 354–55, 357
Crosby, Mary, 159
Crosby Mysteries The, 423
Cross My Heart, 430
Crossing Delancey, 258
Crossing Jordan, 310
Crossings, 423
Cry in the Wild, A, 425
C.S.I., 428
Curley-Kerner, Joanne, 233, 427
Curtis, Jamie Lee, 144
Cutout, The, 320
CyberJustice, 301, 427
Cybill, 224, 424

Da, 425
Daisy Miller, 50

Dallas, 119, 151, 159, 224, 425
Daly, Bob, 317
Daly, Tyne, 252
Danger in Paradise, 229
Daniel Boone, 93
Daniels, Sean, 304
Danilovic, Mariana, 298–99, 425
Dante, Joe, 52
Dark Holiday, 225, 425
Darling, Joan, 32–34, 128, 144, 425
Davenport, Dorothy, 40
David Meyer Is a Mother, 430
David Off and On, 132
Davids, Hollace, 425
Davidson, Karla, 72–73
Davis, Frank, 72–73
Davis, Geena, 313
Davis, Madelyn Pugh, xi, 27
Davis, Marvin, 152, 157
Davis, Ossie, 162
Day in the Life of America, A, 260
Days of Our Lives, 116, 328
Days of Thunder, 261, 262, 265
De Luca, Michael, 293
De Niro, Robert, 220, 339
De Passe, Suzanne, 52, 120, 157, 161, 199
Dead Zone, The, 427
Dean, Dixon, 225, 226
Dean Martin Show, The, 14
Death in the Family, A, 430
Death-Defying Acts, 426
Decline of Western Civilization Part II: The Metal Years, The, 258
Decline of Western Civilization, The, 258
Decoration Day, 225, 430
Dee, Ruby, 354, 357
Deep Blue, 430
Deep Impact, 269, 349, 428
Deer Hunter, The, 161
Defenders, The, 425
Defending Our Daughters, 428
DeFina, Barbara, 302
Deknatel, Jane, 194, 195
Demme, Jonathan, 52, 209
Democratic Party, 121–22
depression, 7
Designing Women, 224
Desperately Seeking Susan, 171–72
Despres, Loraine, 118–19, 159, 425
Deuce, 431
development, 72–74, 81, 92–93, 225, 288–90
D-girl, 71, 321
DeVito, Danny, 358
DGA (Director Guild), 114, 129, 159, 192, 222, 242, 247, 252, 339–41, 348, 357, 374, 425
Diagnosis Murder, 423
Diamond, Janis, 315–18, 425
Diamond, Selma, 27, 91
Diary of a Mad Housewife, 145
Dick Van Dyke Show, The, 102
Die Hard, 184
Different World, A, 225, 235, 250, 427
Diff'rent Strokes, 26
Digital Media X LLC, 425
Diller, Barry, 15, 80–82, 183, 185, 198, 276
Dillon, Melinda, 35
Dingilian, Bob, 199–200
Dinner with Friends, 432
DiNovi, Denise, 278, 320, 322
directing, xi, xiv, 16, 40, 126, 250, 293, 369, 373, 240216

directing (*cont.*)
  in the 70's, 32–34, 104, 126–36,
    137–39, 144, 346
  in the 80's, 159–60, 165–69, 214,
    224, 242–69, 257–58, 259,
    264, 369
  in the 90's, 6, 279, 322, 323,
    327, 329, 334, 342–52, 354–
    59, 374
  American Film Institute (AFI)
    Directors Workshop for
    Women for, xiv, 126, 323,
    325, 326
  assistant (AD), 215, 217, 218,
    219, 228, 248, 323, 339–41
  documentary, 132–36, 258, 357
director of photography. *See*
    cinematographers
Disney, 203, 204, 205, 259, 272,
    285, 297, 299, 306, 366
Disney Channel, The, 299
distribution. *See* marketing
distributors, 55, 180–83, 199
Dixon, Dianne, 288–90, 425
Dixson, Alyss, 288–90, 371, 425
D.O.A., 210, 305
Doctor Doolittle, 155, 431
Doctor, The, 306, 426
Doctors, The, 92
documentary, 132–36, 191–93, 240,
    247, 258, 259, 323–24, 324–
    25, 327, 347, 357
Doel, Frances, 53, 54
Dog Day Afternoon, 45, 46, 423
Donner, Lauren Shuler, 312, 319,
    358
Doran, Lindsay, 365
Dore, Bonny, 88–89, 119, 425
Doris Day Show, The, 37
Dororetz, Wendy, 311
Double Indemnity, 103
Double Jeopardy, 291–92, 308
Double Take, 288, 428
Douglas, Michael, 152
Dowd, Nancy, 365
Dr. Kildaire, 228
Dragon and the Pearl, The, 426
Dream On, 427
DreamWorks SKG, 187, 203, 205,
    348, 426
Dreyfuss, Richard, 353
Driving Miss Daisy, 153, 266, 267,
    268, 432
Driving Under the Affluence, 430
drugs, 43
Dubrow, Donna, 312
Dudes, 258
Duke, Patty, 124
Dunaway, Faye, 69, 105
Duncan, Michael Clarke, 108
Dunston Checks In, 431
Duvall, Robert, 196
Dynasty, 83, 119, 151, 152, 224,
    243, 425, 426

Echo of Thunder, The, 430
Edgework Productions, 428
editors, 40, 44–47, 71, 127, 131,
    254, 255, 265, 302, 351, 366
  sound, 261–66
Educating Peter, 429
Edwards, Marion, 293–97, 425
Eight Is Enough, 430
Eight Men Out, 171, 424
Eisner, Jane, 231
Eisner, Michael, 15, 82–83, 189,
    198, 203, 231
El Salvador, 428

*Eleanor and Franklin: The White
    House Years*, 423
Eleanor, First Lady of the World,
    225, 240, 425
Elephant Man, The, 45, 137
Eliot, Alison, 98
Elmes, Fred, 256
Emigrants, The, 342
Empire of the Sun, 210
Empire Strikes Back, The, 156
Empty Nest, 91, 224
Emshwiller, Ed, 132
End of the Affair, The, 430
End of the Game, The, 132
Engelhardt, Ruth, 101–3, 106,
    425
English, Diane, 224, 237
Entertainment Industry Affairs,
    428
Ephron, Nora, 249, 279
Equal Employment Opportunity
    Act (1972), 2, 72, 86, 89, 225–
    26, 237, 269
Equal Rights Amendment, 2, 11,
    14, 30, 56, 167, 282
ER, 339, 348, 363, 428
Erin Brockovich, 358
Escapade, 161
Escape from L.A., 427
Escape from New York, 145
ESPN, 151, 296
Estrin, Jonathan, 237
E.T., 45, 151, 210
"Evergreen," 431
Everybody's All American, 210, 305
Exactly 3:30, 312, 429
Execution, The, 429
executive producer, 42, 87, 119,
    229, 240, 285, 347, 363, 364,
    366, 373
executive, studio
  in the 70's, 42, 51, 57–61, 65–
    70, 73, 79, 87, 106, 126
  in the 80's, 155–59, 170–89, 203,
    210, 211, 239, 248
  in the 90's/2000, 272, 276–77,
    280–82, 291–93, 301–5, 307–8
  head, 277–79, 306
Eyes of Laura Mars, 305

F/X, 171
Face in the Rain, 431
Face to Face, 432
Facts of Life, The, 26, 240, 427
Fail Safe, 432
Faithless, 343, 345, 432
Falcon and the Snowman, 152
Falcon Crest, 429
Falcon, Ellen, 235
Falkenhagen, Pat, 71–72
Fallen Champ, 428
Falling Lessons, 426
False Witness, 432
Fame, 161, 201, 250
family
  linked to film/radio/TV
    industry, 61, 90–91, 162–63,
    232, 280, 348
  not linked to film/TV industry,
    xiii, 28, 33, 41, 43, 59, 67,
    109, 128–29, 165, 177, 191,
    216, 227–28, 233, 240–41, 252–
    53, 262, 287, 303–4, 311, 319,
    325, 335, 338–39, 350
Family, 118
Family Affair, 26
Family Feud, 87
Family Law, 310, 366

Family Ties, 250, 316
Fantasy Island, 183, 430
Far Harbor, 327
Farinacci, Tony, 85
Fast Times at Ridgemont High, 258
Fatal Attraction, 196, 210, 369, 428
Fatal Passion, 426
Father for Charlie, A, 425
Fatherland, 430
Fatso, 137–38
Favor, The, 311–12, 429
Fear of Flying, 42
Fearless, 432
Fehrle, Phil, 236, 237
Feldman, Ed, 37, 92
Feminine Mystique, The (Friedman),
    2
feminists, 5, 14, 17
Ferrara, Lorraine Senna, 224
Ferrell, Tyra, 251, 252
Field, Fern, 31–32, 240–41, 246,
    425
Field of Dreams, 304
Field, Sally, 40, 136, 146, 148–49,
    210, 305, 430
Fields, Freddie, 42, 162, 164, 206–
    7
Fields, Verna, 3, 40, 44–47, 65,
    120, 130, 158, 262, 267
15 Minutes, 339
Fight Club, 432
film(s)
  blockbuster, 1, 56, 58
  chick, 255–57, 257–58, 278, 291–
    92, 321–22, 368–69
  desert experience (20's to 70's)
    for women in, xii–xiii
  family, 151
  foreign markets for, 272
  independent, 15, 51–56, 116,
    127, 142, 348
  perseverance needed for, 227,
    259–61, 301, 374
  revenue in 90's for, 272
  sacrificing effort for, 48–49, 55,
    217
  studio head, 272, 276–77, 279,
    306
Film Czar, 427
film(s). *See also* executive, studio
film studios, 1
Filmways, 92
Finestra, Carmen, 231
Finnegan, Patricia, 224, 228–30,
    231, 425
Finnegan, William, 228–29
Fires Within, 320
First Do No Harm, 366
First Impressions, 425
First Love, 34, 128
First Wives Club, The, 308, 428
Fisher King, The, 210, 213, 427
Fisher, Lucy, 59, 67, 113, 120, 157,
    158, 170, 199, 201, 277, 279,
    282, 286, 316–17, 425
F.I.S.T., 69
Five Easy Pieces, 150
Five Finger Discount, 137
Flashdance, 261, 262
Fleiss, Heidi, 272
Flintstone Kids, The, 88
Fog, The, 145
Fogwood Films, 210, 305, 429
Fonda, Jane, 40, 41, 120, 136, 145,
    163, 307, 364
Fontana, D. (Dorothy) C., 6, 425
For My Daughter's Honor, 426
Ford, Harrison, 313

Forrest Gump, 200, 428
Fortunate Pilgrim, The, 425
Foster, Christine, 177, 426
Foster, Jodie, 88, 210
Fox 2000, 105, 175, 305, 432
Fox Broadcasting, 272
Fox International TV, 425
Foxfire, 98
Frances, Anne, 81
Frank, Harriet, Jr., 426
Frankie and Johnnie, 430
Franklin, Michael H., 8, 10
Frankovich, Peter, 226–27
Frank's Place, 247, 250
Freak City, 357, 428
Free to Be You and Me, 2, 39
Freeman, Morgan, 267
French Connection, The, 155, 266
Friday Dinner on Middleneck Road, 426
Friedan, Betty, 2, 375, 376
Friendly Fire, 160, 427
Friends, 26, 361
Friends for Life, 428
From Script to Screen, 431
From the Earth to the Moon, 268, 432
Fuchs, Michael, 192, 194–95
Fun and Games, 45
Funny Lady, 45
Funny, You Don't Look 200, 353
Fuzz, 92

Gabor, Zsa Zsa, 151
gaffer (CLT), 265, 323, 327, 332–35
Gainey, Celeste, 327
Gallo, Lillian, 80–82, 88, 89, 94–96, 112–13, 117, 426
Garner, James, 103
Garner, Todd, 272
Garnet, Tony, 277
Garrett, Lila, 6, 104, 426
Gas Food Lodging, 358
Gavin, John, 124
Geffen, David, 198, 205
Geller, Phylis, 173–75, 369, 426
gender discrimination, 174, 204, 278, 375–76. *See also* sexism
  employment ads, opportunity and, 1–2
  women's writer's statistics, employment discrimination and, 10–11
General Electric, 18, 152
General Hospital, 328, 429
Generations, 328
Gentle Ben, 29
Gentleman's Agreement, 155, 266
George Wallace, 432
Gere, Richard, 312, 351
Ghost, 199, 308
Ghost and the Darkness, The, 427
Gia, 430
Gibson, Mel, 264
Gielgud, John, 353
Gilbert, Melissa, 124
Giles, David, 217
Gilliam, Terry, 303
Gimbel, Roger, 17–18, 19, 20, 97, 225
Gimme Shelter, 191
Gimmie a Break!, 231
Girl, 327
Girl in the Cadillac, 327
Girl Interrupted, 425
Girl Who Couldn't Lose, The, 104, 426
Girlfight, 358

Girlfriends, 128
Girls Club, 315
Gish, Lillian, 335
Giving Up the Ghost, 431
Gladiator, 425
Glass House, The, 16
Gleason, Michael, 128, 129
Gless, Sharon, 237
Glory, Glory!, 425
Godard, Jean Luc, 203
Godfather, The, 5, 56
Going All the Way, 431
Gold Star Productions, 429
Gold, Sylvia, 198
Goldberg, Gary David, 316
Goldberg, Len, 30, 183, 257, 428
Goldberg, Whoopi, 285, 329, 353
Golden Girls, The, 29, 37, 91, 152, 224, 430
Goldenson, Leonard, 83, 90
Goldman, Mia, 45
Goldrich, Sybil Niden, 233
Goldsmith, Elaine, 106
Goldsmith, Gloria, 8, 117, 118, 194, 426
Goldwyn, Tony, 98
Good News, The, 424
Good Times, 427
Goodbye Charlie, 424
Goodbye, Miss 4th of July, 425
Goodwin, Bob, 254
Gordon, Barbara, 134
Gordon, Chuck and Larry, 231, 304
Gordon, Margie, 231
Gossett, Louis, Jr., 103
Gould, Diana, 5, 16–17, 113–14, 127, 426
Governor and J.J., The, 428
Grace of My Heart, 358
Grace Under Fire, 224, 225, 235, 427
Graduate, The, 137
Grafton, Sue, 5
Grant, Lee, 40, 45, 126, 128, 257, 258
Grazer, Brian, 301, 303
Great Performances, 174
Greely, Bill, 10
Green Mile, The, 108
Greer, Germaine, 13
Gremlins, 210
Grey Gardens, 191
Greystoke, 210
grip, 22, 221, 245, 265, 323, 339–40
Gross, Marcy, 238
Grossman, Iris, 196, 197–98, 363, 426
Guber, Peter, 15, 42, 57, 280, 282, 317
Guiding Light, 116, 431
Guillaume, Robert, 91
Gunsmoke, 99

Haas, Lukas, 98
Haber, Bill, 250
Hackford, Taylor, 135
Hackman, Gene, 197, 305
Haggar, Paul, 262
Hahn, Helene, 203–5, 426
Haines, Randa, 128, 243–46, 255, 306, 368–69, 426
Hairspray, 358
Haley, Jack, Jr., 62, 77
Hall, Cecelia, 261–66, 426
Haller, Dan, 54–55
Halloween, 144–45, 427

Hallowell, Todd, 144
Halpern, Amy, 22, 334, 426
Hamburger Hill, 429
Hamilton, Nancy, 132
Hampton, Tim, 218
Hanging Up, 279, 430
Hank Aaron: Chasing the Dream, 284, 424
Hanley, William, 245
Hannah and Her Sisters, 45
Hansen, Tom, 304
Hanson, Curtis, 55
Harden, Nancy, 61
Harlan County, U.S.A., 132–34, 191, 428
Harper, Valerie, 34–36, 96, 426
Harris, Barbara, 35
Harris, Ed, 209
Harris, Susan, 24, 26, 37, 91, 224
Harrison, Joan, xi
Harron, Mary, 358
Hart to Hart, 131, 183, 257, 423
Haunts of the Very Rich, 81, 426
Having Our Say: The Delaney Sisters' First 100 Years, 354–58, 366, 427, 428
Hawaii Five-O, 228
Hawn, Goldie, 24, 40, 136, 158, 159, 164, 207–8, 209, 374
Hayden, Tom, 163
Hayes, Helen, 241
HBO (Home Box Office), 1, 151, 176, 191, 192, 193–96, 349, 366, 374, 430
Head of the Class, The, 232
Head Over Heels, 128
Healy, Patt, 75
Heartbreak Hotel, 210
Heartbreak Kid, The, 40
Heart's Desire, 431
Heartsounds, 160, 225, 425
Heaven & Earth, 424
Heaven's Gate, 161, 163, 164
Heckerling, Amy, 152, 258, 373
Helen Keller in Her Story, 132
Heller, Rosilyn, 42, 57–59, 61, 158, 210, 248, 251, 307, 426
Hellman, Jerome, 365
Hellman, Lillian, 125, 135–36
Hello, Dolly!, 155
Hemdale Film Corporation, 214, 215, 216
Henderson, Maggie, 107
Henry, Buck, 209
Henry, Gale, 40
Here on Earth, 331, 428
Hershey, Barbara, 53
Hester Street, 128
Heston, Charleton, 98, 124
Hewitt, Don, 191
Hiad, Charles, 212
High Art, 327
Higher Learning, 431
Hijacking of the Achille Lauro*, The*, 423
Hi-Line, The, 424
Hill, Debra, 45, 98, 143–45, 210, 213, 249, 371–72, 427
Hill, George Roy, 41
Hill Street Blues, 34, 110, 244, 253, 254, 255, 426, 431
Hill, Walter, 217
Hirsch, Sylvia, 102, 110
Hirshfield, Alan, 157
Hizzoner, 425
Hoblit, Greg, 244, 348
Hochman, Sandra, 13
Hoffman, Leslie, 335–38, 427

Hollywood Reporter, The, 9, 86, 115–17, 424
Hollywood Vice Squad, 258
Hollywood Women's Political Committee, 121–22
Hombre, 147, 426
Home Improvement, 225, 231, 429
homosexuals, 196
Honey Dust, 424
Hooperman, 253, 254
Hopkins, Ann, 226
Horberg, Bill, 313
Horner, James, 146
Horowitz, Lou, 226
Horowitz, Mitchell, 29
Hot Fudge, 88
Houston, Whitney, 285
How Green Was My Valley, 266
Howard, Tony, 102, 106–7
Hubley, Faith, 127
Hud, 147, 426
Huggins, Roy, 80
Hugo, Michel, 224
Hunt for Red October, The, 261, 264, 426
Hunt, Helen, 225
Hunter, Tab, 55
Hurd, Gale Anne, 54, 142–43, 170, 214–23, 362, 427
Hurt, William, 246
Hustler, The, 423
Hustling, 94, 427
Hutson Management, Inc., 430
Hyams, Joe, 67
Hyams, Nessa, 42, 126
Hyler, Joan, 102, 103, 105–7, 111, 196, 213, 427
Hyler Management, 107, 427

I Am a Promise, 429
"I Finally Found Someone," 431
I Heard the Owl Call My Name, 16
I Know Why the Caged Bird Sings, 16
I Love Lucy, 8, 27, 99
I Love You, Goodbye, 16, 17, 426
I Saw What You Did, 320, 424
I Shot Andy Warhol, 358
I Spy, 102, 431
I Wanna Hold Your Hand, 430
IATSE (International Alliance of Theatrical Stage Employees), 21–22, 144, 222, 332
Ice Castles, 210, 426
Ice Cube, 330
ICM (International Creative Management), 102, 105–7, 105–97, 107, 109–10, 163, 164, 196–98, 236, 363, 424, 426
If These Walls Could Talk, 366
If These Walls Could Talk 2, 424
If You Believe, 431
I'll Do Anything, 210
I'll Take Manhattan, 426
Ilson, Saul, 287
I'm Dancing As Fast As I Can, 223
Imagine That, 427
Immigrants, The, 429
In Broad Daylight, 193–94
In Country, 320, 424
In Her Own Time, 357, 428
In Love and War, 430
In Pursuit of Honor, 430
In the Line of Fire, 45
In This House of Brede, 16
incubators, 15

Indiana Jones and the Temple of Doom, 210
Instinct, 424
Internet, 271, 272, 294, 297–301, 369, 428, 433
interviews, genesis/attitudes of, xiii–xv
Introducing Dorothy Dandridge, 424
Invasion of Privacy, An, 426
Invisible Child, 238
Iron-Jawed Angels, 374, 427
Ironside, 5, 430
Ironweed, 429
Irreconcilable Differences, 210
Isaacs, Cheryl Boone, 44, 198–201, 427
Island, The, 266
It's a Living, 250
It's My Turn, 128

Jackson 5, 161
Jacksons: An American Dream, The, 423
Jacobson, Nina, 272
Jacoby, Nancy, 325
Jaffe, Stanley, 50, 58, 196, 210
Jaffe/Lansing Productions, 261, 429
Jaguar, 213
Jakob the Liar, 45
James, Judith, 175–76, 330, 353–57, 366, 370, 427
James, Monique, 14
Jarvis, Lucy, 259
Javier, Mary Delia, 256
Jaws, xiii, 43, 45, 56, 266
Jeffersons, The, 225
Jeffries, Georgia, 235–39, 309–10, 374, 427
Jenkins, Billie Beasley, 183–85, 245, 427
Jenny, 426
Jerusalem Within These Walls, 260
Jewell, Isabel, 55
Jewison, Norman, 69
Jhabvala, Ruth Prawer, xii
Jill Ireland Story, The, 425
Jilting of Grammy Weatherall, The, 243
John Q, 423
Jones, James Earl, 162
Jones, Shirley, 62
Jones, Tommy Lee, 197, 292
Josephson, Nancy, 107
Joy of Sex, 257
Judd, Ashley, 292
Judging Amy, 310, 366
Julia, 69, 202, 428, 431
Jumanji, 280, 303
Jumpin' Jack Flash, 258
Just the Ticket, 327

K-9, 304
Kahn, Bernie, 104
Kaizen Heron Group, 427
Kalish, Austin "Rocky," 26, 28, 428
Kalish, Irma, 26–28, 427
Kanbar Institute, 425
Kane and Abel, 225, 240, 425
Kane, Carol, 257
Kaner, Mark, 296
Kanin, Fay, 16, 19–20, 39, 94–96, 120, 123, 160, 369, 376, 427
Kanin, Michael, 20
Kaplan, Jonathan, 52
Karloff, Boris, 48
Kasdan, Lawrence, 211, 212

Katzenberg, Jeffrey, 15, 187, 188, 203, 204, 205, 301, 306
Katzman, Len, 159
Kavurick, Deborah, 45
Kay O'Brien, 426
KCET, 135, 174
Keaton, Diana, 279
Keeping On, 258
Keeping Secrets, 425
Kelley, Paula, 252
Kelly, Marcy, 120, 427
Kennedy, Beth, 45, 65–67, 300–301, 427
Kennedy, Florynce, 14
Kennedy, Kathleen, 210, 302
Kenney, Ann, 366
Kerkorian, Kirk, 70, 152, 206
Kernochan, Claire, 132
Killers Inside, 426
Killing in a Small Town, A, 320, 424
Killing of Randy Webster, The, 426
King, Billie Jean, 14
King, Perry, 61
Kinski, Nastassia, 334
Kirgo, George, 104
Kissinger and Nixon, 427
Klausner, Manny, 68
Klausner, Willette, 67–68, 428
Klute, 145
K.M.A., 158
Knight, Viva, 238
Knots Landing, 119, 128, 237, 425, 429
Koffler, Pam, 358
Kojak, 24
Kolb, Mina, 35
Koplovitz, Kay, 190
Kopple, Barbara, 128, 132–34, 148, 191, 258, 428
Kozak, Harley Jane, 312
Kramer vs. Kramer, 79
Krim, Arthur, 60, 171, 215
Krim, Matilda, 60
Kristin Lavransdatter, 343–44, 345
Kristofferson, Kris, 140
Kulik, Buzz, 240
Kull the Conqueror, 338, 339, 428
Kuras, Ellen, 327

Ladd, Alan, Jr., 155, 157, 162, 200, 202, 267
Ladd Company, 162, 199–200
Ladd, Diane, 227
Lady Beware, 130–31, 258
Lady in Red, The, 145–46, 425
Lady Sings the Blues, 161
Ladyhawke, 210
Lahti, Christine, 209
L.A. Law, 224, 239, 243, 254, 348
Lancaster, Bill, 50
Lane, Andrew, 256
Lansing, Sherry, 72, 74–79, 92–93, 106, 155–59, 161, 196, 199, 200, 210, 249, 265, 267, 272, 276, 291, 308, 428
Laramie, 5, 430
Larsen, Tambi, 49
Last Action Hero, 431
Last Emperor, The, 249, 350, 424
Last Man Standing, 430
Last Picture Show, The, 48, 49, 430
Last Temptation of Christ, The, 45
Late Shift, The, 431
Laurents, Arthur, 141
Lauzen, Martha M., 362, 428
Lavar, Bob, 138–39
Laverne & Shirley, 338

Law & Order, 315, 317–18, 425
Law, Lindsay, 15, 366–67
Lawrence of Arabia, 45
Laybourne, Geraldine, 272, 296–97, 300
Lazarus Syndrome, The, 119
Leachman, Cloris, 81, 227
League of Their Own, A, 430
Lear, Norman, 15, 26–27, 28–32, 92, 240, 241, 242
Ledding, Mary, 72–73, 75–76, 78–79, 179–80, 189, 375, 428
Leder, Mimi, 269, 347–50, 428
Lee, Joanna, 6, 39, 79, 104–5, 428
Left-Handed Gun, 46
Legacy, 45, 129, 131, 131sc, 423
Legends of the Fall, 322
Legrand, Michel, 168
Lehman, Robin, 132
Leonard Goldberg Co., The, 245, 427
Leoni, Téa, 349
Letter to My Grandchild, 432
Letters from Three Lovers, 429
Levien, Sonya, xi
Levin, Gerald, 306
Levine, Joe, 84
Levine, Johnna, 84–86, 88, 176, 429
Levinson, Barry, 433
Levy, Norman, 157
Lifetime, 251, 297, 298, 423
Lightspan, Inc., 432
Like Mom, Like Me, 136–37, 429
Like Normal People, 428
Lily, 25–26, 39, 431
Lion's Love, 134
Lipman, Jonathan, 326
Lipton, Dina, 328–31, 428
List, Shelley, 237
List, The, 312, 429
Listen for the Fig Tree, 247, 253
Little Flower, The, 350
Little Gloria, 223
Little Havana, 424
Little Women, 278, 308, 321–22, 431
Little Women in Transit, 327
Littleton, Carol, 45, 128–29, 257–58
Littman, Lynne, 126, 128, 323, 354–58, 364, 366, 428
Liu, Grace, 338–3341, 428
Living in New York, 29
Living Sands of Namib, The, 259
Living Treasures of Japan, The, 259, 424
Living with AIDS, 428
Loesch, Margaret, 199
Logan's Run, 425
Lone Star, 145
Long Hot Summer, The, 18
Long Kiss Goodnight, The, 358
Longest Day, The, 266
Look Who's Talking, 152, 258
Lords of Flatbush, 60, 61
Lorimar Telepictures, 151–52, 226
Lost in Yonkers, 424
Love, 344
Love and Lies, 194
Love at First Sight, 199
Love Boat, The, 118, 335, 425, 427
Love Is Never Silent, 225, 227, 430
Love Letter, 327, 431
Love, Sex & Murder, 424
Love Story, 8
Loveless, The, 258

Loves of a Blonde, 165
Lowe, Rob, 213
Lucas, George, 56, 58, 139
Lucas, Marcia, 40
Lucas Tanner, 92
Lucchesi, Gary, 248
Lumet, Sidney, 197, 266
Lupino, Ida, xi, 129
Lynch, Ed, 132

MacArthur, 266
MacLaine, Shirley, 137, 327
MacMillan, 426
Mad Dog Time, 428
Madalone, Dennis, 336
Madden, David, 156, 313
Madeline, 281
Madigan, Amy, 354, 357
Madonna, 171
Maffeo, Gayle, 230–33, 429
Mafu Cage, The, 45, 129, 257, 423
Magruder, Betsy, 215, 217
Main Event, The, 430, 431
Maine, 210, 427
Making a Good Script Great, 431
Making a Good Writer Great, 431
Malone, John, 306
Malone, Nancy, 16, 18–19, 62, 82, 115–17, 119, 128, 137–38, 224, 429
Maltese Falcon, The, 152
Mambo Kings, The, 45, 424
Man Who Loved Cat Dancing, The, 18, 429
management company, 107, 108
Mancuso, Frank, 187, 248
Mandabach, Caryn, 235, 297
Mann, Emily, 354, 357
Manning, Michelle, 242, 265
Mannix, 430
Manoogian, Haig, 131
Map of the World, A, 430
Marshall, Frank, 210
Marcus, Ann, 6, 29–30, 363–64, 429
Marcus, Ellis, 29
Marcus Welby, M.D., 5
Margolis, Wendy, 211
Marian Rees Associates, 431
Marion, Frances, xii
Marjoe, 132
Marked for Murder, 425
marketing, 67–68, 199–200, 214, 278, 302–3, 322, 365
Marriage: Georgia O'Keeffe and Alfred Stieglitz, A, 212, 423
Mars Needs Women, 143
Marshall, Frank, 49
Marshall, Penny, 152, 258, 179
Martin, Dick, 24
Martin, Pamela Sue, 146
Martin, Quinn, 10
Marva Collins Story, The, 225
Marvin, Nikki, 236
Mary, 232
Mary Hartman, Mary Hartman, 28, 30, 32–33, 425, 429, 430
Mary Jane Harper Cried Last Night, 428
Mary Tyler Moore Show, The, 5–6, 8, 24, 33–39, 125, 424, 425, 426, 431
Masala Productions, 427
M*A*S*H, 24, 25, 62, 125, 224, 425
Mask of Zorro, The, 281
Masterpiece of the Gods, 260
Match Made in Heaven, A, 429

Matilda, 431
Matlin, Marlee, 246
Matter of Sex, A, 258
Matthau, Walter, 50
Maude, 24, 26, 31, 92, 427
Max Is Missing, 425
May, Elaine, 33, 35, 40, 69
Mayer, Louis B., 70, 75, 78, 212
Maysles, David and Albert, 191
MCA, Inc., 14, 67–68, 302
McAnelly, Jac, 146
McCall, Mary, Jr., 124
McElwaine, Guy, 211
McFadden, David, 231
McGibbon, Josann, 311–14, 429
McGovern, Elizabeth, 312
McGraw, Ali, 97, 106
McKeand, Carol Evan, 97
McQueen, Steve, 97
McRaney, Gerald, 252
McTiernan, John, 185
Me and My Hormones, 427
Mean Streets, xiii, 52
Meara, Ann, 104
Mechanic, Bill, 295
Medavoy, Mike, 15, 58, 60, 61, 163, 171, 215, 365
Mediascope, 427
Medical Story, 8
Medoff, Mark, 246
Meir, Golda, 32
Melnick, Daniel, 74, 76–79, 93, 158
men
 (old) boy's club of, 63–64, 213, 217, 277, 281, 293, 347, 374, 375
 difference in working between women and, 229–30, 363–64, 372
 insecurity of, 13, 92, 218, 353
 mistakes of women and, 202, 293, 334–35, 340, 358–59, 362, 368, 375
 power of, 229, 237, 238, 312–13, 363–64, 370, 373
 swearing of, 12, 28, 29, 37, 68, 207, 326, 371
 women helped by, 15, 30, 34–35, 47, 194–95, 198, 203, 218, 224, 237, 262, 277, 292, 295, 348, 350, 363, 366–67, 374
Mengers, Sue, 3, 106, 109, 197
Menke, Sally, 45
Meredith, Burgess, 61
Merians, Judith, 123, 186–89, 372, 429
Merzbach, Susan, 70–73, 75, 77–79, 156, 157, 429
Messenger, The, 144
Meyers, Nancy, 158, 164, 210
MGM, 70–79, 93, 110, 149, 151, 152, 155, 156, 162, 164, 167, 179, 201, 206, 351, 428
MGM-UA Communications, 152, 162, 206
Mickey Spillane's Mike Hammer, 5, 430
Midnight Cowboy, 365
Midnight Express, 247
Miller, Harvey, 158, 164
Millett, Kate, 13
Mills, Steve, 14, 185, 226, 227
minorities, 162, 199, 201, 203, 242, 287–88, 319–20, 325–26, 338–39, 341, 351–52. *See also* African Americans; racism

Mirror Has Two Faces, The, 347, 431
Miss 4th of July, 426
Miss All-American Beauty, 226–27
Miss Rose White, 430
Mission: Impossible I & II, 244
Mitchell Camera Car, 429
Mitchell, John, 104, 225
Mitchum, Robert, 302
Mod Squad, The, 327
Money Talks, 288
Monkees, The, 431
Monsters, 427
Montalban, Ricardo, 103
Monty Nash, 430
Moore, Mary Tyler, 34, 232
Moore, Susan, 45
Moore, Thomas W., 16, 18
Morgan, Robin, 13
Motion Picture Group, 429
Motion Picture Sound Editors, 426
Motown Productions, 157, 161, 199
Mr. Holland's Opus, 330, 355, 427, 428
Mr. President, 235
MRA, 227
Mrs. Munck, 424
Mrs. Soffel, 152
MTM Enterprises, 15, 26, 29, 34, 36–39, 80, 226, 232, 363
MTV, 151, 152, 210, 297
Mulholland Falls, 45
Mulligan's Stew, 428
Mummy, The, 144
Murder by Moonlight, 423
Murder, She Wrote, 243
Murdoch, Lachlan, 91
Murdoch, Rupert, 152, 306
Murphy, Brianne, 14, 21–23, 136–49, 327, 429
Murphy Brown, 224
Murphy's Romance, 147, 210, 305, 426
Muse, The, 329–30, 331, 426, 428
My Best Friend's Wedding, 281, 425
My Bodyguard, 199
My Generation, 428
My Sister Sam, 243
My Three Sons, 26, 292, 427
Mystic Midway, 315

Naked City, 18
Naked Gun, 427
Nasatir, Marcia, 58–61, 74, 76, 97, 158, 170, 171, 180, 202, 210, 211, 253, 307, 364–66, 429
Nash Bridges, 338
National Committee on Working Women (NCWW), 243
National Endowment of the Arts, 272, 423
National Geographic Society Specials, 258–61, 424, 434
Natural, The, 173
NBC, 1, 21, 22, 24, 62, 63, 80, 84, 152, 194, 286–87, 432
Neighbors, 266
Neill, Sam, 240
Neisser, Winifred White, 286–88, 429
Nelson, Anne, 99–101, 362, 375, 429
Nelson, Donie, 71, 74–79, 429
Nelson, Jessie, 329
Nelson, Judd, 256
Nelson, Kathy, 272

networking, 63–64, 82, 112, 114–20, 232, 268, 277, 281, 293, 375
Nevins, Sheila, 191–93, 372, 429
New Directors Program, 249–50
New Guy, The, 428
New Kind of Family, A, 231, 232
New Leaf, A, 33, 40
New Line Cinema, 200, 278, 288, 325, 427, 430
New Maverick, The, 430
new media. *See* Internet
New World Pictures, 15, 51–56, 116, 127, 142, 172, 209
New York University (NYU), 52, 131, 256
Newirth, Tom, 258
Newman, Paul, 42, 120, 164, 266
Next Friday, 330, 428
Nice Girl, 431
Nicholl, Don, 225
Nichols, Mike, 40, 69
Nicholson, Jack, 51, 70
Nickelodeon, 296, 297
Nickelodeon, 50
Nicksay, David, 223
Nicky, 33
Night Call Nurses, 54
Night Hawk Productions, 427
Nightmare on Elm Street, 292, 337
Nimoy, Leonard, 189
9 to 5, 156, 202
No Place Like Home, 258
No Way Out, 210, 305, 432
Nobody's Child, 258
Nolan, Kathleen, 114, 123–24, 429
Nolte, Nick, 346
Norma Rae, 145–49, 202, 209, 376, 423, 426, 430
Norman Star Media, 426
Normand, Mabel, 40
North Carolina School of Arts, 328
Not a Pretty Picture, 131–32, 255, 424
Nothing in Common, 430
Notting Hill, 272
Nowhere to Run, 333, 425, 431
NRW, 225, 226
Number Our Days, 428
Nuts, 263, 264, 431
Nutty Professor, The, 303

Obst, Lynda, 58, 210, 212–13, 249, 261, 305, 307, 369
O'Connor, Carroll, 26
Odds Against Tomorrow, 46
Off the Minnesota Strip, 430
Old Fashioned Women, 132
Olivier, Larry, 197
Once Upon a Time in America, 200
One Flew Over the Cuckoo's Nest, 60, 215, 429
One from the Heart, 201
One More Hurdle—The Donna Cheek Story, 246–47, 423
O'Neal, Ryan, 49
O'Neal, Tatum, 49–50
Ophelia Learns to Swim, 427
Oppewall, Jeannine Claudine, 329
Ordeal of Patty Hearst, The, 229
Original Programming, 430
Orion Pictures, 92, 157, 164, 171–73, 194, 211, 215, 216, 217
Orphan Train, 96–97, 225
Ostroff, Dan, 312, 313
Other Sister, The, 149, 430
Other Woman, The, 104, 426
Out of Africa, 278

Out to Sea, 424
Overboard, 209
Ovitz, Michael, 302
Owen Marshall, 32, 425
Oxygen Channel, The, 272, 296–98, 424

Paddy, 55
Paley, William, 99–101
Paper Chase, The, 431
Paper Moon, 44, 47, 48, 328
Pappas, Irene, 144
Paramount Decree, 180
Paramount Studios, xii, 42, 61, 81, 152, 187, 188, 199, 200, 201, 203, 234, 242, 245, 248, 256–57, 262, 265, 272, 308, 316, 425, 429
Parent, Gail, 6, 24, 28–29, 35, 36, 430
Parker, Rod, 31
Parriott, Sara, 311–14, 429
Partridge Family, The, 8
Party of Five, 339
Pascal, Amy, 105, 272, 277–79, 282, 284, 307–8, 321–23, 375, 430
Passer, Ivan, 165
Passion Fish, 145
Patton, 155
Pay It Forward, 428
Peacemaker, The, 348, 428
Peck, Gregory, 302
Peirce, Kimberly, 358
Pelican Brief, The, 284
Penalty Phase, 423
Penn, Arthur, 46–47, 128
Perez Family, The, 431
Perfect Storm, The, 432
Perfect Tribute, The, 98
Perlman, Nancy Hutson, 122–23, 150, 376–77, 430
Perry Como Show, The, 231
Perry, Eleanor, 119
Perry, Joyce, 5, 7, 8, 9–10, 430
Peter and the Wolf, 318
Peters, Barbara, 56
Peters, Brock, 162
Peters, Jon, 140, 280, 282, 305
Petrie, Dan, Jr., 96–97, 197, 212
Petrie, Dorothea, 96–98, 225, 227, 430
Phenomenon, 424
Philbin, Regis, 87
Phillips, Julia, 40, 41–44, 45, 61, 121, 153, 266, 430
Phillips, Lee, 229
Phillips, Michael, 40–43
Photoplay, 256
Pickford, Mary, xii, 40, 60
Pierson, Frank, 140
Pillsbury, Sara, 171, 172, 312
Pink Panther, 60
Pinky, 155
Piranha, 145
Pitt, Bill, 312
Place, Mary Kay, 24, 125
Place for Annie, A, 238
Places in the Heart, 45
Plan 9 from Outer Space, 104
Platoon, 45, 171, 230
Platt, Polly, 47–51, 52, 54, 210, 328, 430
Players Club, The, 330
Playing for Time, 423
Pleasance, Donald, 144
Please Don't Eat the Daisies, 29
Pleskow, Eric, 60, 171, 173, 217

Plumley, Barry, 214
Pocket Filled with Dreams, 105
Poitier, Sidney, 42, 164
Polanski, Roman, 69
Police Academy, 200
Pollack, Sydney, 141
Pollock, Tom, 304–5
Ponder Heart, The, 424
Portrait, The, 128
Power, Ilene Kahn, 176, 193–96, 430
Power's Play, 431
Powers, Stefanie, 257–58
Practical Magic, 431
Preacher's Wife, The, 284, 424
Precht, Bob, 25
Prehistoric Woman, 424
Pretty Baby, 430
Pretty in Pink, 210
Pretty Woman, 308, 432
Price, Frank, 181, 211, 212, 283
Pride and Prejudice, 423
Prince of Tides, The, 346, 431
Princess Daisy, 426
Princess Diaries, The, 424
Prisoner of Honor, 427
Private Benjamin, 158, 164
Private Confessions, 344, 432
Prizzi's Honor, 189
producer, 112, 121, 123, 166, 205, 206, 209, 210–23, 214, 224–41, 235–36, 237, 238, 244, 247, 248, 255
    documentary, 191–93
    line, 223, 239
    movie, in 70's, 31, 40–44, 51–56, 61, 68, 70, 105, 129, 132, 142–50, 346
    movie, in 80's, 163, 209, 257–58
    movie, in 90's, 279, 284, 302, 304, 305–6, 312, 313, 339, 344–46, 350–51, 357, 358
    TV, in 70's, 12, 18–19, 103–4, 117–18, 363
    TV, in 80's, 193–96, 224–41, 240
    TV, in 90's, 309–10, 324, 363, 364, 372
    TV-movie, in 70's, 80–81, 89, 93, 94–98, 103, 104, 137–38, 225, 228
    TV-movie, in 80's, 242–53
    TV-movie, in 90's, 205, 285, 347, 353–56, 366, 374
production, 206, 304–5, 331, 334–35, 339, 340–41, 346, 355–56
production companies, 40, 42, 55, 79, 136, 140–41, 164, 178, 199, 208, 209, 210, 211, 214, 215, 220, 224, 225, 226, 229, 234, 242, 259, 266, 284, 285, 297, 305, 311, 312, 351, 374, 430
production companies. *See also* MTM Enterprises; Tandem Productions; Tomorrow Entertainment
production designer, 48–49, 97, 229, 256, 328–31
production manager, 216, 221–22, 228, 331, 339
Prospecting for Planets, and Stardust: "The Astronomers," 432
Protocol, 209, 431
Protozoa, 432
Pryor, Richard, 25
Public Broadcasting System (PBS), 24, 128, 135, 173, 367

publicists, 3, 44, 75–76, 91, 199–200, 249
Pullman, Bill, 312
Pulp Fiction, 45
Puttnam, David, 247, 248, 249, 253
Pygmalion, 279

Quicksand: No Escape, 225, 425
Quigley Down Under, 430
Quinn, Anthony, 144
Quiz Show, 427

racism, 185, 200–201, 213, 228, 287, 289, 352–53
radio, 99–100
Raging Bull, 45, 161, 222, 262
Raiders of the Lost Ark, 151
Rambling Rose, 345, 424
Rape of Richard Beck, The, 131, 423
Rat Entertainment, 425
Ratner, Brett, 288
Ravetch, Harriet Frank, Jr. and Irving, 146–50, 426
Reagan, Ronald, 2
Real McCoys, The, 25, 429
Reason for Living, 425
Reckless, 223
Red Corner, 339
Red Shoes, The, 136
Red Wagon Productions, 59, 426
Redford, Robert, 41, 141, 152
Reds, 45, 46, 423
Rees, Marian, 16, 19, 20, 82, 97–98, 225–28, 366, 430
Refugees from Hollywood, 431
Reid, Tim, 247
Reiker, Tami, 327
Reiner, Rob, 26
Reivers, The, 426
Relic, The, 427
Remick, Lee, 95
Remington Steele, 34, 131, 258, 335, 423
Renzi, Maggie, 358
Rescue, The, 210
Rescuers: Stories of Courage: Two Couples, 428
Reservoir Dogs, 45
Resurrection Blvd., 429
Return with Honor, 432
Reynolds, Burt, 18, 92
Rhoda, 34, 125, 363, 424, 425, 426
Rich, Elaine, 224
Rich Man, Poor Man, 129, 130
Richie Rich, 88
Riding in Cars, 279
Riggs, Bobby, 14
Right Stuff, The, 200
Risher, Sara, 278, 288, 430
Riskin, Victoria, 27, 124
Ritchie, Michael, 50, 209
Ritt, Martin, 147, 149, 263
Ritter, John, 254
Rivals, 432
River, The, 264
River's Edge, 171
Roadie, 161
Robards, Jason, 98, 213
Roberts, Julia, 284, 312
Robin Hood, 162
Robinson, Dolores, 107–9, 430
Robinson Entertainment, 108, 430
Rocco, Nikki, 181–82, 272, 301–3, 430
Rock and Roll Mystery Tour, 432
Rockford Files, The, 33, 103, 110, 430

Rocky, 60, 147, 220, 429
Rocky II, 221, 222
Roddenberry, Gene, 6
Rodgers & Hammerstein's Cinderella, 285
Rodman, Howard, 8
Roe v. Wade, 2, 26
Rookie of the Year, 88
Room 222, 5, 430, 431
Room with a View, A, xii
Rooney, Mickey, 70
Roots, 89, 107, 151, 176
Rose, Alexandra, 54, 146–50, 209, 376, 430
Rose, Kay, 264
Roseanne, 224, 225, 230–33, 424, 429
Rosen, Arnie, 28
Rosen, Deborah, 200
Rosen, Marjorie, 13
Rosenberg, Mark, 161, 320
Rosenberg, Meta, 33, 103–4, 430
Rosenfeld, Michael, 250
Rosenfelt, Frank, 72, 201
Rosenfield, Jonas, 199
Rosenman, Howard, 43
Rosenthal, Ann, 102, 103
Rosenthal, Jack, 164
Rosenthal, Jane, 194
Rosenzweig, Barney, 93, 236–37
Roswell, 430
Rothman, Marion, 45
Rothstein, Freyda, 193
Rouverol, Jean, 5, 7, 8, 431
Rowan, Dan, 24
Ruby Bridges, 366
Rudin, Scott, 223, 279
Rule, Elton, 83
Run for the Dream: The Gail Devers Story, 423
Runaway Bride, 313, 429
Rush, 268, 432
Rush Hour, 288
Russell, Kurt, 209
Ryan, Meg, 291
Ryder, Winona, 213, 278, 351

Saban Entertainment/International, 429
Sachs, Andrea, 431
Sacova, Nancy, 359
SAG (Screen Actors Guild), 5, 114–15, 123–25, 151, 222, 336, 425, 429
Sage, Karin, 280
Salhany, Lucie, 200, 272
Salkowitz, Sy, 62
Sandrich, Jay, 250
Sands, Diana, 162
Sanford and Sons, 24, 25, 37
Sanford, Midge, 171, 172, 312
Sapphire Films, 162
Sargent, Joe, 95, 227
Save the Panda, 258, 260, 424
Say Anything..., 210
Sayles, John, 51, 145–46, 358
Scacchi, Greta, 320
Scandal, 431
Scandalous Summer of Sissy LeBlanc, The, 425
Scenes from a Marriage, 342, 432
Schell, Max, 98, 349
Schenck, Joseph, 155, 266
Scherick, Edgar, 223
Schlatter, Geroge, 24
Schoomaker, Thelma, 45
Schrader, Paul, 197
Schreiber, Nancy, 327

Schwartz, Nancy Lynn, 137
Schwartz, Terri, 263, 264
Schwartz, Terry, 54
Scooby Doo, 88
Scorsese, Martin, 43, 45, 51, 52–54, 105, 131, 139, 222, 262, 302
Scott Free, 430
Scott, Jan, 97
script supervisors, 3, 45, 131, 143–44, 231, 243, 244, 323, 347
Search for Signs of Intelligent Life in the Universe, The, 431
Search for the Great Apes, 259, 432
Search for Tomorrow, 29, 429
Sears, Fran, 234
Second City, 35
Secondari, Helen, 259
Secret Life of Kathy McCormick, The, 426
Secret of Roan Inish, The, 145
Seger, Linda, 431
Segue Productions, 429
Seidelman, Susan, 171, 172
Seidman, Lisa, 237
Senior Year, 92
Serpico, 46, 47, 423
Serving in Silence: The Margarethe Cammermeyer Story, 347
Sesame Street, 173
Sex and the City, 366
sex, lies and videotape, 152
sexism, 74–75, 100, 118, 127, 131–32, 265, 287, 288–89, 356, 358–59, 369, 371
sexuality
  fear for marriage and, 113
  harassment, 78–79, 117–18, 182–83, 186–87, 189, 326, 340, 370–71
  use of (flirtations with), 13, 31, 256, 314
Shabe, Donna, 250
Shag, 431
Shakespeare in Love, 291
Shamberg, Michael, 212
Shampoo, 58
Shane, Alan, 177
Shapiro, Esther, 8, 83, 224
Shapiro Lichtman, 426
Shapiro, Lisa, 106
Shapiro, Richard, 224
Shatner, William, 189
Shaw, George Bernard, 47
Shawshank Redemption, The, 236
Shaye, Robert, 292
Shearer, Moira, 136
Sheehy, Gail, 94, 95
Sheila Levine Is Dead, 29
Sheinberg, Sid, 14, 302, 305
Shepherd, Cybill, 48
Sheppard, Dick, 78
Sher, Stacy, 358
Sherlock Holmes in New York, 62
Sherry, Valentine, 165
Shilliday, Susan, 322
Shipman, Neil, 40
Shire, Talia, 61
Showtime, 151, 152, 252, 423
Shuler, Lauren, 210
Shutt, Buffy, 200
Shyer, Charles, 158, 164
Sidney, Sylvania, 62
Silent Crime, The, 247, 423
silent movies, xi–xii, 126
Silkwood, 189, 278
Silver Bears, 165
Silver, Casey, 302, 304, 305

Silver, Joan Micklin, 32, 128, 258, 369
Silver, Joel, 184–85
Silver, Susan, 15
Silverado, 45
Silverman, Fred, 15, 25–26, 33, 86–88
Silverman, Treva, 35, 36, 37–39, 91, 125, 364, 431
Simpson, Claire, 45
Simpson, Don, 189, 261, 262, 264–65
Singer, Isaac Bashevis, 164–65
Single White Female, 280
Singletary, Tony, 247
Sinking of the Rainbow Warrior, The, 425
Sins, 425
Sioux City, 426
Six Sense, The, 291
Skin Game, 430
Sky Captain, 246, 247
Slap Shot, 46, 423
Slaughterhouse-Five, 423
Sleepless in Seattle, 279
Smith, Donna, 215–23, 303–5, 370–71, 431
Smith, Gordon, 220, 221
Smith, Howard, 132
Smith, Jaclyn, 236
Smith, Leslie, 373, 431
Smithereen's, 171
Smits, Jimmy, 320
Smoke and Mirrors, 428
Smokey and the Bandits, 68
Smokey Bites the Dust, 142, 216
Snider, Stacey, 180, 272, 276–77, 279, 280, 282, 375
Snodgrass, Carrie, 145
So Young, So Bad, 431
Soap, 37, 91
social transformation (of '60's and '70's), xiii, 13–14, 113–14, 143, 167
Sofie, 342–43, 346, 432
Sold Out, 431
Solms, Kenny, 29
Something About Amelia, 183, 245, 426
Something in Common, 194
Something to Talk About, 45, 374, 431
songs, 121, 140
Song of the Lark, The, 98, 423, 430
Sony/Columbia Pictures, 152, 249, 277, 280, 317, 322
Sophisticated Ladies, 203
Sorvino, Paul, 20
Soul Food, 432
Soul Man, 225, 429
Soul of Saints, The, 424
Sound of Music, The, 155, 266
SpaceCamp, 183
Spacek, Sissy, 264
Spelling, Aaron, 30, 119, 183, 224, 257
Spheeris, Penelope, 258
Spielberg, Steven, 15, 41, 43, 45, 56, 108, 139, 205, 210, 264, 335, 348–49, 369
Spirit Lost, 423
Spitsville, 339
Spring Creek Pictures, 432
Square Dance, 212, 213, 423
St. Elmo's Fire, 210
St. Elsewhere, 423
Staircase, The, 423
Stalin, 196, 430

Stallone, Sylvester, 60–61, 220, 221, 257
Stand and Deliver, 426
Stanfill, Dennis C., 62, 157
Stanley & Iris, 426
Stanwyck, Barbara, 308
Stapleton, Jean, 225
Stapleton, Maureen, 20
Star Is Born, A, 140, 305, 346, 431
Star Trek, 188, 189, 263, 425
Star Trek: Deep Space Nine, 336, 425, 427
Star Trek: The Next Generation, 336, 425
Star Trek: Voyager, 336, 427, 429
Star Wars, xiii, 56, 150, 155, 156, 198, 202
Starger, Martin, 82, 83
Stark, Ray, 41
Starman, 45
Starsky & Hutch, 183
Steel, 325
Steel Chariots, 429
Steele, Dawn, xii, xiii, 106, 120, 152, 158, 187–88, 189, 200, 242, 248–50, 261, 277, 279, 282, 284, 287, 301
Steelyard Blues, 41–42
Steinem, Gloria, 251
Stepford Wives, The, 13
Sting, The, 40–42, 44, 150, 266, 430
Stock Cars for Christ, 321
Stoddard, Brandon, 83, 88, 94
Stoltz, Eric, 256
Stone, Noreen, 5, 8–9, 431
Storm in Summer, A, 432
story consultant
  executive, 37
story editor, 104, 201, 202, 226.
  See *also* development
  in the 70's, 41, 53, 59, 60, 70–79, 89
  in the 90's, 280
Story of Adele H, The, 54
Strange Voices, 426
Stranger Than Paradise, 152
Stranger, The, 45
Stranger Who Looks at Me, The, 426
Strauss, Peter, 240
Straw Dogs, 13
Streep, Meryl, 105, 278, 366
Streets of San Francisco, The, 6, 24
Streisand, Barbra, 40, 41, 42, 106, 121, 136, 140–42, 152, 164–69, 263, 305, 307, 345, 346–47, 431
Striptease, 272
Struthers, Sally, 26
Stuart Little, 425
Studs Lonigan, 45, 46
Stuntman, The, 199
stuntwomen, 335–38
Sugarland Express, The, 41
Sugartown, 358
Sum of All Fears, The, 428
Summer of Sam, 327
Summer School Teachers, 56
Sundance Film Festival, 152
Supreme Court, 2, 26
Survivor, 432
Susskind, David, 15, 104, 173
Sutherland, Donald, 41
swearing, 12, 28, 29, 36, 68, 207, 326, 371
Swedlin, Rosalie, 280
Sweet Kill, 55
Swicord, Robin, 278, 321–23, 431

Swing Shift, 208, 209, 210
Switch, The, 429
Switchback, 427
Swofford, Beth, 280
Sylbert, Anthea, 68–70, 121, 159,
    161–62, 163–64, 166, 205, 206–
    10, 363, 374, 431

Tai-Pan, 350, 424
Talalay, Rachel, 358
Talented Mr. Ripley, The, 313
Talmadge, Norma, xii, 40
Tandem Entertainment, 240
Tandem Productions, 15, 19, 26,
    29–30, 31, 37, 80, 225, 226,
    426
Tandy, Jessica, 98, 267, 268
Tannen, Ned, 15, 130, 245, 248
Targets, 48
Tarses, Jamie, 272
Tart, Carola, 39
Taxi, 128, 425, 431
Taxi Driver, 41–44, 58, 220, 430
Taylor, Elizabeth, 227
Teenage Mutant Ninja Turtles, 45,
    292
television (TV), 367. *See also*
    producer
  in 80's, 191–93, 205, 224–41,
    233, 239, 240, 243–46, 257–61
  in 1973, 7
  cable, 190, 210, 271, 296–98
  hits important for, 82
  international, 294–96
  leading society, 14
  miniseries for, 89, 117, 151, 176,
    258, 287
  movies separated by big divide
    from, 40
  networks becoming old-
    fashioned for, 151
  producer's back-end from, 226
  social themes for, 225, 258
  social transformation (of '60's)
    influence on, xiii
  woman in 90's as executives in,
    272, 286–88, 293–96, 297, 362
  woman promoted in 70's to
    executives/vice president in,
    11–12, 11–14, 15, 16, 62–64,
    80, 83–84, 85–89, 93–94, 104
Tell Me Where It Hurts, 19–20, 39,
    94, 427
Tellem, Nancy, 101
Terminator 2, 358
Terminator, The, 142, 143, 214–20,
    308, 427
Terms of Endearment, 261, 430
Terraces, 104, 426
"Terror Times Two," 426
Testament, 356–57, 423, 428
Tewkesbury, Joan, 144
Thalberg, Irving, 70
That '70s Show, 424
That Girl, 34, 210
That's Television, 62
Theater in America, 173
Then Came Bronson, 425
There Were Times, Dear, 429
Theresa Saldana Story, The, 258
They Call Me Sirr, 430
*They Can Kill You but They Can't
    Eat You* (Steele), xii, 187
Thin Red Line, The, 432
Things Behind the Sun, 358
Third Rock from the Sun, 424
Third World Cinema, 162, 246, 255
This Child is Mine, 225

This Nation Israel, 259
This Tiny World, 132
Thomas, Betty, 253–55, 279, 291,
    431
Thomas, Danny, 102
Thomas, Marlo, 2, 9, 34, 39
Thomas, Richard, 98
Thomopoulos, Tony, 93
Thornburgh, Donald W., 100
Thunder Alley, 225, 429
Time, Inc., 152
Tin Wife, 239
Tinker, Grant, 15, 33, 34
Tisch School of the Arts, 425
Titanic, 428
Title, Barbara, 195
TNT, 370
To Dance with Olivia, 425
To Die For, 307
Tomlin, Lily, 24, 25, 39, 120, 431
Tommy, 58
Tomorrow Enterprises, 225, 226
Tomorrow Entertainment, 15–19,
    62, 80, 82, 97, 98, 225, 236
Top Gun, 261, 262–63, 264, 426
Tortellis, The, 424
Towering Inferno, The, 155
Towne, Robert, 210
Townsend, Claire, 122, 156, 199
Tracy Takes On, 430
TransAmerica, 171
Trial of the Catonsville Nine, The,
    429
Tricks of the Trade, 431
Trigger Happy, 330
Tri-Star, 152
True Confessions, 430
True Lies, 358
Truman, 431, 432
Turner Network Television
    (TNT), 198, 426
Turner, Ted, 151, 152, 306
Turning Point, The, 137, 202
Turtle Beach, 424
12 Monkeys, 303, 305
Twelve O'Clock High, 266
20th Century Fox, 59, 62–64, 112,
    151, 152, 155–58, 161, 183–
    85, 198, 199, 201–2, 211, 217,
    218, 249, 266, 267, 276, 294,
    296, 311, 367, 427, 428
28 Days, 279, 431
24-Hour Pass, 433
Twilight Zone, The, 80, 210
Twin Peaks, 350, 424
227, 427
Two Women, 426
Tyson, Cicely, 2, 39, 120, 225

UCLA, 51, 116, 128, 276, 279, 311,
    317
Ullmann, Liv, 169, 342–46, 432
Under the Sky, 243
union, 21–22, 162, 257, 327, 333,
    335. *See also* IATSE
    (International Alliance of
    Theatrical Stage Employees)
Union City, 258
United Artists, xii, 58–60, 76, 97,
    152, 157, 161, 162, 163–64,
    165, 166, 167, 171, 202, 205,
    206, 211, 364–65, 429
Universal Studios, 14, 45, 64, 65–
    67, 81, 124, 129, 130, 180–81,
    267, 279, 276, 294, 301–3, 304–
    5, 370, 425, 428, 429, 431, 432
Untold Story of Mike Tyson, The,
    428

USA Network, 190, 426
USC, 305, 337, 425

Vachon, Christine, 358
Valente, Renée, 12, 104–5, 116,
    158, 248, 432
Valerie, 424, 426
Valley Girl, 132, 256, 424
Van Der Linden, Martina and
    Charles, 132
Van Doren, Mamie, 544
Van Upp, Virginia, xi
Varda, Agnes, 16, 131, 134–35
Variety, 10, 159, 160, 242–43
Velvet Goldmine, 358
Verdict, The, 266
Verno, Helen, 286
Vertical Limit, 429
VH1, 432
Viacom, 152, 251
Victims for Victims, 258
Viking Club, 7
Vincent, Duke, 257, 258
Visions of Eight, 47
Voices of Leningrad, 424
Voight, Jon, 364

Wagner, Janet, 24, 25, 433
Wagner, Paula, 244, 280
Wagner, Ray, 77
Waiting Room, The, 327
Wald, Jeff, 121
Wall Street, 45, 152
Wallerstein Company, The, 432
Wallerstein, Michele, 109–11, 362,
    432
Walters, Barbara, 125
Waltons, The, 24, 39, 119, 426, 428,
    430
War of Children, A, 16
War of the Roses, The, 210, 430
Ward, David, 41
WarGames, 167, 183, 206
Warhol, Andy, 105
Warner Bros., 42, 46, 61, 69–70,
    78, 86, 152, 158, 161, 163,
    177, 179, 189, 199, 201, 202–
    3, 209, 210, 232, 277, 316–17,
    320, 428
Warner Communications, 152
Warner, Frank, 262
Warner, Jack, 47
Warshaw, Chris, 189
Washington, Denzel, 284
Wasserman, Lew, 68, 121, 124,
    181, 305
Waterdance, The, 427
Watkins, David, 346
Way We Were, The, 41, 46, 121,
    141–42
Weathers, Carl, 61
Weaver, Sigourney, 217, 219
Weber, Billy, 262
Weber, Lois, xii, 40
Webster, 234
Wechsler, Winnie, 298–300, 432
Weill, Claudia, 128
Weinberger, Ed, 38
Weinstein, Hannah, 61, 113, 162,
    196, 307
Weinstein, Lisa, 199, 206, 308
Weinstein, Paula, 61, 113–14, 121–
    22, 155, 157, 158, 161–63,
    167, 168, 199, 201, 202, 206–
    7, 279, 320, 369, 373, 432
Weintroub, Bernie, 239
Weir, Peter, 264
Weitz, Julie, 198

Weitzman, Lew, 110
Welles, Orson, 263
Wells, Frank, 15, 69–70, 203
Wells, John, 348
Weltman, Phil, 102
Weltman, Wally, 89–90
Weng, Jude, 323–26, 432
Werner, Tom, 93, 224, 235, 297
West Wing, The, 428
Weston, Ann, 238
Weston, Jack, 92, 187
WETA, 426
WGAw News, 10
What About Bob?, 306, 432
What Are Best Friends For?, 426
What's Happening Now, 247
What's Up, Doc?, 48, 430
When Women Call the Shots, 431
Where in the World Is Carmen Sandiego, 315
White, Jane, 300, 364, 431
White Mile, 430
White Sands, 431
Who Gets the Friends?, 426
Who's That Girl?, 426
Who's Who, 191
Wigan, Gareth, 202
Wilbur, Claire, 132
Wilcox, Deanna, 75
Wild Racers, The, 54
Wild Side, The, 258
Wildcats, 209
Wilder, Billy, 103
Wilkerson-Miles, Tichi, 9, 115–18
William Morris Agency, 101–3, 105–7, 196–98, 425, 427
Williams, Matt, 231
Willis, Bruce, 303, 320
Wilmar 8, The, 258
Winant, Ethel, 11, 15, 35, 36, 64, 99, 158, 248, 432
Winfrey, Oprah, 226, 297–98
Winner Take All, 62
Winningham, Mare, 227, 251, 252
Wise, Robert, 46, 263
Wiser, Christine Zurbach, 259, 432
Witness, 261, 263, 264, 426
wives, 63–64
Wizan, Joe, 97
Wolper Organization, 89, 177
Woman, 307
Woman of the Year, 125
Womanspeak, 426
women, 268–269, 265–266, 236.
    See also networking; sexism; sexuality
on being heard, 166, 175–76, 213
believing in themselves, 156, 200
climbing ladder, 170, 172, 192, 237
communication/creativity of, 364, 366–67, 376–77
competition among, 77–78, 89, 106, 161–62, 170, 200, 205, 329
consumer spending controlled by, 297
daycare for, 316–17
difference in working between men and, 229, 363–64, 372
with difficult reputations, 363–64
dress code and, 321

emotions of, 219, 366
employment restrictions for, 1–2, 10–11, 192–93, 204, 205, 242, 249, 269, 273, 306–7
exploitation in films of, 55, 204, 217, 256, 258
glass ceiling and, 77, 190, 232, 273, 275, 290, 298–99, 301, 362
groups, 114–21, 203, 238, 255
on illusion of control, 236
marriage and, 156, 192–93, 195, 236, 330–31
men helping, 15, 30, 34–35, 47, 161, 187, 197, 203, 224, 237, 262, 277, 292, 295, 348, 350, 363, 366–67, 374
mentoring/nurturing of, 15, 201–3, 205, 229, 267, 269, 279
mistakes of, 202, 255, 293, 334–35, 340, 358–59, 362, 368, 375
motherhood, children and, 82, 163, 180, 194, 195–96, 198, 228, 234, 235, 238, 239, 240, 248, 275–16, 280, 282, 286, 295–96, 306, 307, 313–14, 316–18, 320, 331, 352, 364
as second-class citizens, 74–75, 100, 118, 149, 273
single, 63–64, 259
statistics in entertainment for, xi, 7–9, 26–27, 86, 242, 273, 310–11, 323, 367–68, 374
on taking credit, 174, 267
violence against, 13
women helping, 38–39, 45, 93–94, 162, 187, 194, 198, 200, 217, 232, 238, 277, 280, 281, 311–12, 330
younger generation of, 361–62, 371–75
Women at West Point, 429
Women Filmmakers Summit, 358
Women in Film, xiii, xiv, 114–20, 122, 137, 159, 185, 194, 196, 236, 275, 276, 278, 373
women's movement, 2–3, 6, 11, 114, 282
consciousness, 19–20, 39, 121, 140–41, 150, 352, 353–54, 377
literature of, 2, 13
Los Angeles, 9, 61
men's support for, 30, 32
New York, 9, 61
post, 375–76
Wood, Bob, 101, 225
Wood, Ed, 104
Woodward, Lydia, 363
World Boys, 423
World Where Everyone Gets What They Deserve, The, 301
Worth Winning, 311, 429
Wrestling Ernest Hemingway, 426
Wright, Hillary, 215
writer(s), 123, 144, 197, 205, 225, 234, 235, 259. *See also* Writers Guild of America
blacklisted, 16, 103, 162
comedy, 25–34, 36–39, 91–93, 104, 125, 363
dramatic, 94–95, 146–48, 159–60, 279, 309–10, 315–20, 342, 345, 354

Emmy award winning, 19–20
female sensibility for, 36, 364, 366, 368–69
importance of, 277–78
interactive CD-ROM, 315, 318
minority, 203, 253, 319–20, 325–26
percentage gross points for, 278, 322
pitches of, 6, 312, 325, 371
reality show, 324–25
re-writing writers, 17
romantic comedy, 279, 311–14
structure for, 319–20
women protagonists for, 310, 321–22
women re-writing of women, 38–39
women's statistics as, xi, 7–9, 26–27, 86, 273, 310–11, 323, 367
Writers Guild of America (WGA), xi–xii, 37, 92, 160–61, 222, 238, 239, 374
pressure on women's 70's statistics from, 9–10, 10
support for writer's vision by, 322–23
women as president of, 27, 124
Women's Committee of, xiv, 5, 6–9, 17, 24, 114, 426
women's statistics for, 7–9, 26–27, 86, 273
women's statistics leaked without permission of, 9–10
women's statistics of 70's for, 7–9, 26–27, 86
Writing for Daytime Drama, 431

X-Files, The, 254
Xiu-Xiu: The Sent Down Girl, 350–51, 424
X-Men, 358

Yentl, 152, 164–69, 210, 264, 346, 431
Yordan, Phillip, 45
Yorkin, Bud, 14, 92
Yorty, Mayor, 14
You Don't Have to Die, 429
You Ruined My Life, 431
You'll Never Eat Lunch in This Town Again (Phillips), 43–44, 430
Young, Burt, 61
Young, John Sacret, 348
Young, Kac, 432
Young, Loretta, 31
Your Blues Ain't Like Mine, 427
Your Friends & Neigbors, 327
Youth, 350
You've Got Mail, 358

Zanuck, Darryl F., 155, 266
Zanuck, Lili Fini, 152, 157, 266–69, 374, 432
Zanuck, Richard, 41, 153, 266
Zarky, Norma, 117, 119
Ziegler, Everett, 59, 60
Zimbert, Dick, 188
Ziskin, Laura, 105, 175, 176, 210, 305–8, 377, 432
Zoetrope Studios, 202, 203
Zoos of the World, 432
Zora Is My Name!, 423